Lever of Empire

TWENTIETH-CENTURY JAPAN:
THE EMERGENCE OF A WORLD POWER

Irwin Scheiner, Editor

1. *Labor and Imperial Democracy in Prewar Japan,* by Andrew Gordon
2. *Complicit Fictions: The Subject in the Modern Japanese Prose Narrative,* by James A. Fujii
3. *The Making of a Japanese Periphery, 1750–1920,* by Kären Wigen
4. *The Abacus and the Sword: The Japanese Penetration of Korea, 1895–1910,* by Peter Duus
5. *Authenticating Culture in Imperial Japan: Kuki Shuzo and the Rise of National Aesthetics,* by Leslie Pincus
6. *Splendid Monarchy: Power and Pageantry in Modern Japan,* by T. Fujitani
7. *Marketing the Menacing Fetus in Japan,* by Helen Hardacre
8. *Japan's Total Empire: Manchuria and the Culture of Wartime Imperialism,* by Louise Young
9. *Mirror of Modernity: Invented Traditions of Modern Japan,* edited by Stephen Vlastos
10. *Hiroshima Traces: Time, Space, and the Dialectics of Memory,* by Lisa Yoneyama
11. *MAVO: Japanese Artists and the Avant-Garde, 1905–1931,* by Gennifer Weisenfeld
12. *Reconfiguring Modernity: Concepts of Nature in Japanese Political Ideology,* by Julia Adeney Thomas
13. *The City as Subject: Seki Hajime and the Reinvention of Modern Osaka,* by Jeffrey E. Hanes
14. *Perfectly Japanese: Making Families in an Era of Upheaval,* by Merry Isaacs White
15. *The Social Sciences in Modern Japan: The Marxian and Modernist Traditions,* by Andrew E. Barshay
16. *Reasonable Men, Powerful Words: Political Culture and Expertise in Twentieth-Century Japan,* by Laura Hein
17. *Lever of Empire: The International Gold Standard and the Crisis of Liberalism in Prewar Japan,* by Mark Metzler

Lever of Empire

The International Gold Standard and the Crisis of Liberalism in Prewar Japan

Mark Metzler

UNIVERSITY OF CALIFORNIA PRESS
Berkeley Los Angeles London

University of California Press, one of the most distinguished university presses in the United States, enriches lives around the world by advancing scholarship in the humanities, social sciences, and natural sciences. Its activities are supported by the UC Press Foundation and by philanthropic contributions from individuals and institutions. For more information, visit www.ucpress.edu.

University of California Press
Berkeley and Los Angeles, California

University of California Press, Ltd.
London, England

Library of Congress Cataloging-in-Publication Data

Metzler, Mark, 1957–.
Lever of empire : the international gold standard and the crisis of liberalism in prewar Japan / Mark Metzler.
p. cm. — (Twentieth-century Japan ; 17)
Includes bibliographical references and index.
ISBN 0–520–24420–6 (cloth : alk. paper).
1. Money—Japan—History. 2. Currency question—Japan—History. 3. Gold standard—History. 4. Monetary policy—Japan—History. 5. Liberalism—Japan—History. 6. Inoue, Junnosuke, 1869–1932. 7. Takahashi, Korekiyo, 1854–1936. I. Title. II. Series.

HG1274.M45 2005
332.4'222'095209041—dc22 2005005397

14 13 12 11 10 09 08 07 06
10 9 8 7 6 5 4 3 2 1

To my parents

CONTENTS

LIST OF ILLUSTRATIONS *ix*

LIST OF TABLES *xi*

PREFACE *xiii*

ACKNOWLEDGMENTS *xix*

NOTES ON TERMS *xxi*

PART ONE: GLOBAL MONEY AND EMPIRE

Prologue: London, 1898 *3*

1. Japan and the British Gold Standard, ca. 1715–1885 *14*

2. Gold and Empire, 1885–1903 *29*

3. The Sinews of War, 1904–1914 *45*

4. The "Positive" and "Negative" Policies *67*

5. "Divine Providence," 1914–1918 *91*

PART TWO: GLOBAL MONEY AND THE DOCTRINE OF INDUCED DEPRESSION

6. The Great Divide, 1918–1921 *115*

7. "The Contractionary Tide," 1921–1926 *138*

8. The Theory and Practice of Induced Depression *159*

9. "The Two-Party Principle," 1927–1929 *175*

PART THREE: THE CRISIS OF LIBERALISM

10. The Liberal Triumph, 1929–1930 *199*

11. Opening the Door to a Hurricane, 1930–1931 *217*

12. Capitalist Recovery in One Country, 1932–1936 *240*

Epilogue: Money and Hegemony *257*

APPENDIX: REFERENCE INFORMATION *273*

NOTES *281*

BIBLIOGRAPHY *319*

INDEX *353*

ILLUSTRATIONS

FIGURES

1. Idealized operation of the gold standard in adjusting a nation's trade balance *19*
2. Yen-tael and yen-dollar exchange rates, 1882–1920 *33*
3. Japan's external bonded debt, 1897–1914 *69*
4. The World War I price wave *116*
5. Profitability of large Japanese corporations, 1914–1943 *117*
6. Wartime inflation and postwar deflation in Japan, Britain, and the United States, 1913–1933 *161*
7. The ups and downs of sake consumption, 1909–1938 *208*
8. Wholesale price indices for Japan, the United States, and Britain, 1929–1931 *223*
9. Wholesale price movements in interwar Japan *249*
10. Bank of Japan notes issued and specie reserve, 1885–1940 *251*

PHOTOGRAPHS

1. Inoue Junnosuke and Hijikata Hisaakira, 1897 or 1898 *xxiii*
2. Inoue Junnosuke at the time of his trip to London, 1924 *xxiv*

TABLES

1. Japanese specie and foreign-exchange holdings, 1903–1914 *70*
2. Overseas bond issues by the central and local governments, 1870–1915 *72*
3. Overseas bond issues by companies, 1906–1914 *78*
4. Overseas bond issues, 1923–1931 *150*
5. Number of countries going onto and leaving the gold standard, 1919–1936 *162*
6. Gold outflows, 1930–1931 *238*
A.1. Bank of Japan specie reserve and note issue, 1885–1940 *273*
A.2. Money supply, 1888 – 1941 *276*
A.3. Yearly inflows and outflows of gold, 1893 – 1941 *278*

PREFACE

In early 1920, during the full rush of the May 4 movement in China, Thomas Lamont of Wall Street's J. P. Morgan and Company traveled to Asia to promote an American-led international banking consortium that would monopolize foreign loans to China. The greatest obstacle to American plans was Japan, which had aggressively pushed its own unilateral loans in China during the great European war. Consequently, an important part of Lamont's trip (and the only part that would bear commercial fruit) was his visit to Japan in February 1920.

On his return to America, Lamont was treated as an authority on Asian matters and was several times called to speak on the subject. In a short piece for *The Nation* magazine in February 1921, Lamont wrote about "The Two Japans":

> There are two schools of thought in Japan and the cleavage is a deep one. In general the men of affairs—manufacturers, great merchants, and bankers—are liberal in their ideas. . . . The other party in Japan, the militarists . . . still think the world is ruled by force rather than by ideas.[1]

For Thomas Lamont, the liberal, idea-driven Japan was personified by his chief Japanese contact, Inoue Junnosuke, governor of the Bank of Japan. In a March 1922 letter to Inoue, Lamont repeated his "two Japans" idea, with the flattering specification that Inoue's group was like Lamont's own elite Wall Street circle ("representing in each instance, we will say, the great commercial interests of our two countries").[2] Inoue too was working for a world ruled not by force but by ideas. And among the great ideas that ruled the world envisioned by Inoue and Lamont was that of a worldwide web of credit and debt, with accounts settled in a unitary global money—gold—which should flow freely across international boundaries.

Like the rest of the world, Japan had suspended the gold convertibility of its national currency and embargoed the export of gold during World War I. At the same time, the European war was a boon for Japanese industry, the occasion for Japan's industrial debut on a world stage. The war boom culminated in a speculative financial bubble, and in February 1920, just at the time of Lamont's visit, the bubble burst. The twelve years that followed were the most extended period of economic malaise in Japan's modern history: an era of falling prices, persistent trade deficits, repeated banking crises, and chronic overcapacity in the nation's new heavy industries, all against the backdrop of a deflationary global environment characterized by efforts in one country after another to stabilize their currencies in line with the Anglo-American gold standard. Successive Japanese cabinets in the 1920s tried and failed to restore the yen to a gold basis, as domestic economic policy lurched back and forth between austerity and expansionism. Liberalism and militarism developed side by side, coexisting in an increasingly uneasy balance of social forces.

In January 1930, with the help of American loans arranged by Thomas Lamont, the liberal Japan appeared to triumph, when Inoue Junnosuke, now finance minister in the Minseitō party cabinet of Hamaguchi Osachi, lifted the embargo on gold exports and restored the gold convertibility of the yen at the old prewar par. Inoue's policy required more deflation, and the government launched an all-out effort to force domestic prices back down to their prewar levels. Seen from without, Japan's return to the gold standard appeared virtually to complete the reconstruction of the prewar monetary order. At home, the "lifting of the gold export embargo" (*kin yūshutsu kaikin,* or *kin kaikin* for short) generated the greatest economic controversy yet in Japan's modern experience,[3] and critics like journalist Ishibashi Tanzan of the *Tōyō keizai shinpō* called Inoue's policy a grave mistake.

As Ishibashi predicted, Inoue's triumph turned into a tragedy. World commodity prices were collapsing in the wake of the New York stock market crash, and Inoue's gold-restoration policy augmented the deflationary downdraft. The social effects were brutal. Bankruptcies mounted, unemployment soared, and the already bitter agrarian crisis intensified greatly. The political reaction was equally brutal, and in the face of right-wing terror campaigns and the Japanese army's invasion of China's three eastern provinces, the liberal government fell in December 1931. Liberal internationalist economics was discarded in favor of nationalist and expansionary policies, followed shortly by the assassination of Inoue himself and the repudiation of English-style parliamentary democracy as a whole system.

The logic of the disastrous gold-restoration policy—perhaps the greatest economic policy mistake in Japan's modern history—was the logic of Japan's international position. In pushing their program of free international gold flows, monetary constraint, budgetary retrenchment, and arms limitation, Hamaguchi Osachi and Inoue Junnosuke were on the front lines of the global campaign to perfect a liberal world order largely drawn after Anglo-American conceptions. They were also among the early casualties of the world war between liberalism and its enemies. Thus, the dry and technical details of monetary politics became a matter of life and death in newly industrializing Japan. Monetary questions were central to the inner operations of political and economic power and were intertwined with virtually all of the greatest questions of Japan's external relations. War, imperialism, and the character of Japan's national development were all implicated in the fight over adherence to the gold standard.

The main character in this drama was Inoue Junnosuke. But more than a biography of Inoue, the present study is a "biography" of the international gold standard in newly industrializing, newly imperialist Japan, the story of a transnational institution to which the life of the Japanese financier became fatally fixed. In the same way, more than Japanese history, this is a study in international history with Japan's experience placed at the center. The primary focus is on the period from 1919 to 1932: the era of deflation and the deflation policy in Japan, which is coterminous with the years that Inoue stood at the top of Japan's financial world. *Deflation* was a new word in the economic vocabulary of the 1920s, and deflationary policies had a newly globalized scope. Deflation was also conjoined with larger projects of social and political stabilization. Among the chief tools of monetary stabilization was the "stabilization crisis"—that is, the theory and practice of deflationary stabilization was the theory and practice of policy-induced economic depression.

The present book originated as part of a larger, ongoing study of economic stabilization policies in Japan since the Tokugawa period. Early in my research, as I looked into the unpublished papers of Thomas W. Lamont to investigate his relationship with Inoue Junnosuke and Japan, I realized the extent to which Lamont personally served as a central command post for coordinating the stabilization policies of the 1920s—policies of a global scope in which Japan's vicissitudes had only a small place. As I pondered the seeming inappropriateness of Inoue's ideas for Japan's situation, in light of the country's pressing social need—and soon-to-be proven ability—for rapid economic growth, I found a story that was at once human and personified as well as structural and systemic. This was the story of the global failure of post–World War I stabilization and the story of Japan's great depression and radical turn against the West. The fact that Japan's depression was to a significant degree an *induced* depression further raised the question of the evitability of these historical outcomes—of the place of human choice in what turned out to be a great transformation of the whole political-economic system.

Japan's experience is also a case study in the problem of economic stabilization in the twentieth-century world, as seen in the specific context of an Asian society undergoing an unprecedentedly rapid industrial revolution. In the post-1970s context of stabilization depressions sponsored by the International Monetary Fund (IMF) across much of the developing world, I became convinced that this was a subject of great comparative significance. As Japan's postbubble stagnation verged into actual price deflation in the mid-1990s—the first significant deflation in any country since the Great Depression—this conviction was sharpened. It was sharpened further as "stabilization" crises unfolded across East and Southeast Asia in 1997 and 1998—crises which, in the context of American pressure for economic liberalization, began to look like yet another confrontation between "Japanese" and "American" economics, now on a regionalized scale.

I'll make a final point about monetary history at the outset. A core question of monetary (and political) history is, *Who* defines and creates money, and how? The answers have wide implications for the governance of political and economic structures, both domestically and internationally. The question is made more problematic by the slippery nature of money itself, as something seemingly substantial that can, at certain moments of social crisis, suddenly change quality or even vanish entirely. Gold, because of the antiquity and generality of its use as money, has been valued in Western countries as a monetary standard precisely because it seemed beyond this realm of social createdness—although, significantly, this latter argument was not part of Japanese monetary debates. But the very scarcity that made gold useable as money in the first place also created great pressures to create substitutes for it, which is where much of the present story lies.

The story of the international monetary standard is a story of international hegemony, and if abstractly conceived processes such as hegemony are constructed anywhere, they are constructed by the actions of particular individuals belonging to particular organizations. It is this interaction between world-systemic dynamics and actual individual policy makers that the present study explores.

This book is made up of three smaller books that look, in turn, at Japan's place in the construction of the global gold-standard system, Japan's place in the reconstruction of that system after World War I, and its place in the collapse of that system after 1929. Part 1 begins with Japan's adoption of the gold standard in 1897. In the context of Japan's new international position as of 1898, the prologue introduces the main protagonists: Takahashi Korekiyo, who was then opening up the channels of Western capital into Japan, and Inoue Junnosuke, who was then beginning his career in international finance. In the years after World War I, these colleagues in high finance would come to typify the opposing "positive" and "negative" lines in Japanese economic policy.

A partial national gold standard had existed in "closed country" Japan in the early nineteenth century but was destroyed when Japan was turned into a monetary periphery of the West in 1859, as chapter 1 explains. In the 1870s a truly global system of international credit was created, centered on the city of London and monetarily based on the unitary gold standard. In 1897, as chapter 2 relates, Japan succeeded in joining this system and gaining access to the London financial markets, just as it succeeded in joining the imperialist club of otherwise white, Christian powers. At the same point, both Japan and the United States began building their own spheres of monetary influence.

Chapter 3 looks at the new gold standard in action, as it was employed to fund the construction of Japan's Asian empire in the years before 1914. At the same time, the gold standard also imposed pressures that seemed to threaten chronic recession at home, as described in chapter 4. Within this context, two policy lines in economics, the so-called positive and negative policies, took shape. These policies of expansion and retrenchment were linked to Japan's external financial position and became partisanized within the new framework of two-party politics that developed simultaneously.

As chapter 5 details, the contradictions of finance and empire were reaching a critical point when Japan's position was "saved" by the great war between the European powers. During the subsequent boom, Japanese leaders attempted to make Japan the political and financial core of Asia. At the same time, ambitious spending policies inadvertently created the straitened financial circumstances of the 1920s.

Part 2 opens with the culmination of the pro-spending, pro-inflationary "positive" policy in 1919, when Takahashi Korekiyo was minister of finance and Inoue Junnosuke was governor of the Bank of Japan. The break point between boom and bust came in 1920, and the great divide represented by that year is the subject of chapter 6. This was the beginning of Japan's interwar depression. It was a reaction, Inoue had said three years earlier, that was bound to come. Chapter 7 explores the "contractionary tide" that then began to run as, at Inoue's urging, economic policy turned toward austerity and retrenchment.

Inoue's policies were part of a worldwide stabilization movement in which, as described in chapter 8, Morgan and Company institutionally and Thomas W. Lamont personally played a leading role. The central place of American finance stands out as a novel feature of the times, and the stabilization programs carried out around the world under Morgan and Company auspices form the prehistory of the stabilization policies of the IMF in more recent times.

Chapter 9 picks up the account of postwar policy swings in 1927, when the logic of restoring the gold standard led to a great banking crisis.

Takahashi Korekiyo and Inoue Junnosuke jointly presided over the cleanup. Subsequently, as other countries returned to the gold standard, international pressure to follow suit came to bear on Japan.

Part 3 of the book explores the subsequent crisis of Japanese liberalism. Chapter 10 relates how the Minseitō cabinet led by Hamaguchi Osachi succeeded in returning Japan to the global monetary standard in January 1930. With this monetary reopening to the West, Japan's domestic crisis became a microcosm of the global crisis of the gold-standard system, and chapter 11 outlines the shape of the deflationary breakdown that followed.

The reaction to this failure of economic liberalism shaped the new policies of the 1930s, which are introduced in chapter 12. Japan's new economic course was charted by Takahashi Korekiyo, now a great elder statesman, who in December 1931 returned to office as finance minister. Takahashi's pathbreaking policy of "Japanese Keynesianism" led Japan out of the Great Depression ahead of any other major country and created the financial foundations of a new kind of state-led industrial policy. Yoked to a militarist policy of expansion on the Asian continent, these economically nationalist policies also helped lead Japan "out of" the West and into a bloody contest for hegemony in East Asia.

The epilogue surveys Japan's reintegration into the Western world order. After Inoue's failure, American-style liberal economics did not return to Japan for eighteen years. When it did, with the orthodox "Dodge line" stabilization program of 1949–50, monetary stabilization was directly implemented by American bankers but now serving as officials of the United States government and practicing a public proconsulship, not a private diplomacy. Seen from without, the new Japan was recemented into a reconstructed liberal international economic order by 1952, and the yen was relinked to a new kind of international gold standard, the U.S. dollar standard. At the same time, however, the international and domestic realms of money were successfully delinked, and within Japan, the "positive" nationalist economics that had taken shape in response to the failure of liberalism in 1931 were about to reveal a new potential for high-speed growth.

ACKNOWLEDGMENTS

This book could not have been made without help from many quarters, and it is a pleasure to acknowledge that here. This study began as an essay on liberalism and national economics in interwar Japan, written in 1994 for Professor Irwin Scheiner at the University of California, Berkeley. Further ideas on postwar stabilization were developed in a seminar with Professor Andrew E. Barshay, who then directed the project as a Ph.D. thesis. During my two-year residence at the Economics Faculty of Osaka City University, the project came to be codirected by Professor Ōshima Mario, who graciously guided me through the world of Japanese economic history and offered helpful criticism at every turn. Professor Thomas R. H. Havens took the entire manuscript in hand and was generous and untiring in his criticism and support. The wide-ranging and humanistic scholarship of these teachers has shaped this project at many points. Needless to say, errors remain my own.

Numerous others have contributed their ideas and criticism—so many that I must apologize to those whose names I leave out here. The manuscript has been read and commented on by Simon James Bytheway, Katalin Ferber, William Miles Fletcher III, Richard Smethurst, and an anonymous reader for the University of California Press. I have also benefited from discussions with and suggestions from Akita Shigeru, Sheldon Garon, Itō Masanao, Kagotani Naoto, Kazusaka Takashi, and Karen A. J. Miller. Many others have provided comments and criticism on parts of this project, as have audiences at numerous scholarly venues. I am grateful finally to the late Thomas C. Smith for his advice and encouragement.

Portions of chapters 9 and 10 have been published in the summer 2002 and summer 2004 issues of the *Journal of Japanese Studies,* to whose able editors (and to Martha Walsh in particular) a further thank you. This book would not be a book without the professional team at the University of

California Press, where special thanks go to Steven Baker and Suzanne Knott.

Research for this study has been done in the libraries and archives of Osaka City University; the University of California, Berkeley; the National Diet Library, Tokyo; the Ministry of Finance, Tokyo; the Bank of Japan, Tokyo; Baker Library at the Harvard Business School; and the Federal Reserve Bank of New York. Particular thanks are due to Mr. Terai Jun'ichi of the Ministry of Finance Policy Research Institute and to Mr. Ōmiya Hitoshi and the helpful archives staff at the Institute for Monetary and Economic Studies at the Bank of Japan (where yet more thanks are due to Professor Itō Masanao). I have also used the libraries of the University of Texas at Austin; the University of Michigan, Ann Arbor; Columbia University; the University of Tokyo; the Detroit Public Library; the Hoover Institution at Stanford; and Oakland University, where special thanks go to the resourceful interlibrary loan staff.

The monetary sinews of scholarship have been provided by a dissertation research grant from the Japan Foundation; thanks especially to the kind members of the foundation's Kyoto office. Additional research grants have been provided by Oakland University; the Northeast Asian Council of the Association for Asian Studies; the University of California, Berkeley; the Harvard University Graduate School of Business; and the American Numismatic Society, where special thanks are due to Dr. Michael Bates and Dr. John Kleeberg. Research was made possible by the institutional homes provided by the History Department of the University of California, Berkeley; the Faculty of Economics at Osaka City University; and the history departments of Oakland University and the University of Texas at Austin.

Most important of all has been the constant support of my parents, Robert Eldredge Metzler and Violet Borkholder Metzler; of my parents-in-law, Matsumoto Shigeo and Matsumoto Keiko; and not least of my wife, Taeko.

With acknowledgements should go a general *apologia:* Fiscal and monetary history, with institutional history more generally, is in many ways more fully developed in Japan than in the United States, whether at the level of published compilations of documentary materials, or the writing of official institutional histories and biographies, or the number of university professorships and official positions devoted to the subject, or the volume of secondary scholarship. As the first narrative history in English of core elements of that history, the present book necessarily touches on only a small subset of the vast body of available materials, necessarily leaving most of the scholarly debates to one side and much work to the future.[1]

NOTES ON TERMS

JAPANESE NAMES AND WORDS

Names of Japanese people are given in the Japanese order (family name first), except in bibliographic citations for English-language works in which they were originally listed in the Western order. Japanese names, especially the personal names of public figures, often have alternate readings. For example, Prime Minister Hara Takashi is also called Hara Kei. In such cases, following the practice of most Japanese biographical dictionaries, I use the standard Japanese-style version of the name. I do include the alternate Chinese-style (*on*) reading on first introduction and in the index. Many Japanese family names, such as *Takahashi* and *Inoue,* are very common, and no family relationship should be assumed between bearers of the same family name. Speakers of Japanese will find it unnecessary, but to clarify names (following the example of Marshall Hodgson in his *Venture of Islam,*) I frequently add redundant English identifiers. For example, "Minseitō party," even though the element *tō* itself means party. When rendered into the Latin alphabet, Japanese words are pronounced more or less as they would be in Spanish or Italian.

MONEY

The symbol ¥ in the text means Japanese yen; $ means U.S. dollars; £ means British pounds. *Billion* means 1,000 million. Under the system of par values prevailing from 1897 to 1931, a conventional rule of thumb in Japan was to reckon £1 = ¥10 and $1 = ¥2. In expressing currency equivalences, I also follow that convention here. Under the former British system, one pound (£) = 20 shillings (*s.*), and 1 shilling = 12 pence (*d.*).

DATES

Dates in citations are given in month/day/year format. Modern Japanese era names (which since 1868 have been imperial reign names) are as follows:

Meiji	1868–1912
Taisho	1912–26
Showa	1926–89
Heisei	1989–

ABBREVIATIONS

For abbreviations used in the citations, please see the bibliography.

BOJ	Bank of Japan (Nihon Ginkō)
FRBNY	Federal Reserve Bank of New York
IBJ	Industrial Bank of Japan (Nihon Kōgyō Ginkō)
MOF	Ministry of Finance (Ōkurashō)
ODC	Oriental Development Company (Tōyō Takushoku Kaisha)
SMR	South Manchurian Railway Company (Minami Manshū Tetsudō Kaisha)
YSB	Yokohama Specie Bank (Yokohama Shōkin Ginkō)

ROMANIZATION OF CHINESE NAMES

Except for a few names that are very well known in other forms (e.g., *Kwantung Army, Chiang Kai-shek, Mukden,*) Chinese names are rendered in their Mandarin forms using pinyin romanization. Alternative romanizations in the Wade-Giles system can be found in the index listings.

代 時 學 留 敦 倫

PLATE 1. Inoue Junnosuke (standing) and Hijikata Hisaakira as trainees in London, 1897 or 1898. From IJD.

外遊途上倫敦

PLATE 2. Inoue Junnosuke at the time of his trip to London, 1924. From IJD.

PART ONE

Global Money and Empire

Prologue

London, 1898

The road that led to the crisis of 1931 began in the late 1890s, when Japan's Asian empire, gold standard, and foreign borrowing got underway simultaneously. These three historical processes were linked from beginning to end. The odd thing was that the linkages were forged on the other side of the world, in the city of London.

Japan's modern gold standard was born out of war. In the aftermath of military victory over China in 1895, the Japanese government exacted an indemnity of 230 million silver taels, a sum equal to about one-quarter of Japan's entire national income.[1] The Chinese indemnity was deposited in the Bank of England, to the account of the Yokohama Specie Bank, the quasi-governmental exchange bank that was the overseas financial agent of the Japanese government. This fund was converted in turn into the Bank of Japan's gold reserve; with it, by the Currency Law of March 1897, the Japanese yen was made convertible into gold as of October 1, 1897. The results of this transfer of wealth were profound, and as Sakatani Yoshio of the Ministry of Finance later saw it, abundant karmic connections were thereby established between Japan's financial destiny and China's.[2] Japan's new gold standard would now be put to the use for which it was intended—borrowing money on the London financial markets.[3]

On February 11, 1898, on the secret orders of Finance Minister Inoue Kaoru, Takahashi Korekiyo, vice president of the Yokohama Specie Bank, embarked at Kōbe for a two-month voyage to London. His mission was to investigate the possibility of Japan's raising a large foreign loan of ¥200 million.[4] Takahashi's task of increasing Japan's international financial leverage was a delicate one. The Empire of Japan was still an unknown quantity in the London financial markets. Moreover, the newly minted gold yen coins were flowing rapidly out of the country, and the London financial press was reporting that Japan's new gold standard was already in danger of collapse.[5]

Takahashi's voyage carried him through a world under British sway. Long before he reached England, Takahashi entered England's empire, and in Hong Kong and Singapore, Colombo, Bombay, Aden, and Suez he passed through the junctures of an Asian trading world under direct British dominion.[6] These were the channels of seaborne trade and seaborne military power, of financial and cultural exchange, that connected peripheral Asia to the core of the world system in London, and in 1898 London enjoyed a kind of global centrality unprecedented in world history.

At the same time, a series of challenges to British hegemony were erupting. In China, Japan's recent victory had provoked a rush by the various European powers to lend money to the troubled Qing empire and establish new colonial outposts on its shores. This scramble for concessions came to a head just as Takahashi sailed for London. In November 1897 imperial Germany had made the opening move by landing marines at Jiaozhou Bay (Qingdao). Imperial Russia followed suit in December, dispatching warships to Lüshun (soon to be renamed Port Arthur). With French backing, the Russians also offered to lend the Chinese government £16 million at low (4 percent) interest, to pay off the balance of the indemnity to Japan.

Nevertheless, as the new year dawned in 1898, the London *Economist* surveyed these developments and professed to find little cause for British alarm:

> The Governments of the Continent are nervously alive to the fact that Great Britain controls the situation [in the Far East]. . . . They are perfectly aware that England possesses the most powerful fleet in the Far East, and might even defeat a general combination. They know that she holds every coaling station on the road to China, and could arrest reinforcements by the simple expedient of refusing to sell coal to their steamers, or blocking the Red Sea mouth of the Suez Canal.

Not least, the *Economist*'s writer added, Britain could, if need be, dispatch an Indian army to the coast of China, "as she has done so often before." And in a struggle, Japan would side with Britain, "thus giving her, besides a second fleet and a second army, an incomparable base of operations."[7] This view from the global metropole is as clear a statement as could be given of the hoped-for place of Japan in the London-centered world order. The *Economist* also asserted that were China to be broken up, "commercial opinion" would insist on "a large slice of the derelict empire"; in the event, Britain did join the scramble. On February 23, while Takahashi was stopping over in the foreign concession of Shanghai, he received a cable from the London office of the Yokohama Specie Bank telling him that China had gotten an Anglo-German loan of £16 million to pay the last installment of the indemnity to Japan.[8] The business was conducted by the Hongkong and

Shanghai Bank, the British government's official agent in East Asia, in partnership with the quasi-governmental German-Asiatic Bank.

Eleven days later, on March 6, the German government took a ninety-nine-year leasehold on Jiaozhou Bay and began to treat Shandong as its own sphere of influence, at once sending out prospectors to look for coal.[9] When Takahashi arrived at Colombo at the end of March, he learned that the Russian government had extracted its own leasehold on Lüshun and Dalianwan (Dairen) in South Manchuria, the same territory that Japan had been forced to relinquish three years earlier under combined Russian, French, and German threat. British warships were steaming north from Hong Kong.[10] In April the British took their own leasehold on the northern Shandong port of Weihaiwei, where they replaced, by cordial mutual arrangement, the Japanese garrison that had occupied the city pending the final payment of the Chinese indemnity.

Thus the partnership between Britain and Japan took shape as part of the campaign to seize "rights" in China. British financial backing for Japan's imperial ambitions also became a central feature of the dawning era of East Asian international relations.

It was at this moment of feverish empire-building that Takahashi arrived in London. If Britain remained, despite new challenges, the hegemonic power in maritime Asia, it was equally hegemonic in the realm of international finance; and the London financial district stood at the core of the institutions of "gentlemanly capitalism" that governed both Britain's empire and its globalized finances.[11] Not only was the gold-backed pound sterling the main currency of international trade, and London the place where other countries settled their international trade accounts, but—more to the point for Takahashi—London was the site of the world's greatest market for foreign investment, and London bankers coordinated the annual export of tens of millions of pounds in capital.

Takahashi Korekiyo was himself relatively new to the business of banking. His mastery of English was a fundamental part of his expertise: like England's gold money, its language was gaining a universal currency at this point.[12] Almost uniquely among those born of his generation, Takahashi's familiarity with the English-speaking world went back to his adolescence.

The son of an elderly artist of the samurai class and his sixteen-year-old maid, Takahashi was born out of wedlock in Edo on the twenty-seventh day of the seventh month of 1854 (September 19 by the Western calendar) and adopted by a lower-class samurai of the Sendai domain.[13] In 1864 the Sendai government sent young Takahashi to study English in the newly opened treaty port of Yokohama, where he worked as a student-servant (*shosei*), or "boy," in the house of the Scottish banker Alexander Allan Shand (1844–1930). The connection was fortuitous: Shand later advised Japan's Ministry of Finance on establishing a Western-style banking system, and in the spring of 1898 he was instrumental in helping Takahashi make connections in London financial circles.[14] In the meantime, Takahashi's path took him in directions other than high finance.

In 1867, at age thirteen, Takahashi and one of his fellows from Sendai were sent to study in the United States. In the seventh month of the year, after acquiring a motley outfit of Western clothes and getting a Western-style haircut, Takahashi sailed for San Francisco, traveling with a few Japanese comrades in steerage, together with several hundred Chinese laborers. His overseas study experience in post–gold rush California was of a different sort from that experienced by the generation of up-and-coming managers and bureaucrats whom Japanese institutions were sending abroad in the 1890s. Aboard ship, Takahashi squandered his and his comrade's travel funds (two $20 gold pieces) on liquor, and in San Francisco they went to work as household servants. The boys' first employer was Eugene Van Reed, who had an appointment as U.S. consul to the Kingdom of Hawaii. Van Reed is now best remembered for his deal with the shogunal government to bring the first Japanese contract workers to the cane fields of Hawaii—where they were bonded by three-year indentures and treated like slaves in conditions so harsh that some committed suicide, as young Takahashi heard the story.[15]

At the Van Reeds' home in San Francisco, Takahashi and his comrade were taken in with kind words but then found that they were given only table scraps and told to eat in the same place that the dogs ate. Because it was a waste of oil, they were forbidden to burn a lamp to study by at night. Takahashi began to slack off at his work and thus got himself transferred to a new post with the family of a young banker on a farm in the small town of Oakland. After quarreling with a Chinese servant and threatening to quit, Takahashi learned that he was not free to leave, having unwittingly signed a contract that sold him as a "slave" (*dorei*) for three years.

On hearing the news of the Meiji Restoration, the senior members of the Japanese group that Takahashi had traveled with returned to San Francisco from New York, where they had gone to study, and they now helped Takahashi negotiate a way out of his predicament.[16] The group sailed to Japan in December 1868. Already, as a result of their Western knowledge, their status had advanced relative to the Chinese laborers with whom they voyaged: as Takahashi boasted, the ship's Caucasian crew members now recognized the Japanese, who used their ability in English to mediate between the crew and the Chinese, whom they mercilessly bullied.

Home in Japan, young Takahashi's knowledge of the West also placed him in a special position. Threatened by the anti-foreign faction that had taken power in Sendai, Takahashi and two of his fellows from Sendai were taken under the protection of the twenty-three-year-old Mori Arinori of the Satsuma domain, then a foreign affairs official. Takahashi continued to study English, and from age sixteen began to teach the language and translate as well, bouncing from job to job. He also drank freely and lived wildly, at one point serving as the attendant to an apprentice geisha slightly older than himself, accompanying her to parties and other events. At age eighteen Takahashi briefly held his first official position, as a translator at the Ministry of Finance, where he shocked coworkers by ordering sake from a neighboring restaurant and drinking at his desk. He irritated them further by arranging to work at home and then disappearing entirely for days, and he finally left on bad terms. He later excised this experience from his résumé. Like many other young Westernizers of his generation, Takahashi also converted to Christianity but then backslid into his former ways.[17]

After numerous posts as a teacher and translator, Takahashi began his first career in government in earnest in 1881, at age twenty-seven, entering the Ministry of Agriculture and Commerce, where he translated Western patent laws, took a study tour of Europe, and became the first head of the new Patent Bureau in 1887, at the age of thirty-three. At the Ministry of Agriculture and Commerce, Takahashi was greatly influenced by the "industrial promotion" (*shokusan kōgyō*) ideas of Maeda Masana of Satsuma, and he worked closely with Maeda in editing Maeda's famous thirty-volume report on the encouragement of industry in Japan. Takahashi later credited Maeda with helping him realize the oneness of the self and the state—what he called a "state standard" (*kokka hon'i*).[18] These ideas became foundational to Takahashi's later economic policies.

In 1889 Takahashi resigned from the government to try his hand at business. His initial undertaking, which he later called the first Japanese overseas business venture, was a partnership with a German businessman to open a silver mine in the Peruvian Andes. The two ended up being defrauded, and the venture failed. After returning from Peru, Takahashi also tried and failed in the ventures of managing a farm in Fukushima and a coal mine in Fukuoka. By age thirty-six, in the depression year of 1890, Takahashi was broke and burdened with debt, forced to move his family into a back-alley tenement (*ura no nagaya*).[19]

Takahashi's luck may have crashed, but he retained friends in high places, including Maeda Masana and Matsukata Masayoshi. In 1892 they told him to go see Bank of Japan governor Kawata Shōichirō, who had formerly been a top executive at Mitsubishi.

It was an unusual job interview. Visiting Kawata at his home, Takahashi regaled him and other Bank of Japan officials who had stopped by with the story of his Peruvian misadventure. Finally Kawata asked him, "What will you do now?" Takahashi replied that he was thinking of seeking a quiet life in the countryside. Kawata advised him to pursue a career in the business world instead—"Entrust yourself to me" (*kimi no karada wa watashi ni makasetara yokarō*). Takahashi agreed. Some days later, Kawata offered to arrange a job for Takahashi as the president of a railroad company. Still new to the business world, Takahashi was afraid of failing again and ruining his chance. He asked Kawata to start him out at the bottom instead. Understanding that Takahashi was requesting a job with the Bank of Japan, Kawata replied that because the memory of the Peru business was still fresh, "I can't immediately use you as a regular employee in a bank where trust counts so heavily." He could, he said, use Takahashi as his "doorkeeper" (*genkanban*). Just then, the new Bank of Japan headquarters was being constructed at the site of the old Tokugawa gold mint (*kinza*) in Tokyo's Nihonbashi district. The project was under the general direction of Shibusawa Eiichi, the greatest of all the entrepreneurs of the Meiji era. Kawata arranged for Takahashi to work there as the business manager at a salary of ¥1,200 per year.[20] Takahashi's immediate supervisor was one of his own former students.

In this way Takahashi entered the banking world through the side door. After the construction project, Takahashi was sent to the Bank of Japan's Shimonoseki branch, where he was present for the negotiations that ended the war with China. In 1895 Takahashi joined the Yokohama Specie Bank, becoming managing director in 1896 and vice president in 1897 and overseeing the transfer of the Chinese indemnity funds from London.

Thus, Takahashi finally found his métier in the world of high finance. Even in the wide-open world of early Meiji Japan, Takahashi's career to this point had been remarkable, a tale of "ten-thousand foot waves" (*haran banjō*) that would scarcely be imaginable for the career-oriented young men of the 1890s.[21] At the Yokohama Specie Bank, Takahashi championed Finance Minister Matsukata Masayoshi's adoption of the gold standard in 1897, and thus it was that in the spring of 1898 Takahashi went to work to open the doors of foreign credit for Japan.

When Takahashi arrived in London in April 1898, there were only about thirty Japanese stationed there, and they naturally formed a close and friendly community.[22] Among these mostly young men was a remarkable collection of future national leaders who would play leading roles in the construction of a pro-Western liberal order in Japan in the 1920s and in its fateful collapse in 1931. The foundations of that order were now being laid, and these men were receiving their on-the-job training. In the process, nearly all became Anglophiles.

The senior figure in London was the Japanese minister to Britain, Katō Takaaki (Katō Kōmei, 1860–1926). Katō had discovered an affinity for the gentlemanly English manner when he first came to London as a Mitsubishi employee in 1883. As a diplomat, he became the foremost advocate of an Anglo-Japanese alliance, which was realized in 1902. Katō was later to be foreign minister, founding president of the liberal Kenseikai party, and prime minister in the mid-1920s.[23] Shidehara Kijūrō (1872–1951), himself later foreign minister and prime minister, now recently graduated from Tokyo Imperial University, was also posted to the Japanese legation in London in 1899. Shidehara later remembered his time in London as one of the happiest of his life.[24] While there, the novice diplomat was introduced to Iwasaki Masako, the younger sister of Minister Katō's wife; by their marriage four years later, Shidehara not only became Katō's younger brother-in-law but also the son-in-law of the deceased founder of the Mitsubishi *zaibatsu,* Iwasaki Yatarō.

After the government, it was the banks that were best represented abroad. The Yokohama Specie Bank had an office in London. The Bank of Japan did not, but in 1897 it for the first time sent two young trainees to London, Inoue Junnosuke and Hijikata Hisaakira (1870–1942). Both were later governors of the Bank of Japan. Mitsui and Company also sent two young executives to London in 1899: Dan Takuma (1858–1932) and Ikeda Shigeaki (Ikeda Seihin, 1867–1950), both later heads of the Mitsui group.[25]

An abundance of karmic connections could also be thought to be at work here. In the 1920s Katō Takaaki, Shidehara Kijūrō, and Inoue Junnosuke would, respectively, direct Japan's liberal party politics, liberal diplomacy, and liberal financial policy. Dan Takuma and Ikeda Shigeaki would govern the giant Mitsui group and stand at the pinnacle of Japan's business world. As the culmination of his life's work, Finance Minister Inoue Junnosuke would follow England's lead and restore Japan's gold standard at the prewar par in 1930, with the loyal support of BOJ governor Hijikata. As chief executive of Mitsui Bank, Inoue's erstwhile friend Ikeda would do more than anyone else to loot the Bank of Japan of its gold reserves and destroy Inoue's project. Inoue and Dan would be murdered by comrades from the same band of ultranationalist fanatics.

Recognizable institutional and temporal structures gave form and rhythm to these tightly interwoven life courses. Inoue and Hijikata took up their posts at the Bank of Japan just as a new era of international relations was dawning for Japan, and they were leading members of Japan's first generation of international financiers.[26] As career paths became standardized by the new educational and occupational bureaucracies, members of this new generation rose straight through the elite ranks of Japan's modern meritocracy, following a career pattern very different from the diverse and varied careers of the first Meiji generation.[27] Tokyo Imperial University ("Teidai"), particularly its law school, was the prestigious training ground for Japan's new bureaucratic ruling class, and the leaders of the pro-Western government team that restored the gold standard in 1929–30 all passed through its gates in close company. They included Inoue and Hijikata (both graduated 1896), Shidehara (graduated 1895), and Hamaguchi Osachi, who led the cabinet (also graduated 1895). These men were part of a larger generational cohort that would govern the country in the decade after World War I.

The star of this new generation of international financiers was Inoue Junnosuke, born on the twenty-fifth day of the third month of 1869 (May 6 according to the new Western calendar) to a locally prominent sake-brewing family in Ōzuru village of Hita (or Hida) county, an inland valley in Kyūshū's Ōita prefecture. (It was then Hita prefecture, headed by a young governor named Matsukata Masayoshi, who was already gaining fame for his far-reaching local reforms.) It was a place that Inoue became eager to leave behind.[28]

The unwanted youngest of six children, Inoue was adopted out at age seven to a schoolmaster uncle, who began to give him an education but then died two years later, leaving young Inoue as family heir. Inoue excelled in his studies but then lost two years due to a serious illness. During his long hospitalization, his biographer reported, his birth mother, who ran the family business while his father dabbled in local politics, never visited nor even wrote. Afterward, she grudgingly took him back in, but because of his constant reading, Inoue proved inattentive in his work at the family brewery. At age sixteen, with the help of an older brother who had entered the Japan Shipping Company (Nippon Yūsen Kaisha), Inoue got the chance to study in Tokyo, where he sat for the test to enter the elite First Higher School. Failing because of his lack of preparation in English and mathematics, Inoue studied hard to remedy these deficiencies and, in 1887, at age eighteen, entered the Second Higher School (Daini Kōtō Chūgakkō) in Sendai, which had just opened the year before.

Like Takahashi, Inoue had bounced from place to place in his childhood, learning at a young age to rely on his own abilities. Unlike Takahashi, he was from the point of his entry into the Second Higher School working within a clear institutional framework that placed him on the high road to success. He thereafter pursued this path with great single-mindedness.

At the Second Higher School, Inoue rose to the top of his class of ten, and in an age when students were notorious for their wild and unconventional behavior, he was distinguished by his maturity, careful dress, and sense of moderation and regularity. In 1893 Inoue was admitted to the English Law department of Tokyo Imperial University, although he chose to study commercial law, less prestigious than administrative law, thinking that it would be useful to his older brother who was supporting him in his studies. Inoue graduated a close second in his elite class.

An episode later well remembered by his classmates is revealing of Inoue's uprightness and austere sense of decorum: As a leader of his class, Inoue helped organize the banquet that the graduating students gave to honor their teachers. Thinking that a party attended by traditionally arrayed geisha and apprentice geisha was lacking in dignity, Inoue conducted trying negotiations with the "women's general" (*joshō*) in charge of the entertainment, getting her to agree that the geisha attendants would dress as "amateurs" rather than wear their full makeup. When, just before the event, Inoue noticed that she had not complied with his request, he insisted that she do so, and the party was conducted in an appropriately simple and dignified style.[29]

Upon graduation from the Imperial University in 1896, Inoue, following his brother's intercession, entered the Bank of Japan under the sponsorship of BOJ director Yamamoto Tatsuo (1856–1947), a fellow Ōita native. Inoue did this despite the fact that his professors thought him suitable for a career in the upper bureaucracy (the banking world being viewed as a cut below that). Inoue later did come to view the career choice as a strategic one, seeing banking as holding a central and mediating position between government and the world of business. At the Bank of Japan, Inoue was immediately groomed for the track to the top, and after a brief stint at the bank's Osaka branch, the bank sent him together with Hijikata Hisaakira to London for two years of training in October 1897, just as Japan's gold standard went into effect.[30]

In 1897 the Bank of Japan did not yet have a regular office in London and was not a recognized member of the international banking fraternity. The bank attempted to place Inoue as a trainee at the Bank of England, but the Japanese request was without precedent and was "refused with one word."[31] Instead, Inoue and Hijikata were placed at a branch of Parr's Bank in London, owing to the help of Takahashi's old employer A. A. Shand, who since his return from Japan had become manager of the bank's Lombard Street branch.[32]

Takahashi himself arrived in London in April 1898. Soon after, he met with Shand, recording that the latter in his gentlemanly way never alluded to the fact that Takahashi had been his houseboy (Takahashi once brought it up, but Shand said he had forgotten).[33] The two men became close, and Takahashi's son subsequently lived with the Shand family for eight years while pursuing his studies in London.

However, Takahashi's first effort at raising a foreign loan was less than a complete success. With Shand's help, the Japanese government did succeed in putting together a banking syndicate, which in June 1899 issued £10 million (roughly ¥100 million) in bonds, then a very large sum. The sale of the bonds was a flop, and only 10 percent of the loan was subscribed on the open market.[34] But connections had been made and lessons learned, and the next time that Takahashi Korekiyo put the gold standard to work, it would help Japan to win an imperial war.

In October 1898 Inoue's sponsor, Yamamoto Tatsuo, was appointed governor of the Bank of Japan. Yamamoto's appointment was divisive, and eleven Bank of Japan directors, bureau heads, and branch managers opposed to him resigned in February and March of 1899. As a consequence, there was talk in the government of replacing Yamamoto. Takahashi Korekiyo defended him, visiting, among others, Finance Minister Matsukata Masayoshi, senior statesman Inoue Kaoru, and Army Minister Katsura Tarō to argue that if the government gave in to this "strike" (*dōmei higyō*), it would be an international disgrace. Yamamoto was retained, and in the midst of the uproar, on February 28, 1899, Matsukata appointed Takahashi to fill the previously vacant post of vice governor of the Bank of Japan.[35] Takahashi held this post until 1911.

Because of the wave of resignations, Yamamoto recalled Inoue Junnosuke and Hijikata Hisaakira from England in March 1899.[36] Yamamoto personally traveled to Kōbe to greet them on their arrival. Inoue now began his extraordinarily fast rise through the ranks of the Bank of Japan. The close working relationship of Takahashi and Inoue also dated from this time.

If the late 1890s was a formative time personally for the generation who would lead Japan in the 1920s, it was also a pivot in social time for Japan's international position, as twenty-five years of Western-style modernization began to pay off. In the five years from 1895 to 1900, Japan acquired the beginnings of an overseas empire, renegotiated its treaties with the Western countries on the basis of equality, and began to handle most of its own international trade (previously conducted mainly by foreign merchants). At the same time, the country went from exporting mainly primary products to exporting mainly manufactured goods and launched a heavy industrialization program with the building of the state-owned Yahata Iron Works. It adopted the gold standard and began to borrow abroad. It also made its first significant loans abroad. All of these changes were perceived as important national-developmental mileposts. More simply, one could say that this was the threshold of Japan's industrial revolution, with all the transformations that accompanied it.[37]

These years were also pivotal for the world political-economic system as a whole, as they were for the United States in particular. The imperialist scramble continued in the spring and summer of 1898 as imperial armies were set marching from Cuba to the Sudan. At the end of April, an American naval squadron steamed from Hong Kong to Manila Bay, and the American occupation of Manila was completed in August. With the American seizure of Guam in June and the formal annexation of Hawaii in the same month, the United States emerged as a trans-Pacific empire. American initiatives were also underway in China, as the American China Development Company gained the concession to build a rail line from Hankow to Canton in April 1898.[38] The American railroad deal failed to come off in the end, but the Hankow-to-Canton (Huguang) rail project would in the next several years become a central object of financialized imperial competition in China.

Of more enduring significance were the informal beginnings of a new Anglo-American alignment. As recently as December 1895, there had been threats of an Anglo-American war over the Venezuela-Guiana boundary, but by the spring of 1898, the two countries had "drawn together in a remarkable way."[39] This new "Anglo-Saxon" partnership, whose core was in many ways financial, would form the central axis of world power into the twenty-first century. At the same time, Britain's monetary standard was also nearly universalized, as Austria-Hungary, India, Russia, and Japan all joined the gold-standard system. The "classical" gold standard that ended in August 1914 now entered its final, truly globalized phase.

ONE

Japan and the British Gold Standard, ca. 1715–1885

As it came to Japan in 1897, the gold standard was a Western, originally British institution, and its institutional life story reflects the long rise to worldwide financial ascendancy of Great Britain and its more sudden fall. Japan's engagement with the gold standard was from beginning to end a story about international hegemony, integrally connected to the many questions of Japan's relationship to Britain and to the United States. To understand that story, it is necessary to begin with the prior monetary history of both Britain and Japan.

At its most basic level, the "classical" British-style gold standard consisted of two linked practices. First, a nation's standard money was given a fixed value in terms of gold. Thus, both paper money and subsidiary bronze and silver coins were denominated in terms of gold. The issuing authorities were committed to convert these representatives of gold, on demand by the bearer, into gold coins. Second, private individuals had the right freely to import and export gold. In practice, national gold standards were operated by national treasuries or central banks of issue, which held a stock of gold as a reserve for convertibility and issued paper money backed by that gold. This set of monetary practices, in a variety of national permutations, spread to most of the world in the late nineteenth and early twentieth centuries, and its use had profound economic, social, and political consequences.[1]

These two aspects of the gold standard—unification of the national currency in terms of gold, and free cross-border gold flows—have distinct origins, and their development reveals, respectively, a state-centered and a market-centered aspect of the gold-standard system. These elements came together in Britain over the course of the eighteenth century and formed a complete system, fixed in British law, in 1816. With the companion doctrines of free trade and laissez-faire, the gold standard became a central pillar of classical British liberalism. This latter story has received ample attention from historians. It is less well known that at the same time, Japan's Tokugawa shogunate also developed essential elements of its own national gold standard. The most immediate effect of open trade between Japan and the West was the sudden ruination of Japan's gold-based monetary system.

THE BAKUFU GOLD STANDARD

For several centuries, Japan's monetary circulation depended mainly on the import of Chinese bronze coins, making Japan a peripheral zone in a China-centered monetary sphere that extended across East and Southeast Asia. In the Tokugawa period (1600–1867), a nationally independent monetary system was created, as the shogunal government (Bakufu) issued its own bronze, silver, and gold coinages. Up to the 1770s, the Tokugawa coinage system functioned as a triple monetary standard. Each of the metallic coinages had its own system of denominations, and despite Bakufu efforts to fix rates between them, the gold, silver, and copper coinages in effect floated against each other in the exchange markets. Like other aspects of the Tokugawa order, the currency system was highly segmented socially and geographically; and in its multifariousness, complexity, and lack of overall rationalization into a single system, the Tokugawa currency was typical of early modern currency systems, including that of Britain in the eighteenth century and that of China until 1935.[2]

At the outset of the Tokugawa period, when Japanese society was very incompletely monetized, Japanese mines produced gold, silver, and copper in abundance. Much of it was shipped to China to pay for the import of manufactured goods. In one sense, Japan as a nation was simply trading locally produced commodities—metal for monetary use—for foreign goods. However, as rapid commercialization and monetization demanded an increasing volume of money, this trade of bullion for goods came to be viewed as a national loss for Japan—as a trade deficit, even if that conception itself was not yet available. Thus, by the early eighteenth century, the Tokugawa government's famous restriction of foreign trade had come to be motivated mainly by the fear that foreign trade was causing the loss of irreplaceable gold, silver, and copper. These trade restrictions became increasingly effective after the specie export embargo imposed by shogunal adviser Arai Hakuseki in 1715. At different points in the eighteenth century, they were combined with conscious import-substitution and export-promotion policies, as Japan moved toward an increasingly managed monetary system.[3]

National closure allowed the development of an independent monetary regime with some very modern features. Among the most striking innovations was the creation of a system of token (or fiduciary) silver coins denominated in terms of gold. This principle of monetary leverage—"overvalued" token coins whose face value exceeds the market value of the metal that they contain—is the essential principle of every modern system of coinage. Thus, for example, the metal contained in a quarter-dollar U.S. coin must have a market value of less than twenty-five cents, or else quarters would be minted at a loss and would end up being melted for other uses and vanishing from circulation. Simple as it appears in retrospect, this principle was only arrived at after centuries of monetary experience. It is usually regarded as a principle that was first instituted in England with the full enactment of the gold standard in 1816.[4]

In Japan such a principle was first implemented in 1772 by the government of Bakufu minister Tanuma Okitsugu, which began to issue overvalued silver coins—valued not by the weight in silver that they contained, but given a face value (an exchange value) in terms of gold *ryō*. Seen by generations of Japanese historians as a matter of straightforward debasement of the coinage motivated by simple cupidity, Tanuma's reform was in retrospect a monetary revolution: fifty years before the world's first unitary gold standard was fully realized in Britain—the very definition of monetary modernity for most specialists—the Tanuma administration independently created a partial gold standard in Japan.[5] Tanuma's "gold standard" remained partial in that these gold-denominated silver coins circulated side by side with the old silver-by-weight currency. However, over the final ninety-six years of Tokugawa rule, the new gold-denominated silver coinage occupied a progressively more dominant place in the national stock of currency.[6]

A primary dynamic of general monetary evolution was at work here. Abstractly, economic growth and commercialization demanded a greater circulation of money, but the national stock of specie was more or less fixed. As monetary historian Angela Redish has described it, a specie standard is like a ship on a finite anchor chain in rising seas.[7] More concretely, the difference between the face value of the token coins and their intrinsic metallic value constituted a source of seigniorage—a lord's profit. Such monetary leverage was a wellspring of state power, as seigniorage profits came to constitute a great part of Bakufu revenues.

Thus the "anchor chain" was lengthened—or, to employ a second metaphor, a given national stock of silver was leveraged into an even greater volume of "gold." The result was two distinct sets of gold-to-silver ratios. If Tokugawa gold coins were exchanged for the old-style silver-by-weight coinage, the market rate in 1858 was around 1:10. By contrast, if the actual silver contained in the Bakufu's widely used token coins were compared to their face value in gold, the ratio would have been as low as 1:5. As this difference provided an important source of seigniorage revenues to the Bakufu, it likewise tempted counterfeiters, who, as Takahashi Korekiyo wrote as a young student of English, "used to be crucified but now they are hanged." Outside Japan, gold-to-silver ratios in the world market were 1:15 or 1:16, and this difference would prove a temptation to foreign merchants.

Japan's closed, leveraged monetary system was shattered by the treaties imposed by the Western powers. In 1858, while Britain and France jointly warred against China to extend their economic rights there, U.S. consul Townshend Harris took advantage of the occasion to induce the Bakufu to accept a commercial treaty that required free trade and free monetary flows. Britain and the other European powers signed similar treaties soon after. Applying as a model the system that the powers had forced on China,[8] these treaties opened designated ports to foreign trade and residence, fixed Japanese tariffs at relatively low levels, and provided that the volume of trade should be unlimited. Thus, the Japanese government lost control over both tariffs and foreign exchange.

Many things have changed since 1858, but the respective economic policy positions of the U.S. and Japanese governments have shown some surprising continuities. In August 1929 Finance Minister Inoue Junnosuke, also responding to U.S. pressure, prepared to lift the embargo on gold exports that the Japanese government had imposed during World War I. In this connection he warned the Japanese people: "If we were to lift the gold embargo with things as they now stand, Japan's gold coins would at once go out to foreign countries, exactly like a great flood when a dam breaks." Before the monetary door could be opened, Inoue explained, Japan's foreign-trade accounts must be brought more nearly into balance.[9] Inoue's *kin kaikin,* the lifting of the gold export embargo, was an effort to restore Japan's economic equilibrium by relinking the country to the international gold-standard system. But his warning could have applied equally well to the Tokugawa Bakufu's predicament seven decades earlier. Under the terms of the 1858 Treaty of Amity and Commerce, "all foreign coin shall be current in Japan and pass for its corresponding weight of Japanese coin of the same description. . . . Coins of all description (with the exception of Japanese copper coin) may be exported from Japan."[10] The acceptance of these American demands meant the lifting of the specie export embargo that had been emplaced after 1715. It also meant that foreign silver dollars must be accepted weight-for-weight for the Bakufu's gold-denominated silver coins, as if the latter were a straight silver bullion coinage.

With this, the dam burst. Western traders rushed to convert foreign silver dollars weight-for-weight into the token silver coinage of Japan. They then tripled their money by converting these token coins at their face value into Japanese gold coins and shipping the gold out of the country. Once it began to operate, this circuit worked very quickly, as every available ship was pressed into service for the Yokohama-to-Shanghai run. An estimated 4 million *ryō* of gold coins flooded out of Japan in 1860, and gold rapidly began to disappear from circulation. The Bakufu responded by radically debasing the gold coinage, reducing its gold content by two-thirds in order to match the value of the actual silver content of the subsidiary coinage, at the international gold-to-silver ratio.[11] This "lifting of the gold embargo" in 1859 thus delivered a shock that destroyed Japan's native gold standard and forced the Tokugawa Bakufu to return its coinage to a straight bullion standard based on international rates of exchange. In the process, the Bakufu lost its freedom to finance itself by recoinages and finally resorted to issuing unbacked paper money. A great inflation also got underway, which did much to wash away the Tokugawa social order and make ready the way for the Meiji revolution of 1867.

THE PARLIAMENTARY GOLD STANDARD

The origins of Britain's gold standard are conventionally dated to 1717. Then, just as Bakufu policy makers were attempting to stanch the outflow of bullion from Japan to China, British policy makers were trying to stem the flow of silver from Britain to the European continent (and thence on to India and China), and Sir Isaac Newton, master of the mint, refixed the mint price of silver in an attempt to keep silver in circulation. Gold, however, remained relatively overvalued in England. Silver continued to flow out and gold to flow in, and thus, England became the first country in modern times to have a gold-centered coinage.[12] The result may have been accidental, but as the virtues of a monometallic standard later came to be consciously regarded, Newton's name did provide a convenient authority for the new doctrine. And in fact there was something Newtonian about the equilibrium conception of the gold standard as it came to be imagined by British philosophers like David Hume in the course of the eighteenth century.

In his 1752 essay "Of the Balance of Trade," Hume likened the power of trade to that of gravity: "All water, wherever it communicates, remains always at a level." In a like way, when countries traded freely with one another and did not attempt to dam the free outflow of gold and silver, then money and prices should remain at a common international level.[13] Here, in an ideal form, is the second core element of the classical British gold standard: free international gold flows.

Following Hume's conception, the self-equilibrating mechanism of the gold standard was supposed to keep a nation's trade in automatic balance, as represented in figure 1. In short, if a nation imported more than it exported, it would have to settle its international debts in gold. As gold flowed out of the country, the domestic money supply would contract, which would raise the domestic value of money (gold) relative to goods. To put it another way, the money price of domestically made goods would fall. Domestic goods would thus become cheaper compared to foreign goods, discouraging imports and

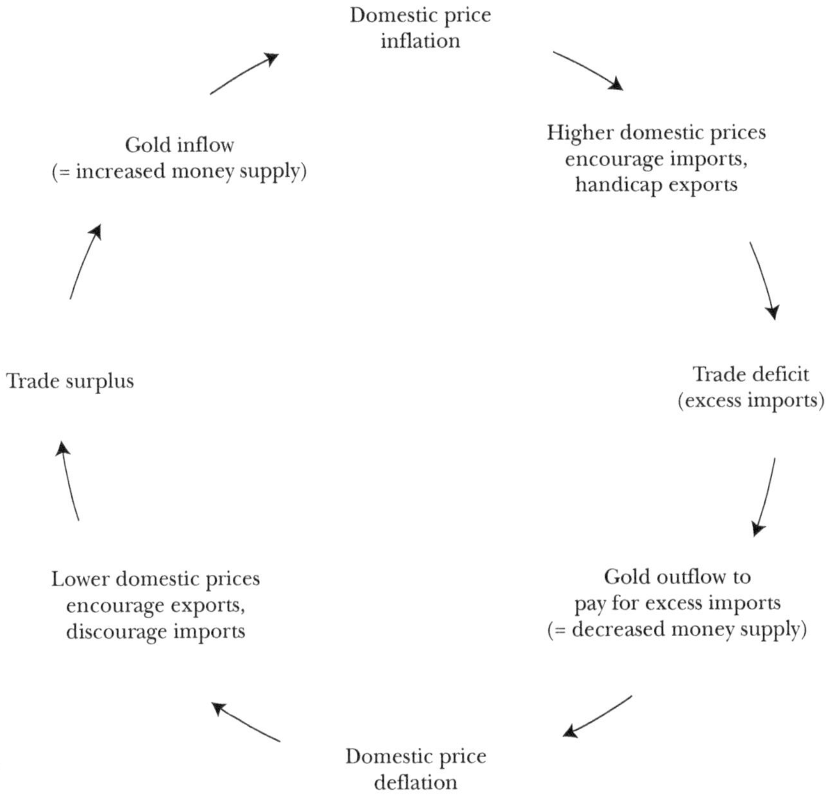

FIG. 1. Idealized operation of the gold standard in adjusting a nation's trade balance.

promoting exports, thus correcting the original trade imbalance. Conversely, a country with an export surplus would receive gold inflows, enlarging the domestic money supply and causing the value of money (gold) to fall relative to goods. This inflation of domestic prices would make domestically produced goods less competitive internationally, thus ending the trade surplus. In modern times, Hume thought, the one thing capable of disrupting this natural balancing mechanism was the issue of paper money and credit. In actuality, even in its late-nineteenth-century heyday the international gold standard never worked in the automatic way that many of its proponents imagined.[14] Nevertheless, the grand simplicity of Hume's naturalistic conception retained a power to convince, and in arguing for a return to gold convertibility in the 1920s, Ishibashi Tanzan, Inoue Junnosuke, and many others presented this theory in its classic, idealized form.

The specie flow system thus appeared as a closed hydraulic system, except for irregular "injections" of newly mined gold and "leakages" of gold lost to circulation. To the extent that adjustment was unobstructed and rapid, the entire mechanism should never be far out of balance. In the common conception of the gold standard, the value of gold itself was held not to fluctuate: gold was the standard relative to which all else fluctuated. Thus, a nation's currency, if held constant relative to gold, should neither appreciate nor depreciate, although the price of goods might—indeed must—fluctuate. The important point here is that under such a regime, the whole burden of trade adjustment falls on domestic prices: net inflows of gold should bring domestic inflation, net outflows should bring deflation. An alternative but presumably temporary way to balance a trade deficit—which would be central to the actual operation of Japan's gold standard—was to borrow money from abroad.

In its actual operation, the gold standard has historically been associated with price deflation. At the most fundamental level, the sheer fact of limited world gold stocks, relative to the long-run expansion of the gold bloc and the rapid economic growth of its member economies, created a pronounced deflationary bias—a finite anchor chain in a rising sea. The fact that creditors thoroughly dominated Britain's political economy and that Britain, the historic center of the gold-standard system, was the world's great creditor nation was not incidental to this arrangement: creditors preferred to be repaid in "heavier" rather than "lighter" money. In the 1920s the United States inherited the role of global creditor, and American bankers became the world's leading promoters of the revived, deflationary gold standard.

In the eighteenth century, however, the neat symmetries of Hume's system remained a kind of utopia, and despite the new centrality of gold, British coinage remained extraordinarily chaotic. It was only after 1821 that Britain became the first European country fully to solve the old problem of keeping gold, silver, and copper coins all in circulation. The solution was the creation of a truly token (that is, overvalued) silver and copper coinage denominated in terms of a single gold standard.[15] This unification of the coinage under a single standard was the essence of the modern monetary revolution. The gold standard thus represented a grand simplification and, in the reckoning of most monetary theorists, a great step forward in monetary progress. Like paper money and like the token silver coins issued by the Tokugawa Bakufu, the value of Britain's new token coins was determined not by their intrinsic metallic content but by their face value as denominated in gold—they were "banknotes printed on silver," to paraphrase J. M. Keynes.[16] Indeed, the logic of paper money and fractional-reserve banking—the creation of banknotes or deposit money in excess of currency reserves—could be thought to be the mental model for this system.

This line of thinking leads finally to a consideration of the central-banking aspect of the gold standard. At the same time that Britain's metallic coinage was being unified, a related development was by stages reducing metallic coinage itself to the trivial monetary importance it has today, for Britain also led the way in the use of cheques and paper banknotes, convertible into gold. In fact, from the beginning, the British gold standard was a gold-and-paper system, as the unitary gold standard and modern paper money took form together, linked by the institution of modern central banking, which also received its first great development in Britain. As central banking evolved in Britain, an ideology developed as well—of the central bank as the guardian of the currency, neutral, expert, above politics, and largely hidden from view.

The specific conjunctural context of Britain's original enactment of the modern gold standard is also relevant to Japan's experience after World War I. In the first instance, the British government was forced to suspend the convertibility of bank notes into specie during the costly and inflationary world war to contain revolutionary France. With the war's end in 1815, the British parliament voted to terminate the wartime fiat currency and to institute gold monometallism formally into law. Britain's gold standard was thus legislatively instituted as a *restoration,* both moral and economic, and as a reaction to the experience of a wartime paper-money inflation.[17] The gold standard guaranteed that the paper banknotes issued by the Bank of England would be backed by "real" money—gold. It also rendered the creation of this real money into a completed fact dating back to the third day of biblical creation—a fact well beyond the reach of secular authorities who might be inclined to inflate the currency. The new gold standard was also highly deflationary.

Herein lies a great difference between the partial Tokugawa gold standard and the unitary gold standard established by the British parliament. The Tokugawa gold standard instituted by Tanuma Okitsugu was essentially an inflationary institution and a step in the direction of a fiat currency. Initially resisted by merchants, it reflected the increased monetary capacity of the Tokugawa state. The British gold standard likewise represented the increased capacity of the British state-bank complex, and notably, it was fully realized only after a successful, if inflationary, wartime experiment in paper money. But it was also conceived, like British constitutionalism in general, as a *limitation* of state power. As such, it reflected the power of the private, creditor interests who dominated the British state.[18]

Britain's unitary gold standard came to have a nearly religious hold on British financial circles. There was, after all, a natural economy and symmetry to the system: there were exactly as many standards of absolute value as there were gods in heaven; Gold was God with a fungible "£" in the middle. These were alike treasures that neither rust nor moths could destroy, and the spiritual dangers inherent in serving two masters were resolved by making them one. Bimetallism, continuing on the Continent until the 1870s, came to appear in Britain as a foolish and dangerous heresy, immoral and unscientific. By the 1840s, support for a "double standard of value" had simply become inconceivable to most British economists and lawmakers, the monetary issue being regarded as settled once and for all.[19] In Japan such quasi-religious monetary convictions were lacking, but in the early 1870s, as Japan's new leaders grappled with the problem of establishing a new monetary standard, Britain's example became influential. Japan's first attempt to join the London-centered gold zone in 1871 failed, and after a wrenching process of deflation and depression, currency stabilization was achieved on a second-best silver-standard basis in 1885.

POSTREVOLUTIONARY MONETARY STABILIZATION IN MEIJI JAPAN

At the same time that Japan was being incorporated into the Western system of trade and diplomacy, Britain's monometallic gold standard was gaining a position of primacy in a world economy that had traded since the sixteenth century primarily on the basis of an international silver-dollar standard.[20] Like the diffusion of the British factory system and the British notion of constitutional government, this was an epochal transformation. And like the popularity of eating beef, wearing neckties, and erecting public buildings in the lumpy Victorian style, this diffusion was not merely a matter of the efficacy of the gold standard as an institution but also a matter of adopting the civilizational markers of prestige and first-class status that attended national wealth and power. It was also a question of linking Japan economically with Europe or with Asia.

As the new Meiji government debated how to unify and modernize Japan's currency system, opinion at first leaned toward a system based on the silver dollar, the de facto trade standard of East Asia. In 1868 the Japanese government purchased the equipment of the British mint at Hong Kong and in 1871 began minting its own version of the silver dollar.[21] Itō Hirobumi, vice minister of finance, was then studying fiscal and monetary systems in America. He swung back and forth between favoring a bimetallic standard and a gold standard, finally recommending the latter "in accordance with the best teachings of modern times."[22] Following Itō's advice, the New Currency Law of May 1871 created the yen (*en*) and made it equal to 1.5 grams of pure gold. This action made Japan one of the very first countries, after Britain, to legally enact a gold standard. The value chosen made the gold yen nearly identical in value to the Mexican silver dollar, the standard trade dollar of the day, which was also the model for the U.S. dollar.[23] At the same time, however, the Meiji government also minted a full-weight silver yen modeled on the Mexican dollar for foreign-trade purposes, giving Japan in practice a bimetallic currency system.

Foreshadowing the wave of foreign borrowing after 1897, the new government also approached the London capital markets for a loan. The Meiji government's first foreign loan, raised in London in April 1870, was for £1 million at 9 percent, to construct Japan's first railroad, an eighteen-mile line from the newly renamed capital, Tokyo, to the new treaty port of Yokohama. With the success of this enterprise, the government took out a second loan of £2.4 million in January 1873, also in London, for the commutation of samurai stipends into interest-bearing government bonds. Thus, the new government borrowed money from British capitalists for the purpose of dissolving feudal obligations at home (very literally, for capitalizing them). Many former samurai in turn used their bonds as capital for founding Japan's first national banks.

Itō's gold-standard plan, however, did not work. First, the government lacked the gold reserves necessary to back up a gold standard. Further, the policy of minting both full-weight gold and silver yen coins, at a time when silver prices were beginning to drop, encouraged foreign traders to exchange their silver yen for gold ones, and thus Japan, like other bimetallic countries, experienced an outflow of gold and was pushed onto a de facto silver standard.[24] Western criticism of Japan's failed gold-standard aspirations is also revealing of the status dynamics of international monetary relations. "So long as silver is and remains the great medium of exchange throughout the East, Japan is only placing herself in an entirely false position in adopting a gold standard," opined the *Japan Mail,* a newspaper of Japan's treaty port community in 1876.

> Doubtless the Finance Minister of the time thought that what England and America had done, could not be wrong; and his successor has been fortified in that belief by the example of Germany and Holland [in adopting the gold standard]. And if Japan were an European country, they might have done well in thus deciding. But it is an Oriental country, and—in all probability—will remain so. Many curious things are and may be done in countries despotically governed, but it might have been better to realize once for all that Japan, whatever else it may do in the future, is obstinately a geographical fixture. . . . Japan was, we fear, too much influenced by the desire to do what England and America had done because she wished to place herself on some imaginary footing with England and America.[25]

In a hierarchically ranked world of colonizers and colonized, Japan thus entered the European world order with a peripheral, nearly semicolonial status. It became the great mission of the statesmen of the new Japan to remove the disabilities of that status and gain parity with the Western imperial powers. Domestically, the new Meiji government also issued its own paper money, which became increasingly disconnected from the worlds of either silver or gold. In effect, inconvertible paper money was used internally, and international money—silver dollars—was used for external payments.[26]

At this point, there occurred a monetary cycle of a sort that would be repeated after the Sino-Japanese War, after the Russo-Japanese War, and—on an international scale—after World War I. In 1877 the government financed the "Southwest War" against rebellious former samurai in Kyushu by a further issue of inconvertible paper money. The national banks, recently established on the U.S. model, also increased the issue of their own private banknotes, helping to fuel an inflationary boom. A debate arose within the government over how to adjust the inflated paper currency and restore specie convertibility. Finance Minister Ōkuma Shigenobu (1838–1922), drawing on the ideas of the Westernizing intellectual Fukuzawa Yukichi, proposed in late 1879 to establish a "specie bank" that would purchase silver coins and bullion and issue silver certificates in their place, thereby concentrating Japan's specie resources in the hands of the government. The semigovernmental Yokohama Specie Bank was accordingly established in February 1880.[27] Ōkuma also proposed a positive policy of raising foreign loans to finance industrial development, which would in turn strengthen exports and balance Japan's foreign-trade accounts. In the early part of 1880, he proposed to stabilize the currency by raising a gigantic loan of ¥50 million in London (at a time when the entire national budget was ¥63 million).

Ōkuma's foreign-loan plan was rejected as dangerous to national independence. This was not an idle fear: British creditors, backed by military force, were just at the moment seizing control of Egypt under the pretext of collecting the debts owed them, most of which had accrued as part of a disastrous deal to underwrite the construction of the Suez Canal. As a youthful Sakatani Yoshio saw it in 1881, if Japan's government by some financial mismanagement were to fail to repay foreign loans, "then we [would] have no alternative but to be the Turks or Egyptians."[28] Thus, after the 1873 loan, Japan did not borrow abroad again until 1897. By that time Japan was itself undertaking a campaign of financial imperialism—on the Egyptian model—in Korea.

In place of Ōkuma's scheme the government adopted an alternative plan put forward by Inoue Kaoru, who called for the government to cut spending and promote exports. Contained within Inoue's proposal was a call, similar in intent to Ōkuma's intentions for the Yokohama Specie Bank, to establish a "Bank of Japan," which would promote exports and attract specie by lending money in paper yen to exporters and then taking payment in the specie they received from the sale of their goods abroad.[29] As Ōkuma was forced by stages from his position of influence, the Specie Bank itself became, in line with a proposal of Maeda Masana, an institution for promoting exports and dealing in foreign exchange, which had previously been controlled by foreign banks. In this it was successful. The Specie Bank immediately began to create an international branch network by setting up offices in Japan's New York and London consulates in 1880 and 1881. The government lent paper money to the Specie Bank, which lent it in turn to exporters on the security of their exported goods. The bank returned the specie received in payment to the government.[30]

Ōkuma was calling at the same time for the immediate establishment of British-style constitutional government, and in October 1881 the Chōshū and Satsuma oligarchs forced him from the government.[31] Matsukata Masayoshi was appointed finance minister, thereafter retaining the finance portfolio for most of the next nineteen years—by far the longest tenure of any cabinet minister in Japan's modern history. Matsukata also completed the policy turn from inflation to deflation by implementing a currency stabilization policy and returning Japan to a hard-money standard, at the cost of a severe depression.

To address Japan's lack of capital and the efflux of specie due to the trade deficit, Matsukata proposed in March 1882 to establish a Bank of Japan, to act as a sole bank of issue and to coordinate and oversee the private banking system, "somewhat in the same way as a head office looks upon its branch offices." That is, the Bank of Japan would take direction from the Ministry of Finance, and the Specie Bank and all other banks would take direction from the Bank of Japan. Matsukata's vision of the function of central banks was also distinctly bullionist: the Bank of Japan would follow the example of "foreign governments," which "are all the time making very strong efforts through their Central Banks to absorb the specie that might otherwise never return."[32] This concern to concentrate specie (that is, foreign exchange) goes back to the original "statist" side of the gold-standard system; and while finding no place in the orthodox market-oriented theory of automaticity and free gold flows, it has historically been at the heart of the story. In June 1882 the Bank of Japan was established by imperial ordinance, and it opened for business in October.

By withdrawing the existing paper money from circulation, Matsukata forced down domestic prices and restored the value of the paper yen to a par with silver. Matsukata officially placed the yen on a silver-standard basis in May 1885, when the Bank of Japan began to issue banknotes, redeemable in silver.[33] The "Matsukata deflation" ended, and a renewed, moderate inflation got underway. In 1893 Finance Minister Matsukata took the first steps to prepare for a transition to the gold standard. In 1897, as the culmination of years of financial institution building, he completed the project, following a German precedent.

DEFLATION IN THE GOLD BLOC

The historiography of the Western economies in the late nineteenth century presents dueling images. On one hand, there is the long-established idea of the "Great Depression," which before it came to signify the global crisis of the 1930s, referred to the period from 1873 to 1896, an age of almost continual price deflation and deep, intractable depressions.[34] On the other hand, many economic historians tend instead to take as a unit the age of the "classical" gold standard from circa 1870 to 1914, foregrounding high levels of international trade, free capital flows across international boundaries, and a smoothly working system for settling international payments, to yield an image of a golden age of globalism and stability, irreparably shattered by the tragic "exogenous shock" of 1914. Partly, the difference of view depends on one's choice of periodization: depression set the international tone for much of the period from 1873 to 1895, and prosperity from 1896 to 1913.[35] The view also depends on whether one looks at things from the standpoint of the metropolitan financial hubs of the global system or from its agrarian peripheries. But remarkably, at the center of both of these opposed views is the fact of the generalization of Britain's gold standard during this period.

Britain adopted a unitary gold standard in 1816, and the eighty years that followed were an age of systemic deflation in the increasingly British-centered world economy.[36] Major gold discoveries in the late 1840s and in the 1890s interrupted this long-run tendency, and World War I, when the gold standard was universally suspended, brought another great inflation, comparable to that of the Napoleonic Wars. With the general restoration of the gold standard in the 1920s came renewed deflation. In this sense as in others, the "restoration" of the 1920s was the final, jangled reprise of the long nineteenth century.

It was during the final phase of the long nineteenth-century deflation, from 1873 to 1896, that the fall of prices in the gold bloc became most continuous and systematic. What happened then was in several ways a preplay of the final deflationary crisis of the global gold-standard system in the 1920s and early 1930s.

At the beginning of the 1870s, most of the core countries had bimetallic standards, and Britain was the only large country to use a monometallic gold standard. By the end of the decade, all of the core industrial countries operated unitary gold standards. Prussia's defeat of France and establishment of the German empire in 1871 set in train a sequence of monetary events. Seizing the chance presented by victory, Germany imposed on France a great indemnity of 5 billion francs—about one-third of France's gross national product (GNP) at the time. The German government used these funds to provide the gold reserve needed to switch to the gold standard.[37] This leveraging of military power into financial power became a model for Japan's adoption of the gold standard a quarter century later. It also set off an international economic crisis. In the short run, the inflow of French money fueled a speculative postwar investment boom in Germany and Austria. In May 1873 the bubble burst when the Vienna stock market crashed, and Germany was immediately swept up into the panic. In September, bank failures and financial panic also erupted in New York.[38] This was the abrupt beginning of what later became known as the Great Depression.

Germany's move from silver to gold also depressed silver prices at a time when world silver production was already increasing rapidly, setting off a general move away from the use of silver as a monetary standard. France and the United States both restricted the coinage of silver in 1873. Other countries went onto the gold standard one after another, further intensifying the scramble for gold and reducing the demand for silver.[39]

Thus, the deflation of 1873–96 was specifically a *gold* deflation. In England the purchasing power of gold in terms of real goods increased by more than 80 percent during the twenty-three-year deflation. At the same time, the purchasing power of silver actually fell by 6 percent.[40] Monetary politics accordingly came to the forefront of popular concern in a way that would happen again in the 1920s, and precisely because of its deflationary effects, the gold standard became the target of populist attack and the subject of a vast polemical literature. Farmers were typically the group worst affected by deflation, as crop prices and land prices fell year after year, while mortgages and other debts grew heavier in real terms. By the same token, bondholders saw the real value of their returns increase year by year. Thus, the gold standard, as anti-gold activists such as William Jennings Bryan saw it, squeezed "the struggling masses" to benefit "the idle holders of idle capital."[41] This social dynamic was recapitulated at the international level, with England appearing as the world's great creditor power.

Silver-standard Japan, however, was insulated from the gold-bloc deflation: instead of Japanese domestic prices deflating, the value of the silver yen depreciated for twenty-three years relative to the gold-backed Western currencies.[42] Thus, the yen began life in 1871 at a level of ¥1 = US$1. By 1896 the yen had lost one-half of its value relative to the U.S. dollar (which returned to gold convertibility in 1879). Japan's adoption of the gold standard in 1897 then fixed yen-dollar rates at a new level of nearly fifty U.S. cents to the yen. This level would be maintained, with interruptions, until the final crisis of Japan's gold standard in December 1931.

As the silver yen depreciated, Japanese domestic prices increased by almost 40 percent from 1873 to 1896.[43] The increased price of Western goods in Japan provided de facto protection for domestically oriented Japanese producers, and the decreased price of Japanese goods in the gold bloc stimulated Japanese exports. A similar combination of inflation internally and deflation externally would appear again in 1932 and 1933, when Finance Minister Takahashi Korekiyo cut the yen loose from gold and allowed it freely to depreciate, helping Japan to recover early from the world economic crisis.

In 1897, as Japanese luck would have it, the long gold-bloc deflation had come to an end. One reason for the upturn in prices was a series of new gold finds in the 1890s, in South Africa, Australia, and the Yukon. As British luck would have it, these were all within—or about to be within—the British Empire.[44] Another reason was that the form of the gold standard that spread in the 1890s to the peripheral regions of the world—including Japan—was a qualitatively new institution, the *gold-exchange standard,* that represented a new extension of the principle of monetary leverage.

TWO

Gold and Empire, 1885–1903

In 1885 Fukuzawa Yukichi, the Meiji era's most famous Westernizer and a leading advocate of liberalism and constitutional government, wrote an editorial asserting that Japan should "leave Asia" (*datsu-A*) and join the West. To associate with neighboring China and Korea would invite Westerners to view Japan as backward and Asian: "The person who is close to bad friends cannot avoid getting a bad name."[1] Fukuzawa's slogan has become well known, and it serves to encapsulate a whole set of systemic changes.

Japan's war with China in 1894–95 was the great turning point. In 1894, before the war, Ikeda Shigeaki, who as managing director of Mitsui Bank later led the speculative run on his country's gold reserves, went to study at Harvard College. He recalled how Japan was still undifferentiated from China in Western minds. "People would say things like, 'Which part of China is Japan in?' When I walked on the street, children would follow after me chanting 'chin, chin, Chinaman!' It was very unpleasant." Japan's defeat of China began to clarify the status distinction, "and for the first time, people understood that Japan was a different country." Rejoicing at news of a Japanese victory in the summer of 1894, Ikeda and his Japanese comrades, on holiday on the Maine coast, "gave a dollar to some Chinese guys who were around there and pretended we were chopping off their heads by the seaside."[2] China's humiliation was the culmination of a long-term shift in Japanese images of China[3]—China's displacement from civilized core to semicivilized periphery.

Monetarily too, Japan moved to join the West. This policy turn was part of a comprehensive regime shift in the late 1890s that encompassed the character of Japan's foreign trade, monetary system, industrial structure, and diplomatic relations. At the same time, Japan, like the United States, moved to leverage its international financial power by setting up its own nationally based gold-exchange standards in newly subordinated neighboring countries. Japan's new monetary regime was also part of a larger shift to gold in the 1890s, the beginning of the second wave of the universalization of the gold standard, which now extended to Asia.

"ENTERING EUROPE"

In 1892 Austria-Hungary took out a large foreign loan to place its currency on a gold-standard basis. In 1893 the colonial government of India demonetized silver and moved to adopt a gold standard tied to the British pound. These actions accelerated the appreciation of gold (or, as it was usually understood at the time, the downward slide of silver prices). In October 1893 Finance Minister Matsukata established the Currency Investigation Commission (Kahei Seido Chōsakai) to consider a gold standard for Japan.[4]

Opposition to the gold standard came especially from the export-oriented business community. For twenty-five years, silver had continually depreciated relative to gold, increasing the prices of Western goods in Japan and by the same token making Japanese exports cheaper abroad.[5] The pro-silver group was led by Shibusawa Eiichi. The gold standard was a symbol of first-class, European-style nationhood, but for most of Japanese business opinion, this symbolic value did not justify giving up the concrete trade advantages provided by a depreciating exchange rate.

On the other side, Ministry of Finance officials, led by Matsukata Masayoshi's chief lieutenants Tajiri Inajirō and Sakatani Yoshio, together with officials in the navy (also dominated by Matsukata's Satsuma clique), were dismayed by the rapid depreciation of silver because it raised the price of warships, munitions, and machinery, practically all of which were ordered from Britain and other gold-standard countries. They therefore favored the gold standard.[6] After nearly three years of deliberation, the Currency Investigation Commission remained divided. In its final report of July 1896 a majority of eight to seven recommended that Japan should change the present currency system. Six of those eight favored a gold standard, to be implemented at "some opportune moment in the future."[7] For Matsukata, that moment had already arrived.

As Matsukata later explained, the immediate obstacle to adopting the gold standard was the lack of sufficient gold reserves. In the 1895 peace negotiations at Shimonoseki between Prime Minister Itō Hirobumi and Grand Secretary Li Hongzhang, the size and conditions of the indemnity were among the most contested issues. Both men recognized that China would have to borrow abroad to raise the money. Half in jest, Li asked Itō at one point if Japan itself would be willing to lend China the money. Itō said no.[8] In the final treaty of April 1895, the amount of the indemnity was set at 200 million Kuping taels. The form of payment was not specified, and

Matsukata Masayoshi took advantage of this ambiguity to attach a new condition, proposing to Itō in May 1895 that the indemnity be made payable in British money—that is, gold—on London. As Takahashi Korekiyo understood Matsukata's intentions, "the Count wanted absolutely to take the indemnity in British pounds, and following the former example of Germany to seize the occasion for implementing the gold standard." China acquiesced to this condition in October. A further 30 million taels was then added to the indemnity to compensate for Japan's retrocession of the Liaodong peninsula.[9]

The total indemnity of 230 million silver taels was equal to £38 million, or ¥356 million—entirely covering the Japanese government's war expenses of ¥233 million and yielding a profit of ¥123 million. Payment in gold compounded the profits: from October 1895 until the payment of the last installment in May 1898, the price of silver on the London market fell 20 percent. Sakatani Yoshio reckoned the added gain for Japan (and loss for China) to be ¥65 million.[10]

The Bank of England had previously refused to open an account for the Yokohama Specie Bank. Now that the Japanese came with the Chinese money in hand, it did so. In fact, the money itself had been raised in London and other European capital markets. The final installment of the Chinese debt was by far the largest check ever drawn on the Bank of England up to that time.[11] British financiers were nervous about the effects of Japan's shipping so much in gold out of London at once, and so the Japanese government accommodated them by stretching out the gold shipments until 1903. In the interval the Bank of Japan issued yen notes in Japan backed by the money on deposit in London. Although considered a temporary expedient at the time, this fact also indicated Japan's new financial orientation toward London, and it created a precedent for Japan's de facto sterling-based gold-exchange standard as it developed after 1905.[12]

The Chinese indemnity provided the fund not only for Japan's gold standard but also for its first great heavy-industrial project, the state-owned Yahata (or Yawata) steelworks. It also enabled Japan's own overseas lending in Korea and later in China itself, as funds were directly transferred from the indemnity account to provide for foreign loans. At the same time, the Japanese government also began to borrow abroad after a twenty-two-year hiatus, by selling in London ¥43 million in domestically issued war bonds held by the Deposit Bureau of the Ministry of Finance. For the Qing government the indemnity meant the beginning of massive borrowing abroad, as the European powers scrambled to lend gold in exchange for new concessions and claims on Chinese government revenues.

Thus, after the fact, Japan's war against China was *entirely funded by the European capital markets.* This was done in a small way via Japanese borrowing and in a great way via Chinese borrowing to pay the indemnity to Japan. For all of these reasons, Sakatani Yoshio, looking back twenty years after, said that the Chinese indemnity "in every way still continues to circulate in the history of the Far East." Later, Sakatani went so far as to say that Japan owed its advance over China to the adoption of the gold standard.[13]

In September 1896 the second Itō Hirobumi cabinet resigned, and Matsukata Masayoshi formed his own second cabinet, serving concurrently, for the sixth and final time, as minister of finance. He now moved to adopt the gold standard. Thanks to Matsukata's deflationary currency stabilization policy fifteen years before, Japan already had an internally stable, silver-backed currency. Thus, Japan did not adopt the gold standard as England had done after the Napoleonic Wars, to stabilize an inflated currency and guarantee sound money domestically. Rather, as stated in an English-language report written primarily by Soeda Juichi and issued under Matsukata's name, Japan adopted the gold standard to enlist foreign capital in its national campaign of economic and military development.

> Since now [that Japan has adopted the gold standard,] the capitalists of the gold standard countries have become assured that they will no longer be in constant danger of suffering unexpected losses from investments made in this country, on account of fluctuations in the price of silver, they seem to show a growing tendency to make such investments at low rates of interest. This tendency, if encouraged, will doubtless bring about a closer connection between this country and the central money markets of the world.[14]

That is, for Japan as for other peripheral countries, the gold standard was desirable chiefly because it opened access to the European capital markets. In this, Count Matsukata was also responding directly to the move of his Russian counterpart, Count Sergei Witte, who adopted the gold standard in January 1897 in order to better obtain foreign financing for Russia's own industrial and imperial development.[15]

In its origins, Japan's gold standard therefore appears as an expansionary, or "positive," economic measure. Takahashi Korekiyo, then a director of the Yokohama Specie Bank and manager of the bank's head office, conspicuously backed Matsukata's gold-standard project. That is, the same man who in 1931 earned enduring fame for suspending the gold standard and closing Japan against the tides of global finance was working in 1896 to bring Japan into the mainstream of international capital flows. Takahashi at the same time expressed a characteristic nationalism, arguing against the pro-silver faction within the Ministry of Finance which said that advice should be sought from D. F. Jackson, head of the Shanghai office of the Hongkong and Shanghai Bank (the largest bank in East Asia and the British government's official financial representative in the region). "I absolutely opposed that," Takahashi later wrote. "In determining Japan's system, it is not necessary to listen to the opinion of foreign bankers."[16]

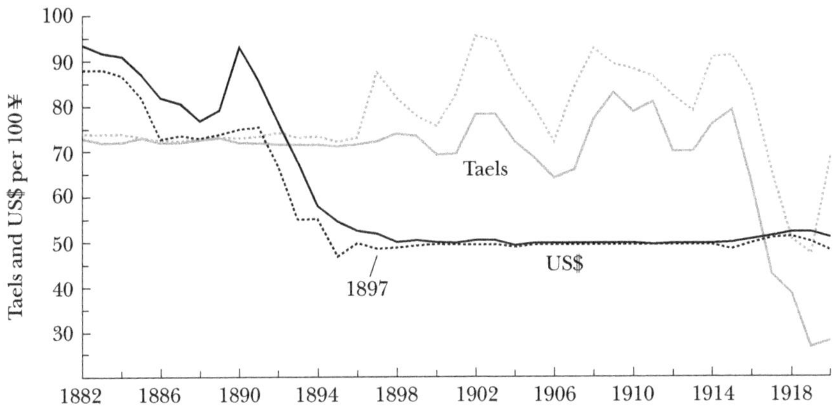

FIG. 2. Yen-tael exchange rate on the Shanghai market, 1882–1920, showing highest and lowest prices of each year, together with yen-dollar rates. The yen was effectively fixed to the gold dollar and unfixed from the silver tael in November 1897.

SOURCES: Asahi Shinbunsha 1930: 414; Nihon Ginkō Tōkeikyoku 1966: 319–321.

NOTE: It was conventional during the pre–World War II period for the dollar-yen rate to be quoted as the dollar price of one hundred yen. Thus, the gold parity fixed in 1897 meant a dollar-yen rate of $49.85 per ¥100.

In March 1897 the new Coinage Law put the yen on a gold standard as of October 1897, with a value of 0.75 grams of gold. This fixed the yen to a value of about one-tenth of a British pound, or very close to fifty cents in U.S. money—almost exactly 50 percent less than the value of the yen issued under Japan's first attempt at a Western-style gold standard in 1871. Bank of Japan notes now bore a legend indicating that they were convertible into gold instead of silver as formerly. "The reform was undertaken at a most favorable moment," as the Japanese government reported to its new foreign creditors, and owing to careful research and planning and to beneficial external circumstances, the monetary changeover was accomplished smoothly. In contrast to the disastrous restoration of the gold standard in 1930, the gold par was fixed at the yen's existing exchange rate, and so domestic prices were little affected.[17]

Fixing the yen in 1897 to the same standard as the British pound and the U.S. dollar also indicated Japan's new orientation to a worldwide trading area centered on London. By the same token, it meant unfixing the yen from its previous stable relationship to China's silver currency, and from 1896 to 1897 the fluctuation of the yen-tael exchange leaped by an order of magnitude (Figure 2). Japan's trade with the United States was also stabilized—henceforth subject to less violent annual fluctuations than its trade with China. This was the monetary aspect of Japan's "departure" from Asia.

As we have seen, Japan's adoption of the gold standard came at a moment of structural shift in Japan's industrial, diplomatic, and monetary regimes, and it was part of a new flurry of financial institution building that included the creation of five specially chartered semigovernmental banks between 1897 and 1902. Among these new public-policy banks were the Bank of Taiwan and the Industrial Bank of Japan, which would be key institutions in the extension of Japanese financial power overseas and in the mobilization of foreign capital for building Japanese industry and empire.[18] The Bank of Taiwan (Taiwan Ginkō) was also Japan's first colonial central bank, approved by the Diet at the same time that it passed the gold standard into law and actually established in 1899. Its charter was to act as Taiwan's bank of issue, to handle commercial banking business in Taiwan, and to further the advance of Japanese business into South China and Southeast Asia.[19] The Bank of Taiwan would later be at the heart of the great financial crisis of April 1927.

The Industrial Bank of Japan (Nippon Kōgyō Ginkō; IBJ), established in 1902, was designed specifically to import Western capital. Concrete planning for the project began in the spring of 1898, when Kaneko Kentarō, then minister of agriculture and commerce, proposed the creation of a government-backed bank to provide long-term industrial financing, which it would fund by issuing its own bonds overseas. Such intermediation would provide access to foreign capital without the danger of foreign control. It would also let the government control, at a step's remove, a new stream of industrial financing, to be directed to strategic infrastructure projects such as railroad building (especially for Taiwan and Hokkaidō), shipbuilding, steelworks, and port construction.[20]

The IBJ project also led to a first, failed approach to J. P. Morgan and Company. In March 1898, just as Takahashi Korekiyo was on his own parallel mission to London, Kaneko sent his own emissary to New York to seek Morgan and Company funding for the IBJ project. Kaneko's representative got no farther than a meeting with Morgan's general counsel, who informed him that Morgan was not interested in a Japanese loan.[21]

Takahashi Korekiyo had been promoted to vice president of the Yokohama Specie Bank in March 1897, the point when the gold standard was enacted into law, and at the beginning of 1898 he was sent by Inoue Kaoru to London to raise Japan's first really large loan. The Japanese government's foreign borrowing before the adoption of the gold standard totaled less than ¥20 million. To this could be added the ¥43 million in yen-denominated war bonds sold overseas in May 1897, although London bankers failed to take up the latter until the Japanese government agreed to put them on a gold basis.[22] The ¥100 million bond issue that Takahashi negotiated in London in 1898 was thus a new departure. The loan was ostensibly for neutral, nonmilitary purposes: railway construction, the extension of the telephone system, and the expansion of the Yahata steelworks, which had begun operations in 1897. These projects, however, were conceived of by the Japanese government as justified by military needs.

The timing of the loan, issued in June 1899, turned out to be poor. With war impending in the South African goldfields, British financial authorities were laying aside huge gold reserves, interest rates were rising, and bond prices were falling. Less than 10 percent of the Japanese loan was taken up in the initial public subscription, and so the Japanese government, assisted by the Bank of Japan, was forced to buy up some 45 percent of its own bonds, while the underwriting banks were stuck with the rest. Evidently, the Japanese government had overestimated its own credit status in London when it claimed that "Japan is now rated between Germany and Italy."[23] In September 1899 the underwriters attempted to interest J. P. Morgan and Company in the Japanese bonds, again without success. The British government itself was borrowing heavily to pay for its South African war, even to the extent of taking out its first major loan in the United States in 1900—which was handled by Morgan and Company. This too was a new departure, as the first great overseas loan conducted by American bankers, as a new phase in a long-running Anglo-American financial partnership, and as a first step foreshadowing the shift of international financial primacy from London to New York.

MONETARY LEVERAGE: THE GOLD-EXCHANGE STANDARD AS AN IMPERIAL SYSTEM

Part of the attraction of the classical gold standard to later generations of admiring economic historians has been the associated image of a whole, seamless world under the reassuring sway of British civilization. Keynes's famous invocation of the world that had been lost, in the opening chapter of his 1919 polemic, *The Economic Consequences of the Peace,* has been quoted many times. It is also highly pertinent and bears repetition here:

> What an extraordinary episode in the economic progress of man that age was which came to an end in August, 1914! . . . The inhabitant of London could order by telephone, sipping his morning tea in bed, the various products of the whole earth, in such quantity as he might see fit, and reasonably expect their early delivery upon his doorstep; he could at the same moment and by the same means adventure his wealth in the natural resources and new enterprises of any quarter of the world, and share, without exertion or even trouble, in their prospective fruits and advantages; or he could decide to couple the security of his fortunes with the good faith of the townspeople of any substantial municipality in any continent that fancy or information might recom-

> mend. He could secure forthwith, if he wished it, cheap and comfortable means of transit to any country or climate without passport or other formality, could despatch his servant to the neighboring office of a bank for such supply of precious metals as might seem convenient, and could then proceed abroad to foreign quarters, without knowledge of their religion, language, or customs, bearing coined wealth upon his person, and would consider himself greatly aggrieved and much surprised at the least interference. But, most important of all, he regarded this state of affairs as normal, certain, and permanent, except in the direction of further improvement.[24]

Here is the idea, and ideal, of global money. It is also the description of the money of one nation—the British pound. In the years around 1900 the gold standard that had originated in England was indeed becoming nearly universal, having spread in the 1870s to the other industrialized core countries and then on to the countries of the world's economic periphery. However, the great majority of people in this newly enlarged gold zone never saw gold coins. Nor could most of them, had they wanted to, have exchanged the gold-denominated silver coins and banknotes that they did use for gold coins. Gold (but in practice, mostly commercial bills drawn on London) was for international transactions, and gold coins actually circulated in a few of the core countries only.

That is, the form of the gold standard that was adopted in the peripheral countries of the former silver zone was the *gold-exchange standard,* a system pioneered in British India, in which foreign-exchange reserves, in this case sterling, substituted for actual gold reserves. In practice if not in name, this was also the form of the gold standard that was adopted in Japan. The gold-exchange standard was also the form of the gold standard adopted by most countries during the monetary restoration movement of the 1920s.

The gold-exchange standard was, significantly, the subject of Keynes's first book, *Indian Currency and Finance,* published in 1913. In that study Keynes was mainly concerned with the technical question of how a small amount of gold could be made to perform the monetary labor of a large amount of gold. The essence of the gold-exchange standard was that gold-backed foreign currency, such as the British pound, could replace gold as the reserve against note issue. Thus, in the case of India, British gold was doubly and trebly leveraged. In the first place, the Bank of England held gold reserves and fiduciary reserves (that is, statements of government and other debts payable to itself) that covered its own note issue. In turn, Bank of England notes, or credit instruments deemed to be readily convertible into Bank of England notes, were held—in London—as the reserves against which rupee notes and token silver coins were issued in India. These rupees in turn formed the reserves of Indian banks, which lent money (and created deposit money) on this basis.[25]

Historically, most of the countries that adopted gold-exchange standards before World War I had formerly been on a silver standard, and after these countries went over to gold-exchange standards, tokenized silver coins, now denominated in gold, remained the mainstay of domestic use. Charles A. Conant, a pioneering American international financial adviser who helped establish colonial gold-exchange standards in the Philippines and other American dependencies, explained it simply: "The gold exchange system may indeed be said to be an extension of the banknote system to token coins. The token coin is, in effect, a metallic banknote."[26]

The gold-exchange standard thus represented a further extension of the principle of financial leverage embodied in the orthodox gold standard itself. Existing national gold standards operated like fractional-reserve banking—also developing rapidly at the same time—in that governments (or their central banks) issued an amount of convertible banknotes greater than the amount of gold they held in reserve. This difference between the amount of reserves held and the amount of banknotes (or deposits) created also constituted a form of seigniorage—free money for those who could make the arrangement work.[27] Far greater than the direct profits that governments made out of this arrangement were the profits metropolitan banks could make by lending money (and creating deposit money) in newly incorporated monetary peripheries. Thus, what we may call "first-order" money in this system—gold—was leveraged into a larger supply of gold-based national monies, such as the British pound—"second-order" money. This second-order money in turn constituted the monetary base for banks that leveraged it into a much greater volume of money by making loans and creating bank deposits—"third-order" money. In a like way, gold-exchange standards in peripheral countries pyramided gold-based foreign exchange money such as the British pound into third-order or fourth-order money. While such a description is too simple and schematic to capture the complexity of many actual monetary arrangements, it suggests the leveraged, multilayered structure of the international gold-standard system.[28]

As with fractional-reserve banking, the leveraged gold standard was also a confidence game, depending on the trust of those who held the bank deposits or convertible paper notes—an extension of banking logic to entire countries. Thus, any nation could figuratively be viewed as a bank, as Morgan and Company economist Russell Leffingwell advised the Japanese government in 1928; accordingly, a country needed to be prepared "to pay all depositors in full on demand."[29] And as a bank might be subject to a run on its reserves if depositors doubted that it could continue to redeem its deposits on demand, so too an entire country could be subject to a run on its national gold reserves if holders of the national currency doubted that the country could continue to maintain gold convertibility. As specie-backed gold standards were leveraged into gold-exchange standards so that a given amount of gold could support a progressively greater volume of money and credit, the possibilities of systemic crisis became greater. These possibilities would become manifest, to a degree no one had imagined, in the summer and autumn of 1931, when the British-centered world monetary order abruptly collapsed.[30]

To guard the leveraged private banking system against bank runs, central banks, following the model of the Bank of England, began to operate as lenders of last resort, ready to supply emergency loans of currency to banks in distress. To guard the leveraged national gold standards that central banks themselves operated, international gold loans might be required. Thus the British financial system, historically much more highly leveraged than the French (that is, operating on a larger scale with slimmer reserves), could work because, in moments of crisis, the Bank of England could call on the Paris capital markets.

Although first developed for application in colonial and peripheral contexts, the gold-exchange standard was also the monetary wave of the future, proving to be more economical in the use of specie and, as Keynes explained, more "elastic" (capable of expansion) than the old-fashioned gold-coin standard. The profits of converting a silver-standard system over to a token coin system could also be substantial. Keynes put the gains on the coinage of rupee token coins at about 42 percent of their nominal value in 1910–12.[31] And of course paper money was much more profitable than that. These gains naturally accrued to the issuers rather than the users of the money. China especially, with its enormous circulation of silver, seemed to Conant and other foreign monetary engineers to offer dazzling possibilities.

The gold-exchange standard was also a question of empire. As he would not do in his later analyses of European affairs, Keynes in the case of India ignored the international power politics involved. Viewed from the more peripheral countries, these politics appear front and center. In particular, gold-exchange standards would prove an effective mechanism for draining specie from the colonies for metropolitan use—an extension internationally of the mercantilist logic that Ōkuma and Matsukata had perceived in domestic central banking.[32] The extension of gold-exchange standards after 1900 thus meant that the gold-standard world, which appeared so seamless from the vantage point of London financiers, came to be divided internally into subblocs—monetary spheres of influence based on the British pound, the French franc, the German mark, the U.S. dollar, and the Japanese yen. This fundamental fact has not been well reflected in the anglophone literature on the gold standard.[33] In fact, the politics of international monetary hegemony were played out most plainly in the construction of these monetary subblocs. China, as the world's last great silver frontier, became a battleground for competing gold-exchange standard schemes.

On paper, Japan's new gold standard was an orthodox gold standard such as existed in Britain. (The legal rules are summarized in appendix A below.) Bank of Japan reserves were to be held mainly in gold, and to prepare for the inauguration of gold convertibility in 1897, ¥74 million in new gold yen coins were minted in Osaka. In actuality, as Inoue Junnosuke later explained,

> Gold coins have never been placed in circulation [in Japan]. What actually circulated was convertible notes issued by the Bank of Japan. Gold is used only in the payment of foreign accounts, in exchange for the bank notes in question, flowing out usually direct from the holdings of the Bank of Japan to foreign countries,—a condition which marks the experience of Japan in the use of coin as entirely different from that of western countries.[34]

The name was not used, but Japan's usage, especially after 1905, was essentially similar to the new gold-exchange standards of Russia, India, the Philippines, and other peripheral countries, which either found it convenient, or were compelled, to maintain gold and foreign-currency reserves in London, Paris, or New York. In this way, the geography of the various gold-exchange standards reflected the geographical hierarchies of imperialism. As Charles Conant explained in 1909, gold-exchange standards using silver token coins were appropriate for the less advanced countries of the Orient. "In the advanced countries," however, "gold and gold alone is the proper form of the full legal tender coin."[35] The cultural signs of power and prestige were formed by these asymmetries. Inoue Junnosuke's career is a case study of this process at work, as Inoue strove not only to introduce to Japanese banking the best British and American practice but also to transmit to Japanese bankers Britain's gentlemanly ethos and style.[36]

After returning from England in 1899, Inoue worked at the Bank of Japan's main office in Tokyo until 1901, when he was sent again to the bank's Osaka office, now as an inspector (*chōsayaku*). In Inoue's case, this position made him, at age thirty-two, virtually the branch manager of the Bank of Japan's second largest office.[37] Inoue arrived during the construction of the new Bank of Japan building (still standing today) at Nakanoshima, and he personally managed the details of the construction, even going out to the mountains to select the timber to be used. The local branch staff was then meagerly educated, and Inoue insisted that they read books and attend his lectures. A great believer in the healthful effects of British-style sport, Inoue himself had taken up golf, tennis, and bicycling, and he had a tennis court built behind the bank. His most visible reform, if one poorly suited to the tropical heat and humidity of Osaka summers, was to insist against considerable resistance that the bank staff abandon Japanese dress, still the predominant style in the Osaka business community, in favor of Western-style suits. Implicitly, Inoue's clothing reform marked Japanese customs as private if not inferior and British customs as modern, public, and superior. His concern for proper, British form also marked an early episode in his relationship with Kansai industrialist Mutō Sanji (1867–1934), who later became one of Inoue's harshest critics. In sending out invitations to the formal opening of the new bank building, Inoue specified that frock coats were to be worn. Mutō, who was stopping by on his way back from a trip to Tokyo, showed up wearing a morning coat and was turned away at the door.[38]

GOLD-STANDARD IMPERIALISM

Building a Yen Bloc

Even as the Japanese yen came to be based on a British sterling standard, Japanese policy makers were working to extend the circulation of the yen on the Asian mainland, creating the beginning of a yen-based gold-exchange standard in Korea. This was a new extension of the principles of monetary leverage.

Efforts to establish a Japanese financial presence in Korea had begun in the wake of Japan's forced opening of Korea to foreign trade in 1876, when the Japanese government lent money to Shibusawa Eiichi's Dai-Ichi (First) Bank so that it could establish a branch at Pusan in 1878. This was the first step overseas by a Japanese bank. Twenty-seven years later Dai-Ichi Bank would assume complete control over the Korean monetary system.

In September 1882 the Japanese government imposed a ¥550,000 indemnity on Korea in the Treaty of Chemulpo. Directly thereafter, with Inoue Kaoru's support, the Japanese government also made its first overseas loan. It was also a kind of extortion: ¥170,000 lent to the Korean government via the Yokohama Specie Bank, in part so that the Korean government could pay the Japanese indemnity. A Japanese mission that included followers of Yukichi Fukuzawa went to Korea to attempt to oversee the loan expenditures.[39] This first initiative ended in failure following a botched Japanese-backed coup in December 1884, after which the dominant Min faction at the Korean court rejected further foreign loans and elected instead to exercise its own, domestic means of monetary leverage by debasing the coinage and issuing a new nickel cash. Japan's failure to reform Korea via the use of financial leverage left a bad taste in Fukuzawa's mouth and resulted in his famously sour editorial on "leaving Asia."[40]

A second effort, undertaken during the Sino-Japanese War, was more nearly successful. In July 1894, shortly before hostilities broke out with China, Japanese forces occupied Seoul. In October Inoue Kaoru, having been made minister to Korea at his own request, arrived in Seoul and directed a frank effort to seize financial and administrative control. His model was the British seizure of Egypt twelve years earlier:

> What was England's pretext for intervening in Egypt? Was it not in the fact that England had obtained a position of real interest there by supplying Egypt with capital? I firmly believe that if we wish to solidify our position in Korea and establish a pretext for intervention in its internal affairs, we must obtain real interests there, whether through railroads or through loans, and by financial means create pretexts for extending our intervention to other kinds of relationships.[41]

In line with this thinking, Inoue staffed the Korean government with Japanese advisers and created a de facto protectorate for the duration of the war. He also began a flurry of efforts to arrange Japanese loans to the Korean government. During the war, local payments of military scrip by Japanese forces had created a temporary yen circulation in Korea; Inoue now tried to make this permanent. Inoue had great authority inside the Mitsui group, and Mitsui Bank made an offer, not taken up, to lend money to the Korean government in exchange for the right to act as the government's treasury and circulate the bank's own gold-denominated notes in Korea. Another deal was agreed to, though never realized, for the Bank of Japan to make a loan to the Korean government in yen notes, which would then circulate as legal tender in Korea for the term of the loan.[42]

These efforts at creating a yen-based currency standard collapsed when Japan's imperial advances provoked further European advances, especially by Russia, as the struggle to dominate Korea merged with the larger scramble for concessions in China. On April 23, 1895, at the instigation of Russian finance minister Sergei Witte, the governments of Russia, Germany, and France jointly demanded that Japan return to China the Liaodong peninsula in South Manchuria, over which Japan had assumed the same rights of perpetual sovereignty that it had in Taiwan. Simultaneously, Witte organized the Russo-Chinese Bank, funded by French capital, and arranged to lend money to China to pay the Japanese indemnity. The so-called triple intervention was followed on May 5 by a quadruple intervention, when the United States joined Germany, Britain, and Russia to protest Japan's efforts to gain exclusive concessions in Korea.[43]

The embattled Korean government attempted to use the Western powers against Japan, and Russian influence advanced to the point that in November 1897 a Russian fiscal adviser, Kir Alexeiev, was appointed by the Korean government, where he was "practically the Korean minister of finances," according to Witte. He set up a new bank, the Russo-Korean Bank, and attempted to end the local circulation of the Japanese silver yen. Then, at the height of the scramble for concessions in March 1898, when the Russians took a leasehold over the same South Manchurian properties they had forced the Japanese to vacate, they attempted to placate Japan by retreating from Korea. Thereafter, the extension of Japanese influence in Korea by means of railroad and financial concessions became a continuous march.[44] In the process, Japan established the foundations of its first colonial gold-exchange standard.[45]

British and Japanese imperial goals also began to harmonize into what would become a twenty-year military and financial alliance. In October 1897 Britain had sent a squadron of warships to Inchon to warn the Russians off their efforts to take over the Korean customs administration (hitherto headed by an Englishman). From the time of the 1898 crisis, and particularly in the latter half of 1901, Britain and Japan moved toward an alliance, finalized on January 30, 1902. Under Article I of the agreement, Britain recognized that Japan "is interested to a peculiar degree politically as well as commercially and industrially in Corea." For both island empires, the Anglo-Japanese alliance ended the historic policy of diplomatic "isolation" (as the British called their own policy), and it signified the entry of Japan into the alliance politics of the European state system.[46] The British alliance also opened financial doors. Matsukata Masayoshi himself visited London in 1902. Not long afterwards, with the quiet support of the British Foreign Office, the Japanese government raised ¥50 million by reselling domestically issued war bonds in London. Other loan issues followed.[47]

Japanese moves to create a yen zone in Korea were paralleled by the initiatives of another new Asian-Pacific empire, the United States, to establish a dollar zone in its own new dependencies. This colonial initiative was the fountainhead of the American-led campaign to restore the international gold standard in the 1920s—a movement to which Japan would itself become subject in 1929.

Building a Dollar Bloc

The gold standard originated as a core institution of British finance, and the gold-exchange standard was invented for British India, but American ambitions entered the story of its international diffusion after 1900. In the 1950s the U.S. dollar would eclipse the British pound as the world's money, and the story of the origins of the international use of the U.S. dollar is a remarkable one. It is also remarkable that this story has until recently been all but untold.[48]

Unlike Britain, where the gentlemanly creditor class was indisputably in political control, the half-agrarian, half-industrial United States was deeply divided over its de facto gold standard during the long deflation of the late nineteenth century. Only in 1900, with assistance from monetary expert Charles Conant, was the gold standard formally enacted into U.S. law. At the same time, the U.S. War Department's new Bureau of Insular Affairs sent monetary reform missions to Puerto Rico and the Philippines, where Charles Conant directed the establishment of a dollar-based gold-exchange standard with the advice of Professor Jeremiah Jenks of Cornell University.

The Philippine gold-exchange standard, enacted into U.S. law in 1903, provided the model for the monetary reforms that followed in other American-controlled territories.[49] These missions became the training ground for the first generation of U.S. overseas financial advisers, just now beginning their careers. Preeminent among them was Jenks's Ph.D. student Edwin Kemmerer, who later advised the governments of a dozen countries on the installation of gold-exchange standards.

The goal of the American initiative was to create a gold-dollar bloc centered on New York, on the model of the gold-sterling bloc centered on London. This was the first step toward a more concerted monetary rivalry with Britain. The essential idea was that dependent countries, under American fiscal supervision, would use U.S. gold dollars for external payments, while a tokenized silver coinage, denominated in terms of American gold dollars, would be minted for internal use. The currency reserve of the dependent country would be deposited in private banks in New York City.[50] One of the most important effects of the Philippine monetary reform was to help reorient Philippine trade toward the United States and away from the Asian silver-dollar sphere centered on maritime China—the Philippines' own "departure from Asia."

The silver bloc was now contracting rapidly. In October 1903 British authorities instituted an Indian-style gold-exchange standard in the Straits Settlements, over the uniform opposition of the Chinese and Malay business communities, which stood to lose by the disruption of their silver-based Asian trade.[51] The abandonment of silver standards further depressed the value of silver against gold, and the remaining silver-standard countries grew alarmed by the increasing burden of their external gold payments. In January 1902 the governments of Mexico and China, the chief silver-standard countries, requested U.S. help in finding a way to stabilize the exchanges between the gold- and silver-standard countries. The U.S. government accordingly sponsored a Commission on International Exchange consisting of Conant, Jenks, and New York banker Hugh H. Hanna, who led missions to Panama, Cuba, the Dominican Republic, Mexico, and China between 1903 and 1905. They adopted as their charter the task of inducing these countries to convert their silver standards to gold-exchange standards.[52]

British practice served as a model—so much so that Keynes disdained the new American gold-exchange standards as an "almost slavish" imitation of British practice in India, unworthy of study.[53] For Conant the methods "which have made Egypt blossom as a rose under British authority" were an inspiration, and after the Philippine currency reform, the U.S. government sent Edwin Kemmerer to Egypt to study British practice there.[54] The Egyptian model of fiscal control without formal annexation suggested itself especially in Panama, where the projected canal was to be America's Suez, enabling commercial and naval expansion in the Pacific. To secure the canal site, Panama was separated from Colombia and set up as a U.S. protectorate in November 1903. Charles Conant directed a Philippine-style currency reform which provided that the new Panamanian government would set aside gold paid by the United States for the canal franchise as a currency reserve, in a New York bank. J. P. Morgan and Company subsequently served as the dependent government's Wall Street agent.[55]

The point at which U.S. ambitions would directly contact those of Japan was China, to which Jeremiah Jenks led a mission in January 1904, on the eve of the Russo-Japanese War. A Chinese gold-exchange standard based solely on New York would stand no chance of international acceptance, and Jenks's initiative was characterized by the sort of multilateral cooperation that later materialized in the famous China consortium. Commission members thus traveled first to the capitals of Europe, where they met with representatives of the imperial banks that served their respective governments in East Asia—the Hongkong and Shanghai Bank, Banque de l'Indochine, German-Asiatic Bank, and Russo-Chinese Bank. To them Jenks proposed that China's projected overseas specie reserve be held jointly by all. Jenks also went to Tokyo, where he met with a committee chaired by Vice Minister of Finance Sakatani Yoshio, who would later, in rivalry with the international consortium, attempt his own monetary reform in China.

In China itself, Jenks's project met with disinterest and resistance on the part of the Qing government, in part because a renewed rise in the price of silver had removed the former pressure on gold payments. His mission ended in failure in August 1904.[56] In the meantime, with the help of both British and American capital, Japan established a new imperial position in Korea and in China itself.

THREE

The Sinews of War, 1904–1914

The Anglo-Japanese alliance became effective in January 1902. Its result was to ensure that Japan could fight a war with Russia without fear of another European power intervening. By October 1903 war appeared imminent, and in December the Japanese minister in London approached the British government for a war loan.[1] On the night of February 8, 1904, Japanese naval forces launched the war with a surprise torpedo attack on the Russian warships stationed at Lüshun (Port Arthur) in southern Manchuria and landed troops at Inchon in Korea. Korea was militarily occupied and a great land campaign was begun in Southern Manchuria. The war lasted until May 1905, fifteen months. It cost the Japanese government the previously unimaginable sum of ¥1.9 billion—almost six times the central government's total spending in 1903.[2] Forty percent of the expenses were paid by overseas borrowing.

LONDON, 1904: PUTTING THE GOLD STANDARD TO WORK

Maintaining its neutrality, the British government declined to guarantee a Japanese war loan, and so the Japanese government turned directly to the London financial market.[3] In February 1904, at Matsukata Masayoshi's initiative, Takahashi Korekiyo, now vice governor of the Bank of Japan, was dispatched as the Japanese government's special financial commissioner.

Traveling via Honolulu, San Francisco, and New York, Takahashi first discussed the possibility of a war loan with Wall Street bankers but found them uninterested. In late March, he proceeded to London. Again, A. A. Shand was instrumental in arranging meetings with British bankers, but Takahashi's negotiations ran into a series of difficulties. Initially, as Takahashi recorded in his diary at the time, "the bankers doubted the capability of the [Japanese] government in holding up the gold-standard."[4] Takahashi reassured them on this account—though in fact, BOJ authorities were growing alarmed that heavy gold outflows would force them to suspend the gold standard. Takahashi also heard rumors that the British were reluctant to be the only "members of the white race" to support Japan in a "yellow-white race war." Less abstractly, the British bankers also insisted that any loan be secured by pledging Japanese railroad revenues or customs duties as security, as was routinely done in loans to China and other peripheral borrowers at the time. They further demanded that a British administrator be sent to Japan to oversee the customs administration, as Sir Robert Hart did in China. "You gentlemen are mistaken in equating Japan and China," Takahashi told them—the Japanese government had never failed to repay even one penny of its public debt.[5] The bankers also suggested that the money that Japan borrowed should be retained in London, as part of the Bank of Japan's gold reserve for convertibility—in effect, that Japan begin to operate a sterling-based gold-exchange standard as India did.

Takahashi was also advised that he needed a truly well connected adviser and that "the Jews are the first-rate financier[s], and [Ernest] Cassel is most influencial in London. He can invite Rostchild as well as Morgan and so on." It was further suggested that Japan take out a big loan "so as to make [it an] Anglo-American concern."[6] Takahashi did establish a relationship with Cassel, who later assisted his efforts in a variety of ways and arranged for Takahashi to have an audience with King Edward VII.[7]

Takahashi's break came at the beginning of May. On May 2 came the news of a Japanese victory on the Yalu River, in the first land engagement of the war. On May 3 Japanese bond prices in the secondary market were up and Russian bonds down, and at a dinner that evening Takahashi met a "1st rate financier in America," Jacob Schiff of the New York investment bank Kuhn, Loeb and Company. As Takahashi recorded at the time, "The first victory on land has brought out the new idea of [the] American market." In fact, Cassel and Baring Brothers had already approached Schiff, who apparently was ready to get involved in the deal before he met Takahashi.[8]

Under Jacob Schiff's leadership, Kuhn, Loeb and Company had become a powerful force in American finance and lent especially actively to what would now be called "emerging markets." J. P. Morgan and Co., the lords of American finance, had grown rich by importing British capital into the United States; Kuhn, Loeb had begun to rival them by serving as a conduit for German investment into the United States. The rivalry was ethnic as well as commercial: the German-Jewish Schiff was viewed as an upstart by the Anglophile Morgan firm, where anti-Semitism was a deep and self-conscious part of the corporate culture, reflecting the pervasive prejudice of the U.S. eastern establishment of the time as well as the concrete circumstances of competition in the investment banking business.[9] At dinner on May 3 Takahashi was seated next to Schiff, who listened with great interest to Takahashi's account of Japan's struggle with Russia and, it seemed to Takahashi, then and there decided to lend his power to Japan's cause. As Takahashi later recalled, "[Mr. Schiff] had a grudge against Russia on account of his race. He was justly indignant at the unfair treatment of the Jewish population by the Russian government, which had culminated in the notorious persecutions. . . . He felt that if defeated, Russia would be led in the path of betterment, whether it be by revolution or reformation, and he decided to exercise whatever influence he had for placing the weight of American resources on the side of Japan."[10]

The entry of the Americans greatly strengthened the loan issue, and on May 8 Takahashi recorded, "In the City Chats in this morning's *Sunday Times,* the Japs beat Russ in finance also." The next day, Shand and Schiff informed Takahashi that everything was settled, and Schiff told of his own royal audience: "the King was satisfied to the American participation. That shows Anglo-American combination in the far East." Financially, London could have underwritten Japan's war effort independently, but, Schiff related, "the king was glad that his country alone was not to supply money to Japan."[11]

The London bankers would ordinarily have brought the French into any equally big undertaking, but because of France's support for Russia, the Paris capital market was closed to Japan, and so the British turned instead to New York. From its side, American finance at this stage of the Anglo-American partnership was not yet ready to operate independently of the British.[12] As the *Wall Street Journal* enthused, the Japanese war loan was New York's "first big step toward the position of an international market." Offering an effective yield at issue of 6.4 percent, the combined Anglo-American loan of May 1904, for a total of £10 million, was oversubscribed by five times in New York and by thirty times in London. Frantic would-be subscribers at the London office of the Hongkong and Shanghai Bank pushed aside the police, bent bank railings, and caused the bank management to call out its staff rugby players to maintain order.[13]

The Anglo-American loan also saved Japan's gold standard. Bank of Japan governor Matsuo Shigeyoshi had been imploring Takahashi by letter and telegram to issue a loan absolutely as soon as possible—gold had left the country in unexpected volume after the war began, and it was increasingly difficult to maintain gold convertibility. With the news of the Anglo-American loan, the gold outflow stopped. To Takahashi the loan thus came as "divine providence" (*ten'yū*).[14]

Takahashi had also been compelled to accept terms extremely favorable to the lenders. These had included securing the loan "by a first charge on the customs receipts of the Empire," although, unlike the conditions placed on loans to China, the administration of those revenues was not placed in foreign hands. As the *Bankers' Magazine* of New York editorialized, "The pledge of specific revenues is usually made as security for loans by nations of second rate credit, and this perhaps is the galling feature to Japanese pride."[15] For these reasons, the loan was criticized in Japan.

In the meantime, Takahashi had entered actively into the social life of British banking circles, deliberately putting off negotiations for a second war loan until the autumn in order to maintain Japan's "dignity in financial matters." In the September negotiations, the foreign bankers again insisted on a loan secured by Japanese railroad revenues. This time Kuhn, Loeb held out for more onerous terms than did the British, to such a degree that Takahashi proposed to the British not to invite American participation in the second loan. Kuhn, Loeb then came around, and the £12 million deal, secured by a second charge on the Japanese customs receipts, was finalized in early November. With £22 million on tap, "the interest as well as the sympathy of the British and American groups, with the wide investing public behind them, was now firmly interwoven with the destiny of Japan," as Takahashi later wrote.[16] His business in London concluded, Takahashi left for New York in December 1904.

In 1924 J. P. Morgan and Company would become the Japanese government's American bankers, but in December 1904 approaching the great Morgan was still perceived to be a very delicate operation. Exhausted by his mission, Takahashi did not even attempt it, despite efforts to arrange a meeting by Japanese minister Uchida Yasuya (Uchida Kōsai) and by Baron Kaneko Kentarō, who was in the United States as the prime minister's personal representative. Kaneko further warned Takahashi that Morgan was "antagonistic to Japan" and had even tried for a Russian loan in New York. Takahashi "told him not to perplex much, Kuhn Loeb is strong enough to prevent any mischief that might come from Morgan." In fact, Russian finance minister Sergei Witte later recounted that when he came to America for the peace talks in 1905, he was graciously hosted by Morgan, who "offered me his services" in regard to a postwar loan, while "insisting that I should not enter into any negotiations with the Jewish group of bankers headed by Jacob Schiff."[17] Despite Morgan's perceived antagonism, Kaneko nevertheless suggested other people through whom Takahashi could arrange to meet with Morgan.

Takahashi did enjoy a cordial visit with the Schiff family in New York and then returned home in January 1905, after eleven months abroad. After the successful conclusion of the war, Mr. and Mrs. Schiff and friends visited Japan in 1906, where they were hosted by the Takahashi family. Takahashi's only daughter then accompanied the Schiffs back to America and lived with them for three years, becoming like a member of the family. Until

Schiff's death in 1920, Takahashi and he carried on a warm and sympathetic correspondence.[18]

Ultimately, with Jacob Schiff's help, Takahashi raised four great war loans between May 1904 and July 1905 in the financial markets of London, New York, and Berlin, for a total of £82 million (¥800 million). Of this, £36 million, or some $175 million, was raised in the United States.[19] This sum, ¥800 million, was double the government's annual revenue at the time. It also exceeded the combined deposits of all Japanese banks.[20] Foreign money, as Takahashi saw it, made the difference between victory and defeat, and the British and American banking groups saw the giant loan issues of 1905 as a message to dissuade Russia from continuing the war. Writing in an English-language memorial on the occasion of Schiff's death, Takahashi (or Fukai Eigo writing for him) quoted the just-published memoirs of Sergei Witte, "We had exhausted all our means and had lost our credit abroad. There was not the slightest hope of floating either a domestic or foreign loan. We could continue the war only by resorting to new issues of paper money." "The financial support of our foreign friends and the foreign investors," Takahashi concluded, "largely contributed to our success in the war and the consummation of the peace." Schiff, he said, had been "unfailing in meeting the needs of the Japanese Government in respect of the sinews of war."[21]

The flow of foreign funds was not infinite, however, and at the appropriate moment, Schiff applied pressure to force the consummation of the peace, warning plenipotentiary representative Takahira Kogorō that "the money markets of the United States, England, and Germany will, with the belief of a war *à outrance,* no longer be prepared to finance Japan's requirements to any great extent."[22] In Japan the financial burden was causing great pressure, and the government maintained gold convertibility through the war only with great difficulty.

To cover the war expenses, the Japanese government demanded an indemnity of ¥1.2 billion ($600 million) from Russia. But having lost the war, Russia was winning the peace. The United States again seemed to hold the balance, as President Theodore Roosevelt personally brokered the final settlement at Portsmouth, New Hampshire. Immediately perceiving the pivotal American role, Russia's plenipotentiary representative Count Witte skillfully suspended his aristocratic manners and played to American public opinion and racial prejudice. "If England and America cease rendering Japan material assistance and side morally with us," he cabled the Russian foreign ministry, "we shall come out victorious."[23] When the peace treaty was finalized on September 5, 1905, Russia paid no indemnity. The Japanese people would have to pay their own war expenses, plus interest. In Tokyo, outraged crowds rioted in the streets. Again it seemed to aggrieved nationalist opinion that Japan had won on the battlefield but had lost in the Western-controlled international political arena.

There were, however, other spoils of war. Japan took over Russia's twenty-five-year leasehold of the Liaodong peninsula, as the Guandong (Kwantung) Leased Territory. It also acquired the four-hundred-mile line of the Russian-owned Chinese Eastern Railway that ran from Changchun to Lüshun (Port Arthur). Renamed the South Manchurian Railway, this original expropriation immediately formed the greater part of Japan's overseas investments.

The Russo-Japanese War loans, critical in securing a continental empire for Japan, would continue to shape Japan's financial situation for the next twenty-five years. Two of the 1905 loans, with a combined value of £60 million, were due to mature in 1925. In 1931 the immediate postwar loan of £25 million would mature. It was the need to refinance the former two loans that led the Japanese government to turn to J. P. Morgan and Company in 1924, initiating a new era of Japanese borrowing from New York financial markets. It was the need to refinance the latter loan that helped force the schedule on Japan's return to gold convertibility, at Morgan and Company insistence, in the bitter depression year of 1930.

In the meantime, with the shooting war over in Manchuria, a new phase of financialized imperial rivalry got underway.

DEPENDENT FINANCIAL IMPERIALISM

During the breakneck contest to extend European empires in the late nineteenth century and the simultaneous explosion of European overseas investment, there developed the idea that modern imperialism was driven by modern capitalism's need to export capital. In the late-nineteenth-century context of gold-bloc deflation, constrained domestic demand, "overproduction," and sharp class conflicts, Western advocates of imperialism such as Charles Conant presented the creation of new markets overseas and the sale of surplus production there as the necessary solution.[24] The English radical J. A. Hobson reversed these pro-imperialist arguments, prefiguring J. M. Keynes in finding the crux of the economic problem to be oversaving by capitalists and underconsumption by workers. Lenin subsequently inflated Hobson's idea into a foundation for his theory of capitalism in its final stage.

But if the Hobson-Lenin theory that modern imperialism is driven by surplus capital seeking foreign outlets may tell us something about the character of British or French imperialism in the decades before World War I, it can have no relevance to the case of Japan's imperialism.[25] As we have seen, newly industrializing Japan suffered from a persistent capital shortage and went into debt to European and American capitalists in order to build its European-style empire. Nevertheless, the Japanese government made early efforts to establish itself as a creditor power in China. Japan's position in this regard was parallel to that of imperial Russia, which also went deeply in debt to France, Britain, and other Western European countries at the same time that it aggressively pushed its own loans on China. This debt-leveraged lending is a case of what has been called Japan's "dependent imperialism" of the early twentieth century.[26] The disintegrating Manchu empire provided the field of action.

As the Chinese indemnity of 1895 provided the ante for Japan's entry into the European gold game, it simultaneously brought China into Europe's financial orbit. Europeans had directed the administration of the Chinese customs since the 1860s, but prior to the Sino-Japanese War, the Chinese government had negligible foreign debt. The indemnity of 230 million silver taels changed this. Not only was the amount beyond the means of the Qing government, but, as Matsukata Masayoshi had arranged, the indemnity was to be paid in British money. The Chinese government also had to go to foreign lenders because Chinese merchants, having no recourse against their government, would not voluntarily lend money to it.[27] As they had done in the Ottoman Empire and elsewhere, the European powers took advantage of the situation by extending loans, in the process gaining increasingly direct control of Chinese government revenues. The Boxer indemnities in 1900 added a further burden of 450 million taels, also reckoned as a gold debt, to be paid over forty years and bearing an interest rate of 4 percent.[28] Japan's victory also opened China to direct foreign investment. In part to enlist British support for its cause, Japan wrote into the Treaty of Shimonoseki the right to engage in manufacturing in China;[29] by the most-favored-nation clauses that were a part of their treaties with China, the several European powers thus gained the same rights automatically. Japan was not yet financially able to invest substantially in China, but the Europeans were.

Acting through ostensibly private agencies, the Japanese government itself got into the business of lending money to China. The first of these loans was made on the eve of the Russo-Japanese War, in January 1904, when the Industrial Bank of Japan (Nippon Kōgyō Ginkō), acting under government instructions, lent ¥3 million at 6 percent to the Daye Mining Company in Hubei. Coming at a time when the Japanese government was not spending lightly on nonmilitary purposes, this loan was no ordinary business venture. Rather, it was intended to support politically directed heavy-industrial development at home by securing a source of iron ore for the state-owned Yahata steelworks, which had gone into operation in 1901 (and which itself had been funded in part by the Chinese indemnity and in part by the 1899 sterling loan). In 1908 the Daye Mining Company merged with the Hanyang Steel Company and the Pingxiang Coal Mining Company to form China's only steel company, the Hanyeping Coal and Iron Company. The Hanyeping Company subsequently became the biggest destination of Japanese lending to China in the years before World War I. Accordingly, it fell under Japanese financial control and became a dedicated supplier of iron ore for the Yahata plant.[30]

But the greatest prize of war was Korea. Japan's 1894 war with China had been fought to separate Korea from the pretensions of Chinese suzerainty, much as Britain had earlier removed Egypt from its nominal suzerainty to the Ottomans. The full protectorate that the Japanese government sought to establish in 1894 was achieved during the war with Russia, when the incipient yen zone was suddenly enlarged by the monetary and financial incorporation of Korea.

LEVERAGING THE GOLD STANDARD IN OCCUPIED KOREA

In 1902 the Japanese government gave the Dai-Ichi Bank permission to issue its own banknotes in Korea, under the direction of the Japanese minister of finance. The power to create money in Korea was at stake. The Korean government, backed by Russia, twice attempted to ban the use of banknotes, and was twice forced to rescind its move by Japanese government pressure. In February 1903 the Japanese government introduced a new set of rules to govern Dai-Ichi Bank's note issue in Korea and fixed a note issue limit of ¥5 million. By the end of 1904, ¥3.37 million in Dai-Ichi banknotes, backed by a reserve of Japanese currency, were circulating in Korea, signifying the beginnings of a yen-based gold-exchange standard there.[31]

Japanese forces occupied Korea in the opening weeks of the war with Russia. As in 1894, the Japanese government imposed a partial protectorate in a protocol signed by the Korean government on February 23, 1904. On the same day, the Korean emperor's financial adviser, Yi Yong-ik, who had attempted several times to set up a Korean central bank, was arrested and taken to Japan. At the end of May, shortly after the Japanese victory at the Yalu River and the conclusion of Takahashi's first big war loan, the Katsura cabinet approved a comprehensive plan for the complete political and economic takeover of Korea. They proceeded to execute it in a highly systematic way.[32]

The financial management of the seizure of Korea was carried out by Megata (or Mekata) Jūtarō, one of Matsukata's right-hand men at the Ministry of Finance, who under an agreement forced upon the Korean government on August 22, 1904, was made Korean financial adviser, with authority over all fiscal and monetary matters. As such, he also replaced the British chief commissioner of Korean imperial customs, John McLeavy Brown, who had been responsible for seeing to it that Korea's foreign creditors were properly paid. Megata arrived in Korea on October 14 and immediately took charge of compiling the Korean government's 1905 budget. He also terminated the Korean government's ability to create money, by ordering the closing of the Korean mint in November. On January 8, 1905, he ordered the implementation, as of June 1, of a gold standard.[33] A Japanese imperial ordinance authorized the Dai-Ichi Bank to implement the gold-standard reform, which it did in June and July of 1905.

Japan's reform of the Korean currency system meant the establishment of the first yen-based gold-exchange standard.[34] Its implementation is a case study in monetary leverage. On the one hand, the Dai-Ichi Bank arranged loans to the captive Korean government, issuing the first Korean government treasury bonds in June 1905, in Tokyo. Despite the tight wartime financial situation, the ¥2 million in bonds were oversubscribed by five times. Other bond issues followed shortly. Simultaneously, the bank directly lent ¥3 million to the Korean government at 6 percent interest. In turn, the Korean government gave ¥3 million back to the Dai-Ichi Bank to pay for the costs of the currency reform.

The monetary alchemy was only beginning. In July the Dai-Ichi Bank began to act as the Korean government treasury, making itself the repository of all these newly conjured-up funds. In the same month, it gained the right to issue full legal tender banknotes, backed by a reserve of Bank of Japan notes and securities (which consisted in part of the Korean government's new debts to the Dai-Ichi Bank). The existing Korean coinage was abolished at this point, and a Japanese-style token coinage was issued. Simultaneously, the Korean banking system was organized under Dai-Ichi Bank supervision. The Dai-Ichi Bank was thereby established as Korea's de facto central bank.

The 1905 monetary reform thus unified the Korean monetary system with the Japanese—with the significant difference that it was established not on the basis of reserves of the world money, gold (or sterling), but on the basis of the Japanese yen. As we have seen, gold functioned as a kind of fundamental, or first-order, money, and sterling banknotes, leveraged on the basis of a gold reserve, were a second-order money. As we will see shortly, the Japanese yen, leveraged on the basis of sterling reserves, became third-order money. The Korean yen, leveraged on the basis of Japanese yen notes, became fourth-order money. This monetary pyramiding thus represented and helped to constitute the hierarchies of international power.

As with the Bank of Japan itself, the Dai-Ichi Bank's reserve for convertibility was theoretically to provide 100 percent backing for the note issue. But up to ¥10 million of the Dai-Ichi's note issue could be covered by a reserve consisting of negotiable securities, and banknotes could be issued over the statutory limit at the discretion of the Japanese resident-general. Thus, as of December 1907, with ¥12.8 million in Dai-Ichi banknotes outstanding, the bank's reserve against note issue was formed as follows:[35]

"Specie" reserve	¥4.6 million. Of this, ¥0.9 million consisted of actual gold coins and bullion, and ¥3.6 million were Bank of Japan notes.
Security reserve	¥8.2 million. Of this, ¥4 million consisted of debts owed by the Korean government to the Dai-Ichi Bank. ¥6.2 million consisted of Japanese government bonds and other securities.
Total	¥12.8 million

Thus, a unified, modern, and stable currency system was created in Korea. It was at once a means of economic development and a means of Japanese expropriation of Korean resources. The Korean currency came to be based on a specie reserve held in Tokyo, which itself depended on a reserve held in London. Here was a textbook version of the principle of monetary leverage via the gold-exchange standard. Japan's successful utilization of the gold-exchange standard in Korea has been considered a foundation of the Japanese advance into Northeast Asia.[36]

Under the terms of the July 1905 monetary reform, Koreans were compelled to trade in their old Korean money (nickel and copper cash), mostly at half or less of its face value. The first result was to wipe out many Korean fortunes. In August 1905, there was a commercial crisis in Seoul, and the Chon-Il Bank, one of two Korean-owed Western-style banks, was forced to suspend payments. Korean commerce was thrown into a severe depression.[37]

The political takeover was completed in November 1905, when Itō Hirobumi led a carefully orchestrated coup d'état. Korea became a formal protectorate, with Itō as the first resident general. Korean fighters kept up a war of resistance until 1911. In November 1909 the Dai-Ichi Bank in Korea was reconstituted as the semiofficial Bank of Korea (Kankoku Ginkō), the central bank of still ostensibly independent Korea. After Japan annexed Korea as an outright colony in August 1910, the bank's name was changed to the Bank of Chosen (Chōsen Ginkō), but otherwise the bank continued as it was.[38]

Korea was thus incorporated into the Japanese monetary system after 1905. It was simultaneously removed from the field of imperial competition. The Japanese government guaranteed that Korea's existing foreign debts would be paid and that existing foreign concessions would be preserved. In line with assurances made by U.S. president Theodore Roosevelt in January 1905, Secretary of War William H. Taft visited Japan in July 1905 and signed a secret agreement with Prime Minister Katsura that recognized Japan's position in Korea in exchange for Japanese recognition of the American position in the Philippines. Britain provided much stronger assurances, extending the term of the Anglo-Japanese alliance for another ten years on

August 12. The renewed alliance now specified that if one party were attacked by any single power, the other party would join the conflict. It also extended the scope of the alliance to British India: in effect, Britain would defend Japan's colonial position in Northeast Asia, and Japan would defend Britain's colonial position from India east.[39] Under Japanese pressure, foreign diplomatic missions were withdrawn from Korea.

YEN DIPLOMACY AND DOLLAR DIPLOMACY IN CHINA

Manchuria became another frontier of Japan's new economic imperialism. Here again, British capital provided vital support for Japan's continental advance. After the costly war with Russia, the Japanese government was strained to pay even for the upkeep of the newly acquired South Manchurian railroad, which was in great disrepair and in need of double tracking. American businessmen immediately saw an opportunity. In August 1905, even before the peace treaty was concluded, American "railroad king" E. H. Harriman, a close business associate of Jacob Schiff, arrived in Japan to negotiate a deal for joint U.S.-Japanese control of the South Manchurian Railway, seeing it as a key link in his plan to create a round-the-world steamship and rail line under American management.[40]

In Tokyo Harriman's plan was favored by senior statesman Inoue Kaoru, who was close to the Mitsui interests, and by Soeda Juichi of the Industrial Bank of Japan. In line with their recommendation, Prime Minister Katsura signed a memorandum of understanding with Harriman in October that provided for joint U.S.-Japanese ownership and management of the South Manchurian Railway, although with continued Japanese control for the present. The Japanese government would provide the physical assets of the existing railroad itself and take half of the shares in the projected company, while Harriman would provide the money capital and take the other half of the shares. On returning from the Portsmouth conference, however, Foreign Minister Komura Jutarō vehemently opposed the alienation of Japan's hard-won gains and had the plan stopped. Harriman had already departed, and on arriving in San Francisco, he learned that the Japanese government had repudiated the deal. When Jacob Schiff visited Japan in the spring of 1906, he attempted to revive the deal for Harriman, without success.[41]

After taking office in January 1906, the new cabinet headed by Saionji Kinmochi set up a Manchuria Management Committee to determine a policy for Japan's new Manchurian properties. The committee's decision was that a single semigovernmental corporation, the South Manchurian Railway Company, should be established "to handle all of the economic rights in Manchuria."[42] Companies already doing business in South Manchuria—the

Yokohama Specie Bank, the Ōkura Group, Mitsui—would continue to do so, but otherwise no competition with the new company would be allowed. The organization of the company reproduced the fifty-fifty conception discussed with Harriman, but with direct foreign participation excluded. To capitalize the new company, the government would provide the physical assets gotten from Russia, in return for stock valued at ¥100 million. For operating capital, another ¥100 million in stock was to be sold to the Japanese public. Company management would be appointed by and receive direction from the government.

The first president of the enterprise was Gotō Shinpei (1857–1929). A German-trained medical doctor and the first civilian governor of Taiwan (1898–1906), Gotō was a man of high ambition who consented to take the job only after he had been convinced that the railway company was destined to be the institutional fountainhead of the whole colonial development of Manchuria. Brilliant and capable, unpredictable, full of grand schemes that were at once progressive, reactionary, and above all imperial, Gotō was as remarkable a symbol of his age of empire as were Cecil Rhodes or Theodore Roosevelt in their respective spheres. Following a policy that he called "military preparation in civilian clothing" (*bunsōteki bubi*), Gotō was also adamant that the South Manchurian Railway should not fall under American influence.[43] To guard Japan's new South Manchurian properties, ten thousand soldiers of the Japanese occupying forces were organized on August 1, 1906 as the Kwantung Army.

Raising money for the company remained a problem. At the initial public offering, made in the midst of the giddy boom that followed the war with Russia, applications for shares came to one thousand times the ¥100 million on offer. But this was ¥100 billion in dreams, and in the end a scant ¥2 million was actually paid in for company stock. Gotō's solution to the capital shortfall was to raise a huge foreign loan. In this he had the support of Finance Minister Sakatani Yoshio, and they jointly formed a plan to borrow money in the European and U.S. markets under Ministry of Finance management.[44] Because the Japanese government had broken its deal with Harriman, the American banking group organized by Kuhn, Loeb rejected the loan business. With the exception of one loan issued jointly with London and Paris in 1912, Japanese borrowers would raise no further long-term loans in America until 1923. The entire amount thus had to be raised in London. The South Manchurian Railway issued its first foreign bonds in London, in July 1907 and in June 1908, for a total of £6 million, or some ¥60 million. The actual work of raising the loan was carried out by Soeda Juichi of the Industrial Bank of Japan, with the cooperation of Wakatsuki Reijirō, now overseas financial commissioner, and his assistant Mori Kengo.[45]

Even with this foreign funding, lack of capital remained an obstacle to the realization of Gotō's expansive plans. Borrowing abroad was one method of raising money. Another was to leverage Japan's own slender monetary reserves by promoting the circulation of Japanese yen notes in Manchuria. Having helped lead the movement to establish the Bank of Taiwan in 1899, Gotō now began to lobby for the establishment of a new central bank in Manchuria.

The Yokohama Specie Bank, now under Takahashi Korekiyo's leadership, had begun to play such a role to a limited degree. The Specie Bank opened its first branch in South Manchuria in January 1900 at the port of Niuzhuang, and began to issue its own silver-backed banknotes there in January 1903. During the war with Russia, in the wake of the military advance, the Specie Bank opened new offices in the former Russian concession at Dalian (Dairen) and in Liaoyang, Mukden (Shenyang), and Tieling, where it handled the financial business of the Japanese army. After the war, the bank established additional offices at Kaiyuan, Changchun, and Harbin. Thus the Yokohama Specie Bank came to hold the same position, as a forerunner of direct colonial control, that the Dai-Ichi Bank occupied in Korea. During the war with Russia the Japanese government issued military scrip, declared to be redeemable in silver yen, for army use in South Manchuria. After the war the Yokohama Specie Bank was made responsible for redeeming these notes, which totaled ¥15 million. To help compensate the Specie Bank for this burden, the government also gave it the right to issue silver yen notes in Manchuria and ordered it to take steps to unify the Manchurian currency on the basis of a Japanese silver-yen standard.[46]

In October 1907 SMR president Gotō Shinpei met with Specie Bank president Takahashi Korekiyo concerning the financing of Manchurian development. Gotō proposed that the Specie Bank engage in agricultural and industrial financing and issue gold notes—that is, operate a gold-exchange standard as in Korea. Takahashi resisted, insisting that the Specie Bank was basically an exchange bank. As Takahashi reported their conversation, Gotō then suggested, as an alternative to the Specie Bank taking on this developmental role, that a new "colonization bank" (*takushoku ginkō*) be established instead. This latter suggestion, which Gotō never succeeded in realizing, can be considered the original plan behind the Manchurian Central Bank that eventually was established in June 1932, when Takahashi Korekiyo himself was finance minister. Gotō's suggestion for a Japanese institution to issue yen notes in China can also be considered the origin of the scheme for an East Asian yen bloc. At the time, fearing that the Specie Bank would only lose gold if put in the middle of China's speculative gold-silver trade, Takahashi recommended a silver-based currency for Manchuria.[47]

Gotō's plans for a Manchurian bank went no further at this point, but in the second Katsura cabinet (July 1908–August 1911), Gotō served as communications minister and president of the Railway Bureau, which again gave him oversight of the South Manchurian Railway. In 1909 he again tried to promote his Manchurian financing schemes. Takahashi Korekiyo, the Ministry of Finance, and the Yokohama Specie Bank continued to oppose Gotō's plans, and Gotō became more combative, warning heatedly of "Manchuria's postwar economic warfare" and the "boycott fever" directed against Japanese businesses there and asserting the need for a "Manchuria standard" (*Manshū hon'i*) as against the Yokohama Specie Bank's "Tokyo economy standard."[48]

Manchuria also remained a field for American ambitions. Directly after his visit to Japan in 1905, E. H. Harriman had made a survey trip to the continent. In Seoul, then falling rapidly under Japanese sway, he met U.S. vice consul Willard Straight, a young Cornell University graduate, and recruited him to assist in his grand railroad enterprise. In 1906 Harriman arranged for President Roosevelt to appoint Straight as U.S. consul general in Mukden. Maintaining close communication with Harriman, Straight attempted to arrange a project remarkably similar to Gotō Shinpei's own plan. In the summer of 1907 he signed an agreement proposed by Fengtian governor Tang Shaoyi to seek an American loan of $20 million to fund the establishment of a Manchurian Bank that would handle provincial government business, reform the Manchurian currency, issue its own banknotes, and finance development projects. This was a direct counter to Japanese initiatives and was connected also to Harriman's new plan to build a rail line to bypass the Japanese-owned South Manchurian Railway. Kuhn, Loeb later agreed to handle the loan. An American proposal to repurchase the SMR on China's behalf was also floated in 1908.[49]

In the fall of 1908 Tang Shaoyi was appointed special minister to the United States and proceeded to Washington, D.C., ostensibly to thank the American government for its partial remission of the Boxer indemnity but in fact to request a gigantic American loan of $300 million. Secretary of State Elihu Root and President Theodore Roosevelt supported the idea, but Tang's initiative fell through when the Empress Dowager Cixi died in November 1908 and Tang's patron Yuan Shikai lost influence at the Qing court.[50] E. H. Harriman also died in 1909.

The American initiative pushed Japan and Russia toward détente, and France used its financial leverage to promote this movement. In June 1907 a secret Russo-Japanese agreement divided Manchuria into Russian and Japanese spheres of influence. The Paris capital markets were now opened to Japan, and several loans followed after 1908.[51] This rapprochement and division of imperial spheres in Manchuria was paralleled by the rapprochement between Britain and Russia. In April 1906 Britain participated in a "loan that saved Russia" (as Witte called it) from its severe postwar financial crisis. The loan certainly saved the Russian gold standard. The Anglo-

Russian Convention of August 1907 divided Persia into Russian and British spheres of influence.[52] These were further steps in the formation of the tensely balanced European alliance system that would be in place in August 1914.

The American initiative in Manchuria also arose from a specifically American context of financial empire building. The United States' age of formal overseas colonialism was brief, not extending beyond the immediate aftermath of the 1898 war. Domestic critics attacked the new imperialism, on the grounds both that it was anti-democratic and that it would incorporate large nonwhite populations into the American body politic. This attack was carried on by many of the same people who had attacked the gold standard, again with William Jennings Bryan placing himself in the van. Formal colonialism was succeeded by a new round of gold-standard diplomacy that began with the "fiscal protectorate," as Theodore Roosevelt called it, established over the Dominican Republic between 1904 and 1907. The key elements of this new model of semiprivate fiscal control were American supervision of customs and other revenues, control over client government spending, and the establishment of a dollar-based gold-exchange standard. The funding, and political leverage, was provided by a "controlled loan" (provided in the case of the Dominican Republic by Kuhn, Loeb).[53] In the experience of American bankers, the controlled loans made in colonial and semicolonial contexts were the predecessors of the more broadly conceived "stabilization programs" of the 1920s with which the present study is centrally concerned.

Between 1909 and 1912 the Republican administration of President William H. Taft systematized its so-called "dollar diplomacy" and made efforts to apply it in Honduras, Nicaragua, Guatemala, Liberia, and China. To evade congressional criticism, these reforms were structured as private-sector undertakings. In fact, as would also be true in the 1920s, these controlled-loan plans featured close cooperation between the State Department and American bankers. They were also frequently backed up by the dispatch of U.S. military forces.[54]

China continued to appear as the great monetary prize. In June and July 1909, at State Department behest, J. P. Morgan and Company joined with Kuhn, Loeb and Company, the National City Bank of New York, and the First National Bank of New York to form a syndicate to lend money to China. This "American group" (sometimes called simply "the Morgan syndicate") also constituted themselves as a consortium to lend money to Latin America. The same group handled the $1.7 million loan that enabled American fiscal control in Liberia in 1911.[55] Twenty years later, the same American group would provide the credits to enable Japan's restoration of the gold standard.

COOPERATIVE FINANCIAL IMPERIALISM: THE CHINA CONSORTIUM

American efforts became part of an international campaign to extend and perfect financial control in China. Sakatani Yoshio later traced the origins of this international movement to 1896, when Britain, France, and Germany planned a "three-country loan" to China, to pay the indemnity to Japan. Separate Anglo-German and Franco-Russian loans were floated instead, but in May 1909 a combined Anglo-French-German loan was arranged to finance the building of the "Huguang" (Hukuang, or Hubei-Guangdong) Railroad, which included the Hankow-Canton line first negotiated by the Americans, together with a line from Hankow to Sichuan. Henceforth, the three European powers agreed to cooperate rather than compete, so as not to "spoil" the Chinese government, as Morgan and Company's Thomas W. Lamont put it.[56]

Willard Straight explained it less condescendingly: backed by the agitation of the Young China party, the Chinese government in 1908 was able to negotiate an easing of European "control" conditions in the Tianjin-Nanjing railway loan agreement. Unhappy with this, the British, French, and German groups decided in the winter of 1908–09 to combine so that they could jointly set the terms of control. It was at this point that the U.S. State Department demanded a share for U.S. bankers and requested Morgan and Company to organize the American banking group mentioned above. The group was formed on June 11, 1909, and "the very capable American [Willard] Straight," as Sakatani Yoshio called him, resigned from government service to become the American group's representative in China.[57] In May 1910 the American bankers reached an agreement to join with the British, French, and German banking groups to form the Four-Power Consortium for lending to China, signed in London in November.

The American consortium initiative was connected to continued efforts to extend U.S. influence in Manchuria. In partnership with the British firm Pauling and Company, Willard Straight pushed forward Harriman's railroad plan by negotiating a deal in October 1909 with the viceroy of Manchuria and governor of Fengtian to build a parallel line to the west of the South Manchurian Railway, projected to run from Jinzhou near the Liaodong Bay to Aigun on the Russian frontier. Secretary of State Knox then attempted to use the offer of participation in this venture, combined with the offer of U.S. funding, to induce Japan and Russia to join a general agreement to "neutralize" all of the Manchurian railroads and place them under a single international administration. Knox's vision of Manchuria as "an immense commercial neutral zone" was not to be, however, as the British scuttled the effort, while Japan and Russia renewed their own agreement in July 1910.[58] It was also in August 1910 that Japan annexed Korea.

The American initiative was connected to plans for reforming China's monetary system as earlier represented by the Jenks mission in 1904. In the fall of 1910 the Chinese government asked the U.S. government to arrange a loan to reform the currency (which China had pledged to do in treaties with the United States, Britain, and Japan). Again, the monetary project was combined with the idea of a loan for Manchurian economic development. The U.S. government then asked that the European consortium partners be included in the deal.[59] The currency loan negotiations thus became connected with the Huguang railroad loan, and in April and May 1911, contracts were signed for a railroad loan of £6 million, with an option on another £4 million, and a currency loan for another £10 million. The Manchurian land tax and other Manchurian concessions were pledged as security. Article 16 of the loan agreement provided that the Four-Power Consortium would have a first claim to the financing of any future development in Manchuria that required a foreign loan. This, said Sakatani Yoshio, was an instance of China's policy of "using barbarians to control barbarians" (*i o motte i o seisuru*): the point of giving the consortium countries a mortgage on Manchurian concessions was to engage their self-interest there and use them to restrain Japanese and Russian initiatives. Article 16 quickly drew protests from Russia and Japan.[60]

At this point, in March 1911, at Takahashi Korekiyo's initiative, Inoue Junnosuke ended his career at the Bank of Japan, joined the Yokohama Specie Bank, and became involved in negotiating Japan's entrance into the international consortium. Initially, Inoue's departure from the Bank of Japan seemed a reversal in a career that had moved only from success to success. His rapid rise through the ranks had also come under the watch of BOJ vice governor Takahashi Korekiyo, who largely ran personnel matters during the term of governor Matsuo Shigeyoshi. During the war with Russia, Inoue headed the bank's Kyoto agency and then the Osaka branch office, distinguishing himself by his success in raising domestic war bonds. At a time when Osaka was still Japan's commercial and industrial capital, Inoue was very young, at age thirty-six, to be branch head, and his direct and self-confident manner caused some resentment among Osaka business leaders as well as the local Bank of Japan staff. Inoue returned to the bank's head office as chief of general affairs (*eigyō kyokuchō*) in August 1906, when Kimura Seishirō left the post to become a BOJ director. This placed Inoue at the very heart of Bank of Japan business. Inoue could thus be considered the first of the succession of BOJ leaders later dubbed "princes"—"true-born" Bank of Japan men designated from very early in their careers for the bank's topmost posts.[61] In 1919 Inoue would become the first BOJ governor to have risen through the ranks of the organization, the first eight governors having all been drawn from the business world.

After these early successes, however, Inoue's career seemed to falter. As chief of general affairs, Inoue was responsible for implementing the postwar monetary tightening in 1908. He also continued to butt heads with senior business leaders and came out on the losing side. In November 1908 he was transferred from the center of the action in Tokyo to take charge of the bank's New York office, where he directed a staff of two clerks. His wife was ill at the time and so Inoue went abroad alone and unhappy. A devoted husband and father, he wrote to his family every day, telling of the difficulties of his situation and of how he made the best of it by taking the opportunity to closely study American banking practices. His weekly routine during his two years in New York was highly regular, according to his official biographer, who reported that Inoue exercised great self-control and never resorted to the women or drunkenness that one might expect.[62] In December 1910 Inoue was transferred back to Tokyo, returning by way of London and the Trans-Siberian Railway.

Soon after Inoue's return, in March 1911, Takahashi Korekiyo, who was simultaneously vice governor of the Bank of Japan and president of the Yokohama Specie Bank, arranged for Inoue to leave the Bank of Japan and become a director of the lesser-regarded Specie Bank. To Inoue, this seemed a grave career setback. To Takahashi, the Specie Bank was a key institution in need of someone of Inoue's international expertise. In June 1911, when Takahashi became governor of the Bank of Japan, Inoue was elected vice president of the Specie Bank. In September 1913 he was appointed president, a post he held until March 1919. At the Specie Bank, Inoue became responsible for assuring the financing of Japan's overseas trade. He also became one of the chief financial administrators for Japan's semicolonial holdings in Manchuria, and soon after his selection as Specie Bank vice president, in September 1911, he left on a two-month tour of the bank's Manchurian offices.[63]

It was also in September 1911 that provincial gentry and merchants in Sichuan staged the opening act of the Chinese revolution by rebelling openly against the Qing government's use of the Huguang railroad loan proceeds to forcibly purchase a regionally owned railroad being constructed there. On October 10 the Qing army in Wuhan mutinied, and the government rapidly lost control of the country. China's political disintegration only intensified the international financial maneuvering. In November Yuan Shikai was called back from retirement and appointed premier; he compromised with the revolutionaries and turned his efforts to raising emergency foreign loans. The dynasty abdicated on February 12, 1912.

One of Inoue Junnosuke's first orders of business at the Specie Bank thus involved lending money to China. In February 1912, acting on government orders, the Yokohama Specie Bank lent ¥3 million to the Hanyeping Company. The loan was to be repaid in the form of ore delivered to the Yahata steelworks. The loan was secured by a second mortgage on the mines, railroads, and entire property of the Hanyeping Company. In 1913 Inoue made a personal visit to the Hanyeping Company to negotiate another loan. By this time the Yokohama Specie Bank had made eight loans to the Hanyeping Company for a total of ¥29 million plus 2.5 million silver taels. All of these funds were provided by the government, the yen funds coming from the Ministry of Finance's Deposit Bureau (*Yokinbu*) and the silver funds coming from the national Treasury (*Kokko*).[64]

Inoue's next major task was to get Japan into the Four-Country Consortium. In January 1912 the Ōkura Group had made a railroad loan to the revolutionary government in Nanjing. This provoked Western protests and a Western effort to bring Japan into the international consortium. On February 29, soldiers of the former Qing army, who had not been paid, rioted in Beijing and began to burn and loot. The four powers became even more concerned, fearing, as Sakatani Yoshio interpreted it, that there might be a repeat of the Boxer Rebellion in North China, which would open a new field for action for the Japanese and the Russians. The Western powers therefore invited both Japan and Russia to join the consortium.[65] Acting on government orders, the Yokohama Specie Bank as Japan's representative, together with a Russian banking group, thus joined the British, French, Germans, and Americans to form a six-country consortium. The final agreement was signed in Paris on June 18, 1912.[66]

Amid the tumult of 1912, relations between Yuan Shikai and the consortium shifted from week to week. The consortium's initial plans for a "Reorganization Loan" in May 1912 called for a virtual fiscal protectorate, with foreign control of Chinese government revenues and detailed oversight of the expenditure of the government's various military and civil bureaus by the military attachés and consular officials of the consortium powers. This idea was rejected by the Chinese, and in December 1912 a more lenient control plan was agreed to that provided for the appointment of fiscal advisers from Britain, Germany, France, and Russia, but not from the United States or Japan.[67]

As it worked out, however, the consortium lent very little to China—its actual function was to foreclose "wildcat" loans to China while attempting to hold in its own hands the financial reins. In the end, the currency reform loan agreed to in May 1911 also failed to materialize. Nonetheless, one condition of the loan was the appointment of a foreign monetary adviser, Dr. Gerard Vissering, former president of the colonial Javasche Bank of Batavia. In 1912 Vissering arrived in Beijing, where as Jeremiah Jenks had done before and as Sakatani Yoshio would do after, he conducted a study and wrote a report recommending that the new republican government establish an overseas specie reserve and issue "gold" notes—to be redeemable only overseas and only in foreign currency. Vissering also considered the full transition to a gold-exchange standard to be a twenty-to-thirty-year process for China.[68]

Shortly after Japan entered the China consortium, the United States pulled out. Wall Street had come under sharp political attack, as the congressional "Money Trust" hearings convened in December 1912 sensationally revealed the extent of Morgan and Company's influence over American industry.[69] On taking office in March 1913, the new Democratic administration of Woodrow Wilson, with William Jennings Bryan as secretary of state, declared the "dollar diplomacy" of the Taft administration abhorrent to democratic principles and terminated American participation in the China consortium. The American bankers learned of the decision when they read about it in the newspapers, and, said Thomas Lamont, they suffered a great loss of face in the eyes of their European colleagues.[70] This ended the first period of active American financial diplomacy in East Asia.

The plan for the Chinese reorganization loan went ahead without the Americans, and in April 1913 the newly quintuple consortium signed a £25 million deal for the Chinese Government 5% Reorganization Gold Loan. Each national group was to provide £5 million. Lacking the spare funds, Japan and Russia ceded their shares of the loan to the British, French, and Germans. This division of business was an internal matter among the consortium partners, however, and in relation to the Chinese government, the Yokohama Specie Bank received customs revenues for loan repayments just as did the other partners.[71]

The Japanese government also continued to advance funds covertly through the Yokohama Specie Bank to the Hanyeping steelworks, with a loan for ¥15 million in 1913. (Such "industrial" loans fell outside the scope of the consortium agreement.) According to an internal Ministry of Finance report, this was done as a matter of "highest state policy" in order "to develop our ironworks." The money was supplied by the Ministry of Finance's Deposit Bureau beyond the scope of legal and budgetary provisions (that is, outside of Diet oversight).[72] In the summer of 1913, Inoue Junnosuke made another trip to China to investigate conditions surrounding lending there.

THE YEN'S CONTINENTAL ADVANCE

The Japanese government took further steps toward incorporating South Manchuria into its new yen bloc. In line with the Chinese "rights recovery" movement, Western-style Chinese banks had begun to issue silver notes to compete with the YSB silver notes, whose use declined after 1911. In July 1913 the government gave the Yokohama Specie Bank the right to issue yen notes in Manchuria that were backed by gold coins or by Bank of Japan notes.[73] The Japanese Bank of Chosen also began to promote the use of its own gold yen notes in Manchuria.

The Bank of Chosen's motivations and actions reflected its dual character as a colonial central bank and as a profit-making commercial bank (a divided character it shared with the Bank of Taiwan). Korea's trade with Manchuria was consistently in deficit. Specie therefore flowed from Korea to Manchuria, making it difficult for the Bank of Chosen to maintain its specie reserve. The bank's advance into Manchuria was thus motivated by a desire to protect its specie reserves: by establishing branches in Manchuria, the bank was able to bring both sides of this trade into its own monetary sphere.[74] The bank had inherited from the Dai-Ichi Bank a Manchurian bridgehead in Andong, on the north side of the Yalu River. In July 1913 the government also allowed the Bank of Chosen to open a branch in Mukden, and branches at Dairen and Changchun were established in August and September. Thus, in the context of half-bureaucratic, half-commercial rivalries between the Specie Bank and the Bank of Chosen, a yen-based gold-exchange standard was extended into the Japanese-controlled zones of South Manchuria. Japanese practice was paralleled by the Russian use of ruble notes in North Manchuria.

One idea behind setting up separate colonial banks of issue—rather than simply letting Japanese coins and Bank of Japan notes themselves circulate as the sole colonial currency—had been Matsukata Masayoshi's idea of buffering Japan from financial crises that might take place in the colonies.[75] In the case of the Bank of Chosen, what was really enabled was monetary expansion, as the bank leveraged its semi-independent money creation power into a basis for "continental advance." In contrast to the Bank of Taiwan, the existence (or fuller realization) of the gold-exchange standard in Korea has been considered a foundation of this expansionist capability.[76] This monetary leverage was one outward face of Japan's gold-standard diplomacy.

The other "imperial" face of the gold standard was its instrumentality in mobilizing European capital. The linkage between Japan's new dependence on European capital and its new investment in Asia was most direct in the case of the semi-governmental colonial development companies. The South Manchurian Railway Company, itself acquired as a result of a war financed by ¥800 million in foreign capital, was an especially prominent foreign borrower, issuing £14 million (¥140 million) in bonds in London between 1907 and 1914. The Oriental Development Company (Tōyō Takushoku) was established in 1908 to promote Japanese colonization in Korea. To this end, it bought up lands formerly owned by the Korean royal family and government, and became Korea's largest landlord. It too borrowed abroad (in 1913), as did the Industrial Bank of Japan (in 1908). Both companies helped to finance Japan's industrial development in Manchuria. (Details of the loans are given in table 3, page 78.) The Yokohama Specie Bank did not borrow abroad, but it helped raise foreign loans for other Japanese agencies. It was also used by the government to channel loans to China.

Thus, acting on its own account or acting indirectly through its state policy companies, the Japanese government very literally borrowed in Europe in order to lend in Asia. Japan's imperial choice also implied a profound financial contradiction. Even as China's chaotically unfolding national revolution offered new openings for Japanese expansion overseas, at home the financial logic of Japan's international situation began to bind increasingly tightly.

As for the gold standard itself, while it first came to Japan, as it did to Russia, as a "positive" tool for industrial and imperial expansion, it was valued by Western bankers and bondholders precisely as a kind of restraint—a restraint in particular on governmental currency expansion and inflationism. The gold standard did become such a restraint in Japan, and in men like Inoue Junnosuke and Hamaguchi Osachi, Japan found financial leaders who came to believe in it as such a restraint.

FOUR

The "Positive" and "Negative" Policies

After the war came the postwar, and even as the Japanese government leveraged the gold standard to build an empire overseas, the contractionary logic of postwar adjustment under gold-standard rules began to bind at home. This contradiction was at the heart of the government's policies for "postwar management" (*sengo keiei*).[1] That is, colonial, military, and heavy-industrial development required continued high government spending. But to repay Japan's foreign debt and maintain the gold standard required fiscal retrenchment. These contrary tendencies also tended to succeed each other in time, in a policy cycle that would be repeated, with a greatly magnified amplitude, after World War I. Thus, the postwar decade began in 1905–06 with an excess of the "positive" expansionary policy. By 1914, however, it was the logic of the "negative" policy of balance through retrenchment that seemed most compelling.

In their economic dimensions the so-called "positive" and "negative" policies (*sekkyoku seisaku, shōkyoku seisaku*) could be rendered in English, slightly anachronistically, as "Keynesian" and "monetarist" policies, if we understand the latter terms as a shorthand for expansionary and stabilization-oriented policies such as can be seen across centuries of fiscal and monetary history.[2] It is not always appreciated how deeply constitutive these processes are of politics as a whole. As the logic of these conflicting drives developed in the decade after the war with Russia, they also took on an increasingly partisan cast.

On one side, Japan's first great political party, the Rikken Seiyūkai (Constitutional Society of Political Friends) became identified with an expansionist positive spending policy. In opposition to this, a policy of retrenchment or reconstruction (*kinshuku, tatenaoshi*) was adopted by the rival Rikken Dōshikai (Constitutional Society of Comrades), which was later reorganized as the Kenseikai (Constitutional Government Society) and then as the Rikken Minseitō (Constitutional Popular Government Party). The retrenchment policy was derided by the Seiyūkai as a "negative" or passive policy. For convenience, I continue to label these the "positive" and "negative" policy lines, even though it should be understood that the latter was a pejorative term applied by its opponents. In the 1910s and 1920s the back-and-forth swings between these policies became a central, structuring element of party politics.

DILEMMAS OF DEVELOPMENT UNDER THE GOLD STANDARD

Japan's turn to empire and to the Western capital markets meant a sudden worsening in the balance of trade. From 1882, when Matsukata Masayoshi stabilized the yen on a silver basis, to the eve of the Sino-Japanese War in 1893, Japan ran a merchandise trade surplus in every year but one (the depression year of 1890, when the U.S. Silver Purchase Act temporarily sent world silver prices and hence the Japanese yen soaring). The Sino-Japanese War initiated a great turn, and in the twenty years from 1894 to 1914, Japan ran a trade deficit in every year but 1906 and 1909.[3]

Expensive wars in 1894–95 and 1904–05 were one cause of the new trade gap. A second cause—and a fundamental reason that the gold standard had been adopted in the first place—was a state-promoted shift in industrial structure toward military-oriented heavy industry. This choice required heavy imports of raw materials and machinery without producing any corresponding export revenues.[4] A third cause of Japan's new trade deficits was the gold standard itself, which ended twenty-four years of currency depreciation relative to the gold bloc. For all of these reasons, the era of the gold standard was an era of chronic trade deficits for Japan.

The twenty years after 1894 were dominated by a cycle of two wars and two "postwars," during which Japan's net foreign payments were managed as follows:[5]

I. During the ten years between the beginning of the war with China and the beginning of the war with Russia (1894–1903), Japan's total current account deficit added up to ¥311 million. It was paid for mainly by running down the indemnity funds received from China.

II. From the Russo-Japanese War to World War I (1904–1914), Japan had a total current account deficit of ¥930 million (nearly half of it incurred during the war itself). This deficit was paid for out of foreign borrowing.

The proceeds of the war loans were so great that Japan ended the Russo-Japanese War with a greater reserve of specie than it had at the beginning of the war. This fund too was steadily run down, and still more money was borrowed, raising Japan's foreign debt to a peak of nearly ¥2 billion in 1914 (Figure 3). Interest payments on the foreign debt, which reached a yearly total of ¥80 million in 1914, added to the balance-of-payments shortfall.

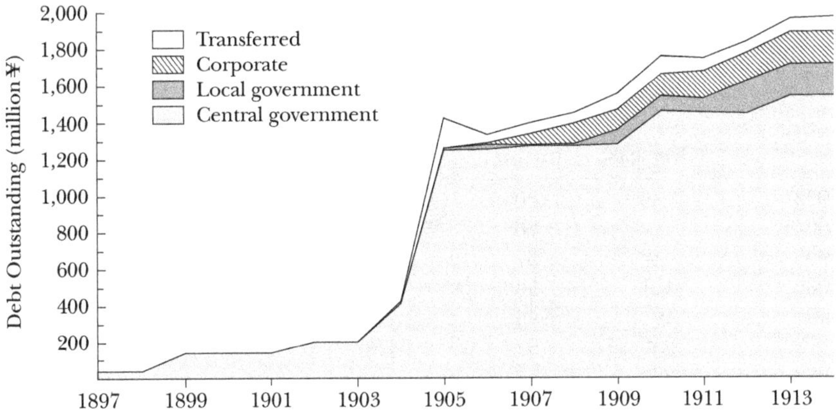

FIG. 3. Japan's external bonded debt, 1897–1914.

SOURCE: Ministry of Finance data given in Nihon Ginkō Tōkeikyoku 1966: 317. Details of the loans are given below in tables 2 and 3.

NOTES: (1) From 1897 to 1909 central government debt totals include specially endorsed domestic government bonds sold overseas. (2) "Transferred" refers to domestically issued government bonds held abroad, as estimated by the Ministry of Finance.

On the eve of the Russo-Japanese War in 1903, total foreign debt came to about ¥200 million. By the end of the war, the total had swollen to ¥1.4 billion, or some 40 percent of GNP. In 1915 foreign debt still equaled more than 36 percent of GNP. Moreover, up to World War I, the greater part of Japan's bonded debt of every description was overseas debt. That is, the majority of Japanese government bonds, local government bonds, and corporate bonds were issued overseas.[6] The domestic bond market developed only later.

The gold standard had been instituted to enable borrowing, but its maintenance seemed to require further borrowing. As chief of general affairs (*eigyō kyokuchō*) at the Bank of Japan, Fukai Eigo confronted the problem directly: "Because the gold raised by overseas bond issues became [Japan's] overseas gold funds, one could even say that that we floated overseas bonds in order to maintain the gold standard."[7]

Japan's Gold Standard as a Gold-Exchange Standard

The fund referred to by Fukai, the so-called "overseas specie reserve" (*zaigai seika*), reflects the in-between character of Japan's international position. These funds, the proceeds of loans taken out in London, were not in fact specie but rather British money in the form of demand deposits and short-term British government sterling bills. Much of this money was placed on deposit with the Bank of England itself. Part of this "overseas specie" was owned by the government and part by the Bank of Japan (table 1). "Thus,"

TABLE 1. Japanese specie and foreign-exchange holdings, 1903–1914
(year-end figures; ¥ millions)

Year	*Location*		*Held by*		*Total*
	Overseas	Inland	Bank of Japan	Government	
1903	19	120	133	6	139
1904[a]	71	26	96	1	97
1905	442	37	116	363	479
1906	441	54	203	292	495
1907	401	44	208	237	445
1908	330	62	226	166	392
1909	329	117	302	144	446
1910	337	135	270	202	472
1911	231	133	251	113	364
1912	214	136	268	82	350
1913	246	130	285	91	376
1914	213	128	292	49	341

SOURCE: Ministry of Finance figures, given in Nihon Ginkō Tōkeikyoku 1966: 169.
[a]Beginning in 1904, silver holdings were no longer counted as part of the Bank of Japan's specie reserve. Thus, Japan seemingly completed the transition to a full gold standard just at the point that it began in fact to operate a sterling-based gold-exchange standard.

former overseas financial commissioner Wakatsuki Reijirō explained, "even though England lent gold to Japan, not one ounce of gold went from England to Japan."[8]

In this way, after 1905 the greater part of Japan's gold (or foreign-exchange) reserves came to be held in London. Although the practice was not provided for by law and was not openly discussed by Japanese financial authorities, these London funds formed part of the Bank of Japan's reserve for convertibility. Inoue Junnosuke traced the origins of the practice to the initial deposit of the Chinese indemnity in London. The usage became institutionalized from the time of the Russo-Japanese War.[9]

Thus, even as Japanese leaders worked to extend yen-based gold-exchange standards in Korea and Manchuria, Japan itself began to operate a sterling-based gold-exchange standard similar to the type operated by India. This was done in part for reasons of convenience and profit and in part at the request of Japan's British bankers, for whom the deposit of loan proceeds in their own London banks was often an informal condition of the loan.

Japan's London balances were not insignificant from the side of London itself. A modern parallel can be drawn: in the same way that, since the 1980s, Japan's immense holdings of U.S. dollars have helped maintain the international dollar standard in the face of mounting U.S. trade deficits, so in the years leading up to World War I, Japanese and Indian holdings of sterling helped to maintain the central place of the British pound and of the London capital markets in the face of mounting British trade deficits.[10] In fact, it appears that Japan held larger sterling reserves than did India.[11] Via its new partnership with the Bank of Japan, the Bank of England used the large Japanese funds on deposit in London as it used Indian funds, to help regulate the money markets. Thus, the Bank of England itself repeatedly borrowed the Bank of Japan's own borrowed funds.[12] This was another financial face of the Anglo-Japanese alliance.

Table 1 reveals the dominant position of overseas specie holdings after the war of 1904–05. It also reveals the great decline of those reserves during the postwar decade despite heavy foreign borrowing. Crises were averted in 1904 and 1908, but by the end of the Meiji emperor's reign in 1912, the whole system was in obvious trouble and was being maintained only by continuous foreign borrowing, which postponed and magnified the basic contradiction in Japan's international financial position.

This actively managed "overseas specie" system was also far from the ideal of an automatic gold standard. In any case, Japan was physically distant from and relatively unknown in the financial capitals of Western Europe, and it was never possible for the Bank of Japan to defend the gold standard by using the "orthodox" (Bank of England) method of raising interest rates in order to induce the inflow of short-term foreign funds. (By the same token, the Bank of Japan was largely untroubled by the problem of capital flight.) Gold (that is, sterling, dollars, and francs) could be attracted only by the slower and more political process of raising overseas bond issues.

Japan's Foreign Borrowing

Like the Sino-Japanese War before it and World War I after it, the Russo-Japanese War was followed by a two-step movement of boom and bust. As would happen again in the decade after World War I, postwar recession seemed to become a chronic condition, with lengthy recessions in 1907–09 and 1913–15.[13] The ongoing drive to build up the military and heavy industry meant high taxes and a deepening balance-of-payments deficit, the latter problem compounded by the immense war debt.

Foreign direct investment into Japan might have provided one solution to the trade gap, but the Japanese government always preferred portfolio investment that implied no ownership rights. Consequently foreign direct investment remained small in absolute volume.[14] Before World War II almost all foreign investment into Japan was in the form of bonds. Central-government bond issues were joined by the foreign bond issues of municipal governments as well as those of public utilities, private companies, and the semigovernmental colonial corporations the Oriental Development Company and South Manchurian Railroad. Tables 2 and 3 summarize government and private borrowing to 1914.

TABLE 2. Overseas bond issues (foreign borrowing) by the central and local governments, 1870–1915

Date of Issue (yr./mo.)	*Face Amount[a] (in millions)*	*Place of Issue*	*Interest Rate (%)*	*Issue Price*	*Maturity (term in years)*	*Name, Details, [Intermediary],[b] and Issuing Firms*
1870/4	£1.0[c]	England	9	98	1882 (13)	Japanese Government 9% Foreign Bonds. For railway construction. Schrõder.
1873/1	£2.4[c]	England	7	92.5	1897 (25)	Japanese Government 7% Foreign Bonds. For commutation of feudal stipends. Oriental Bank.
1897	£4.389	England	5	101.5	1950 (53)	Resale of Japanese government domestic war bonds. Capital & Counties Bank, Hongkong & Shanghai Bank (HSB), Chartered Bank, Yokohama Specie Bank (YSB).
1899/6	£10.0	England	4	90	1953 (55)	Japanese Government First 4% Sterling Bonds. For railway, government steelworks, telephone. Parr's Bank, Chartered Bank, HSB, YSB.
1899/7	£0.24	England	6	92	1910 (11)	Kōbe City Waterworks Bonds. Morles (Yokohama).

1902	£5.104	England	5	100	1957 (55)	Resale of Japanese government domestic bonds (war bonds, steelworks, telephone, tobacco monopoly bonds). Baring Bros., HSB, YSB.
1902/5	£0.922	England	6	98	1925 (23)	Yokohama City Waterworks Bonds. M. Samuel, Capital & Counties Bank.
1902/10	£3.16	England	6	99	1981 (79)	Osaka City First Harbor Construction Bonds. [Third (Dai-San) Bank, Yasuda Bank]; M. Samuel, Capital & Counties Bank.
1904/5	£10.0	England-U.S.	6	92	1911 (7)	Japanese Government First 6% Sterling Bonds. Russo-Japanese war bonds. London: Parr's Bank, HSB, YSB. New York: Kuhn, Loeb. 50–50 Anglo-U.S. participation.
1904/11	£12.0	England-U.S.	6	90.5	1911 (7)	Japanese Government Second 6% Sterling Bonds. Russo-Japanese war bonds. Same as May 1905 group; 50–50 Anglo-U.S. participation.

(continued on next page)

TABLE 2 *(continued)*

Date of Issue (yr./mo.)	*Face Amount*[a] *(in millions)*	*Place of Issue*	*Interest Rate (%)*	*Issue Price*	*Maturity (term in years)*	*Name, Details, [Intermediary],*[b] *and Issuing Firms*
1905/3	£30.0	England-U.S.	4.5	90	1925 (20)	Japanese Government First 4½% Sterling Bonds. Russo-Japanese war bonds. Same as May 1905 group; 50–50 Anglo-U.S. participation.
1905/7	£30.0	Eng.-U.S.-Ger.	4.5	90	1925 (20)	Japanese Government Second 4½% Sterling Bonds. Russo-Japanese war bonds. Same as May 1905 group, with addition of German group; three-way U.S., British, and German participation.
1905/11	£25.0	Eng.-U.S.-Ger.-Fr.	4	90	1931 (25)	Japanese Government Second 4% Sterling Bonds. Taken out shortly after the war, to redeem 6% domestic war bonds. Same as Nov. 1905 group, with addition of London and Paris Rothschilds. London share: £6.5 mil.; New York: £3.25 mil.; Germany: £3.25; Paris: £12 mil.

1906/1	£1.4				1921/1926	Overseas railway bonds taken over by government at the time of nationalization. (See Table 3, below.)
1906/8	£1.5	England	5	100	1936 (30)	Tokyo City Public Works Bonds. For harbor works, street improvements. [Industrial Bank of Japan (IBJ)]; HSB, Parr's Bank, YSB.
1907/2	£0.317	England	5	99	1936 (29)	Yokohama City Public Works Bonds. For harbor works. M. Samuel.
1907/3	£23.0	England-France	5	99.5	1947 (40)	Japanese Government 5% Sterling Bonds. To redeem 6% foreign loans of 1904, plus £1 mil. new loan. Parr's Bank, HSB, YSB, London and Paris Rothschilds; 50–50 Anglo-French participation.
1909/4	£0.66	England	6	97.5	1917 (8)	Yokohama City Gasworks Bonds. HSB.
1909/5	£3.085	England	5	97	1939 (30)	Osaka City Electric Railway & Waterworks Bonds. [IBJ]; HSB, Parr's Bank, YSB.
1909/6	£0.8	England	5	95.5	1943 (34)	Nagoya City Bonds. For waterworks. Lazard Bros.

(continued on next page)

TABLE 2 *(continued)*

Date of Issue (yr./mo.)	*Face Amount[a] (in millions)*	*Place of Issue*	*Interest Rate (%)*	*Issue Price*	*Maturity (term in years)*	*Name, Details, [Intermediary],[b] and Issuing Firms*
1909/7	£0.716	England	5	98	1953 (44)	Yokohama City Second Waterworks Bonds. [IBJ]; HSB, Parr's Bank, YSB.
1909/7	Fr. 45.0	France	5	99	1919 (10)	Kyoto City Public Works Bonds. For water, electric, and other works. [Mitsui Bank]; Banque de l'Union Parisienne.
1910/5	Fr. 450.0	France	4	95.5	1970 (60)	Japanese Government 4% Franc Bonds. To redeem 5% domestic bonds. Paris Rothschilds.
1910/5	£11.0	England	4	95	1970 (60)	Third 4% Sterling Bonds. To redeem 5% domestic bonds. Parr's Bank, HSB, YSB.
1912/1	Fr. 5.0	France	5	98.5	1919 (7)	Kyoto City Public Works Bonds. For water, electric, and other works. [Mitsui Bank]; Banque de l'Union Parisienne.
1912/2	£5.175	England-U.S.	5	98/97.75	1952 (40)	Tokyo City Electric Works Bonds. [IBJ]; London group: HSB, Parr's Bank, YSB; New York: Kuhn, Loeb.

1912/2	Fr. 100.88	France	5	96.75	1952 (40)	Tokyo City Electric Works Bonds. [IBJ]; Société Générale. (Jointly issued with Anglo-U.S. loan.)
1912/4	£0.189	England	5	97.5	1929 (17)	Yokohama City Second Gasworks Bonds. Law Debenture Corp.
1913/3	£3.0	England	5, 5.5	—	1914–15	First Japanese Government short-term railway bonds and bills.
1913/4	Fr.200.0	France	5	98	1923 (10)	Japanese Government Franc Treasury Bills. To redeem foreign loans.
1914/2	£2.5	England	4.75	—	1915	Japanese Government second short-term railway bills.
1915/2	£3.0	England	5.75	—	1915	Japanese Government third short-term railway bills.

SOURCES: Nihon Kōgyō Ginkō Gaijibu 1958: 6–7, 18–22; Suzuki 1994: 198–201; Inoue J. 1926, IJR 1: 520–521; Moulton 1931: 376–377; loan prospectuses reprinted in YSGS; various other sources, including Tsushima 1963, vol. 2.

[a] *Face value* = Japanese debts. The actual proceeds of the loans were generally 6 to 12 percent less than the face value. (Calculated by discounting the loan by its issue price [e.g., for an issue price of 98, multiply by 0.98] and then subtracting the commission [often not publicly known, but generally in the range of 4 to 7 percent of the face value of the loan].) The best guide to the nuts and bolts of these operations is Suzuki 1994. *Yen equivalents:* Under the post-1897 system of par values, the rule-of-thumb conversion rate was £1 = ¥10 and $1 = ¥2. Fr. 1 = ¥0.387.

[b] If specified in the source materials, the intermediary firm is listed in brackets.

[c] Total before 1897 = £3.4 million; fully repaid in 1896.

TABLE 3. Overseas bond issues by companies, 1906–1914

Date of Issue (yr./mo.)	*Face Amount (in millions)*	*Place of Issue*	*Interest Rate (%)*	*Issue Price*	*Maturity*	*Name, Details, [Intermediary], and Issuing Firms*
1906/1	£1.0	England	5	98.5	1921/1926	Hokkaido Colliery & Coal Railway Co. Bonds. Chartered Bank. (Taken over by government at the time of nationalization.)
1906/3	£1.0	England	4.5	97.5	1921/1926	Kansai Railway Co. Bonds. M. Samuel. (Taken over by government at the time of nationalization.)
1907/7	£4.0	England	5	97	1932	First South Manchurian Railway Bonds. Government guaranteed. [IBJ]; HSB, Parr's Bank, YSB.*
1908/6	£2.0	England	5	98	1911	Second South Manchurian Railway Bonds. Government guaranteed. [Panmure Gordon]; privately placed.*
1908	¥2.0	France	7.5	—	—	Kanegafuchi Cotton Spinning Co. Bonds. [Mitsui Bank]; Banque Française pour le Commerce et l'Industrie.

1908/11	£2.0	England-France	5	97	1933	Thirteenth Industrial Bank Bills. Government guaranteed. London: Panmure Gordon, HSB, Parr's Bank, YSB. Paris: Société Générale.
1908/12	£2.0	England	5	97.5	1932	Third South Manchurian Railway Bonds. Government guaranteed. [IBJ]; HSB, Parr's Bank, YSB.*
1909/4	¥0.25	France	6.5	100	1912	Matsui Muslin Spinning & Weaving Co. Bonds. [Hundredth (Daihyaku) Bank]; A. Gysin.
1909	¥0.2	England	6.5	92	—	Keihin Electric Railway bonds. Sale & Frazer Co.
1910/6	¥5.0	England	5	97.875	—	Eighth Hokkaido Development Bank Bills. Sale & Frazer Co.
1911/1	£6.0	England	4.5	98	1932	Fourth South Manchurian Railway Bonds. Government guaranteed. [IBJ]; HSB, Parr's Bank, YSB.*
1913/3	Fr. 50.0	France	5	96.75	1924	First Oriental Development Co. Bills. Government guaranteed. [IBJ]; Banque Franco-Japonaise.

SOURCES: Nihon Kōgyō Ginkō Gaijibu 1958: 18–22; Moulton 1931: 378; Tsushima 1963, vol. 2; Yamamoto Yoshihiko 1978: 198–201.
*In 1920, £7.1 million in South Manchurian Railway Co. bonds issued between 1907 and 1911 were taken over as a direct government obligation.

The Japanese government's resort to the New York capital markets in 1904 and 1905 proved to be temporary. Borrowing costs remained lower in London and Paris, and after the French-brokered rapprochement between Japan and Russia in 1907, the Japanese government made repeated use of the Paris markets. London's place remained preeminent, however, as it remained for the world at large.

Despite Japan's new prominence as an international borrower, the nation's borrowed ¥2 billion (£200 million) did not loom large on the mental world maps of most metropolitan capitalists. The global numbers are worth reviewing. On the eve of the world war, British overseas investment totaled £4 billion (¥40 billion), and Britons were investing abroad £160 million (¥1.6 billion) per year. After Britain came France, with about half as much in overseas investments, followed by Germany, the United States (with £700 million invested overseas), and Belgium, the Netherlands, and Switzerland.[15] In this view, Britain in particular and northwestern Europe more broadly was unmistakably the world's financial center of gravity.

Japan's new foreign debts did loom large in Japan itself, and in effect, foreign borrowing enabled the Japanese government to maintain an expansive economic and international policy where otherwise the rules of maintaining the gold standard would have forced a contractionary deflation policy.[16] Pressures to turn to an outright deflation policy became increasingly compelling.

THE ECONOMICS OF TAISHŌ DEMOCRACY

Ishibashi Tanzan (1884–1973) joined the staff of the business weekly *Tōyō keizai shinpō* (*The Oriental Economist*) as a reporter in 1911, and he remembered his early years there as a time "when pretty much all of society was turning to liberalism." After World War II this liberal tide was conceptualized historically as the age of "Taishō democracy," and while it is difficult to identify any single essence that unites the diversity of Taishō-era social and intellectual movements, nevertheless Taishō democracy appears in retrospect as a distinct historical moment, if only because of the countervailing right-wing reaction that followed in the 1930s.[17]

Politically, the outstanding feature of the new era was the movement of the political parties to the center of the political stage. With the resolution of the "Taishō political crisis" in February 1913, a political party system dominated by two major conservative parties took form. From its inception, this new partisan politics turned on the question of the "positive" and "negative" policies of economic expansionism and retrenchment—in fact, this economic issue was the most persistent policy element in the parties' policy opposition. In the 1920s the conflict between these partisan lines became linked in turn to the issue of the gold standard, which worked to make

Japan's domestic confrontations over economic policy conform in detail with the question of Japan's relationship to the Anglo-American-centered world economic order as a whole.

In the first two decades of the twentieth century, the development of party politics was driven above all by the rise of the Rikken Seiyūkai, founded by Itō Hirobumi in 1900. The Seiyūkai developed in opposition to the army-bureaucratic clique that had formed around Itō's Chōshū comrade and political rival Yamagata Aritomo, and from 1901 to 1913, the old pattern of alternation in office by prime ministers from Chōshū and Satsuma was replaced by a new alternation between the Itō-Seiyūkai group, represented by Itō's protégé Saionji Kinmochi, and the Yamagata clique, represented by Yamagata's protégé Katsura Tarō. In this context, the Seiyūkai moved by stages closer to the center of government.

As the new party politics developed, new civilian spending demands also developed, and they found an institutional form in the "positive" or active policy (*sekkyoku seisaku*) of Hara Takashi (Hara Kei, 1856–1921). As Seiyūkai party secretary, Hara came to dominate the Seiyūkai organization, brokering the compromises between it and Katsura Tarō that assured the Seiyūkai a turn in office. As home minister in the first and second Saionji cabinets (1906–08, 1911–12) and in the Yamamoto Gonnohyōe cabinet (1913–14), Hara gained the power to appoint prefectural governors and to promote his "positive" regional development plans. He thereby built the party's regional power base and created a new kind of development-oriented, pork-barrel politics, which became the Seiyūkai's hallmark.[18]

Hara's self-styled positive program cannot be called a consistent or theoretically conceived economic policy. It originated as a vote-getting policy, tied to the demands of regional elites, and it changed form as the Seiyūkai's bases of political support changed. But in time, the positive policy did receive some explicit and increasingly theorized formulations, most famously in the financial program implemented by Takahashi Korekiyo in the early 1930s.

Postwar Adjustment: From the Positive to the Negative Policy

The Russo-Japanese War was followed by a two-step movement of boom and bust. Thanks above all to Takahashi Korekiyo's efforts, the Japanese government ended the war loaded with debts, both foreign and domestic, but flush with cash. National gold reserves stood at more than three times the level of 1903, creating the conditions for a speculative boom. Backed by the Seiyūkai, the first Saionji cabinet (January 1906–July 1908) maintained the high wartime spending levels and, under the name of "positive postwar management" (*sengo sekkyoku keiei*), increased both military and civilian spending. The latter went especially to rail and telephone construction and public works, all helping to sustain the investment boom that followed the war. Vigorous foreign demand for Japanese goods contributed to the prosperity, pushing Japan's trade into a surplus position for the first time since before the war with China.[19]

The government funded this spending by what at the time was also called a positive policy of raising capital through foreign loans. Another part of the positive policy was the nationalization of the rail system in 1906, done in response to a long-held desire of influential businessmen, against determined resistance within the Ministry of Finance. From the standpoint of the owners of private railroads, the government thereby replaced their fixed investments with ¥450 million in new liquid capital. This huge charge of cash supported further business investment. Not incidentally, nationalization also placed the rail system under direct political control, creating a vast new field for patronage and for the future operation of the positive policy. For this reason, Foreign Minister Katō Takaaki strongly opposed it and ultimately resigned from the cabinet in protest. Takahashi Korekiyo supported nationalization, and the Bank of Japan followed an easy money policy.[20]

The postwar boom was followed by a postwar depression. Early signs of trouble came in January 1907, when shares of the benchmark Tokyo Stock Exchange Company declined. A wave of bank runs began in April. In October the so-called "rich man's panic" struck Wall Street; the economic downturn that followed hit Japanese exports to the American market, which were mainly raw silk, a luxury good highly sensitive to the U.S. business cycle. In November, silver prices fell sharply and exports to China, Japan's second-largest overseas market, fell accordingly. Thus, twenty-seven months after the end of the war with Russia, a delayed postwar reaction hit Japan with full force.[21]

The postwar recession occasioned a major shift in economic policy as the government turned to budgetary retrenchment to conserve specie. Looking back in July 1914, Gotō Shinpei saw this as the first in a two-step movement from a fully "positive" to a fully "negative" financial policy.[22] At this point, however, the keynote still remained the positive policy of solving the economic imbalance via economic expansion, to be funded by raising foreign loans. The Bank of Japan also continued to maintain low interest rates. Further tightening followed in 1908, when the Saionji government adopted a retrenchment budget and the Bank of Japan (where Inoue Junnosuke was chief of general affairs) contracted its note issue.

In July 1908 the Saionji cabinet was replaced by the second Katsura cabinet, and the Seiyūkai went into opposition. Wakatsuki Reijirō, who had been in London since April 1907 as overseas financial commissioner (succeeding Takahashi Korekiyo), returned home to serve again as vice minister of finance and as de facto finance minister from July 1908 to September 1911. (Officially, Prime Minister Katsura acted as his own minister of finance.)[23] In line with the "negative" policy for which Wakatsuki would be known from this point until the debacle of December 1931, the second Katsura cabinet adopted another retrenchment budget in 1909 and continued the policy of monetary constraint. The result was recession and outright price deflation in 1908 and 1909.

Fiscal and monetary restraint was joined with a program of moral retrenchment, as the Katsura cabinet mounted an ideological campaign of a sort that, in a much elaborated form, would be deployed again in the retrenchment campaigns led by Wakatsuki Reijirō and Hamaguchi Osachi in 1924–27 and by Hamaguchi and Inoue Junnosuke in 1929–1930. The tone of this movement was articulated in an imperial rescript issued in October 1908, the Boshin Year Rescript (*Boshin shōsho*) on diligence and thrift. The themes were at once traditionalistic and designed to respond to Japan's postwar balance-of-payments difficulties. Political radicalism seemed to have sprung up in the wake of the war. The emperor's rescript deplored the moral disarray of the postwar situation, which was compared in the official commentary on the rescript to the aftermaths of the Southwest War and the Sino-Japanese War. It urged the Japanese people to remember their social stations, leave off luxury, and return to the path of diligence and thrift, mindful of the problems of debt and postwar industrial adjustment. Thus, fiscal retrenchment and the deflation policy went hand in hand with a reaction against liberalism and radicalism. This moral-economic linkage appears repeatedly, associated with phases of the "negative" retrenchment policy.[24]

Despite budgetary retrenchment, the second Katsura cabinet continued to borrow abroad, floating a large overseas bond issue in London and Paris for some ¥285 million in May 1910. The Ministry of Finance also directed the issuing of overseas bonds by municipal governments—precisely, Wakatsuki explained in his memoirs, to evade the credit limits imposed by the central government's heavy borrowing to support the yen exchange under the gold standard.[25] The proceeds of these loans, about ¥60 million in foreign exchange, went directly into the government's overseas specie reserve, and the borrowing municipalities were supplied not with gold (sterling or francs) but with Bank of Japan notes. Overseas bond issues by private companies were used in the same way to support the gold standard.[26] These included a further £8 million in bonds issued by the semigovernmental South Manchurian Railway and £2 million by the semigovernmental Industrial Bank, for another ¥100 million.[27]

In June 1911, near the end of Katsura's second cabinet, Takahashi Korekiyo was appointed governor of the Bank of Japan. Despite heavy borrowing in London and Paris, the problem of maintaining Japan's specie reserves was pressing. The only short-term solution seemed to be further borrowing. In July the Bank of Japan confidentially reported to the government, in line with the "positive" borrowing policy as then conceived: "What we lack most is capital; the basic solution to the balance-of-payments problem is to develop exports; we need to continue the policy of bringing in foreign capital." In August the BOJ warned that "if we continue at this rate, the [specie] reserve will be gone by 1915" and declared that it was thus inevitable that Japan would have to borrow, even though this added further to the burden of overseas payments in the long run.[28]

In August 1911 the Katsura cabinet resigned and was replaced by the second Saionji cabinet. The Seiyūkai again functioned as the government party, and party secretary Hara Takashi was again home minister. Former BOJ governor Yamamoto Tatsuo became finance minister in the new cabinet, the first businessman, as he was regarded, ever to become a cabinet minister. (Despite taking direction from the minister of finance, the Bank of Japan was formally a private institution, and as Takahashi Korekiyo once put it, its governor was "the number-one representative of the business world.")[29] Hara and the Seiyūkai wanted to conduct a positive spending policy, but the combination of revenue shortfalls and declining specie balances compelled a continuation of the Katsura cabinet's austerity policy. Hara perceived Finance Minister Yamamoto as being opposed to the Seiyūkai and its positive policy, noting in his diary that Yamamoto was stopping all new spending plans and following "an extreme negative policy." Yamamoto was backed in this by senior statesmen Inoue Kaoru and Matsukata Masayoshi. Thus, despite the prominent role of Hara and the Seiyūkai, the second Saionji cabinet continued to retrench, making a partial exception for Hara's rail projects.[30]

It was in the context of this lost battle for the positive policy that Hara Takashi and BOJ governor Takahashi Korekiyo became political friends and that an opposition between Takahashi and Yamamoto Tatsuo began to develop. In line with his retrenchment policy, Yamamoto in 1911 asked Takahashi to raise interest rates. Takahashi resisted the finance minister's request, writing an opposing position paper and then meeting with cabinet power broker Hara. Hara agreed with Takahashi but said that for now, nothing could be done about it. The close working relationship between Hara and Takahashi began at this time.[31] In 1912 the Saionji cabinet also began to restrict foreign borrowing and floated no overseas loans except for three municipal bond issues that were already in the pipeline.

The conflict within the Saionji cabinet over the positive and negative policies persisted to the end. In late 1912 Home Minister Hara proposed an extremely large overseas bond issue of ¥300 million to ¥400 million for rail projects and for filling the specie reserve. The scheme was shot down by strong opposition from Finance Minister Yamamoto and from senior statesman Matsukata Masayoshi.[32] In line with the retrenchment policy, the Saionji cabinet also rejected the army's plan to create two new divisions that the army argued were needed because of the revolutionary situation in China. The cause of military expansion was championed by Major General

Tanaka Giichi, the future prime minister, at the time chief of the Army Ministry's Military Affairs Bureau and a leading member of the Yamagata faction.[33] This budget battle sharpened the antagonism between the Saionji cabinet and the Yamagata-army group, and on December 2, 1912, in the opening months of the reign of the new Taishō emperor, the army minister resigned. By refusing to appoint a successor, the army brought down the cabinet, opening the "Taishō political crisis." Within the context of this constitutional crisis, the divide over the positive and negative financial policies took full shape in party politics.

The Two-Party System

Katsura Tarō had been thinking for some time of forming his own political party to fight the Seiyūkai for control of the House of Representatives. In July 1912 Katsura made a well publicized trip to Europe via the Trans-Siberian Railway, accompanied by his followers Gotō Shinpei and Wakatsuki Reijirō, who had resigned from the Finance Ministry in 1911 and been appointed to the House of Peers. As Wakatsuki later told it, Katsura was pursuing "three dreams." His first dream was to forge better relations with Russia. His second, in response to the invitation of Kaiser Wilhelm II, was to join the kaiser on vacation in Germany. His third dream was to investigate political parties in England.[34]

Another purpose of the trip, Katsura reportedly told Sun Yat-sen, was to meet secretly in Moscow with German representatives to negotiate an alliance that would "topple British hegemony" in Turkey, India, and China. Gotō Shinpei and Tanaka Giichi likewise favored dumping the British alliance for an alliance with Germany.[35]

Katsura's trip was cut short by the news of the death of the Meiji emperor on July 30, after which the project of forming a political party went no further. During his absence, Katsura was appointed lord privy seal in the imperial household, which should have ended his career on the front lines of politics. When the army brought down the Saionji cabinet in December, however, Katsura was able to return to power as prime minister, defying an understanding that Hara and the Seiyūkai thought they had reached to the effect that the Saionji cabinet's tenure would be long enough to let it carry through a one-year retrenchment plan and then return to a full-fledged "positive" policy.[36]

Katsura's third cabinet lasted only fifty-one days and is best remembered for the storm of popular outrage that it provoked. Brief as it was, however, the cabinet had transformative results in that it brought together the political team that, as the core of the later Kenseikai and Minseitō parties, would champion the "negative" retrenchment policy and direct what came to be Japan's liberal party.

Wakatsuki Reijirō was the new minister of finance. The communications minister was Gotō Shinpei. Hamaguchi Osachi, who headed the MOF's Monopoly Bureau, also entered politics at this time. Wakatsuki wanted Hamaguchi as vice minister of finance, but Katsura told him to pick Shōda Kazue instead. During his tenure as civil governor of Taiwan, Gotō Shinpei had gotten to know Hamaguchi, whom he chose as his own vice minister. Katō Takaaki joined the cabinet as foreign minister. Katsura also created the party that Katō, Wakatsuki, and Hamaguchi would, in succession, lead for the next twenty years, naming it the Rikken Dōshikai.

The specie crisis did not let up, and Finance Minister Wakatsuki continued the retrenchment policy and tried to push it further by asking the Bank of Japan to raise interest rates. Bank of Japan governor Takahashi again prevented this from happening.[37] The cabinet adopted a principle of not issuing bonds, but nevertheless, to maintain the gold standard, Wakatsuki did try to raise foreign loans for the Oriental Development Company and for railroad projects. The war in the Balkans had made international capital markets cautious, however, and the political furor at home delayed the cabinet's plans, so the bonds were not issued until March 1913, when Takahashi Korekiyo was finance minister.

Katsura himself gained nothing from what turned out to be his final political effort, as the opposition parties organized a "movement to protect constitutional government," led by Ozaki Yukio and Inukai Tsuyoshi. Crowds of thousands demonstrated outside the Diet, where the opposition politicians were greeted as heroes. Katsura prorogued the Diet three times. In the climax of the movement, on February 10, 1913, tens of thousands of people surrounded the Diet and fought with police, and on February 11 Katsura resigned. A new Seiyūkai-backed cabinet was formed on February 20.[38]

Katsura Tarō had built his political career as a master of the old clique politics and was not liberal by anyone's definition. But despite its illiberal origins, the Dōshikai was the source of what came to be known as Japan's liberal party. In essence, Katsura's party was an anti-Seiyūkai, uniting a broad spectrum of politicians antagonistic to Hara and his party. One main stream that fed into the party was the conservative, pro-government Chūō Club. Another was the Kokumintō (National Party), which carried on the progressive political party tradition associated with Ōkuma Shigenobu, the old champion of British-style parliamentary government. Like Ōkuma's previous parties, the Dōshikai attracted a variety of business and liberal supporters and had a more urban orientation than the landlord-backed Seiyūkai.

Not least, the Dōshikai had a strongly bureaucratic flavor, with former officials from the Finance and Home ministries being especially prominent in the party leadership. Katō Takaaki joined Katsura's party, bringing with him a close connection to the Mitsubishi zaibatsu, which also had longstanding close ties to Ōkuma Shigenobu and his party. Gotō Shinpei also joined. The most prominent former MOF officials were Wakatsuki Reijirō and Hamaguchi Osachi, who between them defined the new party's line in economics as one of orthodox, MOF-style retrenchment. When Katsura died in October 1913, Katō Takaaki assumed the party presidency. Gotō Shinpei and others split from the party at this point, and Katō reorganized it as the Kenseikai in October 1916.[39]

Thus, from 1913 two elite-based conservative parties alternated in power, and the tension between the positive and negative policies became a matter of partisan dispute.

THE RULES OF THE GAME

In the short run, it was the Seiyūkai who gained by the Taishō political change, as the party rode the wave of popular discontent to gain more governmental authority than ever. Saionji declined to serve again as prime minister and instead backed Admiral Yamamoto Gonnohyōe (Yamamoto Gonbei, 1852–1933) of the Satsuma faction. Seiyūkai party boss Hara Takashi was again home minister. Hara himself called the Yamamoto cabinet the "third Saionji cabinet"[40]—which was almost to say, a Hara cabinet. Having discovered his like-mindedness with Hara concerning the positive policy, Takahashi Korekiyo resigned as governor of the Bank of Japan to become finance minister. He also joined the Seiyūkai. In age Takahashi was Hara's senior by two years, but henceforth he followed Hara's lead in party politics.

It would also be little exaggeration to say that from this point forward Takahashi's policy *was* the Seiyūkai party line in economics. Takahashi himself served as finance minister in every subsequent cabinet ever formed by the Seiyūkai, in 1918, 1921, 1927, and 1931. When Hara was assassinated in 1921, it was Takahashi who succeeded him as Seiyūkai party president and prime minister. Yamamoto Tatsuo, who as finance minister had stood in the way of Hara's positive policy, himself joined the Seiyūkai in 1913 and entered the new cabinet as minister of agriculture and commerce. Mishima Yatarō, who also came down on the side of fiscal restraint, succeeded Takahashi as Bank of Japan governor. At this point, Takahashi still remained unable to implement the positive policy. His first step as finance minister was to implement the fiscal year (FY) 1913 retrenchment budget already put together by the Katsura cabinet, and he carried retrenchment a step further by implementing further cuts in the working budget via administrative retrenchment. He also reduced the income tax.[41]

Takahashi also made ambitious plans for raising overseas bonds. Foreign capital was "extremely necessary" for capital-poor Japan, he thought, and borrowing was acceptable if it were for productive enterprises that would pay for themselves over time. He optimistically reckoned that his proposed projects would increase national productive power and solve the chronic trade gap by 1920. This strategy of debt-leveraged development was surrounded with risks, but given the understood necessity of competing in the imperial financial game, the options seemed limited. A few months earlier Takahashi had informed senior statesman Inoue Kaoru of his fears concerning the foreign-currency Russo-Japanese War bonds coming due in 1925. He reminded Inoue that Japan's leasehold on the Kwantung Territory would expire in 1923, and that in 1924 China would gain the right to purchase the Mukden-Andong railroad that connected Japan's Manchurian and Korean rail networks. If Japan failed to refinance the bonds coming due in 1925, it would be extremely pressed financially, allowing the Western powers to move in to lend money to China and buy out Japan's rights in Manchuria. If that happened, "all of East Asia would inevitably come under the superintendence of the [Western] Powers, and it would fall into the same situation as Eastern Europe and the various countries surrounding Turkey." Thus, Takahashi thought Japan must borrow now to expand the economy, expecting that future increases in exports would solve the problem of redeeming the war loan.[42]

There was further monetary tightening in 1913, but Takahashi prevented BOJ governor Mishima from raising interest rates. In drawing up the 1914 budget, Takahashi continued the retrenchment policy but also planned a big overseas issue of railroad bonds, to include ¥10 million for Korean rail development. Matsukata Masayoshi, Yamamoto Tatsuo, and Mishima Yatarō opposed the plan because it would mean a large increase in the BOJ note issue, but with Hara's backing, Takahashi got the proposal approved by the cabinet in late 1913. But in the end, the positive rail policy again failed to materialize, as the Yamamoto Gonnohyōe cabinet left office much as the Katsura cabinet had.[43] In January 1914, while the Diet was in session, the newspapers published stories of bribes paid by the Siemens and Vickers companies to secure Japanese naval contracts. The opposition united in attacking the cabinet. Again, great crowds of protesters surrounded the Diet and the government called out the troops. The House of Peers joined in the attack on the cabinet, which was forced to resign in late March 1914, before having passed Takahashi's budget.

There followed a fundamental shift in policy. The next cabinet was formed by Ōkuma Shigenobu and backed by the Dōshikai. Dōshikai party president Katō Takaaki was foreign minister and acted as vice premier for the seventy-six-year-old Ōkuma. Inukai Tsuyoshi, president of the remnant Kokumintō, called it simply a "Katō cabinet."[44] Wakatsuki Reijirō was again minister of finance, and Hamaguchi Osachi was his vice minister.

Since the Russo-Japanese War, the government had borrowed abroad to tide the country over the worsening specie crisis, but now Wakatsuki and Hamaguchi implemented a doubly negative policy of cutting both government spending and foreign borrowing.[45] The Bank of Japan's Fukai Eigo put the problem succinctly: Japan's policy of foreign borrowing had reached a state of "deadlock" (*gaisai seisaku no ikizumari*). In fact, the shortage of foreign exchange had reached the point that the government had to pull money from the Bank of Japan note reserve in order to pay its foreign debts.[46] Finance Minister Wakatsuki reasoned that to continue to fill the specie reserve via foreign loans would cause currency expansion leading to inflation, a greater trade deficit, and a new outflow of gold. He therefore halted Takahashi's rail bond deal that was already in the works and announced that the specie problem would be dealt with in the orthodox Bank of England manner, by raising interest rates. In July 1914 the Bank of Japan tightened credit and raised interest rates to the highest levels since 1908–09. The specie reserve would no longer be "artificially adjusted" but rather would reflect the "actual economic situation" of the international balance of payments.[47] That is, Japan would now follow gold-standard rules and adjust via deflation.

Foreshadowing his later analysis of the 1920s, Yokohama Specie Bank president Inoue Junnosuke gave the following accounting: Japan was running annual trade deficits of some ¥40 million per year and was borrowing abroad to cover them. But borrowing abroad also promoted imports and thus increased the trade deficit further. Japan's accumulated foreign debt approached ¥1.8 billion, and the annual interest payments alone were ¥80 million. Following normal gold-standard logic, foreign payments would be paid out of the Bank of Japan's gold holdings, forcing the BOJ to contract the note issue correspondingly. The resulting scarcity of money would force up interest rates, which would cause business difficulties and shutdowns, which would reduce imports. For example, "if [cotton-spinning] companies were to shut down, people importing spinning machinery and so on would disappear"—that is, adjustment via depression. But "since the Russo-Japanese War, Japan's finance has departed from normal financial principles and gone off the right track," as overseas borrowing had allowed the currency to increase despite the trade gap. When war broke out in Europe, as Inoue later recalled, there was a real danger that Japan would default on its external debt.[48]

Despite the new turn to the negative policy, plans were still afoot for raising further overseas bond issues. Shōda Kazue (1869–1961) was a career Ministry of Finance official who had graduated from Tokyo Imperial University and joined the ministry in the same year as Hamaguchi. By 1912 he had risen to the post of vice minister. Party influence had extended to the point that vice-ministerial-level officials were joining the governing party, and Finance Minister Takahashi had several times asked Shōda to join the Seiyūkai. When the Ōkuma-Katō cabinet took office in April 1914, Shōda was pressed to join the Dōshikai. He chose to resign instead, and Hamaguchi Osachi became vice minister of finance. In the summer of 1914, accompanied by Tsushima Juichi, who had graduated from Tokyo Imperial University and joined the Ministry of Finance in 1912, Shōda took on a new task for the government, sailing to the German concession of Jiaozhou (Qingdao) and thence traveling on to Europe by rail. Their mission, again, was to investigate a foreign loan to build up Japan's critically depleted gold holdings. While on the Trans-Siberian Railway, they heard the news of the assassination of the Austrian archduke.[49] No more long-term borrowing was possible, and in late 1914 Japan's economy slid into the sharpest price deflation since the Matsukata deflation of the early 1880s.

FIVE

"Divine Providence," 1914–1918

Between 1904 and 1913 the Japanese government financed the building of a continental empire with more than ¥1 billion in borrowed British and American funds. During the same period, Japan's national balance of payments ran a deficit that totaled some ¥850 million. If viewed as a national enterprise, Japan invested heavily in two lines of expansion, overseas empire and militarily oriented heavy industry, neither of which brought a net return in terms of foreign-exchange earnings.[1] Gold was paid out to foreign countries to fund this expansion, while profits gotten within the new Japanese empire came mostly in the form of yen. This gold gap was filled by more foreign borrowing. By 1914 total foreign debt came to more than one-fourth of national income,[2] and as European lenders became reluctant to extend further loans to Japan, there was talk of an impending financial crisis. The external imbalance forced domestic monetary constraint. Recession followed, intensified after April 1914 by the Ōkuma cabinet's "negative" financial policy.

The opening of the European war in August 1914 was a great economic shock, disrupting trade and deepening the recession. Prices rose immediately for goods produced by the belligerent powers. A few Japanese industries also benefited immediately. Beet sugar, for example, mostly produced in Central and Eastern Europe, disappeared from the world market, sending cane sugar prices soaring and profiting Taiwan sugar producers—above all the giant Suzuki sugar interests and their bankers, the semigovernmental Bank of Taiwan. But the war's first effects on most branches of industry were negative, as European sources of supply were cut off and prices were hiked up for key industrial inputs including metals, machinery, chemicals, and dyes. The suspension of gold exports by the belligerents froze Japanese gold holdings abroad and throttled trade financing. "Throughout the world, finance and economy moved around the pivot of London, and when the machinery in London stopped, even in Japan things became dark," as Inoue Junnosuke recalled. As Inoue labored at the Yokohama Specie Bank to make the international financial ends meet, it seemed to him as if there was not a ray of light for weeks.[3] The result of these circumstances was that the wholesale price index actually fell in the latter half of 1914 and the first half of 1915.

Despite the economic gloom, it was also immediately perceived that Europe's war provided a historic opportunity for Japanese expansion—"divine providence" (*ten'yū*), in the famous phrase of elder statesman Inoue Kaoru.[4] Not only was a way opened out of the financial deadlock, but for the first time in its history, Japan emerged as a financial power, and embarked directly on a program of financial imperialism in China.

JAPAN'S OPPORTUNITY

After 1925 the financial and diplomatic policies espoused by the two major political parties came to be aligned along a common "positive-negative" axis: the Seiyūkai advocated a nationalist and expansionist "positive" policy in both economics and in its policy toward China, while the Kenseikai-Minseitō followed the so-called "negative" policy of fiscal retrenchment, military restraint, and international conciliation. In the Dōshikai-backed cabinet of Ōkuma Shigenobu, in contrast, a negative policy of fiscal restraint was joined with an aggressive positive policy toward China, directed by Foreign Minister Katō Takaaki.

The aggressive China policy of the liberal, gentlemanly, and pro-British Katō has sometimes been difficult for liberal historians to explain. The apparent inconsistency arises when one loses sight of the fact that Japan's British alliance historically enabled rather than restrained Japanese expansion. It was for this reason that the U.S. government later insisted on its termination. The Ōkuma-Katō foreign policy took the strengthening of the British alliance as its first point. Receiving the British request for aid on the afternoon of August 7, Katō had by the end of the evening convened the cabinet and moved to commit Japan to war against Germany, without bothering to consult the senior statesmen until after the fact. Public and political opinion was divided over the Anglo-Japanese alliance, and Katō's peremptory action may have been meant to preempt pro-German moves backed by members of Yamagata Aritomo's Chōshū clique.[5] Japan's intention was conveyed to the German minister on August 15, and war was formally declared eight days later.

Like the Russo-Japanese War ten years earlier, the German-Japanese War (*Nichi-Doku sensō,* as it was often called in Japan) was fought primarily in China for control of Chinese territory. Unlike the war with Russia, it cost

Japan relatively little. Three hundred Japanese soldiers and sailors lost their lives in the fighting. Special war expenses for 1914–18 came to ¥226 million, a scant 4 percent of total central government spending.[6] The military phase of the war was also brief, essentially concluding on November 7 with the occupation of the German concession at Qingdao.

The military campaign was directly succeeded by a political campaign for hegemony in China. On January 18, 1915, again before consulting the senior statesmen, Foreign Minister Katō had a detailed list of twenty-one demands presented to the government of Yuan Shikai in Beijing. The story is historically notorious as an early revelation of Japanese ambitions to dominate all of China. Starting from the demand that Japan succeed to German rights in Shandong and extending to the demand that China accept Japanese advisers in designated central government bureaus and local police forces, the Twenty-one Demands were in essence a magnified version of the policy already practiced on Korea.[7] Their full acceptance would have turned China into a de facto Japanese protectorate.

The financial aspects of the demands also laid bare the Japanese government's understanding of the real meaning of international lending and concession hunting in China. The third set of demands, which appear to have derived from Inoue Kaoru's initiative, called for Japan to assume joint control of the Hanyeping Company, which had fallen deeply into debt to Japanese lenders since the first loan of 1904.[8] Other demands required China to recognize Japan's priority or veto rights in regard to any projects for rail construction and foreign lending in Shandong, Manchuria, and Fujian, and called on the Chinese government to engage Japanese financial, as well as military and political, advisers. The implied principle was that the extension of credit meant the extension of control.

The Twenty-one Demands were negotiated on the Chinese side by the Japanese-educated vice minister of foreign affairs Cao Rulin (Ts'ao Ju-lin, 1876–1966), who subsequently directed the Beijing government's financial policies while assembling one of China's greatest personal fortunes. Four years later Cao would also become the first object of attack by the students who protested their government's giveaways to Japan at the Tiananmen Gate, on May 4, 1919. In May 1915 Cao agreed to a subset of Katō's demands, including the extension of the Kwantung leasehold to 1997 (the same year to which Britain's leasehold on the Hong Kong New Territories had been extended), the extension of the South Manchurian Railway lease to 2002, and the extension of the Andong-Mukden railway lease to 2007. Most of Japan's other economic demands were also agreed to. Journalist Ishibashi Tanzan warned that the Japanese policy would generate Chinese enmity and become a "root of evil" for the next hundred years.[9] An early, unintended economic consequence of the demands was to provoke a vigorous anti-Japanese trade boycott.

Katō's aggressive China policy thus moved along substantially the same lines favored by the militaristic clique led by Yamagata Aritomo, but Katō's unilateral conduct infuriated Yamagata and the other senior statesmen, who forced Katō from office in July 1915. Katō, who had seen himself as the next prime minister, was thereafter shut out of government for the next nine years.[10]

While Foreign Minister Katō pushed a "positive" foreign policy, Finance Minister Wakatsuki and his vice minister Hamaguchi Osachi implemented the "negative" policy of gaining external economic balance through fiscal and monetary restraint, and they did so to the fullest extent yet since the opening of the long post–Russo-Japanese War retrenchment drive in 1907. Wakatsuki had begun in the spring of 1914 by implementing the retrenchment budget put together by Takahashi Korekiyo in 1913. But Takahashi had joined budgetary retrenchment with ambitious plans for raising large foreign loans in order to fund Hara Takashi's railroad and infrastructure projects. Wakatsuki abruptly stopped these loan initiatives, initiating a "doubly negative" policy of cutting both government spending and the raising of foreign bonds.[11] The 1915 budget continued the retrenchment process, and although the Seiyūkai and Kokumintō joined forces to defeat the budget in the Diet, the government effected retrenchment anyway in its working budget.

In September 1916 the Dōshikai was re-formed as the Kenseikai (Constitutional Government Society), with Katō Takaaki as president. Wakatsuki Reijirō was vice president. The Ōkuma cabinet resigned in October 1916, when Ōkuma gave up his effort to pass the premiership to Katō and yielded his office to the Chōshū general Terauchi Masatake, governor general of Korea and the leading member of the Yamagata clique. Shōda Kazue, who had been governor of the Bank of Chosen since November 1915, became finance minister. Gotō Shinpei became home minister.

At this point a national realization seems suddenly to have dawned that Japan was in the midst of a spectacular boom. The depression and price deflation of 1914 had continued into 1915, but by the summer of that year, war orders to Japanese factories had begun to lift the depression. In the middle of November 1916, just after the Terauchi cabinet took office, newspapers one after another began to report stories of the boom.[12] European war demand combined with the withdrawal of European competition from Asian and other markets to create huge export opportunities, which Japanese manufacturers rushed to fill. For the first time, Japan sold volumes of manufactured goods to Europe as well as to new markets in Asia, Africa, and South America, all of which prospered as a result of Europe's war. This surge of Japanese exports to "third world" markets, which subsequently receded in the 1920s, foreshadowed the later export boom of the 1930s. The United States enjoyed its own war boom, and the American market absorbed more Japanese exports than ever. So did the Chinese market, which was further buoyed by the wartime appreciation of silver. In the Japanese home market, domestic manufacturers of metals, machinery, and chemicals now supplied many of the high-technology goods formerly imported from Europe.

By whichever index of trade or industrial production, the results were astounding. Between 1914 and 1918 total manufacturing output increased by 54 percent in inflation-adjusted terms. The heavy and chemical industries grew by much more, with especially great increases in steel production and shipbuilding. Exports increased by three times in money terms and by 47 percent in volume. Equally important from the standpoint of Japan's balance of payments was the great expansion of Japanese shipping. The tonnage of ships built in 1919 was more than ten times that built in 1914, and the capacity of Japan's merchant fleet grew by 80 percent over the period. The last year of the war, 1918, was the peak year in foreign receipts, with more than half of the net proceeds coming from "invisible" receipts, mostly profits from shipping and shipping insurance.[13] Industrial profits were extremely high, and dividend levels surpassed 100 percent in many industries. Inoue Junnosuke summed up the process succinctly: "enlargement, expansion, increase, and advance" (*zōdai, kakuchō, zōka, zōshin*).[14]

The boom in exports and shipping and the progress of import substitution converted Japan's payments deficit into a great surplus, making Japan a creditor nation for the first time. Payments surpluses totaled ¥2.4 billion over the years 1916, 1917, and 1918. After net outflows in every year since 1910, gold poured into the country: ¥77 million in 1916 and ¥236 million in 1917. The inflow of gold combined with a great increase in Bank of Japan lending for trade financing to increase the volume of both currency and bank deposits by some four times between 1914 and the end of 1919. Prices increased only slightly more slowly.[15]

Rapid social changes followed, with the conspicuous growth of the industrial working class on the one hand and the rise of nouveaux riches, or *narikin*, on the other. The latter term comes from Japanese chess and means a pawn turned into a much more powerful "*kin*," or gold piece. Tales of *narikin* extravagance were sensationally reported in the press and became the object of the near-Confucianistic opprobrium of government officials, many of whom saw the feverish expansion of the war years as unnatural and destabilizing. Extravagance seemed to extend to the fast-growing salaried class as a whole; as Inoue Junnosuke later lectured an audience of middle-class housewives, it was "an age that produced a lot of so-called *narikin*, an age when all of you lived extremely luxuriously, an age when the prices of everything rose greatly, an age when everywhere Japan was full of an atmosphere of pleasure-seeking."[16] To the formulators of the negative policy, the boom later appeared to have given rise to a consumption bubble that never deflated, and the "luxury" and "looseness" of the times appeared as the great source of Japan's economic problems of the 1920s.

THE GLOBAL FINANCIAL SHIFT

"*Narikin*" powers were also rising in the international arena, and if Europe's bloodbath was providential for Japanese business, it was even more so for American business. In October 1917 the results seemed clear to Inoue Junnosuke: "America is becoming England's successor, which is to say, New York is becoming the central market of world finance."[17]

In later scholarly analyses, most influentially in that of Charles Kindleberger, this global shift has been adduced to explain the magnitude of the global depression that followed in the 1930s. In Kindleberger's conception, international hegemony (or "responsibility") is something carried out by a single country and consists of (1) maintaining an open market for imports, (2) policing the world economic system by coordinating international exchange rates and macroeconomic policies, and (3) acting as the world banker to provide stable, long-term lending and serve as a lender of last resort. Given such a framework, the market mechanism will sort out dislocations that arise in the system. Kindleberger's formula is an idealized picture of the hegemonic role of the United States after World War II and of Britain in the era before World War I. And while Britain did not actively "police" the world economic system, the operation of the international gold standard was thought to do much the same thing. Accordingly, the era between the world wars appears as a hegemonic interregnum, and "British inability and U.S. unwillingness" was the root cause of the severity of the great interwar depression.[18] The story that follows will present numerous points of contact with Kindleberger's thesis.

In less abstract terms, the question of the loss of Britain's primacy in global finance was much discussed at the time, with some saying that it was a temporary wartime phenomenon and others that it was the dawn of a new American age. Thomas Lamont was typically diplomatic and evenhanded, saying that only time would tell. This debate was noticed and reported in Japan.[19] For Japan, Britain's new financial inability presented both difficulties and opportunities, though initially more of the former.

London had been the central marketplace both for Japan's long-term borrowing and for its international trade finance. As of 1914, out of forty overseas bond issues, thirty-two were raised wholly or partially in London. Eleven issues were wholly or partially raised in Paris (many jointly with London). New York came in third, involved with six issues (including the great Russo-Japanese War loans); these were all sterling loans issued jointly in London.[20] Thereafter, owing largely to conflicts over who would manage

Manchurian development, the New York capital markets had been closed to Japanese borrowing.

Most of Japan's foreign trade accounts were also reckoned in sterling and settled in London, whether it was the export of Japanese raw silk to America, the import of raw cotton from India, or the export of cotton yarn and various consumer manufactures to China.[21] (The Japan-China trade was subject to the fluctuating price of silver, but the price of silver itself was set in the London markets, as was the price of virtually every other globally traded commodity.) In settling their trade accounts through banks in London, Japanese merchants (acting chiefly through the agency of the Yokohama Specie Bank) were only doing what the traders of other countries did. It was undoubtedly advantageous to world commerce to have a central place where transactions between any two countries could conveniently be settled. It was also highly advantageous to the place of London as the world's money market and to the place of sterling as a global money to have a great percentage of the world's trading capital parked at any given time in the London markets. According to one estimate, half of the sterling bills in London were for the financing of interforeign trade, that is, trade in which Britain itself was not a party.[22]

New York, not to mention Tokyo, still lacked the facilities to take on such a mediating role.[23] In particular, neither New York nor Tokyo had a developed market for rediscounting trade bills. As the first governor of the newly established Federal Reserve Bank of New York, Benjamin Strong strove to build a powerful central bank on the model of the Bank of England, to turn the U.S. dollar into an international currency on the model of sterling, and to make New York City into a world financial center rivaling London. In line with his plans, Strong worked to build a market for discounting commercial bills in New York. In this as in other respects, Inoue Junnosuke later strove to follow Strong's lead.[24]

With the opening of the war in August 1914, Britain alone among the European combatants had the financial strength to maintain gold convertibility. Britain employed its financial might to extend war loans to its allies, and the British government assumed the power of approving or denying all foreign loans issued in London. Remarkably, as late as February 1915, when Japan's international finances were still extremely constrained, London banks issued a short-term loan to roll over Japanese National Railroad bills that were coming due. As the war ground on, however, London became unable to carry out its functions as an international financial center.[25] Informally, the British government embargoed the export of specie, trapping Japan's large overseas specie reserves overseas. The practice of issuing Bank of Japan notes against the overseas specie reserve had hitherto been done quietly. It now became the subject of increasing controversy and criticism in the Diet, and the practice was compared to that of the legendary "Ninben" *katsuo-don* (bonito and rice bowl) shop, which had issued its own bills on the security of its reserves of fish swimming in the sea.[26]

The New York gold market did remain open, and from Japan's viewpoint, as YSB president Inoue Junnosuke explained, New York now became the safest and most convenient place to deposit gold and settle trade accounts.[27] After December 1916 London's intermediate role broke down altogether. Thus, for the first time, dollar and yen bills of exchange were used to finance the U.S.-Japan trade. But there remained serious limits to U.S. financial capabilities. The U.S. dollar did not function as an international currency outside of a relatively small sphere of influence in the Caribbean and the Philippines. Nor could New York handle Japan's vital trade with India, which had to be settled by the more awkward expedient of direct gold shipments. Thus, gold flowed from America to Japan and from Japan to India.

At the same time that New York began to function as a center for settling international trade accounts, the United States also, suddenly, became the world's greatest creditor nation—a status subsequently maintained for some seventy years, until Japan itself became the world's greatest creditor, during the final phase of the Cold War in the 1980s. America's wartime trade surpluses ballooned from some $470 million in 1914 to more than $3 billion (¥6 billion) per year in 1916, 1917, and 1918, dwarfing the very large surpluses of Japan. To finance their purchases of American goods, Europeans sold their American bonds back to Americans and took out new, American loans. J. P. Morgan and Company took on "the burden of leadership," as Thomas Lamont put it, in this historic operation, handling $3 billion in wartime purchases and issuing some $1.5 billion in war credits for Britain and France.[28] With America's declaration of war in April 1917, Morgan and Company also took a leading role in financing the U.S. war effort. Japanese fears also grew over the potential advance of American economic power into East Asia.

YEN DIPLOMACY

Japan too emerged as an international creditor for the first time. In November 1915 the Banque Franco-Japonaise (Nichi-Futsu Ginkō) arranged a first yen loan to France. In February 1916 the Yokohama Specie Bank, acting on government orders, took the lead in forming a syndicate of Japanese banks to raise a bond issue of ¥50 million for the Russian government, to finance goods purchased in Japan. However, only ¥2.5 million of the Russian bonds were taken up in public subscriptions, and the issuing banks themselves had to take up most of the issue. These were the first Japanese loans to Western countries.[29] Additional bond issues for the European allies followed, all conducted under government direction by the syndicate led by the Yokohama

Specie Bank. Another ¥70 million was lent to Russia in August 1916, ¥100 million to Britain in November, and ¥50 million to France in June 1917. That Japan was lending money—in yen—to Britain and France so that they could buy Japanese goods was a remarkable turnaround, and it registered as a kind of positive shock to business sentiment.[30]

Loans to China also began to flow in volume. Between April and July of 1916 Inoue Junnosuke made another tour of China, again visiting the Specie Bank's offices in Manchuria as well as the new YSB agency in the former German concession of Qingdao. In June the Specie Bank and the Tōzai Bank floated a ¥5 million railroad loan for the Chinese government. The Chinese government bond issue was almost entirely taken up in the public offering and was followed by additional direct lending by the Specie Bank to the Chinese government. Prime Minister Terauchi publicly criticized the luxurious trend of the times, but the Japanese state itself was also a kind of *narikin,* and with national finances floating on "the flood of gold," his cabinet after October 1916 adopted a new policy toward lending to China that could be called the "yen diplomacy."[31]

As we have seen, Japan's gold standard operated substantially as a sterling-based gold-exchange standard after the Russo-Japanese War. This arrangement was inarguably convenient; nor was it externally imposed, as were the outright gold-exchange standards operated by India, the Philippines, and other colonized countries. But Japan's London-centered gold-exchange standard was, like Russia's Paris-centered gold-exchange standard, an expression of financial weakness and peripherality. At the same time, the Japanese government also constructed Japan as a monetary center in its own sphere of influence by imposing new yen-based gold-exchange standards in Taiwan and Korea. As Japan gained financial strength during the war boom, a variety of schemes for extending a yen-based gold-exchange standard to China also took shape.

The versatile Gotō Shinpei functioned as vice premier and power broker in the Terauchi cabinet, serving first as home minister and then as foreign minister. Gotō had also become a kind of apostle for the yen bloc. As civil governor of Taiwan, Gotō had been involved in the establishment of the Bank of Taiwan. As president of the South Manchurian Railway Company—that is, as virtual civil governor of Japan's informal empire in South Manchuria—Gotō had developed, against the opposition of Takahashi Korekiyo and the Yokohama Specie Bank, a series of proposals for a special bank with the authority to issue gold notes, fund Japanese development projects, and assist Japanese colonists. In 1914 Gotō enlarged this idea into a scheme for a special "Bank of the Orient" to cover all of China.[32] On joining General Terauchi's cabinet in October 1916, Gotō at once began to cook up plans for a new financial initiative in China, again invoking his slogan of "military preparation in civilian clothing." This, according to Gotō's biographer Tsurumi Yūsuke, was the

Terauchi cabinet's starting point: Gotō's first and greatest concern "was to break out of the situation of deadlock in China policy which had been the greatest reason for the Ōkuma cabinet's collapse."[33]

Gotō's core conception, established as the new cabinet's unannounced policy, was to bring China into a Japanese-led "East Asian Economic League" (Tō-A Keizai Dōmei) and to make large loans to China outside the framework of the international consortium.[34] The Japanese people had "grown drunk" on the great wartime surplus, Gotō thought. They would suffer a correspondingly great shock when the war ended, the trade gap reappeared, and specie again began to flow out. Now, before the war was over, was the time to act: ¥100 million invested now would have the effect of ¥500 million or ¥1 billion after the war, when Japan would again have to compete with the "European and American economic invasion policy." In this way as in others, Gotō also anticipated the worldview of the 1930s: not only was he an original architect of Japanese Manchuria, but he also perceived the world around him as one of competing economic blocs. Gotō's idea of a marriage of Japanese capital and Chinese labor was behind the Nishihara loans to China.[35]

While Gotō Shinpei played the role of visionary, the actual work of financial expansionism was directed by a "Korean group" centered around Prime Minister Terauchi himself and including Finance Minister Shōda Kazue and businessman Nishihara Kamezō (1873–1954). All were experienced empire builders. Terauchi had overseen Japan's annexation of Korea and served a brutal tenure there as governor general from 1910 to 1916. Shōda, after retiring as vice minister of finance in 1914, had agreed to become the second governor of the Bank of Chosen in November 1915, at the combined urging of Governor General Terauchi, Sakatani Yoshio, and Terauchi's friend and confidante Nishihara Kamezō. Nishihara told Shōda, "The mission of the Bank of Chosen is not merely to be the central bank of Korea; it is the fountainhead of Korean industrial development, and it must be the central axis for our economic advance into Manchuria and China."[36] This was a mission that Shōda pursued aggressively. The Bank of Chosen's mission also built on prior work by Nishihara, who had first gone to Korea as a patriotic activist at the opening of the Russo-Japanese War. He remained for the next twelve years and had his hands in a variety of enterprises. His Kyōekisha (Mutual Benefit Society), begun as a kind of trading cooperative, established trading offices in Manchuria that also served as exchange offices for Bank of Chosen notes and helped to spread their use there.[37]

In July 1916, even before Terauchi formed his cabinet, Nishihara was proposing to him a plan to lend money to the Chinese government and introduce a yen-based gold-exchange standard there. Two days after the formation of the cabinet in October, he was suggesting the "economic territorialization" of Manchuria and Mongolia.[38] Nishihara subsequently became

Prime Minister Terauchi's personal representative in China, where he liberally dispensed yen loans to the Chinese government.

The Terauchi-Shōda-Nishihara policy in China was also directed against the previous control of policy by the Foreign Ministry, where Katō Takaaki's younger brother-in-law, Shidehara Kijūrō, was now vice minister, and the Yokohama Specie Bank, where Inoue Junnosuke was president. Up to this point the Specie Bank had handled some ¥100 million in loans to China, about 60 percent of Japan's total lending to China (or 80 percent, if the ¥49 million Japanese government loan for the Boxer Rebellion indemnity is not counted). But the Specie Bank was a party to the Four-Country Consortium (now, with the removal of Germany as a partner, an Allied body), and consortium membership limited the bank's freedom of action. During the Terauchi cabinet the Specie Bank made only one major loan to China.[39]

To bypass the Specie Bank and the Allied consortium, Finance Minister Shōda in December 1916 secretly directed three semigovernmental banks, the Industrial Bank of Japan, Bank of Taiwan, and Bank of Chosen, to form a group to make "economic" (that is, nonconsortium) loans to China.[40] The so-called Nishihara loans formed the greater part of the bond issues they subsequently organized. Of at least ¥277 million lent in the years 1916–1918, more than half was arranged by Nishihara, who between January 1917 and September 1918 funneled eight loans totaling ¥145 million to the Beijing government, all outside regular Foreign Ministry and Yokohama Specie Bank channels. Nishihara's key contact was Cao Rulin, now communications minister, who secretly recognized Japan's succession to German railroad rights in Shandong as a condition for the loans. From the beginning, Nishihara's loan projects were connected to a scheme for establishing a yen-based gold-exchange standard for China. The Terauchi cabinet's tenure also represented the high point of Japanese lending to China. Lending fell back drastically after the end of the European war, and a smaller surge of lending in 1921–24 was primarily to refinance previous debt.[41]

Inoue Junnosuke disliked the Terauchi cabinet's policy of unregulated political lending, but as YSB president, his first responsibility was to keep trade finance flowing during the abnormal wartime conditions. At the time, the Specie Bank handled almost all of Japan's foreign-exchange business. Inoue showed great technical skill in the task, and his reputation rose to the point that he was being written of in the popular press as a future governor of the Bank of Japan.[42] Trade finance also became the main channel for the inflationary increase in the Bank of Japan note issue.

ANTICIPATING THE POSTWAR DEPRESSION

Even as the wartime boom unfolded, Inoue was pessimistic about its durability. In a speech given in July 1917, Inoue tried to anticipate what economic changes the war would bring. He stressed in particular the inevitability of a postwar economic reaction. While avoiding the word *depression* (*fukyō* and others) in describing this coming reaction, Inoue anticipated up to five years of "extreme financial stringency" after the war. Such a reaction was the general rule after wars and had been the case after the Franco-Prussian War, the Boer War, and the Russo-Japanese War.[43]

Like virtually all modern wars, the European war had been financed by debt, and Inoue perceived that this would have important postwar consequences. The world's war debts in the form of (mostly domestic) government bonds currently added up to nearly ¥120 billion (or roughly US$60 billion), he estimated—a phenomenal amount to have run up in only three years. All countries had multiplied their domestic money supplies: Britain, France, and Germany by six times, Italy by two times, and Russia by twelve times. In Japan the volume of currency had nearly doubled. If the victors demanded a large indemnity from Germany, world debt loads would increase still further. Inoue thus foresaw a debt-burdened postwar world where scarce capital and high interest rates would put great pressure on business. The reconversion of factories to civilian production would also demand large amounts of capital. At the same time, the expanded wartime circulation of currency would naturally be curtailed after the war, bringing price deflation.

Inoue also viewed Japan's need to borrow from Europe as a continuing structural feature. Before the war, he explained, interest rates had been very high in Japan—domestic funds were insufficient, and Japanese business borrowed a great amount from England. These debts were repaid during the war, but if conditions reverted to the prewar situation, Japan would again have to borrow from Europe, and it would take great volumes of borrowed funds to maintain Japan's newly expanded industry. The wartime growth of industry also appeared to Inoue as a strictly temporary gain. Once the war ended, there would be an economic struggle with foreign countries—for this reason too, a postwar reaction must be expected. Because industry had expanded more in the United States and Japan than anywhere else, Inoue reasoned that in trying to maintain these new production levels, Japan, like the United States, would likely suffer worse financial pressure than Europe.

The way out of such a postwar impasse, Inoue suggested, was for Japan to export capital while the war boom lasted, investing especially in foreign bonds. In this he differed with those who argued that Japan's new funds should be used at home for industrial development rather than being invested overseas. American financiers faced the same problem, and so Inoue proposed to follow their example. First, Japan could make direct foreign investments, as the United States had done in South America and China. However, it was impossible productively to make extremely large direct foreign investments overnight, so it was more practical to buy foreign bonds and then sell them after the war, when the money was needed. The United States, having done this, would be able to call in its debts from foreign countries when it faced its own postwar financial stringency. If Japan, like America, could call in the money lent abroad, then even amidst global economic weakness, Japan alone would be able to enjoy easy finance and continue to expand its industry.[44] Inoue did not grasp the fundamental contradiction presented by this "American" solution when it came to the sources of global demand: if America were to call in its credits to Europe, it would choke European demand and come at the expense of American exports to Europe.

Under the Terauchi cabinet, private banks and the Ministry of Finance's Deposit Bureau did extend more than ¥600 million to Japan's European allies, primarily by purchasing Allied government bonds. All but £10 million of this lending was done in yen. It offered the twin advantages of helping to finance Japanese exports and helping to limit the increase of the Japanese money supply and thus curb domestic inflation.[45] However, like most of the roughly ¥300 million in loans to China, the ¥222 million lent to the imperial Russian government was never repaid. As of June 1918 Japan's total overseas investments stood at ¥1.58 billion (about US$800 million)—a great amount of money in Japan's experience, Inoue Junnosuke said, but slightly less than what Britain had invested abroad in just a single average year before the war. It was also slightly less than Japan's ¥1.6 billion in accumulated foreign debt.[46]

Like Inoue, Sakatani Yoshio anticipated worldwide problems of postwar adjustment. In November 1917, at a celebration of the twentieth anniversary of Japan's gold standard, Sakatani presented a wide-ranging set of ideas about the postwar world order to an audience of Japan's top political and business leaders, including almost all of those whose names appear in the present book.[47] The war was being funded by immense paper money issues, Sakatani told them, and Europe's postwar problems of currency and debt disposal would be beyond the power of existing financial institutions. Sakatani had represented Japan at the Allied Economic Conference in Paris in June 1916, and one idea raised there, though not taken up for discussion, was to establish a "world bank" (*bankoku ginkō*). This vision, Sakatani said, was in the minds of Western financiers, and Japanese leaders needed to be aware of it. International financial leaders were now saying that rather than conducting postwar adjustment country by country, it would be better to do so as a league (*rengō*), establishing a world bank for the task. Connected to this was the idea of creating a world currency.

The internationalist vision Sakatani described would, with intellectual leadership from John Maynard Keynes, take form in the Bretton Woods institutions established after World War II. But after World War I, stabilization programs in all of the larger economies would be financed by existing, private financial institutions; and as Sakatani foresaw, the task would ultimately be beyond their power. Although no one anticipated it in 1917, Japan too would be subject to one of these internationally coordinated programs of postwar monetary adjustment.

Sakatani's was one of a series of speeches given to celebrate the success of Japan's gold standard by such eminences as Matsukata Masayoshi and Shibusawa Eiichi. And although the Japanese gold standard seemed to those assembled to be securely established beyond question, in fact it had just been suspended. This appeared at the time purely a temporary wartime expedient, but it would shape Japanese history for the next fifteen years and beyond.

THE GOLD EMBARGO

The world war generated sudden, large international specie movements unlike anything seen in Japan since 1859, when the lifting of the Tokugawa shogunate's embargo on specie exports had been followed by catastrophic gold outflows that destroyed Japan's closed currency system. The European combatant countries had effectively stopped gold exports in 1914 and 1915. By 1917 the United States and Japan were the only economic powers that still permitted gold exports; thus everyone else had to get gold from these two countries. The United States entered the war in April 1917 and stopped gold exports on September 7, cutting off Japan's source of gold supply. Japan's Ministry of Finance followed suit on September 12, issuing a ministry order to embargo gold exports, effective immediately.[48]

The gold embargo effectively dammed up the great gold reserves accumulated in the previous two years. In the years that followed, this wartime emergency measure, never passed as a law, became virtually a fixed aspect of Japan's political economy that was later very painful to change. Policies relative to the lifting of the gold embargo became part of the partisan divide over the "positive" and "negative" policies.

In the government's public explanation, relations with China were again placed at the center of Japan's monetary politics. As Finance Minister Shōda explained it, from the beginning of 1916 until August 1917 Japan had sent ¥64 million in gold to China; now, that outflow would no longer be balanced by an inflow from the United States. Gold was also flowing out to India.[49] This explanation raises several questions. In its trade with India, Japan regularly shipped out gold to pay for a large excess of imports, consisting mainly of Indian cotton purchased for Japanese spinning mills. But with China, Japan had enjoyed a consistent export surplus since the time of the Sino-Japanese War. Thus, one might expect that China would send specie to Japan. However, the flow of Japanese capital into China was now even larger than China's trade deficit—in effect, gold was flowing into

China in the form of Japanese loans and investments or to be traded on the speculative Shanghai exchange. A decade after the fact, Shōda revealed that his primary concerns in imposing the gold embargo were "political and military":

> With the great unease in the whole world due to the chaos of the World War situation, the Russian Revolution and so on in the background, it was a situation in which every country was prohibiting the export of gold and so on, and so the truth is that *in order to prepare for future emergencies,* our country too acted decisively to prohibit the export of gold.[50]

"And especially," Shōda recalled, "there were those among our country's governmental authorities of the time who hoped some day to invest in China." Shōda's explanation was still less than direct. Japan's leaders of the time were busy generating emergencies in East Asia. And as for investment, "some day" had already arrived.

THE LONDON OF THE EAST

The gold embargo did not slow the Terauchi cabinet's overseas financial advance, and "Korean" institutions continued to extend their reach into Chinese territory. In October 1917 the Oriental Development Company (ODC) extended its colonization activities from Korea to South Manchuria by setting up branches in Mukden and Dairen, where it began to supply long-term industrial and agricultural finance to local Japanese enterprises, in place of the Yokohama Specie Bank.[51] In January 1918, by imperial decree, Bank of Chosen notes replaced Specie Bank notes as the sole legal tender in the Kwantung Leased Territory and in the South Manchurian Railway Zone. All YSB gold notes in circulation were to be replaced by Bank of Chosen gold notes. The Bank of Chosen also took over four YSB branches, in Andong, Port Arthur, Liaoyang, and Tieling, and by the end of the war period had thirteen branches in Manchuria and eastern Inner Mongolia. The Bank of Chosen likewise took over the government treasury business formerly handled by the Yokohama Specie Bank in Manchuria. In effect, the Bank of Chosen was now the central bank for Japanese Manchuria.[52] Outside the railway zone, the bank's yen notes functioned as a foreign trading currency alongside the multifarious local currencies, thus operating regionally in the way that the British pound had operated internationally. The Bank of Chosen's business also grew explosively during the wartime boom: from 1914 to 1919 the bank's lending and deposits increased by sixteen and eighteen times, respectively. The bank's note issue increased by more than six times, to a peak of ¥164 million in 1919. By then 30 to 40 percent of the Bank of Chosen's business was in Manchuria.[53]

Japanese lending to Russia in 1916 also promoted a Japanese economic advance into the Russian sphere of influence in North Manchuria.[54] The Russian government used the Japanese credits to buy ¥64 million worth of Japanese goods in 1916 and 1917; these goods were shipped via the South Manchurian Railway through Harbin. After April 1916 the Suzuki Trading Company and other Japanese companies set up offices in Harbin. The Bank of Chosen opened a Harbin office in July. The February and October revolutions in Russia damaged the credibility of Russian ruble notes, which had circulated in North Manchuria in the same way that Japanese yen circulated in South Manchuria, and in 1918 Bank of Chosen notes began to circulate widely in their place. As Russia's international trading relations broke down, Japanese goods began to pile up in Harbin. However, the Russian revolution also opened the way for Japanese military intervention, which led to a further boom for Japanese businesses in North Manchuria after August 1918.

For Inoue Junnosuke, Japan's new financial power kindled a more internationalist vision, of Tokyo as the London of the East. "For the first time, we had created the qualifications to leap out into the world," he later recalled. That those qualifications—¥4 billion in wartime gains—were subsequently frittered away became a great source of personal regret. But in October 1917, after the Yokohama Specie Bank had taken the leading role in the new Four-Power Consortium loan to China, Inoue saw Japan's new position as a fact: "If I speak from my own point of view, I think that Japan is now probably the central financial market of the Orient."[55]

In fact, wartime lending did mean the beginnings of a market for overseas bonds in Japan. In February 1916 the eighteen-bank syndicate led by the Yokohama Specie Bank had attempted to market over ¥300 million in foreign government yen bonds. For the most part, the results of the public subscriptions had been very poor, however, with the issuing banks taking up the bulk of these issues. Private capital was enlisted more successfully in the Nishihara loans, in which the Specie Bank did not participate. This too was an operation initiated by the government; but, attracted by good returns and the government's guarantee, private capital followed.[56] Thus the state worked to develop a market, using low-interest Deposit Bureau (postal savings) funds to prime the pump. At this point, however, the logic of foreign lending remained primarily political. In fact, some of the ostensibly private lending in China by Mitsui Bussan and other companies was merely a facade, with private companies providing covert channels for government policy loans to the Beijing government for weapons purchases.[57]

In connection with its efforts to pull in Japanese loans, the Beijing government also revived the idea of a foreign-assisted monetary reform. In September 1916 the Chinese government had asked the Four-Country Consortium for a £10 million loan to be secured by the salt tax. Because of the war, the idea went nowhere, and in March 1917 the Chinese government approached the Japanese government directly and asked that it send an adviser on monetary reform. The idea now was that a Japanese loan of £10 million would be used to create an overseas specie reserve to enable the adoption of a gold-exchange standard once the European war had ended. In July 1917 Finance Minister Shōda appointed Baron Sakatani Yoshio, now a great senior figure in Japanese finance, as China's adviser on monetary reform. Accordingly, Cao Rulin, now chancellor of finance (*zaisei sōchō*) for the Beijing government, formally invited Sakatani to serve as monetary adviser.[58]

Sakatani's appointment in China was not yet known publicly when he spoke at the celebration of the twentieth anniversary of Japan's gold standard on November 1, 1917, but the question of reforming China's currency was at the center of his remarks. The currency question in China was a very great one, Sakatani said, "and if we ask about the origins of it, it is karmically connected (*innen o nashite*) to the [1895 Chinese indemnity of] 230 million taels; that is, to the fund for the implementation of Japan's gold standard." Now, twenty years after that, China was asking Japan for a currency reform loan, and Japan was putting its efforts into establishing a gold standard for China. Here too, Sakatani said, it could be thought that the karmic connections were abundant. In this morning's newspaper, Sakatani continued, it was reported that America was "shoving its way in" and insisting that a Japanese loan fell under the framework of the past multilateral currency loan negotiations. The opportunity for Japan was an immediate one. The present situation in which East Asian trade was conducted on a sterling or dollar basis was very painful (*kutsū*) to Japan. This problem would continue if a future international currency were created and the yen merely continued to function as before. At the moment, power—we might specify, money-creation power—resided only with London and New York; but if East Asian trade could be settled in yen, Japan would gain a very advantageous position. Under the present gold embargoes, no one could get gold from London or New York, and if Japan could seize the chance to develop the yen's use as an international currency, it would greatly profit Japanese commerce. Even if financial sacrifices were necessary to create this international role for the yen, one must think of the interests of the Japanese people one hundred or two hundred years in the future, he said. Now was the time for both government and business to establish great plans and prepare for the postwar world.[59]

In late March 1918 Sakatani toured China for two months to investigate monetary and economic circumstances and then presented a report to Premier Duan. As Gerard Vissering had done in 1912, Sakatani recommended a gradual transition to a unified national monetary system based on a gold-exchange standard.[60] The Beijing government itself appears to have intended to give Sakatani an ornamental post and a generous salary, using him to facilitate loans from Japan. Sakatani asked instead for real authority to reform the Chinese monetary system, but the other powers protested and the Chinese government refused.

Sakatani was fighting not only to establish the yen as an international currency but also against Nishihara Kamezō's alternative proposal to immediately issue gold notes in China. On his return from China in June 1918, Sakatani moved to kill Nishihara's gold-note plan, meeting in short order with Foreign Minister Gotō, Finance Minister Shōda, senior statesmen Yamagata Aritomo and Matsukata Masayoshi, top officials of the Finance Ministry and Bank of Japan, and Inoue Junnosuke of the Yokohama Specie Bank. Sakatani thereby placed Shōda, his junior, in a position where Shōda himself could no longer recommend Nishihara's plan.[61]

Despite this setback the Beijing government attempted to go ahead with a gold-note plan. In August 1918 Finance Chancellor Cao Rulin himself, arguing that silver-price fluctuations were hurting China's trade and that one-third of the Chinese government's expenditures were gold-denominated payments on indemnities and foreign loans, proposed to move to a gold standard. Accordingly, the government authorized the Bank of China and the Bank of Communications to issue gold notes in preparation for a transition to a gold-exchange standard based on a gold dollar (yuan) worth virtually the same amount of gold as the Japanese yen. Cao intended his project to be funded by Japanese loans arranged by Nishihara and the Bank of Chosen, with the currency reserve to be held overseas in Japan. The project was stopped by domestic opposition and by protests from the foreign bank groups (including the Yokohama Specie Bank), which, backed by their governments, insisted that no currency reform in China be undertaken without their own participation. Moreover, the rising price of silver was now relieving the burden of China's external gold payments and reducing the perceived utility of a gold standard, even had it been capable of realization.[62]

In December 1918 the Chinese government did appoint Sakatani as financial adviser but owing mainly to U.S. opposition, nothing came of it. The effect was rather to motivate the American project of organizing a new China consortium.[63] The Sakatani affair also placed the Japanese ambassador to Washington, Ishii Kikujirō, in an embarrassing position and forced him to resign, to be replaced by Shidehara Kijūrō, who would direct the conciliatory diplomacy of the 1920s.

In the meantime, New York came more and more to seem the London of the West, as America's own dollar diplomacy continued to extend itself. As Woodrow Wilson took America into the war in Europe, he also conducted a rapprochement with Morgan and Company. In June 1918, alarmed about the Nishihara loans and the prospect of Sakatani's appointment as Chinese currency adviser, the Wilson administration forgot its former qualms and asked Morgan and Company to make a loan to the Chinese government. Morgan and Company did not want to act without its British and French partners, and the Wilson administration concluded that a new, American-led international consortium was needed. The dollar diplomacy was back. Again the government turned to Morgan and Company, and Morgan partner Thomas Lamont took on the job.[64]

The American policy reversal paralleled Japan's shift from the confrontational policy of the Ōkuma cabinet to the yen diplomacy of the Terauchi cabinet. For the United States also, the opening of the European war had presented opportunities for unilateral action, and the initial moves of the Wilson administration had been in the vein of gunboat diplomacy. Haiti presented the clearest case of this process: having already fallen under multilateral Euro-American financial control, Haiti was placed under direct U.S. control in late 1914 and 1915.[65] U.S. forces also occupied the Dominican Republic in 1916, and American financial and military controls were greatly tightened in Nicaragua and Liberia in 1916 and 1917. With their arrays of foreign-administered budgetary and military controls and their teams of private U.S. advisers, government in these countries came under the kind of semicolonial control that China might have had had Katō Takaaki's Twenty-one Demands been implemented in full. Not unlike Gotō Shinpei's plan for an East Asian yen bloc, Edwin Kemmerer in 1915 and 1916 developed bold plans (later dropped) for a dollar-based Pan-American monetary union.[66] Revolutionary Mexico also became the stage for U.S. efforts to extend financial controls and a gold-exchange standard, and after an unsuccessful mission led by Edwin Kemmerer, the State Department asked Morgan and Company to organize an international banking consortium for Mexico. Thomas Lamont took on this task also, simultaneously with his effort to revive the China consortium.[67]

Even as the United States began to organize its initiative in China, Inoue Junnosuke began to qualify his earlier idea that the world's financial centers had shifted. "It is true that Britain's power is diminishing and America's power is growing," he said in June 1918, "but after the war America cannot immediately take the position that Britain occupied before the war." For Japan itself to become an international financial center would be even more difficult. To do so, Inoue saw several requirements: Japan must become a clearing center for international settlements; it must become a credit center with abundant capital for overseas investment; it must accumulate large overseas investments and surplus investment capital; and it must have abundant foreign trade. Finally, "as the first absolute condition," it must maintain a free market for gold. To become a true international financial center would require the efforts of fifty or sixty years. In terms of national wealth, the volume of foreign trade, and the volume of the Bank of Japan's note issue, Inoue said, Japan's present economic scale was approximately what England's had been in the 1840s and 1850s. If Germany could be said to be fifty years behind England, then Japan was sixty or seventy years behind.[68]

PRICE REVOLUTION AND POPULAR REVOLT

The boom of the war years was a highly strained and uneven one. Supply bottlenecks and commodity speculation made markets fragile and prone to panics. Exporters accumulated great volumes of trade bills due them, but their profits often existed only on the books and could not be collected due to the Allies' specie embargoes, which threatened to choke off the money needed to fund the continued flow of exports. After the United States embargoed gold exports in September 1917, the problem became acute. The Yokohama Specie Bank accommodated exporters by discounting their trade bills in volume, and the Bank of Japan in turn supported the Specie Bank with generous credits. Thus, to compensate for companies' inability to repatriate gold from overseas, the Bank of Japan lent freely on the basis of trade bills, in effect monetizing those bills. By the second half of 1918, BOJ loans on foreign bills had reached ¥444 million—more than the entire circulation of Bank of Japan notes in 1914. The Bank of Japan's note issue increased correspondingly, growing from ¥386 million at the end of 1914 to ¥1,145 million at the end of 1918.[69]

Monetary expansion, high wartime demand, and wartime shortages of goods resulted in price inflation, and inflation brought its own set of social changes. The cautious businessman, as Inoue Junnosuke later recounted again and again, was overtaken by the speculator and the promoter. Unsound, debt-based enterprises mushroomed. The greatest beneficiaries of the inflation, besides the state itself, were those businessmen engaged in war-oriented production and trade, especially those in a position to set prices and manipulate supply shortfalls.

Consumers suffered the consequences. Price inflation ran far ahead of wage increases up to 1920; only after that did real wages rise. The inflation in rice prices pressed most on people's livelihoods. In 1917 rice prices rose nearly 50 percent. From January 1918 to the denouement of the rice riots in September, they rose by another 80 percent. Such inflation levels had not been seen since the eve of the Meiji Restoration, and, as in the 1860s, shortages and currency inflation combined to provoke a wave of urban riots and disorder. The pressure of the inflation also drove a wave of union organizing and of strikes, as more than 180,000 workers took part in more than 1,300 strikes in 1917–19, a many-fold increase over past levels. While notably moderate by comparison with contemporary Europe, this strike wave was unprecedented in Japanese industrial experience. It was also the beginning of a heightened level of labor organization and protest that would last into the 1930s.[70]

Thus, by early 1918, as Japan's international financial situation again seemed to become deadlocked, domestic political troubles were piling up for the Terauchi cabinet. Again, revolution in a neighboring country—this time Russia—seemed to offer an opportunity "to direct domestic trouble outward," as Finance Minister Shōda suggested to Terauchi in January 1918. Grandiose dreams of a Japanese sphere of influence in eastern Siberia now opened up, as the government prepared to dispatch troops to Siberian ports and along the Trans-Siberian Railway, ostensibly to protect the Czech troops retreating east after Russia's separate peace with the Central Powers.[71]

The crisis point was reached in the inflationary summer of 1918. On July 23 fishermen's wives protested high rice prices in the town of Uozu in Toyama prefecture. Their protests spread along the Japan Sea coast and were reported in national newspapers before the government imposed a news blackout. On August 8 angry consumers rioted in Okayama and then in one after another of the booming industrial cities of the Pacific coast. The rioters expressed few political demands, but government offices and the homes of newly rich *narikin* were among their targets. The greatest of the wartime *narikin* was Suzuki Shōten, a trading company that had originally dealt in sugar and camphor from Taiwan and that had expanded during the war boom to the point that it rivaled Mitsui itself. On August 12 mobs wrecked Suzuki's head office in Kōbe; they appear to have been instigated by agents working for Mitsui and the Seiyūkai party, presaging Suzuki's destruction, at Mitsui's hands, in the great financial crisis of 1927.[72]

Continuing into early October, the rice riots constituted the largest mass disturbances in Japan's modern history. More than a million, perhaps several million, people took part in riots in forty-nine cities, 217 towns, 231 villages, and twenty-nine mining areas, where the bloodiest battles took place. Police and soldiers killed more than thirty protesters.[73] Thus, just as the government began the dispatch of 70,000 troops to combat Bolshevism in Eastern Siberia, it also deployed nearly 100,000 troops to put down civil disorder at home. The riots were suppressed, but they greatly discredited the Terauchi cabinet. As in February 1912 and in April 1914, popular action helped to force a cabinet change, as the senior statesmen sought to manage the situation by inviting Seiyūkai president Hara Takashi to form a cabinet. Thus Hara, the "commoner premier"—the first untitled sitting member of the House of Representatives to serve as prime minister—formed Japan's first durable party cabinet on September 29, 1918. Takahashi Korekiyo again became finance minister and began actively to implement the positive policy. With Takahashi's support, the great boom of the late 1910s now entered its final and most exaggerated phase.

PART TWO

Global Money and the Doctrine of Induced Depression

SIX

The Great Divide, 1918–1921

After the triumphs and turmoil, excesses and grand visions of the late 1910s, Japan, as Inoue Junnosuke had foreseen, entered a new age of limitation in the 1920s. It was an uneasy, in-between era. Contending political forces seemed to stand in a fragile state of balance. In the eyes of conservatives, degenerate customs flourished. Business conditions were chronically depressed, and the entire decade could easily be characterized as a reaction to the inflationary wartime boom.

EXPLAINING THE "DEADLOCK" OF THE 1920S

The 1920s was perceived as a time of economic stagnation in Japan. It was also a time of sharp social and economic dualism. Tokyo, especially as rebuilt after the 1923 earthquake, became the showplace for an American-style consumer culture of department stores, coffee shops, and jazz bars, populated by flapper-style "modern girls" (*mo-ga*) and "modern boy" (*mo-bo*) dandies. In industry, it was a time of giant electrification projects and the stirrings of a new industrial revolution in the heavy and chemical industries. But in the aggregate, like Europe and unlike the United States, Japan saw no mass-market consumer revolution and no roaring twenties. Economic growth, at perhaps 2 percent per year, was distinctly slow compared to the periods before and after. With population growing at rates that approached 1.5 percent per annum—this was precisely the peak of Japan's historic population explosion—income growth was almost nonexistent in per capita terms. Agriculture, which still employed half the population, was especially distressed. As the postwar decade progressed, the idea that Japan was stuck in a kind of "deadlock" (*ikizumari*) was increasingly repeated.[1] Industrial overcapacity, falling prices and profits, mounting debt levels, and repeated

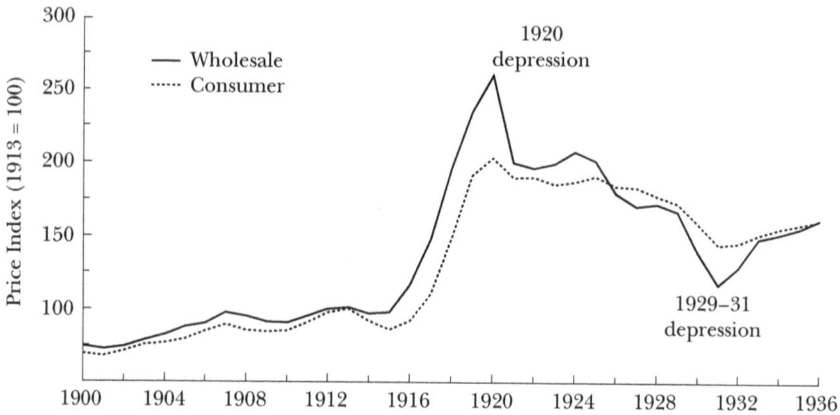

FIG. 4. The World War I price wave: wholesale prices and consumer prices from 1900 to 1936

SOURCE: Nihon Ginkō Tōkeikyoku 1966: 76–77.

banking panics were all part of this picture, lending support to the newly popular Marxist notion that the capitalist system had now entered its final stage. By the end of the decade, the sense of entrapment had become intense.

Most analyses of Japan's chronic recession of the 1920s, then and since, have traced the problem to the imbalances created by the great wartime boom. Thus, in a nationwide radio address to launch his new cabinet's gold-restoration campaign in August 1929, Hamaguchi Osachi explained that with the "extreme prosperity" of the war years,

> both government finances, the management of private enterprise, and the way of life of our people in general suddenly swelled. . . . And whether we may say that it was owing to a weak point in human nature or that it was owing to the carelessness of the politicians of that time or of the people in general, before we knew it, the economy had run loose. . . . The reaction arrived with the 1920 panic, and before that wound had mended, the great 1923 earthquake came, . . . and finally our business world sank into the depths of depression that we see today.[2]

Hamaguchi's finance minister, Inoue Junnosuke, traced a similar cycle of decline: "Continuing since the economic reaction [*zaikai no handō*] of 1920 and the great earthquake and fire of 1923, Japan's business world has gradually been sinking deeper and deeper into an abyss of stagnation and depression."[3]

The logic of this perception of deadlock is instantly clear if we look at the course of prices and industrial profits. Wholesale prices, as figure 4 indicates,

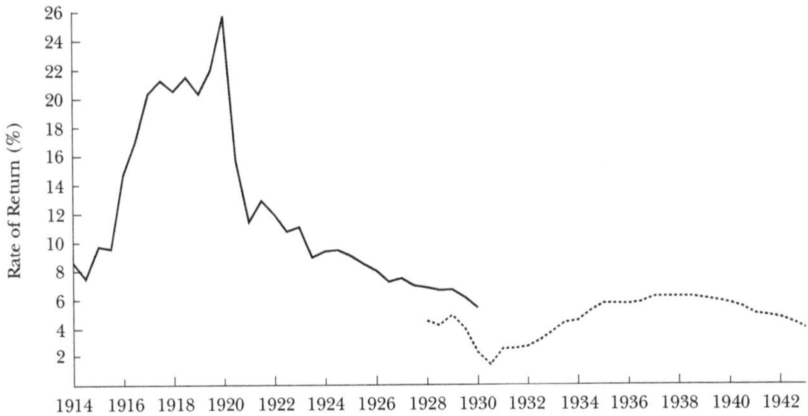

FIG. 5. Profitability of large Japanese corporations, 1914–1943. Rate of return (after tax), relative to total capital used. Two different indices; values shown are for the first and second halves of each year.
SOURCE: Nihon Ginkō Tōkeikyoku 1966: 335–337.

rose to unprecedented heights in early 1920 and then crashed. Price deflation continued for the next twelve years. Industrial profits traced out a similar cycle: profits soared during the war years and leaped even higher in late 1919, then fell very sharply in the second half of 1920 and declined almost without interruption for ten years (figure 5). Different industries experienced different trajectories, but in all industries profits fell after 1920 or at latest after 1921. Investment rose and fell in tandem with profits.[4] Thus, despite the sudden expansion of Japan's industrial base—or because of it—prosperity seemed impossible to maintain in the 1920s. Economic conditions recovered somewhat in the middle of the decade, but profits continued to decline and investment remained weak. Sustained recovery began only in 1932, under the influence of Takahashi Korekiyo's reflation policy.

In the ups and downs of both prices and profits, then, the great divide in the spring of 1920 stands out in sharp relief. Inoue Junnosuke later described it topographically: the wartime boom had been like a long climb to a mountain pass, succeeded by a sudden descent when the war ended in November 1918. Then, like a sudden rush up Mount Fuji, came the ten-month postwar boom whose peak was attained in March 1920—followed by a great fall to a point something like the bottom of Lake Biwa.[5] This break point was the crest of a worldwide economic wave. In Japan, which in relative terms had profited more from the war than any other large country, that crest was traced most sharply. But before the crash came the finale of the boom, presided over by Takahashi Korekiyo.

"THE BOOM BEYOND THE BOUNDS OF COMMON SENSE"

In 1929 Ishibashi Tanzan, who would himself gain fame for his inflationary policy after World War II, looked back at the post–World War I inflation with a critical eye:

> The World War ended in November 1918. Then, on June 26, 1919, America lifted its embargo on gold exports. If, on that occasion, we too had lifted our embargo on gold exports, our business world would have resolved this [gold embargo] problem without any shock, and doubtless could then have returned to the situation of normal times, avoiding the boom beyond the bounds of common sense that lasted from 1919 to the spring of 1920.[6]

The Seiyūkai cabinet led by Hara Takashi took office at the end of September 1918, at the point when the social strains brought about by the inflationary war boom had intensified to the point of crisis. In November the armistice caused a postwar economic panic in Japan, as in the United States. The new cabinet was thus faced almost immediately with what seemed to be the end of the boom, and their challenge became one of reviving prosperity.

For the munitions industries, the end of the war was in fact the end of prosperity. For most other industries, however, the postarmistice reaction turned out to be only a pause in the good times. In April and May 1919 as the United States and Britain recovered, a postwar boom began, and prices resumed their rapid rise. Reconstruction needs and the release of pent-up consumer demand in Europe, amid continuing production shortfalls during the reconversion to civilian production, meant continued demand for Japanese goods. The simultaneous boom in China was a further source of demand. Businessmen thought they were seeing a repetition of the postwar booms that had followed the Sino-Japanese and Russo-Japanese wars.[7] At the same time, encouraged by the yen's appreciation, imports boomed even more than exports, and from the beginning of 1919 Japan's merchandise trade balance slid back into deficit.

By June 1919 the boom took on the aspect of a speculative bubble. Speculation in commodities and the manipulation of materials shortages pushed commodity prices to unheard-of heights. Driven by the boom in America, prices for raw silk increased by almost 50 percent from August to December 1919. Prices for future deliveries of cotton yarn nearly doubled in 1919. Easy credit and the expectation of superprofits led to the creation or enlargement of many joint-stock companies in the "enterprise fever" from June 1919 to March 1920. Share prices soared, and new public offerings were hugely oversubscribed. Projected capital (*keikaku shihon*) grew from ¥200 million in May 1919 to ¥1 billion in February and March 1920, while the ratio that was actually paid in fell to as low as 6 percent in February. Commodity traders began to deal in share futures, and "people of every social class" took part in the speculation, as Inoue Junnosuke later recounted. Even in rural whistle-stops, he said, people bought and sold shares on the basis of a daily telephone call to check the market in Tokyo.[8] There was land speculation as well in both cities and villages. When the monetary tide later receded, many inflated enterprises were left with unsellable stocks of goods, excess productive capacity, and immense debts.

The period 1919–20 was also the full tide of the "positive" policy. The war boom greatly increased the government's tax receipts and made it easy to float public bonds. Total government spending came to more than ¥3 billion in 1919, a 55 percent increase over 1918, and spending in 1920 increased by another 23 percent.[9] In an extraordinary ¥800 million expansion program, the Hara cabinet doubled railroad spending from 1919 to 1921, part of a grandiose thirty-year plan to extend the rail network to every corner of the country that even today has not been fully realized. It adopted a highway law in 1919; initiated a huge, regionally oriented school-building campaign; and provided central-government funds to regional governments to help pay teachers' salaries. The Seiyūkai cabinet likewise boosted public spending on harbors, farmland reclamation, and dams and riverine works.

The greatest increase, starting before the Hara government took office, was in military spending. In 1914 military spending had accounted for 30 percent of the general account budget. By 1920 regular military expenses were 47 percent of a greatly enlarged budget; adding in the specially budgeted war expenses for the Siberian expedition, military spending actually came to 69 percent of total central-government spending.[10] Thus, as after the Sino-Japanese and Russo-Japanese wars, government spending was ramped up to an entirely new level. Once established, these new spending programs were politically difficult to curtail, and the Seiyūkai government's guns-and-butter spending policies thus created the conditions for the straitened government finances of the 1920s.

In March 1919, just as the postwar boom was getting underway, Bank of Japan governor Mishima Yatarō died. Inoue Junnosuke was an obvious candidate for the post, but Finance Minister Takahashi instead recommended BOJ director Kimura Seishirō, who was Inoue's senior at the bank, with Inoue to be vice governor. Prime Minister Hara then reversed the order, and Inoue returned to the Bank of Japan that he had left eight years before.[11]

Inoue immediately set to work to create an active market for the discounting of trade bills, an institution that he had described in 1917 as a prerequisite for making Tokyo an international financial center and the yen an international currency. In this, Inoue sought to do in Tokyo what Governor Benjamin Strong had been doing for several years at the Federal Reserve

Bank of New York, as part of his own drive to make the U.S. dollar a major international currency and New York City a world financial center to rival London.[12] To this end, Inoue introduced two new credit instruments, bankers' acceptances and stamped trade bills, in May and August, explaining them as a means to ease the financing of trade—an expansionary measure—and as a means to contract credit and make the BOJ's interest rate policy more effective. Mutō Sanji later charged that Inoue's encouragement of the use of bankers' acceptances in 1919 was a major cause of the panic in 1920. The Bank of Japan also began to insist that Japanese merchants and banks use yen-denominated trade bills for payments in China and other Asian countries and recommended their use to pay for imports from the United States. However, none of these reforms was really successful.[13]

On taking office, Inoue initially muted his warnings of an inevitable postwar reaction. In his first speech as central bank governor, he spoke on the subject of postwar "adjustment" (*seiri*) to the Osaka convention of the National Bill Brokers Association on April 22, as he did on the next day to the Kansai Bankers' Convention, where he shared the platform with Finance Minister Takahashi. Every branch of industry had expanded greatly during the war, Inoue explained, and the challenge now was to maintain these advances in the postwar world. "Japanese financial markets have gained a conspicuously advanced position in East Asia," he said. "It is truly necessary to maintain and preserve from decline Japan's [new] financial position." The challenge was clear: the balance of trade had already reverted to a deficit position (although, for the moment, the trade deficit was still covered by large surpluses on shipping and other nontrade exchanges). Due to the insufficient development of Japanese trade organization and the poor quality of Japanese goods, Japanese businesses could not expect to maintain their newly developed export markets in China, India, Southeast Asia, and South America. With the trade surplus already gone, one could expect a reversal of the movement of the past four years: that is, the volume of currency would decrease, prices would fall, and consequently the volume of production would decline. In response, Japan could follow a "negative" adjustment policy, passively letting falling demand shrink the level of industrial activity. Or, after the example of American businesses, which were considerably more aware of the problem, Japanese business could pursue a positive policy of actively promoting the export of goods that had piled up in excess of domestic demand. America was now insisting on the postwar overseas development of its trade, and Japan could only do the same.[14]

Inoue's stance on the question of postwar adjustment thus seemed more optimistic than it had been. Speaking to the same convention, Finance Minister Takahashi Korekiyo went considerably beyond Inoue with his own optimistic rhetoric. This "happy talk" (*rakkanron*) was later made notorious by the Kenseikai's Hamaguchi Osachi, who charged that Takahashi had recklessly provoked the speculative boom and thereby worsened the inevitable bust that followed. In 1922 Kansai industrialist Mutō Sanji also singled out Inoue's own speech for sharp criticism, as he opened a bitter political campaign against Inoue that would last until Inoue's death.[15] But on the question of restraining the inflationary boom, Inoue and Takahashi began to come down on opposite sides.

Japan's economic relations with the United States were decisive in the events of 1919 and 1920. Booming American demand was an initial factor that promoted the Japanese boom. The inflation of Japan's speculative bubble after June 1919 was further promoted by America's lifting of the gold embargo.

After the suspension of specie convertibility during the Civil War, America's era of inconvertible greenback money had lasted for seventeen years. In the ensuing half century, the United States had gone from being the world's greatest debtor (or recipient of foreign investment) to being the world's greatest net creditor. The United States was flush with gold reserves after World War I, and only seven months after the armistice, a presidential order on June 26, 1919, lifted the U.S. embargo on gold exports, "except as to those parts of Russia controlled by the so-called Bolshevik government." The first effect of America's return to the gold standard was to promote a continued world boom. The great flow of gold that had been dammed in September 1917 now resumed, and by the end of the year, $94 million (¥188 million) in gold had been shipped from America to Japan in settlement of wartime debts, far more than to any other country.[16] These flows of pure "high-powered money" added fuel to the inflationary flames, creating what was called a "gold inflation" in Japan.

By the summer of 1919, Inoue was lobbying the cabinet to permit him to raise interest rates and warning of the speculative nature of the boom, which he characterized as a "grass fire" (*ryōgen no hi*). For his part, Finance Minister Takahashi thought that Japan must seize the present once-in-a-lifetime chance for rapid economic development relative to the rest of the world. The increase in the amount of currency, he insisted, was a consequence rather than a cause of price increases, which in the present circumstances were unavoidable. Prime Minister Hara himself simplistically attributed the price increase to "foreign trade," and because "Japan can't stop trading," the implication was that the increase in prices had to be accepted.[17] Concerned that monetary restraint would provoke a recession more destructive than the inflation, the Hara government therefore adopted a supply-side approach of trying to meet the increased level of demand with increased production. The government worked especially to increase the rice supply. It also hoped to absorb excess currency in circulation by encouraging savings and selling government bonds in the post offices.[18]

Thus, Takahashi Korekiyo resisted the pressure to raise interest rates until the fall of 1919, and despite the continued speculative rise in prices, the Bank of Japan's interest rate hikes of September and November 1918 were not followed by further increases. We could therefore call this "boom beyond the bounds of common sense" the "Takahashi boom." Privately, Mitsui Bank managing director Ikeda Shigeaki urged his friend Inoue to raise interest rates. Inoue said that if he tried to do so, he would be asked to resign.[19] Finally, Inoue appealed directly to Prime Minister Hara to allow him to raise rates.

MAINTAINING THE GOLD EMBARGO

America's gold-export embargo had been strictly a wartime emergency measure, lasting only twenty-one months. Why didn't Japan, which had built up great gold reserves during the war, also lift its own gold embargo in 1919, when it could have been done without great difficulty? This question was forcefully raised at the time by economic journalist Ishibashi Tanzan of the *Tōyō keizai shinpō,* who by his own account, "made every effort to urge such a policy upon the government." In September 1919 the *Tōyō keizai shinpō* was warning of the "empty" character of the boom. In October the journal made the first public call for an immediate return to the gold standard.[20]

In the early 1930s, Ishibashi Tanzan would strongly advocate Keynesian demand-stimulus policies, and Finance Minister Takahashi Korekiyo would decisively implement such policies. When Ishibashi himself became finance minister in 1946, he would emulate and surpass Takahashi's example in pushing a pro-inflationary positive policy. But Ishibashi came to this view only after the experience of the Great Depression of the 1930s, and in early 1929, he continued to hold to the idea he had expressed in 1919, a year that he now saw as having been a crucial moment of choice:

> Today [March 1929], as the only one of the great powers to ban the export of gold, our country is left behind by all the other countries. But in 1919, our country was, together with America, one of the two great international credit-surplus countries and had prepared very favorable conditions for ending the gold-export embargo, [far better than] those of England and other countries. . . . Our restriction of gold exports should have been abolished after the November 1918 armistice, or, at the least, soon after America lifted its own gold embargo. Once the opportunity was lost due to the government's negligence or delusion, it ultimately departed forever.[21]

Far from taking advantage of the high yen to restore gold convertibility, Ishibashi wrote, the government in 1919 was most concerned to check the yen's rise, which threatened Japanese exports. Afterwards, high domestic prices and the depreciation of the yen meant that the return to the gold standard was bound to be very difficult. By preventing the outflow of gold and trying to hold onto the gold surplus obtained during the war, the government ultimately lost that surplus.[22]

In fact, opinion within the Bank of Japan also appears to have favored lifting the gold embargo in 1919. Inoue Junnosuke himself later called the boom "empty," and at the time, he discussed with Finance Minister Takahashi the question of lifting the embargo in order to restrain the boom. Economically speaking, the case for doing so was clear, he later said. The problem was political, and the government held off out of fear that in an international emergency, Japan's overseas gold would be in an uncertain situation.[23] Therefore, Takahashi wanted to repatriate Japan's overseas specie reserves, and with Inoue's agreement, he rejected an early return to the gold standard in 1919. Ten years later, it seems that Inoue, too, thought that an opportunity had been lost in 1919.[24]

Takahashi's reasons for retaining the gold embargo were largely strategic. As Ishibashi Tanzan reported it, Takahashi held the "truly surprising delusion" that because of Japan's continuing military operations in Russia and because of "the threatening situation in the Orient," the country could not risk lifting the gold embargo and losing specie.[25] In fact, Takahashi's reasons went beyond a prudential concern for military preparedness to include a vision of economic expansionism in China in the context of the imperialist competition for financial leverage. As Takahashi later explained:

> At the time of the Hara cabinet, for our reference in establishing a basic policy in regard to China, we assembled a group of military men who were stationed in every part of China and asked about the situation there. If we consider it now, the attitude of our government and people toward China was rather active [*sekkyokuteki*] and aggressive at that time. However, I was against invasion by military force. An invasion by military force will certainly at some time be reversed by military force. Accordingly, it was my opinion that in order to develop our national power in regard to China, [the means] *had* to be economic.
>
> At present, China is disordered and chaotic, but sooner or later, a time of national stabilization must come. Then, in order to govern the country and pacify the people, the first thing you will need is gold, for laying railroads, establishing industry, and so on. Thus, I thought that China would be seeking a large amount of funds from overseas in the not very distant future. In that case, Japan must definitely be ready to lend at once as much as ¥500 or ¥600 million in gold. If we were not, considering the current world situation, England or America, one or the other, would certainly monopolize the lending. Once England or America had conquered China economically, unlike a conquest by military force, it would be no easy task to reverse it. Japan had to go before the [other] powers, and even if the powers formed a loan consortium, we had to take the leading position in that consortium.
>
> Thinking in this way, I thought that somehow we must set aside domestically an extra ¥500 or ¥600 million of gold. If something happened, our gold

> that was held overseas had to be completely on the spot. Therefore, I strove to the utmost to increase the amount of gold held domestically, even as America lifted their embargo on gold exports (June 1919), and after that, even as gold successively came into our country. I didn't feel like acting to lift the gold embargo.[26]

There are several points to note in Takahashi's remarkable statement. First, Takahashi was talking about lending immense sums of money, dwarfing the ¥145 million in loans arranged during the war by Nishihara Kamezō. In fact, ¥500 million to ¥600 million (US$250 million to US$300 million) was roughly the entire amount by which the government's specie holdings had grown from 1915 to 1918. It was equal to one-third of Japan's combined central-government budget in 1918.[27] Such giant loans were not a matter of prudent international investment but of audacious international power games. Politicians on all sides assumed that lending money to China meant the ability to dominate China. Like the other powers, Japan seemed to be aiming at a kind of economic conquest in China. Thus, strategic considerations remained at the center of the government's reasons for not permitting gold exports.

As a foundation for raising funds overseas, the gold standard was at its inception part of a "positive" and expansionist military and industrial policy.[28] The essential point was to get money for heavy-industrial development, war, and empire building—as Takahashi Korekiyo had done during the Russo-Japanese War. In this sense Takahashi's support for the gold standard in 1897 and his maintenance of its suspension in 1919 were both consistent expressions of his positive-policy stance. Finally, the Hara cabinet's positive policy of delivering government money to the regions required a large budget—restoration of the gold standard would have imposed fiscal retrenchment. Thus, for a tightly linked series of international and domestic reasons, Takahashi Korekiyo did not lift the gold embargo during the flush days of 1919. The boom continued.

FINANCE AND EMPIRE IN EAST ASIA: THE AMERICAN INITIATIVE

As the postwar boom was getting underway, Japan's wartime position in China began to unravel. On January 18, 1919, the Paris Peace Conference opened, with Japanese military and diplomatic leaders expecting to consolidate their wartime gains at the conference table. Secret Allied agreements to support Japan's takeover of the German concession in Shandong were now revealed. So too was the Beijing government's secret acquiescence, in exchange for a loan arranged by Nishihara Kamezō, to demands by Gotō

Shinpei that would in effect create a new Japanese railway zone from Jiaozhou to Jinan. That is, it appeared that Shandong would be turned into a second South Manchuria. As the news became public, Chinese students, intellectuals, and businessmen organized a campaign to demand the removal of all foreign concessions from China.[29] This would burgeon into the May 4 movement. At the same time, the enunciation of Woodrow Wilson's principle of national self-determination encouraged new hopes among Koreans living in exile, and activists in Shanghai sent their own delegates to Paris to demand an end to the Japanese occupation. Patriotic leaders declared national independence on March 1, and a wave of public meetings and demonstrations spread across occupied Korea. Japanese forces responded by massacring thousands, and a fresh wave of Korean activists fled abroad, mostly to China.

At the beginning of May, news reached students in Beijing that the Allies had ignored China's claims at the Paris conference. Together with this came fresh evidence of the Beijing government's complicity with Japan, and on May 4 students gathered in front of the Tiananmen Gate. Charging that Cao Rulin had sold the country to the Japanese, they marched to his house and set it on fire. Cao escaped in disguise and resigned the next day, and the patriotic, anti-imperialist movement spread across the country.[30] The Nishihara loans went into default. In the long view of Chinese history, the tide had begun to turn. It would henceforth increasingly appear, even to its promoters, that time was not on the side of Japanese imperialism.

At the same point, a new American challenge took shape. A week after the May 4 incident, at the headquarters of the Banque de l'Indo-Chine in Paris, Thomas Lamont, financial adviser to the U.S. delegation to the peace conference, chaired a meeting of bankers from the various powers to determine a common strategy toward China. Chinese representatives were not invited. The operation of the first China consortium had been interrupted by the European war, and Japan had aggressively pushed its own loans in China. Concerned to prevent future unilateral—which was to say, Japanese—efforts to seize financial control in China, the U.S. government formally invited the British, French, and Japanese to join a revived consortium in October 1918. The new consortium was to pool all lending to China, including existing investment commitments and options, except those "upon which substantial progress has been made." As before, it was to concentrate on the financing of large public projects such as railroad building and currency stabilization.[31]

The Japanese government held back. Tanaka Giichi, army minister in the Hara cabinet, was adamant that Manchuria and eastern Inner Mongolia be excluded from the scope of consortium activities, even at the risk of Japan's own exclusion from the consortium. Tanaka reasoned from the classic "defensive" logic of imperial expansion—to stop pressing forward could cause the whole venture to disintegrate. If Japan backed down in Manchuria, he warned, Japan's Korean subjects might also revolt.[32]

To induce the Japanese to retract the reservation of Manchuria and Inner Mongolia, Thomas Lamont, at the request of the U.S. State Department, visited Japan and China in early 1920. A further American goal—one that went back to 1905—was to gain access to Japanese railway options in Manchuria. Simultaneously, the State Department began moving to bring an end to the Anglo-Japanese alliance.[33] Bank of Japan governor Inoue, who was about to become greatly distracted by the domestic market panic, was named the chief Japanese negotiator. Lamont's relationship to Japan and to Inoue thus began at this time. Traveling in a party that included Mrs. Lamont, two of her friends, Morgan and Company publicity director Martin Egan, lawyer Jeremiah Smith Jr., a consulting engineer, a secretary, a maid, and a doctor, Lamont arrived in Japan on March 2. Jeremiah Smith, a friend from Lamont's Harvard days, had been counselor for the U.S. Treasury at the Paris Peace Conference and would, with Lamont, play a prominent role in the international stabilization programs of the 1920s.

In the negotiations, Inoue was bound by the instructions of his government, which insisted on the point first enunciated in the Twenty-one Demands, that Japan would exercise veto power over any foreign ventures in Manchuria and eastern Inner Mongolia.[34] Inoue also attempted, without success, to interest Lamont in issuing an American loan to the South Manchurian Railway Company. On both sides, internationally oriented banking interests and nationally oriented political ones could also be seen to diverge. In fact, at the height of the postwar bubble, Wall Street seems suddenly to have discovered Japan. Coincidentally with Lamont's mission, Frank Vanderlip, recently retired as president of National City Bank, was leading a large private mission to Japan at the invitation of Shibusawa Eiichi and other business leaders who were interested in friendship with the United States. FRBNY governor Benjamin Strong was himself in Japan for a private visit.[35] During the consortium negotiations, Lamont was in regular contact with the U.S. State Department as well as with British bankers, chiefly Charles Addis of the Hongkong and Shanghai Bank—more "Anglo-American combination in the Far East," as Takahashi had called it in 1904. Disliking the idea of independent loans by either their Japanese or their American allies, the British were more inclined to compromise with the Japanese conditions.[36] American bankers too were willing to compromise and do business with Japan, while the U.S. State Department opposed any recognition of Japan's claims to preeminence in Manchuria. This divergence of views between Wall Street and Washington would reappear at every later point at which the issue of Manchuria came up in U.S.-Japan financial talks. To rationalize the difference, Lamont suggested that the Western *bankers* recognize Japan's primacy in Manchuria, involving no statement by the U.S. government. Despite direct urging from J. P. Morgan Jr., the State Department rejected this solution, to the irritation of Lamont, who came to see Manchuria as already being within Japan's sphere of influence and therefore saw such objections as merely legalistic. In the end, the Japanese government, while fostering public ambiguity on the subject, largely dropped its demands in regard to Manchuria, but only after Lamont threatened openly that Japan could expect no capital from the United States unless it joined the consortium.[37]

Resistance to the new consortium was much stronger in China, where a great wave of nationalist feeling was sweeping the country in the wake of the May 4 incident. Lamont met with Guomindang leaders including Sun Yat-sen in Shanghai, with the northern government in Beijing, and even with leaders of the student activists who protested outside his hotel. In the end, he persuaded none of them of the need for a new consortium. Returning by rail across Manchuria and Korea, Lamont was back in Tokyo by May 7, and, after a last-minute effort by the Japanese government to reattach special conditions to Japan's entry, Japan's accession to the new Four-Power Consortium was announced on May 13.[38] The new consortium was hailed in the United States as the dawn of a new era, criticized in Japan as a national derogation, and not recognized by the Chinese government, to whom it was supposed to be lending.

As an effort to coordinate activities by the wartime Allies and prevent their competing with one another for financial control in China, the reorganized Four-Power Consortium was an expression of the new postwar multilateralism in East Asia. Lamont even called it "a little league of nations."[39] It was just as clearly an imperialist financial cartel. In both aspects, it appeared as the financial component of the new "Washington system," the network of multilateral agreements created at the Washington conference of 1921–22 to prevent a naval arms race and to enshrine the "open door" in China. But from the standpoint of actual lending, the results of the second consortium were purely negative, and even more than the first consortium, its chief function was to place China under a financial embargo. British participants frankly called it a financial "blockade," and Lamont and Addis intervened repeatedly to block foreign loans to the Chinese government.[40] Japan's unilateral financial initiative in China was stalemated for a decade; but in any case, the economic difficulties that Japan fell into after 1920 would have precluded any major financial initiatives. The major positive result of the negotiations was to open relations between Morgan and Company and Japan.

Lamont ended his first Asian trip with a distaste for the chaos of revolutionary China and with a favorable regard for Japan and for the Japanese merchant aristocracy. From his side, Inoue Junnosuke gained in Thomas

Lamont a very influential connection, placed even more highly in the firmament of international finance than Takahashi's friend Jacob Schiff, who because of his "race," remained outside the Anglo-Saxon Protestant inner circles of power in his adopted homeland. Moreover, World War I had been damaging to Kuhn, Loeb, with their German connection, while the great enterprise of providing wartime credits to Britain and France raised the status of the pro-British Morgan firm from one of national to one of international financial primacy. For his part, Takahashi remained loyal to the memory of Jacob Schiff (who died in 1920).

Takahashi also regarded Morgan and Company's awesome resources more as a threat than as an asset.[41] Whereas Inoue stressed partnership and cooperation with the Western powers, Takahashi stressed competition, and despite the consortium agreement, he continued to envision a highly independent Japanese financial policy toward China. At least incipiently, then, international financial policy during the Hara administration included both a "Takahashi line" and an "Inoue line."

Inoue too recognized the American challenge, but with no great sense of alarm, explaining to an audience of peers in February 1921 that America was now in a very strong position, having ¥4 billion ($2 billion) in debts and ¥10 billion in credits. "From before," he said, the United States "has regarded South America as its own economic domain" and, during the war, "using that reserve power, also wanted to expand in the Orient." So far this had been only talk, however, and that ambition had not been realized. On the other hand, while Inoue recognized that Britain's current situation was poor, he retained his pro-British sensibilities—"as a race, the English are first rate," and they would overcome their postwar difficulties as they had overcome so many difficulties in their history.[42]

Takahashi laid out his own strategic thinking in a top-secret report, "Views concerning the Establishment of East Asian Economic Power," in the spring of 1921.[43] Britain and America, Takahashi wrote, were the two great economic powers that dominated world trends. Japan could now be considered the third great power. However, although militarily strong, Japan was conspicuously lacking in economic power—and in the final analysis, economic power was the fundamental fact, military power being just one aspect of economic power. Japan's current position as one of the three great powers was also based on temporary factors, a primary one being that after the war, Japan held ¥2 billion in specie, while Russia, Germany, France, and Italy suffered severe postwar problems. The only way to make Japan permanently one of the three great powers was for Japan to work with China "as one unit" to jointly develop East Asia's economic power, "harmoniously joining Japan's financial power and China's natural resources, Japan's industrial abilities and China's labor power."[44] If Japan failed to do this, the Western powers would dominate East Asia as they already dominated the rest of Asia.

To develop China, Takahashi thought that Japan must change its policy toward that country to one of true cooperation. Hitherto, Japan's "consistent policy through successive governments" had been, "more than the other powers, a territorial, invasive, exclusive policy of taking concessions and interfering in internal politics." These aggressive policies had yielded poor results and created an anti-Japanese atmosphere in China. Japan should now withdraw its troops and military bases from Shandong and Manchuria-Mongolia. Also, Japanese lending must be done not as in the past, to gain rights or to place advisers, but for the mutual benefit of both countries. The great problem was China's dangerously unstable political situation. To help stabilize China, Japan should undertake to lend ¥5 million to ¥6 million annually to support the Chinese administration.[45] Thus, Takahashi advocated an economically oriented, nationally independent policy of cooperation toward China.

In fact, as Ishibashi Tanzan later asserted, the reality of circumstances was making Takahashi's ideas of leveraging Japan's new financial power seem delusional. At the same time that Thomas Lamont was bringing Japan into the China consortium, panic selling overtook Japan's financial and commodity markets, in the opening chapter of the global interwar depression. Acting from within the Bank of Japan, Inoue Junnosuke took the lead in containing the positive financial policy, while Hamaguchi Osachi led the parliamentary attack from without.

THE 1920 CRASH

As Inoue had stressed in 1917, depressions generally follow major wars, which are almost invariably funded by debt. The greater the debt, the greater the problems of postwar adjustment. The brief postarmistice panic was not the financial reaction Inoue had forecast, and as the war boom inflated into a speculative postwar bubble in 1919, there were new reasons for expecting a great reaction. But whether an economic reaction was ultimately inevitable or not, the depression that began in March 1920 was also the product of deliberate deflationary policies.

When he was finally allowed by the Ministry of Finance to contract credit in the autumn of 1919, Inoue did so forcefully, raising the Bank of Japan's discount rate in two steps, on October 4 and November 19, from 6.57 percent to 8.03 percent. The central bank also issued warnings to financial institutions that it considered overextended.[46] The rate of 8.03 percent—the highest rate seen since 1907—was maintained until April 1925. The Bank of Japan did not reimpose such high rates on a sustained basis until the inflationary 1970s.

On January 22, 1920, Diet representative Hamaguchi Osachi, speaking for the opposition Kenseikai party, launched a vigorous attack that established his reputation as the leading critic of the Seiyūkai cabinet's "loose" spending policies. As against the administration's bland statements on Japan's economic outlook, Hamaguchi asserted that an economic crisis was near. Hamaguchi's interpellation concentrated on the great rise in prices, which, he charged, Prime Minister Hara and Finance Minister Takahashi had ignored. High prices were pressing the people's livelihood everywhere, leading to the wave of "strikes, slowdowns, and workers' riots" in 1919 and causing psychological disturbances that opened the door to "dangerous thought from abroad." Together with this had come a conspicuous rise of luxury and extravagance among the newly rich *narikin*. This new social divide threatened the very basis of society. In their own speeches the day before, Prime Minister Hara had warned against luxury, and Finance Minister Takahashi had warned against unproductive consumption and talked of the need to restrain speculation. However, the thrust of Takahashi's speech had been to insist that the supply of capital and materials to industry must be assured. Hamaguchi responded that Takahashi's "productionism" (*seisan bannō shugi*) did not answer the immediate problem facing the nation. Although the Bank of Japan had raised interest rates and warned against speculation, at the same time it had greatly increased its lending to the private sector and its note issue.[47] Nor, said Hamaguchi, could circumstances in other countries be used as an excuse, as Takahashi had tried to do. In 1919, prices had increased 4.5 percent in New York and 15 percent in London. In Tokyo they had increased 33 percent.

Takahashi defended himself equally vigorously. What Hamaguchi was calling for, he said, was to provoke a recession, which would bring about lower prices. "That's not our policy." What was needed instead was for the Japanese people to promote production more than ever and to make more goods. As for the recent interest-rate hikes, Takahashi claimed they had not been done to restrain prices and were undertaken by the Bank of Japan under its own authority. Takahashi also dismissed the importance of the recent rise in Japanese prices relative to other countries: rather than looking at rates of increase, one must compare the actual levels of particular prices. In fact, except for China, Japanese rice was the cheapest in the world.[48]

A few days after this well-publicized exchange, Inoue Junnosuke clarified his own standpoint, explaining that the boom in share and commodity prices in 1919 was only the aftereffect (*yoha*) of the export boom, which had now been replaced by a large trade deficit. Exports to Europe had fallen greatly, with no immediate prospect of revival, and European competition had returned in China, India, and Southeast Asia. Japan's exports now depended on the demand for raw silk in the United States, which was experiencing its own speculative boom. But unless the necessary capital could be found for European recovery, America's own exports to Europe would decline, American industry would contract, and recession would follow, with direct effects on Japan. It was only with this speech that Inoue was perceived in the press as having definitely exchanged his "optimistic talk" for "pessimism."[49] His remarks were followed by a temporary fall in stock prices.

The movement for "deflation" was international. Indeed, the economic usage of the word *deflation* itself, as the opposite of *inflation,* appears to have come into use in English only in 1919. The first references given by the *Oxford English Dictionary* are for that year, when deflation was being spoken of as a necessity, and for 1920, when it became a fact.[50] Inoue's deflation policy was closely in step with those of the Federal Reserve Bank of New York and the Bank of England, both of which raised interest rates in late 1919.

Immediately after the war, the U.S. and European central banks kept interest rates low because of their governments' needs to finance gigantic war debts. Low interest rates helped fuel a speculative bubble in commodity and financial markets. A series of coordinated interest rate hikes followed. The Bank of England, concerned to rein in inflation and "extravagant living" and to prepare for a return to the gold standard "at the earliest possible moment," began pushing for higher rates in August and September 1919.[51] At the same time, Inoue Junnosuke began to push for rate hikes in Japan. In October and November the Bank of England raised rates, and in early 1920 raised them further. Aiming "to check expansion" and "to induce healthy liquidation," the Federal Reserve Bank of New York likewise raised its rediscount rate in several steps from 4 percent in late 1919 to 6 percent in January 1920.[52] Thus, the Bank of England, the Federal Reserve Bank of New York, and Inoue's Bank of Japan led the way into world deflation. In late 1919 the U.S. and British governments also cut spending and began to run budget surpluses.

If British interest rate hikes were preparation for a return to the gold standard, a primary reason for the Federal Reserve's interest rate hikes was to *defend* the United States' newly restored gold standard. Accordingly, the international depression of 1920 was in one aspect America's own gold-restoration depression—as the world crisis of 1930–31 would be for Japan.

U.S. prices had doubled during the war, but the United States nevertheless returned to gold convertibility at the prewar parity and again allowed the free export of gold in June 1919. At this point, America was the only country to lift its wartime gold embargo. Other countries, led by Japan, cashed in their accumulated dollar claims for gold, and gold rapidly began to flow out of the United States. The U.S. Treasury Department therefore changed course in January 1920, itself suggesting steep interest rate increases to the Federal Reserve in order to keep gold at home. "We [are] dangerously near leaving the gold standard," Assistant Treasury Secretary Russell Leffingwell warned the FRBNY on January 21. "Soon a new gold embargo [will] have to be put in." Dismissing worries that high interest rates would provoke panic selling in the markets, Leffingwell answered that "if a panic in N.Y. should break out he would be glad of it."[53] Later, as chief economist at Morgan and Company, Leffingwell would advise the Japanese government on its own return to the gold standard. For his part, having moved decisively to induce "liquidation" in the United States, FRBNY governor Benjamin Strong left for a round-the-world vacation. He began his trip with a three-month stay in Japan, where he became friends with Inoue Junnosuke and brought him into the international central banking fraternity led by the Bank of England's Montagu Norman and himself.[54] This personal connection followed rather than preceded the de facto coordination of Japanese with British and American interest rate hikes, but it was an important further step in establishing the policy framework of the following decade.

The Federal Reserve maintained high interest rates until May 1921, presiding over a fall in U.S. prices of more than 40 percent and a general depression. This price decline was one of the steepest in the entire U.S. record, comparable only to the declines that followed the War of 1812 and the American Civil War. U.S. GNP fell an estimated 17 percent in terms of current prices, and unemployment in 1921 is estimated to have reached 12 percent, or 5 million people, five times the level of 1919.[55] The sudden loss of American demand had depressionary effects in the rest of the world. These were magnified by a sudden drop-off in U.S. overseas lending. In this regard 1920–21 was a "preplay" of the great suspension of U.S. capital outflows in 1928–29. On the other hand, the global effects of America's "gold restoration depression" were moderated by the fact that other countries had not yet returned to fixed gold parities and could adjust by letting their currencies depreciate rather than resorting to deflation to the extent of the United States. The ongoing inflation in Central Europe also constituted a source of world demand.[56] The choice of adjustment via deflation, Inoue style, or via currency depreciation, Takahashi style, would be a fundamental international question of the decade that followed.[57]

The American depression was also relatively short, as the U.S. economy hit bottom in the summer of 1921 and then recovered very rapidly. The entire stabilization episode was thereafter regarded by American financial leaders as a signal success. Inoue himself later described America's "liquidation" depression in 1920 as a superficial matter, like pus running from a boil on an otherwise healthy body.[58] America's presumed success became a baseline for the later analyses of Russell Leffingwell and Thomas Lamont as to what was wrong with Japan in the 1920s, and it became a model for the stabilization recession engineered by Inoue in 1929.

The 1920 depression thus had one origin point in the United States, but in fact the worldwide panic appeared first in Japan.[59] Its proximate cause appears to have been the sudden fall in world silver prices, which meant a violent reaction in the yen-tael exchange.

Wartime surpluses and booming demand in China and India had caused a great increase in world silver prices. After May 1919, simultaneous with Japan's own postwar bubble, this movement accelerated, and silver prices doubled between then and March 1920. The corresponding appreciation of the Chinese tael against the yen meant a boom for Japanese goods in China. Soaring silver prices also meant that Britain's token silver coins were now being minted at a loss. The British government reacted in early February by announcing that it would reduce the silver content of its subsidiary coinage from the long-established standard of 92.5 percent pure silver to a standard of 50 percent, effective March 20, 1920. This was a big step forward in the tokenization of the British coinage that had begun with the original adoption of the gold standard in 1816, and it suddenly reduced world silver demand. On February 11, 1920, silver prices reached a peak of 89½ pence per ounce on the London exchange and then began to decline. Traders in Shanghai who had accumulated very large stocks of silver now began to unload them. In April the decline of silver prices turned into a collapse, and by mid-June silver had fallen to a low of 44 pence, less than half the February peak. Silver prices dropped sharply again later in the year and especially in 1921, causing the yen to appreciate relative to the Chinese and Indian currencies and suddenly worsening the outlook for the export of Japanese yarn and other cotton goods to China and other Asian countries. Gold also flowed into Japan from those countries, reversing the situation that had prompted the gold embargo in 1917.[60]

On February 26, as silver prices were beginning their great decline, the Hara cabinet dissolved the Diet, and on the news, stock prices and rice prices reached new highs in the week that followed. The speculation then broke. On March 11, share prices and rice prices both fell sharply. News on March 12 of the massacre of Japanese at Nikolayevsk on the Amur added to the negative sentiment, and on March 15 the Tokyo stock market crashed. Shares in the benchmark Tokyo Stock Exchange Company fell ¥100, 27 percent off their March 1 high. Shares of cotton-spinning companies also fell heavily, and the stock market was closed for two days.[61]

This first wave of the panic was largely confined to the Tokyo stock exchange, with little effect on the commodity markets or on the Osaka stock exchange. Then on March 27, rice prices plummeted, and price falls began to spread to other commodities. On April 7 the panic hit western Japan when Osaka's Masuda Bill Brokers Bank suspended payments. Share prices began to fall everywhere, and that afternoon, all stock exchanges were closed. A wave of company bankruptcies followed. The Bank of Japan responded to the panic on April 10 by providing emergency credits, and Osaka's syndicated banks made emergency loans to support the stock market. On April 12 cotton yarn and silk thread prices also began to dive. Stock exchanges reopened on the 13th, but on the 14th, panicky sell-offs hit the stock markets in both eastern and western Japan. The stock markets again closed without a definite plan for when to reopen and remained closed for one month. The Osaka "three commodities" (*sanpin*) market was also closed until May 15. Bank runs broke out in many places, mostly at small regional banks.[62]

Inoue Junnosuke now greeted the arrival of the expected postwar economic reaction—a reaction he himself helped to author. Speaking again to the meeting of the National Banks Clearing House Association on April 22, 1920, when the major stock and commodity markets were closed, Inoue had an audience that was inclined to listen carefully.

"The reaction has arrived" (*genji wa handōki nari*), Inoue declared at the opening of his speech. The advance and retreat of the business world, he said, was "exactly like the cycle of the four seasons": after the unprecedented boom of the past five years, the great expansion of credit, and the speculative fever that went with it, the present reaction was inevitable. To the extent that the boom had been long and the expansion great, the reaction could be expected to be long and severe.[63] There was no opposing this natural process. Rather, each businessman must recognize the current situation and carry out "adjustment" (*seiri*) in his own sphere. In this connection Inoue addressed the special role of bankers. "Unlike other businesses," he told his audience, banking had a "public" character. Bankers must naturally guard their own profits, but at the same time, they must consider the situation of the entire business world. During the boom, the Bank of Japan had warned against speculation and had recommended retrenchment; its attitude had now not changed in the least. The Bank of Japan would provide as much help as possible for "honorable" enterprises that were decisively "adjusting" their operations. But banks could not continue as in the past to lend on the expectation of high profits.[64]

At this point, Inoue saw the depression as a purely domestic reaction. He therefore saw the development of exports as the only way out: "Particularly in such a time of economic reaction [*zaikai no handōki*], purchasing power must decline due to the domestic depression, and accordingly, a surplus of domestic goods will arise. In [such] inescapable circumstances, there can be no other solution but to export the surplus goods overseas."[65] The Bank of Japan, Inoue affirmed, could be counted on to use its credit to support exports as much as possible.

The day after Inoue's speech, on April 23, the BOJ decided to extend ¥120 million in emergency loans to the banks. On April 27 a bank syndicate was formed and was given a BOJ credit line of ¥50 million in order to support the stock market.[66] This was the beginning of a bailout of record scope—¥240 million altogether—which was later blamed for having prevented Japan's 1920 depression from having its full purgative effect *à la américaine.*

Despite Inoue's bailout efforts, a third wave of panic struck in May. On May 1 prices on the Yokohama silk exchange collapsed, and trading was suspended. In mid-May the stock and commodity markets reopened. Then came rumors of huge losses at the Yokohama trading company Shigeki Shōten, and panicked depositors rushed to withdraw their savings from Shigeki's "house bank," the 74th Bank, which was forced to close on May 24. Bank runs spread to the Kansai region, and commodity markets also suffered large price falls on the news of economic slowdown in the United States. By the Bank of Japan's count, there were 169 bank runs between April and July. By June the stock market index had fallen more than 60 percent from its January highs.[67]

Bubbles had arisen on top of bubbles in 1919, and most of them burst in 1920. At the peripheries of Japan's empire, the effects of Japan's boom-bust cycles were often magnified. "The speculative fever did not stop at the home islands [*naichi*]," Inoue later explained. "Wherever Japanese people go, they set up exchanges and speculate." They had done so in every Manchurian town, "and speculation there reached an even higher fever pitch than in Japan." By 1919, land prices in Dairen were six times the level of 1917. Even further out, Japan's adventure in Siberia had generated a boom for the Japanese merchants who had flocked to Northern Manchuria in late 1918 to sell goods to the Japanese army. Their trade was fueled by liberal lending by the Oriental Development Company and the Bank of Chosen, which together lent more than ¥120 million to Japanese enterprises in Manchuria in 1918 and 1919. After the inflationary collapse of the Russian ruble, the generous supply of yen notes printed by the Bank of Chosen circulated in a wide region.[68]

America's announcement in January 1920 that it was pulling its troops out of Siberia left Japan's intervention with little diplomatic cover. On March 12 Russian partisans massacred some three hundred Japanese civilians in Nikolayevsk in the northern Maritime Province, and the military intervention that had been intended to carve out a new sphere of influence turned into a bloody fiasco. In June the Japanese government announced its own pullback, and soldiers began to be sent home. As Japanese forces withdrew, the Manchurian bubble burst, and the Bank of Chosen took on a bailout role. This was the beginning of a decade of stagnation for Japanese commerce in Manchuria. "Manchuria is still messed up," Inoue Junnosuke said in 1925, and this was due to the speculative excesses of 1919. For Japanese residents, Manchuria was suddenly transformed from a frontier of opportunity into a frontier backwater. The Bank of Chosen, facing its own financial difficulties, greatly retrenched its lending and note issue and Japanese businessmen in Manchuria began to demand their own, Manchurian central bank.[69] Combined with the advance of Chinese merchants, who did not labor under the high yen exchange, economic recession supplied the context of an aggressive "subimperialist" activism among Japanese residents that formed the background of the Japanese seizure of the entire region in late 1931 and early 1932.

At home the 1920 depression was a "direct hit" to Japan's light industry. Between March and July more than 160 clothing and textile businesses went bankrupt, with the failures centered in the Kansai region. Prices for cotton yarn and silk thread fell especially sharply. By August the price of silk on the Yokohama Silk Exchange had fallen 37 percent from March highs. The postarmistice economic reaction in November 1918 had already delivered a shock to heavy industry, especially steel and chemicals, and the additional effects of the 1920 depression in that sector were thus comparatively mild, although heavy industry later received a further shock with the arms reductions brought about by the Washington naval limitations treaty in February 1922. Thus, light and heavy industry followed different cycles during this period.[70]

The yen had fallen against the dollar at the onset of the panic in March and April 1920, but continued gold imports covered the exchange crisis and a large inflow of gold again lifted the yen after May. Thus the yen was kept higher than the worsening balance of trade should have warranted and, as Ishibashi Tanzan later saw it, was in contradiction to the fundamental situation of the Japanese economy at the time.[71] The high yen encouraged imports to increase still further in 1920, while exports stagnated and nontrade receipts dropped sharply, owing to the return of European competition.

The depression also became international in June 1920, when stock prices fell violently in New York. The American crisis deepened in July and August and extended to Britain and beyond. Japanese exports suffered a further setback, accompanied by yet another wave of failures of trading companies and banks in the summer of 1920. More banking panics followed in November and December, and recession continued in the financial sector until June 1921.[72]

Accordingly, Inoue also shifted his blame for Japan's economic difficulties, telling the National Banks Clearing House Association in April 1921, "the reaction in our business world is just one part of a world trend." This was all the more reason not to expect an early recovery. Rather, the country faced a long process of currency contraction and recession, whereby reduced incomes would depress purchasing power, leading to lower prices, leading to lower production costs, and finally leading to a recovery of exports, upon which all else depended.[73]

As against Inoue's classical "adjustment" view, Takahashi Korekiyo and the Seiyūkai continued their expansionary spending policy into the depression years of 1920 and 1921, making up for the decline in tax revenues by issuing further domestic bonds. Military spending also continued to increase because of the Siberian expedition, rising from 36 percent of government spending in 1918 to a high point of 49 percent in 1921. The continuation of the "positive" policy also helped to keep prices from falling to the extent they did in the United States and Britain.[74]

Ultimately, however, even Takahashi Korekiyo turned to a policy of restraint, issuing a retrenchment budget for the 1922 fiscal year. Thus, Inoue Junnosuke helped to lead a great turn in economic policy, and Takahashi grudgingly acquiesced. In line with the trend of world economic forces, a great ebb tide had begun to run.

SEVEN

"The Contractionary Tide," 1921–1926

At the beginning of 1920, Inoue Junnosuke and Hamaguchi Osachi warned separately of a necessary reaction after the great boom of the late 1910s. More remarkably, ten years later both men continued to see the entire intervening decade as one long drawn-out reaction. They were joined by much of financial and business opinion. Inoue and Hamaguchi also worked to create this reverse movement, and in line with their sense of things, the policy tone of the 1920s as a whole was toward restriction.

Fiscal retrenchment began with Takahashi Korekiyo's reluctant curtailment of the positive policy in 1922. The demands of earthquake reconstruction temporarily interrupted the retrenchment process after September 1923, but then, from June 1924 until December 1931, apart from the twenty-six-month hiatus of Seiyūkai rule in 1927–29, financial policy was dominated by the restrictive line of the Kenseikai and Minseitō. The economic constraints of the time were such that even the Seiyūkai cabinet in 1927 and 1928 could move only in a limited way toward a positive financial policy.[1]

THE TURN TO DEFLATION

The depression that began in 1920 never seemed fully to lift. After the first round of banking crises in March 1920, bank panics continued intermittently until June 1921. An economic recovery began after March 1921, but recovery brought renewed speculation, which ended with another panic on the stock and commodity markets in February 1922. A new round of bank runs followed. A wave of factory "adjustment," or layoffs, began in May 1922, and the renewed fall of rice prices deepened the agricultural recession. Inoue's Bank of Japan stayed the course of monetary restraint. A further wave of bank runs broke out in November and December 1922, and the Bank of Japan stepped in again to bail out the banking system with ¥171 million in lending.[2] There was another round of bank crises in 1923.

Coming amid revelations of political corruption, the economic downturn discredited the big business and political establishment, and the Hara cabinet became the target of fierce political attacks. On September 28, 1921, in an incident that foreshadowed the terror campaigns that ended party government in 1932, a right-wing activist influenced by the national socialist ideas of Kita Ikki stabbed to death Japan's richest businessman, banker Yasuda Zenjirō (to whom Takahashi Korekiyo was close). On November 4 a rightist-minded railroad employee stabbed Prime Minister Hara to death in Tokyo Station. Takahashi Korekiyo succeeded Hara as Seiyūkai party president and prime minister, while continuing to retain the finance portfolio.

Despite the great fall in prices after March 1920, the opposition continued to hammer on the Takahashi government over "the rise in prices" (*bukka tōki*).[3] This was no longer a matter of ending an ongoing inflation—inflation had come to a decisive end in 1920. Rather, it was the idea that prices in Japan had not fallen far enough. A popular political and journalistic catchphrase for explaining social changes since the late 1910s was the "worsening of thought" (*shisō akka*), a term that encompassed the appearance of communism, feminism, the labor movement, and new, revolutionary isms of all kinds. To the Kenseikai's Hamaguchi Osachi, much of this mental unrest was plainly caused by high consumer prices and economic instability. "Since the war," Hamaguchi declared to the House of Representatives in January 1922, "influenced by foreign ideas, the tone of our people's thought has changed." In particular, "people belonging to the working class" had "embraced dangerous, radical thought." To address this crisis, Hamaguchi said, "social policy" was needed, but the most fundamental social policy was to stabilize the people's livelihoods by removing the greatest cause of instability—that is, by "price adjustment," or deflation.[4]

The theme of frugality came not only from the side of politicians and financial bureaucrats. Mainstream business opinion too came to the view that Japan had entered a new age of limits. In November 1921 the National Federation of Chambers of Commerce petitioned the newly formed Takahashi cabinet to lower prices as an urgent necessity. This meant above all "contracting the currency and lifting the embargo on gold exports." The business group further called on the government to reduce spending and likewise for "every one of the Japanese people to economize on living expenses." Repeating this call a month later, the chambers of commerce launched an "Association for National Thrift" in order "to encourage diligence and accumulation" and "to foster a spirit of simplicity." Member chambers of commerce of each locality were to encourage the people to be punctual; to conserve gas, electricity, water, and other natural resources; to become aware of household budgeting; and "to do away with vain social formalities." To disseminate these principles, the chambers of commerce requested the government "to have the executive officials of each locality issue appropriate official orders."[5]

Coming from an old-style Confucianist statesman, such exhortations to frugality would be in character; coming from a modern chamber of commerce, they may appear odd. Manifestly, these businessmen were not viewing domestic demand as a fundamental source of economic growth. In fact, it seems that they regarded the Japanese people more as their workers than as their customers. In any case, they appeared to share the deflationist view that domestic consumption necessarily came at the expense of exports. Business demands for retrenchment continued in 1922. Mitsui's Dan Takuma, Japan's most powerful industrialist, declared that all Japanese must eliminate luxuries and "wasted expenses." Inoue Junnosuke criticized the "positive" policy from a similar standpoint. Such "top-down" demands were matched by the demands of female consumers, as represented by the All-Kansai Women's Federation, a great federation of women's groups in Western Japan, which also called on the government to bring down prices. As Ishibashi Tanzan later put it, "public opinion" in 1921 and 1922 supported deflation, but the Hara and Takahashi governments failed to follow it.[6] Although Ishibashi himself later gained fame for championing a Keynesian policy of stimulating consumer demand, at the time, he continued to argue for deflation and a return to the gold standard. In fact, Takahashi Korekiyo did begin to cut government spending. The Hara cabinet's 1921 budget had showed a large increase over the giant 1920 budget despite the fall of government revenues caused by the 1920 depression. But Takahashi's retrenchment budget for FY 1922 cut general account spending by more than 5 percent.

The framework of international relations in East Asia also continued to shift in a way that seemed virtually to reverse the expansionist initiatives of Japan's wartime cabinets. At the Washington Conference, which met from November 1921 to February 1922, the British and Japanese governments assented to an American plan to replace the Anglo-Japanese alliance with a set of multilateral treaties: the Four-Power Pact, the Nine-Power Pact, and the Washington Naval Limitation Treaty. This "Washington system" of treaties, renewed at the London Conference in 1930, formed the basic diplomatic framework of East Asian relations in the 1920s.[7] The Washington system was an unambiguous victory for American diplomacy, affirming the "open door" in China, restoring Shandong to Chinese sovereignty (while preserving Japan's economic rights there), and setting a ratio of 5:5:3 for the tonnage of capital ships in the British, American, and Japanese navies, respectively. Thus, in the context of its large war debts to the United States, which required refinancing, the British government yielded to American pressure to end its alliance with Japan.[8] The Japanese government was also concerned to refinance old Russo-Japanese War bonds and was simultaneously seeking additional American loans.

Two months after the Washington Conference concluded, the Japanese government also signed on to the recommendations of the international economic conference at Genoa, which called for all countries to return to the gold standard. As a second multilateral settlement that defined a restabilized postwar order—which was largely the status quo ante—the Genoa resolutions were seen in Japan as the monetary counterpart of the Washington system, and they will be considered more fully in the following chapter. Significantly, Japanese representatives also made informal commitments to British and American representatives at the time of the Washington and Genoa meetings, suggesting that Japan would return to the gold standard when Britain did.[9]

Despite this agreement in principle to restore the gold standard, Takahashi continued the foreign-exchange policy that became a hallmark of his positive policy, allowing the yen to fall through his entire tenure in office. By June 1922, when the Takahashi cabinet resigned, the yen was nearly 5 percent below its gold par. Takahashi would repeat this yen-depreciation policy as finance minister in the wake of the financial crisis of 1927. He would repeat it again, in a very big way, after December 1931.

Takahashi's cabinet remained in office for only seven months. After Hara's murder the Seiyūkai split into a pro-Takahashi faction and an anti-Takahashi "reform faction" led by Tokonami Takejirō and Yamamoto Tatsuo (who had preceded Takahashi as BOJ governor and finance minister and had enforced retrenchment against Takahashi's preference for a positive policy). Tokonami and Yamamoto later led their faction out of the Seiyūkai and eventually into the rival Minseitō.

As the Seiyūkai faltered, there was a brief return to the old pattern of nonparty "transcendental" (*chōzen*) cabinets centered on the House of Peers and led by senior members of the old military-bureaucratic cliques. The first of these was formed with Seiyūkai support by Admiral Katō Tomosaburō (1861–1923), who as navy minister in the Takahashi cabinet and chief delegate to the Washington Conference, led the navy's "treaty faction," which favored arms limitation. The finance minister was Ichiki Otohiko. The new government adopted a policy of deflation and general retrenchment, including cuts in military spending. This pairing of military and fiscal retrenchment (*gunshuku, kinshuku*) later reappeared in the ill-fated policy of Hamaguchi Osachi and Inoue Junnosuke in 1929–31. While retaining an absolute majority in the House of Representatives, the Seiyūkai was divided and weak. The minority Kenseikai remained in opposition.

If the 1920s was a time of ascendant "Americanism" and internationalism, for Japan's military it was a time of retreat and consolidation in comparison to the military "booms" that preceded and followed. As in the economic sphere, Japanese military forces had greatly overextended themselves, and the series of economic fiascoes that began in March 1920 were paralleled by the military fiasco in Siberia. Thus, comprehensive overextension in the late 1910s was followed by comprehensive pullback in the early 1920s. With the practical termination in 1922 and 1923 of the Siberian expedition—which militarily was a much bigger operation for Japan than was World War I—military spending was reduced more than 40 percent.[10] The Siberian expedition also brought public discredit to the military that paralleled the postwar anti-militarist reactions in Europe. In absolute terms, military budgets were hardly low in the 1920s—spending more than ¥600 million per year, Japan remained one of the world's most highly militarized states—but there was a lull in spending compared to the periods before and after.

Soon after the Katō Tomosaburō cabinet was inaugurated in June 1922, the National Federation of Chambers of Commerce requested that the new cabinet as its first step undertake to deflate prices. Lower prices would enable the lowering of wages, which were the basis of production. The new cabinet was sympathetic to this idea, and in August 1922 announced a nineteen-point price reduction plan.[11] Among its specific points was the exclusion of overseas gold holdings from the reserve for convertibility. This measure shrank the issue of Bank of Japan notes, although this effect was limited because Takahashi Korekiyo had already caused much of Japan's overseas specie holdings to be repatriated. It also ended the vestiges of Japan's sterling-based gold-exchange standard (although both the British and the Japanese gold standards were at the time suspended.) Thus, the Anglo-Japanese alliance and Japan's London-based gold-exchange standard were terminated simultaneously.

The August 1922 deflation plan was also the beginning of an effort to restore the gold standard. On September 7 and 8, 1922, Finance Minister Ichiki convened a group of "powerful businessmen" from eastern and western Japan to discuss the issue of lifting the gold embargo. Among them was Mutō Sanji, managing director of Kanebō (the Kanegafuchi Spinning Company), and he took the lead in arguing that the gold embargo should be lifted quickly. Finance Minister Ichiki and Bank of Japan governor Inoue, in line with the general sense of those present, also favored lifting the gold embargo but said that more time was needed. A week later, Finance Minister Ichiki announced that the government would allow limited overseas gold payments in order to raise the yen's exchange rate to the old parity so that it could lift the gold embargo. According to the Bank of Japan's 1930 internal history of Japan's long trek back to the gold standard, this was the first statement that made the government's policy clear.[12] Just how clear is conveyed by Ichiki's convoluted statement itself:

> As for the gold export embargo, being that it was originally an abnormal measure adopted during wartime, we need not debate the fact that we should lift it as soon as possible and restore the economy to its normal course. But having said that, we must prudently consider whether now is or is not the appropriate time to lift the embargo. In my opinion, because the world economic situation still lacks stability, most countries have not yet determined their policies in regard to gold, and international gold movements have not yet returned to being free, and furthermore because we cannot yet report that our country's business world is fully stable, I think that the disadvantageous influence that our business world would suffer as a result of lifting the gold embargo would likely not be at all slight. Accordingly, the Government thinks that now is not the appropriate time to lift the gold embargo, but that when the internal and external economic situation is a bit more stabilized, and when we can see that there is no fear that lifting the gold embargo would bring sudden changes to our financial world, then we should make all efforts to carry it out quickly. Although the foregoing is the Government's view in connection to lifting the gold embargo, [in the meantime] in regard to the negative influence of the export embargo on the exchange markets, the Government's policy will be to pay special consideration to making future sale of [our] overseas specie holdings as easy as possible.[13]

Formally, this was a policy of returning to the gold standard in line with the agreement at Genoa—though it was, as Ishibashi Tanzan said, hardly unambiguous as to when and how. The operative part of Ichiki's statement was the decision to sell overseas specie holdings to raise the value of the yen. The government's willingness to sell overseas specie holdings or to ship gold from Japan subsequently varied significantly from cabinet to cabinet over the rest of the decade and became part of the dialectic of the positive and negative policies.

Otherwise, Ichiki's statement well reflects the halfhearted character of the policies followed by every cabinet until 1929.[14] This policy—to pay out specie and thus maintain the yen's value, but not to do so to the point of allowing prices to fall and hurt business—was criticized as an irresolute half measure by Ishibashi Tanzan, who called for immediate resumption of free gold movements. As far as the gold standard was concerned, Ishibashi later concluded, the Katō Tomosaburō cabinet was a period of sideways motion.[15]

From his side, Bank of Japan governor Inoue Junnosuke welcomed the new deflation policy but insisted that more was needed. As he continued to hold the Bank of Japan's discount rate at the historically high level of 8.03 percent, Inoue was explicit about the fact that his deflationary policy was inducing a depression. Addressing the Kansai Bankers' Convention in November 1922, Inoue recalled how, a year earlier, he had told the same forum that the only way "to adjust the business world, bring down prices, and balance trade" was for the government and the people together to practice "thrift and diligence" to "tighten up the lax popular attitude." Early in

1922—that is, during the Takahashi cabinet—the trade deficit had grown even worse, Inoue said. But thereafter the government had moved to curtail spending and bring down prices, and the people had come to recognize the importance of restraining their consumption and diligently exerting themselves. Thus, "a contractionary tide [*kinshuku no fūchō*] is gradually coming about, and as a result, this has added to an extent to the severity of the general depression. Throughout the country, the volume of trade is gradually declining."[16] Prices had already "shown some measure of decline"—in fact, they had fallen by 15 percent in the past year—but they still remained twice the prewar level. In England and America, prices had fallen much further, and Japan must follow suit. More constraint was needed. "This contractionary trend has only become a bit conspicuous since May or June of this year [1922]," Inoue said, "and we have not yet reached the point where we can simply say that we have gone the whole distance. Thus, I believe that hereafter, the distance must be suitably long, and during that time the business world must be adjusted and prices must gradually come down." The moral stakes were clear:

> Despite the fact that the income of the nation in general has fallen remarkably since the economic reaction of 1920, the wasteful habits to which people grew accustomed during the boom period are not easily reformed, and many people are still living off of past accumulation. Despite the decline in sales revenues, there are also companies that continue to pay inappropriate [high] dividends using the profits accumulated during the boom. Such an unhealthy situation cannot go on forever.

If business failed to adjust promptly, exports would fall and the new overseas trade outlets that had been developed during the war would wither. Ultimately, the financial power gained during the war would be lost.[17]

Adjustment (*seiri*) was a catchall often used at the time but rarely defined. Concretely, Inoue mentioned that businesses must curtail their operations and that unemployment would result: "on this point [of dealing with unemployment], other arrangements would have to be awaited, but [unemployment] was something that could not be avoided in undertaking business adjustment." Business must become more efficient, and "the people as a whole must strain to economize on consumption and revive the custom of hard work." A "mood of retrenchment" must be maintained in this way for several months to come. Although England and the United States had lowered their interest rates in April and May 1921, Japan must maintain high rates. One "must be pessimistic about the future."[18]

In the event, the Bank of Japan did not lower interest rates until April 1925. The sixty-five-month phase of high interest rates that had begun in November 1919 was by far the longest that the Bank of Japan had ever held to a single discount rate up to this point. In helping to bring about this "contractionary tide," Inoue Junnosuke was playing his part in a global movement, as the leaders of the world's most powerful central and private banks set about reconstructing an international financial order in which gold and capital would once again flow freely across national boundaries.

By steps, the government thus moved back toward the gold standard. As Inoue saw it, the Washington Conference had reduced political uncertainty in the Asia-Pacific region. By early 1923 the Katō Tomosaburō cabinet's retrenchment policy had lifted the yen to $0.49, near the old par. Thus, favorable conditions had been prepared for lifting the gold embargo. In not having done so, Inoue later said, the government had committed a "great failure of policy." Finance Minister Ichiki himself later stated that he was looking for a chance to lift the gold embargo but had lost the chance with Katō Tomosaburō's death in August 1923.[19]

At the same time, a fundamental economic contradiction had become visible, one that would appear also in Britain and other countries as they sought to restore the prewar monetary order. After an interval of recovery in the spring of 1923, the stronger yen brought on renewed economic recession and a new round of bank panics. Thinking about this dynamic later, after the experience of the great banking panic of 1927, Ishibashi Tanzan reconsidered his earlier calls for immediately lifting the gold embargo. Finance Minister Ichiki's policy of holding off on gold resumption had made sense after all, he admitted. Had the government pushed the yen up to its par value and lifted the gold embargo, Ishibashi wrote, "our business world would likely have fallen into extreme confusion and experienced the panic of Spring 1927 earlier, around 1923; and once again a gold export embargo might have been unavoidable."[20]

In retrospect then, the policy choice was evident by 1922: restore the gold yen at its former parity and thereby cause panic and recession, or continue in an unsatisfactory, unauthorized, in-between state of fluctuating exchanges and repeated, politically determined adjustments.

DEFLATION INTERRUPTED

Prime Minister Katō Tomosaburō died in office on August 27, 1923. While negotiations for forming a new cabinet were still under way, the great Kantō earthquake struck the Tokyo-Yokohama area at 11:58 A.M. on Saturday, September 1, halting the retrenchment policy and ending the chance to restore the gold standard anytime soon. The scale of the shock is hard to imagine. For two days, firestorms raged in Tokyo and Yokohama, destroying most of the capital city and nearly all of the country's largest port city. More than 140,000 people perished—more than in the horrific firebombing of Tokyo on March 10, 1945. The total economic losses were later estimated at ¥5.5 billion, or three times the cost of the Russo-Japanese War. Another comparison is even more telling: the economic damage caused by the earthquake is estimated to have been equivalent to one-quarter of the damage caused to all of Japan during World War II.[21]

The earthquake also constituted another great financial crisis. On its second day the firestorm reached the Bank of Japan building in Nihonbashi, and Inoue Junnosuke, accompanied by BOJ director Eigo Fukai, personally directed the fire-fighting operation at great personal risk, ensuring that the bank's vaults remained safe. The Bank of Japan thus largely escaped the disaster, but of the other banks in Tokyo, 121 head offices and 222 branch offices were destroyed, or three-quarters of the total. All forty-two bank buildings in Yokohama were destroyed.[22]

On the evening of September 2, a new cabinet was hurriedly formed by a second retired admiral, the seventy-one-year old Yamamoto Gonnohyōe. During Yamamoto's first tenure as prime minister, in the aftermath of the "movement to protect constitutional government," he had allied himself with the Seiyūkai—it was as Yamamoto's minister of finance that Takahashi Korekiyo had first entered political life. But in 1923, with Takahashi as party president, the Seiyūkai opposed the Yamamoto cabinet. The Kenseikai took a more neutral attitude. Inoue Junnosuke, after four years and five months as Bank of Japan governor, resigned to join the cabinet as finance minister.

A great effort of rebuilding now got underway, enabled by a new "positive" policy implemented by Inoue Junnosuke. The Ministry of Finance building in Ōtemachi had burned down, so officials were moved into the finance minister's official residence at Nagatachō, and tents were set up to provide additional office space. On September 7, via an imperial edict, Inoue declared a thirty-day moratorium on debt repayments. Tariffs were temporarily lifted on the import of lumber and other materials needed for relief and reconstruction. Emergency tax relief was granted, and emergency aid was again extended to banks.[23]

The earthquake also aggravated the existing debt crisis. To begin with, despite the vast destruction of real wealth, debts survived intact. Moreover, much of the real wealth destroyed in the disaster was turned into debt as a result of another emergency imperial ordinance on September 27 that authorized Kantō-area banks and companies to issue special "earthquake bills" eligible for discount by the Bank of Japan, permitting the financial system to continue to operate on the same scale as before the disaster. Many companies also took advantage of this provision to convert bad debts left over from 1920 into the new earthquake bills. By the end of March 1924, the Bank of Japan had discounted more than ¥400 million of these bills. The limit set for the redemption of the earthquake bills was September 1, 1925. It was subsequently extended two times. In the end, these debts, many of them unrecoverable, triggered the great banking crisis of 1927.[24]

Inoue initially tried to maintain the value of the yen, but a great gap appeared between New York and Yokohama exchange rates. When a government order virtually stopped specie payments on December 5, 1923, the yen exchange plummeted, as the policy of supporting the exchange was temporarily abandoned.

The earthquake confused the economic situation to the end of 1923. A reconstruction boom also got underway. Japanese sawmills could not cut boards fast enough to keep up with the demand, and imports, especially American lumber and other construction materials, were urgently needed. In early October Inoue sent overseas financial commissioner Mori Kengo and his assistant Tsushima Juichi abroad to raise a large foreign loan—opening a new era of heavy overseas borrowing.[25]

Inoue's first tenure as finance minister was brief. On December 27 an anarchist fired a shot at Crown Prince Hirohito, and to express the weight of their responsibility, the Yamamoto cabinet collectively resigned, to be succeeded by a third nonparty cabinet headed by Kiyoura Keigo (1850–1942). The Diet erupted in opposition to what Takahashi Korekiyo and others charged was an unconstitutional maneuver. Shōda Kazue, formerly finance minister in the Terauchi cabinet, replaced Inoue, who was appointed to the House of Peers and left for a trip around the world.

The Seiyūkai itself now split completely, as the larger, anti-Takahashi faction of the party led by Tokonami Takejirō and Yamamoto Tatsuo constituted itself as the Seiyū Hontō (True Seiyūkai) and supported the new cabinet. There were now three major parties. The rump Seiyūkai party remained greatly weakened through the remainder of Takahashi's tenure as party president and regained its former strength only after 1925, under the leadership of General Tanaka Giichi.

After a brief effort to support the yen exchange, the Kiyoura cabinet let the yen fall again, and it slid nearly 15 percent, to a low of around $0.40 in May 1924. Exports surged. By breaking the high-yen policy—that is, the effort to restore the gold standard—the earthquake thus promoted a general economic recovery. But as the cabinet adopted a new retrenchment policy in May and June, the yen again began to rise, bringing a new round of *endaka* (yen appreciation) recession. The tension between economic recovery and restoring the yen to its old par was becoming increasingly plain. The Seiyū Hontō suffered a sharp defeat in the May 1924 general election, and consequently the Kiyoura cabinet resigned in June, having failed to pass the annual budget.[26]

THE BEGINNING OF AMERICAN LOANS

The demands of earthquake reconstruction and the resulting heavy trade deficit meant a great need for foreign capital. This work was arranged by Thomas Lamont.

Postwar efforts to borrow in the United States went back to March 1920, when in conjunction with negotiating Japan's membership in the new China consortium, Inoue Junnosuke had tried to get an American loan for the South Manchurian Railway Company. Capital was not lacking in Japan in the wake of the wartime boom, and the overriding foreign-policy purpose of seeking the SMR loan was to gain indirect U.S. recognition of Japan's position in Manchuria and to enlist the aid and interests of American bankers on Japan's behalf. In 1921 Shibusawa Eiichi pursued the matter in a trip to the United States, where he met American bankers and proposed a loan of $150 million for the SMR. Lamont initially evaded the question, later suggesting to Inoue that as a first bond issue in the United States (that is, the first handled by Morgan and Company), it ought to be something purely Japanese. Lamont was sympathetic, he told Inoue, but politically the time was not yet right. Moreover, the business really belonged to Kuhn, Loeb, not to Morgan.[27] Two years later, Lamont would genteelly steal Kuhn, Loeb's business and make Morgan and Company the American financial agent of the Japanese government.

While the SMR loan was faltering, another Japanese loan was succeeding—a $20 million bond flotation for the quasi-governmental Oriental Development Company, finalized in March 1923. Like the South Manchurian Railway, the ODC was an agent of Japanese colonial expansion in Manchuria. In approving the one but not the other, the U.S. State Department played a balancing act between the desire to withhold recognition of Japan's position in Manchuria and the desire not to shut Japan entirely out of U.S. capital markets and risk provoking a go-it-alone response.[28] Both of these semigovernmental companies also exemplified the process of dependent financial imperialism, having borrowed in London and lent in China. The ODC loan was Japan's first overseas bond issue of the 1920s. It was followed two months later by a £3 million bond issue in London for the Tokyo Electric Light Company (Tōkyō Denkō). Plans were also underway for overseas bond issues by the Tokyo city government, the South Manchurian Railway, the Industrial Bank of Japan, and other electric companies and public utilities.[29]

At the same time, Japan's wartime initiative to establish a hegemonic position in China came to a failed end. On March 10, 1923, the Chinese government unilaterally abrogated the treaty signed as a result of the Twenty-one Demands in 1915. (The Japanese government did not recognize this action.) The "yen diplomacy" initiative was also moribund, and most of Japan's wartime loans to China were now in default. On April 14 the U.S. government abrogated the wartime Ishii-Lansing agreement of 1917, which had, ambiguously, recognized Japan's special position in Manchuria. Recognizing the trend of the times, on May 30, 1924, a joint conference of the Foreign Ministry, army, navy, and Finance Ministry also decided on a China policy of "economic advance" (that is, rather than military advance).

The 4½ percent sterling loan of 1905 was also coming due in 1925. Twelve years earlier, Takahashi Korekiyo had expressed his fears concerning the refinancing of this loan to Inoue Kaoru, fearing that a misstep could open the way to the Anglo-American domination of China. Japan's financial gains during World War I then seemed to solve the problem, and the government set aside funds to redeem the loan. The postwar depression and the earthquake threw Japan back into its prewar financial bind. Takahashi had also expressed fears of an American advance in East Asia, backed by the immense financial power concentrated in J. P. Morgan and Company. As it happened, the Russo-Japanese War loan was to be refinanced by none other than Morgan and Company, packaged together with a loan for earthquake relief. The Japanese government loan for $150 million was also the largest long-term foreign loan yet handled by New York.[30]

Thomas Lamont carefully managed the Japanese bond issue from the start. Soon after the earthquake, saying he had heard that the Japanese government planned to take out large loans in New York, Lamont encouraged Inoue to refrain for the moment, to avoid the effect of a "calamity market." (Lamont himself had helped organize the American relief effort for Japan, and thought it impolitic to ask people for contributions and try to sell them bonds at the same time.) The American loan, issued in February 1924 under the authority of Finance Minister Shōda, then replaced the old 4½ percent bonds with new 6½ percent bonds, issued conjointly with a £25 million loan in London. The total yen proceeds of the American and British loans came to about ¥500 million, of which some ¥200 million went for reconstruction[31]—it was called the earthquake reconstruction loan, but it could well have been called the Russo-Japanese War refinancing loan.

The 1924 loan also meant switching Japanese government business from Kuhn, Loeb to the rival Morgan firm. This was done over the opposition of Takahashi Korekiyo, who considered Jacob Schiff to have been a great benefactor of Japan. On his side, Lamont carefully coached the Japanese negotiator on how to present the matter to Kuhn, Loeb so as not to violate openly the Wall Street taboo against poaching the business of fellow investment banks. Thus, Kuhn, Loeb was included in the loan syndicate as a junior partner, together with the Morgan-linked First National and National City banks—the same loan syndicate that had first been formed in June 1909 to make loans to China and Latin America. Inoue's overseas banking connection was now far more influential in the greater scheme of things than the aging Takahashi's. The domestic reaction to these higher-interest bonds was not wholly positive in Japan, with newspapers calling them "national humiliation bonds" (*kokujoku kōsai*).[32]

The so-called earthquake loan began a new flow of Western, mainly American, capital into Japan (table 4). It was followed in August 1924 by a bond issue for Daidō Electric Power arranged by Dillon, Read and

TABLE 4. Japanese overseas bond issues, 1923–1931

Date of Issue (yr./mo.)	*Face Amount[a] (in millions)*	*Borrower*	*Interest Rate (%)*	*Issue Price*	*Fee (%)*	*Term (years)*	*Issuing Banks, Details*
1923/3	$19.9	Oriental Development Co.	6	92	5	30	National City Bank of New York
1923/6	£3.0	Tokyo Electric Light Co.	6	94	7	25	Whitehall Trust. First overseas bond issue by a Japanese electric power company.
1923/7	£4.0	South Manchurian Railway Co.	5	88	4	25	Industrial Bank of Japan (IBJ)
1924/2	$150.0	Government of Japan	6.5	92.5	5	30	American group (Morgan & Co., et al.)[b]
1924/2	£25.0	Government of Japan	6	87.5	4.5	35	British group,[c] Yokohama Specie Bank. Jointly issued with U.S. loan. Of the combined total, ¥351 million went to convert the 1905 4½% sterling loans, and ¥187 million for earthquake reconstruction.
1924/8	$15.0	Daidō Electric Power Co.	7	91.5	?	20	Dillon, Reed & Co.
1924/8	$22.0	Industrial Bank of Japan	6	96.5	?	3	National City Bank. Fifth Industrial Bank bills, to convert Nishihara loans.

1925/2	£0.6	Tokyo Electric Light	6	82	?	23	Whitehall Trust
1925/3	$15.0	Tōhō Electric Power Co.	7	90.5	?	30	New York Guaranty Trust
1925/3	$14.0	Ujigawa Electric Power Co.	7	91	?	20	Lee Higginson
1925/7	£0.3	Tōhō Electric Power	5	97	?	20	Prudential Assurance
1925/7	$13.5	Daidō Electric Power	6.5	86	?	25	Dillon, Reed
1925/8	$24.0	Tokyo Electric Light	6	98.9	?	3	Guaranty Trust
1926/7	$10.0	Tōhō Electric Power	6	98	?	3	Guaranty Trust
1926/10	£6.0	City of Tokyo	5.5	83.5	4	35	British group
1926/12	$19.74	City of Yokohama	6	93	4	35	American group
1927/3	$20.64	City of Tokyo	5.5	89.5	3.5	34	American group, Yokohama Specie Bank
1927/12	$7.65	Tokyo Electric Power Co.	6.5	93.25	?	25	Dillon, Reed
1928/1	$9.0	Nippon Electric Power	6.5	94	?	25	Harris Forbes
1928/6	$70.0	Tokyo Electric Light	6	90.5	5.75	25	Guaranty Trust[d]
1928/6	£4.5	Tokyo Electric Light	6	90	7.5	25	Lazard Bros., Whitehall Trust. Jointly issued with U.S. loan.
1928/10	$19.9	Oriental Development Co.	5.5	90	3.75	30	National City Bank
1929/7	$11.45	Tōhō Electric Power	6	96.25	3.75	3	Guaranty Trust, Lee Higginson, Harris Forbes

(continued on next page)

TABLE 4 *(continued)*

Date of Issue (yr./mo.)	*Face Amount*[a] *(in millions)*	*Borrower*	*Interest Rate (%)*	*Issue Price*	*Fee (%)*	*Term (years)*	*Issuing Banks, Details*
1930/5	$71.0	Government of Japan	5.5	90	4	35	American group, Yokohama Specie Bank. To redeem 1905 4% sterling bonds.
1930/5	£12.5	Government of Japan	5.5	90	4	35	British group, Yokohama Specie Bank. Jointly issued with U.S. loan.
1931/2	£1.5	Nippon Electric Power	6	87.5	?	25	Chase, Harris Forbes, Schneider
1931/7	$22.8	Taiwan Electric Power Co.	5.5	93.5	?	25	American group. Government guaranteed.

SOURCES: Itō M. 1989: 148–149, 152–153; and various other sources including Tsushima 1963, vol. 2.

[a] All dollar-denominated loans were issued in New York; all sterling-denominated loans in London. For further explanation, see the notes to table 2, in chapter 4 above.

[b] *American group:* Morgan-led group consisting of J. P. Morgan & Co.; Kuhn, Loeb & Co., National City Bank of New York; First National Bank of New York. (This was the same group originally formed in 1909, at State Department request, for conducting loans to China).

[c] *British group:* Westminster Bank (which had merged with the former Parr's Bank), Hongkong & Shanghai Bank, Rothschilds, Baring Bros., Henry Schroeder, Morgan Grenfell (Morgan & Company's London partnership). Panmure Gordon also took part in the February 1924 loan but not in subsequent loans handled by the British group.

[d] The Tokyo Electric Light Co. loans of June 1928 were issued simultaneously in New York, London, and Tokyo. The Tokyo share was ¥60 million of the total ¥245 million (reckoned in yen, ¥140 million in New York, ¥45 million in London).

Company, one of the most aggressive of the rising Wall Street firms that were floating overseas bond issues in the 1920s. Inoue Junnosuke hailed Daidō's president Fukuzawa Momosuke on his return from New York as a "general returning in triumph." Other executives resented the stiff terms extracted by Dillon, Read as having set a bad precedent, and it was joked that the Daidō president had better watch his step when he went out at night.[33]

In fact, interest rates on foreign loans were no longer significantly lower than those on loans obtainable domestically, but domestic borrowing was limited to five- or ten-year terms, while foreign bonds could be issued on twenty- or thirty-year terms. The longer-term loans were especially needed for capital-intensive applications such as electrification, which would take many years to pay off.[34] They were also connected to Japanese purchases from member firms of the "Morgan zaibatsu," such as General Electric. As in the years after the Russo-Japanese War, foreign loans also served to cover the trade deficit and helped restore the value of the yen to close to the old par; and simultaneously with this new inflow of American capital, there was a renewed phase of domestic retrenchment and deflation.

MORE RETRENCHMENT: THE "LIBERAL PARTY" AFTER 1924

Among the parties, only the Seiyū Hontō supported the Kiyoura cabinet. The Kenseikai led by Katō Takaaki, the Seiyūkai led by Takahashi Korekiyo, and the liberal-reformist Kakushin Club (Reform Club) led by Inukai Tsuyoshi all joined forces to launch a self-styled "second movement to protect constitutional government." Takahashi resigned his peerage to run for the House of Representatives (that is, as a commoner) in the May 1924 elections. He chose to represent the home district of his political mentor Hara Takashi in Iwate—running, in effect, as Hara's successor. The Seiyū Hontō was roundly repudiated in the elections, and the Kiyoura cabinet subsequently resigned. After nine years in opposition, Katō Takaaki gained the position he had sought a decade earlier, forming a cabinet based on a coalition of the Kenseikai, the Seiyūkai, and the Kakushin Club in June 1924. This was the first time under the Meiji constitution that an election had brought about a change of cabinets.[35] It was also the last, and in several ways this triumph of the political parties was the high point of 1920s liberalism. The political parties had joined together to oust a reactionary, nonparty cabinet, and as one of their subsequent legislative achievements, universal manhood suffrage was enacted in March 1925.

The formation of the three-party coalition government also opened a new phase of negative, or reconstructionist, policy and a new movement to return to the gold standard. The coalition government was dominated by the Kenseikai, who held all the key posts of prime minister (Katō Takaaki), home minister (Wakatsuki Reijirō), foreign minister (Shidehara Kijūrō), and finance minister (Hamaguchi Osachi).[36] For its part, the Seiyūkai got the ministries of Justice and of Agriculture and Commerce. Takahashi Korekiyo held the latter post. Thus the partisan tension between the "positive" and "negative" policies was incorporated into the cabinet, with Takahashi's positive policy in the minority position.

In his first address to the Diet as finance minister, Hamaguchi announced the new cabinet's retrenchment policy. Government finances, he explained, were burdened by the huge earthquake recovery expenses, virtually all of which had been covered by government borrowing. Reconstruction demands had greatly increased imports, adding to the trade deficit that had reappeared since 1919 and causing an "unprecedented fall" in the yen exchange. To deal with these problems, "the most important fundamental measure" was to economize on consumption. The government must retrench and the people must correct customs of "thoughtless luxury," "cultivate the beautiful customs of self-control and saving, and strive to accumulate capital by thrift and strenuous effort."[37]

The moral necessity of deflation was brought home to the Japanese people in a new ideological campaign. Following meetings in every ministry to discuss the retrenchment campaign, Prime Minister Katō publicly launched a "Diligence and Thrift Campaign" (*kinken shōrei undō*) on September 1, 1924. Home Minister Wakatsuki Reijirō and Finance Minister (later Home Minister) Hamaguchi Osachi took the lead, as the Home Ministry mobilized its considerable resources of persuasion and control to take the message to the public in every corner of Japan. The starting point of the cabinet's message was the imbalance of external payments: since the war, Japan's foreign trade had turned from surplus to deficit, while the country's debts had grown and grown. "The only way to break out of this desperate situation is diligence and thrift," as the Home Ministry's first campaign poster put it.[38] "In line with the Boshin rescript," which had launched the retrenchment drive that followed the Russo-Japanese War in 1908, a new "Rescript Regarding the Spiritual Uplift of the Japanese People" was issued in the name of the Taishō emperor on November 10.[39] The government also mounted a campaign to "cherish Japanese goods" (*kokusanhin aiyō*), inspired by the "Buy British goods" movement—which was meant to better Britain's own chronic trade deficit and support its own restoration of the gold standard at the old, high par.[40]

After becoming home minister in 1926, Hamaguchi Osachi continued the campaign, delivering the message to women in their role as "superintendents of the household" that the goals of the government's campaign were a matter equally of morality and of daily life. With a national debt of more than ¥5 billion and gold flowing out of the country, Hamaguchi explained, the main point that his listeners should take home with them was that "consumption is excessive" and must be reduced. The Home Ministry even worked to publicize the story lines of fifteen feature films that encouraged diligence and thrift.[41] In its rhetoric and techniques of mass mobilization and in the policy content of its message, the "Diligence and Thrift" campaign formed a dress rehearsal for the campaign led by Hamaguchi Osachi and Inoue Junnosuke that accompanied the return to the gold standard in 1929.

The retrenchment campaign went beyond rhetoric, and in putting together the 1925 budget, Finance Minister Hamaguchi proposed to cut spending by 17 percent and lay off twenty thousand officials. These cuts were scaled back in the face of general resistance, including that of Agriculture and Commerce Minister Takahashi, Army Minister Ugaki Kazunari, and Communications Minister Inukai Tsuyoshi, but in the end, the budget passed in February 1925 still represented a 6 percent cut. Earthquake-related expenses continued to entail some spending increases, but budget cuts and the retrenchment of domestic bond issues were carried further in the 1926 budget.[42]

Despite these moves back toward the gold standard, Hamaguchi initially continued the previous policy of nonintervention in regard to foreign exchange.[43] Expectations that the new government would restore the gold standard briefly boosted the yen exchange during the summer of 1924, but after August the yen again began to fall, dropping to $0.38 in October. This was the bottom of the yen's postearthquake slide, and at this point, a turn in exchange policy came.

At the same time, late 1924, Ishibashi Tanzan of the *Tōyō keizai shinpō* took up a new monetary cause and began to argue that the yen should be restored to gold convertibility at a new, devalued par—that is, at the existing price level. Here, Ishibashi was influenced by the "purchasing power parity" idea of foreign exchange developed by the Swedish economist Gustav Cassel, who in a privately commissioned study widely distributed in Japanese policy circles, also concluded that the Japanese yen was significantly overvalued.[44] Confirming Ishibashi's contention, the low yen brought welcome relief to Japan's export trade and promoted a strong business recovery during the late spring and summer of 1925. At the time, however, Ishibashi's proposal received little attention.[45] It was from the banking community that the new direction of policy got its impetus.

In November 1924, with the yen some 22 percent below par, the annual bank clearing houses' conference called on the government to "thoroughly implement its announced policy of administrative adjustment, fiscal retrenchment, and balancing the budget" and further declared that it "was urgent to devise a fundamental remedy against the great fall of the foreign exchange."[46] This declaration shocked the government into action, according to Ishibashi Tanzan, and Finance Minister Hamaguchi, attending the bankers' convention, responded that the government would use its overseas specie balances to help support the yen exchange. Making good on this statement, the government began to ship gold and pay out money from the overseas specie reserve in January 1925, and the yen began to rise again.[47]

A political movement to restore the gold standard also began in early 1925, when businessman and Diet member Mutō Sanji and veteran liberal politician Ozaki Yukio—backed by Mutō's own small political party, the Jitsugyō Dōshikai, as well as by the Chūseikai and Seiyū Hontō—presented an unsuccessful resolution in the Diet calling for an end to the gold embargo, "the source of the disease in our financial world." Contending that the only way to balance Japan's trade was to reduce domestic prices, they urged lifting the gold embargo and shrinking the currency. Hamaguchi agreed in principle, he said, but in present circumstances, an appreciation of the yen would hurt exports, and a gold outflow and consequent credit squeeze would be a great shock to the business world. In Ishibashi Tanzan's estimation, this on-again, off-again policy left plenty of room for doubting Hamaguchi's actual intentions, and the markets did not take his professions at face value.[48]

"POSITIVE" COUNTERCURRENTS

In the meantime, Takahashi Korekiyo was further developing his own "positive" brand of economics. Financial policy was only part of the picture of the confrontation between the positive and negative policies, and while the retrenchment-minded Kenseikai held the Ministry of Finance and dominated the cabinet's financial policy, the expansion-minded Takahashi held the Agriculture and Commerce portfolio, heading a ministry in which he had last served, with Maeda Masana, in the 1880s. This partisan divide accentuated the usual split between the restraint-minded Ministry of Finance and the development-minded Ministry of Agriculture and Commerce, and under Takahashi's auspices the beginnings of an activist industrial policy began to take shape.[49]

As opposed to the more liberal and urban-based Kenseikai, the Seiyūkai, with its historic base in the rural landlord class, was the more conservative party. The Kenseikai, for example, with Inukai Tsuyoshi's Kakushin Club, had supported the cause of universal male suffrage. The Seiyūkai had opposed it, agreeing to support a suffrage bill only on joining the three-party coalition movement in 1924. The Kenseikai also adopted an activist, reform-oriented social policy, while the Seiyūkai took a hands-off attitude to social problems; in cooperation with leading business organizations, Takahashi took the lead in obstructing the passage of labor bills backed by the Kenseikai.[50] In regard to social policy, it was thus the Seiyūkai whose policy was passive, or "negative."

In regard to business unions, however, Takahashi was an activist, sponsoring legislation to establish government-funded export associations, opposed by the cost-conscious Ministry of Finance under Hamaguchi. Countering arguments that only a return to the gold standard could solve Japan's chronic trade imbalance, Takahashi maintained that Japan lacked the gold reserves to adopt such a course and argued instead that exporters suffered from excess competition. In January 1925 the measures proposed by Takahashi were enacted as the Export Associations Law (Yushutsu Kumiai Hō) and the Important Export Goods Associations Law (Jūyō Yushutsuhin Kumiai Hō), which created provisions for establishing export cartels, although without government financing. These laws constituted a departure point for Japan's modern industrial policy.[51] At the end of his brief tenure, in April 1925, Takahashi also presided over the split of the Ministry of Agriculture and Commerce into separate ministries of Agriculture and of Commerce and Industry. The latter ministry became the institutional fountainhead of the national-protectionist and economically expansionist industrial policies that took shape in the 1930s and was the direct ancestor of the post–World War II Ministry of International Trade and Industry (MITI).[52] Economically, Takahashi's position thus represented a positive countercurrent within the negative tide: in the context of the coalition cabinet's retrenchment-oriented macroeconomic policy, Takahashi began to build an activist and expansionist policy at the microeconomic level.

On April 4, 1925, Takahashi, now seventy-one years old and ailing, retired from political life, resigning from the cabinet and from the post of Seiyūkai president. Under the new presidency of General Tanaka Giichi, formerly minister of war in the Hara and Takahashi cabinets, the Seiyūkai asserted an aggressive new political course antagonistic to the Kenseikai.[53] In May, Inukai Tsuyoshi also merged his Kakushin Club into Tanaka's Seiyūkai. The new Tanaka line was adumbrated in a June 1925 Seiyūkai communiqué that lamented the present state of "industrial stagnation" and called for a policy of "building an industrial state" (*sangyō rikkoku*), which became one of the Seiyūkai's chief slogans. The Seiyūkai's new vision of industrial policy was teamed with a new nationalism and militarism, evident in the party's demands for an "independent diplomacy" (*jishuteki gaikō*), and joined with various measures of military buildup including the promotion of military training for youth.[54]

As a result of the Seiyūkai's new hostility, the three-party coalition cabinet broke up at the end of July, and Katō Takaaki formed a second, Kenseikai-only cabinet. Wakatsuki Reijirō continued as home minister, and Hamaguchi Osachi continued as finance minister. The Kenseikai now had a freer hand to implement many of the policies it had long promoted, and the 1926 budget was put together in line with the "negative" policy.[55]

THE MOVEMENT TO RESTORE THE GOLD STANDARD

On April 28, 1925, shortly after Takahashi's retirement, British Chancellor of the Exchequer Winston Churchill announced to the House of Commons that Britain would restore the gold standard at the old par as of the beginning of 1926. A dozen other countries directly followed Britain's lead, and in Japan the movement to restore the gold standard picked up steam.

After the Seiyūkai quit the coalition, the Kenseikai government took concrete steps toward restoring the gold standard by beginning regular gold shipments in September 1925. Expectations of an impending return to the gold standard led to speculative yen buying in Shanghai, boosting the yen to $0.43 by the end of 1925. In a process that was becoming routine, the higher yen again brought recession. In the face of complaints from the business community, Hamaguchi's Ministry of Finance therefore announced on February 20, 1926, after shipping a total of ¥26 million in gold, that the gold shipments were not meant as preparation for lifting the gold embargo, and it abruptly canceled a gold shipment scheduled for the next day.[56] On February 23 Hamaguchi told the Diet that it was too early to lift the gold embargo. The yen briefly halted its rise, but new foreign loan issues by Japanese electric power companies meant an influx of foreign exchange (that is, gold), causing the yen to resume its upward movement. By April 1926 it had risen above $0.47, an increase of nearly 25 percent from the low point in late 1924. The recession in the silk and cotton trades worsened.

Katō Takaaki died in office in January 1926, and Wakatsuki Reijirō formed a successor cabinet. Hamaguchi Osachi at first remained as minister of finance and then, in June 1926, assumed the powerful post of home minister. He was succeeded as finance minister by Kenseikai politician Hayami Seiji, who died in office in September 1926, and then by businessman and Diet representative Kataoka Naoharu (1859–1934), who continued Hamaguchi's financial policy and took further steps to prepare for a return to the gold standard. While disclaiming an intention to lift the gold embargo soon, Kataoka renewed gold shipments almost immediately after taking office and had the Bank of Japan lower interest rates on October 4, to help businesses "prepare for the financial blow caused by lifting the gold embargo."[57] Fatefully for Kataoka's career and for the finances of dozens of banks and tens of thousands of individual depositors, he also moved to clean up the bad debts represented by the outstanding earthquake bills.

EIGHT

The Theory and Practice of Induced Depression

The theme of restoration was widely sounded in the post–World War I world, and restoration was deeply connected to the questions of deflation and the gold standard. This connection forms a recurring theme in monetary history.

Britain's original legislative enactment of the gold standard in 1816 was itself intended as a restoration of hard money—the "old par"—after the inflationary Napoleonic Wars, and it was a central plank in a larger program of conservative restoration policies. A thirty-year deflation followed. In the 1870s, after episodes of paper-money inflation that accompanied wars of national unification in the United States and continental Europe, the gold standard was adopted by the other core Western countries. This internationalized gold standard helped to drive the twenty-three-year deflation of 1873–96. The world war of 1914–18 brought a new round of internationalized paper-money inflation. It too was succeeded by a new round of hard-money restoration.[1] Thus, the gold standard became the centerpiece of a program of deflationary social-economic restoration in the world as a whole. Japan was drawn into this global process.

THE GLOBAL POSTWAR: WORLD STABILIZATION AND WORLD DEFLATION

Internationally, the decade of the 1920s was dominated by the working out of the economic consequences of Europe's great war. This was also the case in Japan. While the postwar political trend seemed to be one of peace and of a turning away from high politics to economic issues, the economic situation itself appeared grim, and economics became filled with the language of war. In his first (and only) New Year's message as prime minister in 1922,

Takahashi Korekiyo told the Japanese nation that as a result of the world war, "armed competition has become obsolete, but economic competition is growing in intensity." For Inoue Junnosuke, "the war fought with weapons" was over, but an "economic war" was underway. Thomas Lamont also described the postwar decade as a time when "an economic war" was waged in Europe, "more devastating in its effects perhaps than the armed conflict itself." Economic wars over tariffs, German reparations, and boycotts in China all contributed to these perceptions.[2]

Viewed from the twenty-first century, the period from 1920 to 1929 appears as a clearly demarcated era in world economic history. Among the distinctive and constitutive elements of this interval were the following:

- Worldwide preparations for and implementation of the deflationary gold standard, accompanied by a series of gold-restoration depressions
- A corresponding reorientation to austerity in domestic fiscal and monetary policies. This was the case worldwide with the end of the inflations of the early 1920s and was true of Japan for the whole period. Conservative analyses of the times often delineated an extravagant and bloated state sector, but these analyses themselves were part of the campaign to cut back the enlarged state apparatus inherited from the wartime era.
- Chronic overcapacity and "overproduction" relative to effective demand in agriculture and in many branches of industry
- Very large but unstable capital flows out of the United States
- The ascendancy of finance capital: the leading role of private financial institutions in the domestic political-economic arrangements of Britain and America in particular and their domination of international economic arrangements in general

All of these conditions changed dramatically in the "great transformation" of the 1930s.[3] As for the working out of the war's financial consequences, the short-term fix was a great wave of international, chiefly American private lending. The ultimate solution came in the global debt crisis of 1930–31, with the wholesale repudiation of debts and the practical collapse of the international financial system.[4]

Just as Japan's inflation of the late 1910s was part of a worldwide inflationary wave, so deflation was a global phenomenon in the 1920s. Its political and social significance is hard to exaggerate. The inflationary boom of 1919 was most strongly marked in Japan, and Japan led the way into world deflation in March 1920. In Britain, the United States, and the countries closely connected to them, prices began to fall in the summer of 1920. Through the autumn of 1931, Japanese, British, and U.S. prices followed a similar deflationary course (figure 6). In most of continental Europe, high

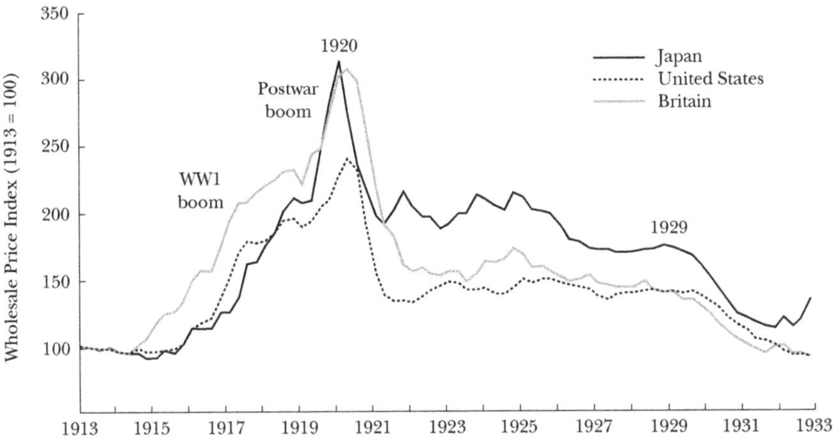

FIG. 6. Wartime inflation and postwar deflation in Japan, Britain, and the United States, 1913–1933. Worldwide depressions began in 1920 and 1929.

SOURCE: Quarterly averages, calculated from table IV (book pocket) of E. B. Schumpeter 1940 (citing, for Japanese prices, Bank of Japan index; U.S. prices, Bureau of Labor Statistics index; British prices, Sauerbeck-Statist index).

inflation persisted into the early 1920s, and there was hyperinflation in the defeated countries. Currency stabilization in Europe subsequently followed staggered national timetables but was largely accomplished by 1926, by which point deflation became a global process.

To gain a wider sense of the meaning of the deflationary world trend, we must again shift our vantage point to the places where world currency stabilization policies were planned and coordinated: the dual financial capitals of the world economy in London and New York. The London-centered imperial system had entered an age of structural crisis. Commercial, naval, and industrial power had been the bases of Britain's financial supremacy; but as British techniques were successfully adapted elsewhere, Britain's advantages inevitably disappeared. In the late nineteenth century, British consumers began persistently to purchase a greater value of goods than British producers made. The deficits in merchandise trade were covered by the profits from British overseas investment. Thus, even as Britain's industrial advantage progressively slipped, the great financial superstructure that had originally been built upon colonial, trading, and industrial profits continued to extend itself, and British finance reached the apex of its global predominance.

The critical turning point in this process of incipient hegemonic decline was the worldwide commercial and industrial boom of 1915–20, whose benefits only the warring states of Europe failed to share. Japanese financial authorities such as Inoue Junnosuke and Sakatani Yoshio began to imagine

TABLE 5. Number of countries going onto and leaving the gold standard, 1919–1936

Years	*Number Returning to Gold*	*Number Leaving Gold*
1919–20	6	—
1921–22	2	—
1923–24	5	—
1925–26	15	—
1927–28	16	—
1929–30	2	5
1931–32	4	31
1933–34	0	6
1935–36	0	8

SOURCE: Tabulated from Eichengreen 1992a: 188–191.

Tokyo as the London of East Asia. New York bankers began to challenge London for global primacy. Even after the war, however, Britain retained enormous financial advantages, even if it was now in debt to the United States. Thus *restoration*—of the gold standard and of London's central place in world finances—appeared as the great priority to British financial policy makers. But the idea of restoration gained a global currency, also appearing as a goal to many leaders in the rising powers of America and Japan.

Every country suspended gold convertibility during World War I. The process of return was more gradual, as enumerated in table 5. The first postwar currency stabilization was undertaken by the United States, which restored the gold convertibility of the dollar on June 26, 1919, two days before the signing of the Versailles Treaty. The United States was joined by its satellite states Cuba, Nicaragua, Panama, and the Philippines, which operated dollar-based gold-exchange standards. Except for Japan and a few of the neutral countries that had likewise accumulated large wartime surpluses, the rest of the world could not easily have followed the American lead. In Japan's case Takahashi Korekiyo held off on restoring gold convertibility in view of the situation in China and Siberia.

The worldwide depression of 1920, as we have seen, was in one aspect the United States' own "gold restoration" depression. Although Britain and Japan did not restore gold convertibility at the time, the Bank of Japan and the Bank of England both raised interest rates and presided over a sharp deflation in 1920 and 1921, as wholesale prices fell nearly 40 percent in Japan and nearly

50 percent in Britain. Inflation thus ended abruptly in America, Britain, and Japan, and prices were stabilized thereafter. Gold-restoration crises followed in Czechoslovakia, Austria, Hungary, and Germany in 1923–24, in Britain after 1925, France after 1926, Italy in 1927, and Japan in 1929–30. In the case of the runaway inflations in Central Europe, these induced depressions were indeed "stabilizations," but even there the continued enforcement of the deflation policy has been criticized as ultimately destabilizing.[5] Elsewhere, the term *stabilization* is much less appropriate.

A dozen or more countries went through comparable "stabilization" experiences, making the story of the restoration of the gold standard a great unifying theme in the international history of the 1920s. Once one steps away from specialized monetary and financial histories, it is also a story perceived by few present-day historians. Most of these stabilization crises, offset in time, were national rather than international in scope; but at the end of the decade, divergent national trajectories of prosperity and depression were resynchronized in the universal crisis of 1929–31. It was Japan's bad fortune that its national gold-restoration depression coincided fatefully with the world depression.

European monetary stabilization began as a chiefly British initiative. In January 1920, as the British, American, and Japanese central banks implemented deflation, financial "power holders," as Tsushima Juichi called them, from the United States and seven European countries met in Amsterdam and proposed an international economic conference. In September, as the waves of the postwar depression spread around the world, an "experts meeting" of representatives from thirty-nine countries was convened under League of Nations auspices in Brussels, where representatives agreed to deflation along the lines being taken by the Bank of England and the Federal Reserve Bank of New York. Overseas financial commissioner Mori Kengo reported the conclusions of the conference to the Ministry of Finance: "The most urgent common task is to contract the expanded structure of money and credit. Therefore, central banks should be free of government pressure. All banks should increase interest rates to bring about adjustment [*seiri*]. The best way to bring about currency and exchange stabilization is a speedy return to the gold standard. Artificial means of regulating foreign exchange should be ended." The Brussels meeting resulted in the creation of the Financial Committee of the League of Nations, which later directed the first of the currency stabilization programs in Czechoslovakia, Austria, and Hungary.[6]

The international stabilization program was carried further at Genoa in April and May of 1922 in a conference attended by cabinet-level representatives from twenty-nine countries. Japan was again represented by Mori Kengo and by BOJ director Fukai Eigo, just arrived from the Washington Conference. They now signed on to a second multilateral settlement, whose financial resolutions were as follows:[7]

1. Every country should stabilize its currency.
2. Every country should have a central bank, "free of political pressure."
3. Central banks should cooperate continuously.
4. All European countries should adhere to a common gold standard, to be adopted as rapidly as possible. [Japan figured here, as it did throughout the international financial diplomacy of the 1920s, as a kind of "honorary" European country.]
5. Government budgets must be balanced. "The true remedy" for this was to reduce expenditure, which "will go far to remedy an adverse balance of external payment *by reducing internal consumption.*" In some cases, an external loan may be necessary to accomplish this.
6. Depending on economic circumstances, it may be advisable for a country not to return to its prewar gold parity but to adopt a new (devalued) parity.
7. An international convention should be held to centralize and coordinate the demand for gold. Gold use should be economized by maintaining foreign-exchange reserves as partial backing for a country's currency issue (that is, by adopting a gold-exchange standard).

Thus, the proposed (British) solution for making the world's given supply of gold go further was to extend the use of the kind of gold-exchange standards that had been employed before the war in colonial and peripheral countries, including Japan. The effect would be to leverage the world's gold supply by establishing certain gold-linked currencies—chiefly the British pound and the U.S. dollar—as substitute gold. So-called "gold center" countries would hold the actual gold. Privately, British policy makers saw the gold-exchange standard as a way to restore London's financial centrality and boost the British pound. In fact, the competition to extend nationally based gold-exchange standards had entered a new phase.[8] This point reflects a fundamental difference between the prewar and postwar gold standards (and a point of difference between British and American visions).[9] Gold itself now stayed in the vaults of central banks and national treasuries—even in Britain and the United States, the prewar gold-coin standard was a thing of the past. Thus, already in 1922, with only the United States and a few other countries back on the gold standard, the world's supply of gold appeared insufficient for global monetary needs.

The problem of limited gold stocks was exacerbated after the war by what could be called the *gold gap.* About 40 percent of the world's gold was now in the United States,[10] and both agricultural and industrial exports flowed one-sidedly from North America to Europe—the United States' abundant production was not matched by Europe's ability to pay. (Japan, thanks to silk exports, ran a consistent trade surplus with America, but had an even larger trade deficit with India and Europe.) This "gold gap" was in essence a dollar gap, as the U.S. dollar was now the only major currency on the gold standard and had become a vital means of international payment. In regard to this global balance-of-payments problem, the Genoa conference's committee of experts recognized that creditor countries (that is, the United States) must absorb exports from debtor countries in order to recycle the means of payment. That this did not happen was a fundamental cause of the global financial imbalances of the decade that followed.[11]

Another aspect of this problem was the "sterilization" of gold inflows by recipient countries—above all, the United States—a new factor that gave the restored gold standard a further deflationary bias. Thus, gold outflows, in accordance with Hume's specie flow model, were deflationary (i.e., reduced the monetary base) for countries that lost gold. But on the other side of the international balance sheet, anti-inflationary central banks "sterilized" gold inflows by refusing to allow "excess" gold to be monetized. "Our great problem is dealing with the continued addition to our mass of gold," Benjamin Strong confided to Fukai Eigo in 1924. "[We must] put it away temporarily until the world comes to its senses and readjusts its monetary systems. It is a menace to us in presenting the possibility of inflation." More particularly, Strong feared "a repetition of the mistakes of the whole world in the years 1919–1920." The result was that neither the United States nor France, the two biggest recipients of gold flows in the late 1920s, acted as great sources of world demand, as they "should have."[12] This violation of the rules of the gold-standard game has appeared as a central problem of the interwar gold-standard system to many modern scholars. Ironically, Japan's great inflation of 1919–20 was substantially based on gold inflows: although the Bank of Japan did take limited sterilization measures, it largely followed the rules of the game at this point.

As the representative of the sole creditor state, New York Federal Reserve Bank governor Benjamin Strong declined to participate in the Genoa conference altogether. American nonparticipation, French resistance, and the failure of the political side of the conference has tended to overshadow the significance of its financial resolutions. In fact, although an international gold standard convention was never held, the ideas outlined at Genoa were largely in line with the private-sector stabilization policies subsequently supported by J. P. Morgan and Company and by Benjamin Strong. At Genoa, Japan was reckoned to be one of the four countries (along with Britain, the Netherlands, and Switzerland) that could directly return to the gold standard. Finance Minister Ichiki's abortive effort to return to the gold standard—in effect, to constitute Japan as a gold-center country—was undertaken directly after.[13]

At Genoa the old themes of gold restoration and retrenchment were also linked with a new vision of the quasi-sovereign role of central banks. This ideal was epitomized and championed by Inoue Junnosuke's colleagues Montagu Norman of the 228-year-old Bank of England—the "great head temple [*dai honzan*] of the international financial world"—and Benjamin Strong of the eight-year-old New York Federal Reserve Bank. Together, these two banks "grabbed the powers by the ears and led them to cooperate," as Inoue expressed it. Inoue was the Japanese counterpart of these central bankers, and he greatly valued his personal connections with them.[14] The sense of clubbiness was strong. So too was the sense of central banking as a world apart from government, and when Inoue left the Bank of Japan in September 1923 to join the government as finance minister, his friend Benjamin Strong reacted as if Inoue were going over to the other side.[15] In the 1920s, this new, semiprivate banking technocracy was in the driver's seat of the international financial system.

THE PRACTICE OF CURRENCY STABILIZATION

In line with the recommendations of the Genoa conference, gold-based currency stabilization programs in the 1920s followed a prescripted pattern, with the script written largely by the financial "power holders" of New York and London. These programs were not unlike the reforms directed by Matsukata Masayoshi in the early 1880s, or those directly managed by the International Monetary Fund in recent decades. Typically, restoration of a country's gold standard was combined with monetary contraction and deflation; cuts in government spending (especially in unemployment and social insurance, frequently joined with the privatization of state-owned enterprises); and strengthening of the independence of central banks from finance ministries and parliaments. These measures were typically tied to a private "stabilization loan" to the state in question, usually combined with a line of credit provided to its central bank, to safeguard the newly convertible currency against speculative attacks. For industrialized states, the stabilization loan was generally in the range of $100 million to $200 million and was put together by an international consortium of private New York and London banks. The central-bank credits were provided directly by other central banks, led by the FRBNY and the Bank of England. The "stabilization loans" of the 1920s also partook of the character of the so-called "controlled loans" used to implement gold-exchange standards in semi-colonial countries before the war. This aspect of control was strongest in the case of the defeated and newly independent countries of Central and Eastern Europe.

European currency stabilization programs began with the stabilization of Czechoslovakia, Austria, and Hungary under League of Nations auspices in 1922–24. In each case, international loans were provided on the condition of extensive fiscal controls. In Hungary the League of Nations resident commissioner was an American with close Wall Street connections, Jeremiah Smith Jr., who had accompanied Thomas Lamont as legal counsel on his spring 1920 trip to Japan and China. Morgan and Company and Kuhn, Loeb handled the $25 million American portion of the stabilization loan.[16] These stabilization programs, especially that of Austria in 1923 became a model for Germany's stabilization a year later by means of the American-brokered Dawes Plan.

Germany's ill-defined and anomalous position was at the heart of the post-war monetary mess, and Germany's was the biggest "stabilization" job of the decade. Hyperinflation had erased most domestic debts and had reduced the German mark and the savings of most Germans to nothing by 1923. At the same time, a great foreign debt existed in the form of a vast, still unspecified war indemnity. Like France in 1870 and like China in 1895, Germany would have to borrow to pay the indemnity.[17] Also like China, Germany lost control over its tariffs, became subject to foreign fiscal supervision, and had part of its national territory fall under temporary foreign occupation. This is not to say that Germany had become a semicolonized country or was, at this point, in real danger of national dismemberment. It is to point out Germany's remarkable demotion in the international system of the 1920s.[18] The "stabilization" experience of Weimar Germany also highlights aspects of the operation of the interwar political economy that are highly pertinent to a consideration of Japan's own in-between position, as the initially dissimilar international positions of the two countries came to seem increasingly parallel.

In Germany, Morgan and Company and the U.S. government took the lead in the international project to stabilize the German mark on a gold-standard basis and regularize German indemnity payments, which was enabled by a massive Anglo-American loan. Thus, notwithstanding received images of American isolationism in the 1920s, U.S. economic diplomacy was extended as never before, although the official American role was masked from the American public and the U.S. Congress by sending an ostensibly private representative group led by Chicago banker Charles Dawes, the former director of the U.S. Bureau of the Budget and future vice president of the United States.[19] The Dawes Plan required the appointment of an American financial commissioner to oversee the German government's finances. The initial plan was to employ a partner from the Morgan firm, but to avoid the charge that Wall Street bankers were controlling Germany, the committee appointed instead a young protégé of Russell Leffingwell, S. Parker Gilbert of the U.S. Treasury Department. Leffingwell himself had already left the treasury to become a Morgan partner.[20] On retiring from his post in Berlin in 1930, after overseeing the transfer of US$2 billion in indemnity payments funded by U.S. loans, Gilbert himself became a Morgan partner.

The Dawes plan also made the German Reichsbank independent of the German government and placed it under partial foreign control. Reichsbank governor Hjalmar Schact subsequently enforced a deflationary policy of high interest rates. The contradictions of Germany's restored gold standard were thus parallel to those faced by Japan after the Russo-Japanese War: external balance could ultimately be achieved only via deflation and depression, and without continuing imports of American and British capital, Germany would have been forced off the gold standard.[21]

Germany's monetary reconstruction was the keystone of a new, American-centered international financial architecture. Inoue Junnosuke saw it, along with stabilization programs in Austria and Hungary, as a triumph of multilateral diplomacy and believed that the League of Nations should next undertake a stabilization program in China, where foreign lending, he said (echoing Takahashi's opinion), had up to now been motivated by a selfish effort to secure special rights and advantages.[22] Coming seven months after Morgan and Company's $150 million earthquake bond issue for Japan, the issue of the $110 million U.S. portion of the Dawes Plan loan also set off a boom in American overseas lending. Germany, which had been a creditor nation before the war, subsequently became the decade's biggest international borrower. Japan was not far behind. A wave of European stabilization programs followed the German operation, with the decisive step coming eight months later, in April 1925, when the British government announced its own return to gold. The Netherlands returned to the gold standard at the same time, and other countries quickly followed.

PRACTITIONERS: THOMAS LAMONT AND COMPANY

The name of Thomas W. Lamont appears repeatedly in any survey of the international financial history of the 1920s, as it has already appeared here. Remarkably, Lamont's name is not mentioned at all in many standard histories of the international political relations of the era—further testimony to the invisibility of the financial sinews of power to most historians, and perhaps also to the discretion with which financial power was exercised even in this age of bankers' hegemony. In fact, were a populist conspiracy theorist of the time to have wholly invented a personification of the international money cartel that pulled the strings of the governments of the world, he could hardly have done better than the actual Mr. Lamont. And as friend and adviser to every Democratic and Republican president from Woodrow Wilson to Franklin Roosevelt, Lamont could have satisfied the requirements of conspiracy theories of either the right or the left. The liberal internationalist Lamont had met with Lenin and Trotsky and was a champion of the League of Nations and of international supragovernmental arrangements in general. At the same time, the versatile financier helped dismantle pro-labor policies in numerous countries, actively bankrolled the Italian inventor of fascism, and championed U.S. partnership with Japan in the colonial development of Manchuria. The position of Lamont and his firm also points to an important reality obscured in modern economic-historical accounts that turn "markets" themselves into reified, impersonal actors, for the market for giant international loans in the 1920s can be located with far greater personal and institutional specificity than such rhetoric suggests. Tracing Lamont's progresses around the world will help us to trace in detail the workings of international finance capital during this period.

Financial control of industry was (and remains) highly concentrated in the United States. The most powerful group of U.S. financial institutions in the 1920s was the Morgan "zaibatsu" (as it was understood in Japan), which was centered around Morgan and Company and included, with varying degrees of closeness, Guaranty Trust, Bankers Trust, and the First National Bank of New York.[23] Morgan and Company first came to prominence in the late nineteenth century as a pipeline for British capital into the United States. Especially in the 1920s, as this flow was reversed, the firm came to serve as the American financial agent for governments around the world. The Morgan group had a controlling interest in numerous industrial companies and controlled the two largest holding companies for electric and gas utilities in the United States, making it the most powerful interest in the new sector of power generation. It was also in the electric power sector that U.S. capital played the most active role in Japan and around the world during the 1920s.[24] In 1929 the eighteen Morgan partners between them held seventy-six directorships in fifty-eight nonfinancial corporations, whose assets totaled $15 billion. Although it was not nearly so tightly integrated as the zaibatsu model suggested, the Morgan group was nothing less than the largest and most powerful business empire in the world.

The two chief partners of Morgan and Company in the 1920s were the Morgan heir, J. P. Morgan Jr. and Thomas W. Lamont. Shy, private, and slightly paranoid, J. P. Morgan Jr. spent much of his time playing at being a benevolent feudal lord on the English estate that he had purchased, complete with deferential villagers. Sunny, urbane, and quick on his feet, Lamont served as the company's spokesman and public face and increasingly made the key decisions. As such, Lamont may be reckoned the single most pivotal figure in the international financial world of the 1920s: "in international finance, the person in the world's highest position of authority," as Japanese overseas financial commissioner Mori Kengo put it.[25] This was not undue exaggeration. From the Paris Peace Conference in 1919, to the Dawes Plan in 1924, to the Hoover moratorium on reparations and war debts in 1931, Lamont had a hand in the pivotal international financial decisions of the decade, as he had a hand in Japan's restoration of the gold standard in 1930.

The new level of American financial influence abroad came in the context of an unprecedented wave of U.S. overseas investment. From 1919 to

1933, Morgan and Company underwrote $6 billion in securities, some $2 billion of which were foreign bonds. Total long-term U.S. foreign lending in the 1920s came to $7 billion.[26] Morgan and Company handled the most political and prestigious of this lending, and following the $150 million loan to Japan in 1924, the firm managed stabilization loans or short-term credits for Germany ($190 million, 1924), France ($100 million, 1924), Britain ($100 million credit, 1925), Italy ($100 million, 1926), Belgium ($100 million, 1926), Japan ($70 million, 1930), and Britain again ($200 million, 1931). These, next to Morgan's wartime loans, were among the largest international financial operations ever conducted. Second- or third-tier firms like Kuhn, Loeb and Dillon, Read participated as members of Morgan-led syndicates or put together loans for less blue-chip clients in places like South America and Eastern Europe—almost all of which later defaulted in the global debt crisis that opened in 1931.

Thus, under Morgan's administration (conjointly with the Federal Reserve Bank of New York), monetary stabilization in Europe was handled multilaterally, in close cooperation with London. At the same time, at the boundaries of America's immediate sphere of influence in South America, stabilization was conducted privately and unilaterally. This latter stream in the new gold-standard diplomacy was associated with the "money doctor" Edwin Kemmerer.[27] "Stabilization" in Japan would fall into the multilateral, "European-style" category. A renewed American attempt to bring a gold-exchange standard to China would fall into the unilateral category.

It was in South America that the new gold-standard diplomacy of the 1920s was most nearly continuous with the United States' prewar gold-standard diplomacy, as the countries of the west coast of South America were brought into the financial orbit of the United States—a step in the shift from British to U.S. economic hegemony in the region. (Unlike the controlled loans administered in the Caribbean basin, however, no military coercion was involved.) As in Europe, the new U.S. lending to South America came on condition of the establishment of currencies backed by gold (or U.S. dollars), free gold flows, and independent central banks. These gold-exchange standards were instituted according to guidelines laid down by Edwin Kemmerer, who helped install liberal financial regimes in Colombia (1923, on the heels of Colombia's recognition of the cession of Panama), South Africa (1925), Chile (1925), Poland (1926), Ecuador (1926), and Bolivia (1927).[28] Besides maintaining close informal ties with the U.S. government, Kemmerer also maintained a sub rosa consulting arrangement with the Wall Street investment bank Dillon, Read, which subsequently lent to the newly stabilized states—it was especially this latter connection that governments were paying for when they invited Kemmerer to advise them.[29] Unlike the Anglophile Morgan firm, Kemmerer was highly jealous of British influence and took every opportunity to shut out British participation in his undertakings. Kemmerer's South African mission challenged British financial primacy within the British Empire itself, helping to force the timetable on Britain's return to gold in 1925. Kemmerer was also a Dawes mission adviser in Germany, where his unilateralist approach, based on a plan by Jeremiah Jenks, was rejected for a plan based on cooperation between Morgan and Company and the Bank of England.[30] At the end of the decade, Kemmerer attempted the most monumental "stabilization" job of all, retracing the path of his teacher Jeremiah Jenks to China.

The year of Britain's return to gold, 1925, marked the high point for the world prices of a number of important export commodities, as a second round of international price deflation—that is, appreciation of the value of gold—got underway.[31] The fall in the prices of farm goods after 1925 opened the second chapter in the worldwide agrarian crisis that had begun in 1920. Deepening agrarian depression was accompanied by a consumer boom in the United States and the rise of a speculative financial bubble in the new international financial center of New York.

Renewed deflation after 1925 was thus connected to a second round of contractionary austerity policies in Britain, which, like Japan, underwent a "second" stabilization. That is, the price stabilization of 1920–21 and the exchange-rate stabilization (return to the gold standard) later in the decade were two distinct operations. This second, exchange-rate stabilization also differed from the first round of price stabilization in that it did not reverse an inflation but rather intensified an existing deflationary trend. In Italy too, although a new, devalued parity was adopted in December 1927, it was deliberately overvalued for purposes of national prestige, generating a recession as in Britain. In France inflation was halted (the currency was stabilized domestically) in 1926; and the restoration of the gold standard in June 1928 (external, or exchange-rate, stabilization) was done at the franc's present depreciated value and did not in the short run have further deflationary effects.[32] Elsewhere in continental Europe new parities also lessened the deflationary impact of the return to the gold standard. With the restoration of gold convertibility in France, Belgium, and Italy in 1926 and 1927, the stabilization of the European monetary system seemed largely complete.

JAPAN'S TURN

By the spring of 1926, a return to the gold standard began to seem opportune to Inoue Junnosuke. After twenty-seven years in banking and political life, Inoue had resigned as finance minister in January 1924 and was appointed to the House of Peers. He then spent several months in London, where he visited Bank of England governor Montagu Norman as well as Federal Reserve Bank of New York governor Benjamin Strong and Morgan and Company partner Thomas Lamont, also in London at the time. On his return, Inoue devoted himself to "taking care of the business world," fulfilling this role to the extent that he was called "a second Shibusawa Eiichi."[33]

Inoue had not been among those campaigning for an early return to gold, and when the yen had fallen to its postearthquake lows in 1924–25, he had absolutely opposed the calls for lifting the gold embargo. Thus, it came as a surprise when Inoue declared himself in favor of lifting the gold embargo in a series of university lectures in May 1926.[34] In October 1926 Inoue declared his conversion in a speech at the Tokyo Bank Club and sought to bring the assembled heads of the banking world around to his view: "There is considerable irony in your bringing me here tonight. As you know, I came here early last year and spoke against lifting the gold embargo. However, since about May of this year, when I gave a lecture at Kyoto University, I have become an advocate of lifting the gold embargo."[35] Rather than having changed his own views, Inoue explained, it was the situation that had changed.

In 1926 Inoue was also frank in saying that restoring the gold standard would induce an economic depression. Inoue's model was the British return to gold convertibility at the old par in 1925, and while he recognized that it had deepened Britain's recession, he also regarded it as a success. The increased value of sterling raised the price of British coal in overseas markets, Inoue explained, hurting coal exports, causing unemployment in the British coal industry, and leading to the great coal strike then in progress. For Japan, raw silk was an "exactly analogous" export good, and therefore "the results would be the same for Japan's raw silk [trade]." In fact, Inoue suggested, workers in Japan's silk industry would be hit even harder. English miners could at least expect to pay less for their imported food, because the increased value of the pound reduced import prices. (Unlike Japanese workers, they could also collect unemployment benefits.) Japanese workers, Inoue explained, would not gain this benefit from a higher yen, because they ate food produced in Japan and did not use imported goods.[36] Knowing that restoring the gold standard at the old par would damage the competitiveness of Japan's number-one export good and severely squeeze the farm economy, so dependent on sericulture, Inoue advocated it nevertheless.

The relation between the return to the gold standard and export competitiveness was also discussed by J. M. Keynes in a critique that Inoue ignored but that Ishibashi Tanzan paid serious attention to. Keynes evaluated the process differently than Inoue:

> The minds of [Mr. Churchill's] advisors still dwelt in the imaginary academic world . . . where the necessary adjustments follow 'automatically' from a 'sound' policy by the Bank of England.
>
> The theory is that depression in the export industries, which are admittedly hit first, coupled if necessary with dear money and credit restriction, *dif-*

> *fuse* themselves evenly and fairly rapidly throughout the whole community. But the professors of this theory do not tell us in plain language how the diffusion takes place.

So Keynes clarified the mechanism of deflation:

> Now what does this mean in plain language? Our problem is to reduce money wages and, through them, the cost of living, with the idea that, when the circle is complete, real wages will be as high, or nearly as high, as before. By what *modus operandi* does credit restriction attain this result?
>
> *In no other way than by the deliberate intensification of unemployment.* The object of credit restriction, in such a case, is to withdraw from employers the financial means to employ labour at the existing level of prices and wages. The policy can only attain its end by intensifying unemployment without limit, until the workers are ready to accept the necessary reduction of money wages under the pressure of hard facts.[37]

To this it could be added that there was little expectation on the part of monetary authorities that when the whole process of deflation was completed, real wages would be as high as before. Rather, gold resumption was part of a strategy to roll back real wages, to restore the "sound" and "moral" living standards that had prevailed before the world war.

In calling now for a return to the gold standard at the old par, Inoue's own restorationist thinking was clear. In the years since 1920, he said, Japan had merely "fumbled along" while things had gotten worse and worse. The gold embargo was "perverse" and a great obstacle to recovery—"with this abnormality [*hentai*] called the gold export embargo as it is now, we will not be able to accomplish anything we try to do." But before the gold embargo could be lifted, further sacrifice was needed, and the business world would have to be "adjusted" for one and a half or two years. Then, the government could "lift the gold embargo and get rid of all the abnormal things" and finally "return our country to the situation of the old Japan."[38]

Implicitly, Inoue Junnosuke also recognized that the yen would be overvalued at its old par value—that the yen's "natural" rate, in Ishibashi Tanzan's terms, had fallen considerably below the old par, and that without government intervention, the exchange would fall in the future. In fact, said Inoue, the yen was only as high as it was now because of speculative yen buying abroad, based on the expectation that the government would lift the gold embargo. When this expectation was disappointed, the yen would inevitably fall and would not likely recover to its present level. But without returning to gold convertibility, Inoue said, Japan would never escape this kind of exchange instability.[39]

In line with this realistic view of the dynamics of the yen exchange, Inoue attacked finance ministers Hamaguchi and Kataoka by name for their unrealistic policies. Kataoka's thinking to lower interest rates and then lift the gold embargo was "sloppy" (*yoi kagen*). Hamaguchi's idea that one could think about lifting the gold embargo once the value of the yen increased and trade had improved was "impossible" and "like looking for fish in a tree."[40] Likewise, Inoue declared his opposition to people like Seiyūkai politician Mitsuchi Chūzō, a close follower of Takahashi Korekiyo, who was then arguing that the gold embargo could not be lifted until Japan became an export-surplus country. Rather, Inoue stressed yet again that the chronic excess of imports could not easily be helped: "When I try to think about the situation of the past sixty years and deduce Japan's situation from this, I think that we cannot end the import surplus in three or five years."[41]

Thus, Inoue saw clearly that if the yen returned to the old par, exports would inevitably suffer. In fact, he said, the yen's appreciation already had hurt exports: when the yen was low in 1925, exports had been "extremely convenient," but as the yen approached its par value in 1926, exports had slumped—by some ¥300 million, or more than 10 percent.[42] Inoue therefore anticipated that people in the export industries would resist his call to restore the gold standard: "People in the raw silk trade are probably hoping that the exchange rate will go down again, I think. People in the raw silk trade are probably opposed to lifting the gold embargo. . . . People in the cotton spinning trade probably also think in the same way."[43] As against these sectoral interests—which between them accounted for more than 30 percent of Japan's industrial production and up to 60 percent of Japan's export earnings in the mid-1920s[44]—Inoue stressed the special role of his fellow bankers in "unifying" business opinion: "Because the businessmen concerned have each according to their various standpoints extremely great connections of profit and loss, these people are considering [things] from their own various individual standpoints, and thus find it hard to take this kind of decisive measure [of lifting the gold embargo]. Rather, I think that this is a matter that you gentlemen, who, as bankers, stand at the center of the business world, should deliberate and decide upon."[45] Inoue implicitly ruled out the alternative of devaluation.

In fact, the Wakatsuki cabinet was more in line with Inoue's thinking than he gave them credit for, and the "contractionary tide" that Inoue had hailed in 1922 continued to run. As preparation for lifting the gold export embargo, the Ministry of Finance had already resumed gold shipments to the United States.[46] On November 17 Finance Minister Kataoka met with BOJ governor Ichiki Otohiko, the president of the Yokohama Specie Bank, and Inoue Junnosuke to discuss the gold embargo issue; the following day a Gold Restoration Research Group was established to study the issue. By the end of the year, the yen had risen to $0.49, near the old parity. In this way, after October 1926 Finance Minister Kataoka maintained the high yen exchange for six months, until the great financial crisis of April 1927.

NINE

"The Two-Party Principle," 1927–1929

The Kenseikai's Hamaguchi Osachi, as finance minister in the Katō Takaaki cabinet, had by stages adopted a "negative" retrenchment policy after June 1924. The Kenseikai cabinet of Wakatsuki Reijirō carried the retrenchment movement further in 1926, and notwithstanding Inoue Junnosuke's criticism of the cabinet's approach as sloppy and half-baked, it is clear in retrospect that Finance Minister Kataoka took decisive steps to prepare for the restoration of the gold standard after September 1926. Compounded by the increasingly bitter conflict between the two mainstream conservative parties, this move back toward the gold standard led directly to the financial panic of spring 1927, the greatest banking crisis in Japan's history.

ORIGINS OF THE 1927 CRISIS

It is not always recognized how deeply the 1927 financial crisis was connected to the issues of deflation and the gold standard. At a fundamental level, the 1927 crisis was the banking aspect of a comprehensive domestic debt crisis, which originated in the great overhang of bad debt left over from the collapse of the inflationary economic bubble in 1920. The deflation of prices after 1920 made domestic debts all the heavier. Unrepayable debts were greatly augmented by the effects of the 1923 earthquake, and Inoue Junnosuke's provision of financial relief by means of the "earthquake bills" allowed bubble-era debt to be carried over under a new guise. The Hamaguchi-Kataoka policy intensified price deflation, squeezing profits and increasing the weight of domestic debt. Thus, the renewed fall of prices in 1926 also formed part of the basis for the 1927 banking panic.[1]

Related to the mountain of bad debt was an institutional condition: poorly regulated and collusive banking practices, particularly in the case of the "house" or "organ" banks (*kikan ginkō*) closely connected to particular companies to whom they carelessly overlent. In his later history of the crisis, Ishibashi Tanzan's colleague Takahashi Kamekichi placed great weight on this factor[2]—an early twentieth-century version of "crony capitalism," to use Western commentators' catchall explanation for the financial crisis that swept through newly industrializing Asia in 1997 and 1998. The most famous of these cozy connections was that between the Bank of Taiwan and the Suzuki Trading Company.

These structural sources of crisis were already in place by spring 1920, and they were manifested in the banking panics of 1920, 1922, and 1923. BOJ governor Inoue Junnosuke's policies likely prevented a wider crisis at each of these points, but the bank bailouts that he oversaw also reinforced the temptation of bankers to overlend in the expectation that the Bank of Japan would bail them out should things go wrong. Fukai Eigo later pointed to this problem—"moral hazard" in modern economic parlance—as a key source of the 1927 crisis.[3]

The yen's appreciation after 1925, also caused by the gold-restoration policy, operated as an intermediate-level cause of the financial crisis. At the end of 1924, the yen had fallen to a low of $0.38. Under finance ministers Hamaguchi Osachi and Kataoka Naoharu, gold shipments were resumed, and speculative yen buying, prompted by expectations of an imminent return to gold convertibility, caused the yen's value to rise from the beginning of 1925. By December 1926 the yen had returned to $0.4875, just below the old par, and it maintained that high level until the panic of April 1927. The yen's appreciation reduced the weight of payments on Japan's foreign debt, but it hampered exports, generating what in more recent times would be called an *endaka* (yen appreciation) recession. The problem was fully recognized at the time; for example, by Bank of Japan governor Ichiki Otohiko, who told BOJ branch managers in a closed meeting that because of the yen's appreciation in 1926, trade worsened, prices fell, and commerce and industry "fell into extreme stagnation, compounding the [existing] general recession."[4]

Not only did the yen appreciate relative to the gold-based currencies, but the price of silver—China's currency—also fell in 1926, further hurting Japanese exports to China. The stagnation of trade intensified the banks' difficulties and helped bring on the crisis. Thus, British consular officials Sansom and Macrae, writing in June 1928, blamed the banking crisis on trade disturbances. Japan's industries, they noted, depended on the reprocessing of imported raw materials, above all, cotton. The prices of such commodities fluctuated widely, and their purchase and sale, "perhaps more in Japan than in most countries, is complicated by a strong element of speculation."[5] Moreover, they said, at the present stage of development, Japan's industry itself rested on an often speculative extension of credit. "Therefore any disturbance of trade attacks at once the financial system, and if the disturbance is severe the financial system breaks down, because industry cannot share in withstanding the attack."[6]

The most immediate cause of the crisis was Finance Minister Kataoka's move to clean up the bad debts in the banking system in preparation for lifting the gold embargo, which forced the undercover debt crisis into the open in March 1927. The most notorious of the bad debts—"the cancer of the financial world"—were the uncollected earthquake bills, whose term had been twice extended. From the summer of 1926, major business groups began calling on the government to replace the earthquake bills with low-interest loans. The government adopted this plan but, to limit the carrying over of bad debts under a new name, combined it with a debt adjustment plan.[7]

The matter was delicate: certain banks had recklessly overlent on the basis of worthless assets. To reveal which banks were effectively insolvent could provoke runs by depositors. The banking world was already uneasy, and in January and February 1927 five small banks were forced to close.[8] With these dangers in view, the presidents of the Kenseikai, Seiyūkai, and Seiyū Hontō, proposing to act in the common interest of the business world, met in January and agreed to cooperate. Also in January, Finance Minister Kataoka met secretly with Seiyūkai president Tanaka Giichi to explain to him the need for lifting the gold embargo and adjusting the banking world. As Kataoka later recounted their meeting, he explained further that the financial world was in a very nervous state, and asked the Seiyūkai only to refrain from attacking the government's policy in the Diet. The bluff Tanaka told him, "I don't understand about economics," but said that he did understand Kataoka's explanation and that despite his doubts he would not oppose the government on this issue. Consequently, when the government introduced two debt relief bills related to the earthquake bills on January 26, the atmosphere during questioning was not bad from the government's standpoint.[9]

In late February, however, the newspapers published stories of a tie-up between the Kenseikai and the Seiyū Hontō. The Kenseikai was then the largest party in the Diet but lacked an absolute majority, which it would gain by teaming with the Seiyū Hontō. Angered by this turn of events, or seizing upon it as a pretext, Tanaka told Kataoka that their deal was off, and the Seiyūkai now attacked the government over the issue of the earthquake bills.[10]

The remainder of the Diet session was extremely contentious and was interrupted several times by fighting on the Diet floor. Lower House representative Mutō Sanji attacked the government's plan, opposing a bailout on principle. The Seiyūkai's attacks were less principled, and the most aggressive of its deputies, Yoshiue Shōichirō, continually pressed Kataoka to name the names of those who held earthquake bills, charging that the government was protecting politically connected businessmen. Fearing that there would be runs on any banks identified as holding bad debts, Kataoka refused. Amid near-riot conditions in the chamber, the government's bills passed the House of Representatives on March 4.

In this charged atmosphere the Kenseikai government took another step back toward the gold standard by announcing unofficially that it would ship ¥50 million in gold from the Bank of Japan's reserve for currency convertibility in order to boost its overseas specie holdings. The government had been making shipments of ¥4 million in gold once or twice a month from its own holdings since the beginning of Kataoka's gold-restoration policy in September 1926. Now, by shipping gold from the Bank of Japan, the government was directly shrinking the base for the bank's note issue, thereby reducing the note issue and mimicking the operations of the automatic gold standard. There were rumors that Finance Minister Kataoka would lift the gold export embargo as early as June, and currency traders bid up the yen's value to over $0.49, very near its old par.[11]

Kataoka himself seemed to indicate that action was in the offing. In the budget committee session in the House of Representatives on the afternoon of March 14, the Seiyūkai's Yoshiue Shōichirō pressed Kataoka to say when Japan would return to the gold standard. Kataoka's response was upbeat: the yen had risen almost to par, the trade balance had improved, and "it looks pretty much like the appropriate time has come to lift the [gold] embargo." The earthquake bills law would go into effect in November, he explained, and would also calm the business world. He did not rule out lifting the gold embargo even before that time. Kataoka followed this positive assessment with the usual qualifications, but the thrust of his statement was to suggest an early timetable for gold restoration, and it was reported that way in the newspapers.[12]

THE BANKING PANIC

As the Diet session on the afternoon of March 14 wore on, Yoshiue Shōichirō continued to press his attack, haranguing Kataoka with "poison-tongued" questions over the earthquake bills.[13] Overnight, their exchange became famous as the spark that set off the financial panic. As Kataoka was fending off questions, an assistant handed him a note with the urgent news that the Tokyo Watanabe Bank was at the point of having to suspend payments to its depositors. Kataoka turned to his attackers and disclosed the note's contents. "Actually, around noon today, the Watanabe Bank finally went bankrupt," he said, indicating that more such crises could be expected if the proposed bailout measures were not conducted quickly.[14]

This impromptu revelation has been remembered as Kataoka's famous "misstatement." Tokyo Watanabe Bank had been one of the most regular recipients of Bank of Japan bailouts, receiving aid in 1920, 1922, and 1923.[15] Despite these transfusions of funds, its demise was now imminent. However, as of Kataoka's public statement, the bank was still open. Kataoka's statement was carried in the newspapers, and on the morning of March 15 panicked depositors rushed to pull their funds from Tokyo Watanabe Bank and a smaller sister bank, forcing both to shut their doors. Kataoka was thus excoriated for "having handed down a death sentence on a living bank."[16] The Tokyo Watanabe failure began the first wave of the 1927 financial panic. By the end of March, runs on eleven additional banks forced them to close, after which the panic momentarily subsided. In the first half of April, three further banks were forced to close.

Events in China were coming to a head at the same time. The previous summer, General Chiang Kai-shek had become commander in chief of the Guomindang's National Revolutionary Army in Guangzhou (Canton) and announced the Northern Expedition to unite central China under the Nationalist government. Guomindang (Kuomintang or KMT) forces advanced into the Yangzi valley, and on the morning of March 24, 1927, just as the first wave of Japan's banking panic was cresting, Guomindang forces occupied Nanjing and attacked the foreign legations there, killing six foreigners. British and American gunboats responded by bombarding KMT positions in the city and raking the waterfront with machine-gun fire. Under the noninterference policy of Foreign Minister Shidehara Kijūrō, Japanese forces refrained from joining in the violence, despite the fact that the Japanese legation had been attacked. Vitriolic attacks on Shidehara's "weak diplomacy" mounted, and the partisan conflict in the Diet reached an even higher pitch.

The continuing partisan fight, combined with the covert machinations of the Mitsui group, set off the second and more severe wave of the banking panic. The two measures pertaining to the earthquake bills were finally passed by both houses of the Diet on March 23, but the Seiyūkai attack had already turned to a new topic, the bad debts held by the Bank of Taiwan.

The Bank of Taiwan did business both as Taiwan's central bank and as a commercial bank. In the latter role, during the World War I boom, both the bank's lending on the Japanese mainland and its lending overseas came greatly to exceed its lending within the island of Taiwan itself.[17] In its role as a policy bank, the Bank of Taiwan also came to hold a portfolio of bad loans to the Beijing government arranged by Nishihara Kamezō. Finally, the Bank of Taiwan had become the largest holder of earthquake bills, in connection with its role as the "house bank" for the Taiwan-based trading company Suzuki Shōten. The greatest of the World War I *narikin,* Suzuki had grown to rival the giant Mitsui trading company during the war, but fell on increasingly hard times during the postwar deflation. Suzuki was also close to the Kenseikai. Seeing a chance to bring down its upstart rival, Mitsui now moved to sabotage the bailout by engineering a run by major depositors on the Bank of Taiwan.[18]

The Bank of Taiwan had been the object of a series of restructuring efforts going back to 1922, and a new effort was begun on March 4, 1927, when a special committee chaired by Inoue Junnosuke was set up to investigate the situation.[19] On April 13 Inoue met with Finance Minister Kataoka, Bank of Japan governor Ichiki Otohiko, and vice governor Hijikata Hisaakira (who had left his post as president of the Industrial Bank of Japan in 1926 to return to the BOJ). They agreed to issue an emergency imperial edict (*kinkyū chokurei*) to enable the provision of relief funds to the Bank of Taiwan. Such an edict did not require the approval of the Diet (which had been recessed) but did require the approval of the Privy Council. The Seiyūkai immediately attacked the procedure as unconstitutional, insisting that the Diet be called into special session to deliberate the matter. Conservatives in the Privy Council were violently opposed to the cabinet's China policy, and against expectations, the council denied the issuance of the edict on April 17, thereby blocking the Bank of Taiwan bailout. Seiyūkai influence was at work behind the scenes.[20] Blockaded by the Privy Council, the Wakatsuki cabinet was forced to resign on April 17.

The following day, the Bank of Taiwan was forced to close its branch offices on the Japanese mainland and overseas, and the second wave of the bank panic began. On that day the Bank of Japan issued an unprecedented ¥88 million in loans. The Omi Bank also closed on April 18, and on the 19th, banks were closing one after another around the country. The yen began to fall on the foreign exchanges, foreign banks were refusing to deal with Japanese banks, and Japan's overseas credit was in danger of collapsing.[21] Fourteen more banks closed their doors in the week that followed.[22] Next to the Bank of Taiwan, the largest bank to fail was the Fifteenth Bank. Both the Bank of Taiwan and the Fifteenth Bank had come to be parts of the financial empire belonging to the many descendents of former finance minister Matsukata Masayoshi.

THE RETURN OF THE POSITIVE POLICY

On April 19 Seiyūkai president Tanaka Giichi received the imperial mandate to form a new cabinet. From the imperial palace he preceded directly on foot to the home of Takahashi Korekiyo, his senior as party president and prime minister, and requested that Takahashi serve as finance minister. The seventy-two-year-old Takahashi, now living in retirement, his health not fully recovered, agreed to serve for the thirty or forty days that he thought it would take to stabilize the financial situation.[23] During that time, however, he made some major policy changes in line with his long-held ideas.

At the cabinet meeting on the evening of April 21, Takahashi got agreement to a three-week moratorium on the repayment of debts, to be ordered via an emergency imperial edict. The only previous instance of such a moratorium was the one declared by Inoue after the 1923 earthquake. Takahashi won further agreement that a special session of the Diet be convoked to approve bailout measures for the Bank of Taiwan and the banking world in general. The processing of the imperial edict could not be completed until the 23rd, so he called together Ikeda of Mitsui Bank and Kushida of Mitsubishi Bank and asked them to arrange for all of the private banks to close voluntarily for the intervening two days. This was done as he requested.[24]

Takahashi also discontinued the previous cabinet's policy of shipping gold in order to maintain the yen's value and adopted a policy of laissez-faire, or "leaving it to nature" (*shizen hōnin shugi*) in regard to the yen exchange. The reason he gave for this was that the recent increase in the issue of Bank of Japan notes had brought the note issue to more than twice the amount of the gold reserve. However, as the business press reported, halting gold shipments was also in line with "new Finance Minister Takahashi's cherished belief."[25] The yen, which since 1926 had been over $0.49, near the old par, had already begun to fall after the closure of the Bank of Taiwan on April 18. Over the course of the next month it fell back to the $0.46 level. Also in line with Takahashi's long-time thinking, the yen-depreciation policy was combined with a go-slow policy in regard to restoring the gold standard. Lifting the embargo on gold exports, Takahashi said, would have to wait until Japan's international credit-debt balance was improved.[26]

The Diet passed the Bank of Taiwan measure and the Privy Council approved it on May 7. Thus, the Seiyūkai government enacted essentially the same measures that it had worked to prevent the Kenseikai cabinet from adopting. The fight was not over the content of the bailout policy but over who would hold power.

There was also the question of who would serve as Bank of Japan governor. The governor was then Ichiki Otohiko, who had succeeded Takahashi as finance minister in June 1922 and had presided over the effort to retrench and return to the gold standard in 1922–23. Ichiki had then succeeded Inoue Junnosuke at the Bank of Japan in 1923. Takahashi wanted to replace Ichiki, according to Mitsui Bank president Ikeda Shigeaki, who related the following story.

Seiyūkai counselor Yamamoto Jotarō, himself a former Mitsui executive, called on Ikeda to ask if he would be interested in the Bank of Japan post. "No way [*iya da yo*]," answered Ikeda—Mitsui Bank needed him now. Yamamoto pressed him, asking, "Which is more important, Mitsui or Japan?" "Mitsui," said Ikeda. "Damn fool!" roared Yamamoto, and stormed out. A few days after this exchange, Inoue Junnosuke also came to see Ikeda, saying that Takahashi had asked him to be Bank of Japan governor. Inoue was not eager to take up his old job again, having already served in the higher post of minister of finance, but Ikeda encouraged him to do so. Reassured, Inoue left, but then, mysteriously, heard nothing at all from Takahashi for many days. Then, at the end of one policy meeting, Ikeda observed Takahashi summoning Ichiki to one side; Ikeda surmised that this was when Takahashi "sang him his requiem." It was on the next day that Inoue Junnosuke was reappointed as Bank of Japan governor.[27]

Thus, as in Inoue's original selection as Bank of Japan governor in 1919, Takahashi hesitated in appointing him, despite the fact that Inoue was widely regarded as the man best qualified for the post. But Inoue, who was not yet associated with any political party, continued to follow Takahashi loyally, and in his later retrospective on Inoue's life, Takahashi recalled that "until that time [1927], as Mr. Inoue and I didn't have any differences of opinion, we had never had any arguments."[28] Up to this point, Inoue had moved up the career ladder in step with Takahashi, succeeding him in the posts of vice president and then president of the Yokohama Specie Bank, governor of the Bank of Japan, and minister of finance. Again in 1927, Japan's two preeminent financial statesmen worked together to restore financial confidence.

The bank bailout now began. For the economy as a whole, Inoue had since 1919 consistently prescribed a saturnine regimen of deflation and constraint. When it came to the banking sector, however, Inoue was a beneficent guardian angel, dispensing Bank of Japan credit in an activist, "positive" fashion. As he had done in 1920, 1922, and 1923, Inoue again directed great flows of credit from the Bank of Japan to tide the banks over the panic. Currency was so urgently needed to back up bank deposits that for a time the Bank of Japan issued banknotes printed only on one side. By the time the banks reopened for business, the panic had subsided.[29] Takahashi resigned in August and was replaced by his close follower Mitsuchi Chūzō. Inoue continued in his post for another year.

As a result of the banking crisis, a total of thirty-six banks holding 8.7 percent of regular bank deposits were shut down.[30] Postal savings and the big zaibatsu banks expanded greatly in the wake of the crisis, and bank consolidation proceeded rapidly, promoted by the new banking law, also passed as a result of the crisis, which significantly strengthened the banking system. By the time that Inoue resigned again as BOJ governor in June 1928, when the emergency financial measures expired, a total of ¥879 million in credits had been extended to the banks. Of this, ¥191 million went to the Taiwan banks. These special advances, Inoue reported to Thomas Lamont, were purely to liquidate fixed and frozen assets of the banks (that is, to cover losses due to uncollectable loans), not for actual commercial or industrial requirements. To prevent inflationary effects, the government then sold government bonds to the banks to absorb this new issue of money.[31] The big banks, with their newly enlarged deposit base, now faced a new problem: surplus funds and correspondingly low interest rates. The desire to gain higher returns on their capital by investing abroad now prompted the big banks to push for a speedy return to gold convertibility.

After the Seiyūkai succeeded in wrecking the Kenseikai cabinet and regaining power, the Kenseikai merged with the Seiyū Hontō in June and re-formed as a new political party, the Rikken Minseitō (Constitutional Popular Government Party). Hamaguchi Osachi was party president. An ideologically defined two-party system now took clearer shape than ever. In the meantime, the Seiyūkai implemented a positive policy in both diplomacy and economics.

Prime Minister Tanaka, who served as his own foreign minister, immediately reversed Shidehara's "weak" policy in China. On May 28, to block the further advance of Chiang Kai-shek's Northern Expedition, he ordered units of the Japanese Kwantung Army to Shandong. To promote his positive policy in Manchuria, Tanaka appointed Yamamoto Jotarō as president of the South Manchurian Railway, charging him with the task of stopping Chinese warlord Zhang Zuolin from building competing parallel lines.[32] Matsuoka Yōsuke, who later led Japan out of the League of Nations and into the fascist alliance, was appointed SMR vice president.

In financial policy, ministers Takahashi and Mitsuchi not only halted gold shipments and let the yen depreciate but also returned to a positive spending policy centered on the extension of railroad lines and other development projects, in line with the Seiyūkai slogan of "building an industrial state."[33] These policies in particular were questioned by Japan's new American creditors.

INTERROGATING STATIST DEVELOPMENTALISM: THE MORGAN MISSION TO JAPAN

Like much of Europe and Latin America, Japan too entered (or seemed to enter) the American financial orbit in the mid-1920s, as American banks moved to occupy the position formerly held by the British. As Britain went into debt to the United States in order to pay for the war, most of Japan's overseas bonds that had originally been floated in London also came to be held in the United States.[34] Morgan and Company now became more deeply involved in Japanese developments.

In October 1927 Thomas Lamont made a sixteen-day trip to Japan at the invitation of overseas financial commissioner Mori Kengo, recently retired, whose idea was to strengthen Morgan connections in Japan.[35] Lamont's trip had been planned in the fall of 1926 and was in effect made at Japanese government invitation. The intervention of the financial crisis made it especially timely.[36] Arriving in Yokohama on October 3, Lamont was welcomed as a hero, greeted by crowds of schoolchildren lining his way and by prints in shop windows calling him the "savior of Japan" for his role in arranging the postearthquake loans.[37] He was welcomed at a banquet held on October 4 at the Marunouchi Bank Club and attended by more than eighty of Japan's topmost business leaders. This was followed the next morning by an audience with the emperor and the award of the "Second Class Order of the Sacred Treasure." (Their conversation, Lamont reported, was translated by "a very jolly Japanese admiral," Yamamoto Isoroku, who later directed the attack on Pearl Harbor.)[38] J. P. Morgan Jr. was awarded, in absentia, Japan's highest honor, the "First Class Order of the Sacred Treasure." Three other Wall Street bankers, representing the other members of the Morgan-led international lending consortium, also got medals.[39] The introduction to the emperor was followed by a lunch banquet with Prime Minister Tanaka and a dinner banquet hosted by president Matsunaga Yasuzaemon of Tōhō Electric Power. On the following days, Lamont was hosted by Baron Mitsui, by Baron Iwasaki of Mitsubishi, and by Dan Takuma of Mitsui.

Notwithstanding public declarations by himself and by Inoue Junnosuke to the contrary, Lamont's visit was more than a courtesy call. One immediate purpose was to pursue the possibility of an American loan to the Japanese-owned South Manchurian Railway. The idea had been broached during Lamont's 1920 trip, but he had rejected it in 1921 as too messy politically. Inoue Junnosuke now sought a $30 million loan for the SMR, and Lamont now saw the loan as a good deal for Morgan and Company.[40] The political significance of such a loan was clear, and after Lamont's trip, *The Nation* magazine editorialized against it, because "such a loan would be regarded in Japan, China, and Russia as notice to the world that the United States supports the new 'positive' policy of Japan in Manchuria." Lamont campaigned for the SMR loan on his return to America, but it was blocked by opposition from China and from the U.S. State Department and again came to nothing.[41]

Lamont also discussed electric utility loans with Mori Kengo, who, at the urging of Mitsui Bank director Ikeda Shigeaki, had become financial adviser to Tōkyō Denkō (the Tokyo Electric Light Company) after his retirement in July 1927. Ikeda's goal of thereby facilitating the inflow of long-term foreign capital later materialized in the electric company bond issues handled by Guaranty Trust in 1928.[42]

Lamont and his firm, representing the views of Anglo-American financial circles as a whole, also had a larger agenda. Accompanying Lamont were Martin Egan of Morgan and Company and Jeremiah Smith Jr., who had been Lamont's legal counsel on his first mission to Japan and China in 1920. Subsequently Smith had served as League of Nations commissioner general to Budapest, where he oversaw the Hungarian government's finances and their restoration of the gold standard.[43]

The significance for Japan was hard to miss, and although Inoue Junnosuke denied it, Japanese newspapers carried considerable speculation on this point.[44] Inoue himself suggested the connection in his welcoming speech for the Morgan mission: "You gentlemen know of the power America has contributed to the work of fiscal reform and currency stabilization in Austria, Hungary, Germany, and Belgium, to England's return to the gold standard, and to the work of revival in various other countries, but I especially want to mention the extremely deep relationship that Morgan and Company has with the European recovery movement."[45] Inoue then lauded the roles of Lamont and Smith in that movement. And in fact, Lamont's greatest goal, underlined by the inclusion of Smith in the party, was that Japan return to the gold standard. Before leaving for Japan, Lamont and Smith had conferred with U.S. secretary of state Frank Kellogg, who had okayed the provision of any credits needed to help Japan return to the gold standard. New York Federal Reserve Bank governor Benjamin Strong had also assured his support.[46]

During their trip Lamont and Smith prepared a detailed report for Morgan and Company on Japan's financial situation in the wake of the 1927 crisis. This "Memorandum on Japanese Conditions" summarized the views presented by Lamont to his hosts. It was based mainly on materials provided by Inoue Junnosuke and Mori Kengo. Lamont and Smith began their report by saying that the government needed to retrench. They attributed the great banking panic in spring 1927 not to the financial aftereffects of the 1923 earthquake but to Japan's failure to deflate after the war. This failure to deflate had allowed the continuation of many enterprises that "*ought to have been liquidated in [the depression of] 1920 and 1921*." Thus, banks were left with bad debts and frozen assets. Among banks, a weeding out had proceeded, with the strong ones gaining by getting the deposits of the weaker. The Japanese government's support for banks, the Americans said, was extraordinary—beyond government support to banks in crisis even in Europe. The question of which banks were to be helped was left to the Bank of Japan, though "political pressure" was also present. Further, "the Government is engaged in the ownership and subsidizing of enterprises to an extent quite unknown in Great Britain and the United States," due to historical necessity and to the paternalistic government tradition. These subsidies accounted for the increase in public debt. "Certainly," opined Lamont and Smith, "the country cannot repeat the experiment of guaranteeing commercial losses."[47]

On the credit side of Japan's national balance sheet, Lamont and Smith noted the "sound" opinions of Japanese banking and industrial leaders who agreed that there should have been a more drastic deflation in 1921. Everyone, they said, declared that Japan was committed to return to gold; Inoue had told them that it was the financial panic that had delayed the return. There was, however, a danger that party politics could lead the government away from these sound opinions, and most of the leaders Lamont and Smith consulted were concerned about the effects of the next election, which would be the first to be held under universal (manhood) suffrage.

The bedrock on which Lamont and Smith built their views of the current world financial situation was the presumed success of the United States' own stabilization depression of 1920–21. At that time, Japan had not let prices fall to the extent they had fallen in America, and Lamont and Smith repeated the idea that Japan had needed a "thorough-going deflation in 1921 upon which a sound expansion might have been built." The "Japanese people," they said, echoing a theme that had been persistently sounded by Inoue Junnosuke, had not retrenched but had "kept up their spending spree."[48] (In fact, as their report stated, Bank of Japan note circulation had shrunk from 1920 to the 1927 banking crisis.)

On October 18, at the end of Lamont's visit, a roundtable discussion was held at the Bank of Japan with a dozen banking and industrial leaders who represented "all important financial interests," as U.S. ambassador Charles MacVeagh reported to the American secretary of state. The attendees included Bank of Japan governor Inoue Junnosuke, Dan Takuma (head of the Mitsui holding company), Ikeda Shigeaki of Mitsui Bank, Gō Seinosuke, and Mori Kengo. Lamont and Smith presented them with "a clear-cut and sweeping criticism of Japanese industrial and financial methods and offered suggestions as to means of improving them."[49]

Before the meeting, Lamont and his associates had submitted a list of questions to the Bank of Japan and to Mori Kengo (for the Ministry of Finance).[50] They asked:

- Why was there no policy of retrenchment? (Rather, there had been "expansion and relative extravagance.")
- Why was the government engaged in these broad developmental projects when the financial situation was not good? [That is, why the positive policy, particularly the Tanaka cabinet's railroad development plans?]
- Why subsidize so many businesses—"why so much government in business?" Would not private business be better?
- Was there any change in the paternalistic attitudes of the government and Bank of Japan?
- Was the government spending money and subsidizing business in China?
- Were military expenditures increasing as a result of the China situation?

- Were there not too many banks in Japan? Was the government really carrying through consolidation?
- Were banks still carrying along industry with loans that had become long term?
- Would it not have been "better for the Japanese to have taken their medicine" and acknowledged losses in 1920 and 1921 rather than carrying along an unsound situation "by artificial aid from the big banks and from the Bank of Japan and the Government"?
- Did Japan intend to return to the gold standard?[51]

The Americans also asked questions about the export trade, shipping, and cotton mills. Indicative of a basic oversight concerning the actual character of Japanese industrial development, they asked no questions about the rising heavy and chemical industries, which would shortly be at the center of a new industrial revolution.

Acting for Inoue, BOJ vice governor Fukai Eigo provided Lamont with a response to his questionnaire before the meeting.[52] The Bank of Japan's response began by saying that the government recognized the need to retrench. The problem, Fukai wrote, was that Japan wanted to lay out a foundation for future development and did not want to relinquish enterprises started for that purpose. Fukai thus partially justified past policy by invoking the waste of the business cycle. "It is now recognized," he wrote, "that it would have been better for us to 'take our medicine' not long after the reaction of 1920. But for a country like Japan not rich in resources, the economic structure grown up during the war was too valuable an asset to be left lightheartedly to the natural course of shrinkage."[53] As to government subsidy and control of business, "the success of Government aid and guidance in the early stages of our economic development still lingers in our memory." Because of the scarcity of private resources in newly industrializing Japan, the government had had to take the lead and help in opening up new lines of activity. On the whole, this had been beneficial. "Thus, undertaking or control of business by the Government still remains as a habit." Especially for chartered banks (such as the Bank of Taiwan), the government should indeed try to help, but there was a limit, and "we are learning by experience, that, in the face of changed conditions, the propping up of business by the Government must be gradually dispensed with." Lately, Fukai reported, the paternalistic attitude of the government had been criticized even at home. There was an intention to return to gold, Fukai said, but it was still impossible to say when.

Mori Kengo provided his own answers to the Americans' questions.[54] Everyone favored retrenchment, he reported. But retrenchment was made difficult by "the depression and stagnation from which the business world of this country has suffered for the last eight long years since the trade panic of 1920." For the benefit of the Americans, Mori also specified some of the differences between the Seiyūkai and Minseitō parties: the present Seiyūkai cabinet had as their first plank a "Policy of Nation on Industry" (the *sangyō rikkoku* policy), a policy of trying to restore prosperity by positively promoting industry, which included the improvement and extension of railways. Hence the budget increase. In the infant stage, Mori continued, industry had been much subsidized by the government, and the people "have not yet completely shaken off this [i]nertia obtained in the past years." Now, he said, subsidies were being stopped. Mori also expressed an opinion in favor of privatizing the telephone and armaments industries. The Bank of Japan and the government were now taking a less "paternalistic or interfering attitude, . . . simply on account of the growing influence of powerful city banks and industrial firms." Disasters and panics were exceptional cases, and protective tariffs were purely temporary. Mori also agreed that Japan should have "taken its medicine" in 1920 or 1921. Japan will return to gold, he said, but in 1926, when the yen exchange had recovered to near the old par, it had hurt business.

The answers provided by Inoue and Mori must have been satisfactory, for Thomas Lamont now became an active advocate for Japanese interests. Even as the Tanaka government pushed the most aggressive and militaristic policy in China since World War I, Lamont seemed convinced that the liberal Japan had won out, and he began working to offset what he saw as the pro-Chinese bias in the United States. Thus, soon after returning to New York, Lamont explained in a speech to the Institute of Pacific Relations that Japanese leaders had no imperialistic designs in China and issued a plea for mutual understanding. Before giving this speech, Lamont talked it over with the Japanese ambassador, and later sent him a copy to demonstrate his friendship with Japan.[55] Lamont also met with the editors of the *New York Times* soon after his return from Japan and, in a letter to Inoue, gave it to be understood that it was his influence that had resulted in the "fairness" of subsequent *New York Times* editorials in relation to the China crisis.[56] Lamont began as well to exercise some direct influence inside Japan, working with Mori Kengo, Ikeda Shigeaki, and Gō Seinosuke to bring an end to the cutthroat competition in the new electric power sector by promoting the merger in December 1927 of Tokyo Electric Light (where Mori Kengo was an adviser) and Tōhō Electric Power.[57]

By this point, world monetary trends seemed to be leaving Japan behind. In December 1927 Italy restored the gold standard with the help of credits from the Federal Reserve Bank of New York and Morgan and Company (again, arranged by Thomas Lamont). France officially restored gold convertibility in June 1928, and Europe appeared to have entered a new age of currency stabilization.[58] The countries of the west coast of South America were also drawn into the American financial orbit in these years, adopting gold standards and independent central banks on the basis of conditional loans from Dillon, Read and Company.[59] Japan was now considered lagging in the process of reform, and the need for Japan to return to normality—gold convertibility—was accepted on all sides. There was an argument in the business journals, led by Ishibashi Tanzan and Takahashi Kamekichi of the *Tōyō keizai shinpō*, that Japan should return to gold convertibility at a new, depreciated par in order to avoid deflation and recession. France, Italy, and all of the defeated countries had returned to gold at new, devalued rates, but to Inoue Junnosuke and others this implied a loss of financial honor, and Ishibashi's argument never enjoyed substantial political support.[60] Despite his recent advocacy of lifting the gold embargo, however, Inoue himself continued to hold back from immediate action, and at the National Bill Brokers' Convention on May 15, 1928, he explained that because of its "special accommodation" lending, the Bank of Japan's control over credit conditions was weakened and it was therefore too early to lift the gold standard.

On June 11, 1928, Inoue resigned again as Bank of Japan governor, once again to devote his full time to "taking care of the business world."[61] He was replaced as bank governor by Hijikata Hisaakira, his comrade during his 1898 internship in London. Inoue remained influential among the top councils of international financial relations and continued to provide detailed financial reports to Lamont.

In the fall of 1928, Morgan and Company continued to push the Japanese to deflate. Japanese wholesale prices had fallen by one-third since 1920, and prices were stable or falling in the late 1920s, but an internal Morgan memo that Lamont shared with Mori Kengo in September 1928 nevertheless described Japan's ongoing postwar situation as one of "inflation," in that money circulation and the price level had been kept up near the wartime level, even while prices and currencies in other countries were being deflated. (The memo was apparently written by Morgan economist Russell Leffingwell.)[62] "Japan has been living on her war fat" and despite the trade slump had avoided deflation. This maintenance of an elevated postwar price level relative to deflation elsewhere, said the Morgan memo, was just like a price increase when world prices are stable. The result must be either to depress the yen's value or to cause the export of gold; the latter had happened. Further, the Bank of Japan must be independent so that it could enforce deflation. Big business should get its capital from "the investment public" and not from banks, which should confine their lending to short-term loans. The government's general account was balanced, but via the special accounts the government was running a deficit.[63] Morgan and Company (Leffingwell) did acknowledge that "Japan could not, of course, have made the amazing progress which she has in the sixty years since she embraced western civilization without the most active participation of the government in everything, and that to an extent which to my laissez faire prejudices is rather shocking."[64] But now, the government's role should be limited and government spending cut. At the least, government-owned railroads should be independently incorporated and should live within their own budgets.

At the same time, Leffingwell told Mori directly that returning to the gold standard would of itself eliminate many of the supposed obstacles—that it was best for Japan to "take the plunge." He then explained that, from the point of view of the money system and exchange relations, any nation may figuratively be viewed as a *bank*. Therefore, a nation should open its doors and be ready "to pay all depositors in full on demand." Thus it would gain depositors and trust.[65] Leffingwell's idea was a simple and clear model of international monetary relations: the issuing of money was a form of credit creation; yen held by foreigners were in effect "deposits"; and deposits should be payable in gold. The extension of international credits evidenced the world's trust in "the bank" that was Japan, said Leffingwell: "the world believes in Japan's financial honor." Leffingwell repeated the point that the Bank of Japan should be independent and free to adopt deflationary interest-rate increases. The Bank of Japan should also provide all necessary information to the U.S. Federal Reserve and seek its advice. Morgan and Company, he said, had cooperated with the Federal Reserve in its assistance to many European central banks, providing both advice and credit.

Lamont too encouraged the Japanese government to lift the gold embargo soon, pointing out that England, Belgium, and Italy had recently returned to gold, all with the help of credits from the Federal Reserve and from Morgan, and that Spain was set to follow.[66] In reply, Mori Kengo wrote in September 1928 that the letters from Lamont and Leffingwell had come at just the right time, as Japan was considering the return to gold. He had sent copies to his friends who were playing a leading role in this movement: Mitsui Bank managing director general Ikeda Shigeaki, Bank of Japan governor Hijikata Hisaakira, vice governor Fukai Eigo, and Inoue Junnosuke—although, Mori added, Inoue did not seem to favor an immediate return to gold.[67] There had never been such a consensus on gold as now, wrote Mori, with numerous business organizations coming out in favor of lifting the gold embargo. Ikeda Shigeaki had recently presented a resolution from the Committee of Tokyo Clearing Banks to the Ministry of Finance calling for an immediate return to gold.

External pressure was not the only force that impelled Japan toward restoring the gold standard in January 1930, but it was the one that seemed to bring all of the other causes into line.[68] When France returned to the gold standard in June 1928, Japan became the only major power that had not yet done so. The need to do so seemed beyond debate, and the only real political argument was as to when. As usual, the Seiyūkai continued to favor holding off, while the new Minseitō favored more decisive action.

THE RENEWED MOVEMENT TO RESTORE GOLD

As the earthquake had done in 1923, the banking crisis forcibly interrupted the retrenchment process. The resulting "surgery" (in Fukai Eigo's phrase) removed the banks' bad debts and, moreover, left surplus yen funds sloshing around in the nation's largest and strongest banks seeking some profitable outlet. This situation of monetary ease also meant that the Bank of Japan lost its power over the money markets, which BOJ leaders thought needed to be restored before the gold embargo could be lifted.[69] Elsewhere, with the banking crisis solved by the resultant panic and shakeout, the return to gold seemed opportune.

Leadership now came from the business world. In June 1928 the Kobe Chamber of Commerce called for a return to the gold standard in order to stabilize the yen exchange. The Japan Chamber of Commerce and Industry issued a similar call in October, and one after another, business groups lined up in support of a speedy return to gold. Thus, by the fall of 1928, the demand for lifting the gold embargo had become "the consensus of public opinion" (*tenka no yoron*), as Gō Seinosuke put it.[70]

In the spring of 1929, when the Young Committee meeting again brought world financial leaders to Paris, Ikeda Shigeaki traveled to Europe and then on to America, where he stayed from September until mid-October. He later recalled this moment on the eve of the world economic crisis as, mysteriously, "a year when there were no troubles in the world . . . whether politically or economically, there were no problems. . . . Pretty much everyone was bullish, and many said that this was just the usual state for America."[71] But invisibly to people's common sense of things, even as the American-sponsored reconstruction of the international gold-standard system was being completed, the end game of that system was already in play.

After Britain lifted its own gold embargo in 1925, gold had begun to flow out from London to New York, forcing the Bank of England to maintain high interest rates in order to attract mobile capital to London and preserve the gold standard. The effect was to deepen Britain's depression. Shortly before Lamont's mission to Japan, in July 1927, New York Federal Reserve governor Benjamin Strong acceded to urging from the governors of the Bank of England and the Bank of France to reduce U.S. interest rates in order to take pressure off of Europe. The New York Fed's fraternal support for the British gold standard had the unanticipated result of promoting a historic stock market bubble on Wall Street.[72]

The year 1927 was also the high point of the American capital outflows, to Japan as to the rest of the world. After June 1928 the booming New York stock market was sucking in most of the funds available for investment. New American fears concerning the reliability of foreign bonds compounded the problem, and U.S. lending to other countries dropped off sharply, resulting in a reverse flow of capital into the United States.[73] Interest rates increased across Europe, and depression began to spread around the peripheries of the world economy. Two years later, in analyzing the onset of the world depression, Inoue Junnosuke would point especially to the importance of this abrupt withdrawal of U.S. overseas investment.[74] Borrowing abroad also became more difficult for Japan, as overseas financial commissioner Tsushima Juichi learned in October 1928, when he went to New York to negotiate a bond issue for the Oriental Development Company.[75]

When viewed from the center, however, the great enterprise of global monetary stabilization seemed to be drawing to a successful close. From February 11 to June 6, 1929, a "Committee of Experts" chaired by General Electric president Owen D. Young met in Paris to arrange a "final and definitive settlement" of the German reparations issue. Mori Kengo was the Japanese representative and was assisted by Tsushima Juichi.[76] J. P. Morgan Jr. and Thomas Lamont attended as American representatives, and private conversations between Mori and Lamont turned again to the need for Japan to restore the yen to gold convertibility.

Especially pressing was the fact that £25 million (¥250 million) in Japanese government sterling bonds issued to help finance the Russo-Japanese War were coming due in January 1931. With overseas specie holdings down to ¥86 million at the end of 1928, Tsushima saw no option but to refinance the loan. To do so would require the cooperation of U.S. and British bankers. The American bankers said that Japan must first stabilize its currency—that is, restore the gold standard.[77] By the end of February 1929, overseas specie holdings had fallen to the lowest level since 1904 and were sufficient to cover only one year's foreign payments by the government. The government grew so alarmed that after April, it stopped announcing the level of its specie reserves.[78]

The Ministry of Finance therefore concluded that restoring the gold standard was an urgent necessity, and on April 12, 1929, the Seiyūkai cabinet's finance minister, Mitsuchi Chūzō, announced that the government was committed to lifting the gold embargo—the very policy that had embarrassed his predecessor with a banking crisis and had brought down the Kenseikai cabinet. Stock prices sagged at the news and there was an outright panic in the markets in May. Mitsuchi therefore kept his further preparations secret. Thus, the initial decision to return to gold was actually taken under the expansion-minded Seiyūkai government of Tanaka Giichi.[79] Adherence to the gold standard had been and became again a central and symbolic element in the struggle between the Seiyūkai's "positive" policy and the Minseitō's "negative" policy, but by the spring of 1929 the need to return to gold convertibility seemed to be a matter of objective, external constraints, independent of the domestic policy dialectic.

There remained, however, a lack of confidence within the financial world that the Seiyūkai in general and the militaristic Tanaka in particular could really put through a retrenchment policy. As Inoue Junnosuke bluntly put it in a speech in April 1929, "Mr. Tanaka's face is a face which is incapable of financial retrenchment."[80] Accordingly, Inoue continued to say that the time was not yet right for lifting the gold embargo. All the same, under the Tanaka government, the economic side of the Seiyūkai's positive policy was relatively restrained, as international economic circumstances seemed to require steps in the direction of the "negative policy" that the Seiyūkai had long decried.

Concrete measures were now taken. On May 4, 1929, Finance Minister Mitsuchi ordered Tsushima home for urgent consultations; Tsushima at once knew that this meant the lifting of the gold embargo.[81] Mori and Tsushima also discussed the matter with Lamont, who reported to Morgan and Company on May 7:

> In part because of discussions that have taken place recently in London and Paris as Sir Mori Kengo explains to me the Japanese Government seems now about to undertake early and vigorous consideration of return to the gold standard. Tsushima has received cable instructions to proceed West and will probably cross over to New York by the same steamer as Mori, possibly it may be the same one I shall be on, and upon arrival in New York will wish to receive advices as to the whole stabilization job from our leading firm economist, Mr. R. C. Leffingwell. The latter has already written out a book on the matter which he can turn up and paraphrase for Tsushima's benefit.[82]

These side discussions at the Young committee meetings occurred during what was in retrospect the end of an era in international financial history. The result of the committee's work, as Tsushima put it, was that "Europe had entered a new age of currency stability."[83] The solution agreed to by the assembled experts was, as Thomas Lamont explained, that the question of German reparations "should be transferred for all time from politics to commerce"[84]—the culmination of a decade of concerted international stabilization efforts mainly directed by central and private bankers. Reparations payments would no longer be handled government-to-government but via the newly created Bank for International Settlements (BIS).

Projected as a central bankers' central bank, the BIS was the object of high hopes among its framers, who included Thomas Lamont and Jeremiah Smith.[85] The proposed organization of the BIS was also a new source of pressure on Japan: membership was to be restricted to "countries with stabilized currencies" (that is, gold-standard countries). It thus appeared that Japan might suffer the "extreme dishonor," as Tsushima saw it, of being excluded from the prospective world central bank. Mori Kengo negotiated an exception to the rules: Japan would be included as a member on the grounds that it was one of the recipients of German reparations. It was understood that Japan would soon return to gold.[86]

On May 16 Tsushima received another secret telegram from the Ministry of Finance telling him to look into obtaining a credit to support the lifting of the gold embargo (that is, a credit that could be drawn on to protect the yen against possible speculative attacks).[87] Throughout these preliminary negotiations, restoration of Japan's gold standard was connected to the refinancing of the Russo-Japanese War bonds, and Tsushima had already suggested that the credit and the bond refunding be combined into a single operation. Lamont insisted they be kept separate.[88] In further discussions with Lamont "and with those who had recent experience in restoring the gold standards in France, Italy, Belgium, and Britain," Tsushima got the same answer: lift the gold embargo first, then handle the bond refinancing separately. Thus, as Lamont reported Tsushima's plans, the U.S. Federal Reserve Bank could provide a credit to the Bank of Japan, and Morgan and Company could provide one to the Ministry of Finance. (This formula of the Federal Reserve providing credits to central banks while Morgan provided credits to governments was the standard pattern seen in numerous international currency stabilization operations.) Then there was the matter of re-funding the Japanese government bonds.[89]

Proceeding to New York, Tsushima discussed plans for restoring the gold standard with Morgan's Russell Leffingwell as well as with Charles Mitchell of National City Bank, Mortimer Schiff of Kuhn, Loeb, and George Harrison of the FRBNY. But after having pushed for further deflation in Japan in 1927 and 1928, Morgan and Company now took the position that deflation had proceeded sufficiently and that it would be best to return the yen to gold convertibility at a depreciated parity. That is, Japan should "stabilize" (return to gold) as soon as possible, but at or below the present depreciated exchange value of the yen, because serious deflation would be too drastic in the face of the existing depression in silk, cotton, and shipbuilding; the more or less closed market in China; and higher world interest rates[90] (which were being caused by the pressure of the New York stock market boom). Ishibashi Tanzan had been arguing the same point since 1924.

Tsushima himself later said that he agreed that a new, depreciated par was best. Finance Minister Mitsuchi, the longtime follower of Takahashi Korekiyo, appears to have held the same view.[91] The succeeding finance minister, Inoue Junnosuke, did not favor a new parity, and Tsushima therefore kept his opinion in favor of a new par to himself. More than further deflation, Morgan and Company now emphasized the importance of assuring the independence of the Bank of Japan, especially in view of its domination by the Ministry of Finance during and since the war.[92] "Most important of all," the Bank of Japan should get the advice of central bank governors George Harrison, Montagu Norman, and Emile Moreau of the United States, Britain, and France.[93] His preliminary consultations completed, Tsushima left for home on June 14, 1929.

Meanwhile, the excesses of the "positive" policy of military adventurism and intrigue in China had set in motion a chain of events that ended up bringing down the Tanaka cabinet. An archexpansionist in his own prime, General Tanaka had been surpassed in zeal by the young officers of the Japanese Kwantung Army, who had attempted to force the issue of Japanese control in Manchuria by dynamiting the military train of the Manchurian warlord Zhang Zuolin on June 4, 1928.[94] The facts of Zhang's assassination began to emerge in the press, and finally, faced with the emperor's loss of faith over his handling of the affair, Tanaka was forced to resign. Thus Tsushima learned while crossing the Pacific Ocean that the Seiyūkai cabinet had been replaced with a Minseitō cabinet led by Hamaguchi Osachi, who was committed to lifting the gold embargo as quickly as possible. The Hamaguchi cabinet was inaugurated on July 2, and it lost no time in implementing the negative policy to the fullest extent yet.

PART THREE

The Crisis of Liberalism

TEN

The Liberal Triumph, 1929–1930

> Inouye speaks the same financial language as Norman, Strong and all of us. I have never found him to deviate from a straight line.
>
> THOMAS LAMONT TO J. P. MORGAN, JR., APRIL 19, 1927

> If I am killed, quickly lift the gold embargo.
>
> STATEMENT OF INOUE JUNNOSUKE TO A TRUSTED OFFICIAL, AS REPORTED BY TAKAHASHI KOREKIYO ON THE DAY AFTER INOUE'S MURDER

In Western terms, it is perfectly unproblematic to describe the Inoue financial policy as orthodox. In the words of economic historian G. C. Allen, who lived in Japan in the 1920s, Inoue was "the nearest approach to an orthodox liberal financier that Japan has produced."[1] For Thomas Lamont, Inoue was a regular member of the international central bankers' club. In line with such judgments, the Minseitō party was described in the Western press as the "Liberal" party as against the "Conservative" Seiyūkai. The new Minseitō government's announced policy of free gold movements, the central plank of the liberal economic project, was warmly received in Anglo-American financial circles—"exceedingly welcome" to the London *Economist*.[2] Theoretically grounded in the certainties of orthodox economic statecraft, Inoue's policy was in actuality a bold leap into the unknown.

THE INOUE LINE

By the time Inoue Junnosuke was made finance minister in the Hamaguchi cabinet, he was an experienced, senior government figure, who could have had every expectation of becoming prime minister in a future cabinet. Inoue had been thinking of entering politics for several years and had even discussed the matter with his foreign friends Benjamin Strong and Montagu Norman as early as 1924. (Strong's advice was to stay out of politics.)[3] But in forming his cabinet, Hamaguchi had kept his choice of Inoue a secret to the end, and Inoue joined the Minseitō only a week after being appointed minister of finance, much as Takahashi Korekiyo had joined the Seiyūkai on first becoming finance minister sixteen years earlier. Moreover, Inoue was a peer, and his most recent tenure as Bank of Japan president, in 1927–28, had been in association with Takahashi Korekiyo and a Seiyūkai government; so his appointment initially caused some resentment within the Minseitō party ranks. Hamaguchi's choice also caused some wonderment because of Inoue's recent statements that it was best to hold off on returning to the gold standard.[4]

In any case, on joining the Minseitō, Inoue pursued party politics with his usual single-mindedness, becoming an active party man and a renowned political campaigner. In line with his belief in the rectitude of the gold standard, he forcefully took the lead in restoring it, to the extent that the English epithet *strong man* (*sutorongu man*) was applied to him. Inoue's old friend Ikeda Shigeaki later evaluated Inoue's transformation into a politician more negatively: Inoue was at bottom a weak person who now overcompensated by being too severe. Ikeda's comments surely reflect his own subsequent conflicts with Inoue, which came to a head in the "dollar-buying" speculation of 1931. But before that time Inoue worked closely with bankers such as Ikeda and was seen as representing the big-business wing of the Minseitō, bringing both business and international support to the new cabinet.[5]

The new cabinet spelled out its goals in the "Ten Point Program," the classic statement of the liberal party's policy line as it developed in the two-party context of the 1920s:[6]

1. Clean government
2. Arousing the people's spirit (which had been running to "frivolity and self-indulgence")
3. Enforcement of discipline among officials
4. Improvement of relations with China
5. Promotion of arms limitation
6. Adjustment and financial retrenchment
7. A balanced budget ("not floating bonds") and reduction of government debt
8. Lifting the gold embargo
9. Establishment of social policy
10. Renovation of education

Points 1 through 3 of the Ten Point Program were banalities that might have been found in any party's platform. Points 4 and 5, noninterfence in China and naval arms limitation in cooperation with the Western powers, were core ideas of the Shidehara diplomatic policy so reviled by the political right. Point 9 of the program, social policy, was another characteristic Minseitō concern, and in the usage of the time meant primarily a law recognizing trade unions, an unemployment relief law, and a farm tenancy law. Social policy extended to an effort to give women the right of political participation on the local level.[7] Points 6, 7, and 8—public and private retrenchment, and the lifting of the gold embargo—were the economic core of the Minseitō program and the essence of the "negative" policy championed by Hamaguchi Osachi and Inoue Junnosuke.

The psychological effects of the new cabinet's announcements were immediate. Convinced that austerity was on the way, speculators began to sell off shares in July, and the stock market fell. By the same token, convinced that a return to the old par was imminent, speculators bought yen, and the yen began to rise. But the yen could not simply be returned to gold convertibility as is. "If we were to lift the gold embargo as things now stand," Inoue Junnosuke explained in an August 1929 appeal to Japan's housewives, "Japan's gold coins would at once go out to foreign countries, exactly like a great flood when a dam breaks. If that happens, Japan's business world would be destroyed."[8] That is, before removing the gold embargo, Japan's trade deficit must be remedied by reducing imports and bringing export prices down to levels where they could be competitive under a high yen exchange rate—the policy that Inoue had described on the eve of World War I as the "negative" policy for fixing a nation's trade gap. Thus, Inoue aimed to produce a preparatory deflation by means of budget cuts, monetary restraint, and moral exhortation to encourage the Japanese people to reduce their consumption and purchase domestic products.

The choice of a full-blown deflation policy requires explanation, because radical deflation was not a necessary part of returning to the gold standard as such. The key decision that necessitated Inoue's vigorous deflation policy was the choice to restore the gold standard at the old 1897 par, which overvalued the yen by almost any measure. Ishibashi Tanzan and Takahashi Kamekichi had been arguing for a new, depreciated par precisely to avoid these deflationary effects. But the new cabinet never seriously considered the idea, and Inoue was almost vituperative in his denunciation of Ishibashi's alternative "new parity" version of gold-standard resumption.[9]

In arguing against devaluation, Inoue's fundamental ideas concerning the utility and meaning of the gold standard were revealed more clearly. Lifting the gold embargo was needed "to break the deadlock of our financial world, which has been sunk in depression for many years, and to fundamentally reconstruct our business world." Some, Inoue said, had argued that a return to the prewar par would put pressure on industry and cause financial disturbances, but it was Inoue's firm conviction that his was the "proper path [*jōdō*]. . . . To change the parity of the currency is a kind of economic revolution, and its influence will extend generally to the nation's credit, the national economy, and the national spirit."[10] As it was for British policy makers, this was a matter of honor—Inoue's personal honor as a central banker and Japan's honor as a first-class nation. Moreover, to adjust via devaluation would make Japan's external debts heavier: if the value of the yen fell, Japan would be pressed for the funds to pay foreign countries.[11] Different sectoral interests were represented here, as Ishibashi's concern for exporters and industrial growth contrasted with Inoue's concern for stable finances and the nation's foreign credit.

On top of this was a practical political consideration. To lift the finance ministry's gold embargo order of September 1917 and return to the old par, established by law in 1897, was a simple matter of the Ministry of Finance issuing a second administrative order and would not require Diet approval. To change the par would require a new law, and the Seiyūkai still held a plurality in the Diet.[12]

The new government acted on its principles quickly and forcefully. At the new cabinet's first meeting on July 5, Hamaguchi and Inoue chose not to wait for next year's budget but began unilaterally to cut the current year's budget, which had already been approved by the Diet. Such extraordinary steps were needed, Hamaguchi Osachi said, to "restore the nation's credit and rescue Japan from a position of economic isolation." The Seiyūkai opposition attacked the procedure as unconstitutional and demanded that the Diet be called into special session to consider the matter. Under the Meiji constitution, the Imperial Diet was convened for a few days in late December, recessed for the New Year's holiday, and reconvened in January to conduct the actual business of passing the budget and other legislation in a session that lasted into the spring. Extraordinary Diet sessions could be called at the discretion of the cabinet, which had broad powers of temporary legislation by decree while the Diet was recessed. Lacking a Diet majority, the Minseitō cabinet refrained from calling the Diet into special session, and under the rubric of a "working budget" (*jikkō yosan*), simply mandated an overall budget cut of 5 percent. Inoue's dramatic cuts included the halting of construction of government buildings in Tokyo. In the October 15 cabinet meeting, Inoue also proposed to cut 10 percent from the salaries of officials who earned more than ¥1,200 annually. The latter attempt had to be withdrawn in the face of a storm of political and bureaucratic opposition.[13]

But this was resistance to Inoue's methods more than to his goals, and as an idea, the panacea of the gold standard seemed to carry all before it. Even Seiyūkai criticism remained muted for a time. This uncharacteristic reticence was largely due to the discredited Seiyūkai's reluctance to face an election that it was sure to lose. After resigning as prime minister, Tanaka Giichi had returned to his hometown of Hagi, and in September he died of heart failure—perhaps, it was said, because of the heartbreak of being rejected by his sovereign, or perhaps because of excessive drinking, feasting, and fornicating on the occasion of his homecoming. Inukai Tsuyoshi, now seventy-four years old, became the new Seiyūkai president. For the first time, the presidents of both the governing party and the main opposition party were sitting members of the Diet. In late October the Seiyūkai called the Minseitō policy "dangerous," saying that Japanese industry needed to be rebuilt before the gold embargo was lifted.[14]

The cabinet also launched a preparatory barrage of ideas. To enable industries to keep exporting under the high yen exchange, the Minseitō cabinet proffered the solution of "industrial rationalization" (*sangyō gōrika*), which served as a general-purpose slogan and fashionable replacement for the previous catchall "adjustment" (*seiri*), which Inoue had promoted since the beginning of the 1920s. Combining cost cutting and layoffs with the ideas of technical improvement and industrial cooperation (including cartelization and production curtailment), rationalization thus appeared as a strain in both the "positive" and "negative" policies, a response to the problems of overproduction, excessive competition, and rapid technological change.[15]

The Minseitō cabinet also organized another great propaganda offensive to encourage the Japanese people to curtail their consumption and reform the culture of extravagance that they perceived to have developed since the World War I boom. Relentlessly, Hamaguchi and Inoue repeated the message that Japan's season of retrenchment was at hand, and hammered away at the theme of how luxury and loose living had brought Japan to its present impasse. Restriction was the only way forward. In doing so, they also inadvertently opened a great debate on the meaning of consumer demand in a modern economy, pitting their old-fashioned austerity views against the "Keynesian"-style views being developed by people like Takahashi Korekiyo and Ishibashi Tanzan.

"THE GOLD STANDARD AS SEEN FROM THE KITCHEN"

There is a long history of government campaigns to promote popular frugality in Japan, and the major campaigns of recent years had been associated with phases of "negative" retrenchment policies, building from the 1908 "Boshin year" campaign of the second Katsura cabinet to the "Diligence and Thrift" campaign mounted by the Katō and Wakatsuki cabinets. Even in this context, the Minseitō cabinet's "Public and Private Retrenchment Campaign" (*kōshi keizai kinshuku undō*) stood out in intensity and scope, as the new cabinet took its message directly to the people via lecture tours and the new technologies of radio, phonograph recordings, and motion pictures. In the new age of mass advertising—the technologies for creating consumer desire—the government deployed the same techniques to throttle back demand.

"A really spectacular effort," was how overseas financial commissioner Tsushima Juichi described the campaign to Japan's British creditors, and one that "bore very fruitful and satisfactory results."[16]

Prime Minister Hamaguchi announced his policy directly to the nation in an extraordinary radio address on August 28, 1929. This was followed in the first week of September by the distribution "to every household" of 13.5 million copies of the tract *Appealing to All of the Japanese People* (*Zen kokumin ni uttau*). In the following nine months, more than 800,000 copies of twenty-three other publications were also printed and distributed to government offices, schools, police stations, youth groups, and other civic organizations nationwide.[17] A total of 8,168 live and motion-picture lectures were given on the subject, attended, according to the Ministry of Finance's count, by 4,076,358 people. Local governors enthusiastically cooperated, reported Tsushima, as did "almost all the public and private organizations, including ex-soldiers' associations, schools and other educational and religious institutions, women's societies, business firms, factories, etc." Via a "moral education general mobilization" (*kyōka sōdōin*), the national education system also went to work to give schoolchildren the message of curtailing consumption and imports.[18] Five feature films were made that featured retrenchment themes.[19] "Even popular songs and performances by professional artists contained the slogans 'Retrenchment and economy' and 'Lifting the gold embargo,'" explained Tsushima. The popular geisha-style singer Fumikichi-san was mobilized to record the song "Retrenchment Ditty" ("Kinshuku kouta") in 1929, which became a hit as the theme song for the movie *Number-one Woman* (*Ichibanme no onna*).[20]

"Retrenchment Ditty"

Saita hana de mo shibomanya naranu,
so ja nai ka.
Koko ga saifu no (sō yo danzen),
aketa saifu no shimedokoro.

[Chorus]
Jisei jisetsu ja, te o totte (ha!),
kinshuku sho ya, kinshuku sho.

Hito no kane nara yosomite sumo ga,
so ja nai ka.
Karita 50 oku (sō yo danzen),
kaesu 50 oku wa atamawari.

Mukō hachimaki,
kata ni wa tasuki, so ja nai ka.
Harae Nihon no (sō yo danzen),
tataru fukeiki no binbōgami.

Omae shiodachi, watashi wa chadachi,
so ja nai ka.

Kin no kaikin (sō yo danzen),
ureshi kaikin togeru made.

Even the blooming flower must close,
isn't it so?
Now it's time to close the open purse
(that's right, absolutely).

[Chorus]
It's the time, it's the season,
all together, hand in hand (yes!),
let's retrench, let's retrench.

You don't have to worry about other
people's money, isn't it so?
But the borrowed five billion
[must be] repaid by all together
(that's right, absolutely).

Tie on your headband,
gird up your sleeves, isn't it so?
Drive away the god of poverty and recession
that is cursing Japan
(that's right, absolutely).

You give up salt, I'll give up tea
isn't it so?
Lifting the gold embargo
(that's right, absolutely),
until the joyful lifting of the embargo.

Inoue himself put together the personal and the macroeconomic at the very outset of the campaign, in an August 15 speech to the All-Kansai Women's Federation entitled "Lifting the Gold Embargo as Seen from the Kitchen Economy—Hoping for the Self-Consciousness of Japanese Women." Inoue's speech was also printed separately and distributed, like most of the other retrenchment campaign materials, to "every ministry, the cabinet, every colonial, territorial, and prefectural office and police station, every city, town, and village, every committee officer."[21] His message summed up all of the essential points of the retrenchment campaign.

Women could not vote (although the Minseitō cabinet was working to extend the franchise), but then as now, family budgeting was typically the wife's responsibility. Therefore, Inoue told his audience of middle-class housewives, "as consumers, women are the most influential people . . . more than nine-tenths [of the money spent] in the world is money spent by you. . . . You may even spend more than that, as there are also those who spend to the point of debt." Producers "are only worried about women's tastes," so "one could even say that you are in charge of the country's production." To rationalize Japan's macroeconomy, "the rationalization of the kitchen" (*daidokoro no gōrika*) was necessary. This required "the spiritual improvement of you who are in charge of the kitchen." Put simply, "we cannot [lift the gold embargo] until your way of living—Japan's way of living—is put into good order."[22]

In line with this idea, Inoue proceeded to anatomize "the bloating of a kitchen economy near destruction," retracing the familiar moral history of Japan's gaudy world-war boom and postwar comeuppance:

> If we speak of Japan's national polity [*kokutai*] or of its race, I think we can be proud of that in the whole world. But in terms of wealth, Japan [before the European war] was a country so poor that it almost lacked the qualifications for independence. However, the European War began in 1914 and Japan rose to quite an enviable position. Japan made an immense sum of money, to an extent that you cannot understand by words alone, acquiring the great amount of four billion yen. Up to then, Japan had been borrowing money from foreign countries every year and was buying more from foreign countries than it sold to them.
>
> . . . With that, from the standpoint of the economy, Japan was able to become an independent country for the first time. . . . I was happy that for the first time we had created the qualifications to leap out into the world.

But, Inoue continued, "if we look at the situation since then, Japan ended up luxuriously spending the money earned. Now, without one penny of [our] money remaining overseas, even if we want to borrow money abroad, we cannot even borrow well, and the four billion yen that we had overseas is all spent." That is, Japan's overseas specie holdings had been exhausted, and the country faced an international credit crisis. Spendthrift politicians and wasteful domestic policies—Inoue hardly needed to mention the Seiyūkai by name—had played their part, but "what the government spends is small compared to what you [women] spend," and "women's sin" had done even more to bring the country to its present "sad and ruined state."[23] Japan's housewives were thus directly responsible for Japan's national predicament: "The result of your unreasonable consumption and unreasonable luxury is that, after all of the pains to rise to a good position, Japan is now even worse off than when we started. . . . Today, facing the world, in every sense, Japan's credit is falling to the ground. The biggest cause behind this is the fact that women's understanding in regard to the economy is extremely slight."[24] The parallels were simple and clear: The new government was setting its financial house in order, and each household must do the same. Individual effort and sacrifice were required to rescue Japan's global situation.

For ten years Hamaguchi Osachi had been calling for deflation in order to stabilize the Japanese people spiritually. Through the ensuing decade, retail prices had fallen 15 percent and wholesale prices 35 percent from their 1920 highs. Farm prices had fallen even further, putting Japanese farmers into a severe debt-deflation squeeze. Yet after nine years of deflation and chronic recession, it seemed to Inoue that "luxurious living and the worsening of people's thought" had only grown worse:

> These days, [people's] thought is worsening in various ways, and you are always worrying about your children. Spiritually, Japanese people are gradually becoming degenerate. Much of this arises from the inconsistencies and irrationalities in the economy. Namely, the fact that people cannot get money, cannot get loans, yet still want to live their former luxurious lives is closely connected to Japan's spiritual decay and worsening of thought.[25]

The suspension of the gold standard had buffered the Japanese people from reality:

> Because it came about after the sixth year of Taishō [1917] that gold could not be taken to foreign countries, you do not feel anything. That is, although you take on debts and consume irrationally, in front of your own eyes, the gold coins have not been reduced even by one. Things bought from foreign countries are still increasing as before. Thus, in front of your own eyes you do not understand anything. However, there is one thing you must understand. That is, to buy things, you need money; accordingly we have paid with the money that as an expedient is kept overseas, and today this money is all gone.[26]

It was Inoue's task to make concrete to the Japanese people their own poverty in the cold light cast by the international standard that really counted. The lifting of the embargo on gold exports would make visible the true situation. With the broken link between the Japanese yen and gold restored, Japan's trade deficits would, following Hume's classic model, automatically cause gold to flow out of the country. Gold outflows, in turn, would mean fewer yen in the hands of consumers, which would bring down prices and force up interest rates, thereby bringing national accounts back into balance.

The logic of Inoue's analysis—the old balanced-budget verities that would be jettisoned in the Keynesian revolution—was commonsensical and readily understandable: the concerns of household budgeting were no different from the concerns of public finance. Even though most people had not lived luxuriously during the boom—many had suffered real hardships from the inflation—all were aware of the extravagant excesses for which the newly rich *narikin* were famous. Spendthrift ways had brought Japan to the door of the poorhouse, and only thrift and hard work could remedy the situation. The picture Inoue Junnosuke painted for the Japanese people was one of a nation trudging painfully up a long, steep hill in the summer heat, wasting time and energy by seeking short cuts that turned into dead ends: "Even if you sweat, [retrenchment] is the

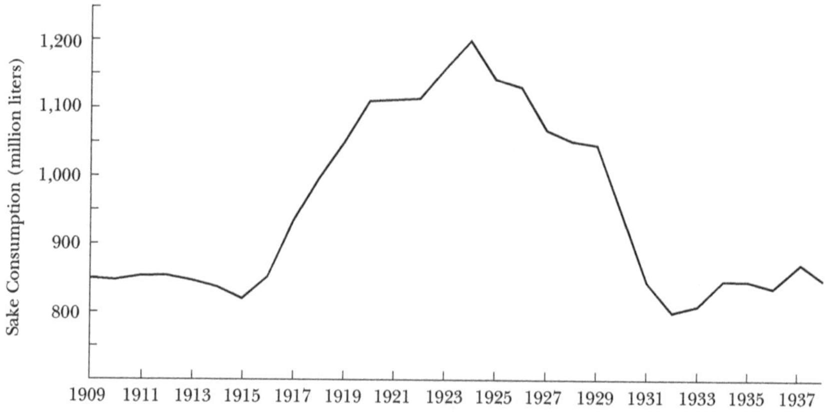

FIG. 7. Drunken boom, sober bust: the ups and downs of sake consumption, 1909–1938.
SOURCE: LTES 6: 208.

right road . . . even if it's bone-breaking, it's the surest and shortest road."[27]

Conventional economic morality plays of the sort outlined by Inoue have frequently been invoked to explain Japan's chronic postbubble recession of the 1990s, and such stories have been mocked by the Keynesian-minded economist Paul Krugman as the "hangover theory" of depression.[28] In fact, whichever may be the direction of causality, Inoue's binge-and-bust story appears to have been as concrete as it was metaphoric. The party spirit was widespread during the inflationary boom, if we judge from the consumption of sake, which grew by 35 percent between 1915 to 1920, to some twenty liters per person per year. Despite the 1920 depression, consumption levels did not fall back, and the sake flowed freely to the end of the 1920s (figure 7). Subsequently, the stabilization depression championed by Inoue Junnosuke appears to have been a nationally sobering experience, as sake consumption fell back (to some twelve liters per capita) in the 1930s.[29] These ups and downs of alcohol consumption thus trace the movements of a great business cycle.

In fact, for consumption in general, when the boom-bust cycle of 1915–22 was over and done, per capita consumption standards had improved considerably, and these new standards were substantially maintained through the 1920s. "I'm definitely not telling you to reduce what you eat and endure to the point of hunger," Inoue assured his female listeners in 1929. But per capita spending on food, which comprised more than half of all personal consumption spending, had already fallen somewhat since the mid-1920s (in line with the decrease of consumption of sake, tea, and tobacco). Under Inoue's austerity policy, spending on food fell further, from a high of ¥102 per person in 1925, to less than ¥93 in 1932 (both reckoned in terms of constant 1934–36 prices).[30]

Inoue's austerity drive also opened up a great debate on the meaning of consumer demand in a modern economy. An argument very different from Inoue's, counterintuitive and foreshadowing a new kind of postdepression economics, was put forth by Takahashi Korekiyo, Ishibashi Tanzan, and others, who argued that in the face of the economic crisis, instead of further constraining domestic demand, the government should actually spend money more freely.

THE GOLD STANDARD AS SEEN FROM THE GEISHA HOUSE

As Inoue Junnosuke took the lead in the Hamaguchi government's nationwide campaign to evangelize for the international gold standard, Takahashi took an increasingly clear counterposition. Takahashi's personal break with Inoue also dated from Inoue's joining the Minseitō cabinet, which according to Takahashi was the last time that the two men met personally:

> It must have been a day or two before the formation of the Hamaguchi cabinet [on July 2, 1929] when Mr. Inoue came by car to see me. . . . He reported to me, "When I conferred with Mr. Hamaguchi, we agreed that in order to reform the present business world, we must force through the lifting of the gold embargo by way of a retrenchment policy, and it was decided that I should undertake to be finance minister." I just listened to his explanation, but when we parted I told him, "Thinking of the nation's future, you probably intend to go forward at all costs in order to accomplish your beliefs, but do not forget to walk straight on the just road."[31]

The ambiguity of Takahashi's statement and the suggestion of disagreement—in the context of an essay memorializing Takahashi's longtime junior colleague shortly after his shocking death—communicate by what they fail to say.

Takahashi had never rejected the gold standard on principle, and his opposition to the Minseitō policy developed in stages. In the autumn of 1929, Takahashi began publicly to criticize Inoue's policy, insisting in a September 1929 magazine article that Japan must follow an independent national course in the matter. "There are those who say that because other countries have lifted the gold embargo Japan must do the same, but the conditions of each country are dissimilar and one cannot claim that they are all the same." Nevertheless, Takahashi concluded on the note of household economy, in tune with the refrain of Hamaguchi and Inoue, noting the admirable example of economizing and using only made-in-Japan goods that had been set by the imperial family. If such an attitude spread among Japan's housewives, it would be safe to lift the gold embargo.[32]

Inoue himself was at pains to demonstrate that his policy was the path of true national independence, which, he concluded in a mass-circulation tract published in September 1929, meant living within one's national means: "If we look at the current situation of each country, they are rather exhausted due to the European war. . . . In such a situation, it is unthinkable that Japan's current depression should be solved by power coming from foreign countries. If we do not break out of today's situation by our own power, it cannot be done. Other than based on one's own power, one's own effort of thrift, there is no other way."[33] At the same time, Inoue awaited Morgan and Company's decision regarding the credit that would enable Japan's return to the gold standard.

Takahashi took a sharper line in the wake of the New York stock market crash, pointedly criticizing "those who become ecstatic saying things such as, because the exchange against America has gone up, or because English and American interest rates have gone down [that is, after the stock-market crash], it has become convenient to lift the gold embargo." The most important thing was to decide the matter independently and to prepare independently for lifting the gold embargo by "establishing the foundation of manufacturing, shipping, and other industries." In terms of international borrowing and lending, Japan must be lending more than it was borrowing. Once this foundation was established, the gold embargo could be lifted. In the absence of such preparation, "lifting the gold embargo thanks to foreign countries" was "a mistaken notion that does not consider the country's permanent interests."[34]

At stake here was a crucial question of the sequencing of developmental and monetary opening measures. Takahashi was arguing that national strength and independence required industrial development first, and only then monetary and financial integration on the basis of a strong balance-of-payments position. In effect, Inoue argued for the opposite sequence—monetary and financial integration first—as global creditor institutions such as the IMF continue to do today.[35] These were two opposing notions of where Japan's national strength lay: in expanding production or in thrift and self-control. This was the old contrast between the expansion and consolidation policies and, at another level, an entrepreneur's versus a banker's vision.

A key aspect of Takahashi's originality was his appreciation of the problem of demand in the economy as a whole. Inoue had posed the decision before the Japanese people as one of luxury and excess versus responsibility and restraint. Instead, argued Takahashi, it was a choice between luxury *and* prosperity on one hand and austerity and poverty on the other. In his criticism of "the so-called retrenchment policy," Takahashi began disputing one of Inoue's major premises, insisting that one must differentiate the logic of the national economy from that of an individual family economy. At the national level, Takahashi said, consumption equals demand, and demand equals productivity. To the degree that demand decreases, national productivity also decreases.[36] (Takahashi was writing at a time of industrial overcapacity and widespread underemployment, when increased consumer demand would have meant increased capacity utilization.)

To show how this was so, Takahashi explained the social utility of luxury, in a passage that has been quoted many times since. "To put the matter in still simpler terms," wrote Takahashi, perhaps recalling his own youthful adventures as an attendant for an apprentice geisha,

> suppose someone goes to a geisha house [*machiai*] and spends two thousand yen by doing things like hiring a geisha and eating luxurious dishes. From the standpoint of order and morality, we don't want to have such things—but just as an example, let us ask how the money used in this way is scattered about. The portion that was spent on food will become part of the salary of the cooks and such; and the costs of the fish, meat, vegetables, seasonings, and other ingredients, as well as the cost of transporting them, will all be paid out as part of the money earned by merchants. Of this, a proportion goes to moisten the purses of farmers, fishermen, and other producers. Moreover, the farmers, fishermen, merchants, and others who receive this money will use it for their own food, clothing, housing, and other expenses. As for the money paid for the geisha's fee, part of that will pass through her hands and be spent on food, taxes, clothing, cosmetics, and other expenses.

Thus, the money spent at a geisha house "passes from hand to hand," working "even twenty or thirty times" in various branches of industry. But "if on the contrary this person should now stop going to the geisha house . . . speaking from the standpoint of individual economics, for the person involved it is truly healthy to save ¥2,000. But for the economy of the country, the other course is desirable. . . . This is where personal and national economies differ."[37] This "twenty or thirty times" we might consider as the "Takahashi multiplier." The idea was integral to his vision of a demand-led economic recovery.

Takahashi naturally followed his parable with the disclaimer that, to illustrate his point, he was giving an extreme example of the most wasteful of expenditures and certainly was not advocating trips to geisha houses. But disclaimers or not, Takahashi's pro-spending line placed him a long way from the almost Confucian moralism of Inoue and Hamaguchi. Takahashi concluded by returning to the question of government-spending policy, describing the deserted construction sites he had seen lately around Tokyo—a consequence of Inoue's budget cuts—and explaining the negative multiplier effects of budget cuts, which exacerbated recession and unemployment.[38]

In the long history of economic thought before Keynes, Inoue's idea of the virtue of thrift was the commonplace view. Views such as Takahashi's of the virtue of spending—or of the virtue of vice—were not only rare but morally suspect and heterodox in the extreme. More jarringly, Takahashi Korekiyo, a proponent of Japan's "beautiful customs" of paternalistic employment and loyal service, drew his example from the industry most highly marked by the persistence of feudalistic, semislave conditions for its female workers.[39] Whereas Inoue had addressed women as consumers, in this "service" industry, women themselves were the objects of male consumption. The ¥2,000 that Takahashi mentioned as the cost of an evening's entertainment was more money than most Japanese families saw in an entire year, and the example was hardly calculated to appeal to the sensibilities of Japan's housewives.[40] In recognizing the importance of demand, economist Takahashi Kamekichi made an argument similar to Takahashi Korekiyo's, as did textile magnate Mutō Sanji and journalist Ishibashi Tanzan. But Inoue's "monetarist" policy would be pursued to its logical conclusion before "Keynesian" alternatives were taken up.

Meanwhile, great changes were underway at the centers of global finance to which Inoue was proposing to yoke Japan more tightly.

"THE HIGHEST BASES OF SOUNDNESS AND CREDIT"

As the New York stock market cruised at record heights in the summer of 1929, Americanism and global economic liberalism appeared triumphant. At the level of ideals, war had been renounced as an instrument of national policy in the Kellogg-Briand pact, which was ratified by forty-five nations including Japan and proclaimed by President Herbert Hoover on July 24, 1928. Thomas Lamont's vision of a world ruled by ideas rather than force seemed a step closer to fulfillment. More concretely, naval arms-limitation talks involving Japan, Britain, the United States, France, and Italy were scheduled to open in London in January 1930, to continue the Washington naval arms-limitation process of 1921–22. With Japan's impending return to gold, the reconstructed international monetary order envisioned in Genoa in 1922 would be practically complete. It also seemed that the gold standard might finally be universalized, as, at the invitation of the Chinese government, a "Commission of Financial Experts" led by Edwin Kemmerer conducted a study of China's monetary system in 1928–29 and wrote up a plan to modernize and unify China's currency system by means of a gold-exchange standard.[41]

Japan's own retrenchment policy had Morgan's nod of approval; Lamont reported to the other Morgan partners on September 11, 1929, that Inoue was "doing very well," having cut the budget and promised further cuts next year. "The whole thing is shaping up to a return to the gold standard in the early months of 1930."[42] But Inoue's foreign friends were beginning to have troubles of their own.

Across the peripheral zones of the world economy, signs of a renewed global downturn were already apparent. World farm prices, after recovering from the 1920 depression, had begun to slide again after 1925, and a worldwide agricultural depression had set in. The American-led overseas lending boom was also short-lived, as U.S. overseas loans dropped off very sharply in mid 1928, coincident with the rise of the New York stock market bubble. As the New York stock market sucked in money capital, interest rates increased across Europe. In Germany the stock market had already turned downward in April 1927, at the time of Japan's great financial crisis, and in 1928 Germany's downturn deepened into depression. Depression also began in Australia, New Zealand, Argentina, Brazil, and other peripheral commodity-exporting countries.[43]

Higher interest rates in New York threatened Japan's plans to lift the gold embargo, presenting the danger that once gold convertibility was restored, Japanese funds would flow out to New York—a fear that Japanese overseas financial commissioner Haraguchi expressed to Lamont. Lamont reassured the Japanese government: he "personally" had "definite knowledge" of the English, German, Italian, Belgian, and French returns to the gold standard; especially in France and Germany, an inflow of foreign funds had followed the return to gold.[44] In fact, the Japanese fears proved to be very well founded.

On October 17, 1929, after weeks of intensive report writing and a long presentation to the cabinet as well as an explanation to the emperor, Tsushima Juichi left again for New York to negotiate with Morgan and Company for the credit that would permit Japan's return to gold.[45] While he was en route, the deepening world crisis reached the financial center of the world economy. The New York stock market had reached a peak in September, and in October, stock prices began a series of abrupt declines. After several record-breaking days of panicky selling, the greatest fall yet came on the morning of "Black Thursday," October 24, 1929, which would be the canonical date for the opening of the Great Depression of the 1930s. At midday on October 24, Thomas Lamont, again at the center of things, hosted an emergency meeting of America's most powerful bankers at Morgan and Company headquarters at the corner of Wall and Broad Streets. Speaking for Wall Street, Lamont then told reporters, "There has been a little distress selling on the Stock Exchange," describing it in an aviation metaphor as a technical problem of "air holes" arising in the market process. The bankers put up money to buy shares and attempt to halt the panic selling, and after Lamont's comments, it did seem briefly that they had succeeded in placing a floor under the price falls.[46] But stock prices continued to slide.

Tsushima Juichi was on the transcontinental train from Vancouver, British

Columbia, when he heard the news of the stock market panic. His confidence fell concerning the upcoming credit negotiations. Arriving in New York on November 1, he found Lamont and other top bankers scrambling to work out countermeasures to the crisis. Lamont joked that Tsushima had brought the stock market confusion with him. None of the actors involved yet perceived the real gravity of the American crisis—or the seismic shift in the financial relations of world power that was now taking place. To Tsushima also, America's boom still appeared very solidly based.[47] In fact, the stock market crash even seemed to ease the way for Japan's return to gold. Inoue Junnosuke saw the deflation of the American bubble as opportune—"even calling it divine providence" (*ten'yū*), Takahashi Korekiyo later charged—as a harbinger, not of the approaching collapse of the whole gold-standard edifice, but rather of lower interest rates in the United States, which would enable Japanese borrowing to support the restored gold standard.[48] In the same way, German borrowers anticipated that the end of the stock market bubble would enable American funds to return to Germany and ease the financial squeeze there.[49]

In these circumstances, Tsushima met on Monday, November 4, with Lamont and Leffingwell to begin the final negotiations for the credit. Lamont advised that London be brought into the deal, and parallel negotiations were conducted there. Tsushima found the negotiations extremely trying. At the outset, he was interrogated as to why, despite Morgan and Company's warning, Japan as a country with a depreciated currency wanted to restore the yen to the old prewar par. Tsushima's answer was, in effect, "Trust Inoue." Tsushima was also painfully conscious of the possible consequences of failing to obtain the credit. When the Belgian government had decided to return to the gold standard in 1926, the U.S. and British bankers with whom it was negotiating (again, with Lamont in the lead) had been dissatisfied with the center-left government's budgetary priorities and had broken off negotiations for the credit, causing the Belgian cabinet to fall. Tsushima feared that failure on his part would bring down the Japanese cabinet. He explained in detail how the new cabinet had made emergency cuts in the 1929 budget, but the American bankers nevertheless held off on signing the contract until the 1930 budget was decided. On November 9 the cabinet held an extraordinary meeting to decide the 1930 budget, which featured a further round of retrenchment. Morgan and Company then agreed to the contract.[50]

Thus, in the final analysis, Japan's lifting of the gold embargo depended on the decision of the "Morgan-led banking group" with whom Tsushima was negotiating. Finance Minister Inoue said as much at the time, indicating to the newspapers that he was awaiting the word from New York so that he could announce the lifting of the gold embargo.[51]

Inoue also appears to have been waiting for the report of his friend Ikeda

Shigeaki. On Ikeda's return from America, Inoue told him that the lifting of the gold embargo had been decided for January but that before announcing it, he wanted to hear what Ikeda thought about foreign opinion. Ikeda assured him that Lamont and others were solidly behind Japan's action. This at least was the version of the story later told by Ikeda, but it is corroborated by Mori Kengo, who told Lamont at the time that Ikeda was "the greatest man in Japan's business world." It was on Ikeda's assurance and suggestion, Mori said, that Hamaguchi and Inoue made the final decision as to when and how to lift the gold embargo.[52] To anticipate the end of the story: it was also Ikeda's Mitsui Bank that would lead the speculative attack that brought down Japan's restored gold standard two years later.

In the meantime, anticipating the yen's appreciation to the old par of $0.4985, the biggest Japanese banks, led by Mitsui Bank, were betting the other way, borrowing foreign currency abroad that they then sold for yen. On the back of this yen-buying speculation, the yen speedily rose from $0.44 in July 1929, when the Hamaguchi cabinet took office, to more than $0.48 in November.

Inoue's quicker-than-expected success in raising the yen to near-par also meant that he felt constrained to act quickly, before currency speculators could doubt him and begin selling off yen again. Feeling pressed by intense public concern, the Hamaguchi government therefore planned to announce the lifting of the gold embargo on November 16. Troubled by the ongoing stock market crisis, the American bankers asked them to wait three days. Then, on November 19, Morgan and Company cabled Inoue that the "American group"—J. P. Morgan and Company; Kuhn, Loeb and Company; National City Bank of New York; and First National Bank of New York—had established a credit of $25 million "for the purpose of yen stabilization" (that is, for defense against speculative attacks). In London the British group simultaneously established a credit of £5 million.[53] The agreement for the credit was signed on November 20, and on November 21 the Japanese government publicly announced that the gold embargo would be lifted on January 11, 1930.[54] The U.S. Federal Reserve Bank and Bank of England made public statements in support of Japan's gold standard, showing the "material and moral support" of international financial circles.[55] Morgan and Company, writing to Inoue on November 19, praised the Japanese government's well-coached action as "still another evidence of the determination of the Japanese government and people" to conduct their currency and finances "upon the highest bases of soundness and credit."[56] Those "highest bases" were none other than the Wall Street banks themselves: for Japanese finance, New York now stood at the financial center of the world, and Japanese finance stood in a satellite relation to it.

The heads of Japan's banking world, led by Ikeda Shigeaki, also declared their support, and Ikeda said, in effect, that there was no danger of an outflow of gold following the lifting of the embargo. Takahashi Korekiyo gave his own grudging support, saying "now that the government has decided to lift the embargo, it is no longer necessary to debate its merits and demerits." All political parties should cooperate in this national policy, and Japan should strive all the more in the sphere of economics, as a first-class country, "to maintain a position not inferior to the [Western] powers."[57]

In May 1926, speaking for himself to an elite audience at Kyoto University, Inoue had frankly recognized that a return to the gold standard at the old par would do to the Japanese silk industry what it had already done to the British coal industry—induce a depression.[58] When he now, as finance minister, touted the gold standard as a panacea to mass audiences, Inoue was less forthcoming about the costs involved, but he did not hide the fact that he was subjecting the country to a deflationary shock. Nonetheless, he said, the only way to break out of the chronic depression of the 1920s was a deliberate step further into depression:

> In such economically unstable times, the Government is retrenching its finances in preparation for removal of the gold embargo; if the people in general will economize on consumption, prices will go down, probably leading to still more depression. However, today's situation is a completely unprecedented depression. It is a depression in which we cannot foresee when recovery might come. If we leave matters as they now rest, we will slide deeper and deeper into the depths of depression. Somehow, we must break out of this situation.[59]

The reintroduction of the gold standard was intended to be that decisive break. The year 1930, Inoue declared in his New Year's greeting published in the newspapers, "will be a year of profound meaning in the history of our nation's business world that will never be forgotten."[60]

ELEVEN

Opening the Door to a Hurricane, 1930–1931

On January 10, 1930, speaking at a luncheon party that he hosted at London's Savoy Hotel, Overseas Financial Commissioner Tsushima Juichi spoke to his elite metropolitan audience of global time and global money: "You, my British friends, may not appreciate [it] so fully as we do, since your London is situated on the Zero Meridian of Greenwich which sets the time of the world," but in fact, nine time zones to the east, it was almost tomorrow in Japan. "In other words, Gentlemen, before we leave this room, the embargo on the export of gold from Japan will be removed." Japan's moment also meant the completion of a global undertaking: "Now that Japan has placed its currency on a gold standard basis, the solution of the world-wide problem of post-war currency stabilization is virtually accomplished."[1]

Former prime minister Wakatsuki Reijirō was also in London, for the first time since he served there as overseas financial commissioner twenty-two years earlier. He had come as Japan's plenipotentiary representative to the naval disarmament conference, and he spoke at the same luncheon, repeating the idea that Japan's return to the gold standard had furthered the cause of "worldwide economic rehabilitation and stabilization."[2] The same message was reported simultaneously to the New York financial community via an article in the *Wall Street Journal* by Kashiwagi Hideshige of the Yokohama Specie Bank: gold resumption meant the return to the "status quo ante" and, economically and financially speaking, "the abolition of the very last of many war measures adopted by the Japanese government during the great war."[3] Remarkably, twelve years after the conclusion of the great European war, in which Japan's military involvement had been marginal, the great concern was still postwar stabilization.

Back in Tokyo, Inoue Junnosuke and Hamaguchi Osachi were occupied with a busy round of celebratory events. The financial and commodity markets took the news in stride, and, as Prime Minister Hamaguchi recorded in his diary, "everything is tranquil and proceeding smoothly, without the least disturbance. Relief. The markets are tranquil, stocks are holding firm. In the cafeteria, champagne was uncorked and we raised a toast."[4] To commemorate the occasion, the government had a special medal featuring the images of Hamaguchi and Inoue struck at the Osaka mint. Inoue's opponent Mutō Sanji, who "was surprised at how they honored themselves," claimed that there were even credulous people who bought the medal and enshrined it on their *kamidana* (family shrine) as if it were "the coming of the god of wealth."[5]

It was also a busy Saturday morning for employees at the Bank of Japan's main office in Tokyo, where from early in the morning, crowds of people gathered, waiting to exchange their Bank of Japan notes for the new gold coins.

THE OPEN DOOR

Amid the celebration over Japan's return to financial normalcy, Inoue again warned the Japanese people what automatic adjustment actually meant: the "unnatural economic situation" that had persisted since 1917 was now over. In effect, there was no longer a difference between internal and external money. If Japan ran a trade deficit, it would be paid for in gold, directly contracting the currency and causing recession. If a great amount of gold suddenly flowed out, it would cause chaos in the business world. To prevent this, the only path was for the government to continue its fiscal retrenchment and for the people to continue to limit their consumption.[6]

To prevent a catastrophic outflow of specie, Inoue had also arranged, when he announced the lifting of the gold embargo on November 21, to have Japanese banks declare their "moral support" for the gold yen and promise to refrain from shipping gold out of Japan until the gold standard was well established. Thus, the Ministry of Finance had been able to assure Morgan and Company that there was no fear of a great gold outflow, in view, "above all, [of] the full understanding secured with the leading banks to the effect that no undue attempt to disturb the market by sudden withdrawal of fund[s] held at home be made."[7]

Despite these provisions, as soon as Inoue and Hamaguchi opened the Bank of Japan's gold window on January 11, 1930, a kind of gold rush began. For days, people continued to line up outside of the Bank of Japan building in Nihonbashi to change their paper yen notes for gold. By the end of January the bank handled almost 19,000 of these personal conversions, distributing a total of ¥1.6 million gold yen.[8] More significant were the financial institutions that now lined up to cash in their paper yen. Because the government had asked the Japanese banks not to buy dollars in excess of their trade and investment needs, truly free trade in gold was for Japan's foreign "depositors." Those foreign banks now scrambled to convert their yen notes into gold.

At 4:00 P.M. on the afternoon of January 21, the *Empress of Canada* left Kōbe loaded with ¥12.5 million in gold yen coins, the first gold shipment under the new monetary regime. Of this, ¥11.5 million was being shipped by the Kōbe branch of the National City Bank of New York, and the remaining ¥1 million by the branches of the two Dutch banks operating in Japan. At Yokohama the *Empress* picked up another ¥3.4 million from the National City Bank and Nederlandsch-Indische Handelsbank and then turned east for San Francisco. Further shipments followed in quick succession, as the speculators who had earlier bid up the yen now took their profits. By the end of the month, foreign banks, led by National City Bank of New York, had converted ¥40 million into gold, and Bank of Japan gold holdings had fallen by ¥128 million, or about 12 percent.[9]

The Mitsui, Mitsubishi, and Sumitomo banks demanded to be let in on the action. After the formation of the Hamaguchi cabinet in July 1929, the Japanese banks had borrowed foreign currency abroad and then bought yen in anticipation of the yen's appreciation—now they too wanted to take their profits.[10] The government permitted Ikeda Shigeaki's Mitsui Bank to ship out ¥4 million in gold as early as January 30. In the first three months of the year, the three zaibatsu banks converted a total of ¥76 million and then stopped again.[11]

In fact, the Bank of Japan had anticipated such an outflow and had attempted to keep track of the speculative yen buying in 1929, calculating that ¥100 million to ¥140 million would flow out when the gold embargo was lifted.[12] Bank officials were surprised by the outflow's continued volume, but subsequently the yen exchange did stabilize. The ¥100 million credit negotiated with the American and British groups did not need to be drawn on during its one-year term. Nonetheless, ¥100 million in backing began to appear small next to the amounts begin withdrawn from the country. By the end of the year, gold shipments totaled ¥309 million as against ¥9 million in inflows (table 5). Foreign banks accounted for 70 percent of the institutional (*ōguchi*) gold conversions in 1930. Of these, the most active was National City Bank of New York. A member of the American group, with close financial links to Morgan and Company, National City Bank had itself participated in the credit to support the gold standard. It then converted and shipped out ¥100 million on its own account. Already, this might begin to look like having employed the wolves to guard the sheep. Takahashi Korekiyo later charged that Inoue had given control of Japan's foreign-exchange market to the foreign banks.[13]

As the Bank of Japan's gold reserves shrunk, the note issue shrunk accordingly, contributing to the contraction of the overall level of economic activity. Well prepared by the great propaganda campaign, the public initially reacted positively to the new policy. The Imperial Diet reopened on January 21 and the government dissolved it on the same day, scheduling a general election for February 20. In the election campaign, the Minseitō ran on the same program of thrift and rectitude promulgated in the Public and Private Retrenchment Campaign. The Seiyūkai could not make its charges stick that the Minseitō policy was bringing about a recession. The result was a great victory for the Minseitō, which took 273 seats as against 174 for the Seiyūkai.

With the successful conclusion of the London naval conference and the correspondingly favorable inclination of Anglo-American financial markets toward Japan, negotiations got underway for re-funding the 4 percent sterling bonds of 1905 that were coming due in January 1931.[14] This was the operation for which Morgan and Company had insisted that Japan's return to the gold standard was a precondition. Japan's gold embargo had been lifted, but in the context of difficulties created by the deepening depression, new conditions appeared.

The Tokyo Electric Light Company (Tokyo Denkō), Japan's largest utility company, had been the greatest overseas corporate borrower of the decade and had been reorganized in 1928 with Morgan backing. It had also fallen into difficulties in the repayment of its foreign debt. In early May 1930 Lamont bluntly warned Inoue that economic depression was no excuse for late payments—after all, Japan's induced depression had been expected by both Inoue and himself. If the situation were not remedied, Lamont indicated that the refunding credits would be delayed, finally softening the threat with a characteristically diplomatic slide:

> As to the general situation in Japan, we fully recognize that the deflation and industrial discomfort which always follows [*sic*] the adoption of a sound money policy were to be expected; in fact they were fully anticipated by your good-self and by those of us who joined in the Credit last January and I am glad to take this opportunity to congratulate you again upon the vigour and courage with which you have continued to meet the situation in a way to comply fully with the expectations of your best friends.[15]

Lamont repeated the message to Tsushima Juichi: the issuance of new loans to the Japanese government hinged on regular loan repayments by Tokyo Electric Light Company.[16]

Morgan and Company's conditions were fulfilled when a reorganization plan for Tokyo Electric Light Company was signed on May 9. On the same day, the agreement was finalized to convert the 1905 Japanese sterling and dollar bonds into a new issue of some ¥260 million in 5½ percent bonds, floated in London and New York. Lamont again congratulated Inoue on manfully meeting things head on, without trying "to disguise or soften the situation."[17] Inoue himself recognized that the current circumstances did not favor Japanese borrowing.

In Japan the conditions exacted by Inoue's "best friends" made it seem to many people that again, as at the London naval conference, Japan was receiving second-class treatment. Mutō Sanji said the whole operation was unnecessary—about half of the sterling bonds had come to be held by the Bank of Japan and the Yokohama Specie Bank, so redemption would in any case have cost only ¥150 million in specie. He called Inoue's bond reconversion a failure—Japan had traded 4 percent bonds for higher-interest bonds, "just like an inferior country." Newspapers even called the new loan the "second national humiliation bonds" (*daini no kokujoku kōsai*)—the first having been the high-interest postearthquake loans negotiated by Inoue Junnosuke in 1924. Because of the higher yield of the new bonds, London quotations of other Japanese bonds fell.[18]

From his side, Lamont now viewed relations with Japan as "excellent," as he told the new American ambassador to Japan, W. Cameron Forbes, a Harvard classmate and former governor general of the Philippines, who had just returned from a mission to Haiti to evaluate the U.S. military occupation and financial stabilization policy there. Japan's foreign policy, Lamont briefed Forbes, was now based on the two cardinal principles of friendship with the United States and reconciliation with China.[19] But the effects of the pro-American financial policy were only beginning to deepen and ramify.

THE HURRICANE

Writing early in 1929, before the installation of the Minseitō cabinet, Ishibashi Tanzan declared that if a government were to make the great mistake of lifting the gold embargo at the old parity, within six months or a year, "our financial world would probably be visited once more by a great confusion comparable to that of spring 1927."[20] The events of 1930 largely bore out Ishibashi's judgment, although this time it was not the banks but the real economy that was at the center of the storm.

Mutō Sanji, now converted to Ishibashi's new parity view, came to hold a like view of Inoue's high-yen policy. In August 1930, in a mass-circulation paperback book entitled *The Illusion of Finance Minister Inoue,* published by Ishibashi Tanzan's Tōyō Keizai Shinpō Company, Mutō wrote: "In a time of such drastic changes coming from outside, Finance Minister Inoue's careless and unprepared lifting of the gold embargo at the old parity has thrown our industry into difficulties and is exactly like deliberately leaving the door open in a storm." The willful failure to protect Japan's economy from the storms of the world economy, said Mutō, was the fault of Inoue Junnosuke, "the person who left the door open."[21]

Inoue's "open door" policy placed Japan's monetary system into unmediated communication with the gold-based U.S. financial system as of January 11, 1930. Coming in the full rush of collapsing world commodity prices that followed the New York stock market crash, the effects were disastrous. In Japan the depression of 1929–32 is known as the "Shōwa panic." Retrospectively, one can date its beginning from the inauguration of the Hamaguchi cabinet in July 1929 and its announcement of austerity measures in preparation for the resumption of gold payments.[22] Severe price deflation was the outstanding feature of the crisis.

Deflation had already lasted ten years, and after the sharp price declines of 1920–21, wholesale prices descended in two further stepwise declines, in 1924–27 and in 1929–31—that is, during the two eras of "negative" policy conducted by the Kenseikai and Minseitō party cabinets. The deflation of share prices had begun in the first half of 1929. Commodity prices also began to slide from the beginning of 1929, and with the stock market crash in New York and the Hamaguchi cabinet's announcement of the definite return to the gold standard in November, the slide turned into a dive. A look at the aggregate wholesale price indices, given in figure 8, shows a single precipitous slide from that point until January 1931, when prices temporarily leveled off. At the most extreme point in the deflation, during the twelve months from November 1929 to October 1930, the wholesale price index fell 24 percent. It can also be seen that the magnitude of the wholesale price deflation in Japan, while slightly greater, was very close to that in Britain and the United States. Export commodity prices fell further in Japan than in any other major country.

A closer look reveals that the deflation came in waves, hitting different sectors in turn. The first wave came in late 1929, before the return to gold convertibility, as cotton yarn prices fell sharply from October 1929 through the first half of 1930, causing great distress in Japan's second-largest export industry. A second deflationary wave hit in the spring and early summer of 1930, as prices for raw silk, Japan's number-one export, collapsed and the yen soared against the Chinese tael. A third wave hit in the fall of 1930, when rice prices abruptly collapsed. Prices subsequently stabilized at the beginning of 1931, but deflation resumed later in the year.

Seen from the side of the domestic economy, the deflation reflected a vicious cycle of falling demand, production curtailment, and wage cuts and layoffs, leading to further declines in demand and intensified at each stage of the process by the government's various deflation and rationalization measures. The Hamaguchi cabinet had intended to compensate for the anticipated decline in domestic demand by selling more goods abroad. In line with Hume's classic theory of the balance of trade, domestic price deflation was supposed to promote exports, and increased exports would solve Japan's trade imbalance and bring gold into the country. But amidst general

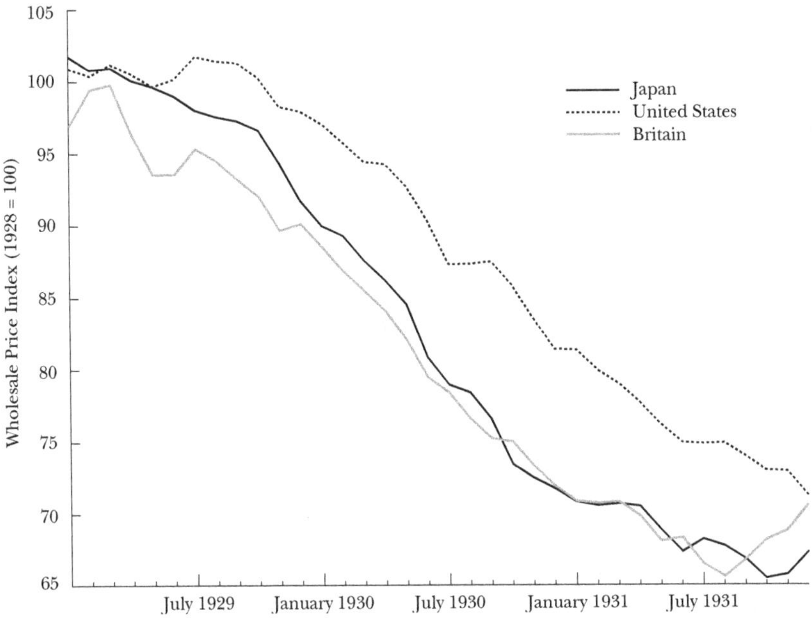

FIG. 8. The deflationary downdraft: wholesale price indices for Japan, the United States, and Britain, January 1929–December 1931.
SOURCE: E. B. Schumpeter 1940: appendix table IV (book pocket).

deflation in the gold bloc—and global deflationary tendencies were magnified each time the membership of the gold bloc expanded—the only way to achieve this goal was to outdeflate other countries. It is notable that price declines were sharpest in sectors closely connected to the international economy, while prices for domestically produced, domestically consumed goods such as foodstuffs did not fall as much.

Japan's deflation also represented the hydraulic logic of the gold standard. In the first year after the gold embargo was lifted, the Bank of Japan's specie reserve fell by about ¥250 million, and the Bank of Japan's note issue fell by ¥150 to ¥200 million, to a level of about ¥1 billion.[23] An increase in loans by the Bank of Japan meant that the note issue did not fall as much as the specie reserve did—in fact, the bands of the gold standard were already being stretched at this point—but the decrease in specie was largely reflected in a decrease in the currency.[24] As Inoue had explained it, the gold coins left the country, and the people of Japan now saw it with their own eyes.

Falling prices created immediate losses for all those who held stocks of goods. The effects of deflation on profits came in the reverse order of the effects of inflation: under rapid inflation, businesses can with little effort sell at higher prices than they bought at. Those with stocks of goods on hand, or crops in the field, will tend to gain. Under rapid deflation, the losses caused by lower sale prices tend to precede the advantage to be gained from lower input prices. When deflation was extreme, as in 1930, farmers and businessmen sold at a substantial loss. This is a story that is not told by macroeconomic indicators when nominal national income estimates are simply inflated into so-called "real" estimates.

This situation was, as in other countries, experienced in Japan as a crisis of overproduction, and Japanese industry responded with cartelization and output cuts. Temporary shutdowns, often industry-wide, often lasting one or two months, became widespread, as did wage cuts. In January 1930 the Japan Cotton Spinners' Association adopted a production curtailment plan and the Raw Silk Commission attempted a buy-up operation to uphold falling silk prices. In February, price- or production-control plans were adopted in the fertilizer, steel, coal, and paper industries. By the end of 1930, thirteen industries were restricting output, with curtailment rates ranging from around 35 percent for cotton spinning and silk reeling to as high as 50 percent for steel and cement. Even umbrella makers curtailed production. The associated movements for "rationalization" and "industrial control" developed rapidly. In terms of holding price levels, cartelization as a whole was a success, and price declines were greatest in noncartelized industries, nowhere more so than in agriculture.[25]

In the context of the 1930 depression, "rationalization" also acquired concrete institutional forms. In the cabinet meeting of November 19, 1929, on the eve of the November 21 announcement of the return to gold, the cabinet had discussed how to suppress the outflow of gold after the lifting of the gold embargo. Restraining consumption would help to limit imports, but the higher yen would reduce the price of imports and work in the opposite direction. Therefore, nationwide industrial rationalization to lower the costs of production was critically necessary, and the cabinet established an Industrial Rationalization Discussion Council to take up the issue. In late January 1930 the cabinet created the Temporary Industrial Rationalization Bureau in the Ministry of Commerce and Industry, and the new bureau went to work at the beginning of June. From a seemingly innocuous start promoting made-in-Japan goods, the Industrial Rationalization Bureau ultimately began to organize mandatory cartels and to control output. As such, "industrial rationalization" represented a step in the direction of a new slogan, "control" (*tōsei*), which later in the 1930s came to be touted as a new economic panacea.[26]

Rationalizing Labor

The brief era of good feelings that attended the restoration of the gold standard in January dissipated in the spring of 1930 as the effects of the first wave of deflation began to be felt. As Inoue had intended, wages fell along with prices. But as it happened—and as Keynes had said of the economic consequences of Mr. Churchill's deflation policy in Britain—the process lacked the appearance of automaticity with which theoretical discussions often endowed it. That is, from the view of the aggregate statistical indices, wages fell. From the view of each individual worker, wages were cut.

The process was played out dramatically at Japan's premier cotton-spinning company, Kanebō. Under Mutō Sanji's direction, Kanebō had gained a high reputation for its policy of "warm treatment" (*onjōshugi*) toward employees, pioneering many of the welfare-oriented employment practices that were later institutionalized in the lifetime employment system practiced by large companies after World War II. With the fall of silver prices that followed Japan's return to gold, Chinese demand dropped off, and cotton yarn prices, already falling since 1929, slumped heavily. On April 5, 1930, Kanebō abolished the special wage allowance granted during the World War I inflation—an effective pay cut of 23 percent, affecting 35,000 workers at thirty-six factories. The cut seemed especially unjust because Mutō Sanji himself had just retired as president in January with a retirement bonus of ¥3 million. Kanebō's new president blamed the fall of silver prices that had followed Japan's return to gold: "We didn't expect the reverberations of the lifting of the gold embargo to be this big."[27]

Kanebō was also an industry leader, and even as the "great wage cut storm at the Kanebō kingdom" raged on, its wage cuts were quickly emulated by other textile companies, soon joined by companies in other industries. There was simultaneously a great drop in Kanebō's share price, and the shares of other cotton spinning companies followed it down. Demonstrations and strikes followed, and the various proletarian parties used the occasion to attempt to form a united front.[28]

A week after Kanebō's wage cut, on April 11, there was general panic on the Tokyo stock exchange. Cabinet ministers met in regard to the panic, and Inoue Junnosuke issued a new statement repeating the need to retrench in the face of the depression. Not only did Japan remain in a chronic depression that had continued since 1920, he said, but England's own long-running depression had recently spread to the United States, compounding Japan's crisis. In these circumstances, the fall of stock prices was inevitable. Kanebō share prices fell further in May, causing another panic in the stock exchanges. By June and July, Kanebō shares, which had traded around the ¥220 level in January and February, hit a low of ¥120.[29]

Having observed Britain's experience in restoring the gold standard, Inoue Junnosuke had anticipated that industrial disputes would follow the return to gold. He likely had not expected to provoke a second strike wave on the scale of that of 1917–19. One reckoning counts more than three thousand strikes from 1929 to 1932, with more than 244,000 workers participating.[30] There was, however, a great difference between the strike wave of 1917–19 and that of 1929–31. In 1917–19, reflecting the conditions of an inflationary boom, more than 80 percent of the strikers' demands were positive demands for higher wages, shorter hours, and the right to organize. During the deflationary bust of 1930, defensive resistance to wage cuts and layoffs accounted for 76 percent of the cases and positive demands for only 13 percent. At least 1 million people were unemployed in 1930[31]—far more than recorded in the official unemployment statistics. These numbers also fail to convey the extent of the dislocation, as many laid-off workers returned to their families in the farm villages, intensifying the burden there and increasing the simultaneous tendency toward agrarian overproduction.

The Second Wave

At this point, in the late spring of 1930, the collapse extended to silk prices. Since the late 1890s, Japan had balanced its trade deficits with Western Europe and India—to the partial degree that it did—by running export surpluses with the United States and China. Imports from Western Europe consisted mainly of machinery, metals, and chemicals. From India came the raw cotton for Japan's spinning mills. Japan's main export to America was raw silk, and to China, cotton yarn and various light manufactured goods. Japanese trade in the 1920s remained highly dependent on these two export markets, and the U.S. market alone took 40 percent of Japan's exports.

Thus, the mainstay of Japan's gold-denominated export earnings, which paid for the flow of raw materials and sophisticated machinery to Japanese industry, continued to be the two million farm families—close to 40 percent of Japan's farm families—who engaged in sericulture and the farm daughters who went to the mills to spin it. This was the "dual structure"—modern industry arising next to, and in many ways built on, a relatively backward and impoverished agrarian sector that was still characterized, to a much disputed extent, by precapitalist landlord-tenant relations.[32] The dual structure was recapitulated within the industrial sector itself, where the great zaibatsu with their modern, highly capitalized plants and skilled, relatively high-paid male workforce produced mainly producer goods, chiefly for the home market, while the medium- and small-scale textile mills and consumer-goods industries that produced most of Japan's export earnings often depended on the superexploitation of less-skilled, low-paid female workers.[33] The pressure of the world depression was greatest on the lower tiers of this dual structure. Silk was also a luxury product highly vulnerable to cyclic swings in U.S. demand. After the American boom collapsed, silk prices began to fall. By June 1930, there were record high stocks on hand in the Yokohama silk market, and between April and July, raw silk prices fell almost 40 percent.

At the same time, monetary factors brought renewed crisis in Japan's trade with China, as the price of silver fluctuated wildly. Japan's return to the gold standard led to speculative yen buying in the Shanghai markets, driving down the price of silver. By the end of February 1930 the yen was trading at record high levels against the Chinese tael. In May and June alone, the tael fell by some 30 percent against the yen, descending from a level of 93.5 taels per ¥100 at the beginning of the year to as low as 140. The yen's appreciation priced Japanese goods out of the Chinese market, and exports to China in 1930 fell by one-third in yen terms from the year before. It also made Chinese silk much cheaper in overseas markets than the Japanese product, and Japan's share of silk exports to the United States suddenly dropped from 85 percent to 65 percent. As a result of its de facto currency devaluation, China enjoyed a temporary boom, while Japan plunged deeper into depression. The simultaneous introduction of rayon was a final factor that combined to ruin Japan's silk industry, which never really recovered.[34]

The economic crisis coincided with a new confrontation over foreign policy. Shidehara's cooperative diplomacy was premised on the idea that access to the China market was essential to Japanese business and that this was best guaranteed not by military means but by peaceful "economic advance." By provoking Chinese boycotts, the militaristic "positive" policy toward China had reacted negatively on Japanese businesses, which had seen their exports to China stagnate through the 1920s.[35] But now Japanese exports to China were in trouble in any case, while the success of Shidehara's arms-reduction policy provoked a fierce domestic reaction.

For the Hamaguchi cabinet, the continuation of the naval disarmament process begun in Washington in 1922 was a centerpiece of both the fiscal retrenchment and international cooperation policies. The arms-control process was carried forward with the signing of the London naval treaty on April 22, and when a special session of the Diet opened on April 21, the Seiyūkai opposition seized on the issue in an effort to arouse nationalist indignation against the government. The Seiyūkai's Mitsuchi Chūzō criticized the government for lifting the gold embargo without proper preparation. Inukai Tsuyoshi and Hatoyama Ichirō (the postwar prime minister) fiercely attacked the government for its supposed violation of the navy's right to supreme command in the conduct of the London talks and for its failure to deal with the unemployment problem. The violence of the Seiyūkai's attacks inside the Diet were soon to be far surpassed by attacks from more dangerous quarters.

As the world economic crisis deepened, Inoue Junnosuke, as he had done in 1920, shifted blame for the crisis to external, global forces beyond anyone's control. "The direct impetus to the present world depression is the overproduction of the main foodstuffs and raw materials throughout the world," he explained in August 1930 in a booklet entitled *The World*

Depression and Our People's Preparedness. Inoue's perception was a general one at the time, shared by U.S. president Herbert Hoover and by their friend in common, Thomas Lamont.[36] In his own analysis, Inoue even recognized that "overproduction" had combined with the decade-long, worldwide process of postwar retrenchment and monetary tightening to decrease purchasing power. This contraction of world purchasing power was aggravated by the decline of U.S. and British overseas lending and by the deflationary gold flows from Europe and "East Asia" to the United States. (In the case of East Asia, the large gold flows were from Japan itself, beginning when Inoue lifted the gold embargo.) Thus, "the decline of [world] purchasing power, accompanying the trend of falling prices and world overproduction of foodstuffs and raw materials, is driving prices still further down."[37]

But having recognized the role of purchasing power, Inoue did not pursue the question of the sources of demand; nor did he pursue the idea that overproduction could alternatively be seen as underconsumption, instead retreating to the reliable verities of retrenchment and reconstruction. This was not a matter for Japan alone, Inoue explained: In regard to the world depression, everything still depended on the U.S. economy. The United States had become the world's great creditor nation during the world war. It also had a persistently large trade surplus. Consequently the United States was absorbing the world's gold. In the late 1920s, the speculative bubble in the New York stock market had sucked in money from around the world, further reducing world purchasing power. America's subsequent stock market crash was "exactly like the reaction in Japan's business world in 1920." World economic recovery depended on the restoration of American overseas investment, which would increase world purchasing power.[38]

Compared to other countries, Inoue reiterated, Japan had been late in adjusting and needed to stay the present course, pursuing "enterprise control" and rationalization as the Western countries were doing. There was no point in thinking that Japan alone could escape the great tide of world depression. Thus, having lifted the gold embargo, Inoue lost his prior sense of the urgency of decisive economic action and took a more philosophical tone: There was always a cycle of boom and bust, like the weather. Prosperity and depression run in a ten-year cycle, so one must take a balanced view of things. To abandon at this point the gold standard that the Japanese people had sacrificed so much to achieve, or to adopt a new, devalued parity (as Ishibashi Tanzan had been urging), "would destroy Japan's business world."[39]

Some members of Japan's business world felt that this was already happening. As early as March 1930, all of the stock exchanges called on the government to lighten the deflation policy. On June 19, Gō Seinosuke and Dan Takuma petitioned Inoue to provide relief for the business world. Mutō Sanji attacked the gold-standard policy directly. In 1925 Mutō had led the political campaign to restore the gold standard. When Mutō's bête noire

Inoue Junnosuke himself actually carried off the task, Mutō switched sides. Whether his conversion was a matter of personal antagonism or of losses in the cotton-spinning business, or purely an intellectual realization, Mutō was won over by Ishibashi Tanzan's arguments, becoming one of the first politicians to support Ishibashi's "new parity" idea.[40] In a personal attack published shortly after Inoue's August 1930 essay, Mutō rebutted Inoue's claim that the depression was due to external causes: "Placing the primary blame for our country's current serious depression on the world depression, Finance Minister Inoue is calmly publishing many writings such as *The World Depression and Our People's Preparedness,* acting as if he did not know that he himself was the person most responsible. . . . More than the influence of the world depression, the main cause of our country's current depression is the mistaken policy of the Minseitō cabinet."[41]

With the terminology of modern monetary concerns subtracted, the rhetoric of the campaign to "economize on consumption" was reminiscent of the repeated austerity edicts of the Tokugawa shogunate, as Mutō suggested: "Premier Hamaguchi's economic conception is the same as the outlook of the age when consumption was thought of as a kind of sin. . . . There have been many cases of our old-fashioned politicians confusing morality and economics . . . if we are speaking of cultivating morality, then to force a sudden curtailment of consumption on the Japanese people and make them experience the bitterness of misery is certainly one method." But this moral-economic vision belonged to the feudal age:

> From the standpoint of the traditional moral conceptions of the Japanese people, the government of the Hamaguchi cabinet can be interpreted as good government. The popularity of the present cabinet is connected to this point. However, if we look at it from the economic standpoint, it is actually extremely illegitimate and the damage done to the Japanese people is so great as to be incalculable. In other words, [the Hamaguchi cabinet] has striven to fulfill the duty of teacher in regard to the Japanese people's thought, which has not tightened up since the wartime [boom]. Regrettably, because economic common sense was lacking, the result has been an opposite effect on the people's thought, and in the end, although Prime Minister Hamaguchi tried to awaken the Japanese people from the many years' dream of the expansion period, on the contrary this goal was not achieved and it only amounted to repeating the oft-attempted failures of the old-fashioned politicians of the feudal era.[42]

"Consumption and production are like the two wheels of a cart," Mutō declared. For the government to suddenly force the curtailment of consumption was like breaking one wheel.

By the summer of 1930, there were already demands that gold be re-embargoed, and speculation increased against the yen—the so-called dollar buying. It now appeared that the credit of the gold-denominated yen was only as good as the credit of the Minseitō government, which was greatly shaken by right-wing agitation over the London naval treaty. Each political disturbance, by promoting the belief that the cabinet would change and that gold would be re-embargoed, brought further speculation against the yen. In August and September Japanese businesses made big purchases of foreign securities in anticipation of a change of the government, which would mean a future fall of the yen. With the treaty's final ratification, the political situation again appeared to be stabilized. Accordingly, on September 18 the Tokyo stock market fell again.[43]

The Third Wave

At this point, after a temporary recovery of the prices of several commodities in August, the third wave of the deflation hit. Unlike wheat and many other crops, rice was not being overproduced relative to demand worldwide. Nevertheless, in 1930 and 1931 the international rice market behaved as if it were. In the Japanese empire, however, after the 1918 rice riots, the Hara cabinet had taken a series of measures to boost rice supplies, with the result that rice was overproduced (relative to effective demand, that is; many poor farmers still could not afford to eat rice on a regular basis and had to subsist on cheaper grains). Rice prices had been sliding since 1925. Amid the price collapses of spring 1930, rice prices held steady but became very volatile in July and August. In September and October rice prices abruptly fell by 40 percent. On October 2 the government announced that the 1930 rice crop was the largest in Japan's history; panic broke out and prices collapsed on the rice exchanges, where trading had to be suspended for two days. The fall of prices in Japan led to panic and price collapses in international rice markets, with effects as far away as Burma and India.[44]

Falling rice and silk prices opened the prospect of ruin for Japan's indebted farm families. It was the same problem experienced by producer-debtors—preeminently farmers—in the great deflation that had occurred in the gold bloc in 1873–96: as prices and incomes fell year by year, loans that had been taken out in "lighter" money had to be paid back in money that had become "heavier" in real terms. This debt-deflation squeeze was repeated around the world in the 1920s and 1930s. When deflation was especially swift, as it was in 1930, the selling price of a crop might not even cover the cost of inputs, and the result of a year's heavy labor could turn out to be a dead loss. Thus 1930 became known as the year of the "bumper crop famine" (*hōsaku kikin*).

Nationalist agitation combined with the rural crisis to produce a deadly mixture. The political right wing had worked itself up into a state of great agitation over the London disarmament conference. Now, radicalized members of the "agrarianist" movement provided the shock troops for the attack on the liberal establishment.[45] One such group was the Aikokusha (Patriotic

Society), led by Iwata Ainosuke, who formed an agricultural commune in Kanagawa, south of Tokyo, where his followers raised vegetables, collected guns, and dreamed of restoring Japan to a state of primal simplicity and virtue. On November 14, 1930, a young Aikokusha member shot and grievously wounded Prime Minister Hamaguchi on a platform in Tokyo station. It was almost exactly nine years since Prime Minister Hara Takashi was fatally stabbed in the same station. The attack had been carefully planned. The assailant, Sagōya Tomeo, who had gone to Manchuria as a "continental *rōnin*" and then joined Iwata's commune, said that he was motivated by the issues of the London naval treaty and the depression. For the next five months, Foreign Minister Shidehara stepped in as acting prime minister. On the day after Hamaguchi was shot, the Tokyo Stock Exchange reacted excitedly, posting the highest levels in nine months.[46]

The attack on Hamaguchi also caused great excitement among ultranationalist activists. Young Kodama Yoshio, the notorious postwar power broker finally brought down in the Lockheed scandal in 1974, was visiting right-wing godfather Uchida Ryōhei when one of Uchida's young disciples rushed in with the news. "I felt like a jolt of electricity ran from the top of my head down my spine," Kodama recalled. The close-mouthed Uchida couldn't contain his satisfaction on hearing that Hamaguchi's wound was to the gut. "If he's shot in the shit-sack, even Hamaguchi can't be helped," he blurted out, with his eyes widening. This was the spark, Kodama concluded, that lit "the fuse of the military and civilian reform movement's attack on the upper and privileged classes."[47]

Nevertheless, the monetary situation seemed to stabilize. Gold outflows had virtually stopped, as Inoue reported in his January 1931 address at the opening of the new year's Diet session. Japan's price index had fallen some 27 percent since June 1929; and while this indicated the severity of the crisis, it also meant that, as in the United States and Britain, prices were nearly down to the prewar level. Thus, "normality had returned," and further price declines should be limited. This process should be furthered by "rationalization and unification of various industries."[48]

THE OPEN DOOR: YEAR TWO

Events seemed to bear out Inoue's judgment. Gold outflows halted at the end of 1930. Price deflation moderated in the last months of 1930 and then stopped entirely, and as the second year of the restored gold standard began, prices even showed some upward tendency in February 1931. At the same time, the gold yen continued to climb to record heights against the silver tael, and on February 4 the price of silver plummeted on the London market, taking the yen to the level of ¥150 per 100 taels.

The political opposition became increasingly violent. The 59th Diet, which convened for regular business on January 22, was an ugly spectacle. The opposition Seiyūkai, with Diet member Hatoyama Ichirō taking the lead in questioning, attacked the government over the prime minister's ongoing absence from his duties. Acting premier Shidehara responded by assuring the Diet that Hamaguchi would appear in the Diet as soon as possible. On the next day, former finance minister Mitsuchi Chūzō attacked Inoue's financial policy, calling the government's optimistic statements about the economy "lying propaganda" (*kyogi no senden*). The Minseitō deputies erupted, and the Diet session devolved into the first of the many brawls that set the tone of the session. The next day, Matsuoka Yōsuke, former vice president of the South Manchurian Railway, now elected as a Seiyūkai representative, insisted that Manchuria and Mongolia were "the lifeline of the Japanese people" and attacked Shidehara over his diplomacy. The Seiyūkai deputies created chaos once again, leaving Shidehara standing helplessly at the podium and forcing the session to adjourn.[49]

Under continual pressure to appear, Hamaguchi formally resumed his post as prime minister and painfully left his sickbed to greet the House of Representatives for five minutes on March 10. The following day, he spent seven minutes in the House of Peers. With that, the government and Minseitō hoped to end the matter. Hamaguchi's condition worsened. The Seiyūkai kept up the pressure, and the government then promised that the prime minister would appear on March 17 and 18 in the budget committee and in the full house to answer questions about the budget. In the afternoon session of the full house on March 18, Hatoyama Ichirō again led off the questioning, challenging Hamaguchi to explain how he could continue as prime minister in his current physical condition. The opposition relentlessly kept up the questioning for three hours. When the exhausted Hamaguchi did not appear for the 9:00 P.M. session, the Seiyūkai members, shouting "bring out Hamaguchi," rushed the podium and prevented the session from continuing. On the next day, the Seiyūkai tabled a no-confidence motion against the government and held two mass protest meetings outside the Diet demanding that the cabinet resign. The protest turned into a riot, with Seiyūkai supporters and hired hooligans fighting with the police who guarded the Diet.[50]

Amid these disgraceful scenes, right-wing activists began to gather their forces and make concrete plans for direct action to bring about a purified, "reconstructed" Japan. Only a year before, the "wage cuts storm" that attended the onset of the gold-restoration depression had provoked a movement among the proletarian parties to try to form a united front. Now it was the turn of the anti-parliamentary ultraright to try to unite. In mid-March 1931 several right-wing organizations came together at the Kōchisha, a Shintō shrine run by Ōkawa Shūmei, to form the All-Japan Patriots' Joint-Struggle Conference. A fifty-man "Youth Vanguard" was selected that included many of those who would be active in a string of assassination and coup plots down to February 26, 1936.[51] Their first action, on the day that Hamaguchi appeared in the Diet, was to parade around the streets of Tokyo with banners calling for a "brocade" (or imperial) revolution. Kodama Yoshio then mingled with the crowd in the visitors' gallery of the Imperial Diet. When Hamaguchi painfully mounted to the podium and began to speak, Kodama began to shout and fling leaflets to the gallery below, before being arrested by the sergeants at arms.

The Seiyūkai hardly needed outside help in the project of disruption, and continued their attack on Hamaguchi. Aggravated by the strain, Hamaguchi's condition deteriorated further, and he and his cabinet resigned on April 13. A new Minseitō cabinet was formed by Wakatsuki Reijirō the next day. It was essentially a continuation of the Hamaguchi cabinet, with Foreign Minister Shidehara, Home Minister Adachi, and Finance Minister Inoue all remaining in office. On August 26, nine months after being shot, Hamaguchi died of his wounds.

The hatred for Inoue himself had become visceral among members of the right wing. Again, Kodama Yoshio: "The cabinet's head clerk, Finance Minister Inoue Junnosuke, had lifted the gold embargo and thrown the country's economy into chaos. In public opinion in general, he was thought of as just like the god of poverty. . . . Especially from our standpoint, he was seen as the running dog of the zaibatsu, or even as the mortal enemy of the national masses."[52]

On the morning of May 2 a dynamite bomb exploded in front of Inoue's house, destroying part of the front gate. It had been placed by a right-wing organization associated with the group who had shot Hamaguchi. Inoue publicly dismissed the incident as beneath his notice (literally, as "less than a fart"). For Kodama, Inoue was "not hearkening at all to the rage of the masses, but rather ignoring public opinion with a sneering attitude." Out of jail after the Diet incident, Kodama wrapped a short sword in a package and mailed it to Inoue, enclosing a brief letter: "Please use it as you will, for self defense, or to cut your stomach."[53] Kodama was arrested and jailed again, afterwards going to Manchuria, where he made his first fortune.

Inoue did not back down. The rules of the international gold standard continued to force deflation, and by March 1931, the Bank of Japan's note issue was shrinking daily, slipping below the ¥1 billion level.[54] The monetary and financial stresses were global, and in May 1931, beginning in the defeated countries of Central Europe, the global monetary crisis proceeded from the stage of deflation to that of institutional collapse.

THE COLLAPSE OF STABILIZATION

In September 1930, with the offer for sale of the German government bonds that "commercialized" the German reparations debt, Thomas

Lamont had reported that the international process of stabilization that began with Austria in 1923 was now complete. This was "the final liquidation of the war."[55] But the process of liquidation was only entering a new stage. It was also in Austria that the collapse of the whole international gold-standard system began, with the bankruptcy on May 12, 1931 of Austria's largest bank, the Credit-Anstalt. As in 1873, the panic spread to Germany, where to defend the gold mark, the Reichsbank raised interest rates from 5 percent in June to a temporary high of 15 percent in early August.[56]

Thomas Lamont again took the lead in trying to contain the financial crisis, and on June 20, at Lamont's urging, President Hoover proposed a one-year international moratorium on war debt and reparations payments. This was the effective end of both. At a stroke, one of the fundamental sources of the global financial imbalances of the 1920s was removed. On June 25 a large international credit was arranged in a last-ditch effort to save the German gold standard. Coincidentally on the same day, the "American group" issued bonds for the Taiwan Electric Company in New York. This was Japan's last overseas bond issue until the 1950s.

Despite the attempt to bail out Germany, the disintegration of the global monetary system had already acquired its own momentum. On July 13 the giant Darmstadter Bank closed and the German government adopted emergency financial measures. On July 18 Germany suspended gold payments de facto. Gold-centered stabilization had failed in its most crucial arena. By this time the vortex of the banking crisis that had swept up Central Europe was sucking in the banking world of London, as the run on Germany turned into a run on the pound sterling. The Japanese yen would be next.

Japan's crisis seemed only to grow worse. Farm families' material reserves had been exhausted by five years of constant deflation of farm prices in a global market environment characterized by "overproduction." Now, in July 1931, poor weather in northern Japan ruined crops, and farmers in Hokkaidō and Tōhoku faced a classic harvest crisis. Newspapers spoke of the advancing "front lines of starvation" (*gashi zensen*) and reported how offices were set up in northern farm villages that specialized in brokering the sale of farmers' daughters to urban prostitution districts such as the Hato no Machi in Tokyo and Tobita in Osaka.[57] Radical agrarianists and young officers from the farm villages knew of such facts firsthand.

Ultimately, the Minseitō government was brought down by two disparate coups. The first took place on the borderlands of the Japanese empire in Manchuria, where army officers bitterly opposed to the cabinet's liberal policies executed a kind of military coup at a distance. The second shock came from the core of the global monetary system, with the collapse of Britain's gold standard and the subsequent attack on Japan's gold standard by some of Inoue's best friends. The coincidence of these twin shocks is ironic but revealing: each announced, in two very different social domains, the crack-up of the liberal international order of the 1920s. Both the Shidehara diplomatic policy and the Inoue financial policy were suddenly placed in an impossible position.

Like Inoue Junnosuke and Hamaguchi Osachi, Lieutenant Colonel Ishiwara Kanji (1889–1949) perceived Japan as being caught in a stifling deadlock in the 1920s. Ishiwara's answer was to gain "breathing space" for the growing nation in Manchuria, and in July 1929, as the Hamaguchi cabinet was launching its "negative" policy in an attempt to break Japan's deadlock, Ishiwara wrote out his own "positive" plan for the occupation of Manchuria and eastern Inner Mongolia by the Japanese Kwantung Army. In May 1931 Ishiwara began concrete planning for the plot that eventuated four months later in what came to be called the Manchuria incident.[58]

Ishiwara's military strike was carefully prepared. It began with a faked incident of Chinese sabotage on the night of September 18 on the South Manchurian Railway line outside Mukden (Shenyang). Immediately, the Kwantung Army attacked local Chinese forces, and on September 19 Japan's newspapers were filled with announcements of war. From this point, stirring photographic scenes of the rising-sun flag waving in the clear autumn sky and of energetic young soldiers on the move across the continent's wide open spaces became daily news images. A way out of deadlock seemed suddenly to have opened, and a great and sudden change took place in the climate of Japanese public opinion. In the months that followed, as Japanese forces won battle after battle on the continent, national unity became the great demand, and "divisive" elements, from leftists to feminists to the establishment political parties themselves, were expected to subordinate their self-centered demands to Japan's national mission. Manchuria now became an overseas outpost of the "positive" policy and subsequently became a testing ground for various ideas of state-controlled economy. At the same time, a new round of economic warfare also began in Shanghai, where a highly effective anti-Japanese boycott was begun on September 22.[59]

Manchuria itself was only the immediate target of the Kwantung Army's coup; the primary target was the "weak," pro-Western government at home. The incident at Mukden was the beginning of a Japanese military takeover by stages of North China, and it was likewise the beginning of a military takeover by stages of the Japanese state. The movement of these national-socialist–minded officers was political and military, but it had an economic aspect, as Ishiwara and his comrades called for military-centered, strategic state planning and rejected economic liberalism and plutocracy. This nationalist line was not completely dissonant from Takahashi Korekiyo's own economic nationalism, and Takahashi and the militarists would seem to ride the same wave for a few years, although by 1935 Takahashi also would appear much too liberal and plutocratic to the radicals of the militarist movement.

Shidehara and Inoue were now in the position of having to explain the

Kwantung Army's actions to their Western friends. Most of what Thomas Lamont knew of the situation in Manchuria came through Inoue, and Lamont responded to his client's new public relations difficulties by orchestrating a newspaper story that justified Japan's position in Manchuria.[60] Lamont remained an apologist for Japanese aggression throughout the first phase of the Manchurian war. From most Westerners, condemnation was much more readily forthcoming. The Kwantung Army's actions thus placed the liberals in the Japanese government in the same kind of predicament in which the attacks of anti-foreign bravos had placed the Tokugawa Bakufu during the 1860s, making the government appear duplicitous to foreigners and weak or treasonous to patriots at home. On October 24 the League of Nations called for Japan to give up its new imperial conquests, and by stages, the hollowness of the post–World War I liberal-imperial international political order was also revealed.

The international financial order on which Inoue had staked his life was also crumbling. Unlike most other countries, Japan had "already had" its banking crisis in the spring of 1927 and was relatively spared the waves of bank failures that swept around the world in the summer of 1931.[61] In other countries, currency and banking crises were combined in 1931. It was the currency crisis that came to Japan. British financiers were heavily invested in Germany, and the German bank panic led to a run on the British pound. The "wholesale liquidation" of sterling assets in international financial markets began in the middle of July, as the British government later explained it to other countries. The U.S. Federal Reserve and the Bank of France organized an emergency credit of £100 million. On September 3 the British government instituted exchange controls. A second Franco-American private loan totaling $400 million (£80 million) was made to the British government on September 10.

Gold outflows from London reached a climax in mid-September, by which point more than £200 million had been withdrawn from the London market.[62] On the afternoon of Friday, September 18—just as Kwantung Army units were moving to seize control of Mukden, eight time zones to the east—the British prime minister was informed jointly by the acting head of the Bank of England and by the head of Baring Brothers that Britain had no choice but to abandon the gold standard. J. P. Morgan and Company—which had just finished organizing a giant $200 million loan for the British government—was informed later that night.[63]

The events of September 1931 reveal both the power that Morgan and Company could hold over governments and the limits of that power. Even British policy makers had become subject to Morgan conditionality in that the $200 million loan was contingent upon the British government cutting unemployment benefits. The result was that the Labour cabinet split and a cabinet of national unity was formed; when the requested budget cuts were made on September 10, the loan came through.[64] However, when it came to the decision to abandon the gold standard a week later, Morgan and Company was left out of the loop, and its last-minute efforts to reverse the decision were unavailing.[65] This sudden loss of leverage was a sign of things to come.

The public announcement of the British government's decision to suspend the 1925 Gold Standard Act was made on Monday, September 21. For a day, it replaced events in Manchuria as the top news story in Japan. England had "fallen from the throne of world finance," as newspaper headlines put it.[66] The British government's official diplomatic notice, in a tone that stopped somewhere short of apologetic, itself suggested the global shift represented by Britain's "fall": "His Majesty's Government in the United Kingdom are fully aware that the step which they have taken is bound to cause serious trouble and confusion especially in those countries which in the past have been particularly dependent upon London to supply them with credit and other financial facilities."[67] Britain's foreign "depositors" could no longer be paid in full, on demand, in gold, and they now watched the value of their sterling holdings suddenly contract as a result of the pound's rapid depreciation. British trade and finance began a historic reorientation toward a closed imperial bloc.

It now appeared that Inoue was sailing on a sinking ship. Other countries quickly put in their own gold embargoes: Denmark on September 22; Norway, Sweden, and Switzerland on the 27th, 28th, and 29th; Finland on October 12; Canada on October 19. Inoue, however, downplayed the importance of Britain's fall, telling the newspapers that "there would not be very much influence on Japan" and telling Thomas Lamont by cable that although the British action was regrettable, "nevertheless I do not think the permanent effect in this country will be serious." On September 25 Inoue made a public statement declaring that Japan would not re-embargo gold, and the London and New York offices of the Bank of Japan were told to instruct the Bank for International Settlements and others to this effect. Inoue's assurances were not taken seriously at Morgan and Company.[68]

The Japanese securities markets, already unsteady on the news from Manchuria, were thrown immediately into chaos by the news of Britain's gold embargo, and Inoue's Ministry of Finance closed stock and bond markets in Tokyo, Osaka, and Nagoya to halt panic selling. When the markets were reopened on Wednesday, there was more panic selling, and they were closed again until the 26th.[69] Prices also fell again on the commodity markets.

The greatest beneficiaries and supporters of gold restoration in Japan, besides the foreign banks, were the great zaibatsu combines, especially their financial arms, which gained greatly from the strong yen and invested hundreds of millions of yen in overseas securities. Proximately, these were the same groups that brought down the gold yen in late 1931. Inoue was one of the best friends that Japan's banking leaders had ever had. However, the nature of their enterprise was to take profits and hedge losses, and once it appeared that the Japanese government could not maintain the gold con-

TABLE 6. Gold outflows, January 1930–December 1931
(¥ millions)

Year	Month	Net Inflow (+) or Outflow (–)
1930	January	–44.80
	February	–85.00
	March	–46.10
	April	–23.40
	May	–19.91
	June	–3.48
	July	+2.84
	August	–18.97
	September	–8.35
	October	–39.46
	November	–14.09
	December	+1.12
Net outflow, 1930		–299.58
1931	January	–0.39
	February	–0.17
	March	–4.30
	April	–2.33
	May	–0.28
	June	–1.30
	July	–29.57
	August	–18.60
	September	+0.24
	October	–135.12
	November	–146.32
	December	–52.50
Net outflow, 1931		–390.64
Net outflow, 1930–31		–690.22

SOURCE: Bank of Japan data given in NGHS 3: 424. Some totals not equal as a result of rounding.

vertibility of the yen, Japanese banks themselves felt constrained to join the speculative attack against it, selling their yen for dollars and in effect looting the Bank of Japan's gold reserves. The run on the "bank" that was Japan was part of a crisis of confidence in the whole international financial system.

By 1931 it was physically possible to ship out ¥50 million of gold in a week and ¥200 million in a month. Massive "dollar buying" began immediately on September 21. Foreign banks began sending out gold, and in October and November alone, ¥280 million in gold was shipped from Japan (table 6). Dollar buying by Japanese banks appeared virtually traitorous to many contemporary observers. Mitsui Bank and its managing director, Ikeda Shigeaki, received the greatest blame in the dollar-buying episode.[70]

Inoue responded to the run on the yen by having the Bank of Japan raise interest rates on October 6 and again on November 5, to discourage speculative borrowing for dollar buying. Inoue's action added to the depressionary effect of the cabinet's policies. In November, there was another round of bank runs and further bail-outs by the Bank of Japan. On November 16 the government abandoned its policy of trying to contain the military action in Manchuria and approved of the campaign. After months of heatedly attacking the Minseitō's depression-inducing economic policy, the Seiyūkai also officially called for a policy of gold re-embargo, and in November, rumors were flying of a new government and an impending re-embargo of gold.[71]

The Minseitō cabinet itself began to split, and its final weeks in office were dominated by a struggle between the jingoistic home minister Adachi Kenzō and the liberal internationalists Inoue and Shidehara. On November 21, Adachi, who had not supported most of the Inoue and Shidehara policies, publicly called for a coalition government with the Seiyūkai, and for the suspension of the gold standard and an end to the conciliatory diplomacy.[72] The opposition of Inoue and Shidehara forced Wakatsuki to table the idea. From New York, Thomas Lamont again attempted to influence the situation, informing Sonoda of the Yokohama Specie Bank that he had read that Inoue might be left out of a bruited coalition cabinet, and that "I trust that there is no truth in this dispatch, because, for your information, any such action would cause a distinct chill in New York and London banking circles."[73] This was a direct message to Tokyo and Sonoda took it as such, immediately cabling Lamont's views to his superiors. After delivering this Olympian warning, Lamont left, as was his custom, on a long winter vacation, and it was in Bermuda that he heard the news of Inoue's fate.

In early December, Adachi publicly broke with the government. On December 11 the Yokohama Specie Bank ended sales of foreign exchange, and the yen-dollar exchange fell sharply. On December 12 the cabinet resigned. Share prices surged, and the stock markets were temporarily closed. The senior statesmen turned to the Seiyūkai to form a new government. Seiyūkai party president Inukai Tsuyoshi, now seventy-six years old, was prime minister. Takahashi Korekiyo, at age seventy-seven, came back from retirement for the second time to serve as finance minister.

The new cabinet was formed on December 13, a Sunday. On that day the cabinet issued a single order, reissuing under Takahashi's authority the same Ministry of Finance order that had embargoed gold exports in 1917, effective immediately. The share and commodity markets rallied on December 14. Takahashi completed the operation on December 17 by having an imperial edict issued that ended gold convertibility "for the time being," except by permission of the finance minister.[74] In fact, the gold standard was dead. Takahashi's return to political life also meant the comeback of the "positive" economic policy, in a form developed far beyond the policies of the 1920s.

TWELVE

Capitalist Recovery in One Country, 1932–1936

When the whole world is in a depression, it is asserted that if only we reimpose the gold embargo, business conditions will improve in Japan alone, but is that common sense? The world is afflicted by depression, but can it be solved as simply as Finance Minister Takahashi says?—There is no simple plan that so easily converts the depression in the world into prosperity.

INOUE JUNNOSUKE, SPEAKING IN THE HOUSE OF PEERS IN RESPONSE TO THE STATEMENT OF FINANCE MINISTER TAKAHASHI, JANUARY 21, 1932

It has been [the Seiyūkai's] conviction that conditions in Japan are dissimilar to those of other countries.

TAKAHASHI KOREKIYO, SEPTEMBER 1932

Under Takahashi Korekiyo's leadership, financial conditions in Japan rapidly did become dissimilar to those of other countries. After December 13, 1931, the yen fell sharply, and by early 1932, Japanese industry was beginning to export its way out of the depression. In 1932 Takahashi also initiated a historic policy of deficit finance, funding government spending projects via the direct creation of money. Domestic prices rose, corporate profits and investment ended the long downward slide that had begun in 1920, and by late 1932 or 1933, prosperous conditions had returned to most branches of industry. Japan came to present the picture of a "lone island of prosperity," even as the depression deepened in most of the rest of the world.[1]

In many ways, Japan's economy thus picked up in 1932 where it had left off in 1920, with the augmented capacities made available by the intervening years of rapid technical progress, electrification, and infrastructural development.[2] As during the World War I boom, the export of light-industrial consumer goods surged, going mainly to Asian and other developing-country markets that Japanese businessmen had first broken into during the European war and in many cases had subsequently retreated from. The invasion of northeastern China generated military demand, driving a new wave of advances in the rising heavy and chemical industries. Takahashi's own presence was another aspect of continuity: having presided over the "grass fire" boom of 1918–20, Takahashi now promoted a new and more macroeconomically attuned version of the "positive" policy in finance.

The continuities between the World War I boom and the "munitions boom" of the 1930s returns us to the fundamentally different evaluations of Japan's potential for rapid growth made by Inoue Junnosuke and Takahashi Korekiyo. Inoue had consistently perceived this potential as limited: economic development was inevitably slow and arduous for a country like Japan, and overrapid progress only begged a reaction. The world-war boom especially appeared to him as no more than a lucky break that had rescued an economy on the edge of a serious foreign debt crisis and deferred the inevitable day of judgment. Lacking such a fortuitous external boost, Japan must rely on its own efforts (*jiriki*) to overcome its persistent balance-of-payments difficulties. Structurally, Japan depended on imports for both raw materials and technology, and thus inherently imported more than it exported. An export surplus was possible only "in the indefinite future." For Inoue it was almost as if recession were the natural state for narrow, constricted Japan: depression was an endogenously generated condition, but recoveries had been fluky and exogenous.[3]

Another lesson could be drawn from the experience of the World War I boom: that Japan had the strength for a tremendous industrial expansion, if only market demand were sufficient. Like Inoue, Takahashi Korekiyo saw the postbellum world as a place of economic stagnation—but this stagnation was brought on less by collective overreaching or by loose living than by mistakenly restrictive gold-based policies:

> Upon the termination of the World War, all nations adopted programmes of financial readjustment and, in their eagerness for a speedy return to gold, the enforcement of fiscal plans which called for radical retrenchment became the order of the day, especially immediately before and after the removal of gold restrictions. A world-wide disparity between the supply of goods and purchasing power ensued, bringing in turn violent declines in commodity prices and ever-increasing unemployment.[4]

In other words, instead of suppressing the supply of goods to achieve balance through contraction, nations needed to expand purchasing power—that is, consumption. Takahashi's "Keynesian" view of the gold standard's constraining effects on global purchasing power was not a functional part of Inoue's analysis. And far from lagging behind Europe, Takahashi thought, "Japan's power for recuperation when the corner is turned will be far greater than that of the nations of Europe, if we consider the crushing debt burdens arising from the World War under which the former are struggling."[5] As Japan's economy revived and the Western economies stagnated, a vision of a new Japan, stronger and more vital than the Western countries, began to be widely expressed.

As for the specific sources of this new purchasing power—the social character of the positive policy—vital questions of political power and social distribution were being decided. Again, Ishibashi Tanzan offered a farsighted solution.

THE ROAD NOT TAKEN

The day after Takahashi reimposed the gold embargo, December 14, 1931, Ishibashi gave the first part of a two-day national radio broadcast on Tokyo's NHK radio station, JOAK. The timing was accidental, the broadcast having been scheduled a month beforehand, but it was apt, as Ishibashi called for growth based on expanded domestic demand—growth that did not require outside dollars or gold. The question of appropriate consumption and woman's place was again symbolically at the heart of things, as Ishibashi addressed his talk, "The Consumption Economy and the Production Economy," especially to Japan's women. In it, he answered Finance Minister Inoue's call to "rationalize the kitchen economy" by curtailing home consumption.[6]

Ishibashi challenged the idea that production and consumption were opposites, the one positive and the other negative. Rather, he argued, as Mutō Sanji had, that they were two parts of a whole process, necessarily entailing and including each other. This simple point had to be emphasized because consumption had been ignored and treated as something outside of economics. The old production-centered idea of economics was an idea of the eighteenth and nineteenth centuries, the era of the industrial revolution. The new economy of the twentieth century was different, and the "second industrial revolution," recently much discussed, was in fact the turn to an economy in which the importance of consumption was recognized. Especially important here was remarkable growth of the "service industry" (Ishibashi used the English word), which was nothing other than the direct consumption of labor power (that is, not intermediated by goods). Inoue himself had deployed the new language of "consumerism," but his point was that consumers (housewives) should exercise their sovereignty to buy and consume less.[7] Ishibashi argued instead that consumption must be increased and enhanced.

There was also a logical problem with Ishibashi's argument. Collectively, increased domestic consumption of domestically producible goods and services was indeed the path out of depression, but from the standpoint of an individual family's budget, especially in a time of frightful economic uncertainty, it was Inoue's logic of frugality that made sense. Ishibashi grappled with this problem of collective action by proposing a new role for the state. Consumption was managed mostly by individual families; and while consumers collectively added up to a great economic power, without an organization to unite them, they were individually weak, he explained. The government had already created production-oriented ministries responsible for agriculture and forestry, commerce and industry, and transportation and communications; therefore, Ishibashi proposed that a Ministry of Consumption should likewise be established. Despite the fact that women could neither vote nor hold office, Ishibashi also proposed on the second day of his broadcast, following the suggestion of a female listener, that the minister should be a woman.[8]

Ishibashi's feminism was ahead of its time. His analysis is also a reminder of just how far Japan was in 1931 from being the mass-consumption society that it became in the 1950s and 1960s, when domestic consumption truly did become an engine of economic growth and social betterment. At a time when Inoue Junnosuke was insisting that domestic markets were "glutted," Ishibashi itemized how much room there was for domestic consumption to increase. Hen's eggs, for example, remained a luxury, and national production came to less than one egg per person per week. Consumption of milk was only one one-hundredth of European and American levels.

> We still want to wear good clothes and to live in good houses, we want good furniture, we want pianos and violins, we want better radio sets, we want to see plays and go to the movies . . . such desires are limitless. To properly satisfy these desires, if we encourage consumption, production will necessarily increase accordingly; and if consumption grows and production increases, the phenomenon of depression will thereby disappear.[9]

Here too was a British model at work—not the deflationary Bank of England logic that had shaped Inoue's thinking, but the counterlogic of John Maynard Keynes, whose writings Ishibashi read with great sympathy. Like Ishibashi's Gladstonian vision of a peaceful "little Japan" without an empire—a Japan that might serve as a model for other developing countries—his Keynesian vision of a prosperous mass-consumption society was the vision of a future that would be realized within his own lifetime. It also came with significant intellectual and political guidance from Ishibashi himself.[10] But in 1931 Ishibashi's ideas were unfortunately out of synch with the militaristic trends of the times, and most political and business leaders continued to see the ability of the Japanese people to endure hardship and deprivation as a vital basis of national strength—even as Japan's edge over the overfed and decadent West. Takahashi's new deficit-spending policy did meet with Ishibashi's partial approval, but it came as part of a package of "military Keynesianism." Takahashi himself made the point clear in a 1935 interview with Ishibashi, relating again his shopworn parable of the spendthrift *narikin* at the geisha house and extending this example of the economic utility of unproductive spending to justify military spending as well.[11] Thus, government spending marched ahead. The civilian economy did recover in the mid-1930s, but the decisive trend of consumption over the course of the decade was toward greater and greater military consumption, at the ultimate cost of harsh austerity for the masses of Japanese people and a bloody holocaust in Asia.[12]

BREAKING THE BANDS OF THE GOLD STANDARD

In fact, Ishibashi failed fully to embrace Takahashi's policy from the start. The two men shared similar views of the gold standard, but even had the Minseitō cabinet continued, Ishibashi wrote in his 1932 New Year's editorial, it was only a matter of time until the nation abandoned the gold standard—"even a three-foot tall child could have done it." The question was what would follow. Here, Ishibashi thought that the most important point was Takahashi's statement on December 13 that the government would no longer artificially support the yen's value by shipping gold or floating overseas bonds. This laissez-faire exchange-rate policy was the same thing Takahashi had done when he was called on to restore confidence in the 1927 crisis. Ishibashi applauded it: let the yen fall as far as it will, he said, imagining that within a few weeks it would find its true level.[13]

The yen did fall far and fast, shedding nearly a third of its value against the dollar in the last two weeks of December. The yen's depreciation meant the final success of the Mitsui group's dollar-buying venture: Inoue had lost and Ikeda Shigeaki had won. It also decided the question of whether to adjust the trade deficit by price deflation, as Inoue and the Minseitō had attempted, or by currency depreciation, toward which Takahashi and the Seiyūkai had been inclined. Linked to this was the question of the sources of capital for development. Inoue's priority had been to maintain Japan's credit abroad. Takahashi's policy was to borrow—or directly create money—at home.

Ishibashi also addressed the question of reflation. If the yen fell but domestic prices failed to increase, he wrote, the economic situation would not improve. To boost prices and stimulate production, the government must either conduct its own public works or provide funds to the business world (as Ishibashi himself would do on a grand scale as finance minister in 1946–47). Here, Ishibashi said, the danger was a return to "chaotic, so-called loose" spending policies—an unmistakable reference to Takahashi's spending policy during the Hara cabinet, which had led to the "boom beyond the bounds of common sense" in 1919 and the crash of 1920.[14] As Ishibashi's less-than-respectful editorial stance makes clear, despite the similarity of their ideas, there was no direct relationship between Ishibashi and Takahashi at this time. Takahashi's anti-depression policies were an expression of Takahashi's own long-held views, Ishibashi wrote many years later, and the similarities between their thinking were accidental: "Mr. Takahashi didn't especially follow my theories and I didn't especially praise what he did."[15]

In fact, Takahashi's reflation policy lived up to Ishibashi's hopes. "Hampered by monetary stringency and credit contraction," Takahashi wrote later in the year, "our trade and industry are at present denied the means of healthy development. The logical remedy is to put into circulation adequate amounts of money."[16] Inoue Junnosuke's policies were being turned on their head. As it happened, Takahashi's second comeback from retirement also coincided with Inoue's final leave-taking, as the career of the older man framed that of his younger colleague in a tragic and ironic way.

INOUE'S DEATH

Inoue did not give up. Despite the failure of his gold-restoration policy, Inoue himself was now widely regarded as a future president of the Minseitō and, by extension, a future prime minister.[17] Prince Saionji, with whom the decision would ultimately have rested, shared this view and accordingly viewed the Seiyūkai cabinet's positive policy as no more than the prelude to an inevitable new round of the negative policy.[18] In fact, the policy cycle of the "two-party" era had been decisively broken.

On January 21, 1932, the 60th Diet session reopened, and in the last Diet speech of his career, Inoue responded in the House of Peers to Finance Minister Takahashi's budget speech and attacked the new cabinet's policy. Inoue was at pains to defend his record on the issue of dollar buying. Speculators had made a killing only because the gold standard was ended, he said; if the gold standard had been maintained, they would have lost. Thus, it was the fault of the new Seiyūkai cabinet. With the renewed gold embargo, all the effort to achieve fiscal balance and establish the gold standard, all the sacrifices of the Japanese people had been rendered vain.[19]

Later the same day, the Seiyūkai cabinet, lacking a parliamentary majority, dissolved the Diet and scheduled elections for February 20. For the remaining nineteen days of his life, as Minseitō general secretary and chairman of the election committee, Inoue ran the party's campaign, which he turned into a referendum on the gold standard. Virtually all of Inoue's speeches and lectures during these days were attacks on the reimposition of the gold embargo. True to form, he doggedly repeated the same arguments again and again.[20]

While Inoue fought to return to the old monetary certainties, Japan's external political and economic position continued to change with extraordinary speed. In Shanghai the anti-Japanese boycott provoked by the invasion of Manchuria began to bite, and relations between Chinese and Japanese residents reached a state of virtual economic war. The seasoned conspirators of the Japanese Kwantung Army also covertly went to work there, deliberately fomenting anti-Japanese disturbances that could serve as a pretext for military action.[21] The denouement came on the night of January 28, 1932, when Japanese marines and "*rōnin*" irregulars attacked Chinese troops and civilians. A Japanese aircraft carrier task force was already standing by, and naval warplanes bombed apartment blocks in the Chinese section of the city in the world's first large-scale terror bombing of civilian targets. The following day, Kwantung Army units began their assault on Harbin in northern Manchuria, whose occupation on February 5 largely completed the conquest of Manchuria. The bombing of Shanghai—the headquarters of Western capital in China—was graphically reported in Western newspapers and newsreels. Amid the general reaction of horror and loathing, Thomas Lamont began to distance himself from the public relations problems of his Japanese clients. Events in Manchuria had been "difficult for American friends to explain," Lamont wrote in a draft letter, perhaps intended for Inoue. The attack on Shanghai was impossible.[22]

At home in Japan the international situation and the worsening agrarian crisis had created a war mentality among young members of the right-wing movements. Fifty miles northeast of Tokyo in rural Ibaraki, Inoue Nisshō (1886–1967), a former "China *rōnin*" turned Nichiren priest, had begun to plot the violent destruction of plutocracy and liberalism. Inoue Nisshō's career personified the conjunction of adventurism in China and reactionary politics at home seen also in the lives of Kita Ikki and Ōkawa Shūmei. Like Kita and like Ōkawa, Inoue returned from China, where he had worked variously for the South Manchurian Railway and as an army spy, to discover his homeland in dire social and spiritual straits. Settling outside Mito city, he practiced sitting meditation until he gained what he considered enlightenment and then began to recruit local youth into his "Blood Pledge Corps" (Ketsumeidan). Adopting the slogan, "One man, one kill," Inoue wrote a death list that included government leaders and the heads of Mitsui and Mitsubishi. Each member of the Blood Pledge Corps pledged to erase the life of one person named on the list.

Inoue Junnosuke's name topped that list. In January 1932 Inoue Nisshō ordered twenty-year-old Onuma Shō (1911–78) to do the job and gave him a pistol and twenty bullets. After test-firing the pistol at a secluded beach, Onuma went to Tokyo to hunt down Inoue Junnosuke. Onuma stalked his victim for several days, once getting close enough to him to jostle him in a crowd at a campaign rally, as he later narrated in his almost obscenely detailed account of the murder. Learning from a campaign poster that Inoue would be speaking in support of a candidate at the Komamoto

Primary School on the evening of February 9, Onuma retrieved his pistol from a friend's house and went to wait at the school gate. As Inoue got out of his car and approached, Onuma stepped forward and shot him. Inoue died in the hospital hours later. The young assassin was sentenced to life in prison but was released in a general amnesty in 1940. One of his first acts on his release was to visit Inoue's grave at Tokyo's Aoyama Cemetery, where it stands next to Hamaguchi Osachi's. Onuma did owe Inoue a strange debt, for the murder established him as a prominent leader of the unreformed ultrarightist movement after World War II.[23]

Again, the worlds of cosmopolitan finance and nationalist resentment had collided. Inoue Junnosuke's sense of the world and of Japan's place in it had few points of contact with the queasy mix of agrarian romanticism, otherworldly spiritualism, social outrage, and bloodlust that inspired his killers, but his do-or-die (*kesshi*) spirit was not entirely different from that of the *kesshitai* members who plotted and executed his assassination. "The gold standard has slain its tens of thousands," William Jennings Bryan had declared during the United States' deflationary crisis of the 1890s. In a moment of high rhetoric of his own, Mutō Sanji charged that Inoue's restoration of the gold standard was like "a general climbing to fame on top of the bodies of thousands of soldiers."[24] Inoue's policies certainly had their thousands and their tens of thousands of victims. But it turned out that Inoue himself was on the front lines of the fight.

Well behind the lines, Thomas Lamont was immediately cabled at his vacation quarters in Bermuda with the news of Inoue's death. Sonoda of the Yokohama Specie Bank wrote to him that he felt as if the North Star had disappeared. Lamont cabled his condolences to Mrs. Inoue. Privately, he concluded that after all, the bad, militarist Japan had won out over the good.[25]

Thus the life of Japan's great liberal financier ended, as the structure of international relations that he had worked so long to build crumbled around him. Liberalism as a whole system was discredited and abandoned. The cause of Inoue's party was also a losing one. In a sharp reversal of the Minseitō's electoral mandate two years earlier, the election of February 20, 1932—the third conducted under universal male suffrage—was a landslide for the Seiyūkai, which won 301 seats in the House of Representatives (up from 174), versus 146 for the Minseitō (down from 243). On March 1 the new state of Manchukuo was announced to the world, greeted by Chinese and Western condemnation and unanimously endorsed by the Japanese Diet. Japan was officially united behind a policy that virtually committed it to a wider war against the Chinese people.

Dan Takuma, head of the Mitsui group, had been another of Thomas Lamont's prominent hosts during his two visits to Japan. On March 5 another young member of the Blood Pledge Corps shot Dan to death in front of Mitsui headquarters. The killer was from the same village as Inoue's assassin. With Dan's murder, Lamont asked Sonoda to inform Finance Minister Takahashi of a cutoff of Western credit. As Lamont put it, it was fortunate that Japan now required no foreign credit: "If it did, of course it would be quite impossible to arrange."[26]

Shocked by Inoue's assassination and their repudiation at the polls, the Minseitō turned to an "opposition" strategy of opposing party government altogether and supporting a supraparty cabinet of national unity. This was not long in coming. On May 15 a group of "superpatriot" naval officers linked to Ōkawa Shūmei, who himself had had previous contact with the Blood Pledge Corps, attacked the Seiyūkai headquarters, Mitsubishi Bank, and Bank of Japan and murdered Prime Minister Inukai. The era of party government ended with him. As he had done after Hara's assassination in 1921, Takahashi Korekiyo briefly stepped in as acting prime minister. It was he who advised Prince Saionji against forming another Seiyūkai cabinet. In any case, a new Seiyūkai cabinet would logically have been led by the new Seiyūkai president Suzuki Kisaburō, a reactionary former police official who himself had long been an outspoken opponent of party government.[27] Thus it was that in both the Minseitō and the Seiyūkai, the party leadership itself no longer supported party government.

"We are passing from an aristocracy to a democracy," Inoue Junnosuke had once told Thomas Lamont. Such transitions were always uncomfortable, he said, but he concluded hopefully, "We have seen the worst."[28] Inoue did not envision that a fascist reaction would be one of the stations along the way.

THE "POSITIVE" TIDE

In its usual usage, "Takahashi financial policy" (*Takahashi zaisei*) refers to Takahashi's final, fifty-month tenure as finance minister, which continued, with a brief interruption, through the Inukai, Saitō, and Okada cabinets, until Takahashi's own murder by "superpatriot" soldiers on February 26, 1936.[29] The two endpoints of Takahashi's tenure, December 13, 1931, and February 26, 1936, are two of the great turning points of Japan's modern political-economic history. Coming after the economic storms of 1930–32 and preceding the wildly unbalanced war economy that took shape after 1937, the period from early 1933 to early 1936 also presents a picture of economic equilibrium that is almost uncanny, as if Japan were sitting for a time in the eye of a great storm. The impression is all the stronger against the background of the global depression and Japan's ongoing "quasi-war" in China. By 1935, while maintaining stable domestic price levels, Japan's economy achieved nearly full employment and factories were operating at close to full capacity. It was a scene of economic activity rivaled among the major powers only by Nazi Germany and the Soviet Union.

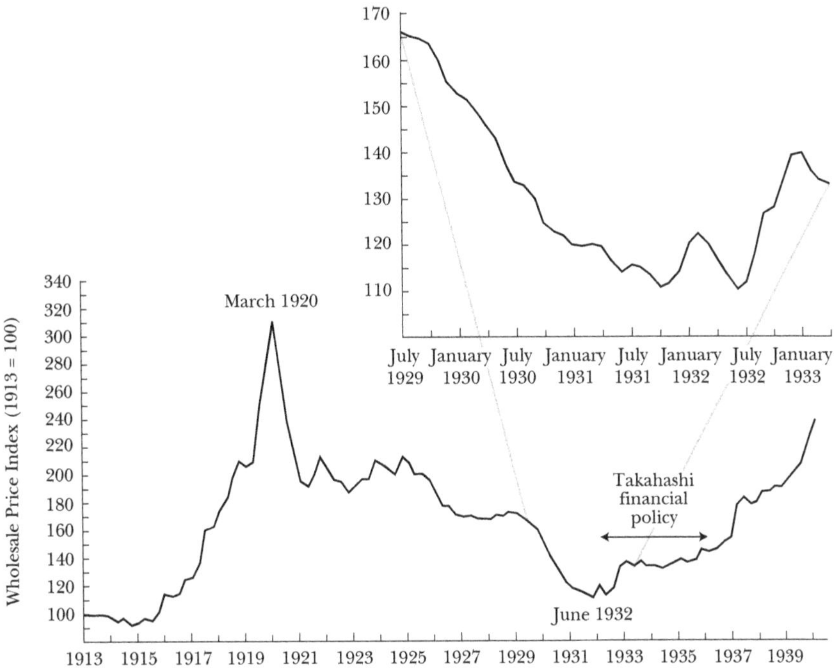

FIG. 9. The big valley: wholesale price movements in interwar Japan, with a close-up view (inset) of the Inoue deflation and Takahashi reflation from July 1929 to January 1933.

SOURCE: E. B. Schumpeter 1940: appendix table IV (book pocket) (Bank of Japan index).

The key points of Takahashi's policy were the resuspension of the gold standard (meaning depreciation of the yen), increased government spending funded by deficit bonds (meaning monetary expansion); and low interest rates.[30] The reimposition of the gold embargo did not lead directly to recovery. As happened in Britain after September 1931, Japan gained a temporary bounce in prices after suspending the gold standard in December, but in March 1932 both British and Japanese prices began to fall again, reaching a new low in June 1932. This was the final trough of the long deflation that had begun in March 1920 (figure 9). The subsequent reinflation of prices from the summer of 1932 to January 1933 was a nationally independent movement. In the United States the long deflation continued without letup until 1933, and sustained reinflation did not come to Britain until World War II.

Both prices and production turned upward after June 1932, and after August prices increased strongly, as Takahashi's policies began to counteract the depression. The yen's slide had the double effect of promoting exports and magnifying exporters' profits when they converted their foreign-currency earnings into yen. As Ishibashi Tanzan had long argued, depreciation was after all the solution to the chronic problem of relatively high Japanese prices in the 1920s. Put in another way, it was not Japanese prices that had been too high—as Gustav Cassel himself had argued, it was only the yen that was too high. Most of these initial price increases stemmed from the decreasing exchange. By the end of 1932 the yen temporarily reached a low point of $0.21, only 40 percent of the old par against the dollar.[31] With the beginning of the dollar's own gyrations in 1933, Takahashi chose to maintain the yen at a de facto parity with sterling, and rates remained steady until his assassination.[32]

On the fiscal side, the government boosted its spending by some 20 percent in 1932 and again in 1933, with especially large increases going to the military. The country had already had too much budgetary economy and could not endure any more, according to Takahashi, and although Manchuria was not part of his positive-policy vision—like Inoue's, Takahashi's approach to military expansion was distinctly negative—nevertheless Takahashi's Ministry of Finance also provided ample funds to pay the expenses of the "Manchuria incident." Public works spending also got money moving in the rural areas.[33] For Takahashi, Japan's "dissimilar conditions" justified covering the resulting budget deficits by issuing bonds rather than raising taxes, and in November 1932 the government began to sell entire issues of its deficit bonds to the Bank of Japan rather than to private institutions. That is, increased government spending was funded by the direct creation of money by the BOJ. Takahashi's idea was first to boost the money supply and stimulate industry, and then, as conditions improved, to have the private sector buy the government bonds from the Bank of Japan, soaking up money from circulation and controlling inflation. In fact, after the price increases of 1932–33, the price level was remarkably stable: as Takahashi anticipated, underemployed people and resources were being put back to work, so the initial effects of his depreciation and deficit spending policies were not inflationary.[34]

With the gold link cut, Japan's monetary "anchor chain" could now be let out at will, and in June 1932 the ceiling for the Bank of Japan's fiduciary note issue was raised from the level of ¥120 million set in 1899 to a new level of ¥1 billion.[35] But the idea of specie backing was not wholly abandoned. During the era of the gold embargo from 1917 to 1929, remarkably, the ratio of the BOJ's specie reserves to its note issue never fell below 60 percent—higher than any period in Japan's modern monetary history including the period of Japan's "classical" gold standard itself. Reserve ratios during the 1920s were also more stable (there were smaller year-to-year fluctuations) than they had been under the classical gold standard.[36] In this way, although the Japanese government restricted gold exports, it con-

FIG. 10. Breaking the bands of the gold standard: Bank of Japan notes issued and specie reserve, 1885–1940. Note again that the "specie" reserve included foreign exchange.

SOURCE: Bank of Japan data (year-end figures), given below in appendix table A.1.

tinued to operate a kind of "shadow" gold standard in the 1920s. The relationship between the gold reserve and the note issue actually broke down when Inoue restored the gold standard, and huge gold outflows forced the ratio down to 35 percent in 1931. Under Takahashi's administration, the reserve ratio was maintained at 28 to 30 percent of the note issue. In this regard, Takahashi's policy ratified a situation that Inoue's policy of free gold flows had inadvertently created (figure 10). Money had become more than ever what the national government said it was, for better and for worse.

Takahashi also ended the high interest rates that Inoue had imposed during the final phase of the gold-standard panic. The Bank of Japan lowered its discount rate in March, June, and August 1932 and again in July 1933, bringing rates from the 6.57 percent rate set in late 1931 to 3.65 percent, the lowest level in the central bank's history to that point.[37] Business investment recovered accordingly.

Thus, Takahashi initiated an expansionary reinflation phase in December 1931. Perhaps he had also learned a lesson from his heedless stoking of the "grass fire boom" of 1919–20, for even before a real industrial recovery appeared, he began to counsel caution, warning his countrymen in tones worthy of Inoue Junnosuke "not to get drunk with the momentary recovery."[38] Takahashi grew more worried about inflation as the recovery progressed, and in 1933 he began working to hold back spending increases, especially in the military budget. This was the second, more anti-inflationary phase of the Takahashi financial policy.

The Takahashi policy was associated with a great extension of state controls over the economy. The reimposition of the gold embargo itself meant the return to a permit system for conversion of the yen into foreign currency: this was the first step in the construction of the extensive financial controls of the 1930s.[39] Foreign-exchange controls were carried further with the Capital Flight Prevention Law of June 30, 1932, and the Foreign Exchange Control Law, put into effect on May 1, 1933. Industrial control laws also followed one after the other in rapid succession, as the development of "Japanese-style" industrial policy accelerated.[40]

Recovery was also based on a developmental transition. The Shōwa panic dissolved the old export structure, and silk production never recovered from the shocks of 1930–31. At the same time, a new export industry, cotton goods, matured, and Japan became a world leader in both weaving technology and in responsiveness to consumer demand in a range of "third world" markets.[41] The enhanced competitiveness of Japanese cotton cloth was due not only to the falling yen but also to the rationalization undertaken during the deflationary period from 1927 to 1931. It can therefore be argued that Inoue's policies of "creative destruction" cleared the way for subsequent growth. Certainly the deflation policy forced down wages and other costs of production. But it is also hard to imagine that its continuation would have brought anything but continued depression, as was experienced by countries that persisted in deflation at the time.

LEAVING THE WEST, ENTERING ASIA

Takahashi's new nationalist line in economics went together with a sudden cooling of the formerly close ties between Japanese and Anglo-American financial circles.[42] In any case, Wall Street had troubles of its own, as the public adulation of business leaders in the 1920s turned to suspicion and anger in the 1930s. Coming into office in the midst of a nationwide bank panic, Franklin D. Roosevelt in his inaugural address on March 4, 1933, denounced the "rulers of the exchange of mankind's goods" and "the unscrupulous money changers." Acting "with great courage and decisiveness," Takahashi Korekiyo thought, Roosevelt announced on the next day a banking moratorium and an emergency embargo of gold exports. This was the end of the U.S. gold standard. The U.S. Congress also launched a new round of investigations of Wall Street, and again, unwillingly, Morgan and Company was at the center of things, only now it was in the process of being split up. Writing empathetically to Thomas Lamont in July 1933, Mori Kengo called the hearings "a Spanish Inquisition on the freedom of financial conscience." The world had become "topsy-turvy," he confided—"like a long bad dream."[43]

In regard to Manchuria, Takahashi also ignored the Four-Power Consortium's "financial blockade" of China negotiated by Lamont: as Manchukuo was an independent country and not part of China, he decided, Japan need not consult the consortium partners concerning loans there. Nonetheless, the Ministry of Finance did not abandon plans for persuading U.S. capital to invest in Manchuria—this idea seemed all the more attractive because increased Japanese investment in Manchuria led to new balance-of-payments shortfalls. And after his shock at Japan's violent behavior had died down, Thomas Lamont, ever adaptable and realistic, again involved himself in a plan to promote American loans to Japanese operations in Manchuria. Again the State Department vetoed it. Fruitless Japanese efforts to gain American capital for Manchurian development persisted until as late as the summer of 1940.[44] Aside from the refinancing in London of £4 million in existing SMR bonds in 1933, Japan did not borrow abroad again until the 1950s.

Thus, the boom of the 1930s was funded entirely by domestic capital. Moreover, a new wave of Japanese overseas investment rose after 1932, in tandem with Japan's stepwise invasion of China: in this view also, the 1930s boom picked up where the World War I boom left off. This new investment went above all to Manchuria, where a new kind of developmental industrial colonialism was taking shape.[45]

In 1930 Inoue had written that world economic recovery depended on a renewed outflow of U.S. dollars. And in the end, the renewed outflow of dollars was to be the ultimate solution to the global capitalist crisis. But this solution came more than fifteen years after Inoue's own death, and after the United States had invested tens of thousands of American lives and tens of billions of dollars to destroy Japan's Asian empire and occupy the Japanese mainland. In the meantime, Japan's recovery of the 1930s came not from American but from Asian markets. This advance in Asia mirrored the decline of the American market. In the 1920s, Japanese exports to the United States had boomed as never before, reaching an annual level of ¥1 billion, more than 40 percent of Japan's total exports.[46] But exports to America crashed in 1930 and 1931, and when Japanese exports recovered and then surged ahead in the 1930s, they went mainly to markets in countries less industrialized than Japan, as consumers in many colonial countries, pressed by the world depression, switched from European cloth and other consumer goods to cheaper Japanese goods. Exports of capital equipment to Manchuria simultaneously made Japan a net exporter of steel and machinery, although Japanese industry still depended on Western countries for higher-technology metals and machines.[47] These shifts in markets thus reflected a structural shift in the composition of Japan's exports toward higher-technology goods.

Monetarily, however, Japan's captive colonial markets could not substitute for Western markets. Much of the increase in exports to the yen bloc was paid for in freshly created yen—"inflation capital," in Itō Masanao's phrase—and did not earn the foreign exchange needed to purchase essential imports from more industrialized countries. For these reasons among others, Takahashi repeatedly tried to restrain the flow of Japanese investment to Manchuria and to restrict the independent money creation power of Japanese authorities there.[48] Despite the creation of an "independent" Manchurian central bank in February 1932, Takahashi, persisting in ideas he had held twenty years before as Yokohama Specie Bank president, overrode the arguments of the Bank of Chosen and the Kwantung Army and insisted that Manchuria's new yen be established on a silver basis—both to maintain Manchuria's linkage with the Chinese economy and to deny the Kwantung Army the power to create at will the virtual equivalents of Bank of Japan notes. In early 1935 Takahashi even threatened to revoke the independent money creation power of the Bank of Chosen and Bank of Taiwan. The Manchurian currency remained on a silver-exchange basis until December 1935, when China itself abandoned the silver standard. Only then was the Manchukuo yen linked directly to the Japanese yen.[49]

In international monetary relations, the 1930s were a different world from the 1920s—"conservative twenties, revolutionary thirties," in Karl Polanyi's formula.[50] But not yet completely different. For much of the world, Britain's departure from the gold standard did not end the international centrality of the British pound, and in some ways it liberated British financiers to undertake new initiatives. One of these was a finally successful attempt to establish a modern monetary system for China.

In the face of mounting Japanese aggression, the Chinese government began a new round of efforts to get British and American loans, and in June 1935 Frederick Leith-Ross, the British government's chief adviser on international financial relations, was named financial adviser to the Chinese government. He aimed to settle the East Asian crisis at a stroke: Britain, preferably jointly with Japan, would lend £10 million to Manchukuo; Manchukuo would pay £10 million as an indemnity to China; Britain would actually deliver the money, in the style of a controlled loan, to the Chinese government; and China would use the funds as a reserve to establish a sterling exchange standard. China, with Britain, would thus recognize Manchukuo's "independence"—along the lines of the Egyptian precedent—and Japan would return to the League of Nations. In effect, Japan would buy Manchuria from China, taking out a loan in London to do so. This was nothing less than a bid to restore the old cooperative imperialism of the era of the Anglo-Japanese alliance. But U.S. representatives declined to meet Leith-Ross, and Japanese officials found the restoration of British financial leverage unnecessary. When Leith-Ross came to meet them in Tokyo in September 1935, Takahashi Korekiyo and BOJ governor Fukai Eigo were not unsympathetic to his plan, although Takahashi insisted that China should retain a silver standard; but the army violently rejected a return to

Anglo-Japanese cooperation. The British and Chinese governments went ahead alone, and in November 1935 the Chinese government demonetized silver and established a fully managed paper currency—in fact, a sterling exchange standard, with Chinese banknotes to be used internally and sterling for external payments. To create a reserve fund, the Chinese government nationalized the nation's silver stock and began selling it to the United States. Despite Japanese efforts, Chinese nation building was proceeding, with the crucial consolidation of national money creation power. Monetary reform led directly, as the Chinese government had hoped, to a negotiated settlement of China's outstanding foreign debts and to arrangements for new currency stabilization and rail loans—the same sort of deal signed in the spring of 1911 but then ruined by the political chaos that followed. Now it was Japan's turn to use the international consortium to try to block unilateral British loans. In early 1937 the British government therefore proposed to the Americans that the consortium be dissolved, and it let the Japanese group know of this intention in June.[51] At this point, Japan's invasion of China intervened.

Takahashi Korekiyo had earned the top posts at the Bank of Japan by his ability to raise the war loans that paid for the first installments of Japan's continental empire. But he had also frequently resisted the more aggressively expansionist plans aimed at China, and the successive fiscal enabling and restraining of Japanese militarism had repeatedly occupied his energies. In the end, Takahashi's efforts to restrain reckless military spending placed him in head-to-head conflict with military expansionists, much as Finance Minister Inoue had been before him. In late 1935 Takahashi forced through a retrenchment budget over bitter opposition from the army. The dissatisfaction reached an extremity among young superpatriot officers of the army's elite First Division, among whom the national-socialist ideas of Kita Ikki had gained influence, and they resolved to destroy the corrupt gerontocracy that stood between the emperor and the masses. At just after 5:00 A.M. on the snowy morning of February 26, 1936, while their comrades occupied the government district of Tokyo, a squad of soldiers from the First Division tramped into Takahashi's house, then shot and hacked to death the eighty-two-year-old finance minister as he lay in bed. Their coup was put down within days and the conspirators purged, but the financial brakes on expansion were now removed.[52] The job of finance minister itself became an unwanted task.

By 1936, there were also signs that the economic expansion that had taken place under Takahashi's watch was finished and that the economy was entering a new phase of deadlock. Monetary expansion was beginning to generate inflation, which became serious after Takahashi's removal. The advance of Japanese exports had provoked new trade barriers in colonial markets controlled by the Western powers. Most fundamentally, runaway military expansion was creating huge fiscal and balance-of-payments disproportions that could be solved only by radical retrenchment—or as self-deluded military planners saw it, by a greater-than-ever commitment to a "positive" policy of military action, to seize by force the resources that Japan lacked. In June 1937 the army's own five-year economic plan, drafted under the direction of General Ishiwara Kanji, now chief of operations on the army general staff, was adopted as government policy, serving to defeat the option of retrenchment in regard to the renewed fiscal crisis.[53] Thus, further microeconomic controls were the only way out—in effect, the restraining function of "negative" budgetary policies was now performed by direct administrative action. With full-scale wartime mobilization after July 1937, production concerns wholly overrode financial ones, and the dialectic of the positive and negative policies ceased to matter for a time, as Japan entered a new era of inflationary finance combined with comprehensive price and production controls.

Epilogue

Money and Hegemony

In the fall of 1951, soon after U.S. occupation authorities lifted the purge restrictions under which they had placed him four years earlier, Ishibashi Tanzan wrote an essay in which he considered the reasons for the disaster that had befallen his country. Ishibashi had made his reputation as an economist by attacking Inoue Junnosuke's restoration of the gold standard at the old par, and he now returned to a familiar theme:

> The profound livelihood difficulties that the Japanese people fell into because of the depression that began in 1929 formed a good basis for extending the influence of the right-wing groups and the young officers who called for national renovation. It would be a mistake to say that things like the Manchuria incident, the May 15 [1932] incident, and the February 26 [1936] incident happened only because of the depression. However, it is probably beyond doubt that the depression supplied the best basis for these things to occur. This, after all, was the same as in Germany, where the severe depression after 1929 ended up by giving political power to Hitler in 1933. Germany was ruined by Hitler, but Japan too was driven by the military to the brink of national destruction. If we consider it like this, we can say that *what placed Japan in the adversity of present days was actually the lifting of the gold embargo in 1930.*[1]

For Ishibashi, one of the most original and influential of the young liberals of the Taishō era, the historical lesson seemed inescapable: the failure of Japanese liberals to adopt a more populist, pro-growth economics helped to provoke the backlash that destroyed liberalism in Japan. "I was worried that postwar Japan might repeat the same mistake," Ishibashi wrote. From the time of the surrender in August 1945, he thus began to anticipate a deflationary postwar depression.[2]

Opinions like Ishibashi's were widely held in the postdepression, postwar world, and they shaped the policy instincts of a generation. Ishibashi also got the chance to make his own economic policy mistakes, when he was appointed finance minister in May 1946. Inspired by Takahashi Korekiyo's example, Ishibashi implemented an ultrainflationary version of the positive policy, which he carried through until his purge by the U.S. occupation authorities one year later.[3]

In fact, like World War I, World War II brought global inflation, not deflation, in its immediate wake. In defeated Japan, with some help from Ishibashi, the inflation verged into hyperinflation. And while this phase of inflationary reconstruction could hardly be considered a boom, it did yield a familiar two-step movement of inflation and deflation. Deflationary stabilization, when it finally came in early 1949, was imposed under direct U.S. orders and directed by American bankers. In the process, the Japanese yen was reestablished on the basis of a U.S. dollar standard.

REPRISE: JAPAN'S GOLD-STANDARD ERA

The fixing of the yen to the U.S. dollar in 1949 provides a view of Japanese history come full circle. The gold standard had originally been adopted in 1897 as part of a larger set of policies that could be called, to borrow Fukuzawa Yukichi's idea, a program of "entering Europe." Shortly after, Western capital began to flow in volume. Japan's gold-standard era was also the era of the Anglo-Japanese alliance and of Japan's entrance, with British sponsorship, into the European system of states as a kind of guest member. Japan's "westward" movement went forward in tandem with its empire building in Asia. Thus, Japanese financial and diplomatic policies operated largely within the frameworks given by the European state system. Many of these policies supported the structures of the British Empire in particular. This was nowhere truer than in Japan's international financial relations.

Seen from the side of London, newly industrializing Japan was a small but not insignificant part of the international system of credit and debt. In fact, from 1897 to 1913, Japan was the single largest state borrower on the London money markets. China was close behind, and together the two East Asian countries accounted for almost one-third of the £489 million in loans issued in London to sovereign borrowers in the final eighteen years of the classical gold standard.[4] Japanese and Chinese borrowing was more "complementary" than parallel, however, as a great part of China's debt was to pay for its own subjugation, while the greater part of Japan's debt was to pay for the building of an Asian empire. Japan also supported London's international financial primacy by maintaining sterling reserves larger than those of any other country, including India. By 1905, Japan was in practice operating not an orthodox gold standard but a sterling-based gold-exchange standard.[5]

The era of Japan's "classical" gold standard was also an era in world history. From 1897, when Russia and Japan joined the gold-standard system, until 1914, when the European war deranged it, virtually the entire industrialized world adhered to a regime of convertible gold-backed currencies with fixed rates of exchange between them. These seventeen years of Anglo-Japanese exchange-rate union were also the culminating phase of the nineteenth-century Eurocentric international system—the retrospectively golden twilight of Europe's "hundred years' peace" that had lasted since 1815.[6] This was Japan's era of cooperative (or "dependent") imperialism, when formal empire building seemed fully compatible with the workings of the liberal international financial order.

Japan's gold standard achieved its purpose of opening access to the international capital markets and enabling national expansion. But as newly industrializing, newly imperial Japan began to run regular trade deficits, the system of fixed parities put increasing strain on the domestic economy. The yen was maintained at its gold par only by repeatedly borrowing abroad and by repeatedly imposing austerity policies at home. By the eve of the World War I, Japan was reaching the limit of its ability to borrow abroad, and the defense of the gold standard had become an economic constraint.

The European war ended the brief era of the classical gold standard and "providentially" rescued Japan's international financial situation. The system of international gold payments was suspended, and while the European powers warred with each other, Japan, with a relatively free hand in China, moved in an independent and aggressive direction. For Japanese leaders, World War I thus offered a new vision of financial independence and of Japanese hegemony in an East Asia devoid of Europeans. By the end of World War I, it was not the harmony but the contradictions between Japan's aggressive imperialism and the demands of international financial cooperation—now championed by the United States—that seemed most salient, and the forces of militarism and finance seemed to outside observers such as Thomas Lamont as if poised in an uneasy balance.

The Japanese initiative in China provoked an American response, and although the U.S. government ended up standing aloof from the multilateral arrangements it had first proposed in Europe, in East Asia the United States took the lead in implementing the new multilateralism. Diplomatically, the Anglo-Japanese alliance that had enabled Japan to expand as a regional partner of the British Empire was replaced after World War I, at American insistence, by a looser set of multilateral cooperative arrangements, including the second China consortium and the Washington system of treaties—arrangements that were intended by Americans to *contain* Japanese expansion. The international campaign to restore the gold standard was likewise an Anglo-American initiative expressing both the cooperation and the rivalry that existed between the declining and the rising hegemonic power.

And while it was not conceptualized as a matter of monetary "containment" vis-à-vis Japan, in fact that is what it was.

Monetarily, the 1920s formed a long interim phase of suspension of the gold standard for Japan. The financial policy of the decade can also be thought of as an unsettled compromise between the evolving policy lines associated with Takahashi Korekiyo and Inoue Junnosuke. Without really planning it, Finance Minister Takahashi established a new and uncertain framework for policy by maintaining the gold embargo after 1919. In effect, this was an effort to maintain the new economic structure that had resulted from the world-war boom.[7] It was also, explicitly, an effort to maintain Japan's financial freedom of action in China in the face of the new financial power of the United States. But at the end of 1919, pressed by the compelling need to rein in inflation—and in line with moves by the U.S. Federal Reserve and the Bank of England—Bank of Japan governor Inoue began using the deflationary policy to "contain" the pro-inflationary positive policy of Takahashi Korekiyo and the Seiyūkai. Thereafter, the restraint policies of the Bank of Japan and of successive Kenseikai and Minseitō cabinets put the brakes on Japanese money growth for more than a decade. The divisions over the monetary issue also became congruent with the domestic political confrontation between the two mainstream conservative parties. Phases of expansionary "positive" and contractionary "negative" policy alternated during this decade, but monetarily speaking, Inoue's "contractionary tide" was the dominant trend. It was carried to its fullest extent in 1930 and 1931, the trough of Japan's interwar depression, when the conflict between the Inoue and Takahashi lines again came to a head. The turn to recovery after 1932 was defined by the return to Takahashi's positive policy.

JAPAN AND THE FAILURE OF POST–WORLD WAR I STABILIZATION

Gold-centered stabilization policy in Japan was of a piece with conservative stabilization policies implemented around the world in the 1920s. These policies were based on a universalist, bankers' vision, and transnational financial institutions promoted and underwrote the effort to attain this vision. The greatest of these institutions was J. P. Morgan and Company, and for Thomas Lamont and his partners at Morgan and Company, Japan was just one piece of an ambitious global strategy. Lamont saw himself as a kind of private statesman who was working to institutionalize a new kind of world peace, and he later described the monetary stabilization campaigns of the 1920s as a "general effort to restore the civilized world."[8]

Post–World War I stabilization was a movement facing at once forward and backward. In many ways, the new international arrangements that Lamont championed in the 1920s were ahead of their time, foreshadowing the more enduring international system created after World War II. In other ways, the rally of the 1920s was a brief and ultimately disastrous attempt to restore the prewar political-economic order. The League of Nations itself expressed the divided character of the postwar international order. In some respects, the League represented a new vision of democratic internationalism. In others, it was an Anglo-French imperialist condominium; and under the mantle of the new multilateralism, the prewar Anglo- and Francocentric world order was not merely maintained in the 1920s: it was precisely at this point, by their annexation of former Turkish and German territories as League of Nations mandates, that the British and French empires reached their final and greatest extent. This was the final reprise for the nineteenth-century European system. A financial view also reveals its fundamental weakness, for this late-imperial rally rested on the quicksand of Wall Street loans, German reparations, and Allied war debt repayments. That is, it was based on the financial presence but political absence of both the United States and Germany. As such, it was ultimately illusory.[9] From this failure arose the Great Depression, the rise of fascism, and World War II.

Even after these cumulative disasters, Thomas Lamont could still insist in 1951, in a restrospective look at his transnational career, that the result of Morgan's private banking operations of the 1920s had been "to stabilize Europe" for a decade, enabling the Europeans to get back on their feet. Then, unfortunately, had come the "rise of the dictators."[10] But more than providing the general good of social-economic stabilization, Lamont's real business was to sell bonds. It afterwards became clear that private capitalists were not up to the task of social stabilization: they poured loans in when business looked good, but cut off the lending when times got tough, intensifying rather than ameliorating the financial whiplash effect at the end of the decade. The destructive effects of the cutoff of American credit were recognized at the time and have been given a central place in subsequent analyses of the causes of the Great Depression.[11] But the story goes further than that: more than an *insufficiency* of private stabilization, it was the active excesses of liberal deflationism that undermined political liberalism in many of the places where it was weakest and most tentative. The financial leverage of the American and British banking groups was the key to implementing the deflation policy around the world. The result was a series of gold-restoration depressions—or, as Thomas Lamont put it to Inoue Junnosuke in 1930, "the deflation and industrial discomfort which always follows the adoption of a sound money policy."[12] Although the finances of creditor interests may have been stabilized by these induced depressions, those of agriculture and export industry were destabilized. Social turmoil and right-wing terror incidents were one consequence of this financially oriented stabilization. For Lamont the rise of the dictators was evidently a process exogenous to economics; but here as so often,

Lamont, who incidentally bankrolled and befriended Europe's first fascist dictator, appears disingenuous.[13]

The Japanese government too formally adhered to the liberal multilateralism of the 1920s, and like the British and French empires, the Japanese empire extended its reach as a result of the European war. But as in Germany and Italy, nationalists in Japan came to consider their nation a "have-not" power—caught moreover in a deadlock that ultimately derived from the constraints of the Western-dominated international system.

The comparison with Europe is revealing. Looking at Germany caught between inflation and depression in the 1920s, William C. McNeil described a situation of "institutions in stalemate."[14] In Charles Maier's influential analysis of the "recasting of bourgeois Europe," this interwar deadlock appears as a trans-European phenomenon, arising as a consequence of a new kind of distributional politics—in essence, a bitter conflict between a now highly politicized industrial working class and the owners and managers of capital.[15] In Japan, however, the new distributional politics driven by the rise of powerful labor unions and social-democratic parties did not appear until after World War II; nonetheless there appeared in the 1920s a deadlock similar to that in Europe. This parallel experience suggests that Maier's analysis of Europe's deadlock needs to be reconsidered in a globalized context—that the widely felt deadlock of the 1920s was part of an international political-economic process that transcended domestic political contradictions. Here, the global constraints on demand, created by the deflation policy, deserve primary consideration.[16] This was the fundamental point argued in Europe at the time by Keynes and argued increasingly clearly in Japan by Ishibashi Tanzan and Takahashi Korekiyo.

It also appears that the hegemony of orthodox Anglo-American *ideas* of economics helped to keep Japan in chronic recession in the 1920s. If "European-style" stabilization programs caused great damage in Europe itself, such programs appear even less appropriate in newly industrializing Japan, which in the 1920s was precisely at the most intense phase of its historic population explosion—even as its industrial revolution was being placed on monetary hold. As the leading practitioner of these Anglo-American financial ideas, Inoue Junnosuke personally embodied the contradictions in Japan's international position. The strong desire among bourgeois Europeans for a restoration of the prewar world requires little explanation. It is less clear why turning back the clock should have appealed to Japanese elites, and the restorationist aspect of the Minseitō program—the effort to return to the world before August 1914—seems more a reflection of European dreams than of Japanese realities. As Takahashi Korekiyo argued, Japan was not Europe and was on a very different developmental trajectory; and as Japanese economic development came to be actualized in the middle decades of the twentieth century, Takahashi's nationalist and mercantilist vision was much closer to the path actually taken than was Inoue's more liberal and universalist vision.

In one view, Inoue's timing was simply unlucky: he planned to deflate domestic prices and thereby to promote exports, but the world depression ruined that plan. But at a deeper level of analysis, the world depression itself was a consequence of the wave of national deflation (demand-reduction) policies that came to a ruinous climax in 1931. Japan was not merely a bystander to an independent global process. Inoue Junnosuke was tragically loyal to the ideas and social forms of the liberal world order. By pushing the logic of that order to its full conclusion, he also helped to destroy it.

From a distance, the history narrated above looks like a movement toward and away from the West. In late 1931 the balance shifted abruptly, in the sharp turn from Shidehara Kijūrō's cooperative diplomacy to the continental invasion schemes of Ishiwara Kanji, and from Inoue Junnosuke's internationalist financial policy to the nationalist policies of Takahashi Korekiyo. Japan abruptly "left Europe" and entered Asia with a vengeance. The turn to a fully managed currency and to comprehensive state controls over trade and industry was one logical outcome of the decisions made at this point. Other results of this new course were alienation from the West, withdrawal from the League of Nations, and finally, war with the United States and Britain. With Japan's defeat came another great reversal. It was now a case not of "*datsu-A, nyū-Ō,*" of leaving Asia and entering Europe, but of "*datsu-A, nyū-Bei,*" leaving Asia and entering America.

In the spring of 1929, Tsurumi Yūsuke, a leading intellectual spokesman of the new 1920s internationalism, finished a speaking tour in the United States, where he was greatly impressed by Los Angeles and the motorcar, and he wrote a book called *The Pacific Age* (*Taiheiyō jidai*). In it, he anticipated the coming of an American age, in which American values and American goods would be the new universal standards. "The phrase, *the Pacific age* is gradually ripening in our ears and becoming a usual expression," he said. No one had thought in this way thirty years ago—the world center was still Europe, and it was the "Atlantic age." Then came the suicidal European war, and world wealth and power had moved to America and, to a degree, to Japan. Not only was America the new center, but henceforth Japan's external relations, even with Asia, would be mediated through Washington: "The diplomacy of the Japanese people is centered upon China, but the center of Sino-Japanese diplomacy is not in China, not in Nanjing nor in Mukden, but rather in the American capital of Washington. Because the center of the entire world is now shifting from London to Washington, the solution of the world's great problems now begins according to discussion with the people in Washington."[17] Like Inoue's vision, this was both a farsighted and a nearsighted view. In 1929, it turned out, the new American standard was not something to bank on. Twenty years later, it was inescapable, and Japan's Pacific age had dawned. Attractive force and coercion were complexly combined.

THE U.S. DOLLAR STANDARD

This study concludes not with the end of a story but with the beginning of one, that of Japan's reintegration into the Western world order after 1952. As part of this process, the yen was reestablished on the basis of the U.S. dollar.

In December 1931 Takahashi Korekiyo suspended the operation of the gold standard without formally creating anything new in its place, and until 1942, Bank of Japan notes continued to bear the now meaningless phrase "convertible into gold." In that year, in line with the needs of wartime finance, the new Bank of Japan Law superseded the 1897 Currency Law. The Bank of Japan itself was placed more directly than ever under Ministry of Finance authority. The distinction between the specie reserve and the fiduciary reserve was also abolished, and although the pretense of 100 percent backing of the note issue was maintained, the BOJ's own advances to the government and its purchases of government bonds could be counted as reserve assets. The size of the note issue was to be determined by the minister of finance. In law and in fact, Japan now had a completely state-managed currency. By this point, 1942, the yen had already lost one-half of its former value against the U.S. dollar, itself now depreciated against gold.[18] Just how far the Japanese currency had evolved from a gold standard is indicated by the minting of the now familiar aluminum yen coins (initially valued at 1 sen) in 1938; by 1945 the government was even preparing to mint tiny ceramic yen tokens.

In the meantime, new yen-based monetary standards were set up in the wake of Japanese military advances, as "Manchukuo," occupied China, and Japan's new satellite states in Southeast Asia were incorporated into the swelling yen bloc. New central banks were set up in Manchuria (1932), Inner Mongolia (1937), Beijing (1938), and Shanghai (1941), with the right to issue banknotes backed by yen reserves. The South Seas Development Fund (Nanpō Kaihatsu Kinkō) was given similar powers in the occupied territories of Southeast Asia and the Pacific, where Japanese planners envisioned the yen taking the former place of sterling and dollars.[19] Such money creation schemes were a more extreme version of the colonial gold-exchange standards preceding them: a lever of power and exploitation, allowing the Japanese occupiers to squeeze capital out of capital-poor societies.[20] They also brought about a series of catastrophic inflations that were increasingly extreme toward the peripheries of the new "Co-Prosperity Sphere," where monetary authority devolved to the occupying military forces, which expropriated local wealth even more directly by issuing their own paper scrip denominated in local currencies.

As the actual realization of Gotō Shinpei's dream of monetary dominion in East Asia became increasingly cruel and grotesque, American and British financial authorities began to plan a restored international monetary order. Serious negotiations to this end began in 1942, and from the outset, the Americans pushed for a new gold- and dollar-based system. The British, led by Keynes, resisted, proposing the creation of a new, elastic international monetary unit, the "bancor," to take the former place of gold. As the United States now held some $22 billion of the world's reported $28 billion in gold, the questions of the gold shortage (or dollar gap) that had arisen after World War I would manifestly be raised to a new power after the second. On Wall Street a few traditionalists promoted a restored gold standard, but the bankers were effectively cut out of the decision-making process by U.S. treasury secretary Henry Morgenthau, who was determined, echoing Franklin Roosevelt's 1933 inaugural address, that the "money-lenders be driven from the temple." The new international monetary institutions, he declared, would be "instrumentalities of sovereign governments and not of private financial interests." Privately, Morgenthau was also determined that the U.S. Treasury in Washington, not London or Wall Street, should be the center of the restored international monetary system.[21]

The result was a global vision that went far beyond the semiprivate Genoa and BIS visions of the 1920s. In April 1944, British and American representatives agreed to the foundational idea for an "International Monetary Fund" (IMF) to help countries stabilize their currencies, and in July delegates from forty-five countries gathered at a resort hotel in Bretton Woods, New Hampshire, to draw up a formal agreement for the postwar international monetary order. Treasury Secretary Morgenthau announced America's expansive global-monetary vision at the conference's inaugural session: "Prosperity has no fixed limits. It is not a finite substance to be diminished by division."[22] Unlike the world's stock of gold, one might add. The old "money doctor," Edwin Kemmerer, rejected the Bretton Woods approach and called for a second return to the gold standard, but what had been orthodox common sense, almost beyond argument, in the decade after World War I seemed faintly ridiculous by 1944. As Keynes quipped, the restoration of "good old 1920–1921 or 1930–1933" had little appeal.[23]

Although it was not clearly stated in the Bretton Woods agreement itself, the U.S. dollar was without question the pivot of the system. The dollar thus assumed the place that British policy makers had envisioned for sterling twenty-two years earlier at Genoa, but the United States was now the great "gold center" country. The new Bretton Woods system could in fact be viewed as the restoration of a highly attenuated gold-exchange standard. Only the U.S. dollar was backed by gold, and gold circulated only among national treasuries and central banks—the "anchor chain" had been let out again.[24]

But the keynote of the conference was not restoration but a new departure, and the new system was designed above all to end the instability and inflexibility that had characterized interwar monetary arrangements. Like the classical gold standard, the Bretton Woods agreement instituted a system of fixed par values (exchange rates) for currencies. But it was also a much more statist standard, with assumptions of automaticity largely abandoned. Until the 1970s, there was no free market in gold, and one could better say that gold had been fixed to the dollar than that the dollar had been fixed to gold. For other currencies, convertibility meant convertibility into dollars. By the mid-1950s, most world trade was settled in dollars, and most countries' currency reserves were held in dollars. This represented the completion of the shift from British to U.S. financial hegemony that had begun in World War I.

When news of Bretton Woods was heard in Japan, economist Ōuchi Hyōe, then working at the Bank of Japan, immediately recognized its importance. Relying on secretly monitored shortwave radio reports and on information sent via submarine courier by the bank's Berlin office, Ōuchi discreetly began to investigate the monetary agreement, and he quickly reached a conclusion that he could not yet voice in public: that postwar Japan must be prepared to join the new U.S.-British monetary system. Almost immediately after Japan's surrender in August 1945, Ōuchi began to publish his findings.[25] But before defeated Japan could rejoin the reconstructed international monetary system, a wrenching process of postwar adjustment was necessary.

Remarkably, Japan largely preserved its monetary independence even under allied military occupation. Tsushima Juichi had risen to the post of vice minister of finance under Takahashi Korekiyo, and he subsequently served as vice governor of the Bank of Japan, president of the North China Development Company, and briefly in 1945, finance minister. He was then purged from public office under U.S. orders. At the outset of the occupation, American authorities had prepared their own yen-denominated military scrip for use in Japan; it was Finance Minister Tsushima who convinced the Americans not to use military scrip by assuring them that all of their needs could be supplied with Bank of Japan notes.[26]

Postwar finance thus continued to depend on inflation, and the inflation policy reached an extreme when Ishibashi Tanzan became finance minister in May 1946. Echoing Takahashi Korekiyo in 1919, Ishibashi reasoned that the greatest problem was the shortage of production. To increase production required expansionary measures, meaning massive credits to industry.[27] The result was that Japan's post–World War II adjustment came via inflation and currency depreciation rather than by deflation. In effect, the government's huge domestic debts were inflated away and the Japanese people's savings vanished. After stabilization, the name of the currency remained the same, but for practical purposes postwar Japan had a new yen, with an internal purchasing power of approximately 1/350th of the prewar yen. Currency stabilization, when it came in 1949, was mandated by U.S. authorities.

Politically powerful during the Republican Party's ascendancy in the 1920s, Wall Street bankers were widely blamed for the depression of the 1930s and lost much of their political influence. During the second world war, however, as during the first, the financial demands of war and of the Anglo-American alliance meant a partial return to influence for the big Wall Street banks. With the Republican sweep in the 1946 congressional elections, Wall Street regained real political influence, and the management of financial policy in occupied Japan also became the domain of American bankers. Unlike their counterparts in the 1920s, however, American bankers now came not as private financiers but as public proconsuls, and in fact, Japan was not subordinated to the private financial interests of Wall Street but rather to the public, strategic interests of Washington, D.C.[28]

After Morgan and Company, Dillon, Read was Wall Street's number-two international lender in the 1920s. In 1947 former Dillon, Read president James Forrestal became the United States' first secretary of defense, and he appointed his vice president at Dillon, Read, William Draper Jr., as army undersecretary with responsibility for overseeing the occupation of Germany and Japan. Draper led two fact-finding missions to Japan in 1947 and 1948, concluding, in line with the orthodox financial logic of the 1920s, that increases in domestic demand would only drain off resources that could otherwise be used for exports and industrial reconstruction. That is, overconsumption was the problem and austerity the solution. A subsequent mission led by Ralph Young of the Federal Reserve Board's Research Division added that Japan needed to fix a single exchange rate and to cut consumption and reduce the real wages of workers (which had already fallen to some 65 percent of their 1934–36 levels). The new stabilization policy, announced in December 1948, was subsequently implemented by Joseph M. Dodge, president of the Detroit Bank, head of the American Bankers Association, future director of the U.S. Bureau of the Budget, and an experienced hand at currency reform in Germany. Draper himself returned to Dillon, Read, and in January 1950 led a third, private mission to Japan to investigate the prospects for American investment there.[29]

The "Dodge line" deflation of 1949–50 was the first real turn to a "negative," or contractionary, economic policy since the abandonment of the gold standard in December 1931. By the spring of 1950, Dodge's policy had stopped inflation cold, at the cost of a grinding stabilization depression. There was, however, no outright deflation in Japan, and in contradistinction to post–World War I stabilization, prices were stabilized at existing levels.

As part of his program, Dodge also abolished the complex system of multiple exchange rates then in use and returned the yen to a unitary, fixed exchange rate of ¥360 to the dollar. The new yen-dollar rate was thus 1/360th of the rate first instituted in 1870, and 1/180th of the yen's 1897 dollar par restored by Inoue Junnosuke in 1930. While there seems to be no basis for the legend that Dodge fixed the 360 rate upon hearing that the word yen (*en*) meant "circle," it surely did seem a nice round number. The new yen-dollar rate held for twenty-two years, two years longer than had the old fixed rate under the classical gold standard.

In May 1950 after a year of austerity and disinflation, Finance Minister Ikeda Hayato and his secretary and translator Miyazawa Kiichi traveled to Washington, D.C., to try to negotiate an easing of the deflation policy with Joseph Dodge. Few Japanese were abroad in 1950—unless as prisoners of war—and Ikeda and Miyazawa were among the first officials to travel to the United States after the war. On the eve of his departure, in April 1950, Ikeda met with the supreme commander for the Allied powers, who chose to talk to him about gold:

> [General MacArthur] said, in short, that "gold" had been the means of trade among human beings for centuries, and accordingly was the means of peaceful accommodation. Now, however, as a consequence of most of the gold being gathered in America, the means of trade among nations was on the verge of being lost, and accordingly, the road of peaceful accommodation was being closed. Moreover, a replacement for gold had not yet been born. As a result of this, in America there was a "poverty due to surplus," making a precise contrast to Japan's "poverty due to poverty." Both were difficult problems, he said.[30]

What MacArthur called America's "poverty due to surplus" was a concern that had driven an American search for overseas markets since the 1890s. The problem reached a new order of magnitude after World War II and was manifest in the form of the "dollar gap": the world lacked the dollars needed to pay for America's abundant production. This was part of the problem of overproduction relative to effective demand that was a fundamental cause of the Great Depression and that was the object of the Keynesian solution. Having served as vice minister of finance under Ishibashi Tanzan, Ikeda also knew something of the facility of credit creation. Listening to MacArthur's soliloquy, an easy answer came to his mind: "I was going to say that the replacement for 'gold' is 'credit.'" But "once [MacArthur] got started, his eloquence did not easily come to an end," and so Ikeda's helpful idea remained unspoken.[31] It was to be practiced and practiced in later years.

In Washington, Dodge was unswayed by Ikeda's pleas to ease the austerity policy, and Ikeda returned home empty-handed. Dodge did convey to Ikeda that the United States would help Japan find overseas markets in

Southeast Asia.[32] In fact, economic salvation was much closer at hand than the impoverished markets of Japan's former Co-Prosperity Sphere. Inoue Junnosuke had once described how depression in Japan had often been "turned to prosperity due to outside forces," especially by the boon of wartime demand. Now again, Japan reaped an economic windfall when war broke out in its former colony of Korea in the summer of 1950. U.S. military procurements in Japan proved to be the functional equivalent of Marshall Plan aid in Western Europe, and a sustained economic recovery at last got underway. With ample historical resonance, Prime Minister Yoshida Shigeru called it *ten'yū shinjo*—"divine providence."[33]

Another aspect of the Korean War boom was described by an internal Bank of Japan report written shortly after Japan's return of independence: as had happened twenty years before, after the "Manchuria incident" and Takahashi's gold re-embargo, Japan was experiencing a great economic recovery. And as after the Manchuria incident, various economic controls, which had been abolished at the time of the Dodge line, had again become necessary.[34]

Thus, the financial controls of the 1930s were quietly reconstructed in a new form, even as Japan itself came to be imagined by Americans as a "Western" island in eastern waters[35]—truly "an incomparable base of operations," as the London *Economist* had hopefully termed it in 1898. Under the terms of the San Francisco Peace Treaty and the jointly negotiated U.S.-Japan alliance, Japan regained its sovereignty as of April 28, 1952, but became, in effect, an American military protectorate.

In the cabinet meeting of the same day, April 28, the formal decision was made to apply for membership in the International Monetary Fund and the World Bank. A year later the Japanese government announced to the IMF in Washington, D.C., that the value of the yen would be fixed at a rate of ¥1 = 2.46853 milligrams of pure gold. At the fixed dollar-gold rate of $35 per ounce, the announced gold par meant a dollar-yen exchange rate of exactly 360 yen to the dollar. In other words, this was a formal commitment to the exchange rate for the yen established by Joseph Dodge in April 1949, and the generalization of that rate as the basis for all of Japan's external financial relations.[36] In fact, it was a dollar rate, and the new yen was never convertible into gold.

NEW YORK CITY, 1952

A familiar balance-of-payments situation also reappeared, as Japan began to run regular trade deficits that had to be covered by foreign credit—a case of "history repeating itself," as Tsushima Juichi saw it. Under Article 18 of the peace treaty, the Japanese government recognized all prewar foreign debts and undertook to begin repaying them promptly. The country also greatly needed capital for postwar reconstruction. Therefore, to rebuild Japan's international credit and bring in foreign capital, Prime Minister Yoshida and Finance Minister Ikeda placed great importance on restarting payments on the prewar foreign debts, now reckoned to stand at $460 million.[37]

Led by Tsushima, a delegation of top Ministry of Finance officials went to Wall Street to meet with Japan's American and British creditors in July 1952. Tsushima had boasted in his prewar bond promotions that Japan had never failed to make a foreign debt payment "since the age of Emperor Jinmu" (supposedly, 600 B.C.)—a sales line picked up by Thomas Lamont. Tsushima thus felt personally disgraced by Japan's cessation of debt payments at the beginning of the Pacific war, which "ruined at a stroke" the credit built up over so many years. The talks, conducted in parallel with negotiations on Germany's foreign debt, were concluded in September, and the Japanese government began repaying the debt in December. American and British bondholders were thus repaid with interest for, among other things, the funds lent to build Japan's vanished empire. Although the arrival of the Japanese delegation rated small mention in the New York newspapers, Tsushima considered the meetings to be among Japan's most important international financial meetings of the new postwar era.[38]

Tsushima did get a reassuring welcome from the Wall Street community, as he was hosted for a long series of luncheons and dinners, first with Morgan and Company and then with National City Bank; Kuhn, Loeb and Company; Guaranty Trust; Chemical Bank; Brown Brothers Harriman and Company; Dillon, Read and Company; and many other Wall Street firms. It seemed indeed that the sunnier circumstances of the 1920s might be revived.

Politically, Japan was thus reincorporated into and resubordinated to a Western liberal-capitalist world order now strongly centered in the United States. Monetarily, the yen was fixed to the dollar. Nevertheless, Japan's financial secession of 1931–32 was not essentially reversed. Unlike Japan's relative financial opening during the gold-standard era, and despite continuing American efforts to open the country to foreign investment, postwar Japan remained largely closed to foreign investment. In line with Ishibashi Tanzan's vision, capital for Japan's high-speed growth was almost entirely self-generated, and it was largely allocated by a system of bank credit centered on the Bank of Japan. Like Japan's prewar gold standard but to a greater extent, the new dollar standard was for external purposes only. Japan's dollar holdings did not govern the volume of the yen circulation; and to govern the use of scarce dollar resources, the government retained a highly centralized system of foreign-exchange budgeting that involved the Ministry of International Trade and Industry, the Ministry of Finance, and the Bank of Japan.[39] Thus, the heritage of exchange controls that went back to Takahashi Korekiyo's reimposition of the gold embargo remained in place. The restored international order itself was less liberal and more statist than in the 1920s, but Japan's post–World War II economic system in particular was significantly more closed and tightly organized than that of the 1910s and 1920s. Japan's national capitalism was skillfully articulated with the reliberalizing world economy but in essential respects was not itself liberal.

Because the yen was not fully convertible, Japan also remained a second-class, "Article 14 country" under the IMF charter. As such, it was subject until 1964 to annual inspections during which IMF officials would ask why Japan was still maintaining foreign-exchange controls—and, as the Bank of Japan's Yoshino Toshihiko remembered it, "we would bow our heads and say, if we end foreign-exchange controls, we will not be able to preserve the exchange rate of $1 = ¥360." Only after 1964 could Bank of Japan officials speak to the IMF inspectors as equals.[40]

The fixing of the yen to the dollar after 1949 also turned out to be the bottom of a long-run depreciation vis-à-vis the U.S. dollar that had begun with the creation of the yen in 1871. Depreciation had been interrupted in 1897 by the institution of the fixed-rate gold standard regime, under which the yen became increasingly overvalued. When the old system of par values finally broke in the latter half of 1931, depreciation resumed. The next time the yen's exchange value was altered, in 1971, it was an upward revision, the beginning of a long-run phase of yen appreciation.

In his 1966 memoirs, Tsushima Juichi noted, without attaching too much importance to it, that just in the past year, Japan had shown a trade surplus. In fact, 1965 marked the end of a long era of recurring trade deficits and the start of the run of ever larger export surpluses that continues to the present writing. Unlike the ephemeral surpluses of World War I, these were indeed what Inoue Junnosuke had hopefully anticipated in 1917—the beginning of a great shift in the relations of international financial power. Japan's new export surpluses added to the stresses on the dollar-denominated world monetary order. Five years after Tsushima's writing, against all Japanese intentions, these new surpluses became the proximate factor in finally cutting another "anchor chain"—ending the gold convertibility of the U.S. dollar itself and with it the last vestiges of the gold standard.

APPENDIX

Reference Information

This appendix contains reference information on the Bank of Japan's specie reserve and note issue, the total money supply, and inflows and outflows of gold. A virtual given of the modern age has been *increase*—in the size of government, the volume of money in circulation, the level of prices, and in economic production more generally. Decline in any of these indicators is more extraordinary, and in line with the present study's concern with the problems of deflation and stabilization, I highlight outright declines in various indicators in the following tables with a downward arrow (↓), indicating a reduction relative to the previous year.

SPECIE RESERVES AND NOTE ISSUE

The Bank of Japan began to issue convertible banknotes in 1885. Until 1897 these notes were convertible into silver, and from 1897 until 1917 convertible into gold (though see the foregoing account for a description of the actual situation). The gold standard was suspended in 1917, restored in January 1930, and resuspended at the end of 1931.

TABLE A.1. Bank of Japan specie reserve and note issue outstanding, 1885–1940
(¥ millions)

Year	*Specie Reserve*	*Note Issue*	*Excess Issue*	*Ratio of Specie Reserve to Note Issue*
1885	3	4	—	0.75
1886	24	40	—	0.60
1887	32	53	—	0.60
1888	45	66	—	0.68

(continued on next page)

TABLE A.1 *(continued)*

Year	*Specie Reserve*	*Note Issue*	*Excess Issue*	*Ratio of Specie Reserve to Note Issue*
1889	57	79	—	0.72
1890	45	103	—	0.44
1891	63	116	—	0.54
1892	81	126	—	0.64
1893	86	149	—	0.58
1894	82	150	4	0.55
1895	60	180	55	0.33
1896	133	198	—	0.67
1897	98	226	47	0.43
1898	90	197 (↓)	24	0.46
1899	110	251	21	0.44
1900	67	229 (↓)	41	0.29
1901	71	214 (↓)	23	0.33
1902	109	232	3	0.47
1903	117	233	—	0.50
1904	84	287	83	0.29
1905	116	313	77	0.37
1906	147	342	75	0.43
1907	162	370	88	0.44
1908	170	353 (↓)	63	0.48
1909	218	353	15	0.62
1910	222	402	59	0.55
1911	229	433	84	0.53
1912	247	449	82	0.55
1913	224	426 (↓)	82	0.53
1914	218	386 (↓)	47	0.56
1915	248	430	62	0.58
1916	411	601	71	0.68
1917	650	831	62	0.78
1918	713	1,145	312	0.62
1919	952	1,555	483	0.61
1920	1,247	1,439 (↓)	73	0.87
1921	1,246	1,547	181	0.80
1922	1,064	1,558	375	0.68
1923	1,057	1,704	526	0.62
1924	1,059	1,662 (↓)	483	0.64
1925	1,057	1,632 (↓)	455	0.65
1926	1,058	1,570 (↓)	392	0.67
1927	1,063	1,682	500	0.63
1928	1,062	1,739	557	0.61
1929	1,072	1,642 (↓)	450	0.65
1930	826	1,436 (↓)	490	0.57

TABLE A.1 *(continued)*

Year	*Specie Reserve*	*Note Issue*	*Excess Issue*	*Ratio of Specie Reserve to Note Issue*
1931	469	1,330 (↓)	741	0.35
1932	425	1,426	1	0.30
1933	425	1,544	119	0.27
1934	466	1,627	161	0.29
1935	504	1,766	262	0.28
1936	548	1,865	317	0.29
1937	801	2,305	504	0.35
1938	501	2,754	553	0.18
1939	501	3,679	977	0.14
1940	501	4,777	2,076	0.10

SOURCE: Bank of Japan data (Nihon Ginkō Tōkeikyoku 1966: 170–172); year-end figures.

RULES GOVERNING NOTE ISSUE

Under the terms of the Convertible Banknotes Law of 1884 and various later revisions, the Bank of Japan's note issue followed a fiduciary model like that of the Bank of England. The formal "rules of the game" were as follows:

1. The note issue was to be entirely covered by a *specie reserve* of silver and gold coins and bullion, later exclusively gold coins and bullion; but
2. A further issue could be made, backed by a *fiduciary reserve* consisting of government bonds and other securities, up to a limit fixed by law at ¥70 million in 1888, ¥85 million in 1890, ¥120 million in 1899, and raised by Takahashi Korekiyo to ¥1 billion in 1932; and
3. An additional issue against securities (the *excess fiduciary issue*) could also be made. If the excess issue extended over fifteen days, it required the finance minister's approval and was taxed at a minimum rate of 5 percent (reduced to 3 percent in 1932).

The amount of the fiduciary issue is not listed in table A.1 but may be calculated by subtracting the specie reserve and the excess issue from the total note issue.

Between 1905 and 1922 a large proportion of the so-called specie reserve was actually British money held in London, mostly in the form of bank deposits and short-term bills. Thus, the ratio of specie to note issue listed above is actually the ratio of specie *and* foreign exchange holdings to note issue.

MONEY SUPPLY

Table A.2 lists the total amount of currency in circulation, including Bank of Japan notes, and the total amount of bank deposits.

TABLE A.2. Money supply, 1888–1941
(¥ millions)

Year	*Currency in Circulation (A)*	*Bank Deposits (B)*	*"M1" (A + B)*	*M1 Percent Change from Previous Year*	*Comments (key policy makers)*
1888	172	66	238		
1889	178	68	246	3.4	
1890	201	63 (↓)	264	7.3	
1891	209	66	275	4.2	
1892	212	85	297	8.0	
1893	231	112	343	15.5	
1894	230 (↓)	134	364	6.1	
1895	260	184	444	22.0	
1896	275	235	510	14.9	
1897	296	305	601	17.8	
1898	279 (↓)	371	650	8.2	
1899	340	536	876	34.8	
1900	317 (↓)	576	893	1.9	
1901	303 (↓)	579	882 (↓)	−1.2	
1902	323	692	1,015	15.1	
1903	325	759	1,084	6.8	
1904	384	811	1,195	10.2	
1905	423	974	1,397	16.9	
1906	469	1,395	1,864	33.4	
1907	509	1,325 (↓)	1,834 (↓)	−1.6	
1908	499 (↓)	1,304 (↓)	1,803 (↓)	−1.7	1908 ("Boshin") deflation policy (Katsura–Wakatsuki)
1909	521	1,506	2,027	12.4	
1910	586	1,649	2,235	10.3	
1911	634	1,776	2,410	7.8	
1912	649	1,941	2,590	7.5	
1913	628 (↓)	2,110	2,738	5.7	
1914	561 (↓)	2,112	2,673 (↓)	−2.4	1914 deflation policy (Wakatsuki)
1915	623	2,569	3,192	19.4	
1916	827	3,464	4,291	34.4	
1917	1,117	5,146	6,263	46.0	
1918	1,576	7,236	8,812	40.7	
1919	2,082	8,734	10,816	22.7	
1920	1,801 (↓)	8,829	10,630 (↓)	−1.7	1920 deflation policy (Inoue)
1921	1,949	9,494	11,443	7.6	

TABLE A.2 *(continued)*

Year	*Currency in Circulation (A)*	*Bank Deposits (B)*	*"M1" (A + B)*	*M1 Percent Change from Previous Year*	*Comments (key policy makers)*
1922	1,858 (↓)	9,551	11,409 (↓)	−0.3	1922 deflation policy (Ichiki, Inoue)
1923	2,195	9,692	11,887	4.2	
1924	2,177 (↓)	10,232	12,409	4.4	1924–26 deflation policy (Hamaguchi, Kataoka)
1925	2,137 (↓)	10,821	12,958	4.4	
1926	2,062 (↓)	11,272	13,334	2.9	
1927	2,199	11,247 (↓)	13,446	0.8	
1928	2,286	11,691	13,977	3.9	
1929	2,179 (↓)	11,972	14,151	1.2	1929–31 deflation policy (Hamaguchi, Inoue)
1930	1,915 (↓)	11,546 (↓)	13,461 (↓)	−4.9	
1931	1,828 (↓)	11,093 (↓)	12,921 (↓)	−4.0	
1932	1,965	11,445	13,410	3.8	
1933	2,130	12,049	14,179	5.7	
1934	2,288	12,775	15,063	6.2	
1935	2,480	13,626	16,106	6.9	
1936	2,596	14,726	17,322	7.5	
1937	3,180	16,405	19,585	13.1	
1938	3,759	20,716	24,475	25.0	
1939	4,940	27,626	32,566	33.1	
1940	6,325	34,284	40,609	24.7	
1941	7,881	41,518	49,399	21.6	

SOURCE: Nihon Ginkō Tōkeikyoku 1966: 166, 195 (year-end data).

GOLD FLOWS

During and after the great boom, from 1916 to 1921, a net total of ¥1.2 billion (US$560 million) flowed into Japan. Gold exports were embargoed in September 1917 (that is, made subject to Ministry of Finance permission), and the embargo was lifted from January 1930 to December 1931. The outflows that followed the lifting of the gold export embargo in 1930 were nearly a negative mirror image of the great inflows of 1916–21. Between 1925, when Finance Minister Hamaguchi had begun limited gold shipments, and 1932, when the final dollar-buying contracts were settled, there was a net outflow of ¥800 million.

TABLE A.3. Yearly inflows and outflows of gold, 1885–1936
(¥ millions)

Year	Gold imports	Gold Exports	Balance
1885	0.6	0.5	0.1
1886	1.2	0.3	0.9
1887	1.3	0.1	1.2
1888	1.2	0.4	0.8
1889	0.7	0.3	0.5
1890	0.4	1.7	–1.3
1891	0.3	0.2	0.1
1892	0.4	8.5	–8.1
1893	0.5	2.3	–1.8
1894	0.6	3.5	–3.0
1895	1.0	2.8	–1.8
1896	10.2	2.0	8.2
1897	64.3	8.9	55.4
1898	37.1	46.3	–9.2
1899	20.2	8.8	11.4
1900	9.2	51.8	–42.5
1901	11.8	11.5	0.4
1902	31.9	0.5	31.4
1903	26.7	16.8	9.9
1904	7.2	107.1	–99.9
1905	22.3	17.2	5.0
1906	38.9	23.1	15.8
1907	8.6	19.4	–10.8
1908	18.3	3.8	14.5
1909	79.8	6.4	73.4
1910	21.8	23.6	–1.8
1911	17.1	23.7	–6.7
1912	20.4	21.4	–1.0
1913	11.8	21.1	–9.3
1914	18.8	26.1	–7.4
1915	37.9	40.7	–2.8
1916	117.1	22.7	94.4
1917	398.3	151.1	247.2
1918	7.6	1.4	6.2
1919	330.5	2.7	327.7
1920	416.6	1.1	415.5
1921	138.2	0.1	138.1
1922	5.6	0.0[a]	5.5
1923	6.1	0.3	5.8
1924	4.3	0.9	3.4
1925	3.6	22.3	–18.6
1926	6.0	32.2	–26.2
1927	4.6	36.3	–31.7

TABLE A.3 *(continued)*

Year	*Gold imports*	*Gold Exports*	*Balance*
1928	3.8	0.4	3.4
1929	6.3	0.1	6.2
1930	35.8	308.7	−272.9
1931	48.4	419.9	−371.4
1932	28.1	122.5	−94.4
1933	24.0	24.5	−0.5
1934	31.4	0.3	31.0
1935	33.5	2.0	31.5
1936	51.2	0.7	50.5

SOURCE: Nihon Ginkō Tōkeikyoku 1966: 298–299.
NOTE: Negative numbers indicate a net outflow.
[a] = ¥47,000.

NOTES

PREFACE

1. Lamont 1921a: 172.
2. Lamont to Inoue 3/20/1922, TWLP 186–14.
3. Tanaka 1969: 357.

ACKNOWLEDGMENTS

1. A review of relevant scholarly debates can be found in Nihon Ginkō Kin'yū Kenkyūjo 1993 (thanks again in this connection to Professor Itō Masanao). A valuable and accessible introduction to Japanese monetary and financial history can be found in the Histor¥ OpenResearch project created by Michael Schiltz of the University of Leuven, at http://akira.arts.kuleuven.ac.be/meijifin/. In the spirit of open research, I also hope that interested researchers will contact me at mmetzler@ mail.utexas.edu.

PROLOGUE: LONDON, 1898

1. Matsukata 1900: 214; LTES 1: 200.
2. Sakatani 11/1/1917 in Kinka Hon'i Jisshi Mannijūnen Kinenkai 1917b: 46; see also chapter 3 below.
3. See Matsukata 1899: xii, and chapter 1 below.
4. Takahashi Korekiyo 1976 [1936], 2: 102–103.
5. E.g., the London *Economist* of January 8, 1898.
6. As recorded in his autobiography (Takahashi Korekiyo 1976 [1936], 2: 107–111). The cultural and literary side of Japan's new Anglotropism is explored by Ioannis Mentzas (1998), who describes the parallel journey to London two years later by Natsume Sōseki, and from whom some of the sense of this paragraph is drawn.
7. *Economist* 1/1/1898, p. 2.
8. Takahashi Korekiyo 1976 [1936], 2: 105; *Economist* 2/26/1898.

9. Esherick 1987: 184–185; Asakawa (1904: 101–134) provides a survey of the scramble for concessions as seen from Tokyo.

10. Takahashi Korekiyo 1976 [1936], 2: 109.

11. The structures of "gentlemanly capitalism" are anatomized by Cain and Hopkins (1993a, 1993b). See also Akita (1996, 1997) for an application of this idea to Japan's experience.

12. See, again, Mentzas (1998) for a provocative discussion.

13. Takahashi Korekiyo 1976 [1936], 1: 15–16; Uetsuka 1976 [1936]: 304–305. The following details are drawn from Takahashi's autobiography (Takahashi Korekiyo 1976 [1936]), which covers the years of his life up to 1906. Richard Smethurst is now completing a book that will tell Takahashi's extraordinary life story.

14. Takahashi Korekiyo 1976 [1936], 1: 31–32; Takahashi Korekiyo 1936a: 61–62. For Shand's career, see Checkland and Tamaki 1997 and NGHS 1: 38–45.

15. Takahashi Korekiyo 1976 [1936], 1: 37–47. Van Reed's operations are discussed in Okahata 1971: 37–62 and Van Sant 2000.

16. Takahashi Korekiyo 1976 [1936], 1: 47–70.

17. Takahashi Korekiyo 1976 [1936], 1: 77–125; Hall 1973: 146; Takahashi's résumé in TKM 138. For the prominent moral and intellectual role of Christian converts, see Scheiner 1970.

18. Takahashi Korekiyo 1976 [1936], 1: 184–197.

19. Takahashi Korekiyo 1976 [1936], 1: 286, 361; 2: 77.

20. Takahashi Korekiyo 1976 [1936], 2: 11–15.

21. The phrase *haran banjō* has been used often in reference to Takahashi's life. Richard Smethurst (1998) attributes Takahashi's later originality in the policy sphere to his wide experience and self-education.

22. IJD: 39–40.

23. For Katō, see Duus 1968.

24. Shidehara 1953: 230.

25. IJD: 40; Ikeda S. 1949a: 50–53; Ikeda S. 1949b: 124.

26. Mitani 1974: 124; Mitani 1980a: 30; Mitani 1996: 154–156.

27. See also Pyle 1969.

28. This and the following details are drawn from IJD: 3–24, Inoue's official biography, written shortly after his death by the Bank of Japan's Aoki Tokuzō.

29. IJD: 29–31.

30. IJD: 31–38.

31. IJD: 39.

32. IJD: 39.

33. Takahashi Korekiyo 1976 [1936], 2: 116.

34. Suzuki 1994: 69–74. See also chapter 2 below.

35. Takahashi Korekiyo 1936 [1976], 2: 127, 132–141; NGHS 2: 101–103; NGHS Shiryōhen: 30.

36. IJD: 42.

37. Ishii Kanji (1997) provides an authoritative survey.

38. Matsuda 1979: 2.

39. *Economist* 5/28/1898: 794; see also Watt 1984: 24–26.

1. JAPAN AND THE BRITISH GOLD STANDARD, CA. 1715–1885

1. The literature on the gold standard is voluminous. For useful introductions, see Drummond 1987; Eichengreen and Flandreau 1997; Gallarotti 1995; Bordo 1999.

2. Surveys can be found in Yoshida 1876 and Tōno 1997. I develop the argument presented in this section in Metzler 1999.

3. Exponents of the bullionist view included Kumazawa Banzan, Miyazaki Antei, and most influentially, Arai Hakuseki (see Totman 1993: 147; Arai 1979 [1717]; Nakai 1988). On the so-called "closed-country" (*sakoku*) policy, see Tashiro 1976, Innes 1980, and Toby 1991 [1984]. For import-substitution policies, see Toby and Ohba 1997. For the export-promotion policy of the 1760s–1780s, see Hall 1955 and Ōishi S. 1991.

4. Cipolla 1956: 27–37. The British state's adoption of this innovation was preceded by a century of private-sector experimentation in the use of token coins (John Kleeberg, personal communication).

5. Mikami 1996: 230–231; Ōishi S. 1991: 107–110; Mikami 1989: 59; Metzler 1999.

6. The numbers can be found in Taya 1973.

7. Redish 1993: 778.

8. Beasley 1991: 304.

9. Inoue J. 1929c: 174, and chapter 10 below.

10. Treaty of Amity and Commerce between the United States of America and Japan, 7/29/1858, Article V (reprinted in Beasley 1955: 183–189). Article X of Britain's August 1858 treaty with Japan contained identical provisions. On the negotiations of the currency provisions, see Mikami 1996: 253–285; Mikami 1989: 85–153; Hanashiro 1999: 5–17; and Frost 1970: 13–24. Western writers have often represented Bakufu officials as not grasping the meaning of this clause. In fact, those officials tried and failed to exempt the token silver coinage from the provision for straight weight-for-weight conversion.

11. Mikami 1989: 85–153; Yamamoto Yūzō 1994: 8–11; Hanashiro 1999: 17–23; Frost 1970: 35–45. One way to convey the logic of this transformation is to imagine that the U.S. dollar were devalued in order to conform to the straight metallic value of four cupronickel quarter-dollar coins.

12. Feavearyear 1963: 154–155. Newton's report is reprinted in W. A. Shaw 1896: 166–171.

13. Hume 1970: 63, 67–68, 75. Hume's trade balance idea was apparently first stated in a letter he wrote to Montesquieu in 1747 (Rotwein afterword to Hume 1970: 188).

14. Drummond (1987: 14, 22) goes so far as to say that in the actual operation of the gold standard, there was no necessary relation between a nation's gold holdings and its domestic money supply.

15. See Feavearyear 1963: 169; Cipolla 1956: 27. I owe several of the ideas in this section to discussion with Dr. John Kleeberg and to his expert tour through the vaults of the American Numismatic Society in New York.

16. Keynes 1971 [1913]: 26.

17. On the linkage of deflation and moral restorationism, see Metzler 2004b.

18. Here again, see Cain and Hopkins 1993a.

19. See Fetter 1980: 96. British debates over bimetallism are surveyed by Wilson 2000.

20. Flynn and Giraldez 2002.

21. Hanashiro 1999: 34–41, 72–75.

22. Sakatani 1912: 103–105; see Shunpo-kō Tsuishōkai 1940, 1: 516–544, for Itō's memoranda of 1870 and 1871 to financial officials Ōkuma Shigenobu, Inoue Kaoru, and Shibusawa Eiichi; excerpts in English translation are given in Matsukata 1899: 2–5; see also Matsukata's speech of 11/1/1917, in Kinka Hon'i Jisshi Manni-jūnen Kinenkai 1917b: 57.

23. Yamamoto Yūzō 1994: 78–85; New Currency Law, reprinted in Matsukata 1899: 6–9. In North America, the term *dollar* referred originally to the Mexican silver dollar, which for many years was the de facto currency standard of American trade. The Mexican dollar in turn traces its origins to the original Central European silver dollar (*taler*, from *Joachimsthaler*). The Japanese term *en* (yen), meaning "round," came into use as a colloquial term for money in the early 1800s and seems also to have originated as a Chinese name for the Mexican silver dollar (Mikami 1996: 288–298).

24. For a comparative perspective, see Flandreau 1996 and Wilson 2000.

25. *Japan Mail*, 9/23/1876, excerpted in Japan Gazette 1882: 18–19. Note the perception that the United States was already an established gold-standard country in the early 1870s.

26. Yamamoto Yūzō 1994: 87–103.

27. YSGS 1: 5–10; Tamaki 2001: 108–119; Tamaki 1990: 193–195.

28. SYM, 908. The details of Egypt's national bankruptcy are summarized in Owen 1981: 127–134; see also Landes 1958.

29. T. C. Smith 1955: 97–98; Yamamoto Yūzō 1994: 104–108.

30. Tamaki 1995: 46–48.

31. Lebra 1973: 37–54.

32. Matsukata memorandum of 3/1/1882, reprinted in Matsukata 1899: 43–67. An official account of the currency stabilization policy is given in Matsukata 1899: 38–144. For the agricultural depression, see Ike 1950: 138–147.

33. Matsukata 1899: 72.

34. For the "great depression," see, among others, Rostow 1948. A strenuous argument against the concept is given by Saul 1985.

35. See Thorp and Mitchell 1926, table 10.

36. I do not mean to argue that the long nineteenth-century deflation was strictly a British-centered or even strictly a monetary phenomenon. Its first phase, the deflation of the 1820s to 1840s, was common to both gold- and silver-standard countries (see Lin, forthcoming). In regard to the century as a whole, Landes (1969: 233–234) has argued that deflation was driven by technological progress: more efficient production and transportation brought lower prices. But as Saul (1985: 13) has pointed out, the great productivity advances of the twentieth century were accompanied not by deflation but by inflation—in fact, by a worldwide price revolution.

37. Kindleberger 1993: 235–245; Flandreau 1996: 873.

38. McCartney 1935.
39. See Gallarotti 1993 and Flandreau 1996.
40. Jastram 1981: 50.
41. Bryan 1896: 205.
42. Nihon Ginkō Tōkeikyoku 1966: 318–320. The one exception to this long-run depreciation of silver was a great upward spike in silver prices in 1890, due to the U.S. Silver Purchase Act, which temporarily boosted world silver prices and helped to cause a depression in Japan.
43. Droppers 1895: xix; wholesale prices from *Asahi shinbun* index, given in Nihon Ginkō Tōkeikyoku 1966: 76.
44. Anglo-American analysts of the gold standard, following Hume, have almost universally treated the physical location of gold reserves as an unimportant matter. Japanese officials, from the very beginning, were acutely aware of this question, seeing it as a source of British strength and Japanese weakness, and as early as the 1870s, the Japanese government made concerted efforts to gain access to Korea's meager gold production.

2. GOLD AND EMPIRE, 1885–1903

1. Fukuzawa 3/16/1885, in Fukuzawa 1958–1964 10: 238–240; see also K. Miwa 1968.
2. Ikeda S. 1949a: 36–37.
3. Harootunian 1980.
4. Accounts can be found in Bytheway 2001; NGHS 2: 3–5; Tamaki 1988; and Matsukata 1899.
5. Garrett Droppers (1895: xix), then a professor at Tokyo Imperial University and later an economic adviser to U.S. president Woodrow Wilson, presented evidence that under the silver standard, prices in Japan had been much more stable than prices in Europe and America, which had experienced great price declines.
6. Nakamura 1990: 36, citing Muroyama 1984. Matsukata's right-hand man Sakatani Yoshio also happens to have been Shibusawa Eiichi's son-in-law. For Tajiri, see Ferber 2005.
7. Matsukata 1899: 164–165.
8. Their conversation is transcribed in Kajima 1976–78 vol. 1.
9. Takahashi Korekiyo 1976 [1936] 2: 58; Matsukata 1899: 168–173; Matsukata 1900: 214–228. The Kuping (Treasury) tael was a silver unit of account, not an actual coin.
10. Ono 1922: 57, 76–77; Sakatani speech of 11/1/1917, in Kinka Hon'i Jisshi Mannijūnen Kinenkai 1917b: 42; Matsukata speech of 11/1/1917 in ibid., 62.
11. Takahashi 1976 [1936] 2: 99; YSGS 1: 174–175; Tamaki 1994: 128.
12. YSGS 1: 173–174; Matsuoka 1936: 486–512, which gives a detailed accounting. See also Bytheway 2004.
13. Sakatani 11/1/1917, in Kinka Hon'i Jisshi Mannijūnen Kinenkai 1917b: 43; SYM, 789 (article series for the *Tōkyō nichi nichi shinbun,* November–December 1929, on the occasion of Japan's impending return to the gold standard).
14. Matsukata 1899: xii, 348.

15. Witte 1921: 59–61. Bordo and Rockoff (1996) call the gold standard "a good housekeeping seal of approval" for gaining foreign credit.

16. Takahashi Korekiyo 1936a: 334–335; Hatano 1992: 353–354; Feis 1930: 436; Matsukata 1899: 277. On Jackson and the Hongkong & Shanghai Bank, see King 1987.

17. Matsukata 1899: 370; English text of the law in ibid., 192–198; Yamamoto Yūzō 1994: 159–184. The legal rules governing the BOJ's note issue are summarized in the appendix to this book.

18. NGHS 2: 7–10; Tamaki 1995. The other special banks (*tokubetsu ginkō*) were the Japan Hypothec Bank (Nippon Kangyō Ginkō), 1897; Agricultural and Industrial Bank (Nōkō Ginkō), 1897; Hokkaidō Development Bank (Hokkaidō Takushoku Ginkō), 1900; and Industrial Bank of Japan (Nippon Kōgyō Ginkō), 1902.

19. Bank of Taiwan Law, cited in Shimazaki 1989: 20.

20. Asai 1985: 5–6.

21. Asai 1985: 7–10.

22. See table 1 below; Nihon Ginkō Tōkeikyoku 1966: 317; and Suzuki 1994: 66–69, where Suzuki gives a detailed accounting of Japan's overseas borrowing before 1914. See also Bytheway 2005.

23. Suzuki 1994: 73–74; *Ginkō tsūshinroku,* 7/15/1899, quoted in ibid.

24. Keynes 1971 [1920]: 11–12.

25. Keynes 1971 [1913]; Kemmerer 1916a: 3–152. Keynes himself defined the gold-exchange standard as follows:

> The gold-exchange standard may be said to exist when gold does not circulate in a country to an appreciable extent, when the local currency is not necessarily redeemable in gold, but when the government or central bank makes arrangements for the provision of *foreign remittances* in gold at a fixed maximum rate in terms of the local currency, the reserves necessary to provide these remittances being kept to a considerable extent abroad. [Keynes 1971 [1913]: 21–22, my emphasis]

The first point in Keynes's definition would actually have described most of the gold-standard countries—only Britain, France, and the United States had a large circulation of gold coins. It was the latter points that distinguished the gold-exchange standard as something new.

26. Conant 1909: 200.

27. In the case of Britain itself, it took several decades before these possibilities were fully realized. The subsidiary (token) coinage instituted in 1816 was not substantially lightened until the 1860s. The Bank Act of 1844 also restricted the Bank of England's note issue. The possibilities of monetary leverage were exploited most fully by commercial banks via the system of cheques, which developed more extensively in Britain and America than anywhere else.

28. See the related consideration of "high-powered money" in Friedman and Schwartz 1963.

29. Leffingwell to Mori 9/10/1928, TWLP 188–30; also see chapter 9 below.

30. See chapter 10 below. Lindert (1969) has demonstrated that as a percentage of total world reserves, holdings of foreign exchange (as opposed to specie) had by 1913 reached a level similar to that of 1931. One great difference between the two

points is that in 1913, Russia, Japan, and India—all operating forms of a gold-exchange standard—between them held some 60 percent of the total foreign-exchange reserves; foreign exchange was much more widely held in 1931.

31. Keynes 1971 [1913]: 26.

32. Regarding India, see Bagchi 1997, De Cecco 1974, and Rothermund 1996: 90–91.

33. But see Ford 1962 for a study of Argentina's sterling-centered system; see also Eichengreen 1992c. De Cecco 1974 is a seminal work on Britain's imperial gold-exchange standard as a system. Lindert's work on key currencies (1969) is also fundamental. The recent work of Emily Rosenberg (1999) surveys American efforts to build dollar-based gold-exchange standards during the early twentieth century. Benjamin Cohen (1998) provides a more general set of reflections on monetary blocs.

In Japan, the character of the gold-exchange standard as a global system, and Japan's peculiar in-between position in this system, was recognized in the 1930s by Matsuoka Koji. Matsuoka himself drew on the work of French analysts who tended to view the gold-exchange standard as a specifically British institution, if not as an outright device for maintaining and extending London's international financial power. My own account draws heavily on Matsuoka's 1936 book, *Kin kawase hon'isei no kenkyū* (Research on the gold-exchange standard).

34. Matsukata 1899: 229; NGHS 2: 5; Inoue 1929d: 5.

35. Conant 1909: 200.

36. Again, Cain and Hopkins's notion of Britain's "gentlemanly" financial capitalism provides an analytical base point for bringing together the political-economic and sociocultural sides of the question (Cain and Hopkins 1993a, 1993b). For some complementary reflections on the gentlemanly ethic of American financial reformers, see Rosenberg 1999, especially pp. 32–39 and 187–218.

37. IJD: 47–52.

38. IJD: 49–50.

39. Conroy 1960: 105–106; Duus 1995: 54–57.

40. K. Miwa 1968.

41. Inoue Kaoru, quoted in Duus 1995: 92; ibid., 134–135; Inoue Kaoru Kō Denki Hensnkai 1934, 4: 392–394.

42. Duus (1995: 66–108) sorts out the extraordinarily fast and furious maneuvering of the time; see also Kim and Kim 1967: 81–84; Conroy 1960: 276–283.

43. Witte 1921: 83–85; Duus 1995: 96–102.

44. Witte 1921: 97–98, 106; Chōsen Ginkō 1919: 10–11; Duus 1995: 125–126 et seq.

45. For the question of Taiwan's gold-exchange standard, see chapter 3 (note 34) below.

46. Nish 1966, chs. 1–11 (pp. 216–217 for the text of the treaty); Chirol 1923: 292.

47. Suzuki 1994: 75–82; Nish 1966: 253–256; Hunter 2004; Bytheway 2004.

48. The subject has been opened up by the pathbreaking work of Emily Rosenberg (1999), upon which much of my own discussion draws.

49. U.S. Government, Commission on International Exchange 1904; Kemmerer 1916a: 245–388; Rosenberg 1999: 4, 13–18. On Conant, see also Parrini 1993.

50. Rosenberg 1999: 5, 24.

51. Kemmerer 1916a: 389–463. For some related considerations, see Hamashita 1983.

52. Conant 1903: 693–694; U.S. Government, Commission on International Exchange 1904: 9; Rosenberg 1999: 18–23; Parrini 1993: 58. The context of Mexican-Chinese cooperation is discussed by Schell 2001: 124–125.

53. Keynes 1971 [1913]: 19.

54. Rosenberg 1999: 29, 53, 84.

55. U.S. Government, Commission on International Exchange 1904: 10, 24–25; Chernow 1990: 111.

56. Conant 1903: 695–699; SYM, 368; Lai and Gau 1999, ch. 2. Thanks to Professor Cheng-chung Lai for providing a copy of his valuable unpublished manuscript.

3. THE SINEWS OF WAR, 1904–1914

1. Suzuki 1994: 84–86.

2. Ono 1922: 88; LTES 7: 162. Nakamura (1990: 6) gives a higher estimate for total war expenses, of ¥2.15 billion.

3. Suzuki 1994: 86–88, 91. The Anglo-Japanese alliance specified that Britain would intervene on Japan's behalf only if Japan found itself facing two enemies.

4. Takahashi journal 4/13/1904, in TKM 135. On arriving in Honolulu, Takahashi switched his journal entries to English, and he used the foreign language to record his business until his return to Japan at the end of 1904. In quoting from the diary, I have retained Takahashi's original spelling and capitalization. Takahashi's journal is held with his papers in the Kensei Shiryōshitsu, National Diet Library, Tokyo; it is discussed in detail and translated into Japanese by Fujimura 1992. The negotiations are also described in Takahashi's autobiography and by Fukai Eigo, who accompanied Takahashi as his secretary (Takahashi Korekiyo 1976 [1936], 2: 190–300; Fukai 1939: 42–95). The recent work of Toshio Suzuki (1994) comprehensively surveys the relevant British archival materials.

5. Takahashi Korekiyo 1976 [1936], 2: 200–202, 205; IKD 5: 70–71.

6. The advice was from financier Henry R. Beeton. Takahashi journal 4/22/1904, in TKM 135.

7. Takahashi Korekiyo 1976 [1936], 2: 213–214, 257–261. On Cassel's role, see Suzuki 1994: 94, 96–98, 106–107.

8. Takahashi journal May 3–4, 1904, in TKM 135; Takahashi Korekiyo 1976 [1936], 2: 203–204; Suzuki 1994: 90, 94, 96–98.

9. See Chernow 1990: 90, 196–200, 216. Schiff was especially close to the Warburg firm, for which, see Chernow 1993.

10. Takahashi memorandum on Schiff (1920), in Adler 1929, 1: 217–227; Takahashi Korekiyo 1976 [1936], 2: 203–204, 210–212. Takahashi entrusted the actual writing of the piece for Schiff's biography to Fukai Eigo (ibid., 213).

11. Takahashi journal 5/8/1904, 5/9/1904, in TKM 135; Takahashi Korekiyo 1976 [1936], 2: 205.

12. As Takahashi was later told by both Jacob Schiff and Takahira Kogorō, who was then Japan's minister to Washington (Takahashi journal 12/11/1904, in TKM 135).

13. *Wall Street Journal* 7/3/1905, quoted in Best 1972: 322; Suzuki 1994: 100–103; Takahashi Korekiyo 1976 [1936], 2: 205.

14. Takahashi Korekiyo 1976 [1936], 2: 205–206.

15. "Prospectus of the Imperial Japanese Government 6% Sterling Loan of May 1904," in YSGS 3: 691–700; *Bankers' Magazine* (New York), 69:1, July 1904: 2–3.

16. Takahashi journal 6/20/1904, 10/31/1904, 11/8/1904, in TKM 135; Takahashi memorandum on Schiff (1920), in Adler 1929, 1: 217–227.

17. Takahashi journal 12/13/1904, in TKM 135; Witte 1921: 169–170.

18. Takahashi's correspondence with Schiff is held in the Kensei Shiryōshitsu, National Diet Library, Tokyo; several letters are also reproduced in Adler 1929.

19. Table 2; Best 1972: 313.

20. Kang 1960: 172–174; Nihon Ginkō Tōkeikyoku 1966: 194, 166, 128.

21. Takahashi (1920), in Adler 1929, 1: 217–227; Witte 1921: 135.

22. Takahashi (1920), in Adler 1929, 1: 231–232.

23. Nakamura 1990: 27; Witte 1921: 139–143, 154, 156, 161.

24. Parrini 1993; Parrini and Sklar 1983.

25. Hobson 1965 [1902]; Lenin 1939 [1916]. See also Duus 1995: 428–438 on this latter point. The character of Japanese imperialism is discussed in Myers and Peattie 1984, Duus and Myers 1989, and Beasley 1991.

26. The term *dependent imperialism* (*jūzoku teikokushugi*) derives from the work of Yamazaki Ryūzō (1978). Asai (1982) reviews the scholarly debate and adds his own important contributions. See also Itō M. 1989: 347.

27. Shaw 1926: 147–148; Feis 1930: 435–442, 460.

28. "Final Protocol for the Settlement of the Disturbances of 1900," 9/7/1901, in MacMurray 1921, 1: 278–308. The total in principal and interest to be paid by the end of 1940 was reckoned to be 982 million taels. The Japanese share of the take was 7.7 percent.

29. Text of the treaty given in MacMurray 1921, 1: 18–25. The motive of enlisting British support is mentioned by Duus 1995: 427.

30. M. Andō 1967; Feuerwerker 1964; Jansen 1954.

31. Chōsen Ginkō 1919: 16–17; Chōsen Ginkō Shi Kenkyūkai 1987: 30; Matsuoka 1936: 520–522.

32. Duus 1995: 180–186.

33. Chōsen Ginkō 1919: 12–14; Residency General [of Korea] 1908: 37–38, 48–49, 102; Matsuoka 1936: 522–524. The Korean government itself had attempted to adopt a gold standard four years earlier but had failed.

34. Matsuoka 1936: 524–527. Matsuoka (1936: 512–514) did not consider Taiwan to have a gold-exchange standard because Bank of Japan notes were counted there as part of the Bank of Taiwan's fiduciary (security) reserve rather than as part of the specie reserve. Other writers did consider it a gold-exchange standard, but it was in this sense a less highly leveraged one.

35. Residency General [of Korea] 1908: 53–54. (Some totals do not match because of rounding errors.) In 1907 the Korean population was just under 10 million, so the circulation of the new Japanese money came to roughly ¥1.7 per person. Of this, ¥12.8 million was in Dai-Ichi banknotes and ¥4.1 million in new coins.

36. Matsuoka 1936: 512–514.

37. Residency General [of Korea] 1908: 50, 55, 59; Eckert 1991: 11–12, 270. By

the end of 1907, nearly ¥9 million of Korean money (reckoned in terms of the new Japanese currency) had been converted.

38. Duus 1995: 188–195, 220–239; Hoshino 1920: 280–281.

39. LaFeber 1997: 84–86; Kim and Kim 1967: 125–127; Gooch 1923: 336–337.

40. Wakatsuki 1950: 87; Kennan 1917; Matsusaka 2001: 43–44.

41. Kennan 1917: 4–27, 37; Wakatsuki 1950: 88, 105–106.

42. Wakatsuki 1950: 84–91; Matsusaka 2001, ch. 2. As vice minister of finance, Wakatsuki Reijirō was a member of the six-man committee.

43. Tsurumi Y. 1937–1938, 2: 814–815. Gotō's biographer, Tsurumi Yūsuke (who was Gotō's son-in-law) emphasized that the intent of the "civilian clothing" policy was to take control of policy from the army, which was in a dominant position in Southern Manchuria following the war with Russia.

44. Tsurumi Y. 1937–1938, 2: 774–775. In his own account, Wakatsuki Reijirō, who came to dislike Gotō, did not mention Gotō's role and emphasized that there had been an idea from the beginning to raise the capital overseas (Wakatsuki 1950: 88–91).

45. Tsurumi Y. 1937–1938, 2: 776; Tsushima 1963, 2: 340–342.

46. YSGS 1: 248–249, 269–273, 286–288; Hoshino 1920: 258–259, 272–273; "Manshū kahei tōitsu ni kansuru tokubetseu meirei," 12/16/1905, in YSGS 3: 756–757. The Yokohama Specie Bank had actually issued its own banknotes in China as early as November 1902, in Tianjin. In 1911 the Specie Bank's issue of silver notes in Southern Manchuria reached a peak of ¥7 million.

47. Tsurumi Y. 1937–1938, 2: 885–889; "Manshū kahei ni kansuru ken," in SYM, 539.

48. Tsurumi Y. 1937–1938, 2: 889–895.

49. Straight 1913: 129; Croly 1925: 238–242.

50. Straight 1913: 126–127; Kennan 1917: 43–45.

51. Suzuki 1994: 131–139, 141.

52. Cain and Hopkins 1993a: 416–417.

53. Rosenberg 1999: 41–47, 59–60.

54. Rosenberg 1999: 62–77.

55. Matsuda 1979: 43; Rosenberg 1999: 65; FRUS 1912: 693.

56. Sakatani 11/1/1917 in [Kinka Hon'i Jisshi Mannijūnen Kinenkai] 1917b: 44; T. Lamont 1933: 154.

57. Straight 1913: 132–134; Sakatani 11/1/1917 in [Kinka Hon'i Jisshi Mannijūnen Kinenkai] 1917b: 44.

58. Straight 1913: 128; FRUS 1910: 231–269, particularly Ambassador O'Brien to Count Komura, 12/18/1909 (pp. 237–238) and Komura to O'Brien, 1/21/1910 (pp. 251–252). The quotation is from the secretary of state's statement to the press on January 6, 1910, in ibid., 243–245.

59. "Message of the President," 12/7/1911, in FRUS 1911, xvii–xviii.

60. Sakatani 11/1/1917 in [Kinka Hon'i Jisshi Mannijūnen Kinenkai] 1917b: 44–45; FRUS 1912: 99–100.

61. IJD: 55–57; Werner 2002.

62. IJD: 68–80.

63. IJD: 83–84; YSGS 1: 400–401.

64. IJD: 84–85; YSGS 1: 405–406, 426–428; Itō M. 1989: 64.

65. Sakatani 11/1/1917 in [Kinka Hon'i Jisshi Mannijūnen Kinenkai] 1917b: 44–45; FRUS 1912: 108–112, 121–122, 128–130, 136–137, 140–141.

66. The text of the consortium loan agreements is given in MacMurray 1921, 1: 841–899.

67. Chan 1971: 364, 368–369.

68. "Chinese Government Currency Memorandum," published in government gazette of 8/12/1918 (in MOF-SZS 5–183: 20); Lai and Gau 1999, ch. 2.

69. Chernow 1990: 149–156.

70. Bryan and Bryan 1925: 361–363; Woodrow Wilson statement of 3/18/1913 in Link et al. 1978: 192–194; T. Lamont 1933: 161–165; Sakatani Yoshio 11/1/1917, in [Kinka Hon'i Jisshi Mannijūnen Kinenkai] 1917b: 45.

71. IJD: 85–88; YSGS 1: 411–414.

72. Itō M. 1989: 73–74. For the Deposit Bureau, see Ferber 2002.

73. Hoshino 1920: 259–260, 268–270; YSGS 1: 418–419. The first Western-style Chinese bank in Manchuria was the Provincial Bank of Mukden, established immediately after the Russo-Japanese War in 1905 and later renamed the Three Eastern Provinces Bank.

74. Hoshino 1920: 284–288.

75. Saitō Toshihiko, in Nihon Ginkō Kin'yū Kenkyūjo 1993: 77.

76. Matsuoka (1936: 512–514) claimed that this difference was a fundamental reason for the greater results of Japan's "northern advance" strategy, monetarily backed by the Bank of Chosen, as opposed to the lesser results of the "southern advance" strategy backed by the Bank of Taiwan. The Bank of Taiwan did serve as a tool of overseas expansion, and it became an aggressive lender in the Japanese business world, to the extent that it was at the center of the 1927 banking crisis. This latter instance, however, related more to its profit-seeking character as an ordinary commercial bank than to its character as a central bank of issue.

4. THE "POSITIVE" AND "NEGATIVE" POLICIES

1. For which see Nakamura 1990.
2. See Kindleberger 1985a.
3. Tōyō Keizai Shinpōsha 1931, sec. 3: 100–104.
4. See Yasuba 1995, 1996.
5. Statistics taken from LTES 1: 192–193.
6. Teranishi 1990: 73; [Kinka Hon'i Jisshi Mannijūnen Kinenkai] 1917a, which gives the following statistics: In 1914, the central government had ¥1.52 billion in foreign bonds outstanding as against ¥1.04 billion in domestically issued bonds (the latter down from a high of ¥1.42 billion in 1909). Local governments had ¥177 million in foreign bonds outstanding as against ¥150 million in domestic bonds. ¥142 million in corporate bonds had been issued overseas and ¥24 million domestically.
7. Fukai 1941: 80.
8. Fukai 1941: 78–82; Wakatsuki 1950: 125. Wakatsuki went on to say that some gold was transferred indirectly via Australia but that the Japanese government, in line with an informal understanding with British financiers, was careful to withdraw its funds so as not to disturb the London financial markets. For more on this point, see Bytheway 2004.

9. Inoue to Kazoku Kaikan, 11/21/1929, in "Nihon Ginkō sōsai enzetsu shū [1915–1923]," materials held at the Bank of Japan; Matsuoka 1936, ch. 19. The overseas specie reserve has been the subject of considerable research and debate; see especially Matsuoka 1936, chs. 18 and 19; Kojima H. 1981: 67–110; Itō M. 1987.

10. India's key role in maintaining London's financial centrality is the subject of a famous analysis by De Cecco (1974). Japan's part has been much less noticed. For Japan's role in maintaining the dollar's centrality in the 1980s and 1990s, see Murphy 1997.

11. Lindert 1969: 10–11, 18–19; Asai 1982: 55–56. According to the figures compiled by Lindert, at the end of 1913, India held sterling balances of approximately £28 million, and Japan held £39 million. The next largest holdings were those of Russia, at about £5 million. (Russia was the only country to hold larger total reserves of foreign currency than Japan, but most of it was in French francs.) Lindert's figures, which include short-term funds held by the Yokohama Specie Bank, are all given in U.S. dollars, and I have reconverted them into sterling.

12. Sayers 1976, 1: 39–41. Sayers cited the following example: at least five times between December 14, 1905, and January 18, 1906, the Bank of England borrowed sums of between £500,000 and £1.6 million from the BOJ. See also Bytheway 2004; Wakatsuki 1950: 125–126; Suzuki 1994: 162–173; and see Lindert 1969: 15–16, 27–28, 31–32 for some related considerations.

13. TKS 6/13/1931: 14–15. Nagaoka (1971) has interpreted the period from 1907 to 1914 as one of chronic recession. A counterargument has been made that precisely because of the inflow of foreign capital, Japan was able to enjoy moderate economic growth during the period. (A review of the scholarly debate is given in Nihon Ginkō Kin'yū Kenkyūjo 1993: 69–74, 78–79.) Both interpretations place foreign borrowing at the center of the dynamics of the period, and whether we evaluate it positively or negatively, the weight of foreign debts came increasingly to condition all economic policy decisions as the postwar decade progressed. In connection with the character of growth during this period, see also Mosk 2001: 119–126.

14. See Mason 1992.

15. Inoue 6/19/1918 in IJR 2: 184, citing Chancellor of the Exchequer David Lloyd George, in United Nations, Department of Economic Affairs 1949: 2.

16. Kang 1960: 209.

17. Ishibashi 1994 [1964]: 3; Shinobu 1954. For a study of Ishibashi Tanzan as a Taishō-era liberal, see Nolte 1987. For English-language studies of Taishō democracy, see Harootununian 1974 and the other essays in Silberman and Harootunian 1974; Duus 1982; Duus and Scheiner 1988; and Minichiello 1998.

18. See Najita 1967.

19. Kamiyama 1989: 48–49, 52–53; Banno 1979: 187–188; Takahashi Kamekichi 1954, 1: 7–10.

20. Nakamura 1990: 28–32; Wakatsuki 1950: 96–100; Inoue Kaoru Kō Denki Hensankai 1934, 5: 164–165; NGHS 2: 191–193. Ericson (1996: 245–373) provides a comprehensive study of the politics of rail nationalization; Ramseyer and Rosenbluth (1998: 123–125) offer related considerations.

21. YSGS 1: 324–325, 328; Takahashi Kamekichi 1954, I: 5.

22. Kamiyama 1989: 79. Kamiyama develops this point in detail, and my discussion here follows his analysis.

23. Wakatsuki 1950: 135; Duus 1968: 44.

24. Yoshikawa Kōbunkan 1908. "Boshin" was the year designation of 1908 in the sixty-year calendrical cycle. See also Gluck 1985: 90–92, 157–162; Garon 1998; and Metzler 2004b for a fuller consideration of the moral-economic issues.

25. Wakatsuki 1950: 146–147; Mochida 1990: 291–292.

26. Fukai 1941: 81.

27. Details of the various loans are given in Suzuki 1994: 128–162 and Tsushima 1963, 2: 339–371. See also Bytheway 2005.

28. NGHS 2: 278–280; see also Fujimura 1992, 1: 293–297.

29. Fletcher 1989: 17; Takahashi Korekiyo 1976 [1936], 2: 74.

30. NGHS 2: 280–281; Kamiyama 1989: 64–66; Najita 1967: 87–89.

31. Takahashi Korekiyo 1936a: 18–20; Kamiyama 1989: 66; Hara A. 1996: 144.

32. Kamiyama 1989: 66.

33. Morton 1980: 23.

34. Wakatsuki 1950: 177–179; Ozaki 2001 [1955]: 259–260; Najita 1967: 93.

35. Dickinson 1999: 274.

36. Najita 1967: 89–90, 103.

37. Kamiyama 1989: 66–67. Once the Saionji cabinet was forced to quit, Katsura himself dropped the issue of army expansion and transferred Tanaka Giichi back to the field (Najita 1967: 100). Tanaka later went over to the Seiyūkai side.

38. Ozaki 2001 [1955]: 264–276. Accounts of the Taishō political change are also given by Najita 1967: 80–184 and Hackett 1971: 250–265.

39. For Katō and the formation of the Kenseikai, see Duus 1968: 42–49, 59–68, 96–97.

40. NGHS 2: 284.

41. Kamiyama 1989: 68.

42. Takahashi statement of September 1912, quoted in Asai 1982: 58; Kamiyama 1989: 68–69.

43. Kamiyama 1989: 66, 69–70; Takahashi Masanori 1980: 478.

44. Ozaki 2001 [1955]: 283–284, 286; Lebra 1973: 117–118.

45. Kamiyama 1989: 71.

46. Fukai 1941: 108; Itō M. 1989: 48–49.

47. Itō M. 1989: 50; NGHS 2: 293–296; Fukai 1941: 112–113.

48. Inoue Junnosuke lecture at Waseda University, July 1914, in IJR 2: 48–52, 59–62; Inoue 1926, in IJR 1: 270.

49. Tadai 1997, 1: 199–200. Shōda Kazue is called Katsuta Kazue in some books.

5. "DIVINE PROVIDENCE," 1914–1918

1. On this point, see Yasuba 1995, 1996.

2. Nihon Ginkō Tōkeikyoku 1966: 28, 32.

3. Inoue 1925, in IJR 1: 7.

4. Inoue Kaoru Kō Denki Hensankai 1934, 5: 367. This idea is discussed in its international political aspects by Dickinson 1999 and Anno 1999: 322–325.

5. See Dickinson (1999: 61–63), whose account is invaluable for understanding the political dynamics of the World War I period.

6. SZS 17: 4 (Table 2); LTES 7: 147–149, 162–163, 168–171.

7. The text of the demands is given in MacMurray 1921, 2: 1231–1234. For discussion of the Twenty-one Demands, see, among others, Dickinson 1999: 85–116; Chi 1970: 28–61.

8. Inoue Kaoru Kō Denki Hensankai 1934, 5: 306–309.

9. The several treaties and exchanges of notes are given in MacMurray 1921, 2: 1215–1230; Ishibashi editorial, in TKS, 5/5/1915, reprinted in Ishibashi 1991: 55–69.

10. Duus 1968: 92–97.

11. Kamiyama 1989.

12. Tadai 1997, 1: 204–205.

13. LTES 1: 229; Allen 1980: 101 (export increase from 1913 to 1918); Nihon Ginkō Tōkeikyoku 1966: 106, 120; Inoue 1926: 233–234.

14. Inoue J. 1925, in IJR 1: 11.

15. Nihon Ginkō Tōkeikyoku 1966: 166, 194, 278, 298–299, 304; *Asahi shinbun* wholesale price index in ibid., 76.

16. Inoue J. 1929c: 164.

17. Inoue 10/27/1917, in IJR 2: 111.

18. Kindleberger 1986: 289–298.

19. Lamont's opinion, with the opinions of other British and American financiers, was reported in an internal Ministry of Finance compilation (Ōkurashō Rinji Chōsakyoku Kin'yūbu 1917).

20. See tables 2 and 3 above. Several of these loans were issued jointly in London, Paris, and New York, so the numbers in the text add up to more than the actual total.

21. Itō M. 1979: 52; Odate 1922: 25–28.

22. Wyse 1918: 389.

23. This was Inoue's own judgment (Inoue 6/19/1918, in IJR 2: 156, 184). See also Odate 1922: 13–14, 37–39, 75–77.

24. Chandler 1958: 86–93; Odate 1922: 37–41, 71–75; Metzler 2004a.

25. Keynes 1914; Tsushima 1963, 2: 361–362; Inoue to Shōgyō Kaigisho Rengokai, 10/27/1917, in IJR 2: 106; Odate 1922: 12, 33–36.

26. Itō Masanao, personal communication; Odate 1922: 51–53.

27. Inoue 10/27/1917, in IJR 2: 111.

28. U.S. Department of Commerce, Bureau of the Census 1960: 537; T. Lamont 1933: 186–230; Chernow 1990: 185–191, 197–203.

29. Bytheway 2004; YSGS 1: 434–436; IJD: 107–112. There were instances of bonds issued in Western countries being marketed in Japan as early as the 1870s (Shinjo 1962: 37–38).

30. Inoue 1925, in IJR 1: 14.

31. IJD: 108–109; Matsuda 1979: 76.

32. Tsurumi 1937–1938, 2: 885–904.

33. Tsurumi 1937–1938, 3: 641–642.

34. Gotō Shinpei, "Tō-A keizai dōmei no kensetsu," 11/21/1916, and "Tai-Shi seisaku no hon'an," 12/19/1916, in Tsurumi 1937–1938, 3: 642–649; Dickinson 1999: 161–162.

35. Matsuda 1979: 77; Shimazaki 1989: 120–121.

36. Quoted in Tadai 1997, 1: 204.

37. Tadai 1997, 1: 202. For Nishihara's career, see Duus 1995: 347–350.

38. Shimazaki 1989: 124–126; Dickinson 1999: 163–164.

39. Itō M. 1989: 63–64, 70–71; IJD: 112–113. The one loan was a ¥30 million advance on the currency reform loan (the "Second Reorganization Loan"), which was issued in three installments in August 1917, January 1918, and July 1918.

40. Itō M. 1989: 64.

41. Itō M. 1989: 63. Shao (1978: 48) listed nearly ¥212 million in loans between August 1917 and September 1918. See also Remer 1933: 539.

42. Inoue 1926, in IJR 1: 303; IJD: 103–106, 115–117; Yoshino 1975–1979, 5: 1057. Itō Masanao (1979) provides a detailed analysis of the Specie Bank's role in foreign-exchange transactions.

43. Inoue 7/27/1917 speech to the Central Hōtokukai, in IJR 2: 104.

44. Inoue 7/27/1917, in IJR 2: 99–102.

45. Inoue J. 1925: end table; Itō M. 1989: 60–62. The total lending to the allies was as follows:

Russia ¥222 million; issued between February 1916 and October 1917
Britain ¥186 million plus a sterling loan of £10 million (¥100 million); issued between December 1916 and January 1919
France ¥133 million; issued between March 1917 and November 1918, rolled over in 1920–21

The terms of these loans ranged from six months to three years.

46. Inoue 6/19/1918, in IJR 2: 184–185. The greatest part of Japan's overseas investments, as Inoue reckoned them, consisted of ¥600 million in overseas specie held by the Japanese government and Bank of Japan, part of which formed the "specie reserve" for the BOJ note issue. Added to this was ¥500 million in total overseas credits, ¥180 million invested in China (not including Manchuria), and ¥300 million invested in Manchuria, most of which was the capital of the South Manchurian Railway Co.

47. Sakatani 11/1/1917 in [Kinka Hon'i Jisshi Mannijūnen Kinenkai] 1917b: 46–47.

48. Ishibashi 1929: 539; *Kanpō* No. 1535, 9/12/1917: 144. Technically, the Ministry of Finance order established a permit system, requiring that anyone who wanted to export gold must get ministry approval (except for those traveling abroad who were taking less than ¥100). In fact, it was a strict embargo.

Six days previously, on September 6, an identically worded ordinance had embargoed silver exports, but with a ¥50 rather than ¥100 limit for travelers. The silver embargo was a response to the outflow of subsidiary silver coins that had followed the great increase of silver prices in 1916, caused by booming demand in China and India, and does not appear to have been directly related to the American gold embargo on September 7 (*Kanpō* No. 1531, 9/6/1917: 105; NGHS 2: 412). The Ministry of Finance's public statement on September 6 mentioned the increased demand for silver in India and China but made no mention of the United States.

49. *Tōkyō nichi nichi shinbun* 9/12/1917, in TNJ 3: 133; Ishibashi 1929: 539.

50. Shōda Kazue, 1928 *Ōsaka asahi shinbun* interview, reprinted in *Asahi keizai nenshi* 1929: 338 (emphasis in original); see also Ishibashi 3/16/1929, in ITZ 6: 246.

51. Hoshino 1920: 275–276. In its first year and a half of operation in Manchuria, the ODC lent more than ¥11 million and bought shares in eighteen local Japanese companies. It also set up a subsidiary financial and trading company, the Tōshō Jitsugyō Kaisha (Eastern Provinces Enterprise Co.).

52. Chōsen Ginkō 1934: 122–124, 155–159; Matsuoka 1936: 577; Hoshino 1920: 257–258, 287–290, 296–298.

53. Chōsen Ginkō 1934: 128–135, 143–150; share of business in Manchuria as reckoned by the location of deposits and lending (ibid.: 160–161, 164–165).

54. Yasutomi 2000.

55. Inoue J. 1929c: 160–161; Inoue speech to Shōgyō Kaigisho Rengōkai, 10/27/1917, in IJR 2: 111.

56. IJD: 107–114; Itō M. 1989: 65–66. Of the total ¥145 million in loans negotiated by Nishihara, ¥40 million was provided by the Ministry of Finance's Deposit Bureau. The rest came from the private sector (¥100 million in government-guaranteed bills issued by the Industrial Bank of Japan and sold to private banks, and the remaining ¥5 million supplied directly by the issuing banks).

57. Itō M. 1989: 69.

58. Shimazaki 1989: 126–127; Tadai 1997, I: 273–275; SYM, 543.

59. Sakatani 11/1/1917, in Kinka Hon'i Jisshi Mannijūnen Kinenkai 1917b: 46–48.

60. Shimazaki 1989: 127–128; Tadai 1997, 1: 272–273.

61. Tadai 1997, 1: 278.

62. FRUS 1918: 159–160; Lai and Gau 1999: ch. 2, appendix 2; Matsuoka 1936: 469. See also FRUS 1918: 147–151, 155–157.

63. FRUS 1919: 556–565.

64. Minister in China (Reinsch) to Secretary of State, 2/7/1918 and 4/27/1918, in FRUS 1918: 141–142, 146–147; T. Lamont 1933: 165–166; W. Cohen 1982: 42–43; FRUS 1918: 169–196.

65. Rosenberg 1999: 81–83; FRUS 1914: 362–382.

66. Kemmerer 1916b; Rosenberg 1999: 102.

67. Rosenberg 1999: 81–93; R. F. Smith 1972: 128–131.

68. Inoue speech to Zaisei Keizai Kōkyūkai 6/19/1918, in IJR 2: 155–156, 184–185, 193–195.

69. Odate 1922: 42–57; Inoue 1925, in IJR 1: 247; see also table A.2 in the appendix to this book.

70. Inoue 1925, in IJR 1: 256–257; historical price data in Shinbo 1978: 282; Garon 1987: 249–250; Anno 1999: 321.

71. Dickinson 1999: 180–203 (Shōda quoted on p. 197).

72. Walton 1976: ch. 8.

73. Lewis 1990: 16–17, 28; Ōishi K. and Miyamoto 1975: 280. For the gendered aspect of the inflation crisis, see Metzler 2004b: 321–326.

6. THE GREAT DIVIDE, 1918–1921

1. I am grateful to Ōshima Mario for pointing out the significance of this idea. The notion of deadlock acquired an almost historical-philosophical status in the late 1920s, for which, see Hoston 1986: 82–88. For English-language accounts of the

depressed 1920s, see Nakamura 1987, 1989b; Patrick 1971; Yamamura 1972, 1974. For aspects of the "modern" boom of the era, see, among others, Tipton and Clark 2000. The "population problem" was widely discussed at the time; Inoue's own discussion can be found in a 1925 lecture, "Jinkō zōka ni tomonau shomondai," in IJR 2: 343–367.

2. Hamaguchi 1929: 183–185.

3. Inoue J. 1929a: 2. The term *zaikai* ("the financial world") came, after the World War II, to refer to the politically organized business world, especially to peak organizations such as Keidanren (the Federation of Economic Organizations). But in the interwar period, there was no real distinction between the term *zaikai,* which I have generally translated as "business world," and *keizaikai* (literally, "economic world"). For a valuable study of the prewar *zaikai* in the first sense mentioned above, see Fletcher 1989.

4. Hara A. 1987: 382–386.

5. Inoue 1925, in IJR 1: 6–7.

6. Ishibashi 1929: 544.

7. IJD: 145.

8. NGHS 2: 531–532; Inoue 1925, in IJR 1: 30–31, 258–259.

9. LTES 7: 147–149, 162–163, 168–171.

10. Nakamura 1993: 34.

11. Yoshino 1975–1979, 5: 1058–1060.

12. IJD: 131–144; NGHS 2: 487–491, 519–530; Odate 1922: 71–77; Chandler 1958: 86–93.

13. Inoue 1926, in IJR 1: 328; IJD: 145; Odate 1922: 63–64; Mutō in the *Tōkyō asahi shinbun* of 8/18/1922, excerpted in IJD: 126–127. Introductions to the scholarly debate on the subject are given by Itō Masanao in Nihon Ginkō Kin'yū Kenkyūsho 1993: 96–98, and in NGHS 2: 491–503.

14. Inoue speeches to Zenkoku Tegata Kōkanjo Rengōkai, 4/22/1919, and to Kansai Ginkō Taikai, 4/23/1919, excerpted in IJD: 123–126.

15. Hamaguchi to House of Representatives, July 1920, and January 21, 1922, in Hamaguchi 1925: 59–60, 132–134. Hamaguchi's criticism of Takahashi went back to the former's entry into politics in 1915 ("Shōkyoku seisaku to sekkyoku seisaku," March 1915, in ibid., 290–294).

16. *Annual Report of the Federal Reserve Board,* 6 (1919): 50, 52–53. See the appendix to this book for statistics of gold flows and money supply.

17. NGHS 2: 512–513, 518; Inoue 1925, in IJR 1: 28; Hara to House of Representatives, in Hara T. 1929: 266, 358.

18. NGHS 2: 509–510, 513.

19. As reported by Akashi Teruo, head of the Dai-Ichi Bank, cited in NGHS 2: 519.

20. TKS 9/25/1919: 354; TKS 10/4/1919: 398–399.

21. Ishibashi 1929: 544.

22. Ishibashi 1929: 547.

23. NGHS 2: 510–511; Inoue 1925, in IJR 1: 198–200; Itō M. 1989: 133.

24. This view is presented in the Bank of Japan's internal history of the gold embargo written in 1930 (Nihon Ginkō Chōsakyoku 1930), which can be thought

to reflect Inoue Junnosuke's viewpoint. Sakatani Yoshio held the same opinion (Sakatani article series in *Tōkyō nichi nichi shinbun,* 11–12/1929, in SYM, 789).

25. Ishibashi 1929: 544.

26. 7/1/1928 interview with Takahashi Korekiyo in OAS 7/21/1928 (emphasis in original). See also Patrick 1971: 232. One fragment of Takahashi's statement—"unlike a conquest by military force, an economic conquest is not easily reversed"—has been picked up and quoted out of context by various Western writers on Japan. (Specifically, the fact that Takahashi specified England and America as agents of economic conquest has been omitted.)

27. From the end of 1915 to the end of 1918, the Japanese government's total gold holdings grew from ¥153 million to ¥855 million. Bank of Japan holdings also grew from ¥363 million to ¥733 million (Nihon Ginkō Tōkeikyoku 1966: 169).

28. This was first pointed out to me by Ōshima Mario.

29. Chow 1960: 86–94.

30. Chow 1960: 99–116 et seq.

31. "Minutes of Meeting at Banque de l'Indo-Chine, May 11, 1919," in YSGS 4: 1175–1178; YSGS 1: 487–489; E. Lamont 1994: 154; W. Cohen 1982: 43.

32. See Matsuda 1979: 276–279. Matsuda's unpublished dissertation, which draws on research in American, Japanese, and British archives, gives the fullest analytical account of the negotiations.

33. T. Lamont 1920: 11; Matsuda 1979: 283; Iriye 1965: 15–20; and for the larger contexts of the Manchurian question, Matsusaka 2001.

34. Matsuda 1979: 318–319.

35. Metzler 2004a.

36. Matsuda 1979: 281–346, 293; Takahashi 5/9/1904, in TKM 135.

37. W. Cohen 1982: 46–47; Matsuda 1979: 333–334; E. Lamont 1994: 158.

38. T. Lamont 1920: 11; E. Lamont 1994: 161; Matsuda 1979: 334–336.

39. Quoted in Matsuda 1979: 315.

40. W. Cohen 1982: 47–48, 51–59; W. Cohen 1978: 61–63; Matsuda 1979: 309–312. On Addis's role, see Dayer 1988. For Lamont, the chief sticking point went back to the Huguang railway loan of 1911. In April 1919 the Chinese government canceled the German-issued portion of the Huguang railway bonds, retroactive to August 1917, when China had entered the war against Germany. During the war, however, many of the German-issued bonds had been bought up by Americans at bargain prices. American banks and the U.S. government protested the Chinese refusal to pay interest on these bonds, and Lamont insisted that payment on the bonds was a condition of any future loan.

41. E.g., in Takahashi, "Tai-Shi keizai keisaku gaiken," May 1921, in TKM 127.

42. Inoue speech at Kazoku Kaikan, 2/18/1921, in *Nihon Ginkō sōsai enzetsu,* materials held at the Bank of Japan.

43. Takahashi, "Tō-A keizairyoku juritsu ni kansuru iken," May 1921, in TKM 127.

44. Takahashi, "Tō-A keizairyoku juritsu ni kansuru iken," in TKM 127.

45. Takahashi, "Tō-A keizairyoku juritsu ni kansuru iken," in TKM 127.

46. Nihon Ginkō Chōsakyoku 1930: 8–9; NGHS 2: 535–540; BOJ discount rates (*shōgyō tegata waribiki buai*) given in NGHS Shiryōhen: 356, 374–382. Interest rates were quoted in *sen* (¥1⁄10) and *rin* (¥1⁄100) per ¥100 per day. Hence the odd numbers when these are converted into annualized rates.

47. Hamaguchi to House of Representatives, 1/22/1920, in Hamaguchi 1925: 2–26, 34–35.

48. Takahashi to House of Representatives, 1/22/1920, in Hamaguchi 1925: 31, 37–38.

49. Inoue speech of 1/27/1920, in "Nihon Ginkō sōsai enzetsu shū" [1915–1923], materials held at the Bank of Japan; *Tōkyō keizai zasshi*, 2/9/1920, excerpted in IJD: 129–130.

50. *Oxford English Dictionary* (Oxford: Clarendon Press, 1989). As late as 1931, Inoue's translator, E. H. de Bunsen, apparently considered the words *inflation* and *deflation* barbarous neologisms and refused to use them in his translation.

51. Eichengreen 1992a: 112, 109; Howson 1974: 97–98, quoting Bank of England memoranda.

52. Friedman and Schwartz 1963: 222, 229; *Annual Report of the Federal Reserve Bank*, 6, 1919: 67.

53. Leffingwell's statement was recorded by Charles S. Hamlin, quoted in Friedman and Schwartz 1963: 230. See also Eichengreen 1992a: 116–121.

54. Metzler 2004a and BSP, various files.

55. Friedman and Schwartz 1963: 231–234; U.S. Department of Commerce, Bureau of the Census 1960: 73, 139. Because prices fell so much, U.S. GNP in deflation-adjusted terms could be said to have fallen only 2 percent (ibid.). Such after-the-fact calculations would have given little comfort to the farmers and business-people who had bought high only to sell low. For further ideas on the unreality of "real" national income estimates under conditions of sudden deflation, see pp. 222–24.

56. Eichengreen 1992a: 121–123.

57. See Keynes 1924 [1923].

58. Inoue 8/1930, in IJR 1: 589.

59. A detailed account is given in TSZH 1: 237–264.

60. *Economist* 1/10/1920; *Economist* 2/14/1920; Spalding 1924: 346; Ishibashi 1929: 545; silver prices given in Jastram 1981: 199; TKS 12/18/1920: 801; and TKS, various issues, 1920.

61. IJD: 158; TSZH 1: 253–257.

62. IJD: 158–159; TSZH 1: 257–267; Inoue 1925, in IJR 1: 62–72; Hara A. 1987: 368.

63. Inoue to Zenkoku Tegata Kōkanjo Rengōkai, 4/22/1920, in ZKN 6: 245–246.

64. Inoue 4/22/1920, in ZKN 6: 247, 246.

65. Inoue 4/22/1920, in ZKN 6: 247.

66. IJD: 160–161; NGHS 3: 10–20.

67. NGHS 3: 7–8; TSZH 1: 267–272, 287–291.

68. Inoue 1925, in IJR 1: 32; Yasutomi 2000.

69. Inoue 1925 in IJR 1: 32; Shimazaki 1989: 103–104.

70. Hara A. 1987: 368; Nakamura and Odaka 1989a: 29.

71. Ishibashi 1929: 546.

72. TSZH 1: 272–279.

73. Inoue to Zenkoku Tegata Kōkanjo Rengōkai, 4/11/1921, in IJR 2: 270, 276.

74. Sakairi 1989, 3: 79–80; Nakamura and Odaka 1989a: 29.

7. "THE CONTRACTIONARY TIDE," 1921–1926

1. This conclusion differs from that of Hara A. (1981: 105), who sees budgetary policy in the 1920s as having been expansionary and countercyclical on the whole. If one looks at monetary and fiscal policy as a piece, however, the "negative tide" is unmistakable. See also tables A.1 and A.2 in the appendix to this book.

2. NGHS 3: 29–36.

3. The English loanword *inflation* (*infureeshon*), conveying a sense of systematic and continuing price increase, appears to have come into general use only in the 1930s.

4. Hamaguchi speech to House of Representatives, 1/21/1922, in ZKN 1: 816–817. For the Kenseikai's social policy program, see Garon 1987.

5. Zenkoku Shōgyō Kaigisho Rengōkai resolutions of 11/16/1921 and 12/16/1921, in ZKN 4: 100–101. For the National Federation of Chambers of Commerce, see Hara A. 1977: 174–177 and Fletcher 1989. The retrenchment campaigns of the era are treated in depth by Garon (1998), to whose analysis should be added the fact that these campaigns waxed and waned in line with the partisan dialectic of the "positive" and "negative" policies.

6. Fletcher 1989: 33, 40; Ishizuka 1980: 166; Ishibashi 1929: 544.

7. Hosoya and Saitō 1978. Iriye (1965: 57–88) dates the end of the "Washington system" to the formation of the Nanjing government in 1927, but from the standpoint of U.S.-Japan relations, the framework of active financial-diplomatic cooperation continued to the fall of the Hamaguchi cabinet in December 1931.

8. Dayer 1976.

9. Fukai to Strong, 6/23/1925, BSP file 1330.1(2); Metzler 2004a.

10. Hara A. 1981: 80–81.

11. Zenkoku Shōgyō Kaigisho Rengōkai 6/28/1922, in ZKN 4: 103; Ishibashi 1929: 548.

12. Nihon Ginkō Chōsakyoku 1930: 32–34; NGHS 3: 142–143.

13. Ichiki statement of 9/16/1922, quoted in Ishibashi 1929: 548; Ichiki, in OAS 1927.

14. See Patrick 1971.

15. Ishibashi 1929: 548.

16. Inoue to Kansai Ginkō Taikai, 11/25/1922, in ZKN 6: 259.

17. Inoue 11/25/1922, in ZKN 6: 259–260.

18. Inoue 11/25/1922, in ZKN 6: 260–261.

19. Inoue 1925, in IJR 1: 201–203; Ichiki interview, in OAS 1928.

20. Ishibashi 1929: 548.

21. Hara A. 1987: 369; Ministry of Foreign Affairs, Special Survey Committee 1992 [1946]. The latter comparison was made in 1946 by a team of Japanese government economists to dramatize not the scale of the earthquake but rather the vast extent of the damage caused by World War II.

22. IJD: 177–181; Fukai 1941: 203–206; NGHS 3: 48. The BOJ's library and archives, kept in the former main building, were destroyed in the fire.

23. NGHS 3: 50–52.

24. NGHS 3: 58–61.

25. IJD: 186–190; Tsushima 1963, 2: 171–173.

26. Ishibashi 1929: 549–550; Kanazawa 1990: 349; Tōyō Keizai Shinpōsha 1931, sec. 3: 15–16.

27. TWLP 186–13; Lamont to Inoue 3/20/1922, in TWLP 186–14. For Shibusawa's mission, see Fletcher 1989: 20 and Kimura 1991.

28. Mitani 1980b. From May 1921, in the context of war debt settlements, the U.S. government assumed the right to veto all foreign loans.

29. Nihon Ginkō Chōsakyoku 1930: 652; NGHS 3: 144.

30. Chernow 1990: 236.

31. Lamont to Inoue, 10/10/1923, TWLP 186–16; IJD: 147–148; loan prospectus in MOF-SZS 1–55: 28.

32. Chernow 1990: 235–236; Ikeda S. 1949a: 97.

33. Tōkyō Asahi Shinbun Keizaibu 1925: 77–78.

34. Teranishi 1989: 213; Horie 1950: 49.

35. Takahashi Korekiyo 1936a: 365; Mitani 1988: 55. Under the Meiji constitution the method of selecting the cabinet was left to the emperor, which is to say, not really specified. In practice, it was done by a small circle of senior statesmen. Control of the Home Ministry in particular conferred immense advantages in the election process, and as a rule electoral success for the governing party followed rather than preceded a cabinet change.

36. See Duus 1968: 193–199. Shidehara never actually joined the party, but he and his policy of cooperative diplomacy became a fixture of Kenseikai and Minseitō politics for the next eight years. Of the Kenseikai ministers, only Hamaguchi was actually a Kenseikai representative in the House of Representatives, while Katō and Wakatsuki were members of the House of Peers (to which Shidehara was also appointed in 1926).

37. Kanazawa 1990: 348–349.

38. Duus 1968: 195; Garon 1998: 324–328; [Naimushō,] Shakaikyoku 1927, which gives the official history of the movement and reproductions of the campaign posters, some of which can also be found in Garon 1998.

39. "Kokumin seishin sakkō ni kansuru shōsho," in [Naimushō,] Shakaikyoku 1927: frontispiece.

40. MOF-SZS 3–41: 1, 4, 7. In the Ministry of Finance's internal documentary archive, reports concerning the "Buy Japanese" movement of 1925–26 were filed under the head "Lifting the Gold Embargo."

41. Hamaguchi 1980 [1926]; [Naimushō,] Shakaikyoku 1926.

42. Duus 1968: 195–199; Kanazawa 1990: 397.

43. Ishibashi 1929: 551.

44. TKS 11/15/1924, 11/29/1924, 12/6/1924; Gustav Cassel, "The Japanese Exchange," in MOF-SZS 3–40: 4; Ikeo 1999: 18–20. (I am grateful to Professor Ikeo for making available a copy of her paper.) A copy of Cassel's 1925 report was given to Ishibashi, who published a summary in the *Tōyō keizai shinpō* in 1926. The report was translated into Japanese and published in the same year in the *Ginkō tsūshinroku*.

45. Nihon Ginkō Chōsakyoku 1930: 76.

46. Resolution of Zenkoku Kōkanjo Taikai, quoted in Ishibashi 1929: 552.

47. Ishibashi 1929: 552.

48. Ishibashi 1929: 552; Hamaguchi to House of Representatives, 6/28/1924, in Hamaguchi 1925: 195, 198–201, 210–212.

49. See Johnson 1982, particularly pp. 93–94.

50. Garon 1987: 35–36, 125.

51. Fletcher 1989: 35–37; Tokyo Institute of Political and Economic Research 1934; Johnson 1982: 98.

52. See, again, Johnson 1982.

53. See Asō 1929: 273.

54. The Seiyūkai's statement is reprinted in Asō 1929: 276–277. On Tanaka Giichi, see Bamba 1972 and Morton 1980.

55. Asō 1929: 277; Duus 1968: 219–222.

56. "Naichi seika no gensō ni tsuite," MOF-SZS 3–40: 29; Ishibashi 1929: 553.

57. Ishibashi 1929: 553–554; internal MOF documents cited in NGHS 3: 116.

8. THE THEORY AND PRACTICE OF INDUCED DEPRESSION

1. For further thoughts along these lines, see Kindleberger 1985b.

2. Takahashi quoted in Iriye 1974: 244–245; Inoue 1926, in IJR 1: 480; Lamont to Arthur E. Post, 10/8/1938, TWLP 62–5; see also Tōkyō Asahi Shinbun Keizaibu 1925.

3. See Polanyi 1957 [1944].

4. Again, there is a vast literature on the international monetary politics of the 1920s, with much of the best of it dating from the era itself. Eichengreen (1992a) provides an index to the literature by a contemporary scholar who has studied the era in great depth and breadth.

5. For the case of Germany, see McNeil 1986 and James 1990, especially pp. 42–44.

The choice of terminology was significant. As Overseas Financial Commissioner Tsushima Juichi pointed out, the Japanese term *lifting the gold embargo* was different from the usual Western terms, which were *restoration of the gold standard* or *currency stabilization* (Tsushima in Andō 1965, 1: 58). Japan already had an internally stable currency, and this difference in terminology points to the fact that for Japan the gold question was fundamentally a matter of external relations.

6. Tsushima 1963, 2: 125–133 (conference resolutions abstracted from pp. 127–133). For the League Financial Committee, see Pauly 1997 and Péteri 2002.

7. Abstracted from Tsushima 1963, 2: 139–146, and Financial Commission Report, in *Federal Reserve Bulletin* 8:6, June 1922: 678 (my italics). See also Hawtrey 1922; Clarke 1973: 4–18.

8. Péteri (1984, 2002) discusses British ambitions to create a new sterling sphere in Central Europe that could in turn serve as a European base for restoring the British pound's global position vis-à-vis the U.S. dollar. Rothbard (1998) views the new gold-exchange standard as an effort to support Britain's own return to the gold standard at the old par under the inflated postwar price structure.

9. But see Lindert (1969) and Matsuoka (1936) for the continuities between the prewar and postwar gold-exchange standards, and see the relevant comments of Eichengreen (1992a: 20, 193–194).

10. Péteri 2002: 48, citing League of Nations data.

11. Falkus 1971; FRB 6/1922: 680; Eichengreen 1992a: 198–203.

12. Strong to Fukai, 3/11/1924, BSP file 1330.1; Friedman and Schwartz 1963: 279–284; Eichengreen 1992a: 205–207, 247–249.

13. Costigliola 1977: 916–920; Fink 1984; Tsushima 1963, 2: 144, 146; and chapter 6 above.

14. Inoue 7/1930, in IJR 4: 265; Metzler 2004a; see also Meyer 1970 and Simmons 1996. The idiom refers to leading a cow by the ear. Inoue discussed his relations with Strong and Norman in Inoue 7/1930, in IJR 4: 266–269. Most of Strong's correspondence with Inoue can be found in BSP.

15. Strong to Inoue, 11/1/1923, materials held at the Bank of Japan; Strong to Inoue, 5/10/1927, BSP file 1330.1(1). On this point, see also Meyer 1970: 12.

16. Pauly 1997: 52–55; Péteri 1984; Chernow 1990: 246–247. Pauly sees these League of Nations stabilization programs as the direct predecessors to the later programs of the International Monetary Fund. However, the League's overall role was minor compared to that of J. P. Morgan and Co., which coordinated the major operations of the decade.

17. The term *reparations* (rather than *indemnity*) was a novelty of the era. I continue to use the prewar term *indemnity* here to highlight the parallels between the German indemnity and earlier indemnity payments, not to imply a judgment about the question of German war guilt.

18. See James 1985: 10.

19. For the place of the Dawes Plan in U.S. domestic politics, see Miller 2001.

20. Chernow 1990: 248–253.

21. James 1985: 60, and for further discussion, McNeil 1986, Schuker 1988, James 1986, and Eichengreen 1992a.

22. Inoue, "Dōzu-an seiritsu no jijō to sono eikyō," 1925, in IJR 4: 184–186.

23. The information in this paragraph is drawn mainly from the summation given by Kotz (1978: 47, 49–50); see also Chernow 1990. Japanese observers perceived (or misperceived) the Morgan group as a banking-industrial *Konzern,* that is, as a larger and more powerful version of the Mitsui and Mitsubishi industrial empires. In line with this idea, Lamont himself was called Morgan's *dai bantō* ("head clerk"), a term used for the non-family-member general managers who ran the actual operations of the Japanese zaibatsu (Tōkyō Asahi Shinbun Keizaibu 1925).

24. Horie 1950: 47–49; Hausman and Neufeld 1988.

25. Chernow 1990: 219, 264; Tsushima 1963, 1: 144; Fitzsimons 1990: 207.

26. Chernow 1990: 257. By way of comparison, America's total surplus on merchandise trade from 1920 to 1929 was $10.6 billion. The total U.S. balance-of-payments (goods and services) surplus over the same period was $14.3 billion. About 21 percent of U.S. foreign lending in the 1920s went to Canada (U.S. Department of Commerce, Bureau of the Census 1960: 537, 564; Mintz 1951: 10).

27. Rosenberg 1999: 154–155, 167–169.

28. Drake 1989a; Eichengreen 1994 [1989]; Rosenberg 1999: 159–164, 177–181.

29. Drake 1989a: 18.

30. Rosenberg 1999: 169.

31. Called "structural deflation" by Kindleberger (1986: 92–94).

32. Cohen 1972; Kemp 1971.

33. IJD: 259–364; Yoshino 1975–1979: 1067. Inoue's name was also proposed as mayor of Tokyo (the post held successively by Sakatani Yoshio, Tajiri Inajirō, and Gotō Shinpei after they had retired from their "front line" official and political

careers). Instead, Inoue assumed the chairmanship of the Great Japan Federation of Youth Groups (Dai Nippon Rengo Seinendan).

34. Inoue to Tōkyō Ginkō Kurabu, 10/26/1926, in IJR 2: 521–522. Inoue's Kyoto lectures were published in July as a book (Inoue J. 1926), which was later translated into English by British vice consul E. H. de Bunsen (Inoue J. 1931 [1926]). Loose and colorful, de Bunsen's translation is accurate on points of fact but often misleading on points of rhetoric.

35. Inoue 10/26/1926, in IJR 2: 488.

36. Inoue 1926, in IJR 1: 460–462; 417–418; Inoue 10/26/1926, in *IJR* 2: 494. Rice was imported from Korea and Taiwan, but monetarily these were part of Japan.

37. "The Economic Consequences of Mr. Churchill," in Keynes 1970 [1925]: 31, 35. Italics in original. In 1928 Keynes's essay was loosely translated into Japanese and published in a book, *Kin kaikin to kokumin keizai* (Lifting the gold embargo and the national economy).

38. Inoue 10/26/1926, in *IJR* 2: 520–522.

39. Inoue 10/26/1926, in *IJR* 2: 494–495, 498, 502.

40. Inoue 10/26/1926, in *IJR* 2: 489, 493. (The expression is from Mencius.)

41. Inoue 10/26/1926, in *IJR* 2: 513–514. Inoue himself described Mitsuchi as an intimate associate of Takahashi (Inoue to Lamont 6/2/1927, in TWLP 186–24). As prime minister in 1921, Takahashi had appointed Mitsuchi as chief cabinet secretary (*shoki kanchō*), and in June 1927 Mitsuchi succeeded Takahashi as finance minister in the Tanaka cabinet.

42. Inoue 10/26/1926, in IJR 2: 493–494; Nihon Ginkō Tōkeikyoku 1966: 280–281.

43. Inoue 10/26/1926, in IJR 2: 500–501.

44. Takamura 1985: 153.

45. Inoue 10/26/1926, in IJR 2: 502.

46. The Finance Ministry's preparations are described in "Kin kaikin jikkō ni taisuru junbiteki shisetsu ni tsuite" and "Kin kaikin no jikkō to shōrai ni okeru wagakuni seika shūshi kankei," both 11/13/1926, in MOF-SZS 3–41: 17, 18.

9. "THE TWO-PARTY PRINCIPLE," 1927–1929

1. Hara A. 1987: 375; Teranishi 1989: 205.

2. Takahashi and Morigaki 1993 [1968].

3. *NGHS* 3: 196; Fukai 1941: 217–220.

4. Takahashi and Morigaki 1993 [1968]: 96–101; Ichiki speech of April 7, 1927, in "Shitenchō kaigi shorui," Spring 1927–Fall 1928, materials held at the Bank of Japan.

5. Sansom and Macrae (1928), quoted in Nitobe 1931: 37.

6. Sansom and Macrae, quoted in Nitobe 1931: 37. On George Sansom's role during this period, see Akita and Kagotani 2002: 150–155.

7. NGHS 3: 185.

8. NGHS 3: 186.

9. Kataoka interview in Ōsaka Asahi Shinbun Keizaibu 1999 [1928]: 88.

10. Kataoka in Ōsaka Asahi Shinbun Keizaibu 1999 [1928]: 89.

11. *Tōkyō Nichi Nichi Shinbun* 3/4/1927, in SNJ 1: 80.

12. *Ōsaka Mainichi Shinbun* 3/15/1927, in SNJ 1: 80.
13. Kataoka in Ōsaka Asahi Shinbun Keizaibu 1999 [1928]: 91.
14. Kataoka to Diet budget committee, 3/14/1927, in NKS-S 25: 432.
15. NGHS 3: 16, 35, 72.
16. Kataoka's defense of his actions is given in his 1928 *Ōsaka Asahi Shinbun* interview and in his subsequent autobiography and history of the period (Kataoka 1934).
17. NGHS 3: 187.
18. Walton 1976, ch. 9.
19. NGHS 3: 40–41; IJD: 314–317. Inoue was also the House of Peers representative on the committee.
20. NGHS 3: 193.
21. Takahashi Korekiyo 1936a: 317–318.
22. NGHS 3: 179.
23. Takahashi Korekiyo 1936a: 317–318.
24. Takahashi Korekiyo 1936a: 321–324.
25. *Chūgai shōgyō shinpō* 4/24/1927, in SNJ 1: 80–81.
26. *Chūgai shōgyō shinpō* 4/23/1927, in NKS-S 21: 761–762.
27. Ikeda S. 1949b: 128.
28. Takahashi 3/7/1932, in Takahashi Korekiyo 1936a: 59.
29. Takahashi Korekiyo 1936a: 329–331.
30. Teranishi 1989: 205.
31. Inoue 5/26/1928 report, TWLP 186–28.
32. Bamba 1972: 315.
33. Hara A. 1981: 85–86, 100–102.
34. This was the judgment of Thomas Lamont (Lamont to H. Kashiwagi 10/16/1923, TWLP 186–16).
35. Tsushima 1963: 141; Lamont to Morgan & Co. 11/1/1927, TWLP 190–6. After sixteen years as Japan's overseas financial commissioner, Mori retired in May 1927 to join the House of Peers. He was replaced by Tsushima Juichi, who had been private secretary to Finance Minister Takahashi in 1920.
36. Mitani 1975: 175.
37. E. Lamont 1994: 232.
38. IJD: 390, 396; E. Lamont 1994: 232–234.
39. These were Mortimer Schiff of Kuhn, Loeb; Charles Mitchell of National City Bank; and George Baker of First National Bank (Mitani 1975: 175).
40. TWLP 189–27, various memos, 9–10/1927.
41. "Mr. Lamont's Duty," *The Nation,* 12/14/1927, p. 671; FRUS 1927, 2: 482–492; Iriye 1965: 187–190.
42. Tsushima 1963, 2: 255–256.
43. Péteri 2002: 95–97.
44. Inoue column in the *Kokumin shinbun* of 10/31/1927, reprinted in IJD: 397.
45. Inoue speech of 10/4/1927, in IJD: 391.
46. TWLP 190–9; Itō M. 1989: 135. Lamont apparently said nothing to the State Department about the SMR loan until after his trip (Kellogg to Mayer, 11/21/1927, in FRUS 1927, 2: 483–484).

47. Thomas W. Lamont and Jeremiah Smith Jr., "Memorandum on Japanese Conditions," TWLP 190–6 (my italics).

48. Lamont and Smith, "Memorandum," TWLP 190–6.

49. MacVeagh to Kellogg, 11/21/1927, in FRUS 1927, 2: 486. MacVeagh's report almost surely reflected Lamont's account of the meeting.

50. Abstracted from Lamont and Smith, "Memorandum," TWLP 190–6.

51. Abstracted from Lamont and Smith, "Memorandum," TWLP 190–6.

52. Fukai to Lamont 10/17/1927, TWLP 190–7.

53. Fukai to Lamont 10/17/1927, TWLP 190–7. Inoue later published an almost identical statement.

54. TWLP 190–8.

55. Lamont speech of December 1927, TWLP 186–26.

56. Lamont to Inoue 6/1/1928, TWLP 186–28.

57. TWLP 186–26; Tsushima 1963, 2: 258–275. The merger was concluded jointly with the international bond issue in April 1928.

58. Tsushima 1963, 2: 327.

59. Drake 1989a; Rosenberg 1999. Other American "stabilization" missions were sent to South Africa, Poland, Persia, Turkey, and China but with less (or no) success.

60. Ishibashi 1994 [1964]: 19–21; Inoue 8/1929, in IJR 4: 254.

61. "Moppara minkan de zaikai sewa yaku o yaru yō ni narimashita," in the words of Takahashi Korekiyo (1936a: 59).

62. Unsigned letter to Lamont of 9/22/1927, TWLP 188–29. A year later, Leffingwell gave a copy of this same letter to Lamont, who sent a copy to Mori Kengo on 9/13/1928. Mori in turn distributed copies to Ikeda Shigeaki, Hijikata Hisaakira, Fukai Eigo, and Inoue Junnosuke.

63. It was not clear to outside observers that the apparent deficits in the special accounts were covered by deposits in the postal savings system (Katalin Ferber, personal communication).

64. Leffingwell (?) to Lamont, 9/22/1927, TWLP 188–29.

65. Leffingwell to Mori 9/10/1928, TWLP 188–30.

66. Lamont to Mori 9/13/1928, TWLP 188–30.

67. Mori to Lamont 10/20/1928, TWLP 188–30.

68. See Miwa 1974.

69. NGHS 3: 369–372. In a closed-door meeting in October 1928, Vice Governor Fukai Eigo told BOJ managers that the bank's control needed to be restored so that it could manage gold outflows in the event of lifting the gold embargo.

70. Miwa 1974: 175–176; Fletcher 1989: 56; NGHS 3: 151–153; "Kin kaikin no mondai ni kanshi shodantai no happyō shitaru ikensho, seimeisho," MOF-SZS 3–41: 19; Gō Seinosuke, *Kin kaikin ni tsuite,* 2/1929, no publication information, held at Zaimushō Bunko.

71. Ikeda S. 1949a: 58.

72. Clarke 1973: 123–125; Kindleberger 1986: 50–53; Eichengreen 1992a: 212–215. Present at the secret meeting, held in the Long Island home of U.S. treasury secretary Ogden Mills, were Strong, Norman of the Bank of England, Rist (for Moreau) of the Bank of France, and Schacht of the German Reichsbank. Despite his connection with Strong, Inoue was informed only later (Metzler 2004a).

73. Kindleberger 1986: 54–61.
74. Inoue 8/1930, in IJR 1: 584–585.
75. Tsushima Juichi, in Andō 1965–66, 1: 60.
76. Kindleberger 1986: 65–68; Tsushima 1963, 2: 298–299; Aritake 1967–68, 1: 281.
77. Tsushima, in Andō 1965–66, 1: 61. Bank of Japan figures give total overseas specie holdings in December 1928 as ¥114 million (NGHS 3: 378). By March 1929 they were down to ¥91 million.
78. NGHS 3: 379.
79. TWLP 186–31; Itō M. 1989: 136–137; Tiedemann 1959: 122–129. In a parallel way, the Tanaka cabinet also retreated to a more cooperative policy line in China in the latter part of 1928 (Iriye 1965: 239–244).
80. Quoted in Tiedemann 1959: 128.
81. Tsushima in Andō 1965–66, 1: 59.
82. Lamont to J. P. Morgan & Co., 5/7/1929, TWLP 186–31. Mori was in London in January 1929, preparing for the Paris conference (Tsushima 1963, 2: 298–299).
83. Tsushima 1963, 2: 327.
84. T. Lamont 1930b: 321.
85. Their hopes for the BIS can be found in Lamont 1929 and J. Smith 1929. See also Costigliola 1972.
86. Tsushima 1963, 2: 327; Aritake 1967–68, 1: 306–308; Tsushima, in Andō 1965–66, 1: 60.
87. Tsushima, in Andō 1965–66, 1: 59; Aritake 1967–68, 1: 282–283.
88. Lamont to J. P. Morgan & Co. 5/7/1929, TWLP 186–31.
89. Tsushima, in Andō 1965–66, 1: 59; Lamont to Morgan 5/24/1929, TWLP 178–27; Lamont to J. P. Morgan & Co. 5/25/1929, TWLP 186–31; Meyer 1970: 13–14. In the event, the Federal Reserve did not participate in the credit but instead offered its "moral support."
90. Unsigned memo of 6/27/1929, probably written by Leffingwell, in TWLP 186–31. This memo, or one like it, was shared with Tsushima (Aritake 1967–68, 1: 284). Why Morgan & Co. changed its position is not fully clear.
91. Tsushima in Andō 1965–66, 1: 62–63; Aritake 1967–68, 1: 331–332.
92. That the Bank of Japan had lost its independence was another misapprehension—it had not been independent in the first place. Americans revived the issue of central bank independence during the Dodge Line of 1949–1952, when the BOJ Policy Board was created in order to give the central bank a more independent and Federal Reserve–like structure (Tsutsui 1988: 73–90). The effects were almost nil, and new reforms to give the Bank of Japan more independence were enacted in 1998.
93. Memo of 6/27/1929, TWLP 186–31.
94. On Tanaka's foreign policy, see Iriye 1965, Bamba 1972, and Morton 1980; on Zhang, see McCormack 1977.

10. THE LIBERAL TRIUMPH, 1929–1930

Epigraphs: Lamont to Morgan, 4/19/1927, TWLP 189–27. Takahashi, "Inoue Junnosuke-kun no shi o kiite" [On hearing of the death of Mr. Inoue Junnosuke],

3/1932, in Takahashi Korekiyo 1936a: 60. Takahashi's report of Inoue's words appeared first in the *Ōsaka asahi shinbun* on February 10. However, unlike later appearances of the same statement, Inoue's words there were printed as "quickly reimpose the gold embargo," which can only be a printer's mistake; both terms (*kin yushutsu kaikin* and *kin yushutsu saikinshi*) were much in the news at the time.

1. Allen 1980: 38.

2. *Economist*, 7/29/1929: 118.

3. Strong: my surmise, based on Inoue 11/1926, in IJR 4: 237–239. In early 1924, when Inoue visited London, he discussed the matter of entering party politics with an unnamed English friend (apparently Montagu Norman) and with another unnamed friend from "a certain New York bank" (probably Strong, but perhaps Lamont, both of whom visited London at the time). Inoue wrote of his relation with Norman in Inoue 7/1930 (IJR 4: 266–269).

4. Tiedemann 1959: 76. Inoue's stance has been interpreted as reflecting his lack of confidence in the Seiyūkai cabinet's ability to pull off the job—the speculation being that Inoue thought that only he himself could do it (Nakamura 1978: 70–71).

5. *Hochi shinbun*, 2/12/1932, excerpted in IJD: 883; Ikeda 1949b: 124–125; Tiedemann 1959: 76.

6. Summarized from *Minsei* 3:8 (August 1929): 2–7; see also the discussion in Tiedemann 1959: 90–94.

7. See Garon 1987, especially pp. 157–186.

8. Inoue 1929c: 174.

9. "Kyū heika kaikin ron" (Lifting the [gold] ban at the old par), 8/1929, in IJR 4. Aligned with Ishibashi as part of the "gang of four" who argued for a new par were Takahashi Kamekichi, Obama Toshie, and Yamazaki Yasuzumi.

10. Inoue 8/1929, in IJR 4: 254–255.

11. Inoue 1929c: 173.

12. Tsushima, in Andō 1965–66, 1: 62; Aritake 1967, 1: 329, 330, 335.

13. Hamaguchi quoted in Tiedemann 1959: 132; Furuya 1990: 68–69. The cabinet cut ¥90 million from the general account budget of ¥1,770 million. An additional ¥57 million was cut from the special accounts.

14. Tiedemann 1959: 167–168; Takahashi Masanori 1980: 489; Declaration of Seiyūkai Diet members, 10/30/1929, ZKN 3: 625–626.

15. For the rationalization movement, see Tsutsui 2001, ch. 2, and Tsunoda 1993, ch. 7, which discusses the uses both Inoue and Takahashi made of the term.

16. "Kōshi keizai kinshuku undō ni kansuru keikaku yōkō," MOF-SZS 1–88: 18; Tsushima speech of 1/10/1930, MOF-SZS 3–40. The senses of the words *public* and *private* differ in English and in Japanese, where *public* (*kō*) historically referred to the government and *private* (*shi*) to the people. An account of the campaign is given in NHK Shuzaihan 1995: 123–137; see also Garon 1998.

17. Hamaguchi 1929; "Insatsubutsu sakusei narabi ni haifu chō," 5/1930, MOF-SZS 1–88: 21.

18. "Kōshi keizai kinshuku dō-fu-kenbetsu kōenkai gaikyo chō," MOF-SZS 1–88: 20; Tsushima in MOF-SZS 3–40. The significance of the term *kyōka* is discussed by Garon (1997: 7, 10–13), who translates it as "moral suasion."

19. Ministry of Finance materials (SZS 1–88: 24) list the following feature films

related to "public and private retrenchment": *Shizuka naru ayumi* (*A Quiet Walk*), produced by Nippon Katsudō Shashin; *Bentō bako* (*Lunch Box*), by Taiyō Kinema Sha; *Itsutsu no chikai* (*Five Vows*), by Fuji Eiga Sha; *Tsuchi wa eien ni iku* (*The Earth Lives Eternally*), by Teishin Kinema Sha.

20. Tsushima 1/10/1930, in MOF-SZS 3–40. The song by Fumikichi-san has been rereleased on Japan Victor no. 60329. Hosokawa Shuhei, personal communication; NHK Shuzaihan 1995: 135. Thanks to Hosokawa Shuhei for kindly providing me with a recording; further thanks to Christine Yano.

With the advantage of hindsight, the retrenchment campaign seems a bitter joke, and the liner notes of the modern compact disc compilation attribute a sense of irony to the song. In fact, it seems the campaign was undertaken in complete earnestness.

21. Speech to the Consumer Economy Discussion Group of the All-Kansai Women's Federation, published in September 1929 in the tract *Kin kaikin—zen Nippon ni sakebu* (Lifting the Gold Ban—Calling Out to All Japan), in Inoue 1929c; MOF-SZS 1–88: 21. For more on the state's use of women and women's organizations in its savings campaigns, see Garon 1998, 2000. Some important comparative considerations are discussed by Kasza 1995: 87–99.

22. Inoue 1929c: 157–158, 164, 174.

23. Inoue 1929c: 160–161, 167.

24. Inoue 1929c: 161–162.

25. Inoue 1929c: 169–170.

26. Inoue 1929c: 172–173.

27. Inoue 1929a: 36.

28. Krugman 1998, 1999.

29. Calculated from statistics given in LTES 6: 208–212. Beer consumption also doubled during the boom of the late 1910s, rising to an annual level of some two liters per capita. The consumption of *shōchū* and other liquors nearly doubled, to some four liters per capita.

30. Inoue 1929c: 179; LTES 6: 141.

31. Takahashi 3/1932, in Takahashi Korekiyo 1936a: 59.

32. From *Gendai,* 9/1929, in NKS-S 22: 536–537.

33. *Kokumin keizai no tatenaoshi to kin kaikin,* in Inoue 1929a: 34–35.

34. Takahashi 11/1929, in Takahashi Korekiyo 1936a: 252.

35. A recent critique can be found in Stiglitz 2002.

36. Takahashi 11/1929, in Takahashi Korekiyo 1936a: 247–248.

37. Takahashi Korekiyo 1936a: 248–249. Notably, Takahashi did not assume that savings equaled investment. This was realistic, given the considerable idle funds in the banks, especially after the 1927 banking panic—banks did not think it profitable to invest in domestic industry at this juncture.

38. Takahashi Korekiyo 1936a: 250–251.

39. Takahashi's views on paternalistic employment relations are given in Takahashi Korekiyo 1938: 121.

40. For a contemporary feminist criticism of the retrenchment policy, see Hiratsuka Raichō's October 1929 essay, in Hiratsuka 1984, 5: 144–151, and the discussion in Metzler 2004b: 342–344.

41. Shen 1941: 151–152; Lai and Gau 1999, ch. 2.

42. Lamont to Morgan partners, 9/11/1929, TWLP 187–1.

43. Kindleberger 1986: 54–61; Rothermund 1996.

44. TWLP 187–1.

45. Tsushima, in Andō 1965–66, 1: 62; Aritake 1967–68, 1, "Nenpyō," p. 7.

46. NYT 10/25/1929, p. 1.

47. Tsushima in Andō 1965–66, 1: 65–66.

48. Ministry of Finance statement of 11/21/1929, TWLP 187–2; Takahashi Korekiyo speech to House of Peers, 1/21/1932, NKS-S 21: 151.

49. NYT 10/25/1929.

50. Tsushima in Andō 1965–66: 1: 64; Aritake 1967–68, 1: 332–334; Furuya 1990: 69–70. For Belgium's experience, see Eichengreen 1992a: 170–172 and Meyer 1970: 16–41.

51. *Tōkyō asahi shinbun,* 11/16/1929, in Ōkurashō, "Kin kaikin ni kansuru kirinuki shinbun," Zaimushō Bunko, Tokyo.

52. Ikeda 1949a: 89; Mori to Lamont, 11/27/1929, TWLP 188–30.

53. Aritake 1967–68, 1: 332–333; Nihon Ginkō, Gaikoku Kawase Kyoku, "Kin kaikin jisshi ni tomonau honkō Yokohama Shōkin Ginkō no kyōtei," materials held at the Bank of Japan; Morgan & Co. to Inoue 11/19/1929, TWLP 187–2.

The British group consisted of Westminster Bank, Baring Brothers, Morgan Grenfell, Rothschilds, J. Henry Schroeder & Co., the Hong Kong and Shanghai Bank, Hambros, and the Chartered Bank of India, Australia, and China. John Rae was the representative of the British group.

Under the terms of the "revolving credit," the Yokohama Specie Bank, acting for the Japanese government, could call on funds up to the maximum of $25 million plus £5 million, to be drawn on equally from the New York and London groups. With each advance, the YSB would deposit with Morgan & Co. and with the Westminster Bank collateral in the form of Japanese government dollar or sterling bonds equal to 120 percent of the advance. No interest would be charged unless an advance was made. An up-front commission of 1 percent of the total credit was paid to the group, with an extra 0.25 percent commission to Morgan & Co. (Nihon Ginkō, Gaikoku Kawase Kyoku).

54. *Kanpō, gogai* (unnumbered), 11/21/1929. The silver embargo order, although it was no longer enforced, was lifted at the same time, as were the specie embargoes in Korea, Taiwan, and Karafuto (Sakhalin). The government chose to implement its plan after the end of the year because of the high demand for money to handle year-end settlements.

55. Tsushima, in SKS 1: 64. Because the Bank of Japan did not participate in the credit, which would have required that it open its books concerning the "special accommodations" made to bail out Japanese banks, the U.S. Federal Reserve and the Bank of England refrained from taking part in the credit.

56. Morgan & Co. to Inoue 11/19/1929, TWLP 187–2.

57. News reports of 11/20 and 11/21/1929, in "Kin kaikin ni kansuru bunken," 11/1929, and "Kin kaikin kankei (sono 3)," Nihon Ginkō hisshoyaku report to Ōkurashō hisshoyaku, 11/21/1929, materials held at the Bank of Japan.

58. See chapter 7, above.

59. Inoue 1929a: 33.

60. MOF-SZS 1–90: 4.

11. OPENING THE DOOR TO A HURRICANE, 1930–1931

1. Tsushima speech of 1/10/1930, in MOF-SZS: 3–40: 15 and 1–86: 5. Tsushima also spoke of a deep debt "of gratitude" owed to Lamont and his associates, to whom he sent a copy of his speech (TWLP 187–4).

2. TWLP 187–4.

3. *Wall Street Journal* 1/11/1930 (copy in TWLP 187–3).

4. IJD: 576–579; *Hamaguchi Osachi nikki* 1/11/1930, in Hamaguchi 1991: 283; NHK Shuzaihan 1995: 183.

5. Mutō 1930: 61–62.

6. Inoue 1/11/1930, in IJD: 573–574.

7. NGHS 3: 425; TWLP 187–2.

8. NGHS 3: 422. Over the course of 1930, individual (*koguchi*) conversions added up to less than ¥3 million, or about 1 percent of institutional (*ōguchi*) conversions.

9. Telegraphic reports of Kōbe Zeikan and Yokohama Zeikan to MOF Shūzeikyoku, 1/20/1930 through 1/23/1930, in "Kinka oyobi kinkai yushutsu-nyūdaka hōkoku," MOF-SZS 3–40: 32; NGHS 3: 423; Aono 1931: 45.

10. Nihon Ginkō Chōsakyoku, "Kinkaikingo ni okeru naichi seika no ryūshutsu gaku suisan," 11/1929, materials held at the Bank of Japan; Fukai 1941: 244–245.

11. NGHS 3: 425, 423; Yokohama Zeikan to Shūzeikyoku, 1/30/1930, in MOF-SZS 3–40: 32.

12. Nihon Ginkō Chōsakyoku, "Kinkaikingo ni okeru naichi seika no ryūshutsu gaku suisan," 11/1929, materials held at the Bank of Japan.

13. NGHS 3: 423–424; Takahashi 1/21/1932, in NKSS 21: 151. After National City Bank, the Mitsui group was second in line, as Mitsui Bank and the Mitsui Trust Company together converted ¥36 million into gold. The Hongkong and Shanghai Bank and the Chartered Bank, which participated in the credit from the London side, together cashed in ¥30 million, and the Nederlandsch-Indische Handelsbank and Nederlandsche Handel-Maatschappij together took ¥42 million in gold.

14. Tsushima to Lamont 4/22/1930, TWLP 187–4.

15. Lamont to Inoue 5/5/1930, TWLP 187–5.

16. Lamont to Tsushima 5/8/1930, TWLP 187–5.

17. Aono 1931: 55; Lamont to Inoue 6/3/1930, TWLP 187–5.

18. Mutō 1930: 18; NGHS 3: 445; Aono 1931: 55.

19. Lamont to Inoue 7/21/1930, TWLP 187–5.

20. Ishibashi 1929: 561.

21. Mutō 1930: 2–3.

22. Hara A. 1987: 391.

23. MOF-SZS 1–88: 9. This does not count the year-end note issue, which was always much higher than in other months, to accommodate demand for money to settle year-end accounts.

24. At the end of November 1929, the ratio of the BOJ's specie reserve to the note issue was 79 percent, and the ratio of the specie reserve to the bank's note issue and deposits was 56 percent. At the end of November 1930, the two ratios were 69 and 54 percent. See figure 10 and appendix table A.1, below.

25. Aono 1931: 45–48, 33, 61; Hara A. 1987: 395–399.

26. *Tokyo nichi nichi shinbun* 11/20/1929, in SNJ 2; Johnson 1982: 102–114.

27. OAS 4/6/1930.
28. OAS issues of 4/8, 4/9, 4/10, 4/11/1930.
29. OAS 4/12/1930; Aono 1931: 37.
30. Garon 1987: 250, citing Miwa Ryōichi. For a close-up look, see Faison 2001.
31. Hara A. 1987: 399.
32. An introduction to the debate is given in Hoston 1986 and Ōshima 1991.
33. Odaka (1989) reviews the "dual structure" of the 1920s. Tsurumi (1990) describes the conditions of women textile workers, which often amounted to indentured bondage. Smethurst (1986) gives a more optimistic picture of agrarian development.
34. Ōkurashō, Kokko Chōsagakari, "Ginkai sōba hōraku no gen'in," 4/17/1930, MOF-SZS 1–87: 17; Aono 1931: 20; Mutō 1930: 6; Ma 1996: 339.
35. Rōyama 1941: 38; Iriye 1974.
36. Inoue, *Sekai fukeiki to waga kokumin no kakugo,* 8/1930, IJR 1: 582; Hoover 1951–52, 3: 61; TWLP 147–9; NYT 11/27/1930; Kindleberger 1986: 70–71.
37. Inoue 8/1930, in IJR 1: 582–583, 585.
38. Inoue 8/1930, in IJR 1: 589, 618.
39. Inoue 8/1930, in IJR 1: 592, 602, 607, 613, 617–618.
40. Aono 1931: 49. Mutō's conversion on the gold-standard question is described by Ishibashi 1994 [1964]: 19–21. Mutō's "bête noire": Fletcher 1989: 40.
41. Mutō 1930: i, 2.
42. Mutō 1930: 66–68, 73–74; see also Metzler 2004b: 319–320, 330.
43. Inoue report, "Recent Financial and Economic Conditions in Japan," TWLP 187–7; Aono 1931: 78.
44. Rothermund 1996: 41–42; Nakamura 1981a.
45. For a history of the broad and multifarious agrarianist movement, see Havens 1974.
46. Hamaguchi 1931: 148–149, 153; Aono 1931: 89.
47. Kodama 1972a: 62–63; Kodama 1972b: 31. Kodama's postwar career is discussed in Kaplan and Dubro 2003.
48. Inoue 1/22/1931, in IJR 3: 474–475; the quotation is taken from an English translation of Inoue's speech that was sent to Thomas Lamont ("Gist of speech by Inoue to Diet," 1/22/1931, TWLP 187–7).
49. Furuya 1990: 89–90.
50. Hamaguchi 1931: 178, 184–185; Furuya 1990: 93–95.
51. Kodama 1972a, 1: 64.
52. Kodama 1972a: 66–67.
53. Shakai Mondai Shiryō Kenkyūkai 1975: 92; Kodama 1972a: 63, 68–69.
54. *Asahi keizai nenshi,* 1932: 283. See also appendix table A.1 below.
55. Lamont 1930b: 321, 325, 326.
56. Kindleberger 1986: 144–153; Nihon Ginkō Kin'yū Kenkyūjo 1988: 145.
57. *Chūō kōron* 1/1932.
58. Peattie 1975: 97, 99, 113.
59. Goto-Shibata 1995: 135.
60. TWLP 187–10.
61. Hara A. 1987: 190.

62. British ambassador to Foreign Minister Shidehara, 11/21/1931, MOF-SZS 1–86: 6; Kindleberger 1986: 154–158.

63. Kunz 1991: 44.

64. Eichengreen 1992a: 283–284.

65. Kunz 1991: 44.

66. OAS 9/22/1931.

67. British ambassador (Lindley) to Shidehara, 9/21/1931, MOF-SZS 1–86: 6.

68. OAS 9/22/1931; Inoue to Lamont 9/20/1931, TWLP 187–9; NKN: 146. Morgan's Russell Leffingwell penned a note to Lamont at the time: "How long before they follow suit?" (TWLP 187–9).

69. NKN: 146.

70. Inoue to House of Peers, 1/21/1932, IJR 3: 578–579; *Chūō kōron* 1/1932: 191.

71. Seiyūkai representatives' meeting 11/10/1931, ZKN 3: 687–688; TKS 11/14/1931: 1430.

72. Berger 1977: 40.

73. Lamont to Sonoda 11/23/1931, TWLP 187–12.

74. *Kanpō, gogai* (unnumbered), 12/13/1931; MOF-SZS 1–88: 26; *Kanpō, gogai,* 12/17/1931. The new gold embargo order was identical to the 1917 edict except that the clause permitting travelers to take out up to ¥100 without ministry permission was omitted. Japan did not abandon the gold standard by law until 1942, after which Bank of Japan notes abandoned all pretense of being convertible into anything but themselves.

12. CAPITALIST RECOVERY IN ONE COUNTRY, 1932–1936

Epigraphs: Inoue Junnosuke speech, 1/21/1932, IJR 3: 588. Takahashi Korekiyo, 1932: 170–171.

1. Hara A. 1987: 406; Takahashi Korekiyo 1936a: 231.

2. For the latter point, see Mosk 2001: 125–134.

3. Inoue 1926: 3, 209, 228–236, 250; see also Inoue 1929a: 34–35.

4. Takahashi to House of Representatives, 1/21/1932, in NKSS-S 21: 151; Takahashi Korekiyo 1932: 169, from which the translation is taken. Takahashi's standpoint here seems to reflect the ideas of Fukai Eigo.

5. Takahashi Korekiyo 1932: 174.

6. ITZ 8: 487–488. NHK was then Japan's only broadcasting system, and broadcasts from JOAK were relayed to branch stations around the country. By 1932, 25 percent of urban families owned a radio receiver, but less than 5 percent of rural families did (Kasza 1988: 88). Ishibashi later published his speech in *Infureeshon no riron to jissai* (The theory and actuality of inflation, 1932), which is reprinted in ITZ 8.

7. Ishibashi 12/14/1931, in ITZ 8: 489–494; Inoue 1929c: 159.

8. Ishibashi 12/14/1931, in ITZ 8: 496. On Ishibashi's feminism, see Nolte 1987, especially chap. 3. On the women-led consumer movement, see Maclachlan 2002.

9. Inoue 1929d: 4; Ishibashi 12/15/1931, in ITZ 8: 497–498.

10. On Ishibashi's "little Japanism," see ITCS 3; on his postwar role, see Nolte 1987: 281–332 and the epilogue below.

11. Takahashi Korekiyo 1936a: 404.

12. For Japan's extraordinary wartime austerity measures, see Havens 1978 and Garon 2000.

13. Ishibashi 1/2/1932, in ITCS 2: 80–81. The course of the yen exchange in the following months is analyzed by T. Ito, Okina, and Teranishi 1993.

14. Ishibashi's exact words were direct to the point of rudeness: "Mata muchakuchana iwayuru hōman seisaku o tottara taihen da" (Ishibashi 1/2/1932, in ITCS 2: 81).

15. Ishibashi 1994 [1964]: 24.

16. Takahashi Korekiyo 1932: 172.

17. For example, by the *Hōchi shinbun* of February 12, 1932 (reprinted in IJD: 882).

18. Harada diary cited in Nakamura 1978.

19. Takahashi to House of Representatives, 1/21/1932, in "Ōkura daijin zaisei enzetsu yōryō," materials held at the Bank of Japan; Inoue 1/21/1932, in IJR 3: 582–583, 586.

20. IJR 3: 574; IJD: 864–867.

21. Goto-Shibata 1995: 135–140; Coble 1991: 33–44.

22. Lamont draft letter in TWLP 187–13. It is unclear whether the letter was sent or not. The name of the recipient was removed before inclusion in the archives.

23. IJD: 870–877; Onuma Shō, "Jōshinsho," in Takahashi M. 1964. For the background to the assassins' ideas, see Havens 1974, esp. pp. 297–302, and for their enthusiastic popular reception, Large 2002.

24. Bryan 1896: 205; Mutō 1930: 62. Whether Mutō Sanji's impassioned attacks on Inoue had affected the murderous intentions of the young men of the Blood Pledge Corps or not, Mutō was clearly sensitive on the matter and in his 1934 autobiography was at pains not to speak ill of his slain antagonist. Mutō himself became a collateral victim of industrial rationalization, assassinated in 1934 by an unemployed worker.

25. Sonoda to Lamont 2/16/1932, TWLP 187–13; Inoue Junnosuke Ronsō Hensankai 1938: 69; TWLP 187–13, 187–14, 187–16.

26. OAS 3/6/1932; Lamont to Sonoda 3/10/1932, TWLP 187–14.

27. Berger 1977: 43, 46–51.

28. Inoue to Lamont 10/4/1927, TWLP 189–27.

29. On July 8, 1934, Takahashi attempted to retire, for the third time, yielding his post to Vice Minister Fujii Shinji. Under the stress of being caught between a national debt that had ballooned to ¥10 billion and the demands of the military for more money, Fujii soon became ill, and Takahashi had to step in again as finance minister on November 27. General discussions of the Takahashi financial policy can be found in Nakamura 1978 and Hara A. 1987; Takahashi is also the subject of a forthcoming study by Richard Smethurst.

30. NGHS 4: 51–53.

31. Hara A. 1987: 404–405; Cassel, "The Japanese Exchange," in MOF-SZS 3-40: 4; Fukai 1937: 391–392. Cha (2003) emphasizes the effects of Takahashi's fiscal policy.

32. Takahashi Korekiyo 1936a: 415–416; Itō M. 1989: 342–343; NGHS 4: 67–70. The yen was maintained at a level of 1 shilling, 2 pence.

33. Nakamura 1981b; Takahashi Korekiyo 1932: 170, 173. Aside from the rural cotton-weaving districts, which benefited from the export boom, prosperity began to reach the farm villages only around 1935. For the continuing agrarian depression, see K. Smith 2001.

34. Takahashi Korekiyo 1936a: 244–245; Itō 1989: 322–334; Ide 2003; Nihon Ginkō Chōsakyoku 1953: 82; NGHS 4: 19–29, 42–51; Nakamura 1981a: 112; budget statistics given in LTES 7: 147–149, 162–163, 168–171.

35. NGHS 4: 128–133. At the same time, the tax on the BOJ's excess note issue was reduced in March and June 1932, from 6 to 3 percent, with a portion of the BOJ's profits now being delivered directly to the government. See also appendix table A.1, below.

36. See appendix table A.1, below. Reserves stood virtually unchanged at just over ¥1 billion from 1922 to 1929, while the note issue remained between ¥1.5 billion and ¥1.7 billion.

37. NGHS 4: 29–42; chronology of BOJ discount rates (*shōgyō tegata waribiki buai*) given in NGHS Shiryōhen: 350–357, 374–383.

38. Takahashi first raised this fear in a speech to the National Governors' Conference (Nihon Chihō Chōkan Kaigi) on January 14, 1932. He repeated it in his Diet address of January 21 (NKSS 21: 153) and expanded on it in an article, "Ichiji no handō keiki youna," reprinted in Takahashi Korekiyo 1936a: 253. Takahashi's January 14 speech is summarized in "Rondon, Nyū Yōku chūzai zaimukan ate junden, 1925–1937," materials held at the Bank of Japan.

39. Nihon Ginkō Chōsakyoku 1953: 82.

40. Tokyo Institute of Political and Economic Research 1934; Johnson 1982, chap. 4; Nakamura 1989b: 312–315; Gao 1997, chap. 4; see also Barnhart 1987.

41. Ma 1996; Shimizu 1986; Kagotani 2002.

42. Nakamura 1989b: 466. Thomas Lamont, for example, maintained an active correspondence with Inoue and exchanged only a few, very formal letters with Takahashi (TWLP, various files).

43. Roosevelt 1938: 11; Feis 1966: 112–131; Takahashi Korekiyo 1936a: 242; Chernow 1990: 355–377; Mori to Lamont 7/27/1933, TWLP 188–31. In an April 1935 interview with Ishibashi Tanzan, however, Takahashi concluded that Roosevelt had so far only been "chasing theories" and had failed (Takahashi Korekiyo 1936a: 401).

44. Chernow 1990: 343–345; Chō 1973; Iguchi 2003, chap. 6; Yamamura Katsurō 1973: 293–294. Morgan & Co.'s Martin Egan went to Japan soon after Inoue's assassination and on his return defended Japan's position in Manchuria. Lamont turned definitely against Japan only in 1934.

45. See, among others, L. Young 1998, chap. 5; Johnson 1982: 124–125, 129–133; Schumpeter 1940.

46. Not counting exports to Korea and Taiwan, which were internal to Japan's monetary system (statistics in Nihon Ginkō Tōkeikyoku 1966: 278–279, 290–292).

47. Schumpeter 1940: 260, 272; Nakamura and Odaka 1989a: 61–69.

48. Itō M. 1989: 305, 308–310, 341–343; Takahashi Korekiyo 1936a: 412–413.

49. Tadai 1997, 2: 204, 211–212; Shimazaki 1989: 105–109; Itō M. 1989: 318. The background to the abandonment of the silver standard in 1935 was the sudden appreciation of silver prices caused by the U.S. Silver Purchase Act of 1934.

50. Polanyi 1957 [1944].

51. Leith-Ross 1968, chap. 15; Endicott 1975: 102–149 (Leith-Ross's reference to Egypt on p. 112); Shimazaki 1989: 141–145; Coble 1991: 261–267; A. Young 1971: 223–252, 362–363. Disliking an exclusive sterling link, the United States insisted on conditions that gave dollar reserves a much bigger place and restored some role for silver in the Chinese reserves. For the curiously restricted money creation power of the early modern Chinese state, see also Lin, forthcoming.

52. Smethurst 2001; Shillony 1973.

53. Nakamura 1994: 79–81; Itō M. 1989: 349; Peattie 1975: 210–216.

EPILOGUE: MONEY AND HEGEMONY

1. Ishibashi 10/1951, in ITZ 15: 203 (my emphasis). Ishibashi was also far from being a one-sided economic determinist, and later in the same essay he placed even greater blame for the rise of militarism on the flaws of the 1889 constitution.

2. Ishibashi 10/1951, in ITZ 15: 203; Ishibashi 1946: 117.

3. Ishibashi's "positive" policy, the Dodge line deflation, and the larger questions of post–World War II stabilization are the subjects of my present research. See also Nolte 1987: 289–305.

4. Suzuki 1994: 10–11, 192–196. From 1894 to 1913 the Chinese government borrowed £82 million in London, and the Japanese government borrowed £84 million (beginning in 1897).

5. See chapter 4, above.

6. "Hundred years' peace": Polanyi 1957 [1944]: 3–19. Europe's domestic peace was, of course, an age of systematic externally directed aggression.

7. Itō M. 1989: 3.

8. Lamont to Arthur E. Post 10/8/1938, TWLP 62–5.

9. See Cain and Hopkins (1993b) for a contrary argument of very broad scope (presented in outline on pp. 3–7).

10. Lamont 1951: 267.

11. See for example Kindleberger 1986: 39–41, 54–61, 292.

12. See chapter 10, above.

13. Lamont's long relationship with Mussolini is detailed by Chernow (1990: 277–285, 403–407, 454–458).

14. McNeil 1986: 6.

15. Maier 1988; see also Eichengreen 1992a.

16. See again Eichengreen 1992a. Maier's work has been the most prominent in an extensive literature on post–World War I stabilization that appeared in the 1970s and 1980s, much of which I have drawn on in the foregoing study. This "new international history" of the post–World War I decade is reviewed by Jacobson (1983). However, the "new international history" remained largely confined to Europe, and it scarcely touched on the dynamics of European empire, which, to repeat the point, reached its ultimate extent precisely in the 1920s. See again Cain and Hopkins (1993b) on this point.

17. Tsurumi 1929: 8–10.

18. NGHS 4: 466–521; see Noguchi 1995: 34 et seq. for related considerations. The yen-dollar rate at the time of the Pearl Harbor attack was ¥4.27 per dollar (¥1

= $0.23). The text of the new Bank of Japan Law can be found in NGHS Shiryōhen: 204–212, and an English translation is given in Shinjo 1962: 179–194.

19. The yen's "invasion history" is detailed by Shimazaki 1989; see also Swan 1989: 314–321.

20. Shimazaki 1989: 426.

21. Van Dormael 1978: 93, 97–98; James 1996: 39. See also Arrighi 1994: 278–279.

22. James 1996: 39–48; Morgenthau quoted in James 1996: 56. The IMF had been called a "Stabilization Fund" in earlier proposals. The idea for a "Bank for Reconstruction and Development" to undertake long-term lending (the World Bank) had been laid out before this.

23. Kemmerer 1944; Keynes quoted in James 1996: 64, 34.

24. James 1996: 50, 60, 66; Redish 1993.

25. Yoshino 1996: 173–180; Ōuchi 1947. Yoshino Toshihiko, later the Bank of Japan's eminent historian, worked as Ōuchi's research assistant. For Ōuchi's wide-ranging influence, see Hein 2005.

26. Yoshino 1996; NGHS 5: 20–21. For the North China Development Co., see Nakamura 1980.

27. Ishibashi to Shūgi'in, 7/25/1946, in ITZ 13: 194–197; Ishibashi 1951: 634.

28. Notwithstanding the argument made by Davis and Roberts 1996.

29. Schonberger 1989: 161–235; T. Cohen 1987: 401–442; Yoshino 1996: 130–147; "Report of the Special Mission on Yen Foreign Exchange Policy" (Ralph A. Young, Chairman), Tokyo, June 12, 1948, held in Allan Sproul papers, Federal Reserve Bank of New York; Iguchi 2003: 222–229.

30. Ikeda H. 1952: 220–221.

31. Ikeda H. 1952: 221.

32. Dodge to Ikeda 6/30/1950, JMDP, "Japan-1950–7." On this point, see, among others, Borden 1984 and Cumings 1993.

33. Inoue 1929a: 34 (see chapter 11, above); Dower 1988 [1979]: 316, 424.

34. Nihon Ginkō Chōsakyoku 1953: 5.

35. See Cumings 1993.

36. "Kokusai Tsūka Kikin oyobi Kokusai Fukkō Kaihatsu Ginkō e no kamei ni tsuite," 4/28/1952, and "Kokusai Tsūka Kikin nado e no kamei ni tsuite," 5/26/1952, in "Kokusai Tsūka Kikin ippan shiryō, 1952–1956," materials held at the Bank of Japan; Yoshino 1996: 181–182.

37. Tsushima 1966: 3, 13–14, 20–22. In 1943 the government had liquidated some ¥650 million ($191 million plus £27 million) in foreign-currency bonds held by Japanese by replacing them with domestic bonds (which soon became worthless). Even during the war, traders in London continued to buy and sell Japanese bonds, though these naturally fell to very low price levels (Tsushima 1966: 8–11).

38. Tsushima 1966: 2, 4–9.

39. "Annual Report on Exchange Restrictions for 1953," in "Kokusai Tsūka Kikin ippan shiryō, 1952–1956," materials held at the Bank of Japan; Hollerman 1967: 225–236, 262–279.

40. Yoshino 1996: 184–185.

BIBLIOGRAPHY

ABBREVIATIONS

The following abbreviations have been used in the citations.

BSP	Benjamin Strong papers, Federal Reserve Bank of New York.
FRUS	*Foreign Relations of the United States*. Washington, D.C.: U.S. Government Printing Office, various years.
IJD	*Inoue Junnosuke den* [Biography of Inoue Junnosuke]. Tokyo: Inoue Junnosuke Ronsō Iinkai, 1935.
IJR	*Inoue Junnosuke ronsō* [Collected works of Inoue Junnosuke]. 4 vols. Tokyo: Inoue Junnosuke Ronsō Hensankai, 1935.
ITCS	*Ishibashi Tanzan chosakushū* [Selected works of Ishibashi Tanzan]. 4 vols. Tokyo: Tōyō Keizai Shinpōsha, 1995–96.
ITKM	Ishibashi Tanzan kankei monjo [Papers related to Ishibashi Tanzan]. Kensei Shiryōshitsu, Kokuritsu Kokkai Toshokan [National Diet Library], Tokyo.
ITZ	*Ishibashi Tanzan zenshū* [Collected works of Ishibashi Tanzan]. 15 vols. Tokyo: Tōyō Keizai Shinpōsha, 1970–72.
JMDP	Joseph M. Dodge papers, Burton Historical Collection, Detroit Public Library.
LTES	*Chōki keizai tōkei, suikei to bunseki* (*Estimates of Long-term Economic Statistics of Japan since 1868*). 14 vols. Edited by Ohkawa Kazushi, Shinohara Miyohei, and Umemura Mataji. Tokyo: Tōyō Keizai Shinpōsha, 1965–88.
MOF-SZS	Shōwa zaisei shi shiryō [Materials on the history of public finance in the Shōwa period], Ministry of Finance, Tokyo. Some Taishō and early Shōwa materials have been microfilmed and are held in the Tokubetsu Shiryōshitsu, National Diet Library.
NGHS	*Nihon Ginkō hyakunenshi* [One-hundred Year History of the Bank of Japan]. 6 vols. Tokyo: Nihon Ginkō Hyakunenshi Iinkai, 1982–86.

NKS-M *Nihon kin'yūshi shiryō, Meiji-Taishō hen* [Materials on Japanese financial history, Meiji and Taishō eras]. 26 vols. Edited by Nihon Ginkō Chōsakyoku. Tokyo: Ōkurashō Insatsukyoku, 1956–1961.

NKS-S *Nihon kin'yūshi shiryō, Shōwa hen* [Materials on Japanese financial history, Shōwa era]. 35 vols. Edited by Nihon Ginkō Chōsakyoku, Tokyo: Ōkurashō Insatsukyoku, 1961–74.

NYT *The New York Times.*

OAS *Ōsaka asahi shinbun* (Osaka).

SNJ *Shōwa nyūsu jiten* [Dictionary of Shōwa news]. 6 vols., Edited by Uchikawa Yoshimi, Matsuo Takayoshi, et al. (Shōwa Nyūsu Jiten Hensan Iinkai), Tokyo: Mainichi Komyunikeshonzu, 1990–91.

SYM Sakatani Yoshio monjo [Sakatani Yoshio papers]. Kensei Shiryōshitsu, National Diet Library, Tokyo.

SZS *Shōwa zaisei shi* [History of public finance in the Shōwa period]. Edited by Ōkurashō Shōwa Zaiseishi Henshūshitsu [Ministry of Finance, Shōwa Financial History Editorial Office]. Tokyo: Tōyō Keizai Shinpōsha, 1959.

TAS *Tōkyō asahi shinbun.*

TKM Takahashi Korekiyo monjo [Takahashi Korekiyo papers]. Kensei Shiryōshitsu, National Diet Library, Tokyo.

TKS *Tōyō keizai shinpō* (*The Oriental Economist*), Tokyo.

TNJ *Taishō nyūsu jiten* [Dictionary of Taishō news]. 7 vols., Edited by Uchikawa Yoshimi, et al. (Taishō Nyūsu Jiten Hensan Iinkai). Tokyo: Mainichi Komyunikeshonzu, 1986–89.

TSZH Takahashi Kamekichi, *Taishō Shōwa zaikai hendōshi* [History of changes in the business world of Taishō and Shōwa]. 3 vols. Tokyo: Tōyō Keizai Shinpōsha, 1954.

TWLP Thomas W. Lamont papers, Baker Library, Harvard Business School. Numerical references are to box and folder numbers.

YSGS *Yokohama Shōkin Ginkō shi* [History of the Yokohama Specie Bank]. 5 vols. Edited by Yokohama Shōkin Ginkō. Tokyo: Yokohama Shōkin Ginkō, 1920.

ZKN *Zaisei keizai 25-nen shi* [Twenty-five-year chronicle of public finance and economy]. 8 vols. Edited by Takahashi Kamekichi. Tokyo: Jitsugyō no Sekaisha, 1932.

MATERIALS HELD AT THE BANK OF JAPAN

In accordance with the advice of the Bank of Japan archivist that the internal numbering system of the archives is undergoing revision, references to materials archived at the Bank of Japan are made by document name and date only.

MINISTRY OF FINANCE ARCHIVES

References to the archival collection, Shōwa Zaiseishi Shiryō, are given in the format: MOF-SZS *series number–volume number*: *item number.*

PERIODICALS

Annual Report of the Federal Reserve Board. Washington, D.C.

Asahi keizai nenshi [Asahi Economic Yearbook]. Osaka: Ōsaka Asahi Shinbun Hakkōsho.

The Bankers' Magazine [*The Bankers' Insurance Managers' and Agents' Magazine*]. London.

The Bankers' Magazine. New York.

Chūo kōron [The central review]. Tokyo.

The Economist [*The Economist, Weekly Commercial Times, Bankers' Gazette and Railway Monitor*]. London.

Ekonomisuto [The economist]. Tokyo.

Federal Reserve Bulletin. Washington, D.C.

Kanpō [Official gazette]. Tokyo.

Kensei [Constitutional government: journal of the Kenseikai]. Tokyo.

Minsei [Popular government: journal of the Minseitō]. Tokyo.

Ōsaka asahi shinbun. Osaka.

Seiyū [Political friends: journal of the Seiyūkai]. Tokyo.

Tōkyō asahi shinbun. Tokyo.

Tōyō keizai shinpō [English subtitle: *The Oriental Economist*]. Tokyo.

BOOKS AND ARTICLES

ABE Takeshi. 1990. "Men kōgyō" [The cotton industry]. In Nishikawa and Abe 1990b, 163–212.

Cyrus ADLER. 1929. *Jacob H. Schiff, His Life and Letters.* 2 vols. London: William Heinemann.

Shigeru AKITA. 1996. "'Gentlemanly Capitalism,' Intra-Asian Trade and Japanese Industrialisation at the Turn of the Last Century." *Japan Forum,* 8:1, 51–65.

———. 1997. "'Gentlemanly Capitalism,' the British Empire and Intra-Asian Trade, 1890s–1930s: An Interpretation of Japanese Industrialisation." Paper for the Eighth Tsukuba Annual Seminar on Canadian Studies, January 24–25.

Shigeru AKITA and Naoto KAGOTANI. 2002. "The International Order of Asia in the 1930s." In Shigeru Akita, ed., *Gentlemanly Capitalism, Imperialism and Global History* (Houndmills, Basingstoke: Palgrave Macmillan), 143–167.

G. C. ALLEN. 1925. "The Recent Currency and Exchange Policy of Japan." *The Economic Journal,* March, 66–83.

———. 1980. *Japan's Economic Policy.* London: Macmillan.

ANDŌ Minoru. 1967. Nihon no tai-Ka zaisei tōshi—Hanyepin Konsu shakkan [Japan's fiscal investment in China, the Hanyeping Company loans]. Ajia no miru me, 8. Tokyo: Ajia Keizai Kenkyūjo.

ANDŌ Yoshio, ed. 1965–66. *Shōwa keizaishi e no shōgen* [Testimony on Shōwa economic history]. 2 vols. Tokyo: Mainichi Shinbunsha.

———. 1979a. *Ryōtaisenkan no Nihon shihonshugi* [Japanese capitalism between the world wars]. Tokyo: Tōkyō Daigaku Shuppankai.

———. 1979b. *Kindai Nihon keizaishi yōran* [Survey of the economic history of modern Japan]. 2nd edition. Tokyo: Tōkyō Daigaku Shuppankai.

Tadashi ANNO. 1999. "The Liberal World Order and Its Challengers: Nationalism and the Rise of Anti-Systemic Movements in Russia and Japan." Ph.D. dissertation, University of California, Berkeley.

Takeo AONO. 1931. *Japan after Gold Ban Removal.* Kobe: Ribunkaku; Tokyo: Maruzen.

ARAI Hakuseki. 1979 [1717]. *Told round a Brushwood Fire: The Autobiography of Arai Hakuseki.* Translated by Joyce Ackroyd. Princeton: Princeton University Press; Tokyo: University of Tokyo Press.

ARISAWA Hiromi et al., eds. 1976. *Shōwa keizaishi* [Economic history of the Shōwa period]. Tokyo: Nihon Keizai Shinbun Sha.

ARITAKE Shūji. 1967–68. *Shōwa Ōkurashō gaishi* [Unofficial history of the Ministry of Finance in the Shōwa era]. Edited by Tsushima Juichi. 3 vols. Tokyo: Shōwa Ōkurashō Gaishi Kankōkai.

Giovanni ARRIGHI. 1994. *The Long Twentieth Century: Money, Power, and the Origins of Our Times.* London: Verso.

Asahi Shinbunsha. 1930. *Nihon keizai tōkei sōkan* [Statistical overview of the Japanese economy]. Tokyo: Asahi Shinbunsha.

ASAI Yoshio. 1982. "Jūzoku teikokushugi kara jiritsu teikokushugi e—gaishi dō'nyū o chūshin to shita Nihon no taigai keizai kankei, 1895–1931 nen—" [From subordinate to independent imperialism—Japan's foreign economic relations centering on the introduction of foreign capital, 1895–1931]. *Rekishigaku kenkyū,* no. 511 (December), 47–66.

———. 1985. "Nisshin sensōgo no gaishi dōnyū to Nihon Kōgyō Ginkō" [The import of foriegn capital after the Sino-Japanese War and the Industrial Bank of Japan]. *Shakai keizai shigaku,* 50:6 (February), 1–24.

Kan'ichi ASAKAWA. 1904. *The Russo-Japanese Conflict: Its Causes and Issues.* Boston: Houghton Mifflin.

Asō Daisaku. 1929. *Takahashi Korekiyo den* [Biography of Takahashi Korekiyo]. Tokyo: Takahashi Korekiyo Den Kankōkai.

Amiya Kumar BAGCHI. 1997. "Contested Hegemonies and Laissez Faire: Controversies over the Monetary Standard in India at the High Noon of the British Empire." *Review* (Fernand Braudel Center), 20: 1 (Winter), 19–76.

Nobuya BAMBA. 1972. *Japanese Diplomacy in a Dilemma: A New Light on Japan's China Policy, 1924–1929.* Vancouver: University of British Columbia Press; Kyoto: Minerva Press.

BANNO Junji. 1979. "The Taishō Political Crisis and the Problem of Japanese Government Finance, 1906–1914." *Papers in Far Eastern History,* vol. 19. Canberra: Australian National University, 181–202.

———. 1994. *Taishō seihen, 1900-nen taisei no hōkai* [The Taishō political change: The collapse of the 1900 system]. Tokyo: Minerva Shobō.

Michael A. BARNHART. 1987. *Japan Prepares for Total War: The Search for Economic Security, 1919–1941.* Ithaca: Cornell University Press.

W. G. BEASLEY. 1955. *Select Documents on Japanese Foreign Policy, 1853–1868.* London: Oxford University Press.

———. 1991. *Japanese Imperialism, 1894–1945.* New York: Clarendon Press.

Gordon Mark BERGER. 1977. *Parties Out of Power in Japan, 1931–1941.* Princeton: Princeton University Press.

———. 1988. "Politics and Mobilization in Japan, 1931–1945." In Duus 1988, 97–153.

Gail Lee BERNSTEIN, ed. 1991. *Recreating Japanese Women, 1600–1945*. Berkeley and Los Angeles: University of California Press.

Gary Dean BEST. 1972. "Financing a Foreign War: Jacob H. Schiff and Japan, 1904–05." *American Jewish Historical Quarterly*, vol. 61 (June), 313–324.

William S. BORDEN. 1984. *The Pacific Alliance: United States Foreign Economic Policy and Japanese Trade Recovery, 1947–1955*. Madison: University of Wisconsin Press.

Michael D. BORDO. 1999. *The Gold Standard and Related Regimes: Collected Essays*. Cambridge: Cambridge University Press.

Michael D. BORDO and Hugh ROCKOFF. 1996. "The Gold Standard as a 'Good Housekeeping Seal of Approval.'" *Journal of Economic History*, 56:2, 389–428.

Dorothy BORG and Shumpei OKAMOTO, eds. 1973. *Pearl Harbor as History: Japanese-American Relations, 1931–1941*. New York: Columbia University Press.

J. Lawrence BROZ. 1997. *The International Origins of the Federal Reserve System*. Ithaca: Cornell University Press.

S. D. BROWN. 1974. "Shidehara Kijūrō: The Diplomacy of the Yen." In R. D. Burns and E. M. Bennett, eds., *Diplomats in Crisis: United States-Chinese-Japanese Relations, 1919–1941*. Santa Barbara: ABC-Clio.

William Jennings BRYAN. 1896. *The First Battle: A Story of the Campaign of 1896*. Chicago: W. B. Conkey.

William Jennings BRYAN and Mary Baird BRYAN. 1925. *The Memoirs of William Jennings Bryan*. Philadelphia: John C. Winston.

Simon James BYTHEWAY. 2001. "Japan's Adoption of the Gold Standard: Financial and Monetary Reform in the Meiji Period." In John McGuire, Patrick Bertola, and Peter Reeves, eds. *Evolution of the World Economy, Precious Metals and India*. New Delhi: Oxford University Press, 79–95.

———. 2003. "Anglo-Japanese Financial Cooperation: 1897–1923." Paper presented at the Bank of Japan Institute of Monetary and Economic Studies, December 12, 2003.

———. 2004. "Japanese Capital Loans and 'Yen Diplomacy': 1915–18." Paper presented at the Asian Studies Conference Japan, Tokyo, June 16, 2004.

———. 2005. *Nihon keizai to gaikoku shihon: 1858–1939 nen* [The Japanese economy and foreign capital: 1858–1939]. Tokyo: Tosui Shobō.

P. J. CAIN and A. G. HOPKINS. 1993a. *British Imperialism: Innovation and Expansion, 1688–1914*. London: Longman.

———. 1993b. *British Imperialism: Crisis and Deconstruction, 1914–1990*. London: Longman.

Rondo E. CAMERON. 1967. *Banking in the Early Stages of Industrialization: A Study in Comparative Economic History*. New York: Oxford University Press.

Edwin CANNAN. 1925. Preface to *The Paper Pound of 1797–1821: A Reprint of The Bullion Report* [1810]. 2nd ed. London: P. S. King & Son.

Myung Soo CHA. 2003. "Did Takahashi Korekiyo Rescue Japan from the Great Depression?" *Journal of Economic History*, 63:1 (March), 127–144.

K. C. CHAN. 1971. "British Policy in the Reorganization Loan to China 1912–13." *Modern Asian Studies*, 5:4, 355–372.

Lester V. CHANDLER. 1958. *Benjamin Strong, Central Banker.* Washington, D.C.: Brookings Institution.

Olive CHECKLAND. 1994. "Juichi Soyeda, 1864–1929: A Chequered Banking Career." In Checkland, Nishimura, and Tamaki 1994: 139–150.

Olive CHECKLAND and Norio TAMAKI. 1997. "Alexander Allan Shand, 1844–1930—A Banker the Japanese Could Trust." In Ian NISH, ed., *Britain and Japan, Biographical Portraits.* Vol. 2. Richmond, Surrey: Japan Library/Curzon Press.

Olive CHECKLAND, Shizuya NISHIMURA, and Norio TAMAKI, eds. 1994. *Pacific Banking, 1859–1959: East Meets West.* New York: St. Martin's Press.

Ron CHERNOW. 1990. *The House of Morgan: An American Banking Dynasty and the Rise of Modern Finance.* New York: Simon & Schuster.

———. 1993. *The Warburgs: The Twentieth-Century Odyssey of a Remarkable Jewish Family.* New York: Random House.

Madeleine CHI. 1970. *China Diplomacy, 1914–1918.* Harvard East Asian Monographs, East Asian Research Center, Harvard University. Cambridge, MA: Harvard University Press.

Valentine CHIROL. 1923. "The Boer War and the International Situation, 1899–1902." In Ward and Gooch 1923: 263–293.

CHŌ Yukio. 1967. "From the Shōwa Economic Crisis to Military Economy—With Special Reference to the Inoue and Takahashi Financial Policies." *The Developing Economies,* 5:4 (December), 568–596.

———. 1973. "An Inquiry into the Problem of Importing American Capital into Manchuria: A Note on Japanese-American Relations, 1931–1941." In Borg and Okamoto 1973: 377–410.

CHŌ Yukio and SUMIYA Kazuhiko, eds. 1969. *Kindai Nihon keizai shisōshi* [History of economic thought in modern Japan]. Tokyo: Yūhikaku.

CHŌSEN GINKŌ. 1919. *Chō-Man keizai 10-nen shi* [10-year history of the Korean and Manchurian economies]. Seoul: Chōsen Ginkō.

CHŌSEN GINKŌ. 1934. *Chōsen Ginkō 25-nen shi* [Twenty-five-year history of the Bank of Chosen (Korea)]. Tokyo: Tōyō Keizai Shinposha.

CHŌSEN GINKŌ SHI KENKYŪKAI. 1987. *Chōsen Ginkō shi* [History of the Bank of Chosen (Korea)]. Seoul: Chōsen Ginkō.

CHOW Tse-tsung. 1960. *The May Fourth Movement: Intellectual Revolution in Modern China.* Stanford: Stanford University Press.

Carlo M. CIPOLLA. 1956. *Money, Prices, and Civilization in the Mediterranean World, Fifth to Seventeenth Century.* Princeton: Princeton University Press.

Stephen V. O. CLARKE. 1967. *Central Bank Cooperation, 1924–31.* New York: Federal Reserve Bank of New York.

———. 1973. *The Reconstruction of the International Monetary System: The Attempts of 1922 and 1933.* Princeton Studies in International Finance No. 33. Princeton: Department of Economics, Princeton University.

Parks M. COBLE. 1991. *Facing Japan: Chinese Politics and Japanese Imperialism, 1931–1937.* Cambridge, MA: Harvard University Press.

Benjamin J. COHEN. 1998. *The Geography of Money.* Ithaca: Cornell University Press.

Jon S. COHEN. 1972. "The 1927 Revaluation of the Lira: A Study in Political Economy." *Economic History Review,* 25:4 (November), 642–654.

Theodore COHEN. 1987. *Remaking Japan: The American Occupation as New Deal.* Edited by Herbert Passin. New York: Free Press.

Warren I. COHEN. 1978. *The Chinese Connection: Roger S. Greene, Thomas W. Lamont, George E. Sokolsky, and American–East Asian Relations.* New York: Columbia University Press.

———. 1982. "America's New Order for East Asia: The Four Power Financial Consortium and China, 1919–1946." In *Essays in the History of China and Chinese-American Relations.* Asian Studies Center, East Asia Series, Occasional Paper No. 7. East Lansing: Michigan State University.

Charles A. CONANT. 1903. "Putting China on the Gold Standard." *North American Review,* 177:564, 691–704.

———. 1909. "The Gold Exchange Standard in the Light of Experience." *Economic Journal,* 19:74 (June), 190–200.

Lesley CONNORS. 1987. *The Emperor's Adviser: Saionji Kinmochi and Pre-war Japanese Politics.* London: Croon Helm and Nissan Institute for Japanese Studies.

Hilary CONROY. 1960. *The Japanese Seizure of Korea, 1868–1910: A Study of Realism and Idealism in International Relations.* Philadelphia: University of Pennsylvania Press.

Frank C. COSTIGLIOLA. 1972. "The Other Side of Isolationism: The Establishment of the First World Bank 1929–1930." *Journal of American History,* 59:3, 602–620.

———. 1977. "Anglo-American Financial Rivalry in the 1920s." *Journal of Economic History,* 37:4 (December), 911–934.

Herbert CROLY. 1925. *Willard Straight.* New York: Macmillan.

Bruce CUMINGS. 1993. "Japan's Position in the World System." In Gordon 1993, 34–63.

Kenneth W. DAM. 1982. *The Rules of the Game: Reform and Evolution in the International Monetary System.* Chicago: University of Chicago Press.

Glenn DAVIS and John G. ROBERTS. 1996. *An Occupation without Troops: Wall Street's Half-Century Domination of Japanese Politics.* Tokyo: Yenbooks.

Roberta Allbert DAYER. 1976. "The British War Debts to the United States and the Anglo-Japanese Alliance, 1920–23." *Pacific Historical Review,* vol. 45 (November), 569–595.

———. 1981. *Bankers and Diplomats in China, 1917–1925: The Anglo-American Relationship.* London: Frank Cass.

———. 1988. *Finance and Empire: Sir Charles Addis, 1861–1945.* New York: St. Martin's Press.

Marcello DE CECCO. 1974. *Money and Empire: The International Gold Standard, 1890–1914.* Oxford: Basil Blackwell.

Margaret Garritsen DE VRIES. 1974. "The Bretton Woods Conference and the Birth of the International Monetary Fund." In Kirshner 1996, 3–18.

Frederick R. DICKINSON. 1999. *War and National Reinvention: Japan in the Great War, 1914–1919.* Cambridge, MA: Harvard University Press.

John W. DOWER. 1988 [1979]. *Empire and Aftermath: Yoshida Shigeru and the Japanese Experience, 1878–1954.* Harvard East Asian Monographs no. 84. Cambridge, MA: Harvard University Press.

Paul W. DRAKE. 1989. *The Money Doctor in the Andes: The Kemmerer Missions, 1923–1933.* Durham, NC: Duke University Press.

———. 1994a. "Introduction, The Political Economy of Foreign Advisers and Lenders in Latin America." In Drake 1994b, xi–xxxiii.

Paul W. DRAKE, ed. 1994b. *Money Doctors, Foreign Debts, and Economic Reforms in Latin America from the 1890s to the Present.* Wilmington, DE: Scholarly Resources

Garret DROPPERS. 1895. "Silver in Japan." *Transactions of the Asiatic Society of Japan,* vol. 23, vi–xxix.

Ian M. DRUMMOND. 1987. *The Gold Standard and the International Monetary System 1900–1939.* Houndmills, Basingstoke: Macmillan Education.

Peter DUUS. 1968. *Party Rivalry and Political Change in Taishō Japan.* Harvard East Asian Series No. 35 Cambridge, MA: Harvard University Press.

———. 1982. "Liberal Intellectuals and Social Conflict in Taishō Japan." In J. Victor Koschmann and Tetsuo Najita, eds. *Conflict in Modern Japanese History: The Neglected Tradition* (Princeton: Princeton University Press), 412–440.

———. 1995. *The Abacus and the Sword: The Japanese Penetration of Korea, 1895–1910.* Berkeley and Los Angeles: University of California Press.

Peter DUUS, ed. 1988. *The Cambridge History of Japan, Volume 6: The Twentieth Century.* Cambridge: Cambridge University Press.

Peter DUUS and Ramon MYERS, eds. 1989. *The Japanese Informal Empire in China, 1895–1937.* Princeton: Princeton University Press.

Peter DUUS and Irwin SCHEINER. 1988. "Socialism, Liberalism, and Marxism, 1910–1931." In Duus 1998, 654–710.

Carter ECKERT. 1991. *Offspring of Empire: The Koch'ang Kims and the Colonial Origins of Korean Capitalism, 1876–1945.* Seattle: University of Washington Press.

Barry EICHENGREEN. 1992a. *Golden Fetters: The Gold Standard and the Great Depression, 1919–1939.* New York: Oxford University Press.

———. 1992b. "Introduction." In B. Eichengreen, ed., *Monetary Regime Transformations.* Hants, UK: Edward Elgar Publishing, ix–xviii.

———. 1992c. "The Gold Standard since Alec Ford." In S. N. Broadberry and N. F. R. Crafts, eds. *Britain in the International Economy, 1870–1939.* Cambridge: Cambridge University Press, 49–79.

———. 1994 [1989]. "House Calls of the Money Doctor: The Kemmerer Missions to Latin America, 1917–1931." In Drake 1994b, 110–131.

Barry EICHENGREEN and Marc FLANDREAU, eds. 1997. *The Gold Standard in Theory and Practice.* 2nd ed. London: Routledge.

Stephen Lyon ENDICOTT. 1975. *Diplomacy and Enterprise: British China Policy 1933–1937.* Manchester: Manchester University Press; Vancouver: University of British Columbia Press.

Steven J. ERICSON. 1996. *The Sound of the Whistle: Railroads and the State in Meiji Japan.* Cambridge, MA: Harvard University Press.

Joseph ESHERICK. 1987. *The Origins of the Boxer Uprising.* Berkeley and Los Angeles: University of California Press.

Elyssa FAISON. 2001. "Producing Female Textile Workers in Imperial Japan." Ph.D. dissertation, University of California, Los Angeles.

M. E. FALKUS. 1971. "United States Economic Policy and the 'Dollar Gap' of the 1920's." *Economic History Review,* 2nd series, 24:4 (November), 599–623.

Albert Edgar FEAVEARYEAR. 1963. *The Pound Sterling: A History of English Money.* Oxford: Clarendon Press.

Herbert FEIS. 1930. *Europe: The World's Banker, 1870–1914.* New Haven: Yale University Press.

———. 1950. *The Diplomacy of the Dollar: First Era, 1919–1932*. Baltimore: Johns Hopkins Press.

———. 1966. *1933: Characters in Crisis*. Boston: Little, Brown.

Gerald D. FELDMAN. 1993. *The Great Disorder: Politics, Economics, and Society in the German Inflation, 1914–1924*. New York: Oxford University Press.

Katalin FERBER. 2002. "'Run the State Like a Business': The Origin of the Deposit Fund in Meiji Japan." *Japanese Studies*, 22:2 (September), 131–151.

———. 2005. "Professionalism as Power: Tajiri Inajiro and the Modernization of Meiji Finance." In Janet Hunter and Cornelia Storz, eds. *Institutional and Technological Change in Japan, Past and Present*. London: RoutledgeCurzon.

Frank W. FETTER. 1980. *The Economist in Parliament: 1780–1868*. Durham, NC: Duke University Press.

Albert FEUERWERKER. 1964. "China's Nineteenth-Century Industrialization: The Case of the Hanyehping Coal and Iron Company, Limited." In C. D. Cowan, ed. *The Economic Development of China and Japan: Studies in Economic History and Political Economy*. New York: Frederick A. Praeger, 79–110.

Carole FINK. 1984. *The Genoa Conference: European Diplomacy, 1921–1922*. Chapel Hill: University of North Carolina Press.

David M. FITZSIMONS. 1990. "Thomas W. Lamont." In Larry Schweikart, ed., *Banking and Finance, 1913–1989. The Encyclopedia of American Business History and Biography*). New York: Facts on File, 207–209.

Marc FLANDREAU. 1996. "The French Crime of 1873: An Essay on the Emergence of the International Gold Standard, 1870–1880." *Journal of Economic History*, 56:4 (December), 862–897.

William Miles FLETCHER III. 1982. *The Search for a New Order: Intellectuals and Fascism in Prewar Japan*. Chapel Hill: University of North Carolina Press.

———. 1989. *The Japanese Business Community and National Trade Policy, 1920–1942*. Chapel Hill: University of North Carolina Press.

———. 1991. "Japanese Banks and National Economic Policy, 1920–1936." In H. James, H. Lindgren, and A. Teichova, eds. *The Role of Banks in the Interwar Economy*. Cambridge: Cambridge University Press, 251–271.

Dennis O. FLYNN and Arturo GIRALDEZ. 2002. "Cycles of Silver: Global Economic Unity through the Mid-Eighteenth Century." *Journal of World History*, 13:2 (Fall), 391–427.

A. G. FORD. 1962. *The Gold Standard, 1880–1914: Britain and Argentina*. Oxford: Clarendon Press.

Milton FRIEDMAN and Anna Jacobson SCHWARTZ. 1963. *A Monetary History of the United States, 1867–1960*. Princeton: Princeton University Press.

Peter K. FROST. 1970. *The Bakumatsu Currency Crisis*. Cambridge, MA: East Asian Research Center, Harvard University.

FUJIMURA Kin'ichirō. 1992. *Takahashi Korekiyo to kokusai kin'yū* [Takahashi Korekiyo and international finance]. 2 vols. Tokyo: Fukubu Shoten.

Takashi FUJITANI. 1996. *Splendid Monarchy: Power and Pageantry in Modern Japan*. Berkeley and Los Angeles: University of California Press.

FUKAI Eigo. 1937. "The Recent Monetary Policy of Japan." In A. D. Gayer, ed. *The Lessons of Monetary Experience*. New York: Farrar & Rinehart.

———. 1939. *Jinbutsu to shisō* [People and ideas]. Tokyo: Nippon Hyōronsha.

———. 1941. *Kaiko 70 nen* [Reminiscences of seventy years]. Tokyo: Iwanami Shoten.

Ippei FUKUDA. 1933. "Korekiyo Takahashi—Japan's Sage of Finance." *Contemporary Japan,* 1:4 (March), 610–618.

FUKUZAWA Yukichi. 1958–1964. *Fukuzawa Yukichi zenshū* [Collected works of Fukuzawa Yukichi]. 21 vols. Edited by Keiō Gijuku. Tokyo: Iwanami Shoten.

FURUYA Tetsuo. 1990. "Kin kaikin • Rondon jōyaku • Manshū jihen—Dai 57-kai Teikoku Gikai–dai 61-kai Teikoku Gikai— [The lifting of the gold embargo; the London treaty; the Manchuria incident—57th Imperial Diet–61st Imperial Diet]. In Uchida, Kanehara, and Yoshiya 1990, 3: 65–125.

Giulio GALLOROTTI. 1993. "The Scramble for Gold: Monetary Regime Transformation in the 1870s." In Michael Bordo and Forrest Capie, eds., *Monetary Regimes in Transition.* Cambridge: Cambridge University Press, 15–67.

———. 1995. *The Anatomy of an International Monetary Regime: The Classical Gold Standard, 1880–1914.* New York: Oxford University Press.

Bai GAO. 1997. *Economic Ideology and Japanese Industrial Policy: Developmentalism from 1931 to 1965.* Cambridge: Cambridge University Press.

Sheldon GARON. 1987. *The State and Labor in Modern Japan.* Berkeley and Los Angeles: University of California Press.

———. 1997. *Molding Japanese Minds: The State in Everyday Life.* Princeton: Princeton University Press.

———. 1998. "Fashioning a Culture of Diligence and Thrift: Savings and Frugality Campaigns in Japan, 1900–1931." In Minichiello 1998, 312–334.

———. 2000. "Luxury Is the Enemy: Mobilizing Savings and Popularizing Thrift in Wartime Japan." *Journal of Japanese Studies,* 26:1 (Winter), 41–78.

Carol GLUCK. 1985. *Japan's Modern Myths: Ideology in the Late Meiji Period.* Princeton: Princeton University Press.

G. P. GOOCH. 1923. "Continental Agreements, 1902–1907." In Ward and Gooch 1923: 294–382.

Andrew GORDON. 1993. *Postwar Japan as History.* Berkeley and Los Angleles: University of California Press.

Harumi GOTO-SHIBATA. 1995. *Japan and Britain in Shanghai, 1925–31.* Houndmills, Basingstoke: Macmillan Press.

Roger HACKETT. 1971. *Yamagata Aritomo in the Rise of Modern Japan, 1838–1922.* Cambridge, MA: Harvard University Press.

Ivan Parker HALL. 1973. *Mori Arinori.* Cambridge, MA: Harvard University Press.

John Whitney HALL. 1955. *Tanuma Okitsugu, 1719–1788, Forerunner of Modern Japan.* Cambridge, MA: Harvard University Press.

HAMAGUCHI Osachi. 1925. *Yūkō yūben, Hamaguchi zōsō enzetsushū* [The eloquence of Yūkō, Collected speeches of Finance Minister Hamaguchi]. Edited by Sawamoto Mōko. Tokyo: Aoyama Shoin.

———. 1929. "Keizai nankyoku no dakai ni tsuite" [Breaking out of the economic predicament], national relay broadcast from the Tokyo Central Broadcasting Station, August 28, 1929. In Inoue 1929c, 182–204.

———. 1931. *Zui kanroku* [Various impressions]. Edited by Hamaguchi Fujiko. Tokyo: Sanseido.

———. 1980 [1926]. "Katei jitsumu shidōsha kōshūkai heikai no sai ni okeru Hamaguchi naimu daijin kunji" (November 1926). In *Jitsumu katei no shishin* (Kyōka Shiryō, 57 [Tokyo: Kyōka Dantai Rengōkai, 1927]). Reprinted in Maruoka Hideko, ed. *Nihon fujin mondai shiryō shūsei,* vol. 7. Tokyo: Domesu Shuppan, 273–275.

———. 1991. *Hamaguchi Osachi nikki • zuikanroku* [Hamaguchi Osachi diary and various impressions]. Edited by Ikei Masaru, Hatano Masaru, and Kurosawa Fumitaka. Tokyo: Misuzu Shobō.

HAMASHITA Takeshi. 1983. "A History of the Japanese Silver Yen and the Hongkong and Shanghai Banking Corporation, 1871–1913." In Frank H. H. King, ed., *Eastern Banking.* London: Athlone Press, 321–349.

Roy S. HANASHIRO. 1999. *Thomas William Kinder and the Japanese Imperial Mint, 1868–1875.* Boston: Brill.

HARA Akira. 1977. "Zaikai" [Financial circles]. In Nakamura Takafusa and Itō Takashi, eds. *Kindai Nihon kenkyū nyūmon* [Introduction to research on modern Japan]. Tokyo: Tōkyō Daigaku Shuppankai, 170–192.

———. 1981. "1920 nendai no zaisei shishutsu to sekkyoku, shōkyoku ryō seisaku rosen" [Government spending in the 1920s and the positive and negative policy lines]. In Nakamura 1981b, 77–109.

———. 1987. "Keiki junkan" [Economic cycles]. In Ōishi Kaichirō, ed. *Nihon teikokushugi shi 2, Sekai dai kyōkō ki* [History of Japanese imperialism, vol. 2, The great depression era]. Tokyo: Tōkyō Daigaku Shuppankai, 367–410.

———. 1989. "Senji tōsei" [Wartime controls]. In Nakamura 1989b, 69–105.

———. 1996. "Zaiseika • seijika toshite no Takahashi Korekiyo" [Takahashi Korekiyo as financial official and politician]. In Satō Hideo and Yamamoto Taketoshi, eds. *Nihon no kin-gendaishi to rekishi no kyōiku.* Tokyo: Tsukiji Shokan, 141–153.

HARA Takashi. 1929. *Hara Takashi zenshū* [Complete works of Hara Takashi]. Edited by Hara Takashi Zenshū Kankōkai. Tokyo: Hara Takashi Zenshū Kankōkai.

H. D. HAROOTUNIAN. 1974. "Introduction: A Sense of an Ending and the Problem of Taishō." In Silberman and Harootunian 1974, 3–28.

———. 1980. "The Functions of China in Tokugawa Thought." In Akira Iriye, ed. *The Chinese and the Japanese.* Princeton: Princeton University Press, 9–36.

HATANO Sumio. 1992. "Kaisetsu" [Afterword]. In Fujimura 1992, 2: 351–392.

William J. HAUSMAN and John L. NEUFELD. 1988. "US Foreign Direct Investment in Electric Power Utilities in the 1920s." In Mira Wilkins and Harm Schröter, eds., *The Free-Standing Company in the World Economy, 1830–1996.* London: Oxford University Press, 361–390.

Thomas R. H. HAVENS. 1974. *Farm and Nation in Modern Japan: Agrarian Nationalism, 1870–1940.* Princeton: Princeton University Press.

———. 1978. *Valley of Darkness: The Japanese People and World War Two.* New York: Norton.

R. G. HAWTREY. 1922. "The Genoa Conventions on Currency." *Economic Journal,* 32:127 (September), 290–304.

Laura HEIN. 2005. *Reasonable Men, Powerful Words: Political Culture and Expertise in Twentieth Century Japan.* Berkeley and Los Angeles: University of California Press.

HIRATSUKA Raichō. 1984. *Hiratsuka Raichō chosakushū.* Edited by Hiratsuka Raichō Chosakushū Henshū Iinkai. Tokyo: Ōtsuki Shoten.

HIGUCHI Hiroshi. 1940. *Nihon no tai-Shi tōshi* [Japanese investment in China]. Tokyo: Keiō Shobō.

J. A. HOBSON. 1965 [1902]. *Imperialism: A Study*. Ann Arbor: University of Michigan Press.

Michael J. HOGAN. 1977. *Informal Entente: The Private Structure of Cooperation in Anglo-American Economic Diplomacy, 1918–1928*. Columbia: University of Missouri Press.

Leon HOLLERMAN. 1967. *Japan's Dependence on the World Economy: The Approach toward Economic Liberalization*. Princeton: Princeton University Press.

Herbert HOOVER. 1951–52. *Memoirs*. 3 vols. New York: Macmillan.

Yasuzo HORIE. 1950. "Foreign Capital and the Japanese Capitalism after the World War I." *Kyoto University Economic Review*, 20:1 (April), 38–59.

HOSHINO Tokuji [Bank of Chosen]. 1920. *Economic History of Manchuria*. Seoul: Chōsen Ginkō.

HOSOYA Chihiro and SAITŌ Makoto. 1978. *Washinton taisei to Nichi-Bei kankei* [The Washington system and Japan-U.S. relations]. Tokyo: Tōkyō Daigaku Shuppankai.

Germaine A. HOSTON. 1986. *Marxism and the Crisis of Development in Prewar Japan*. Princeton: Princeton University Press.

Chi-ming HOU. 1965. *Foreign Investment and Economic Development in China, 1840–1937*. Harvard East Asian Series 21. Cambridge, MA: Harvard University Press.

Christopher HOWE. 1996. *The Origins of Japanese Trade Supremacy: Development and Technology in Asia from 1540 to the Pacific War*. Chicago: University of Chicago Press.

Susan HOWSON. 1974. "The Origins of Dear Money, 1919–20." *Economic History Review*, 2nd series, 27:1 (February), 88–107.

David HUME. 1970. *Writings on Economics*. Edited by Eugene Rotwein. Madison: University of Wisconsin Press.

Janet HUNTER. 1984. *Concise Dictionary of Modern Japanese History*. Berkeley and Los Angeles: University of California Press.

———. 2004. "Bankers, Investors, and Risk: British Capital and Japan during the Years of the Anglo-Japanese Alliance." In Phillips Payson O'Brien, ed. *The Anglo-Japanese Alliance, 1902–1922*. London: RoutledgeCurzon, 176–198.

ICHIMADA Hisato and ŌUCHI Hyōe. 1949. *Nihon keizai no zendō—Taidan, Ichimada Hisato, Ōuchi Hyōe—* [The road ahead for the Japanese economy: A conversation between Ichimada Hisato and Ōuchi Hyōe]. Arisawa Hiromi, moderator. Tokyo: Rōdō Bunka Sha.

Eisaku IDE. 2003. "Policy Debates on Public Finance between the Ministry of Finance and the Bank of Japan from 1930 to 1936." *Monetary and Economic Studies* (Bank of Japan), December, 87–104.

Haruo IGUCHI. 2003. *Unfinished Business: Ayukawa Yoshisuke and U.S.-Japan Relations, 1937–1953*. Cambridge, MA: Harvard University Press.

Nobutaka IKE. 1950. *The Beginnings of Political Democracy in Japan*. Baltimore: Johns Hopkins Press.

IKEDA Hayato. 1952. *Kinkō zaisei* [Balanced finance]. Tokyo: Jitsugyō no Nihon Sha.

IKEDA Shigeaki [Ikeda Seihin]. 1949a. *Zaikai kaiko* [Recollections of the business world]. Tokyo: Sekai no Nihon Sha.

———. 1949b. *Kojin imabito* [People departed and people present]. Tokyo: Sekai no Nihon Sha.

IKEO Aiko. 1999. "Monetary Economics and Policy in Pre-WWII Japan: The International Context." Working Paper, Dept. of Economics, Kokugakuin University.

Robert Leroy INNES. 1980. "The Door Ajar: Japan's Foreign Trade in the Seventeenth Century." Ph.D. dissertation, University of Michigan.

INOUE [INOUYE] Junnosuke. 1925. *Sengo ni okeru waga kuni no keizai oyobi kin'yū.* [Our country's economy and finance in the postwar period]. Tokyo: Iwanami Shoten.

———. 1926. *Waga kokusai kin'yū no genjō oyobi kaizensaku.* [The current state of our international finances and the means of improving them]. Tokyo: Iwanami Shoten.

———. 1929a. *Kokumin keizai no tatenaoshi to kin kaikin* [Rebuilding the people's economy and the lifting of the gold ban]. Tokyo: Chikura Shobō.

———. 1929b. "Kin kaikin no keizaikai ni ataeru eikyō" [The influence of lifting the gold ban upon the business world]. *Chūō kōron,* 44:9.

———. 1929c. *Kin kaikin—zen Nippon ni sakebu—* [Lifting the gold ban—calling out to all of Japan]. Tokyo: Senshinsha.

———. 1929d. *The Economic and Industrial Development of Japan* Western Influences in Modern Japan, No. 14. Tokyo: The Japanese Council, Institute of Pacific Relations.

———. 1930. *Kokusaku keizai o kataru* [Speaking of national policy and economy]. Tokyo: Jitsugyō no Nihon Sha.

———. 1931 [1926]. *Problems of the Japanese Exchange, 1914–1926.* Translated by E. H. de Bunsen. London: Macmillan & Co. Translation of Inoue 1926.

———. 1935. *Inoue Junnosuke ronsō* [Collected works of Inoue Junnosuke]. 4 vols. Edited by Inoue Junnosuke Ronsō Hensankai. Tokyo: Inoue Junnosuke Ronsō Hensankai.

INOUE Junnosuke and MUTŌ Sanji. 1930. *Fukeiki wa dō naru ka?* [What will happen with the recession?]. Edited by Jiji Shinpōsha. Tokyo: Jiji Shinpōsha.

INOUE JUNNOSUKE RONSŌ HENSANKAI, ed. 1938. *Seikei ochiho* [Pure mountain stream gleanings]. Tokyo: Inoue Junnosuke Ronsō Hensankai.

INOUE JUNNOSUKE RONSŌ IINKAI. 1935. *Inoue Junnosuke den* [Biography of Inoue Junnosuke]. Tokyo: Inoue Junnosuke Ronsō Iinkai.

INOUE KAORU KŌ DENKI HENSANKAI (rep. Sakatani Yoshio). 1934. *Segai Inoue-kō den* [A record of the exalted life of Prince Inoue]. 5 vols. Tokyo: Naigai Shoseki.

Akira IRIYE. 1965. *After Imperialism: The Search for a New Order in the Far East, 1921–1931.* Cambridge, MA: Harvard University Press.

———. 1971. "The Failure of Military Expansion." In Morley 1971, 107–138.

———. 1974. "The Failure of Economic Expansion: 1918–1931." In Silberman and Harootunian 1974, 237–269.

Akira IRIYE and Madeleine CHI, eds. 1980. *The Chinese and the Japanese: Essays in Political and Cultural Interactions.* Princeton: Princeton University Press.

ISHIBASHI Tanzan. 1929. "Kin yushutsu kaikin ron shi" [A history of the debate on lifting the gold export ban]. *Tōyō keizai shinpō,* no. 1340, March 16, 1929, 539–562.

———. 1932. *Infureshon no riron to jissai* [Theory and actuality of inflation]. Tokyo: Tōyō Keizai Shinpōsha.

———. 1946. "Danger of Retrenchment Policy." *Contemporary Japan,* 15: 1–4 (January–April), 117–120 (reprint of a December 1945 article).

———. 1951. "Ways for Japan's Economic Survival" (4 parts). *Oriental Economist,* vol. 18 (August 4, 8, 16, 1951), 601–603, 633–635, 648–650.

———. 1970–72. *Ishibashi Tanzan zenshū* [Collected works of Ishibashi Tanzan]. 15 vols. Edited by Ishibashi Tanzan Zenshū Hensan Iinkai. Tokyo: Tōyō Keizai Shinpōsha.

———. 1981. "Zōshō jidai o furikaette." *Jiyū shisō,* nos. 18 and 19 (February and May), 24–45 and 35–57.

———. 1991. *Ishibashi Tanzan hyōronshū* [Collected criticism of Ishibashi Tanzan]. Edited by Matsuo Takayoshi. Tokyo: Iwanami Shōten.

———. 1994 [1964]. *Tanzan zadan* [A conversation with Ishibashi Tanzan]. Tokyo: Iwanami Shoten. (Republication of "Tanzan kaiko." *Keizai hyōron,* January–February 1964.)

———. 1995. *Ishibashi Tanzan chosaku, 2, Ekonomisuto no menboku* [Selected works of Ishibashi Tanzan: vol. 2, The honor of the economist]. Edited by Nakamura Takafusa. Tokyo: Tōyō Keizai Shinpō Sha.

Ishii Kanji. 1997. *Nihon no sangyō kakumei, Nisshin • Nichiro sensō kara kangaeru* [Japan's industrial revolution, considered from the time of the Sino-Japanese and Russo-Japanese wars]. Tokyo: Asahi Sensho.

Ishimoto Shidzue [Katō Shizue]. 1984 [1935]. *Facing Two Ways: The Story of My Life.* Stanford: Stanford University Press.

Ishizuka Shizue. 1980. "Fujin undō no tenkai" [Development of the women's movement]. In Koyama Hitoshi, ed. *Taishōki no kenryoku to minshū.* Kyoto: Hōritsu Bunka Sha.

Itō Masanao. 1979. "Taigai kin'yū no kōzō—1920 nendai no gaikoku kawase • bōeki kin'yū ni kansuru yobiteki kentō—." In Andō 1979a, 51–85.

———. 1986. "Nihon kinhon'isei no hōkai to chūō ginkō seisaku" [The collapse of the Japanese gold-standard system and central bank policy]. In Kaizuka and Ono 1986, 69–86.

———. 1987. "Nichi-Ro sengo no Nihon kinhon'isei to chūō ginkō seisaku" [Japan's gold standard after the Russo-Japanese War and central bank policy]. In Fujise Hiroshi and Yoshioka Akihiko, eds. *Kokusai kinhon'isei to chūō ginkō seisaku.* Nagoya: Nagoya Daigaku Shuppankai.

———. 1989. *Nihon no taigai kin'yū to kin'yū seisaku, 1914–1936* [Japan's external finance and financial policy, 1914–1936]. Nagoya: Nagoya Daigaku Shuppankai.

Takatoshi Ito, Kunio Okina, and Juro Teranishi. 1993. "News and the Dollar/Yen Exchange Rate, 1931–1933: The End of the Gold Standard, Imperialism, and the Great Depression." *Journal of the Japanese and International Economies,* 7, 107–131.

Jon Jacobson. 1983. "Is There a New International History of the 1920s?" *American Historical Review,* 88, 617–645.

Harold James. 1985. *The Reichsbank and Public Finance in Germany, 1924–1933: A Study of the Politics of Economics during the Great Depression.* Frankfurt am Main: Fritz Knapp Verlag.

———. 1986. *The German Slump, Politics and Economics, 1924–1936.* Oxford: Clarendon Press.

———. 1990. "Economic Reasons for the Collapse of the Weimar Republic." In Ian

Kershaw, ed. *Weimar: Why Did German Democracy Fail?* New York: St. Martin's Press, 30–57.

———. 1996. *International Monetary Cooperation since Bretton Woods.* Washington, D.C.: International Monetary Fund; New York: Oxford University Press.

Marius JANSEN. 1954. "Yawata, Hanyehping, and the Twenty-one Demands." *Pacific Historical Review,* 23:1 (February), 31–48.

Marius JANSEN, ed. 1989. *The Cambridge History of Japan,* vol. 5. Cambridge: Cambridge University Press, 569–617.

JAPAN GAZETTE, ed. 1882. *The Currency of Japan: A Reprint of Articles, Letters, and Official Reports, Published at Intervals in the Foreign Newspapers of Japan,* [etc.]. Yokohama: Japan Gazette.

Roy W. JASTRAM. 1981. *Silver: The Restless Metal.* New York: John Wiley.

Chalmers JOHNSON. 1982. *MITI and the Japanese Miracle: The Growth of Industrial Policy, 1925–1975.* Stanford: Stanford University Press.

KAGOTANI Naoto. 2002. "Japan's Trade Penetration in Asia and British Financial Interests in the 1930s." Paper given at the London School of Economics and Political Science, March 5.

KAIZUKA Keimei and ONO Eisuke, eds. 1986. *Nihon no kin'yū shisutemu* [Japan's financial system]. Tokyo: Tōkyō Daigaku Shuppankai.

Morinosuke KAJIMA. 1976–78. *The Diplomacy of Japan, 1894–1922.* 3 vols. Tokyo: The Kajima Institute of International Peace. (English edition of parts of *Nippon gaikō shi.*)

KAMIYAMA Tsuneo. 1989. "Nichi-Ro sengo no seika seisaku to zaisei" [Specie policy and fiscal policy after the Russo-Japanese War]. *Shigaku zasshi* (Tōkyō Daigaku Bungakubu), 98:1, 48–80.

KANAZAWA Fumio. 1990. "Gyō-zaisei seiri • fusen • chi'an iji hō—Dai 49-kai Teikoku Gikai–dai 52-kai Teikoku Gikai" [Administrative and fiscal adjustment, universal suffrage, the Peace Preservation Law—38th Imperial Diet–40th Imperial Diet]. In Uchida, Kanehara, and Yoshiya 1990, 2: 337–407.

KANEHARA Samon. 1990. "'Kaizō' no jidai e no kaimaku to gikai—Dai 38-kai Teikoku Gikai–dai 40-kai Teikoku Gikai" [The Diet and the lifting of the curtain on the age of 'reform'—38th Imperial Diet–40th Imperial Diet]. In Uchida, Kanehara, and Yoshiya 1990, 2: 127–188.

Moon Hyung KANG. 1960. "The Monetary Aspect of the Economic Development in Japan with Special Reference to Monetary Policies: 1868–1935." Ph.D. dissertation, University of Nebraska.

David E. KAPLAN and Alec DUBRO. 2003. *Yakuza: Japan's Criminal Underworld.* Berkeley and Los Angeles: University of California Press.

Gregory J. KASZA. 1988. *The State and the Mass Media in Japan, 1918–1945.* Berkeley and Los Angeles: University of California Press.

———. 1995. *The Conscription Society: Administered Mass Organizations.* New Haven: Yale University Press.

KATAOKA Naoharu. 1934. *Taishō Shōwa seijishi no ichidanmen, zoku kaisōroku* [A section of the political history of the Taishō and Shōwa eras, continued reminiscences]. Kyoto: Nishikawa Momoko-i Bunko.

Edwin Walter KEMMERER. 1916a. *Modern Currency Reforms: A History and Discussion of*

Recent Currency Reforms in India, Porto Rico, Philippine Islands, Straits Settlements and Mexico. New York: Macmillan.

———. 1916b. "A Proposal for Pan-American Monetary Union." *Political Science Quarterly,* 31:1 (March), 66–80.

———. 1944. *Gold and the Gold Standard: The Story of Gold Money, Past, Present, and Future.* New York: McGraw-Hill.

George KENNAN. 1917. *E. H. Harriman's Far Eastern Plans.* Garden City, NY: Country Life Press.

John Maynard KEYNES. 1914. "The City of London and the Bank of England, August 1914." *Quarterly Journal of Economics,* 29:1 (November), 48–71.

———. 1924 [1923]. *Monetary Reform.* New York: Harcourt, Brace & Co.

———. 1970 [1925]. "The Economic Consequences of Mr. Churchill." In Keynes, *Essays in Persuasion.* New York: Macmillan, 1931; reprinted in Sidney Pollard, ed. *The Gold Standard and Employment Policies between the Wars.* London: Methuen, 1970, 27–43.

———. 1971 [1913]. *Indian Currency and Finance.* Vol. 1 of *The Collected Writings of John Maynard Keynes.* London: Macmillan.

———. 1971 [1920]. *The Economic Consequences of the Peace.* New York: Harper & Row.

C. I. Eugene KIM and Han-Kyo KIM. 1967. *Korea and the Politics of Imperialism, 1876–1910.* Berkeley and Los Angeles: University of California Press.

KIMURA Masato. 1991. *Shibusawa Eiichi, minkan keizai gaikō no sōshisha* [Shibusawa Eiichi, the originator of nongovernmental economic diplomacy]. Tokyo: Chūō Kōronsha.

Charles P. KINDLEBERGER. 1985a. *Keynesianism vs. Monetarism and Other Essays in Financial History.* London: George Allen & Unwin.

———. 1985b. "British Financial Reconstruction, 1815–1822 and 1918–25." In Kindleberger 1985a, 105–118.

———. 1986. *The World in Depression, 1929–1939.* Berkeley and Los Angeles: University of California Press.

———. 1993. *A Financial History of Western Europe.* 2nd ed. Oxford University Press.

Frank H. H. KING. 1987. *The Hongkong Bank in Late Imperial China, 1864–1902.* Cambridge: Cambridge University Press.

[Kinka Hon'i Jisshi Mannijūnen Kinenkai], ed. 1917a. *Kinka hon'i jisshi mannijūnen kinenkai* [Twentieth anniversary commemoration of the implementation of the gold coinage standard]. Tokyo: Kinka Hon'i Jisshi Mannijūnen Kinenkai. (Unpublished volume of reference materials, held at Zaimushō Bunko.)

———. 1917b. *Kinka hon'i jisshi mannijūnen kinenkai kiji* [Report of the twentieth anniversary commemoration of the implementation of the gold coinage standard]. Tokyo: Kinka Hon'i Jisshi Mannijūnen Kinenkai. (Unpublished volume of speeches, held at Zaimushō Bunko.)

W. Dean KINZLEY. 1991. *Industrial Harmony in Modern Japan, The Invention of a Tradition.* London: Routledge.

Orin KIRSHNER, ed. 1996. *The Bretton Woods–GATT System: Retrospect and Prospect after Fifty Years.* Armonk, NY: M. E. Sharpe.

Ushisaburo KOBAYASHI. 1922. *War and Armament Loans of Japan.* Carnegie Endowment for International Peace, Japan Monographs. New York: Oxford University Press.

Kenji KODAMA. 1932. "The Trade Outlook." *Contemporary Japan*, 1:1 (June), 30–34.

KODAMA Yoshio. 1972a. *Akusei, jūsei, ransei* [Misgovernment, gunshots, wild times]. Vol. 2 of *Fūun, Kodama Yoshio chosaku senshū* [State of affairs: selected works of Kodama Yoshio]. Tokyo: Nihon oyobi Nihonjinsha.

———. 1972b. *Ware, kaku tatakaeri* [I fought like this]. Vol. 3 of *Fūun, Kodama Yoshio chosaku senshū*. Tokyo: Nihon oyobi Nihonjinsha.

KOJIMA Hitoshi. 1981. *Nihon no kin hon'isei jidai (1897–1917)—En no taigai kankei o chūshin to suru kōsatsu—* [Japan's gold-standard age (1897–1917): A consideration centered on the yen's external relations]. Tokyo: Nihon Keizai Hyōron Sha.

KOJIMA Nao. 1976. "Kaisetsu" [Commentary]. Epilogue to Takahashi Korekiyo 1976, vol. 2, 312–317.

KOKUMIN KEIZAI KENKYŪKAI [Matsuo Keiji]. 1929. *Inoue Junnosuke ron* [Concerning Inoue Junnosuke]. Tokyo: Bunshūdō Shoten.

David M. KOTZ. 1978. *Bank Control of Large Corporations in the United States*. Berkeley and Los Angeles: University of California Press.

Diane B. KUNZ. 1991. "American Bankers and Britain's Fall from Gold." In H. James, H. Lindgren, and A. Teichova, eds. *The Role of Banks in the Interwar Economy*. Cambridge: Cambridge University Press, 35–48.

Paul KRUGMAN. 1998. "The Hangover Theory." *Slate* (http://slate.msn.com), posted December 3, 1998.

———. 1999. "No Pain, No Gain?" *Slate* (http://slate.msn.com), posted January 14, 1999.

Walter LAFEBER. 1997. *The Clash: A History of U.S.-Japan Relations*. New York: W. W. Norton.

Cheng-chung LAI and Joshua Jr-shian GAU. 1999. "Fetters or Lifeboat? The Silver Standard and the Chinese Economy, 1900–1937." Unpublished manuscript, Department of Economics, National Tsing Hua University, Taiwan.

Edward M. LAMONT. 1994. *The Ambassador from Wall Street: The Story of Thomas W. Lamont, J. P. Morgan's Chief Executive*. Lanham, MD: Madison Books.

Thomas W. LAMONT. 1920. "Helping China to Help Herself." *Nation's Business*, September, 11–13.

———. 1921a. "The Two Japans." *The Nation*, February 2, 172–173.

———. 1921b. "Reparations." In Edward Mandell House and Charles Seymour, eds. *What Really Happened at Paris: The Story of the Peace Conference, 1918–1919, by American Delegates*. New York: Charles Scribner's Sons, 259–290.

———. 1929. "Bank for International Settlements." *World Trade* (Paris: International Chamber of Commerce), July, 366–368.

———. 1930a. "The Final Reparations Settlement." *Foreign Affairs*, April 1930, 343.

———. 1930b. "The Reparations Settlement and Economic Peace in Europe." *Political Science Quarterly*, 45:3 (September), 321–326.

———. 1933. *Henry P. Davison: The Record of a Useful Life*. New York: Harper & Brothers.

———. 1951. *Across World Frontiers*. New York: Harcourt, Brace & Co.

David S. LANDES. 1958. *Bankers and Pashas: International Finance and Economic Imperialism in Egypt*. Cambridge, MA: Harvard University Press.

———. 1969. *The Unbound Promotheus: Technological Change and Industrial Development in Western Europe from 1750 to Present.* Cambridge: Cambridge University Press.

Stephen S. LARGE. 2002. "Substantiating the Nation: Terrorist Trials as National Theatre in Early Shōwa Japan." In Sandra Wilson, ed. *Nation and Nationalism in Japan.* London: Routledge Curzon.

Joyce C. LEBRA. 1973. *Okuma Shigenobu, Statesman of Meiji Japan.* Canberra: Australian National University Press.

Frederick LEITH-ROSS. 1968. *Money Talks: Fifty Years of International Finance: The Autobiography of Sir Frederick Leith-Ross.* London: Hutchinson.

Vladimir Ilich LENIN. 1939 [1916]. *Imperialism, the Highest Stage of Capitalism: A Popular Outline.* New York: International Publishers.

Michael LEWIS. 1990. *Rioters and Citizens: Mass Protest in Imperial Japan.* Berkeley and Los Angeles: University of California Press.

Man-houng LIN. Forthcoming. *China Upside Down: Currency, Society, and Ideologies, 1808–1856.* Cambridge, MA: Harvard University Press.

Peter H. LINDERT. 1969. *Key Currencies and Gold, 1900–1913.* Princeton: International Finance Section, Department of Economics, Princeton University.

Arthur S. LINK et al., eds. 1978. *The Papers of Woodrow Wilson,* vol. 27, 1913. Princeton: Princeton University Press.

Friedrich LIST. 1922 [1885]. *The National System of Political Economy.* Translated by Sampson S. Lloyd. London: Longmans, Green & Co.

Stewart LONE. 2000. *Army, Empire, and Politics in Meiji Japan: The Three Careers of Katsura Tarō.* New York: St. Martin's Press.

Debin MA. 1996. "The Modern Silk Road: The Global Raw-Silk Market, 1850–1930." *Journal of Economic History,* 56:2 (June), 330–355.

Patricia L. MACLACHLAN. 2002. *Consumer Politics in Postwar Japan: The Institutional Boundaries of Citizen Activism.* New York: Columbia University Press.

John V. A. MACMURRAY, ed. 1921. *Treaties and Agreements with and Concerning China, 1894–1919.* 2 vols. New York: Oxford University Press.

Charles S. MAIER. 1987. *In Search of Stability: Explorations in Historical Political Economy.* Cambridge: Cambridge University Press.

———. 1988. *Recasting Bourgeois Europe: Stabilization in France, Germany, and Italy in the Decade after World War I.* Princeton University Press.

MARUOKA Hideko, ed. 1980. *Nihon fujin mondai shiryō shūsei,* vol. 7. Tokyo: Domesu Shuppan.

Mark MASON. 1992. *American Multinationals and Japan: The Political Economy of Japanese Capital Controls, 1899–1980.* Cambridge, MA: Harvard University Press.

Takeshi MATSUDA. 1979. "Woodrow Wilson's Dollar Diplomacy in the Far East: The New Chinese Consortium, 1917–1921." Ph.D. dissertation, University of Wisconsin–Madison.

MATSUKATA Masayoshi [Ministry of Finance]. 1899. *Report on the Adoption of the Gold Standard in Japan.* Tokyo: Government Press.

———. 1900. *Report on the Post-Bellum Financial Administration in Japan,* Tokyo: Government Press.

MATSUOKA Koji. 1936. *Kin kawase hon'isei no kenkyū* [Research on the gold-exchange standard]. Tokyo: Nihon Hyōronsha.

Yoshihisa Tak MATSUSAKA. 2001. *The Making of Japanese Manchuria, 1904–1932*. Cambridge, MA: Harvard University Press, 2001.

E. Ray MCCARTNEY. 1935. "Crisis of 1873." Ph.D. dissertation, University of Nebraska. Minneapolis: Burgess Publishing.

Gavan MCCORMACK. 1977. *Chang Tso-lin in Northeast China, 1911–1928: China, Japan, and the Manchurian Idea*. Stanford: Stanford University Press.

William C. MCNEIL. 1986. *American Money and the Weimar Republic: Economics and Politics on the Eve of the Great Depression*. New York: Columbia University Press.

Ioannis MENTZAS. 1998. "Sōseki in London, or, Fetishism, Mimicry & De-nomination." Unpublished manuscript, Columbia University.

Richard Hemmig MEYER. 1970. *Bankers' Diplomacy: Monetary Stabilization in the Twenties*. New York: Columbia University Press.

Mark METZLER. 1999. "A Monetary Revolution in Late Eighteenth-Century Japan." Paper presented at the American Numismatic Society, New York City, August 11.

———. 2002. "American Pressure for Financial Internationalization in Japan on the Eve of the Great Depression." *Journal of Japanese Studies*, 28:2 (Summer), 277–300.

———. 2004a. "Benjamin Strong, Inoue Junnosuke, and the Onset of Deflation in the 1920s." Paper presented at the Bank of Japan Institute for Monetary and Economic Studies, May 18, 2004.

———. 2004b. "Woman's Place in Japan's Great Depression: Reflections on the Moral Economy of Deflation." *Journal of Japanese Studies*, 30:2 (Summer), 315–351.

MIKAMI Ryūzō. 1989. *En no tanjō, Kindai kahei seido no seiritsu* [The birth of the yen: The establishment of the modern currency system]. Enlarged edition. Tokyo: Tōyō Keizai Shinpōsha.

———. 1996. *Edo no kahei monogatari* [The story of currency in the Edo period]. Tokyo: Tōyō Keizai Shinpōsha.

Karen A. J. MILLER. 2001. "Dawes Plan and Republican Politics." Working paper, Oakland University.

Sharon MINICHIELLO. 1984. *Retreat from Reform: Patterns of Political Behavior in Interwar Japan*. Honolulu: University of Hawai'i Press.

Sharon MINICHIELLO, ed. 1998. *Japan's Competing Modernities: Issues in Culture and Democracy, 1900–1930*. Honolulu: University of Hawai'i Press.

MINISTRY OF FOREIGN AFFAIRS, SPECIAL SURVEY COMMITTEE, ed. 1992 [1946]. *Postwar Reconstruction of the Japanese Economy*. Compiled by Saburo Okita. Tokyo: University of Tokyo Press.

Ilse MINTZ. 1951. *Deterioration in the Quality of Foreign Bonds Issued in the United States, 1920–1930*. New York: National Bureau of Economic Research.

MITANI Taichirō. 1974. "Nihon no kokusai kin'yūka to kokusai seiji" [Japan's international financiers and international politics]. In Satō Seizaburō and R. Dingman, eds. *Kindai Nihon no taigai taido* [Modern Japan's attitude to the outside world]. Tokyo: Tōkyō Daigaku Shuppankai, 123–154.

———. 1975. "Uooru Sutoriito to kyokutō, Washinton taisei ni okeru kokusai kin'yū shihon no yakuwari" [Wall Street and the Far East, the role of international finance capital in the Washington system]. *Chūō kōron*, vol. 90 (September), 157–181.

———. 1980a. "Japan's International Financiers and World Politics, 1904–31." Translated by Gordon Berger (translation of Mitani 1974). *Proceedings of the British Association for Japanese Studies*, 5:1. Sheffield: University of Sheffield Centre of Japanese Studies, 29–53. Reprinted in Smitka 1998.

———. 1980b. "Manchuria: American Capital and Japanese Special Interests in the 1920s." In Ian Nish, ed., *Some Foreign Attitudes to Republican China*. International Centre for Economics and Related Disciplines, London School of Economics, 1–25.

———. 1988. "The Establishment of Party Cabinets, 1898–1932." In Duus 1988, 55–95.

———. 1991. "Yo—kokusai kyōchō no jidai kara sensō no jidai e" [Preface—From the age of international cooperation to the age of war]. *Kokusai seiji*, vol. 97 (May), 1–13.

———. 1996. "Inoue Junnosuke no zaisei kin'yū seisaku to tōji no gaikō" [Inoue Junnosuke's fiscal and monetary policy and the diplomacy of the time]. In Satō and Yamamoto 1996, 154–169.

B. R. MITCHELL. 1978. *European Historical Statistics 1750–1970*. Abridged ed. New York: Columbia University Press.

Kimitada MIWA. 1968. "Fukuzawa Yukichi's 'Departure from Asia,' A Prelude to the Sino-Japanese War." In Edmund Skrzypczak, ed. *Japan's Modern Century*. Special Issuc of *Monumenta Nipponica*. Tokyo: Sophia University; Charles E. Tuttle, 1–26.

MIWA Ryōichi. 1973. "Dai-ichiji taisengo no keizai kōzō to kin kaikin seisaku" [The post–World War I economic structure and the policy of lifting the gold ban]. In Andō Yoshio, ed. *Nihon keizai seisakushi ron*, vol. 1. Tokyo: Tōkyō Daigaku Shuppankai, 259–329.

———. 1974. "Kin kaikin seisaku kettei katei ni okeru rigai ishiki" [Consciousness of interests in the process of deciding the policy of ending the gold ban]. *Aoyama keizai ronshū*, 26:1–3 (November), 173–200.

MIYAKE Jun'ichi, ed. 1988. *Nihon kin'yū nenpyō (Meiji gannen~Shōwa 62-nen)* [Financial chronology of Japan (1868–1987)]. Tokyo: Nihon Ginkō Kin'yū Kenkyūsho.

MIYAMOTO Matarō and Kōzō YAMAMURA. 1981. "Ryōtaisenkan-ki kosaku sōgi no sūryō bunseki e no isshiron" [An essay onthe quantitative analysis of tenancy disputes in the interwar period]. In Nakamura 1981b, 389–425.

MIYAZAWA Kiichi. 1956. *Tōkyō-Washinton no mitsudan* [The Tokyo-Washington secret talks]. Tokyo: Jitsugyō no Nihonsha; reprint Tokyo: Bingokai, 1975.

MOCHIDA Nobuki. 1990. "Toshi no seibi to kaihatsu" [The equipment and development of cities]. In Nishikawa and Yamamoto 1990, 271–317.

MORIKAWA Hidemasa. 1969. "Zaibatsu-kata shihon no kakuritsu to zaibatsu no shisō" [The establishment of zaibatsu-style capital and zaibatsu thought]. In Chō and Sumiya 1969, 265–288.

James W. MORLEY, ed. 1971. *Dilemmas of Growth in Prewar Japan*. Princeton: Princeton University Press.

William F. MORTON. 1980. *Tanaka Giichi and Japan's China Policy*. New York: St. Martin's Press.

Carl MOSK. 2001. *Japanese Industrial History: Technology, Urbanization, and Economic Growth*. Armonk, NY: M. E. Sharpe.

Harold G. MOULTON, with Junichi Ko. 1931. *Japan, an Economic and Financial Appraisal.* Washington, D.C.: Brookings Institution.

Harold G. MOULTON and Leo PASVOLSKY. 1932. *War Debts and World Prosperity.* New York: Century Co., for Brookings Institution.

MUROYAMA Yoshimasa. 1984. *Kindai Nihon no gunji to zaisei, Kaigun kakuchō o meguru seisaku keisei katei* [The military and fiscal policy in modern Japan: the process of policy formation surrounding naval expansion]. Tokyo: Tōkyō Daigaku Shuppankai.

R. Taggart MURPHY. 1997. *The Weight of the Yen.* New York: W. W. Norton.

MUTŌ Sanji. 1925. *Kin kaikin mondai hayawakari* [Quick guide to the question of lifting the gold embargo]. Tokyo: Jitsugyō Dōshikai.

———. 1930. *Inoue zōsō no sakkaku, Wareware no fukeiki kyūji jissaku* [The illusion of Finance Minister Inoue: The policy for curing our depression]. Tokyo: Tōyō Keizai Shinpōsha.

———. 1934. *Watakushi no mi no jōwa* [The story of my life]. Hyōgo, Sumiyoshi: Mutō Kinta.

Ramon H. MYERS and Mark R. PEATTIE, eds. 1984. *The Japanese Colonial Empire, 1895–1945.* Princeton: Princeton University Press.

NAGAOKA Shinkichi. 1971. *Meiji kyōkōshi josetsu* [Introduction to the history of Meiji economic crises]. Tokyo: Tōkyō Daigaku Shuppankai.

NAGASU Kazuji. 1967. "Introduction" (Special Issue: The Modernization of Japan III). *The Developing Economies,* 5:4, 551–567.

[NAIMUSHŌ], SHAKAIKYOKU. 1926. *Kinken shōrei eiga sujigakishū* [Digest of movies encouraging diligence and thrift]. Tokyo: Shakaikyoku Shakaibu.

———. 1927. *Kinken shōrei undō gaikyō* [Outline of the movement to encourage diligence and thrift]. Tokyo: Shakaikyoku Shakaibu.

Tetsuo NAJITA. 1967. *Hara Kei in the Politics of Compromise, 1905–1915.* Cambridge, MA: Harvard University Press.

Tetsuo NAJITA and Harry D. HAROOTUNIAN. 1988. "Japanese Revolt against the West: Political and Cultural Criticism in the Twentieth Century." In Duus 1988, 711–774.

Tetsuo NAJITA and J. Victor KOSCHMANN, eds. 1982. *Conflict in Modern Japanese History: The Neglected Tradition.* Princeton: Princeton University Press.

Kate Wildman NAKAI. 1988. *Shogunal Politics: Arai Hakuseki and the Premises of Tokugawa Rule.* Cambridge, MA: Harvard University Press.

NAKAMURA Takafusa. 1978. *Shōwa kyōkō to keizai seisaku, aru ōkura daijin no higeki* [The Shōwa panic and economic policy: The tragedy of a certain finance minister]. Tokyo: Nihon Keizai Shinbunsha.

———. 1980. "Japan's Economic Thrust into North China, 1933–1938: Formation of the North China Development Corporation." Translated by Robert Angel. In Iriye and Chi 1980, 220–253.

———. 1981. "'Takahashi zaisei' to kōkyō tōshi seisaku—'Jikyoku Kyōkyū' nōson doboku jigyō no saihyōka—" ['Takahashi finance' and public investment policy: A reevaluation of the 'Emergency Relief' rural public-works enterprises]. In Nakamura 1981b, 111–133.

———. 1983. *Economic Growth in Prewar Japan.* Translated by Robert A. Feldman. New Haven: Yale University Press.

———. 1985. *Meiji Taishō-ki no keizai* [The economy of the Meiji and Taishō periods]. Tokyo: Tokyo Daigaku Shuppankai.

———. 1987. "The Japanese Economy in the Interwar Period: a Brief Summary." In R. P. Dore and Radha Sinha, eds. *Japan and World Depression, Then and Now.* New York: Macmillan, 52–67.

———. 1988. "Depression, Recovery, and War, 1920–1945." In Duus 1988, 451–493.

———. 1989a. "Gaisetsu, 1937–54 nen" [Outline, 1937–1954]. In Nakamura Takafusa, ed. *"Keikakuka" to "minshuka"* ["Planning" and "democratization"]. Nihon keizaishi 7. Tokyo: Iwanami Shoten, 1–69.

———. 1989b. "Keiki hendō to keizai seisaku" [Business cycles and economic policy]. In Nakamura and Odaka 1989b, 273–322.

———. 1990. "Makuro keizai to sengo keiei" [The macroeconomy and postwar management]. In Nishikawa and Yamamoto 1990, 1–36.

———. 1993. *Shōwa shi* [History of the Shōwa era], vol. 1. Tokyo: Tōyō Keizai Shinpō Sha.

———. 1994. *Lectures on Modern Japanese Economic History, 1926–1994.* Tokyo: LTCB International Library Foundation.

———. 1995. "Kaisetsu" [Commentary]. In Nakamura, ed. *Ishibashi Tanzan chosaku, 2, Ekonomisuto no menboku.* Tokyo: Tōyō Keizai Shinpō Sha, 337–358.

NAKAMURA Takafusa, ed. 1981b. *Senkanki no Nihon keizai bunseki* [Analysis of the Japanese economy in the interwar period]. Tokyo: Yamakawa Shuppansha.

NAKAMURA Takafusa and ODAKA Kōnosuke. 1989a. "Gaisetsu, 1914–1937" [General statement, 1914–1937]. In Nakamura and Odaka 1989b, 1–80.

NAKAMURA Takafusa and ODAKA Kōnosuke, eds. 1989b. *Nijū kōzō* [Dual structure]. Nihon keizaishi 6. Tokyo: Iwanami Shoten.

Dick K. NANTO and Shinji TAKAGI. 1985. "Korekiyo Takahashi and Japan's Recovery from the Great Depression." *American Economic Review,* 75:2 (May) [AEA Papers and Proceedings], 369–374.

Scott NEARING and Joseph FREEMAN. 1925. *Dollar Diplomacy.* New York: B. W. Huebsch; Viking Press.

NHK SHUZAIHAN, ed. 1995. *Kin'yū shōkoku Nippon no higeki* [The tragedy of financial nonsuperpower Japan]. Nihon no Sentaku 6. Tokyo: Kadokawa Bunkō.

NIHON GINKŌ CHŌSAKYOKU (Bank of Japan, Survey Office). 1930. "Kin yushutsu kaikinshi (Taishō 8-nen Beikoku kin yushutsu kaikin tōji yori Shōwa 5-nen kaikin jikkō ni itaru made no keii)" [History of the lifting of the gold embargo (The process from the time of the lifting of the American gold embargo in 1919 to the execution of the lifting of the embargo in 1930)]. Typescript, held at the Bank of Japan.

———. 1953. *Kin yushutsu saikinshi yori shūsen made no wagakuni keizai tōsei no idō* [The movements of economic control in Japan from the reimposition of the gold ban to the defeat]. Chōnai no. 1, August 2. Materials held at the Bank of Japan.

NIHON GINKŌ KIN'YŪ KENKYŪJO (Bank of Japan, Institute for Monetary and Economic Studies). 1988. *Nihon kin'yū nenpyō (Meiji gannen–Shōwa 62-nen)* [Chronology of Japanese finance, 1868–1987]. Tokyo: Nihon Ginkō Kin'yū Kenkyūjo.

———. 1993. *Nihon Ginkō seido • seisaku ron shi* [History of studies of the Bank of Japan system and policy]. Itaku kenkyū hokoku, 5. Tokyo: Nihon Ginkō.

NIHON GINKŌ TŌKEIKYOKU (Bank of Japan, Statistics Office). 1966. *Meiji ikō hompō shuyō keizai tōkei. Hundred-Year Statistics of the Japanese Economy.* [Tokyo:] Nihon Ginkō.

NIHON KAHEISHŌ KYŌDŌ KUMIAI [Association of Coin Dealers of Japan]. (Annual.) *Nihon kahei keiroku* [Catalogue of Japanese Coins and Banknotes]. Tokyo: Nihon Kaheishō Kyōdō Kumiai.

NIHON KŌGYŌ GINKŌ GAIJIBU (Foreign Affairs Department, Industrial Bank of Japan). 1958. *Nihon gaisai shōshi* [Brief history of Japanese foreign bonds]. Unpublished mimeograph, held at Special Collections Room, National Diet Library.

Ian NISH. 1966. *The Anglo-Japanese Alliance: The Diplomacy of Two Island Empires, 1894–1907.* London: University of London, Athlone Press.

———. 1972. *Alliance in Decline: A Study of Anglo-Japanese Relations, 1908–23.* London: University of London, Athlone Press.

Ian NISH, ed. 1982. *Anglo-Japanese Alienation, 1919–1952.* Papers of the Anglo-Japanese Conference on the History of the Second World War. Cambridge: Cambridge University Press.

NISHIKAWA Shunsaku and ABE Takeshi. 1990a. "Gaisetsu, 1885–1914" [Outline, 1885–1914]. In Nishikawa and Abe 1990b, 1–77.

NISHIKAWA Shunsaku and ABE Takeshi, eds. 1990b. *Sangyōka no jidai (jō)* [The age of industrialization, 1]. Nihon keizaishi 4. Tokyo: Iwanami Shoten.

NISHIKAWA Shunsaku and YAMAMOTO Yūzō, eds. 1990. *Sangyōka no jidai, ge* [The age of industrialization, 2]. Nihon keizaishi 5. Tokyo: Iwanami Shoten.

NISHIKAWA Shunsaku, ŌDAKA Kōnosuke, and SAITŌ Osamu, eds. 1996. *Nihon keizai no 200 nen* [200 years of the Japanese economy]. Tokyo: Nihon Hyōronsha.

NISHINO Kiyosaku. 1930. *Rekidai zōsō den* [Biographies of the successive ministers of finance]. Tokyo: Tōyō Keizai Shinpōsha.

Inazo NITOBE. 1931. *Japan's Public Economy and Finance.* Tokyo: Japan Council of the Institute of Pacific Relations.

NOGUCHI Yukio. 1995. *1940-nen taisei* [The 1940 system]. Tokyo: Tōyō Keizai Shinpōsha.

Sharon H. NOLTE. 1987. *Liberalism in Modern Japan: Ishibashi Tanzan and His Teachers, 1905–1960.* Berkeley and Los Angeles: University of California Press.

———. 1986. "Women's Rights and Society's Needs: Japan's 1931 Suffrage Bill." *Comparative Studies in Society and History,* 28:4 (October), 609–714.

ODAKA Kōnosuke. 1989a. "Nijū kōzō" [Dual structure]. In Nakamura and Odaka 1989b, 134–184.

ODANAKA Sōshu. 1990. "Sengō fukyō to Kantō dai shinsai—Dai 45-kai Teikoku Gikai–dai 48-kai Teikoku Gikai" [The postwar depression and the great Kantō earthquake—45th Imperial Diet–48th Imperial Diet]. In Uchida, Kanehara, and Yoshiya 1990, 2: 261–336.

Gyoju ODATE. 1922. *Japan's Financial Relations with the United States.* Faculty of Political Science of Columbia University, ed. Studies in History, Economics and Public Law, no. 224 (vol. 48, no. 2). New York: Columbia University.

Kazushi OHKAWA and Miyohei SHINOHARA, eds. 1979. *Patterns of Japanese Economic Development: A Quantitative Appraisal.* New Haven: Yale University Press.

Ōishi Kaichirō, ed. 1985. *Nihon teikokushugi shi, 1, Dai-ichiji taisen ki* [History of Japanese imperialism: Vol. 1, The World War I period]. Tokyo: Tōkyō Daigaku Shuppankai.

———. 1987. *Nihon teikokushugi shi, 2, Seikai dai kyōkō ki* [History of Japanese imperialism: Vol. 2, The Great Depression period]. Tokyo: Tōkyō Daigaku Shuppankai.

Ōishi Kaichirō and Miyamoto Ken'ichi, eds. 1975. *Nihon shihonshugi hattatsushi no kiso chishiki* [Fundamental knowledge of the history of the development of Japanese capitalism]. Tokyo: Yūhikaku.

Ōishi Shinzaburō. 1991. *Tanuma Okitsugu no jidai* [The age of Tanuma Okitsugu]. Tokyo: Iwanami Shoten.

James H. Okahata, ed. 1971. *A History of Japanese in Hawaii.* Honolulu: United Japanese Society of Hawaii.

Shumpei Okamoto. 1982. "The Emperor and the Crowd: The Historical Significance of the Hibiya Riot." In Najita and Koschmann 1982, 258–275.

[Ōkurashō] Rinji Chōsakyoku Kin'yūbu [Ministry of Finance, Temporary Survey Bureau, Finance Division]. 1917. *Sekai kin'yū chūshin shijō no idō ni kansuru shosetsu yoryō* [Summary of various opinions concerning the shift of the world's central financial market]. [Tokyo: Ōkurashō], August 1917. Held at Zaimushō Bunko.

Ōkurashō Zaisei Kin'yū Kenkyūsho Zaiseishishitsu, ed. 1998. *Ōkurashō shi—Meiji-Taishō-Shōwa* [History of the Ministry of Finance—Meiji, Taishō, and Shōwa eras]. 3 vols. Tokyo: Ōkura Zaimu Kyōkai.

Ono Giichi. 1922. *War and Armament Expenditures of Japan.* New York: Oxford University Press; Carnegie Endowment for International Peace.

Ōsaka Asahi Shinbun Keizaibu, ed. 1999 [1928]. *Shōwa kin'yū kyōkō hiwa* [The behind-the-scenes story of the Shōwa financial panic]. Tokyo: Asahi Shinbun.

Ōshima Kiyoshi. 1967. "The World Economic Crisis and Japan's Foreign Economic Policy." *Developing Economies,* 5:4 (December), 628–647.

Ōshima Mario. 1991. "A Distant View of the Debate on Japanese Capitalism." *Osaka City University Economic Review,* 26:2, 23–34.

Ōuchi Hyōe (Hyoyé Ohuchi). 1927. "Kin yushutsu kinshi shiron" [Historiography of the gold export embargo]. *Keizaigaku ronshū* (Tōkyō Teikoku Daigaku), 5:4, 103–142.

———. 1932. "The Government's Financial Policy." *Contemporary Japan,* 1:3 (December), 349–362.

———. 1947. *Sekai shintsūka seido no kenkyū* [Research on the new world currency system], reprinted in *Ōuchi Hyōe chosakushū* [Selected works of Ōuchi Hyōe]. Tokyo: Iwanami Shoten, 1975, 7: 3–173.

T. W. Overlach. 1919. *Foreign Financial Control in China.* New York: Macmillan.

Ozaki Yukio. 2001 [1955]. *The Autobiography of Ozaki Yukio: The Struggle for Constitutional Government in Japan.* Translated by Fujiko Hara. Princeton: Princeton University Press.

Roger Owen. 1981. *The Middle East and the World Economy, 1800–1914.* London: Methuen.

Carl Parrini. 1969. *Heir to Empire: United States Economic Diplomacy, 1916–1923.* Pittsburgh: University of Pittsburgh Press.

———. 1993. "Charles A. Conant, Economic Crises and Foreign Policy, 1896–1903." In Thomas J. McCormick and Walter LaFeber, eds. *Behind the Throne: Servants of Power to Imperial Presidents, 1898–1968.* Madison: University of Wisconsin Press, 35–66.

Carl PARRINI and Martin J. SKLAR. 1983. "New Thinking about the Market, 1896–1904: Some American Economists on Investment and the Theory of Surplus Capital." *Journal of Economic History,* 43 (September), 559–578.

Hugh T. PATRICK. 1967. "Japan, 1868–1914." In Cameron 1967, 239–289.

———. 1971. "The Economic Muddle of the 1920s." In Morley 1971, 211–266.

Louis W. PAULY. 1997. *Who Elected the Bankers? Surveillance and Control in the World Economy.* Ithaca: Cornell University Press.

Mark R. PEATTIE. 1975. *Ishiwara Kanji and Japan's Confrontation with the West.* Princeton: Princeton University Press.

T. J. PEMPEL. 1998. *Regime Shift: Comparative Dynamics of the Japanese Political Economy.* Ithaca: Cornell University Press.

Louis G. PEREZ. 1999. *Japan Comes of Age: Mutsu Munemitsu and the Revision of the Unequal Treaties.* Madison: Fairleigh Dickinson University Press; Teaneck, NJ: Associated University Presses.

Gyögy PÉTERI. 1984. "'Tying up a Loose End,' British Foreign Economic Strategy in 1924: The Hungarian Stabilization." *Acta Historica Academiae Scientiarum Hungaricae,* 30:3–4, 321–351.

———. 2002. *Global Monetary Regime and National Central Banking: The Case of Hungary, 1921–1929.* Translated by Mario D. Fenyo. Boulder: Social Science Monographs; Wayne, NJ: Center for Hungarian Studies and Publications; New York: Columbia University Press.

Karl POLANYI. 1957 [1944]. *The Great Transformation: The Political and Economic Origins of Our Time.* Boston: Beacon Press.

Kenneth PYLE. 1969. *The New Generation in Meiji Japan: Problems of Cultural Identity, 1885–1895.* Stanford: Stanford University Press.

J. Mark RAMSEYER and Frances M. ROSENBLUTH. 1998. *The Politics of Oligarchy: Institutional Choice in Imperial Japan.* Cambridge: Cambridge University Press.

Angela REDISH. 1993. "Anchors Aweigh: The Transition from Commodity Money to Fiat Money in Western Economies." *Canadian Journal of Economics,* 26:4 (November), 777–795.

C. F. REMER. 1933. *Foreign Investments in China.* New York: Macmillan.

RESIDENCY GENERAL [OF KOREA]. 1908. *Annual Report on Administration of Chosen.* Seoul: Residency General.

Laurel Rasplica RODD. 1991. "Yosano Akiko and the Taishō Debate over the 'New Woman.'" In Bernstein 1991, 175–198.

Franklin D. ROOSEVELT. 1938. *The Public Papers and Addresses of Franklin D. Roosevelt, Volume Two: The Year of Crisis, 1933.* New York: Random House.

Emily ROSENBERG. 1999. *Financial Missionaries to the World: The Politics and Culture of Dollar Diplomacy, 1900–1930.* Cambridge, MA: Harvard University Press.

Henry ROSOVSKY. 1961. *Capital Formation in Japan.* Glencoe, Ill.: Free Press.

W. W. ROSTOW. 1948. *British Economy of the Nineteenth Century.* Oxford: Clarendon Press.

Murray N. ROTHBARD. 1998. "The Gold-Exchange Standard in the Interwar Years."

In Kevin Dowd and Richard H. Timberlake Jr., eds. *Money and the Nation State: The Financial Revolution, Government, and the World Monetary System.* New Brunswick: Transaction Publishers, 000–000.

Dietmar ROTHERMUND. 1996. *The Global Impact of the Great Depression, 1929–1939.* London: Routledge.

Masamichi RŌYAMA. 1941. *Foreign Policy of Japan: 1914–1939.* Tokyo: Japanese Council, Institute of Pacific Relations; reprint, Westport, CT: Greenwood Press, 1973.

SAKAIRI Chōtarō. 1989. *Nihon zaiseishi kenkyū* [Research on the history of Japanese public finance]. 4 vols. Tokyo: Sakai Shoten.

SAKATANI Yoshio. 1912. *Nihon keizairon* [On the Japanese economy]. Tokyo: Maruyama Shosekibu.

S. B. SAUL. 1985. *The Myth of the Great Depression, 1873–1896.* London: Macmillan.

R. S. SAYERS. 1976. *The Bank of England, 1891–1944.* Cambridge: Cambridge University Press.

Harry N. SCHEIBER. 1969. "World War I as Entrepreneurial Opportunity: Willard Straight and the American International Corporation." *Political Science Quarterly,* 84:3 (September), 486–511.

Irwin SCHEINER. 1970. *Christian Converts and Social Protest in Meiji Japan.* Berkeley and Los Angeles: University of California Press.

———. 1998. "The Japanese Village: Imagined, Real, Contested." In Vlastos 1998, 67–78.

Irwin SCHEINER and Peter DUUS. 1988. "Socialism, Liberalism, and Democracy, 1901–1931." In Duus 1988, 654–710.

William SCHELL Jr. 2001. "Silver Symbiosis: ReOrienting Mexican Economic History." *Hispanic American Historical Review,* 81:1, 89–133.

Howard R. SCHONBERGER. 1989. *Aftermath of War: Americans and the Remaking of Japan, 1945–1952.* Kent, OH: Kent State University Press.

Stephen A. SCHUKER. 1988. *American "Reparations" to Germany, 1919–1933: Implications for the Third-World Debt Crisis.* Princeton Studies in International Finance, no. 61. International Finance Section, Department of Economics, Princeton University.

Elizabeth Boody SCHUMPETER, ed. 1940. *The Industrialization of Japan and Manchukuo, 1930–1940: Population, Raw Materials, and Industry.* New York: Macmillan.

SHAKAI MONDAI SHIRYŌ KENKYŪKAI, ed. 1975. *Uyoku shisō hanzai jiken no sōgōteki kenkyū (Ketsumeidan jiken yori 2•26 jiken made)* [Synthetic research on right-wing thought-crime incidents (from the Blood Pledge Corps incident to the February 26 incident)]. Tokyo: Tōyō Bunkasha.

Hsi-ping SHAO. 1978. "From the Twenty-one Demands to the Sino-Japanese Military Agreements, 1915–1918: Ambivalent Relations." In Alvin D. Coox and Hilary Conroy, eds. *China and Japan: Search for Balance since World War I.* Santa Barbara: Clio Books, 37–57.

Kinn Wei SHAW. 1926. *Democracy and Finance in China: A Study in the Development of Fiscal Systems and Ideals.* New York: Columbia University Press.

William A. SHAW, ed. 1896. *Select Tracts and Documents Illustrative of English Monetary History, 1626–1730.* London: George Harding.

L. Y. SHEN. 1941. *China's Currency Reform: A Historical Survey.* Shanghai: Mercury Press.

SHIDEHARA Kijūrō. 1953. *50-nen gaikō* [Fifty years of diplomacy]. Tokyo: Yomiuri Shinbunsha.

Ben-Ami SHILLONY. 1973. *Revolt in Japan: The Young Officers and the February 26, 1936, Incident.* Princeton: Princeton University Press.

SHIMAZAKI Kyūya. 1989. *En no shinryakushi* [The yen's invasion history]. Tokyo: Nihon Keizai Hyōronsha.

Hiroshi SHIMIZU. 1986. *Anglo-Japanese Trade Rivalry in the Middle East in the Inter-war Period.* St. Antony's Middle East Monographs No. 17. London: Ithaca Press.

SHINBO Hiroshi. 1978. *Kinsei no bukka to keizai hatten* [Early modern prices and economic development]. Tokyo: Tōyō Keizai Shinpōsha.

Hiroshi SHINJO. 1962. *History of the Yen: 100 Years of Japanese Money-Economy.* Kobe: Research Institute for Economics and Business Administration, Kobe University.

SHINOBU Seizaburō. 1954. *Taishō demokurashii shi* [History of Taishō democracy]. Tokyo: Nihon Hyōronsha.

———. 1967. "From Party Politics to Military Dictatorship." *Developing Economies,* 5:4, 666–684.

SHUNPO-KŌ TSUISHŌKAI. 1940. *Itō Hirobumi den* [Biography of Itō Hirobumi]. 3 vols. Tokyo: Tōseisha.

Bernard S. SILBERMAN and H. D. HAROOTUNIAN, eds. 1974. *Japan in Crisis: Essays in Taishō Democracy.* Princeton: Princeton University Press.

Miriam SILVERBERG. 1991. "The Modern Girl as Militant." In Bernstein 1991, 239–266.

———. 1998. "The Cafe Waitress Serving Modern Japan." In Vlastos 1998, 208–225.

Beth A. SIMMONS. 1996. "Rulers of the Game: Central Bank Independence during the Interwar Years." *International Organization,* 50:3, 407–443.

Richard J. SMETHURST. 1986. *Agricultural Development and Tenancy Disputes in Japan, 1870–1940.* Princeton: Princeton University Press.

———. 1998. "The Self-Taught Bureaucrat: Takahashi Korekiyo and Economic Policy during the Great Depression." In John Singleton, ed. *Learning in Likely Places: Varieties of Apprenticeship in Japan.* Cambridge: Cambridge University Press, 226–238.

———. 2001. "Takahashi Korekiyo's Fiscal Policy and the Rise of Militarism in Japan during the Great Depression." *Kindai Nihon kenkyū* (Keiō Gijuku Fukuzawa Kenkyū Sentaa), vol. 18, 260–288.

Jeremiah SMITH, Jr. 1929. "The Bank for International Settlements." *Quarterly Journal of Economics,* 43:4 (August), 713–725.

Kerry SMITH. 2001. *A Time of Crisis: Japan, the Great Depression, and Rural Revitalization.* Cambridge, MA: Harvard University Press.

Robert Freeman SMITH. 1972. *The United States and Revolutionary Nationalism in Mexico, 1916–1932.* Chicago: University of Chicago Press.

Thomas C. SMITH. 1955. *Political Change and Industrial Development in Japan: Government Enterprise, 1868–1880.* Stanford: Stanford University Press.

Michael SMITKA, ed. 1998. *The Interwar Economy of Japan: Colonialism, Depression, and Recovery, 1910–1940.* New York: Garland.

William F. SPALDING. 1924. *Eastern Exchange: Currency and Finance.* London: Pitman & Sons.

Robert M. SPAULDING Jr. 1971. "The Bureaucracy as a Political Force, 1920–1945." In Morley 1971, 33–80.

Joseph STIGLITZ. 2002. *Globalization and Its Discontents.* London: Penguin.

Willard STRAIGHT. 1913. "China's Loan Negotiations." In George H. Blakeslee, ed. *Recent Developments in China.* Clark University Addresses, November 1912. New York: G. E. Stechert.

Toshio SUZUKI. 1994. *Japanese Government Loan Issues on the London Capital Market, 1870–1913.* London: Athlone Press.

William L. SWAN. 1989. "Thai-Japanese Monetary Relations at the Start of the Pacific War." *Modern Asian Studies* 23:2, 313–347.

TADAI Yoshi. 1997. *Tairiku ni watatta en no kōbō* [The yen's rise and fall on the continent]. 2 vols. Tokyo: Tōyō Keizai Shinpōsha.

TAKAHASHI Hidetada. 1990. "Hara Takashi naikaku-ka no gikai—Dai 41-kai Teikoku Gikai–dai 44-kai Teikoku Gikai" [The Diet under the Hara Takashi cabinet—41st Imperial Diet–44th Imperial Diet]. In Uchida, Kanehara, and Yoshiya 1990, 2: 189–260.

TAKAHASHI Kamekichi. 1936. "Japan's Finances and Takahashi's Policies." *Contemporary Japan,* 4:4 (March), 519–526.

———. 1954. *Taishō Shōwa zaikai hendōshi* [History of changes in the business world of Taishō and Shōwa]. 3 vols. Tokyo: Tōyō Keizai Shinpōsha.

———. 1963. *Keizai hyōron 50 nen—watakushi no jinsei to sono haikei—* [Fifty years of economic commentary: My life and its background]. Tokyo: Tōshi Keizai Sha.

TAKAHASHI Kamekichi and MORIGAKI Sunao. 1993 [1968]. *Shōwa kin'yū kyōkō shi* [History of the Shōwa financial panic]. Tokyo: Kōdansha.

TAKAHASHI Korekiyo. 1925. *Waga kuni no sangyō ni tsuite* [Concerning our country's industry]. Osaka: Sangyō Shinkō Kenkyūkai.

———. 1932. "The 1932 Budget." *Contemporary Japan,* 1:2 (September), 169–174.

———. 1936a. *Zuisōroku* [Essays]. Tokyo: Chikura Shobō.

———. 1936b. *Takahashi Korekiyo keizairon* [Takahashi Korekiyo on economics]. Tokyo: Chikura Shobō.

———. 1976 [1936]. *Takahashi Korekiyo jiden* [Autobiography of Takahashi Korekiyo]. 2 vols. Edited by Uetsuka Tsukasa. Tokyo: Chūkō Bunko.

———. 1938. *Nihon kokumin e no yuigon* [A final testament to the Japanese people]. Tokyo: Chikura Shobō.

TAKAHASHI Masae, ed. 1964. *Kokkashugi undō (2)* [The ultranationalist movement, vol. 2]. Gendai shiryōryō (5). Tokyo: Misuzu Shobō.

TAKAHASHI Masanori. 1980. *Nihon seiji jiten* [Dictionary of Japanese politics]. Tokyo: Kokusho Kankōkai.

TAKAMURA Naosuke. 1985. "Shihon chikuseki (1), keikōgyō" [Capital accumulation: Vol. 1, Light industry]. In Ōishi K. 1985, 1: 153–197.

TAKEHARA SHŌTEN CHŌSABU, ed. 1921. *Zaikai no zento wa dō naru ka? —tōzai zaikai meishi ni iken—* [What is the outlook for the business world? Opinions of notable figures of the business world of East and West Japan]. Osaka: Takehara Shōten.

Norio TAMAKI. 1988. "Economists in Parliament: The Fall of Bimetallism in Japan."

In Sugiyama Chūhei and Mizuta Hiroshi, eds. *Enlightenment and Beyond: Political Economy Comes to Japan.* Tokyo: University of Tokyo Press, 1988, 223–236.

———. 1990. "The Yokohama Specie Bank: A Multinational in the Japanese Interest 1879–1931." In Geoffrey Jones, ed. *Banks as Multinationals.* London: Routledge, 191–216.

———. 1994. "Japan's Adoption of the Gold Standard and the London Money Market, 1881–1903: Matsukata, Nakai and Takahashi." In Ian Nish, ed. *Britain and Japan: Biographical Portraits.* Folkstone, Kent: Japan Library, 121–132.

———. 1995. *Japanese Banking: A History, 1859–1959.* Cambridge: Cambridge University Press.

———. 2001. *Yukichi Fukuzawa, 1835–1901: The Spirit of Enterprise in Modern Japan.* Houndmills, Basingstoke: Palgrave.

TANAKA Ikuo. 1969. "Kin kaikin ronsō" [The debate on lifting the gold ban]. In Chō and Sumiya 1969, 357–379.

TASHIRO Kazui. 1976. "Tokugawa jidai ni okeru gin yushutsu to kaihei aridaka—1680 nendai ikō Chōsen, Ryūkyū no gin yushutsu o chūshin ni—" [Tokugawa era silver exports and the volume of currency]. In Umemura Mataji et al., eds. *Sūryō keizaishi ronshū 1: Nihon keizai no hatten.* Tokyo: Nihon Keizai Shinbunsha, 223–239.

———. 1982. "Foreign Relations during the Edo Period: *Sakoku* Reexamined." *Journal of Japanese Studies,* 8:2, 283–306.

TAYA Hirokichi. 1973. "Edo jidai kahei hyō no saikentō" [Reexamination of the Edo period currency chart]. *Shakai keizai shigaku,* 39: 3, 261–279.

TERANISHI Jūrō. 1989. "Fukinkō seichō to kin'yū" [Unbalanced growth and finance]. In Nakamura and Odaka 1989b, 185–229.

———. 1990. "Kin'yū no kindaika to sangyōka" [The modernization of finance and industrialization]. In Nishikawa and Yamamoto 1990, 37–84.

Juro TERANISHI and Yutaka KOSAI, eds. 1993. *The Japanese Experience of Economic Reforms.* New York: St. Martin's Press.

TERANISHI Jūrō and UCHINO Yūko. 1986. "Kinhon'isei to geemu no ruuru" [The gold-standard system and the rules of the game]. In Kaizuka and Ono 1986, 55–68.

William Long THORP and Wesley C. MITCHELL. 1926. *Business Annals: United States, England, France, Germany, Austria, Russia, Sweden, Netherlands, Italy, Argentina, Brazil, Canada, South Africa, Australia, India, Japan, China.* New York: National Bureau of Economic Research.

Arthur E. TIEDEMANN. 1959. "The Hamaguchi Government: First Phase, July 1929–February 1930, A Study in Japanese Parliamentary Government." Ph.D. dissertation, Columbia University.

———. 1971. "Big Business and Politics in Prewar Japan." In Morley 1971, 267–316.

Elise K. TIPTON. 2000. "The Café: Contested Space of Modernity in Interwar Japan." In Tipton and Clark 2000.

Elise K. TIPTON and John CLARK, eds. 2000. *Being Modern in Japan: Culture and Society from the 1910s to the 1930s.* Honolulu: University of Hawai'i Press.

Ronald P. TOBY. 1991 [1984]. *State and Diplomacy in Early Modern Japan: Asia in the Development of the Tokugawa Bakufu.* Stanford: Stanford University Press.

Ronald P. Toby and Ohba Osamu. 1997. "The Bitter and the Sweet: Import Substitutions in Sugar and Ginseng in Eighteenth-Century Japan." Unpublished manuscript.

Tōkyō Asahi Shinbun Keizaibu, ed. 1925. *Kokusai shihonsen* (English subtitle: *The World War of Capital*). Tokyo: Nihon Hyōronsha.

Tokyo Institute of Political and Economic Research. 1934. "The Control of Industry in Japan." In Bruno Lasker and W. L. Holland, eds. *Problems of the Pacific, 1933: Economic Conflict and Control* (Proceedings of the Fifth Conference of the Institute of Pacific Relations, Banff, Canada, August 1933). London: Oxford University Press, 254–270.

Tōno Haruyuki. 1997. *Kahei no Nihonshi* [A currency history of Japan]. Asahi shinsho 574. Tokyo: Asahi Shinbunsha.

Conrad D. Totman. 1993. *Early Modern Japan.* Berkeley and Los Angeles: University of California Press.

Tōyō Keizai Shinpōsha, ed. 1931. *Nihon no keiki hendō* [Japanese business cycles]. 2 vols. Tokyo: Tōyō Keizai Shinpōsha.

———. 1935. *Nihon bōeki seiran* (English subtitle: *Foreign Trade of Japan, A Statistical Survey*). Tokyo: Tōyō Keizai Shinpōsha.

———. 1959–60. *Nihon kin'yūshi shiryō: Meiji-Taishō hen.* Vol. 22. Tokyo: Ōkurasho Insatsukyoku.

Vaso Trivanovitch. 1937. *Economic Development of Germany under National Socialism.* National Industrial Conference Board Studies No. 236. New York: National Industrial Conference Board.

Elizabeth P. Tsunoda. 1993. "Rationalizing Japan's Political Economy: The Business Initiative, 1920–1955." Ph. D. dissertation, Columbia University.

E. Patricia Tsurumi. 1990. *Factory Girls.* Princeton: Princeton University Press.

Tsurumi Yūsuke. 1929. *Taiheiyō jidai, to shinjiyūshugi gaikō no kichō* [The Pacific age, and the keynote of the diplomacy of the new liberalism]. Tokyo: Shinjiyūshugi Kyōkai.

———. 1937–38. *Gotō Shinpei.* 4 vols. Tokyo: Gotō Shinpei-haku Denki Hensankai.

Tsushima Juichi [Tsushima Hōtō]. 1931. *Sekai keizai to kokusai taishaku* [World economy and international credit and debt]. Tokyo: Kin'yū Kenkyūkai.

———. 1963. *Mori Kengo-san no koto.* 2 vols. (vols. 11 and 12 of Hōtō zuisō). Tokyo: Hōtō Kankōkai.

———. 1966. *Gaisai shori no tabi kokusai shin'yō no kaifuku, gaisai dōnyū e no michi* [A journey to deal with foreign bonds]. Hōtō zuisō, 16. Tokyo: Hōtō Kankōkai.

William M. Tsutsui. 1988. *Banking Policy in Japan: American Efforts at Reform during the Occupation.* London: Routledge.

———. 2001. *Manufacturing Ideology: Scientific Management in Twentieth-Century Japan.* Princeton: Princeton University Press.

Uchida Hoshimi. 1990. "Gijutsu iten" [Technology transfer]. In Nishikawa and Abe 1990b, 255–302.

Uchida Kenzō, Kanehara Samon, and Yoshiya Tetsuo, eds. 1990. *Nihon Gikai shiroku* [The history of parliamentary government in Japan]. 6 vols. Tokyo: Daiichi Hōki Shuppan Kabushikigaisha.

Uetsuka Tsukasa. 1976 [1936]. "Furoku: Takahashi-ō no jikka oyobi yōka no rakki"

[Addendum: A brief record of the venerable Takahashi's birth family and adoptive family]. In Takahashi Korekiyo 1976 [1936], 2: 301–311.

UNITED NATIONS, DEPARTMENT OF ECONOMIC AFFAIRS. 1949. *International Capital Movements during the Inter-War Period.* Lake Success, NY: United Nations.

UNITED STATES COMMISSION ON INTERNATIONAL EXCHANGE [Hugh H. Hanna, Charles A. Conant, and Jeremiah W. Jenks, Commissioners]. 1904. *Gold Standard in International Trade: Report on the Introduction of the Gold-Exchange Standard into China, the Philippine Islands, Panama, and Other Silver-Using Countries, and on the Stability of the Exchange.* Submitted to the Secretary of State, October 22, 1904. Washington, DC: Government Printing Office.

U.S. DEPARTMENT OF COMMERCE, BUREAU OF THE CENSUS. 1960. *Historical Statistics of the United States, Colonial Times to 1957.* Washington, DC: Government Printing Office.

Armand VAN DORMAEL. 1978. *Bretton Woods: Birth of a Monetary System.* New York: Holmes and Meier.

John E. VAN SANT. 2000. *Pacific Pioneers: Japanese Journeys to America and Hawaii, 1850–1880.* Urbana: University of Illinois Press.

Stephen VLASTOS, ed. 1998. *Mirror of Modernity: Invented Traditions of Modern Japan.* Berkeley and Los Angeles: University of California Press.

WAKATSUKI Reijirō. 1950. *Kofūan kaikoroku, Wakatsuki Reijirō jiden, Meiji, Taishō, Shōwa sekai hisshi* [Autobiography of Wakatsuki Reijirō: The secret political history of the Meiji, Taishō, and Shōwa eras]. Tokyo: Yomiuri Shinbunsha.

Robert D. WALTON. 1976. "The Rising Companies and the Establishment, 1905–1931: The Forerunners of Japanese Expansion and their Struggle for Emergence." Ph.D. dissertation, University of British Columbia.

A. W. WARD and G. P. GOOCH, eds. 1923. *The Cambridge History of British Foreign Policy, 1783–1919: Vol. III, 1866–1919.* New York: The Macmillan Co.

George F. WARREN and Frank A. PEARSON. 1935. *Gold and Prices.* New York: John Wiley & Sons.

D. Cameron WATT. 1984. *Succeeding John Bull: America in Britain's Place, 1900–1975.* Cambridge: Cambridge University Press.

Richard A. WERNER. 2002. *Princes of the Yen: Japan's Central Bankers and Their Battle to Transform the Nation.* Armonk, NY: M. E. Sharpe.

Mira WILKINS. 1973. "The Role of U.S. Business." In Borg and Okamoto 1973, 341–376.

Ted WILSON. 2000. *Battles for the Standard: Bimetallism and the Spread of the Gold Standard in the Nineteenth Century.* Aldershot, Hampshire: Ashgate.

Sergei WITTE. 1921. *The Memoirs of Count Witte.* Translated by Abraham Yarmolinsky. New York: Doubleday & Co.

William D. WRAY. 1984. *Mitsubishi and the N.Y.K., 1870–1914: Business Strategy in the Japanese Shipping Industry.* Cambridge, MA: Harvard University Press.

Maurice WRIGHT. 2002. *Japan's Fiscal Crisis: The Ministry of Finance and the Politics of Public Spending, 1975–2000.* New York: Oxford University Press.

Robert Callander WYSE. 1918. "The Future of London as the World's Money Market." *The Economic Journal,* 28: 112 (December), 386–397.

YABE Yōzō et al., eds. 1996. *Gendai Nihon keizaishi nenpyō* [Chronological tables of modern Japanese economic history]. Tokyo: Nihon Keizai Hyōronsha.

YAMAMOTO Yūzō. 1989. "Shokuminchi keiei" [Colonial management]. In Nakamura and Odaka 1989, 231–274.

———. 1994. *Ryō kara en e—Bakumatsu, Meiji zenki kahei mondai kenkyū—* [From the ryō to the yen—research on the currency question of the Bakumatsu and early Meiji periods]. Tokyo: Minerva Shobō.

YAMAMOTO Yoshihiko. 1978. "Shihon yushutsunyū no suii to kiki gekika" [Changes in the export and import of capital and the intensification of the crisis]. In Yamazaki 1978, 2: 170–254.

YAMAMOTO Yūzō and OKU Kazuyoshi. 1990. "Bōeki" [Trade]. In Nishikawa and Yamamoto 1990, 85–131.

YAMAMURA Katsurō. 1973. "The Role of the Finance Ministry." In Borg and Okamoto 1973, 287–302.

Kozo YAMAMURA. 1972. "Then Came the Great Depression: Japan's Interwar Years." In Herman Van Der Wee, ed. *The Great Depression Revisited: Essays on the Economics of the Thirties.* The Hague: Martinus Nijhoff, 182–211.

———. 1974. "The Japanese Economy, 1911–1930: Concentration, Conflicts, and Crises." In Silberman and Harootunian 1974, 299–328.

Sobun YAMAMURO. 1932. "Economic Depression and the Gold Embargo." *Contemporary Japan,* 1:1 (June), 52–61.

———. 1933. "Japan's Economic Conditions since the Gold Embargo." *Contemporary Japan,* 2:2 (September), 232–239.

Kakujiro YAMASAKI and Gotaro OGAWA. 1929. *The Effect of the World War upon the Commerce and Industry of Japan.* New Haven: Yale University Press.

YAMAZAKI Ryūzō, ed. 1978. *Ryōtaisenkanki no Nihon shihonshugi* [Japanese capitalism between the world wars]. 2 vols. Gendai shihonshugi sōsho 9, 10. Tokyo: Ōtsuki Shoten.

YASUBA Yasukichi. 1995. "Nihon keizaishi ni okeru shigen, 1800–1940" [Natural resources in Japanese economic history, 1800–1940]. *Shakai keizai shigaku,* 62:3.

———. 1996. "Did Japan Ever Suffer from a Shortage of Natural Resources before World War II?" *Journal of Economic History,* 56:3 (September), 543–560.

YASUDA Hiroshi. 1990. "Dai-ichiji taisen-ka no gikai—Dai 32-kai Teikoku Gikai–dai 37-kai Teikoku Gikai" [The Diet in the First World War—32nd Imperial Diet–37th Imperial Diet]. In Uchida, Kanehara, and Yoshiya 1990, 2: 61–125.

YASUTOMI Ayumu. 1997. *'Manshūkoku' no kin'yū* [Finance of 'Manchukuo']. Tokyo: Sōbunsha.

———. 2000. "Siberian Expedition and Bubble Economy in Manchuria." Paper presented at the Asian Studies Conference-Japan, Tokyo, June 19.

YOKOHAMA SHŌKIN GINKŌ. 1920. *Yokohama Shōkin Ginkō shi* [History of the Yokohama Specie Bank]. 5 vols. Tokyo: Yokohama Shōkin Ginkō; reprint, Nihon Keizai Hyōronsha, 1976.

YOSHIDA Kensuke. 1876. *Dai Nippon kaheishi* [Currency history of Great Japan]. Tokyo: Ōkurashō.

YOSHII Ken'ichi. 1990. "Tai-Chūgoku seisaku tenkan to gikai—Dai 53-kai Teikoku Gikai–dai 56-kai Teikoku Gikai" [The turn in policy toward China and the Diet—53rd Imperial Diet–56th Imperial Diet]. In Uchida, Kanehara, and Yoshiya 1990, vol. 3, 1–63.

YOSHIKAWA KŌBUNKAN, ed. 1908. *Kinken shōsho rakkai* [Abbreviated guide to the rescript on diligence and thrift]. Tokyo: [Kunaishō Goyō Shoshi] Yoshikawa Kōbunkan.

YOSHINO Toshihiko. 1976. *Rekidai Nihon Ginkō sōsai ron, Nihon kin'yū seisaku shi no kenkyū* [On the successive presidents of the Bank of Japan, Research in the history of Japanese finance]. Tokyo: Mainichi Shinbunsha.

———. 1975–79. *Nihon Ginkō shi* [History of the Bank of Japan]. 5 vols. Tokyo: Shunjūsha.

———. 1996. *En to doru* [Yen and dollar]. Tokyo: Nihon Hōsō Shuppan Kyōkai.

YOSHIYA Tetsuo. 1990. "Goken undō to Siemens jiken—Dai 28-kai Teikoku Gikai–dai 31-kai Teikoku Gikai" [The movement to protect the constitution and the Siemens incident—28th Imperial Diet–31st Imperial Diet]. In Uchida, Kanehara, and Yoshiya 1990, vol. 2: 5–60.

Arthur N. YOUNG. 1971. *China's Nation-Building Effort, 1927–1937: The Financial and Economic Record*. Stanford: Hoover Institution Press.

A. Morgan YOUNG. 1929. *Japan in Recent Times, 1912–1926*. New York: William Morrow & Co.

Louise YOUNG. 1998. *Japan's Total Empire: Manchuria and the Culture of Wartime Imperialism*. Berkeley and Los Angeles: University of California Press.

INDEX

1890s, as historical pivot, 12–13, 29–30, 34
1920s: as era of chronic recession, 115–17, 216, 241, 262; in Manchuria, 135–36; in world history, 159–60, 163, 168, 260–63
1927 financial crisis. *See* banking crisis, of 1927
74th Bank, 135

Adachi Kenzō, 233, 239
Addis, Charles, 126, 127
"adjustment" (*seiri*), 134, 144, 163, 173, 203
"agrarianist" (*nōhonshugi*) movment, 230–31, 234. *See also* right-wing movements
agricultural depression (1920s–30s): international, 171, 213; in Japan, 115, 138, 224, 226–27, 230–31, 234, 315n33
Aikokusha (Patriotic Society), 230–31
Alexeiev, Kir, 41
Allen, G. C., 199
Allied Economic Conference (Paris, 1916), 103
allies (World War I), 127; Japanese lending to, 98–99, 103, 295n45
All-Japan Patriots' Joint-Struggle Conference (1931), 232–33
All-Kansai Women's Federation, 140, 205
American China Development Company, 12
"American group" (Morgan & Co., Kuhn, Loeb, National City Bank, First National Bank), 59–60, 149, 152, 214–15, 234, 270. *See also* China consortium
"Americanism" and Americanization, 115, 141, 212, 263
Amsterdam financial conference (1920), 163
"anchor chain" metaphor (Redish), 16, 20, 250, 265, 271
Andong-Mukden railway, 88, 93
Anglo-American alignment, 12–13; in finance, 35, 265–66; vis-à-vis Japan, 46–47, 126–28, 140–41, 184, 214–15, 252, 259; wartime alliances, 98, 267
Anglo-American economics, 262
Anglo-American loans: to Germany, 167–68, 170–71, 214, 270; to Japan, 46–49, 73–74, 76 (table), 150–52 (table), 167, 270
Anglo-French imperialism, 261
Anglo-Japanese alliance, 258–59; enabler of Russo-Japanese war, 45, 288n3; ending of, 126, 140–41, 142, 254–55; establishment of, 4–5, 8, 42; extension of, 54–55; opposition to, 85; and WWI, 92
Anglophile feeling: in Japan, 8–9, 128, 281n6; at Morgan & Co., 46, 128, 169, 170
Anglo-Russian rapprochement (1907), 58–59
anti-Semitism, 46–47
Aoyama Cemetery, 247
Arai Hakuseki, 15, 283n3
Argentina, 213
armistice economic reaction (1918), 118
army (Japanese): and budgetary politics, 84–85, 250, 255–56; and China policy, 84, 123, 125–26, 129, 254. *See also* Kwantung Army

Asia: Japanese "leave Asia" view, 29, 40, 263; silver standards in, 36–39
Asian economic crisis (1997–98), xvi, 176
Australia, 28, 213, 291n8
Austria (and Austria-Hungary): stock market crash (1873), 27; gold standard (1892), 30; post-WWI stabilization, 163, 166–67, 168, 185; collapse of stabilization (1931), 234
"automatic adjustment" (under gold standard), 18–20, 71, 89, 172–73, 207, 218, 266; diagram of, 19

bailouts (of financial institutions, by BOJ), 176, 185, 186–87, 310n55; in 1920–22, 133, 134–35, 139; in 1923, 146; in 1927, 179–80, 182–83, 189; in 1931, 239
bakufu. See Tokugawa shogunate
balance of payments (Japan): in Tokugawa era, 15; in 1870s–80s, 24–25; from 1880s to 1914, 68–69, 82–84, 87–89; during WWI, 91, 95, 104–5, 206; in 1920s, 118, 130, 144, 154, 157, 164–65, 206–7, 241; in 1930s, 253, 256; after WWII, 269; after 1965, 271
balance of payments (other countries): Britain, 161; U.S. and Europe, 164–65, 303n26. *See also* "dollar gap"; specie-flow theory
Balkan war (1912–13), 86
"bancor" (Keynes), 265
bankers, as mediate between government and industry, 11, 134, 174
Bankers Trust (N.Y.), 169
Bank for International Settlements (BIS), 193–94
banking: consolidation, 187; practices, 62, 119–20, 175–76
banking crises: of 1907, 82; of 1920–21, 134, 135, 136, 138–39; of 1923, 145, 146–47; of 1927, 111, 174–83, 185; aftereffects of 1927 crisis, 191, 236, 309n37; of 1931, 239; bank runs (in general), 37–38; international, of 1931–33, 38, 234, 236, 252
Bank of China, 108
Bank of Chosen (Chōsen Ginkō), 54, 94, 100; and loans to Beijing government, 101, 108; in Manchuria, 64–65, 105–6, 135, 254, 291n76
Bank of Communications (China), 108
Bank of England: banknotes and gold convertibility, 21, 36, 236; as borrower of last resort, 38; and central bank cooperation, 132, 166, 171; deflation policy after 1919, 131, 144, 162–63; deflation policy after 1925, 172–73, 191; and Japan, 3, 11, 31, 69, 71, 215; as model of central banking, 97, 275
Bank of France, 191, 195, 236
Bank of Japan (BOJ): banknotes and gold convertibility, 33, 39, 218–19, 264, 266, 273; and deficit bonds, 250; dependence on Ministry of Finance, 25, 129, 264, 307n92; establishment of, 24–25; and foreign-exchange budgeting, 270; as "head office" of private banks, 25; and Inoue Junnosuke, 11–12, 61–62, 82; and Korea, 41; management "strike" of 1899, 11–12; Osaka branch, 39, 61; policy stance, 82, 84, 86, 87–89, 120, 121–23, 129–31, 134, 138–39, 143, 144, 158, 165, 239, 249, 251; relations with foreign banks, 71, 187, 215, 271; reserves, 46, 47, 70 (table), 71, 89, 178, 219, 223, 238, 250–51 (graph), 264, 273–75; and return to gold standard, 123, 142, 174, 190, 191, 218–19; and Takahashi Korekiyo, 7–8, 12; and Yokohama Specie Bank, 110; young officers' attack on (1932), 248. *See also* bailouts; note issue; overseas specie reserve
Bank of Japan governors. *See* Fukai Eigo; Hijikata Hisaakira; Ichiki Otohiko; Inoue Junnosuke; Kawata Shōichirō, Matsuo Shigeyoshi; Mishima Yatarō; Takahashi Korekiyo; Yamamoto Tatsuo
Bank of Japan Law (1942), 264
Bank of Korea (Kankoku Ginkō), 54
Bank of Taiwan, 91, 291n76; as colonial central bank, 34, 57, 65, 99, 254; in crisis of 1927, 176, 179–81, 182; and gold-exchange standard, 65, 289n34; lending in China, 101, 179, 254
Banque de l'Indochine, 44, 125
Banque Franco-Japonaise, 98
Baring Brothers, 46, 236
beer consumption, 309n29
Beijing (Peking) government, 93, 101, 106–8, 124–25, 127
Belgium, return to gold standard, 170, 171, 185, 190, 214

bills of exchange: dollar, sterling, and yen, 98, 107; rediscounting, 97, 119–20. *See also* pound sterling
bimetallism, 22–23, 26
"Blood Pledge Corps" (Ketsumeidan), 246–48
Bolivia, 170
bonds: corporate, 69, 78–79 (table), 148–53 (table, 150–52); domestic market for, 106, 119, 121, 291n6; local government, 69, 72–77 (table), 83, 150–52 (table). *See also* Japanese government overseas bond issues
booms: after 1877, 24; after Russo-Japanese war, 56, 81–82; during WWI, 94–96, 99, 105–6, 110–11, 116–18, 240–41; after WWI, 118–22, 130, 134, 160–61 (graph), 208, 241; postearthquake, 147; of 1930s, 240–41, 248–50; U.S., of 1920s, 171. *See also* postwar inflation-deflation cycles
Boshin Rescript (1908) and deflation policy, 83, 154, 276
Boxer rebellion, indemnities, 51, 58, 101
boycotts, Chinese, 58, 93, 160, 227, 235, 246
Brazil, 213
Bretton Woods conference (1944) and institutions, 103, 265–66. *See also* International Monetary Fund; World Bank
Britain: as creditor country, 20, 21, 27, 80; in depression of 1920, 136, 137, 160–62; depression after 1925, 171, 172–73, 191; graph of prices, 161; overseas borrowing, 98–99; after suspension of gold standard, 249. *See also* Anglo-American alignment; Anglo-Japanese alliance; Anglophile feeling; Bank of England; gold standard (British); London
"British group" (Westminster Bank, Hongkong & Shanghai Bank, Rothschilds, Barings, Schroeder, Morgan Grenfell), 150, 152, 310n53
British hegemony, 161–62, 170–71, 263; in Asia, 5, 85; and cultural forms, 5, 39–40, 281n6; financial, 5, 14, 35–36, 96, 237. *See also* London, as international financial center; pound sterling
Brown, John McLeavy, 52
Brown Brothers Harriman and Co., 270
Brussels financial conference (1920), 163
Bryan, William Jennings, 27, 59, 64, 247
bubble of 1919–20, 118–19, 121–22, 126, 129–31, 133–34; in Manchuria, 135; and postbubble debt crisis, 175. *See also* depression, of 1920
budgetary balance, and gold standard, 164, 166
budgetary policy (in Japan), 45, 189, 256; in 1906–15, 81–85, 87–89, 94; in 1919–20, 119; in 1920–22, 137, 140; in 1925–26, 155, 157; in 1929, 202, 212; in 1932–33, 250, 251; in 1935, 255
"building an industrial state" (*sangyō rikkoku*), 157, 183, 188
de Bunsen, E. H., 304n34
Burma, 230
business cycles, 187, 228. *See also* booms; depressions
business organizations, 139–40, 142, 156–57, 191
"Buy British goods" movement, 154
"Buy Japanese goods" movement, 154, 209–10, 301n40

cabinet changes, and elections, 153, 301n35
Canada, 237
Canton (Guangzhou), 179
Cao Rulin (Ts'ao Ju-lin), 93, 101, 107, 108, 125
capital flight, 71, 252
cartelization, 203, 224
Cassel, Ernest, 46
Cassel, Gustav, 155, 250, 301n44
central banks, 21, 131; bullionist conception of, 25, 38; colonial, 34, 64–65, 254, 264; independence of, 163–64, 166, 167, 170, 189, 190, 194–95, 307n92; international cooperation among, 132, 163–64, 166, 191, 194–95, 199, 306n62, 310n55; as lenders of last resort, 38. *See also names of individual banks*
Central Europe: postwar inflation, 132, 163; "stabilization," 166, 233–34. *See also* Austria; Czechoslovakia; Germany; Hungary
chambers of commerce, 191; national federation of, 139–40, 142
Chang Kai-shek (Jiang Jieshi), 179, 183
Chemical Bank, 270

Chemulpo, Treaty of, 40
cheques, bank, 286n27
Chile, 170
China: banks, 64, 108; coinage, 15; financial imperialism in, 123–24; foreign borrowing, 31–32, 51, 60–64, 93, 100–101, 106–8, 124, 254–55, 258, 295n39; gold-exchange standard plans, 38, 43–44, 61, 63, 99–101, 107–8, 170, 171, 212, 254–55; indemnities, 3–5, 8, 30–32, 51, 58, 68, 101, 107; monetary reform of 1935, 254–55, 316n51; revolution of 1911, 62–63, 84; scramble for concessions in, 4–5, 12; in WWI boom, 95, 133. *See also* Japanese relations with China; Manchuria; Sino-Japanese War
China consortium (of international banks), 60–61, 63–64, 100, 101, 106–7, 123; as financial blockade, 127, 252–53, 255, 298n40; U.S. initiative to reorganize, 108–9, 125–28. *See also* "American group"
Chinese Eastern Railway, 50
Chon-Il Bank, 54
Chōshū clique, 81, 92, 94
Chūō Club, 86
Churchill, Winston, 158; "Economic Consequences of Mr. Churchill" (Keynes), 172–73, 304n37
Chūseikai, 156
Civil War, U.S., 121, 132
Cixi (Tz'u-hsi), Empress Dowager, 58
coal, 4–5, 172
coinage, 14–18, 20–21, 36–39, 53, 133, 283n4, 286n27
Colombia, 170
Commission on International Exchange (U.S.), 43
commodity speculation, 119, 133–34, 176–77
communism, 139
Conant, Charles A., 37, 39, 42–44, 50
constitution (of 1889): provisions of, 202, 301n35
constitutionalism, in Japan, 25
consumption, 95, 115, 309n29; efforts to restrain, 140, 144, 154–55, (as international movement, 164), 203–9, 218, 224, 228, 229; encouragement of, 210–12, 229, 241–44; statistics of, 208–9 (graph)
"containment" of Japan in 1920s, 259–60
continental *rōnin;* China *rōnin,* 231, 233, 246
"control" (*tōsei*), 224
controlled loans, 59, 166, 170
Convertible Banknotes Law of 1884, 275
Co-Prosperity Sphere, 264
cotton: raw cotton imports, 97, 176; spinning companies, 133, 174, 224, 225; weaving, 252; yarn exports and prices, 97, 118, 133, 158, 223, 225
counterfeiting, 16–17
credit, Anglo-American, for return to gold standard (1929), 194, 213–15, 219, 220
Credit-Anstalt bankruptcy, 234
"crony capitalism," 176
Cuba, 43, 162
Currency Investigation Commission (Kahei Seido Chōsakai), 30
Currency Law of 1897, 3, 33, 264. *See also* New Currency Law of 1871
currency stabilization. *See* gold standard, restoration; stabilization
Czechoslovakia, 163, 166

Daidō Electric Power, 149, 150, 153
Dai-Ichi (First) Bank: as Korean central bank, 40, 52–54, 57, 65, 289n35
Dalian (Dairen), 5, 57, 65, 105, 135
"dangerous thought," 130, 139
Dan Takuma, 9, 140, 184, 186, 228; assassination of, 247–48
Darmstadter Bank, 234
Dawes, Charles, 167
Dawes plan (1924), 167–69, 171
Daye Mining Co., 51
"deadlock" (*ikizumari*), 89, 92; in 1920s, 115–17, 201, 235, 262
debt. *See* bonds; foreign debt; Japanese government bonds; loans, international
debt crisis, 146, 160, 175, 176, 185, 191, 230
deficit finance, 240, 243–45, 249–50
deflation (in Japan): of 1881–84, 25; of 1908–09, 83; of 1914–15, 90, 92, 94; of early 1920s, 115–17, 129–32, 138–45, 160–63; after 1924, 153–56, 189; of 1929–32, 201, 206–7, 221–31, 234, 240, 249; of 1949–50, 267–68; of 1990s, xvi, 208; as concept and policy, xv, 131–32, 130–32, 159, 172–73, 185–86,

220, 263; as "creative destruction," 252; and debt, 175, 185; table of, 276–77; graphs of, 161, 249; versus depreciation or devaluation, 132, 174, 201–2, 244, 250, 266. *See also* "negative policy"
deflation (elsewhere): of 1873–96, 26–28, 159, 247; of 1920s, 159–71, 186, 189, 213, 249, 262; and farmers, 27, 213, 230, 234; under gold standard, 18–20, 89, 159, 284n36; Lamont on, 220; and profits, 223–24, 240, 299n55
demand. *See* consumption
Denmark, 237
"dependent imperialism" (Yamazaki), 51, 259
depreciation, devaluation. *See* deflation (Japan) versus depreciation; gold par; yen
depressions: of 1890, 68, 285n42; of 1907, 82; of 1920, 116–117, 129–39, 160–61, 162, 185, 208, 228; of 1929–31, 116, 163, 192, 222–40, 257; international, of 1930s, 96, 213, 240, 248. *See also* agricultural depression; deflation; gold-restoration depressions; "Great Depression" of 1873–96; induced depression
Diet, Imperial, 64, 141; parties in, 85, 94, 111, 129–30, 141, 153; length of sessions, 202; sessions: of 1913, 86; of 1914, 88; of 1927, 177–79; of 1931, 231–33; of 1932, 245. *See also* elections; political party system
"Diligence and Thrift Campaign," 154–55
Dillon, Read and Co., 170, 189; lending to Japan, 149, 150, 151, 153; after WWII, 267, 270
"divine providence" (*ten'yū*), 47, 92, 214, 269
Dodge, Joseph M., 267–68
"Dodge line" deflation, 267–69
dollar. *See* silver-dollar standard; U.S. dollar
"dollar buying" speculation (1930–31), 215, 229–30, 237–39, 244, 245, 277
"dollar diplomacy," 59, 109
"dollar gap": after WWI, 164–65; after WWII, 265, 268
Dominican Republic, 43, 59, 109
Dōshikai (Society of Comrades), 67, 85–87, 88, 89, 92. *See also* Kenseikai; Minseitō
Draper, William Jr., 267
Droppers, Garrett, 285n5
"dual structure," 226
Duan Qirui (Tuan Ch'i-jui), 107

earthquake and fire of 1923, 115, 116, 145; economic aftereffects of, 155, 185; as financial crisis, 146–47
earthquake bills, 146, 175, 177–79
"earthquake loan" of 1924, 147, 149–50, 168, 184
"East Asian Economic League," 100
Economist (London), 4, 199
Ecuador, 170
education system, 119, 204
Edward VII, King, 46, 47
Egan, Martin, 126, 184, 315n44
Egypt, as model of financially-led colonization, 24, 40–41, 43, 52, 254
elections: of 1924, 153; of 1930, 220; of 1932, 245, 246–47; under Meiji constitution, 301n35
electrification, electric-power industry, 115, 240; overseas borrowing for, 148, 149–53, 158, 169, 184, 188
employment, full, 248. *See also* unemployment
endaka (yen-appreciation) recessions, 147, 158, 176
English language, 5
export associations, 157
export markets, of Japan, 120, 130, 226–26, 240–41, 252–53, 255. *See also* Japanese relations with China; silk exports

famine, of 1931–32, 234
farm tenancy, 201, 226
fascism, 248, 262. *See also* right-wing movements
fascist alliance, 183
February 26, 1936 coup attempt, 233, 255, 257
Federal Reserve Bank of New York (FRBNY), 97, 166, 170, 188, 236; and deflation policy, 131–32, 144, 163; interest-rate cuts in 1927, 191; and Japan, 185, 190, 194, 215. *See also* Strong, Benjamin
Federal Reserve Board Research Division, 267
feminism, 139, 235, 309n40
Fifteenth Bank, 180
finance capital, 160, 168–69
financial crises. *See* banking crises
Finland, 237

First Higher School (Tokyo), 10
First National Bank of New York, 149, 169
fiscal policy. *See* budgetary policy
Forbes, W. Cameron, 221
foreign borrowing and lending. *See* loans, international
foreign debt: 68–69 (graph), 91, 269–70. *See also* bonds; Japanese government loans
foreign direct investment: into Japan, 71; Japanese outward investment, 102, 253, 295n46
foreign-exchange controls, 252, 270–71
foreign-exchange reserves, 237, 286n30, 292n11. *See also* Bank of Japan reserves; gold-exchange standards; overseas specie reserve
foreign investment: British and other Western, 80; U.S., in 1920s, 169–70
Foreign Ministry (Japan), 101
Forrestal, James, 267
fractional-reserve banking, 20, 37; nation viewed as a bank (Leffingwell), 37, 190
France: as creditor country, 38, 47, 58, 80; overseas borrowing, 98–99, 170; in 1920s, 163, 171; return to gold standard, 188, 189, 190, 213
Franco-German war, 102; indemnity, 26–27
French franc, exchange rate, 77n
Fujian (Fukien), 93
Fujii Shinji, 314n29
Fukai Eigo, 146, 163, 165, 176, 187, 190, 254; on foreign borrowing, 69, 89; and Takahashi Korekiyo, 49
Fukuzawa Momosuke, 153
Fukuzawa Yukichi, 24, 29, 40
Fumikichi-san, 204

geisha, 7, 10–11
geisha house parable (Takahashi), 211–12, 244
General Electric, 153, 192
generational cohorts, 9–10
Genoa conference (1922), 163–66; Genoa financial resolutions, 141, 143, 164, 265
"gentlemanly capitalism" (Cain & Hopkins), 5, 8, 39, 42, 287n36
German-Asiatic Bank, 5, 44
German-Japanese alliance, 85, 183
German-Japanese war (1914), 92–93
German Reichsbank, 167–68, 234
Germany, 109, 261; compared to China and Japan, 167; and concessions in China, 4–5, 41, 93; as creditor nation, 49, 80; as debtor nation, 168; depression after 1927, 213, 234, 236, 257; and gold standard, 23, 26–27, 31, 234; "stabilization" in, 163, 167–68, 170, 171, 185, 262; after WWII, 267, 270
Gilbert, S. Parker, 167
gold: conceived as a monetary standard, xvi, 21, 265; deflation of prices as appreciation of, 171; discoveries and production of, 15, 26, 28, 285n44; free export of, 14, 18; international stock of, 164; in MacArthur's view, 268
"gold center" countries, 164–65, 265
gold export embargo (Japan): imposed (1917), 104–105, 202, 295n48; debate over lifting, xiv, 118, 122–24, 172–74, 207, 302n5; lifted (1930), 215–20, 257; reimposed (1931), 229, 237, 239–40, 244, 249, 252, 313n74. *See also* gold shipments; gold standard, restoration
gold export embargo (U.S.): imposed (1917), 104; lifted (1919), 118, 121, 122, 124, 131; reimposed (1933), 252
gold export embargoes (international), 91–92, 237
gold-exchange standards, 28, 29–30, 264, 286n30, 287n33; and Bretton Woods system, 265–66, 271; defined, 36–39, 286n25; Japan's gold standard as, 31, 46, 69–71, 142, 258, 292n11; sterling-based, 36, 70, 164, 255, 302n8; U.S. dollar-based, 59, 42–44, 162; after WWI, 164, 166, 170; yen-based, 40–42, 52–55, 57–58, 65. *See also* China, gold-exchange standard plans
gold flows. *See* gold shipments
"gold gap." *See* dollar gap
gold par: old versus new (devalued) parity, 155, 159, 164, 189, 194, 201–2, 228–29; par values (yen, pound, dollar, franc), xxi, 77; after WWII, 266, 268, 269
gold-restoration depressions, 160, 162–63, 241, 261, 265; in Japan, 163; in U.S., 131–32. *See also* gold standard (Japanese, etc.), restoration
gold shipments, international, 14, 18–20, 191, 228, 236–37; during gold embargo

(1917–29), 136, 143, 156, 158, 174, 176, 178, 181; to and from Japan, 15, 17–18, 23, 98, 104–5, 218–19, 231, 238–39 (table), 251, 277–79
gold:silver ratios, 17–18, 27–28, 30–31. *See also* silver appreciation and depreciation
gold standard (international): "classical," 13, 14–15, 26, 96, 259, 268; defined, 14, 18–21; divided into subblocs, 38–39; as "hydraulic" system, 20; suspended during WWI, 91, 162 (table); movement to restore in 1920s, 141, 159–173 (table, 162), 259–63; collapse in 1931–33, 234; after WWII, 265–66; and moral-economic restoration, 21, 159; and "negative" policy, 66–67; statist versus market aspects, 14, 21, 25; in U.S. law, 42; final end in 1971, 271. *See also* Germany, gold standard; gold-exchange standards; Russia, gold standard
gold standard (British), 14–15, 16, 18–22; establishment of, 14, 16, 20, 159, 286n27; diffusion of, 26–28, 30, 36–39; suspension of, 97; restoration of, 131, 163, 158, 168, 171, 172–73, 185, 191; collapse of, 234, 236–37; and coinage, 133, 283n4
gold standard (Japanese): attempt to establish in 1871, 22–24; and deflationary "rules," 80, 89–90; establishment of in 1897, 3, 8, 25, 30–33, 107; and foreign borrowing, 32, 45–46, 80, 286n15; and party politics, 80–81; as sterling-based gold-exchange standard, 31, 46, 69–71, 99, 142, 258, 275; movement to restore, 139, 141–42, 145, 153–56, 158, 178, 181, 183, 187, 190–95; restoration of (1930) [a.k.a. gold embargo, lifting of], 50, 116, 199–216, 257, 302n5; of Tokugawa shogunate, 15–18, 21; workings of, 38–39, 250–51
gold yen coins, 39, 218
Gō Seinosuke, 186, 188, 191, 228
Gotō Shinpei, 56–58, 82, 85, 86–87, 94, 99–100, 108, 124–25, 290n43, 303n33
"Great Depression" of 1873–96, 26–28
"great transformation" (Polanyi), 160
greenbacks, 121
Greenwich meridian, 217
growth, economic: in 1920s, 115
Guam, 12
Guandong Army; Guandong Leased Territory. *See* Kwantung Army; Kwantung Leased Territory
Guaranty Trust (New York), 151, 169, 184, 270
Guatemala, 59
Guomindang (Kuomintang), 127, 179

Haiti, 109, 221
Hamaguchi Osachi (Yūkō), 9, 86, 87, 88–89, 94, 129–30, 301n36; on wartime boom and postwar depression, 116, 121–22, 138–39; as finance minister, 154–56, 157–58, 173–76; as home minister, 158; as Minseitō president, 183; as prime minister, xiv, 195, 199–204, 209, 217–18, 222, 227, 229, 232–33; assassination of, 231, 233, 247
"hangover theory" (Krugman), 208
Hanna, Hugh H., 43
Hanyang Steel Co., 51
Hanyeping Coal and Iron Co., 51–52, 62–63, 64, 93
Hara Takashi (Kei), 81, 84–85, 87, 88, 94, 153; as prime minister, 111, 118, 121, 122; assassination of, 139; Hara cabinet, 119, 124, 128, 130, 133, 139, 140
Haraguchi (of MOF), 213
Harbin, 106, 246
Harriman, E. H., 55–56, 58, 60
Harris, Townshend, 17
Harrison, George, 194, 195
Hart, Robert, 46
Harvard College, 29, 126, 221
Hatoyama Ichirō, 227, 232
Hawaii: Japanese workers in, 6; U.S. annexation of, 12
Hayami Seiji, 158
heavy and chemical industries, 91, 95, 136, 241. *See also* munitions industry
hegemony, 96, 259, 263, 266: and international monetary standard, xvi, 38; Japanese, in Asia, 259. *See also* British hegemony; U.S. hegemony
highway law, 119
Hijikata Hisaakira, 9, 180, 189, 190; photograph of, xxiii
Hiratsuka Raichō, 309n40
Hirohito, Emperor, 147, 184, 195, 213
Hitler, Adolf, 257
Hobson, J. A., 50

Hokkaido, 34, 234
Home Ministry (and home minister), 81, 86, 154, 155, 301n35
Honduras, 59
Hongkong and Shanghai Bank, 4–5, 32, 44, 126, 311n13. *See also* loans, overseas, Japanese
Hong Kong mint, 22
Hoover, Herbert, 212, 228
Hoover moratorium on war debts and reparations, 169, 234
"house" banks (*kikan ginkō*), 176, 179
Huguang (Hukuang) railways, 12; loan, 60–61, 62, 298n40
Hume, David, 18–19. *See also* specie-flow theory
"hundred years' peace" (Polanyi), 259
Hungary, 163, 166–67, 168, 184–85
hyperinflation: post-WWI, 161, 163, 167; post-WWII, 258

Ichiki Otohiko: as minister of finance, 141, 142–43, 145, 165; as BOJ governor, 174, 176, 180, 181–82
Ikeda Hayato, 268, 270
Ikeda Shigeaki (Seihin), 9, 29, 181, 184, 186, 188, 190, 191; and dollar-buying speculation, 215, 238, 244; and Inoue Junnosuke, 122, 181–82, 200, 214–16
Illusion of Finance Minister Inoue (Mutō), 221, 229
imperial family, and consumption, 210
imperialism: and extension of gold-exchange standards, 35–44; financial theories of, 50–51; Japanese, funding of, 91
import substitution, 95
indemnities. *See* Chemulpo, Treaty of; China, indemnities; Franco-German war indemnity; World War I indemnity
India, 55, 133, 230; and gold-exchange standard, 30, 36–39, 42–43, 70, 286n25, 286n30; trade with Japan, 97, 98, 104
Indian army, in China, 4
induced depression, xv–xvi, 130–32, 172–73, 220, 261. See also "negative policy"; stabilization
Industrial Bank of Japan (IBJ), 55; foreign borrowing, 34, 56, 83, 148, 150; lending in China, 51, 101, 296n56
industrial policy and "control," 186–88, 203, 224, 228, 235, 269; as "positive" policy, 156–57, 251–52, 256
industrial revolutions, 242
industry, military, 68
inflation: in nineteenth century Japan, 18, 27; in specie-flow conception, 19; during WWI, 102, 103, 110–11; after WWI, 116 (graph), 130–32, 139, 160–63 (graph, 161), 165; "relative" inflation in 1920s, 189; in 1930s, 249 (graph), 250–51, 256; in Japanese-occupied territories, 264; after WWII, 266–67; of 1970s, 129. *See also* "positive policy"
"inflation capital" (Itō), 253
infrastructure, 240
Inner Mongolia, 264
Inoue Junnosuke (career), 95, 97; photographs of, xxiii–xxiv; early life of, 9–11; at BOJ (1896–1911), 11–12, 39–40, 61–62, 82; at YSB (1911–19), 62–63, 89, 92, 96–98, 99, 101, 108; as BOJ governor (1919–23), 101, 119–123, 126–28, 129–37, 138–39, 140, 143–45, 146, 166, 176; as minister of finance (1923–24), 146–47, 171; as patron of business world, 153, 171–72, 180, 189, 190; as BOJ governor (1927–28), 181–83, 184–86, 187, 189; as minister of finance (1929–31), 199–209, 212, 214–16, 217–18, 220–22, 227–29, 231–33, 235–37, 239; assassination of, 246–47; and Minseitō, 199–200, 245; and Takahashi Korekiyo, 12, 61–62, 119–22, 182, 200, 209–10
Inoue Junnosuke (policy and thought): and bank bailouts, 134–35, 176, 182; on causes of world depression, 192; and China, 62–64, 101, 168; on consumption, 205–09, 242; in debate over restoring gold standard, 172–74, 190, 193; de Bunsen's translation of, 304n34; on European stabilization programs, 168; on Japanese gold standard, 39; versus new parity, 189, 201–2, 228; versus "positive" policy, 140, 193; as representative of liberal Japan, xiii, xv, 199, 247–48, 262–63; on requirements of an international financial center, 109–10; on WWI boom and postwar depression, 101–103, 110, 116, 117,

119, 120–21, 123, 130–31, 134–37, 160, 206, 241
Inoue Kaoru, 3, 12, 24, 34, 55, 84, 88, 92, 93; and Korea, 40–41
Inoue Nisshō, 246
Institute of Pacific Relations, 188
interest rates (as tool of central bank policy), 71, 89. *See also* Bank of Japan, policy stance
International Monetary Fund (IMF), 210, 269, 271; establishment of, 265, 317n22; and stabilization/induced depression, xvi, 166, 303n16
interwar era, as hegemonic interregnum, 96. *See also* 1920s
Inukai Tsuyoshi, 86, 88, 153, 155, 156; as Seiyūkai president, 157, 203, 227; as prime minister, 239; assassination of, 248
Ishibashi Tanzan, 19, 80, 93, 118, 136, 143, 156, 172, 221, 316n1; calls for restoration of gold standard (1919), 122–23, 140, 145; calls for new yen parity (1924), 155, 189, 229, 250, 301n44; on antidepression policy, 242–45; criticism of Takahashi, 123, 244–45; as minister of finance (1946–47), 122, 244, 258, 266; post-WWII views of, 257–58
Ishii Kikujirō, 108
Ishii-Lansing agreement (1917), 148
Ishiwara Kanji, 235, 256
isolationism, U.S., 167. *See also* multilateralism
"isolation" policy (Britain), 42
Italy, 262; return to gold standard, 170, 171, 188, 189
Itō Hirobumi, 22–23, 30–31, 32, 54, 81
Iwasaki Hisaya, 184
Iwasaki Masako, 9
Iwasaki Yatarō, 9
Iwata Ainosuke, 231
Iwate prefecture, 153

Jackson, D. F., 32
Japan: as creditor country, 98, 103, 122; as "European" country, 23, 29, 164, 258, 263, 269; stage of economic development compared to Europe, 109, 241–42; as world power, 128
Japan Chamber of Commerce and Industry, 191
Japanese government overseas bond issues, 258; of 1870, 23; of 1873, 23; 1897 gold standard to enable, 32; of 1899, 11, 34–35; of 1904–05, 47–50, 68–69, 88; "deadlock" of by 1914, 89; of 1924, 147, 149–150, 168; of 1930, 220–21; refinancing of Russo-Japanese war bonds, 88, 141, 149, 192, 194, 220–21; tables of, 72–77, 150–52; during and after WWII, 269–70, 317n37. *See also* bonds (corporate, local government)
Japanese names, xxi
Japanese relations with China: diplomacy, 30–31, 51, 93–94, 126, 148, 263; images of, 29; invasion of, 235, 241, 253; investment in, 51–52, 62–63, 64, 93, 105, 123–24, 128–29; military intervention in, 92–93, 148; policy of "economic advance" in, 123–24, 148, 298n26; trade, 33–34, 97, 104–5, 176, 225. *See also* Manchuria
Javasche Bank, 63
Jenks, Jeremiah, 42–44, 63, 171
Jews, as financiers, 46–47
Jiaozhou (Kiaochow), 4–5, 93, 99, 125
Jitsugyō Dōshikai, 156

Kakushin (Reform) Club, 153, 156, 157
Kanebō. *See* Kanegafuchi Spinning Co.
Kanegafuchi Spinning Co., 225. *See also* Mutō Sanji
Kaneko Kentarō, 34, 48
Kansai (Osaka-Kōbe-Kyoto) business world, 133–34, 135, 136
Kashiwagi Hideshige, 217
Kataoka Naoharu, 158, 173–75, 176, 177–80
Katō Takaaki (Kōmei), 82, 86–87, 88–89, 94; in London, 8–9; and "positive" policy in China, 92–94; as prime minister, 153–54, 157, 158, 301n36
Katō Tomosaburō, 141, 145; cabinet of, 142–43
Katsura Tarō, 12, 52, 55, 57, 81, 82–86
Kawata Shōichirō, 7–8
Kellogg, Frank, 185
Kellogg-Briand pact, 212
Keynes, J. M., 20, 50, 243, 265; on gold standard, 35–36, 172–73; on gold-exchange standard, 36, 38, 286n25

Keynesian policy, 67, 203, 211–12, 241–44, 268
Kemmerer, Edwin, 43, 109, 170–71, 212, 265
Kenseikai (Constitutional Government Society), 87, 94, 141, 146, 153–54, 177, 179, 301n36; as liberal party, 85, 156, 248; merger with Seiyū Hontō to form Minseitō, 183; and "negative" retrenchment policy, 67, 92, 129–30, 139, 154–55, 157–58, 175. *See also* Dōshikai; Minseitō
Kimura Seishirō, 61, 119
Kindleberger, Charles, 96
kin kaikin (lifting of the gold embargo): defined, xiv, 302n5. *See also* gold export embargo; gold standard (Japan), restoration of
Kita Ikki, 139, 246, 255
Kiyoura Keigo, 147, 153
Knox, Philander, 60
Kōchisha shrine, 232
Kodama Yoshio, 231, 233
Kokumintō (National Party), 86, 88, 94
Komura Jutarō, 55
Korea, 60, 65, 100, 105, 125, 269; foreign borrowing of, 31, 40–41; gold-exchange standard in, 40–42, 52–55, 289n33; and Russo-Japanese war, 45, 52
Korean central bank, 52. *See also* Bank of Korea; Bank of Chosen
Krugman, Paul, 208
Kuhn, Loeb, and Co., 58, 59, 128, 167, 170; and Japanese government loans, 46–49, 56, 148–49, 270. *See also* Japanese government bonds; Schiff, Jacob
Kuomintang (Guomindang), 127, 179
Kushida Manzō, 181
Kwantung (Guandong) Army, 56, 183, 195, 235–36, 246, 254
Kwantung (Guandong) Leased Territory, 5, 41, 50, 88, 93, 105

labor: legislation, 156, 201; movement, 110, 139, 262
Labour party (UK), 236
Lamont, Thomas W., 96, 98, 160, 168–69, 172, 252; and China consortium, 60, 64, 109, 125–28, 298n40; and Japanese return to gold standard, 190, 192, 193–94, 212–15; and lending to Japan, 147–49, 182, 270; second visit to Japan, 183–88; and stabilization policies, xv, 167, 188, 192, 220, 233–34, 260–61; and Takahashi Korekiyo, 315n42; and U.S.-Japan relations, xiii, 188, 220–21, 236, 237, 239, 246, 247–48, 253, 315n44; and world depression, 228. *See also* Morgan and Company
landlords, 86, 156
land prices, 119
League of Nations, 127, 236, 261; Financial Committee (and stabilization programs), 163, 166–67, 168, 184–85, 303n16; Japanese departure from, 183, 254
Leffingwell, Russell, 37; at U.S. Treasury, 131–32; at Morgan & Co., 167, 189–90, 193, 194, 214
Leith-Ross, Frederick, 254–55
lender of last resort, 38, 96. *See also* bailouts
Lenin, V. I., 50
Liaodong peninsula, retrocession of, 31, 41. *See also* Kwantung Leased Territory
liberalism: Anglo-American economic, 14–15, 21, 212, 261; in Japan, 80, 85–86, 153, 156, 199–201, 235, 247–48, 257; after WWII, 271
Liberia, 59, 109
lifetime employment system, 225
Li Hongzhang, 30
"liquidation" (in U.S. conception), 132, 134, 185, 187, 234
"little Japan" vision (Ishibashi), 243
loans, international: British to U.S., 169; for Chinese indemnity, 4–5; commissions on, 77n; Japanese borrowing of 1920s, 147–53; Japanese to China, 51–52, 168; Japanese to Korea, 31, 53–54; Japanese to wartime allies, 103, 295n45; by U.S. in 1920s, 132, 168, 191–92. *See also* bonds; Japanese government loans; Nishihara loans
Lockheed scandal (1974), 231
London: as international financial center, 3–5, 31, 36, 46–47, 69–71, 80, 91–92, 107, 161–62, 164, 217, 236–37, 258–59; Japanese community in, 8–9; shift of financial business to New York, 96–98, 183
London naval conference (1930), 140, 212, 217, 220; reaction against, 221, 227, 230, 231

Lüshun (Port Arthur), 4–5, 45, 50

MacArthur, Douglas, 268
MacVeagh, Charles, 186
Maeda Masana, 7, 25
Maier, Charles, 262
Malaya, 43
Manchukuo, 247, 252–54
Manchukuo yen, 254
Manchuria and eastern Inner Mongolia, 5, 45, 55–61, 64–65, 88, 93, 99–100, 105–6, 125–27, 129, 195, 231, 232, 247, 252–54; in boom-bust cycle of 1919–20, 135–36; Japanese seizure of (1931–32), 234–36, 237, 239, 246, 250, 257; U.S. interest in, 55–56, 58–61, 97, 126–27, 148, 184, 252–53. *See also* Kwantung (Army, Leased Territory); South Manchurian Railway Co
Manchuria Management Committee (Japan), 55–56
Manchurian Central Bank, 57, 105, 135, 254, 264
Manila, 12
March 1 (1919) movement, 125
Marshall Plan, 269
Masuda Bill Brokers Bank, 133
Matsukata deflation (1881–84), 25, 166
Matsukata Masayoshi, 10, 25, 42, 65, 84, 88, 104, 108, 180; and adoption of gold standard, 30–32; and Takahashi Korekiyo, 7, 8, 12, 45
Matsunaga Yasuzaemon, 184
Matsuoka Yōsuke, 183, 232
Matsuo Shigeyoshi, 47, 61
May 4 (1919) movement, 93, 125, 127
May 15 (1932) incident, 248, 257
McNeil, William C., 262
Megata (Mekata) Jūtarō, 52–53
Meiji: emperor, 85; era, xxii; revolution, 18
Mexican dollar, 284n23. *See also* silver-dollar standard
Mexico, 43, 109
"military Keynesianism," 243–44
military scrip: Japanese, 41, 57, 264; U.S., 266
military spending, 119, 136–37; 1920s as era of retrenchment in, 141–42
mining (of precious metals): in British empire, 28; in Japan, 15; in Korea, 285n44
ministers of finance. *See* Ōkuma Shigenobu; Matsukata Masayoshi; Inoue Kaoru; Sakatani Yoshio; Katsura Tarō; Yamamoto Tatsuo; Takahashi Korekiyo; Wakatsuki Reijirō; Shōda Kazue; Ichiki Otohiko; Inoue Junnosuke; Hamaguchi Osachi; Kataoka Naoharu; Mitsuchi Chūzō; Tsushima Juichi; Ishibashi Tanzan; Ikeda Hayato
Ministry of Agriculture and Commerce (MAC), 7, 156
Ministry of Commerce and Industry (MCI), 157, 224
"Ministry of Consumption" (Ishibashi), 243
Ministry of Finance (MOF), 58, 82, 86, 89, 156, 186, 270; and Bank of Japan, 25, 129, 264, 307n92; decision to restore gold standard, 192–95; Deposit Bureau, 31, 63, 64, 103, 106, 296n56; gold-embargo and re-embargo orders, 104–05, 202, 239. *See also* budgetary policy; ministers of finance (listed); overseas financial commissioner
Ministry of International Trade and Industry (MITI), 157, 270
Minseitō (Popular Government Party), 67, 85, 220, 232, 247; formation of, 141; and "negative" policy, 201; as liberal party, 199–201, 248. See also Dōshikai; Kenseikai
Mishima Yatarō, 87–88, 119
Mitchell, Charles, 194
Mitsubishi Bank, 181, 219, 248
Mitsubishi group, 7, 8, 86, 184
Mitsuchi Chūzō, 174, 227, 232, 304n41; as minister of finance, 182, 183, 192–93, 194
Mitsui, Baron, 184
Mitsui Bank, 9, 41, 181, 219; and dollar-buying speculation, 215, 238, 244, 311n13. *See also* Ikeda Shigeaki
Mitsui group, 9, 56, 106, 111, 179–80, 186, 247
Miyazawa Kiichi, 268
"modern girls" and "modern boys" (*moga, mobo*), 115
monetarist policy, 67, 212
monetary leverage: via gold and gold-exchange standards, 36–38, 286n27; in Japanese-occupied territories, 53–54, 65, 264; practiced by Tokugawa shogunate, 16–17. *See also* fractional-reserve banking; gold-exchange standards

money: creation of, xvi, 244. *See also* coinage; gold; monetary leverage; paper money
money supply (table), 275–77
"Money Trust" hearings, 64
moral and economic retrenchment, 83, 95, 154–55, 203–9, 212, 229
"moral hazard," 176
moratorium on debt repayment: of 1923, 146; of 1927, 181
Moreau, Emile, 195, 306n72
Morgan, J. P. Jr., 127, 169, 184, 192
Morgan and Co., xiii, 44, 46, 98, 132; and China consortium, 59–60, 64, 108–9, 126–28; Congressional investigations of, 64, 252; and Japanese deflation, 185–88, 189–90, 194; and Japanese loans, 34, 35, 48, 50, 148–53, 270; and Japanese return to gold standard, 192, 193–95, 210, 212–15, 220; lending and stabilization programs of the 1920s, 165, 167–71, 188, 214, 260–61, 303n16; mission to Japan (1927), 183–88; splitting up of, 252; and suspension of British gold standard (1931), 236–37; as "zaibatsu," 153, 169, 303n23. *See also* Lamont, Thomas W.; Japanese government loans
"Morgan conditionality," 236
Morgenthau, Henry, 265
Mori Arinori, 6
Mori Kengo: as overseas financial commissioner, 56, 147, 163, 169, 305n35; as financial adviser, 183, 184, 185, 186, 187–88, 189, 190, 192, 193, 194, 215, 252
motion pictures, 155, 204
Movement to Protect Constitutional Government: of 1912–13, 86; of 1924, 153
Mukden (Shenyang), 57, 58, 65, 105, 235
multilateralism, post-World War I, 127, 140–41, 163, 168, 170, 259, 261–62
multiplier (Takahashian), 211
"munitions boom" (*gunju keiki*), 241
munitions industry, 118
Mussolini, Benito, 168–69, 262, 316n13
Mutō Sanji, 40, 156, 177, 225; criticism of Inoue Junnosuke, 120, 121, 218, 221, 228–29, 247; assassination of, 314n24

Nanjing (Nanking), 179
Napoleonic wars, 21, 26
narikin (nouveaux riches), 95–96, 99, 111, 130
national banks (Meiji era), 24
National City Bank of New York, 126, 149, 150, 151, 152n, 194, 270; gold shipments from Japan, 219
"national humiliation bonds" (*kokujoku kōsai*), 149, 221
national income estimates, in times of rapid deflation, 223–24, 230, 299n55
national self-determination (Wilson), 125
national socialism, 139, 235, 255
The Nation magazine, xv, 184
Natsume Sōseki, 281n6
naval arms limitation, 127, 136, 140, 141, 200–201, 212, 227. *See also* Washington, London naval arms limitation treaties
navy, Japanese, 88, 141; and gold standard, 30
Nederlandsch-Indische Handelsbank, 219
"negative" (retrenchment) policy: defined, 67–68; of 1920s, 138–45, 153–56, 158, 222; of Ōkuma cabinet, 91, 94; under "Dodge line," 267. *See also* deflation
Netherlands, 165, 168
New Currency Law of 1871, 22
"new parity" (Ishibashi). *See* gold par
Newton, Isaac, 18
New York City, as international financial center, 43–44, 47, 80, 96–98, 107, 119–20, 149, 161–62, 168, 215
New York stock market bubble, 191–92, 212
New York stock market panics: of 1873, 27; of 1907, 82; of 1920, 132, 136; of 1929, 210, 213–15, 222, 228
New York Times, 188
New Zealand, 213
NHK (Nihon Hōsō Kyōkai), 242
Nicaragua, 109, 162
Nichiren Buddhism, 246
Nikolayevsk massacre (1920), 133, 135
Nishihara Kamezō, 100–101, 108
Nishihara loans (to China), 100–101, 103, 106, 124–25, 148, 150, 179, 296n56
Norman, Montagu, 132, 166, 171, 195, 199, 306n72
North China Development Co., 266
Northern Expedition (1926–27), 179, 183
Norway, 237
note issue (Bank of Japan), 110, 142, 219,

223, 233, 250–51, 264, 273–75; excess, 275, 315n35; fiduciary, 250, 264, 275

Ōita prefecture, 10, 11
Ōkawa Shūmei, 232, 246, 248
Ōkuma Shigenobu, 24–25, 86; as prime minister (1914–16), 88–89, 91–94
Ōkura Group, 56, 63
Omi Bank, 180
Onuma Shō, 246–47
"open door" policy, 127, 140
Oriental Development Company (ODC): activities in Korea and China, 65, 105, 135, 296n51; overseas borrowing by, 71, 79, 148, 150, 151, 192
Osaka business world, 39, 61, 133–34
Ōuchi Hyōe, 266, 317n25
overcapacity and overproduction, 117, 160, 203, 224, 227–28, 234, 268
overseas financial commissioner (Japanese government). *See* Takahashi Korekiyo, Wakatsuki Reijirō, Mori Kengo, Tsushima Juichi
overseas specie reserve: under gold standard, 68–71, 83, 84, 91, 97–98, 275, 286n30; repatriation of, 123–24; table of, 70; after WWI, 142–43, 156, 178, 192; exhausted in 1929, 206
Ozaki Yukio, 86, 156

"Pacific Age" (Tsurumi), 263–64
Pacific war. *See* World War II
Panama, 43–44, 162, 170
Pan-American monetary union plan (Kemmerer), 109
paper money, 14, 20–21, 24, 36–39, 121, 159. *See also* Bank of England notes, Bank of Japan notes
Paris Peace Conference (1919), 124–25, 126
parity; par values. *See* gold par
Parr's Bank, 11. *See also* British group
parties, political. *See* political party system
Pearl Harbor attack, 184
Persia, 59, 306n59
Philippines, 12, 54, 221; gold-exchange standard in, 37, 39, 42–43, 162
Pingxiang Coal Mining Co., 51
planning, economic, 235
plutocracy, 235, 246
Poland, 170, 306n59
Polanyi, Karl, 254
political party system, 67–68, 89, 111, 153, 235; as two-party system, 80–81, 85–87, 92, 183, 245. See also Dōshikai; Kenseikai; Minseitō; Seiyūkai
population growth, 115, 262
pork-barrel politics, 81
Portsmouth (New Hampshire), Treaty of, 49–50
"positive" and "negative" policies: contrasted, 80–90, 92, 120, 154, 156, 245, 256, 260; and gold standard, 104, 143, 192–93
"positive policy": defined, 67–68; of Ōkuma Shigenobu, 24–25; gold standard initially enables, 32, 124; after 1923 earthquake, 146–47; of Ishibashi Tanzan, 258, 266. *See also* Seiyūkai, "positive policy"
postal savings, 182, 306n63. *See also* Ministry of Finance Deposit Bureau
postwar inflation–deflation cycles: after "Southwest war" of 1877, 24–25, 83; after Sino-Japanese war, 68, 83; after Russo-Japanese war, 67–68, 71, 81–85, 89, 94, 102, 292n13; after WWI, 67, 101–4, 115–22, 129, 159–63; after WWII, 257–58, 266–68. *See also* depression of 1920
"postwar management" (*sengo keiei*), 67, 81
pound sterling: as basis for gold-exchange standards, 31, 70, 164, 255, 302n8; as global money, 36, 96–97, 107, 237, 254; run on (1931), 234, 236; depreciation after 1931, 237; and shillings, pence, xxi
price revolution, of World War I, 110. *See also* inflation, of World War I
prices. *See* deflation; inflation
privatization, 166, 188
Privy Council, 180, 181
production curtailment, 203, 223, 224
productionism, 130
productivity, 211
profit rates, 117, 240
proletarian parties, 225
prostitution, 234
"Public and Private Retrenchment Campaign" (1929), 203–9, 220
public works spending, 244, 250. *See also* positive policy

Puerto Rico, 42
purchasing power parity (Cassel), 155

Qingdao (Tsingtao), 4–5, 93, 99, 125
"quasi-wartime" (*junsenji*) economy, 248

race, and international hierarchy, 46, 128
radio broadcasting, 204, 242–43, 313n6
Rae, John, 310n53
railways, Japanese: nationalization of, 82; and "positive policy," 84, 88, 119, 183, 186
"rationalization" (*gōrika*), 203, 206, 224, 228, 231, 252
rayon, 227
recessions, chronic: after Russo-Japanese war, 71, 292n13; of 1920s, 115–17, 188, 207, 216, 241, 262; of 1990s, 208. *See also* depressions
Redish, Angela, 16
reflation, 244–45, 249–50 (graph), 251. *See also* inflation of the 1930s
reparations (World War I), 160, 167, 192, 193–94, 233–34
Republican party (U.S.), 267
restoration, and deflation: after the Napoleonic wars, 159; after WWI, 159, 162, 173, 262, 265. *See also* gold standard, as restoration
"retrenchment" (*kinshuku*). *See* "negative policy"
"Retrenchment Ditty," 204–5
rice prices and production, 110, 121, 130, 133, 138, 223; in 1930–31, 230
rice riots of 1918, 110–11, 230
right-wing movements, 230–31, 232–33, 246–48, 257
Roosevelt, Franklin, 168, 252, 315n43
Roosevelt, Theodore, 49, 54, 58, 59
Root, Elihu, 58
Rothschilds, 46, 74, 75
Russia: and China, 4–5, 41–42, 65, 106, 135; and gold-exchange standard, 32, 39, 58, 99, 286n30, 292n11; imperialism compared with Japan's, 51; Japanese lending to, 98–99, 103, 105–6; revolution of 1917, 105, 106. *See also* Siberian intervention
Russo-Chinese Bank, 41, 44
Russo-Japanese rapprochement, 58, 60, 80, 85
Russo-Japanese war of 1904–05, 45; Japanese war loans, 45–50, 68–69. *See also* postwar inflation-deflation cycles
Russo-Korean Bank, 41

Sagōya Tomeo, 231
Saionji Kinmochi, 55–56, 81, 82, 84–85, 245, 248
Sakatani Yoshio (or Yoshiro), 3, 24, 30, 32, 44, 56, 60, 61, 63, 100, 303n33; on post-WWI adjustment, 103–4; as Chinese government adviser, 106–8
sake consumption, 208
samurai stipends, commutation of, 23
San Francisco Peace Treaty, 269
Sansom, George, 176
Satsuma clique, 30, 81, 87
Schacht, Hjalmar, 168, 306n72
Schiff, Jacob, 46–49, 55, 128, 149. *See also* Kuhn, Loeb & Co.
Schiff, Mortimer, 194
school spending, 119
scramble for concessions in China and Korea, 4–5, 12, 41–42
Second Higher School (Sendai), 10
seigniorage, 16, 37, 38
Seiyū Hontō (True Seiyūkai), 147, 153, 156, 177
Seiyūkai (Society of Political Friends), 111, 118, 139, 146, 153–54, 202–3, 220, 247–48; attacks on Minseitō cabinets, 227, 232–33, 239; attacks on Wakatsuki cabinet, 177–80, 181; as conservative party, 156, 199; and gold standard, 191; split of, 141, 147
Seiyūkai and "positive policy," 67–68, 92; and Hara Takashi, 81, 84–85; and Takahashi Korekiyo, 87–88, 94; under Hara-Takahashi cabinets, 119–22, 124, 130, 136–38; under coalition cabinet, 154, 156–57; under Tanaka cabinet, 183, 188, 192–93, 195; under Inukai cabinet, 239–42, 245
semigovernmental banks (*tokubetsu ginkō*), 34, 286n18. *See also* Bank of Chosen, Bank of Japan, Bank of Taiwan, Industrial Bank of Japan, Yokohama Specie Bank
Sendai domain, 5, 6
senior statesmen (*genrō*), 92, 93, 94
service industry, 242

"shadow" gold standard (of 1920s), 250–51
Shand, Alexander Allan, 5–6, 11, 45, 47
Shandong (Shantung): foreign concessions in, 4–5, 101, 124–25, 140; Japanese occupations of, 93, 125, 129, 183
Shanghai, 4, 125, 235, 264; exchange markets, 17, 105, 133, 158, 227; Japanese attack on, 246
Shibusawa Eiichi, 8, 30, 40, 104, 126, 148, 172
Shidehara Kijūrō, 101, 108; in London, 8–9; as foreign minister, 154, 179, 183, 201, 227, 231, 233, 235, 239, 301n36
Shigeki Trading Co., 135
Shimonoseki, Treaty of, 8, 30–31, 51
shipping and shipbuilding industries, 95
Shōda Kazue, 86, 89–90; as minister of finance, 94, 100–101, 104–5, 108, 111, 147, 149
Shōwa era, xxii
"Shōwa panic" (*Shōwa kyōkō*), 222, 252
Siberian intervention, 106, 111, 119, 123, 135, 136, 142
Siemens scandal, 88
silk exports and prices: in 1907, 82, 97; in 1919, 118, 130, 133; in 1920s, 135, 136, 158, 164–65, 174; in 1930–31, 223, 226–27, 252; compared to British coal exports, 172
silver: appreciation and depreciation of, 27–28, 30–31, 33 (graph), 43, 82, 95, 132–33, 176, 225, 227, 231, 285n42, 315n49; export embargo, 310n54; and London market, 97. *See also* coinage; gold:silver ratios
silver-dollar standard, 22–24, 43, 284n23
Silver Purchase Act, U.S.: of 1890, 68, 285n42; of 1934, 315n49
silver standard: international move away from, 27, 37, 43; in China, 33, 254–55, 315n49; in Japan, 25, 32, 273
silver yen, 41
Sino-Japanese war (1894–95), 29, 40–41, 68; funding of, 31–32; indemnity, 3–5, 8, 30–32, 51, 68, 107
Smith, Jeremiah Jr., 126, 167, 184–86, 193
social-democratic parties, 262
social policy, 139, 156, 200–201
Soeda Juichi, 32, 55, 56
Sonoda (of Yokohama Specie Bank), 239, 247, 248
South Africa, 28, 170–71; South African war, 35, 102
South America, as field of U.S. economic expansion, 109, 128, 170, 189
Southeast Asia, 264, 268–69
South Manchuria. *See* Manchuria
South Manchurian Railway Co. (SMR), 50, 55–58, 93, 99, 183, 235; attempts to borrow in U.S., 126, 148, 184, 305n46; overseas borrowing by, 65, 71, 78–79 (table), 79n, 83, 150, 253; railway zone, 105
South Seas Development Fund (Nanpō Kaihatsu Kinkō), 264
Spain, 190
Spanish-American war, 12
"special banks" (*tokubetsu ginkō*), 34, 286n18
specie-flow theory (Hume), 18–20, 165, 223
"stabilization," xv–xvi; crises, xv, 132, 220; of prices versus exchange rates, 171; programs, 59, 162–63, 166–68, 170–71, 192, 241, 260–63, 303n16, 306n59, 316n16; apparent success in early 1929, 191, 193, 212, 217; after WWII, 267–68. *See also* gold standard, restoration; gold-restoration depressions; induced depression; "negative policy"
state-owned enterprises, 166, 185, 188
"sterilization" of gold inflows, 165
sterling. *See* pound sterling
sterling bloc, 43, 237, 302n8
stock markets (Japanese): boom of 1919–20, 118–19; crash of 1920, 133–35; in 1930–31, 225, 228, 230, 231, 237, 239
stock markets (other countries). *See* New York stock market
Straight, Willard, 58, 60
Straits Settlement, 43
strikes, 110, 130, 225–26
Strong, Benjamin, 126, 165, 166, 185, 191, 199, 306n72; and Inoue Junnosuke, 97, 119–20, 132, 171
"subimperialist" activism, 136
Suez Canal, 4, 24
suffrage: female, 201, 205; universal male, 153, 156, 186, 247
sugar industry, 91
Sumitomo Bank, 219
Sun Yat-sen, 85, 127
supply-side policy, 121. *See also* productionism

Suzuki Kisaburō, 248
Suzuki Trading Co., 91, 106, 111; in 1927 crisis, 176, 179–80
Sweden, 237
Switzerland, 165, 237

tael. *See* yen-tael exchange rates
Taft, William H., 54, 59
Taishō: emperor, 154; era, xxii; political crisis, 80, 85–87
"Taishō democracy," 80–81, 257
Taiwan, 91. *See also* Bank of Taiwan
Taiwan Electric Power Co., 152, 234
Tajiri Inajirō, 30, 303n33
Takahashi financial policy (*Takahashi zaisei*, 1931–36), 81, 117; defined, 248–49
Takahashi Kamekichi, 176, 189, 212, 308n9
Takahashi Korekiyo: and adoption of gold standard, 31, 32; assassination of, 248, 255; at BOJ, 61–62, 82, 83–84, 86; and bubble of 1919–20, 120–22, 244; early life of, 5–8; and Manchuria, 57–58, 99, 129, 252–54; as minister of agriculture and commerce (1924–25), 154–57; as minister of finance, 87;—(1913–14), 87–89, 94;—(1918–22), 111, 119–24, 128–30, 136–39;—(1927), 180–83;—(1931–36), 239–42, 244–45, 248–56, 314n29; and Morgan & Co., 128, 315n42; opposition to army, 123, 129, 235, 250, 255; opposition to Inoue policy, 209–12, 216, 219; as overseas financial representative, 3–5, 45–50, 81; as prime minister (1921–22), 139, 140, 144, 159–60; and Seiyūkai, 84, 87–89, 139, 141, 146, 147, 153, 157; and yen-depreciation policy, 141, 181, 244, 249–50
Takahira Kogorō, 49
Tanaka Giichi, 84–85, 125–26, 292n37; as Seiyūkai president, 147, 157; as prime minister, 177, 180, 184, 192, 193; "positive" China policy of, 183, 184, 188, 195; death of, 202–3
Tang Shaoyi (T'ang Shao-i), 58
Tanuma Okitsugu, 16, 21
tariffs, 160
Terauchi Masatake, 94, 99, 100, 101, 109, 110–11
Ten Point Program (Minseitō), 200–201
textile industry, 136. *See also* cotton; silk
thrift. *See* Diligence and Thrift Campaign; Public and Private Retrenchment Campaign
Tiananmen incident (May 4, 1919), 93, 125
Tōhō Electric Power Co., 151, 184, 188
Tōhoku (Northeast) region, 234
token coins. *See* coinage
Tokonami Takejirō, 141, 147
Tokugawa shogunate (*bakufu*), 236; austerity edicts of, 229; coinage system, 15–18, 21; specie export embargo, 15, 17–18, 104, 283n10
Tokyo, 115; in 1923 earthquake, 145–46; as international financial center, 53–54, 106–7, 109, 119–20; mayorship of, 303n33; municipal bond issues, 148, 151
Tokyo Electric Light Co. (Tōkyō Denkō), 148, 150–51, 152n, 184; merger of, 188; debt crisis at, 220–21
Tokyo Imperial University, 9–10
Tokyo Stock Exchange Co., 82, 133. *See also* stock markets, Japanese
Tokyo Watanabe Bank, 178–79
Tōyō keizai shinpō (*The Oriental Economist*), 80, 122, 189, 221
Tōzai Bank, 99
trade: Japan-China, 33, 97, 104–5, 176, 225; Japan-India, 97, 98, 104; Japan-U.S., 33–34, 121, 147, 153; Japan's trade structure, 164–65, 226–27, 240–41, 252–53
trade balance. *See* balance of payments; specie-flow theory
trade finance. *See* bills of exchange; Yokohama Specie Bank
"transcendental" cabinets, 141
treaties, unequal, 12, 17
Treaty of Amity and Commerce (1858), 17
Tsurumi Yūsuke, 99, 263, 290n43
Tsushima Juichi, 90; as overseas financial commissioner, 147, 163, 192–95, 204, 213–14, 217, 220, 302n5, 305n35; after WWII, 266, 269–71
Turkey (and Ottoman empire), 24, 51, 261, 306n59
Twenty-one Demands (1915), 93–94, 126, 148
"Two Japans" (Lamont), xiii, 247

Uchida Ryōhei, 231
Uchida Yasuya (Kōsai), 48

underconsumption, 228, 241. *See also* consumption; overproduction
unemployment: and "adjustment," 144, 173, 201, 236, 241; in 1930, 226, 227
unequal treaties, 12, 17
United States: boom of WWI, 94; as creditor country, 20, 80, 96–98, 121, 122, 147–53, 165, 191–92, 228; in depression of 1920, 135, 136, 137, 160–62; and Korea, 41, 54, 58; and Manchuria, 55–56, 58–61, 97, 126–27, 148, 184; occupation of Japan, 257, 258, 266–69; post-WWII hegemony, 263–64, 266, 270; restoration of gold standard, 118, 121, 122, 124, 131, 162; trade with Japan, 33–34, 121, 147, 153; as trans-Pacific empire, 12. *See also* Federal Reserve Bank of NY; loans, international; New York City
U.S. dollar, 22, 284n23; as international currency, 70–71, 97–98, 164–65; as post-WWII standard, 258, 265–66, 269; end of gold convertibility in 1971, 271. *See also* yen-dollar exchange rates
U.S. dollar bloc, 42–44, 59, 162. *See also* gold-exchange standards
U.S. government: Bureau of the Budget, 167, 267; State Department, 59, 60, 109, 126, 184, 185, 253; Treasury Department, 126, 131–32, 167, 265
U.S.-Japan alliance, 269

Vanderlip, Frank, 126
Van Reed, Eugene, 6
Versailles Treaty, 162. *See also* Paris Peace Conference
Vickers scandal, 88
Vienna stock market crash (1873), 27
Vissering, Gerard, 63, 107

wage cuts, 173, 223, 224–26, 267
Wakatsuki Reijirō, 217, 301n36; as MOF official, 56, 82–83, 85; as minister of finance, 86–87, 88–89, 94, 290n44; as home minister, 154, 157; as prime minister (1926–27), 159, 174–75; as prime minister (1931), 233, 239
Wall Street, 267, 270. *See also* New York City as international financial center
War of 1812 (U.S.), 132. *See also* Napoleonic wars
wartime economy (after 1937), 248, 256
Washington Conference (1921–22) and naval arms limitation treaty, 127, 136, 140–41, 145
"Washington system," 127, 140, 300n7
Weihaiwei, 5
Weimar Republic. *See* Germany
Wilhelm II, Kaiser, 85
Wilson, Woodrow, 64, 108, 125, 168; Wilson administration, 108–9
Witte, Sergei, 32, 41, 48, 49, 58
women: as consumers, 205–8, 212, 242–43; political participation of, 201, 205, 243; as producers, 226
women's organizations, 140, 205
World Bank, 103, 269, 317n22
World Depression and Our People's Preparedness (Inoue), 227–28, 229
World War I: economic effects of, 91–92, 94–111, 159–165; German indemnity (reparations) for, 160, 167, 192, 193–94, 233–34; Japanese military participation in, 92–93, 142; war debts, 98, 102, 103, 140, 241–42. *See also* postwar inflation-deflation cycles
World War II (Asia-Pacific war, 1937–45), 255, 256, 263, 264

Yahata (or Yawata) Iron Works, 12, 31, 35, 51–52, 62, 64
Yalu River, battle, 46
Yamagata Aritomo, 81, 85, 94, 108; Yamagata clique, 81, 92, 94
Yamamoto Gonnohyōe (Gonbei), 81, 87, 88, 146, 147
Yamamoto Isoroku, 184
Yamamoto Jotarō, 181, 183
Yamamoto Tatsuo, 11–12, 87; versus Takahashi Korekiyo, 84, 88, 141, 147
Yasuda Zenjirō, 139
yen: establishment of, 22–24, 284n23; exchange policy during 1920s, 143, 146–47, 155–56, 181, 301n44; exchange rate and prosperity, recessions, 147, 158, 176; overvalued in 1920s, 155, 250, 301n44; run on in 1931, 238–39
yen appreciation (*endaka*), 122, 145, 147, 158, 178, 201, 215, 271
yen bloc: in China, 57, 64–65, 99–101; in Korea, 40–42, 52–55; during WWII, 253–54, 264–65. *See also* gold-exchange standards

yen depreciation (*enyasu*), 27–28, 33 (graph), 68, 141, 147, 154, 155, 239, 244, 249–50, 271
yen-dollar exchange rates, 27, 33, 77n, 136, 239, 250, 264, 268, 269
yen-sterling exchange rates, 77n, 250
yen-tael exchange rates, 33, 132–33, 223, 225, 227, 231
Yi Yong-ik, 52
Yokohama, 135; in 1923 earthquake, 145–46; silk exchange, 135, 136, 226
Yokohama Specie Bank (YSB), 3, 4, 8, 239, 310n53; in China, 56–58, 62–65, 99, 101, 105, 106, 290n46; establishment of, 24; overseas lending, 40, 98–99; overseas offices, 9, 25, 31; and trade finance, 92, 97, 101, 110
Yoshida Shigeru, 269, 270
Young China party, 60
Young Committee (1929), 191, 192–93; Young plan, 233–34
Young, Owen D., 192
Young, Ralph, 267
youth groups (Great Japan Federation of), 303n33
Yoshino Toshihiko, 271, 317n25
Yoshiue Shōichirō, 177–78
Yuan Shikai, 58, 62, 63, 93
Yukon, 28

zaibatsu, 226, 233
zaibatsu banks, 182–83, 219, 237–38. *See also* Mitsubishi Bank; Mitsui Bank
zaikai ("business world"): defined, 297n3
Zhang Zuolin (Chang Tso-lin), 183, 195

Text: 10/12 Baskerville
Display: Baskerville
Compositor: BookMatters, Berkeley

www.ingramcontent.com/pod-product-compliance
Lightning Source LLC
LaVergne TN
LVHW041403100425
808274LV00010B/156/J
* 9 7 8 0 5 2 0 2 4 4 2 0 7 *